Davidson
1990

Medieval English Drama

GARLAND MEDIEVAL BIBLIOGRAPHIES
(VOL. 2)

GARLAND REFERENCE LIBRARY
OF THE HUMANITIES
(VOL. 956)

GARLAND MEDIEVAL BIBLIOGRAPHIES

MEDIEVAL ENGLISH DRAMA
An Annotated Bibliography of Recent Criticism

Sidney E. Berger

GARLAND PUBLISHING, INC. • NEW YORK & LONDON
1990

Library of Congress Cataloging-in-Publication Data

Berger, Sidney E.
   Medieval English drama: a bibliography of recent criticism /
Sidney E. Berger.
     p. cm. — (Garland Medieval bibliographies ; vol. 2)
(Garland reference library of the humanities ; vol. 956)
   ISBN 0–8240–5790–2 (alk. paper)
    1. English drama—To 1500—History and criticism—Bibliography.
2. Mysteries and miracle-plays, English—History and criticism—
Bibliography. 3. Moralities, English—History and criticism—
Bibliography. I. Title. II. Series. III. Series: Garland
reference library of the humanities ; vol. 956.
Z2014.D7B43   **1990**
[PR641]
016.822'109—dc20   89–17114
                                                CIP

Printed on acid-free, 250-year-life paper
Manufactured in the United States of America

This book is for Frances, Joe,
and especially Michèle
who made it possible.

Contents

This bibliography on medieval English drama offers annotated entries for editions, collections, and scholarship of various kinds. It contains about 2,000 entries with appropriate cross-references, and focuses only on work which is not already cited in Carl J. Stratman's *Bibliography of Medieval Drama* (New York: Frederick Ungar, 1972).

I have chosen to interpret the phrase *medieval English drama* loosely, so as to include a wide variety of materials, since all kinds of entertainment in the Middle Ages may well have had some influence on what scholars usually look to when they think of the era's drama: the cycle and morality plays, and also the few surviving miracle plays. I have therefore included many entries on liturgical and folk drama and on other forms of entertainment. There are also a few entries on closely related works--in Welsh or in other languages--which had parallel growth or direct connection with English plays.

I have tried to do the impossible--that is, to be exhaustive. But such bibliographies as this are necessarily obsolete the moment they appear because of the proliferation of scholarship. Also, a few entries here were not available to me, despite what seemed to be herculean efforts to obtain them; these entries are left unannotated. For all the rest I have handled copies, read, and had other scholars to help me with translations, and have produced annotations from the originals.

For this reason I am greatly indebted to a number of people. Patricia Norcott provided simply invaluable help with French, German, Dutch, Italian, and Spanish works. Dr. Michèle Cloonan also helped me with the French works, and a great deal with the proofreading. Mrs. Yasuko Makino, the Japanese Librarian at the University of Illinois Asian Library (in Champaign/Urbana), generously gave many hours translating works from Japanese for me. Ya'acov Ziso helped with an item in Hebrew; Alan Degutis and Ann-Catherine Rapp of the American Antiquarian Society assisted me with works in German and Swedish, respectively.

The most onerous and frustrating task for me was obtaining copies of the materials that I had citations for. Thanks to the kindness of many people, I was able to procure copies of nearly every item listed in the bibliography. David Warrington of Harvard University was immensely helpful. Miriam Skey and Judith May Newton made available to me some very difficult to obtain articles in Japanese. John C. Coldewey kindly provided an advance copy of his and Marianne G. Briscoe's *Contexts for Early English Drama* (see entry # 228), and Indiana University Press sent me page proofs of this book from which I was able to specify page numbers for individual articles. Eckehard Simon likewise sent me the table of contents from his forthcoming collection, *Medieval Theater* (see entry # 1469). Meg Twycross, Alexandra Johnston, Lawrence M. Clopper, Clifford Davidson, Stanley Kahrl, and many others too numerous to mention also offered suggestions on where and how to obtain materials. And Clifford Davidson was especially helpful and kind in informing me about many new publications. Mary L. Robertson of The Huntington Library provided information about one of its forthcoming volumes (see entry # 499). And Ashley Smith of Brown University retrieved many items for me from many different shelves.

A majority of the research was conducted at the University of Illinois (Champaign/Urbana), which either had the items I sought or provided them through its superlative inter-library loan service or its amazing on-line circulation system. I also conducted a good deal of work at the Newberry Library, the library at the University of Iowa, Brown University, Holy Cross College in Worcester, Richland Community College in Decatur, Illinois, Harvard University, the American Antiquarian Society, and Clark University.

A few people deserve special praise and thanks: Marla Wallace and Mary Hartman of Clark University's reference department. They worked ceaselessly for me in obtaining scores of articles and books from the far reaches of academia. And Jacques Bouvard has been generous beyond all measure--from the beginning of my computer work to the end-- with his time and his expertise, helping to shape this bibliography into its present laser-printed form. I owe him these people my deepest gratitude.

I also want to thank Aaron for his love and understanding during the many hours I sat at the computer.

And finally I wish to thank my wife Michèle for her linguistic expertise, her tireless proofreading, her constant encouragement, and her tender patience.

Sources Cited

To save space, extensive use of abbreviations is made for most of the periodicals cited in the bibliography. For some, full titles are given; for others, place of origin is supplied.

AAPSS	*American Academy of Political and Social Science. Annals*
AB	*AB/Bookman's Weekly*
ABR	*American Benedictine Review*
Acad	*Academician*
AHR	*American Historical Review*
AJ	*Antiquaries Journal*
AL	*American Libraries*
Albion	
Allegorica	
AmAnth	*American Anthropologist*
America	
AmJSoc	*American Journal of Sociology*
AmS	*American Scholar*
Anglia	*Anglia: Zeitschrift für Englische Philologie*
AnM	*Annuale Mediaevale*
ANQ	*American Notes & Queries*
Apollo	
ARBA	*American Reference Books Annual*
Archives	
ARS	*The Annual Report of Studies* (Shizuoka Eiwa College)
ArtB	*Art Bulletin*
ArtH	*Art History*
ASNSL	*Archiv für das Studium der neueren Sprachen und Literaturen*
AULLA	*Journal of the Australasian Universities Language & Literature Association (formerly AUMLA--Journal of the Australasian Modern Language Association)*
AWN	*A Wake Newslitter* [sic]
B&B	*Books & Bookmen*
Bamah	*Bamah: Theatrical Review* (Jerusalem)
BBN	*British Book News*
BCGE	*Bulletin of the College of General Education* (Tohoku U., Miyagi)
BestS	*Best Sellers*

BFE	Bulletin of the Faculty of Education (Mie U.)
BkF	Book Forum
BkR	Book Report
BksA	Books Abroad
BkW	Book World
Booklist	
BSUF	Ball State University Forum
BurlM	Burlington Magazine
CahE	Cahiers Elisabethains
Caliban	
C&H	Computers and the Humanities
C&L	Christianity and Literature
C&M	Classica et Mediaevalia
C&RL	College & Research Libraries
CanJH	Canadian Journal of History
CE	College English
Celestinesca	
Cent	Centerpoint
ChauR	Chaucer Review
ChHist	Church History
Choice	
CHR	Catholic Historical Review
ChrCnt	Christian Century
Chronica	
Cithara	
CL	College Literature (Westchester, PA; Westchester State College)
CLAQ	Children's Literature Association Quarterly
Clio	
CLW	Catholic Library World
Come-All-Ye	
Comitatus	
Comm	Communique (Pietersburg)
Commonweal	
CompD	Comparative Drama
CompL	Comparative Literature
CompLS	Comparative Literature Studies
ComQ	Communication Quarterly
Connoisseur	
ContempRev	Contemporary Review (London)
ContempSoc	Contemporary Sociology
CR	Classical Review
Crit	Criticism
CritQ	Criticism Quarterly
CSM	Christian Science Monitor
CSSH	Comparative Studies in Sociology and History
CW	Classical World
DalR	Dalhousie Review
DC	Dutch Crossing
Dorset Year Book	
Drama	Drama: The Quarterly Theatre Review

DramRev	*Drama Review*
EAM	*East Anglian Magazine*
E&S	*Essays and Studies*
EconHR	*Economic History Review*
Economist	
ECS	*Eighteenth Century Studies*
EDAMN	*Early Drama, Art, and Music Newsletter*
EETS	*Early English Text Society*
EHR	*English Historical Review*
EJ	*Essex Journal*
ELN	*English Language Notes*
ELR	*English Literary Review*
ELR (Kyoto)	*English Literature Review* (Kyoto Women's U.)
EM	*Early Music*
Enc	*Encounter*
Engl	*English*
EngStud	*English Studies*
EngStudA	*English Studies in Africa: A Journal of the Humanities* (Johannesburg)
EngStudC	*English Studies in Canada*
ESRS	*Emporia State Research Studies*
EssCrit	*Essays in Criticism*
EssLit	*Essays in Literature* (Macomb, Illinois)
EtAng	*Etudes Anglaises: Grande-Bretagne, Etats-Unis*
ETJ	*Educational Theatre Journal* (subsequently *Theatre Journal*)
Expl	*Explicator*
F&R	*Faith and Reason*
FCS	*Fifteenth-Century Studies*
FJS	*Fu Jen Studies: Literature and Linguistics* (Republic of China)
Flor	*Florilegium*
Folklore	
FR	*French Review*
Fulcrum	
Gamut	
Genre	
GermanQ	*German Quarterly*
GW	*Guardian Weekly*
HandZ	*Handelingen van de Zuidnederlandse Maatschappij voor Taal- en Letterkunde en Geschiedenis*
Historian	
History	
HistT	*History Today*
HLQ	*Huntington Library Quarterly*
HRNB	*History: Reviews of New Books*
HSNPL	*Harvard Studies and Notes in Philosophy and Literature*
HTR	*Harvard Theological Review*
HudR	*Hudson Review*

IJCS	International Journal of Comparative Sociology
ILQ	Illinois Quarterly
Inter	Interpretations: Studies in Language and Literature (Memphis State U.)
IR	Innes Review
JAAC	Journal of Aesthetics and Art Criticism
JAF	Journal of American Folklore
JAMS	Journal of the American Musicological Society
JEconH	Journal of Economic History
JEconS	Journal of Economic System
JEGP	Journal of English and Germanic Philology
JGE	Journal of General Education
JHG	Journal of Historical Geography
JHI	Journal of the History of Ideas
JJQ	James Joyce Quarterly
JLH	Journal of Library History
JMH	Journal of Modern History
JMRS	Journal of Medieval and Renaissance Studies
JPC	Journal of Popular Culture
JPMMS	Journal of the Plainsong and Medieval Music Society
JRel	Journal of Religion
JRMMRA	Journal of the Rocky Mountain Medieval and Renaissance Association
JWCI	Journal of the Warburg and Courtauld Institutes
KPAB	Kentucky Philological Association Bulletin
KPBG	Kliatt Paperback Book Guide
KR	Kirkus Reviews
L&L	Lore and Language
Lang&S	Language and Style
Lib	The Library
LibR	Library Review
Listener	
LitNQ	Literature in North Queensland
LJ	Library Journal
LP	Lettore di Provincia
LQ	Library Quarterly
LRB	London Review of Books
LSE	Leeds Studies in English
MAe	Medium Aevum
M&H	Mediaevalia et Humanistica
M&L	Music and Letters
M&RD	Medieval & Renaissance Drama in England
Manuscripta	
McNR	McNeese Review (McNeese State College, Louisiana)
Markham Review	
MedAe	Medium Aevum

Medi	Mediaevalia
MedS	Mediaeval Studies
MEJ	Music Educators Journal
MET	Medieval English Theatre
MFLAE	Memoirs of the Faculty of Liberal Arts and Education (Yamanashi U.)
MichAc	Michigan Academician. Papers of the Michigan Academy of Science, Arts, and Letters
MiltQ	Milton Quarterly
MLQ	Modern Language Quarterly
MLR	Modern Language Review
MLS	Modern Language Studies
Moreana	
Mosaic	
MP	Modern Philology
MQ	Musical Quarterly
MT	Musical Times
MusAn	Music Analysis
NA	Norfolk Archaeology
N&Q	Notes & Queries
NatCR	National Civic Review
Nation	
NatOb	National Observer
Neoph	Neophilologus
NewLH	New Literary History
NewRep	New Republic
NewS	New Statesman
NewThM	New Theatre Magazine
New York Times	
NM	Neuphilologische Mitteilungen
NMW	Notes on Mississippi Writers
NorH	Northern History (Leeds)
Notes	Notes (Music Library Association)
NotMS	Nottingham Medieval Studies
NYRB	New York Review of Books
NYT	New York Times
Obs	Observer (London)
OldC	Old Cornwall: Journal of the Federation of Old Cornwall Societies
Orb	Orbis (Louvain). Bulletin International de Documentation Linguistique
Oxon	Oxoniensia
P&P	Past and Present
PAJ	Performing Arts Journal
Parergon	Parergon. Bulletin of the Australian and New Zealand Association for Medieval and Renaissance Studies
PBSA	Papers of the Bibliographical Society of America
PCP	Pacific Coast Philology
PIEBC	Proceedings of the International Beast Epic Colloquium

PIMA	*Proceedings of the Illinois Medieval Association*
PLL	*Papers on Language and Literature*
PMLA	*Papers of the Modern Language Association of America*
Poetica	
PPMRC	*Proceedings of the PMR Conference, Annual Publications of the International Patristic, Mediaeval and Renaissance Conference*
PQ	*Philological Quarterly*
PRMA	*Proceedings of the Royal Musical Association*
PS	*Prairie Schooner*
PSIAH	*Proceedings of the Suffolk Institute of Archaeology and History*
PW	*Publishers Weekly*
QFG	*Quaderni di Filologia Germanica della Facoltà di Lettere e Filosofia dell'Università di Bologna*
QJS	*Quarterly Journal of Speech*
RABM	*Revista de Archivos, Bibliotecas y Museos*
REEDN	*Records of Early English Drama Newsletter* [N.B. issues from 1976–1982 (vols. 1-7) are not numbered as such; volume numbers appear for the first time on vol. 8. Numbers for vols. 1-7 are supplied, not in brackets, in this bibliography.]
RefSR	*Reference Services Review*
Ren&Ref	*Renaissance and Reformation*
Renascence	
RenD	*Renaissance Drama*
RenMS	*Renaissance and Modern Studies*
RenP	*Renaissance Papers*
RenQ	*Renaissance Quarterly*
RES	*Review of English Studies*
Revue des Langues Vivantes	
RHT	*Revue d'Histoire du Théâtre*
RORD	*Research Opportunities in Renaissance Drama*
RQ	*RQ, ALA Reference and Adult Services Division*
RRBN	*Reference and Research Book News*
RS	*Religious Studies*
RSR	*Religious Studies Review*
RUO	*Revue de l'Université d'Ottawa*
SAHJ	*Society of Architectural Historians. Journal*
Samlaren	
S&S	*Science and Society*
SB	*Studies in Bibliography*
SchLib	*School Librarian*

Scintilla	
SCJ	*Sixteenth Century Journal*
ScotHR	*Scottish Historical Review*
ScotStud	*Scottish Studies*
SEL	*Studies in English Literature*
SELL	*Studies in English Literature and Language* (Kyushu U., Yamanashi)
SevCN	*Seventeenth-Century News*
SewR	*Sewanee Review*
ShakN	*Shakespeare Newsletter*
ShakQ	*Shakespeare Quarterly*
ShakS	*Shakespeare Studies* (Knoxville, TN)
ShakStud	*Shakespeare Studies* (Tokyo): Shakespeare Society of Japan
Shiron	*Shiron* (Tohoku U., Miyagi)
SLI	*Studies in the Literary Imagination*
SMART	*Studies in Medieval and Renaissance Teaching* (Central Missouri State U.)
SMCOP	*Sewanee Mediaeval Colloquium Occasional Papers*
SN	*Studia Neophilologica*
SoAQ	*South Atlantic Quarterly*
SoCB	*South Central Bulletin*
SocH	*Social History*
Socio	*Sociology: Review of New Books*
SocSR	*Sociology and Social Research*
Sophia	*Sophia: Studies in Western Civilization and the Cultural Interaction of East and West*
SoQ	*Southern Quarterly*
SoTh	*Southern Theatre*
SP	*Studies in Philology*
Spectator	
Specu	*Speculum: A Journal of Medieval Studies*
SSL	*Studies in Scottish Literature*
Statistical Methods	*in Linguistics* (Stockholm)
StudAC	*Studies in the Age of Chaucer*
StudCL	*Studies in Canadian Literature*
StudHum	*Studies in the Humanities*
StudIcon	*Studies in Iconography*
StudMedCul	*Studies in Medieval Culture*
Style	
The Sunday Times (London)	
SUS	*Susquehanna University Studies*
Sylvan	*Sylvan* (Tokyo)
T&C	*Technology and Culture*
TennSL	*Tennessee Studies in Literature*
TES	*Times Educational Supplement*
Text	*Text: Transactions of the Society for Textual Scholarship*
TFSB	*Tennessee Folklore Study Bulletin*
TheolT	*Theology Today*
TheoStud	*Theological Studies*

THES	Times Higher Education Supplement
ThJ	Theatre Journal (formerly Educational Theatre Journal)
ThN	Theatre Notebook
Thought	
ThRI	Theatre Research International
ThSur	Theatre Survey
The Times (London)	
TLS	Times Literary Supplement
Tréteaux	Tréteaux: Bulletin de la Société Internationale pour l'Etude du Théâtre Médiéval Section Française
Trivium	Trivium, Lampeter (Dyfed), St. David's University College, Wales
TxSLL	Texas Studies in Literature and Language
ULR	University of Leeds Review
The Upstart Crow (U. of Tennessee, Martin)	
USFLQ	The USF Language Quarterly (Tampa, Florida)
UTQ	University of Toronto Quarterly
Viator	
VQR	Virginia Quarterly Review
VV	Village Voice
Werk	
WF	Western Folklore
WHR	Western Humanities Review
WLB	Wilson Library Bulletin
WS	Women's Studies
YaleR	Yale Review
YES	Yearbook of English Studies
YWES	Year's Work in English Studies
ZAA	Zeitschrift für Anglistik und Amerikanistik
ZeitK	Zeitschrift für Kunstgeschichte

Editorial Abbreviations

c.	Circa
Co.	Company
col(s).	Column(s)
Comp.	Compiler, compiled
Diss.	Dissertation
Ed.	Edited, editor(s), edition
e.s.	Extra Series
facs.	Facsimile(s)
gen. ed(s).	General editor(s)
Inc.	Incorporated
ll.	lines
ms(s)	Manuscript(s)
n.d.	No date
no.	Number
n.p.	No place; no publisher
n.s.	New Series
p., pp.	Page(s)
pt(s).	Part(s)
rpt.	Reprinted
rev.	Revised; review(s)
ser.	Series
s.s.	Second series; Supplemental series
trans.	Translated, translator
U.	University
vol(s).	Volume(s)

Introduction

Carl Stratman completed the monumental job of compiling his
Bibliography of Medieval Drama in 1969 or 1970 (it was
published in 1972). Despite its many inaccuracies and
omissions and its lack of annotations, it has been the
single most useful source of information on the drama for
the past twenty years. Ian Lancashire's excellent yearly
bibliographies in the late '70s and early 80s were quite
useful, but they covered only a few years. A couple of
other bibliographical works have been done in the field, but
they lacked accuracy, scope, or annotation.
     The present bibliography will serve as a kind of
anniversary volume--appearing approximately 20 years after
Stratman's. It contains citations of works--editions and
collections of plays, and books and articles of criticism--
from Stratman's era which did not appear in his
bibliography, and as many items published since as I have
been able to learn of or acquire.
     No bibliography can be complete, not only because of
the finite nature of the compiler, but also because of the
seemingly infinite number of sources that he or she could
list. Further, the production of criticism and editions
continues, while the published bibliography is static. The
effort here, however, has been to be as thorough, wide-
ranging, and "complete" as was humanly possible, given the
constraints of personal life, employment, finances, and the
ills that flesh is heir to.
     Most of the entries here are to works published since
1969, but many predate this, since they were not in
Stratman's volumes. For instance, Margaret Dean-Smith's
"Folk-Play Origins of the English Masque" (entry # 430) was
published in 1954. This entry indicates that the subject
matter covered by this bibliography is quite broad. The
attempt has been to display not only primary and secondary
materials relating directly to the mystery, morality, and
miracle plays, but also tertiary works parallel to,
preceding, or in some way related to these plays. Hence, a
good number of entries pertain to the liturgical tropes, to
various folk plays and customs, or to related plays in other
cultures. I have entered below a good representation of
articles on music in the Middle Ages, trying to select items
that pertained in some way to the drama. There are dozens
of other pieces on medieval music which I rejected because
they seemed peripheral to the present focus.
     Further, the movement from medieval to renaissance
drama is nebulous territory, especially in the genre of
morality plays. The bibliography includes works on some of

the more prominent transitionary playwrights (Bale, Medwall, Rastell) and some of the plays most treated by scholars (e.g. *Hick Scorner*). Appendix B lists the plays and playwrights from this transitionary period.

I have not listed later editions of works which predate 1970 unless substantial new material has been added since Stratman's volumes were published.

Since Stratman's day there has been a burst of interest in the drama from new young scholars with truly new approaches. The two most vocal of these groups are the REED and EDAM researchers. The Records of Early English Drama series, headquartered at the University of Toronto and set into motion just over ten years ago, offers to scholars a rich resource in each of its volumes. Their editors spend countless hours poring over thousands of records of many kinds contemporary with the drama, looking for references to anything having to do with the plays. The aim is to reconstruct as clearly as possible from the dim past what the plays looked like, how they were performed, what the actors wore, what the staging was like, and so on. By seeing the plays in their actual physical setting, we can interpret and perform them more knowledgeably today. Appendix C lists the projected volumes in the REED series, to accompany the volumes already in print (for York, Chester, Coventry, Newcastle upon Tyne, Norwich, Cumberland/Westmorland/Gloucestershire, Devon).

Emerging from the Medieval Institute at Western Michigan University, the Early Drama, Art, and Music (EDAM) series offers another mine of information, drawn primarily from contemporary non-dramatic arts. The theory of this series is that all the artists of the time were influenced by the same religious and secular phenomena, and that the visual arts could well reveal a great deal of information about the drama, which itself was a visual and auditory art. Hence, the EDAM scholars consider paintings, stained glass, all kinds of carvings, music, sculpture, and the other plastic arts, looking for elements in these which will enlighten us about the drama. They not only observe the physical elements of these arts, they also discuss the iconographic, exegetical meanings that these elements impart to an audience.

Both of these approaches have been tremendously useful to scholars trying to answer the two basic questions about the drama: what did it look like? and what did it mean? Both approaches have spawned journals espousing their causes: *REEDN* and *EDAMN*. But the editors of these periodicals print essays and shorter pieces that do not necessarily focus on these two approaches, recognizing the many other questions contemporary critics are asking about the plays. For example, Who were the actors? were they amateur or professional? Who were the authors? Who was the audience? What influenced the playwrights? What later playwrights were influenced by these plays, and in what way?

The nearly 2,000 entries below address these and scores of
other problems facing critics.

It is worth noting here that the interest in medieval
English drama has grown so much in the last twenty years,
that such journals as *Research Opportunities in Renaissance
Drama (RORD)* have added a "Medieval Supplement" to most
issues, acknowledging the impact that the earlier drama had
on that of the renaissance.

A third scholarly approach worth mentioning here (not
necessarily exclusive of the other two) is that taken by
today's directors and actors. Their criticism is based on
their own experiences in trying to perform the plays. They
look at the dialogue, the vocabulary, the stage directions,
the manuscripts, and many other things to try to reconstruct
as honestly as possible an actual medieval production.
These critics have found that by *doing* they can uncover a
good deal about the plays that theoretical scholars can only
theorize about.

Because of the great interest in the *performance* of the
plays, I have included among the criticism a large number of
reviews of performances, most of which contain at their core
literary analysis of various kinds.

The expanding interest in the drama is reflected in the
great variety of Sources Cited (vi-xiii) publishing articles
about or criticism of works. Reviews or articles have
appeared, for example, in journals devoted to political and
social science, book collecting, religious studies,
anthropology, art, computers, economics, local histories,
music, sociology, folklore (even American folklore),
education, music, geography, popular culture, archaeology,
architecture, science, oriental culture, and even twentieth
century authors who were influenced by or writing in the
same genres as were the medieval playwrights.

In sum, these and other more traditional approaches
(linguistic, literary criticism, symbol analysis, and so on)
have gone a long way to make the plays more accessible to a
modern audience--and ultimately more enjoyable and didactic.
And it is appropriate that such an end should be in sight,
for the playwrights themselves strove for those same two
classical ends--to teach and delight.

. . .

In producing the following bibliography I have read and
rejected perhaps three to four hundred articles or books
whose titles were promising but whose texts were
inappropriate here. I have included a few items intended
for children, partly to warn scholars not to turn to these
if they want something more "elevated," and partly to appeal
to those who wish to present the drama to children.

A number of items beyond my reach wound up in the pages
below unannotated. Several I simply had to remove, thinking
I had found ghosts in the literature. One of my sources
cited an article in issue X of a Japanese journal for a

particular year. I searched through a full run of that
journal from its inception up through the date of my source,
but found nothing. I found citations at Harvard's Widener
Library for microfilm reels for "Three Religious dramas or
miracle plays in Cornish Verse," representing manuscripts at
the Bodleian and at the Library of Wales. These were of
such unobtainable materials that I rejected these from the
bibliography as well. Another item I found in one source
was cited as "Introduction: Historical Inquiry and Formal
Criticism"; this was purported to be the title of an essay
by Alan H. Nelson in the Jerome Taylor/Nelson collection of
essays *Medieval English Drama* (entry # 1573). But my own
paperbound and hardback copies of this book do not contain
anything matching this title, though the 27-page essay by
Jerome Taylor, "Critics, Mutations . . ." (entry # 1572) is
subtitled "An Introduction to the Essays that Follow."
    Two items cited in notes as being on medieval English
drama (by Mikiko Ishi ["Chusei Eikoku-geki Kenkyu no
Kiseki," *Eigo Seinen* 127 {1981}: 357-58]; and by Yoshio Arai
[*Igirisu Engeki to Eiga*. Tokyo: Shinjusha, 1982; 210 pp.
plus a film]) eluded my search for four years. In anger I
jettisoned them from the bibliography. And in the 1974 *MLA
Bibliography* I found under Middle English Drama entry number
1274 followed immediately by number 1276 (on p. 44).
Letters and a series of phone calls finally connected me
with Jerry Coniff, the new managing editor, who--after some
checking--assured me that there never was a 1275.
    In two cases (entries # 1267 and 1654) there are
citations to unpublished papers, included because the
subject matter is of great interest to scholars and I
thought it better to notify others of the papers' existence
than to let others duplicate someone else's work. And in
another instance only incomplete page proofs were available
to me (the Briscoe and Coldewey collection of essays--#
228); hence the styling "252 pp., + index."
    Journals or collections of essays generally will not
appear as separate entries in the bibliography; in a few
cases, however, those volumes were reviewed as collections
by themselves, so they merited individual entry (see, e.g.,
entries 144 and 409). And for dissertations and theses I
have provided no annotations since abstracts are usually
readily available.
    Many studies deemed just too peripheral were simply
excluded, though they might merit perusal. Ian Lancashire
lists a number of them in his fine bibliographies. Hence
the exclusion of Kay Staniland's "Clothing and Textiles at
the Court of Edward III 1342-1352" (*Collectanea Londiniensia
. . .*, 223-34; ed. by Joanna Bird, et al. London and
Middlesex Archaeological Society, 1978; Special Paper No.
2). Also, for the most part, this bibliography does not
include musical texts, recordings, films, or filmstrips.
For a useful bibliography through 1983 see Lorrayne Y.
Baird, et al., "Musical Texts . . ." (entry # 133).

For the most part, this bibliography covers printed sources. Entry 1736, however, is one of a few which cite video productions; this entry also contains a note on other videos from the same source. The Toronto series deserves such coverage because of its breadth and the scholarly quality of these productions. In fact, much of the published scholarship in the field emanates from the writers' experiences in creating these filmed performances. Other inferior video productions have generally been excluded from the bibliography. For example, two fifteen-minute filmstrips ("Mystery and Morality Plays" and "Elizabethan Drama Before Shakespeare"), put out by Films for the Humanities, offered no new scholarship. From the same source was a version of "The Second Shepards' Play" [sic--from their advertisement], a 52-minute movie. If they could not even spell the title correctly, they did not deserve inclusion here.

The annotations do not purport to be comprehensive summaries of the items' scholarship. In some instances, especially for some monographs, I have had to reduce the annotation to little more than a slightly expanded table of contents. No scholar should rely solely on a bibliography for her or his own work, and the annotations are intended to lead readers to appropriate sources, not to be substitutes for these sources. Hence the rather sketchy treatment of some books, which a serious scholar will read in full.

The practice here has been to follow the styling of each author or source in the display of play titles or spelling of names. E.g. where authors use italics or quotation marks for play titles, I follow each author's usage. Where J.J. Anderson hyphenates Newcastle-upon-Tyne in entry # 104 but not in entry # 102, his own styling is followed. The same is true for the presentation of numbers: where one volume designates chapters with roman numerals, another with arabic numerals, I have followed the author's style. Similarly, with play titles, the individual styling of, say, *Fulgens/Fulgence,* or *Lucres/Lucrece* will be kept.

My practice has been, as well, to standardize the presentation of titles of articles and books (except for foreign titles in which I adopt the practice of the original language). Many publishers omit capitalization, italics, or certain elements of punctuation. For the sake of consistency, the styling of titles is regularized here. The entries themselves follow *The Chicago Manual of Style* (13th ed., 1982) in their presentation.

For most of the monographs listed below I have striven to cite a sampling of reviews; naturally it has been impossible to be exhaustive here. Reviews are listed chronologically.

. . .

After teaching medieval drama for twenty years, I have found it remarkably entertaining to prepare this bibliography, a task that could have been deadly. But the subject matter of the essays and books, the diversity and beauty of the plays, and the richness of the medieval period have lightened the task for me. I hope that the product of my efforts lightens the task of others doing research in this rich and rewarding literature.

Sidney E. Berger
Worcester, Massachusetts
April 1989

Editions and Collections

1. Adams, Barry B., ed. *John Bale's* King Johan. San
       Marino, CA: Huntington Library, 1969. ix, 211 pp.

       Introduction covers text, date, sources,
       theatrics, verse, relation of the play to
       sixteenth century drama. Edited text with notes
       and appendixes.

2. Anderson, John, and A.C. Cawley. "Noah's Ark." (The
       Newcastle Play; facsimile). *REEDN* 1 (1977), 11-
       17.

       See under criticism, # 105 below.

3. Astington, John, ed. *Everyman.* Toronto: *Poculi Ludique
       Societas*, 1980. *PLS* Performance Text, No. 2. 105
       pp.

       Introduction discusses the play, the text,
       staging, acting, costume, music, stage history.
       Presents a modernized text with notes, variants,
       and bibliography. Appendixes discuss "This Rodde"
       of line 778, Extreme Unction, music used in the
       1979 *PLS* production, and information about actors
       in this performance. With illustrations.

4. Axton, Marie, ed. *Three Tudor Classical Interludes:
       Thersites, Jacke Jugeler, Horestes.* Cambridge:
       D.S. Brewer; Totowa, NJ: Rowman & Littlefield,
       1982. viii, 237 pp.

       Presents texts of the three plays with
       introduction, bibliography, note on editorial
       procedure, notes to the plays, and glossary. With
       some musical notation and appendixes: I,
       "*Thersites* by Ravisius Textor with parallel
       English translation" [*en face*] (139); II, "Music
       in *Horestes*" (a note; 156).

       Rev. Alasdair A. MacDonald. *EngStud* 66.2 (April
             1985): 162-66 (see entry # 1025 below).

5. Axton, Richard, ed. *Three Rastell Plays: "Four
       Elements," "Calisto and Melebea," "   Gentleness
       and Nobility."* Cambridge and Ipswich: D.S.
       Brewer; Totowa, NJ: Rowman & Littlefield, 1979.
       169 pp.

       Contains texts of the plays, introduction, brief
       bibliography, statement of editorial procedure,
       notes, and glossary.

Rev. *BBN* (Apr. 1980): 245.
   Choice 17 (July 1980): 675.
   David Bevington, *CompD* 15.2 (Summer 1981):
      176-78.

6. Baker, Donald C., and J.L. Murphy, eds. *The Digby
   Plays: Facsimiles of the Plays in Bodley MSS.
   Digby 133 and e Museo 160.* [Leeds]: The
   University of Leeds School of English, 1976.
   Leeds Texts and Monographs, *Medieval Drama
   Facsimiles 3.* Gen. eds. A.C. Cawley and Stanley
   Ellis. xix, 244 facsimile pages, 2 color plates.

   Introduction discusses the mss: description,
   history, people related to them, scribal
   practices. With notes and bibliography. The mss
   in facsimile are of "The Conversion of St. Paul,"
   "Mary Magdalen," "Candelmes Day and the Kyllyng of
   the Children of Israelle," and "Wisdom." [The
   first three and some of "Wisdom" are from Digby
   133; MS e Museo 160 contains "Christ's Burial" and
   "Christ's Resurrection."]

7. Baker, Donald C., John L. Murphy, and Louis B. Hall,
   Jr., eds. *The Late Medieval Religious Plays of
   Bodleian MSS Digby 133 and E Museo 160.* Oxford:
   EETS, Extra series 283. London: Oxford U. Press,
   1982. cix, 284 pp.

   Contains *The Conversion of St. Paul, Mary
   Magdalen, Killing of the Children, Wisdom,
   Christ's Burial,* and *Christ's Resurrection.* With
   introduction and with notes on each play,
   glossary, list of proper names, three plates of
   facsimiles of pages from the mss. Introduction
   covers physical descriptions of the mss and
   discussions of versification, language, sources,
   and staging for each play.

   Rev. Meg Twycross, *Engl* 32.144 (Autumn 1983):
      251-57.
   G.C. Britton, *N&Q,* n.s. 32.4 (230) (Dec.
      1985): 513-14.

8. Barnouw, Adriaan J[acob], trans. *The Mirror of
   Salvation: A Moral Play of Everyman, c. 1490.* The
   Hague: Nijhoff, 1971. Bibliotheca Neerlandica
   extra muros, 2. xvi, 46 pp.

   Translation of the Dutch *Elckerlijc,* with brief
   introduction. No notes, glossary, or commentary.

8a. Barron, Ray, comp. and trans. *Shepherds and Kings.*
   London: Radius, 1981. The Religious Drama Society

2

of Great Britain, Plays for the Eighties, 4.
Series eds. Sylvia Read and William Fry. 72 pp.

Contains a composite text, "made up of whole plays
and parts of plays from the four surviving English
Mystery Cycles; only the final stanza is invented"
(1). With brief introduction covering the text,
set, "suggested staging" (1), dialect, verse,
music, costumes, and casting, and with one drawing
of a possible stage configuration. No notes,
glossary, or commentary.

9. Beadle, Richard, ed. *The York Plays*. London and
    Baltimore: Edward Arnold, 1982. York Medieval
    Texts, second series. vi, 537 pp.

    Contains preface, bibliography, introduction, full
    cycle of plays, notes, appendix on music of play
    XVI (*Assumption of the Virgin*), appendix on
    "Summary of Versification" (475-76), and glossary.
    Introduction considers date, purpose, early and
    late history of the ms, description of the ms,
    development of the cycle, and mode of performance.
    (See Kinneavy, entry # 907 below.)

    Rev. *EDAMN 6.1 (Fall 1983),: 17-18.*
        Miriam Skey, *SEL*, English Number, (1986):
            79-85.
        Daniel F. Pigg, *StudAC* 9 (1987): 175-76.

10. ---, and Pamela M. King, eds. *York Mystery Plays: A
     Selection in Modern Spelling.* Oxford: Clarendon
     Press; New York: Oxford U. Press, 1984. 279 pp.

     Offers 22 plays in modernized spelling.
     Introduction discusses origin and history of the
     cycle. With headnotes before each play, running
     glossary, bibliography, and note on sources.
     Plays include: 1) Fall of the Angels; 2) Fall of
     Man; 3) Building of the Ark; 4) The Flood; 5)
     Moses and Pharaoh; 6) Joseph's Troubles about
     Mary; 7) Nativity; 8) Herod and the Magi; 9)
     Flight into Egypt; 10) Slaughter of the Innocents;
     11) Temptation; 12) Entry into Jerusalem; 13)
     Conspiracy; 14) Christ before Annas and Caiaphas;
     15) Christ before Pilate [1]: The Dream of
     Pilate's Wife; 16) Christ before Herod; 17) Christ
     before Pilate [2]: The Judgement; 18) Crucifixion;
     19) Death of Christ; 20) Harrowing of Hell; 21)
     Resurrection; 22) Last Judgement.

     Rev. Clifford Davidson, *Specu* 60 (1985): 1042.

Meg Twycross, *N&Q*, n.s. 33.3 (231) (Sept. 1986): 404-05.
Darryll Grantley, *StudAC* 8 (1986): 164-66.

11.   ---, and Peter Meredith, intro.; Richard Rastall, note on the music. *The York Play: A Facsimile of British Library MS Additional 35290, Together with a Facsimile of the* Ordo Paginarum *Section of the A/Y Memorandum Book.* [Leeds]: The University of Leeds School of English, 1983. Leeds Texts and Monographs, *Medieval Drama Facsimiles VII*, General eds. A.C. Cawley and Stanley Ellis. lxi, 551 facs. pages, 5 color plates.

Contains introduction, covering history of the ms; collation; state of the leaves; binding; catchwords; pricking and ruling; layout of the text; handwriting; Scribe C, John Clerke; abbreviation; correction; rubrication; punctuation and metrical indications; craft names--headings and running titles; initial letters at the beginnings of pageants, etc.; titles; *Jhc* monogram; stage directions; speakers' names; marginal alterations and additions; names and casual inscriptions; music. Gives full facsimile.

Rev. Clifford Davidson, *CompD* 18.2 (Summer 1984): 179-81.
SEL 62.2 (Dec. 1985): 343-48.

12.   Beamer, Linda, ed. "A Critical Edition of John Redford's Play, *Wyt and Science.*" Ph.D. diss., U. of Toronto, 1973.

13.   Bevington, David, ed. *The Macro Plays:* The Castle of Perseverance, Wisdom, Mankind, *A Facsimile Edition with Facing Transcriptions.* New York: Johnson Reprint Corp.; Washington, D.C.: The Folger Shakespeare Library, 1972. The Folger Facsimiles, Manuscript Series, vol. 1. xxvi, 305 pp.

Contains introduction, notes on the ms and on the edition, bibliography, facsimile of the three plays, and facing transcriptions. Introduction summarizes the importance of the plays with some remarks on dialect, focus of the plays, history of the plays, genre, staging, structure, characterizations, actors, etc.

14.   ---, ed. *Medieval Drama.* Boston: Houghton Mifflin, 1975. xxii, 1075 pp.

Contains introductions to each section (Liturgical Beginnings; Twelfth-Century Church Drama; The

Corpus Christi Cycle; Saints' Plays or Conversion
Plays; The Morality Play; Humanist Drama) as well
as to each play. Gives a note on the language of
the plays, textual notes, glosses at foot of page,
marginal glosses, and bibliography.

Presents the following texts and plays: 1)
"Concerning Tragedies" by Honorius of Autun; 2) "A
Palm Sunday Procession in Fourth-Century
Jerusalem" by The Lady Etheria; 3) "The Service
for the Consecration of a Church" by Bishop of
Metz; 4) "Adoration of the Cross" from the
Regularis Concordia; 5) "The Interment of the
Cross in the Sepulchre" from the *Regularis
Concordia*; 6) "The Raising of the Host from the
Sepulchre" from St. Gall; 7) Antiphons for Easter
Vespers; 8) Antiphons with Responses for the Vigil
of the Most Holy Easter; 9) Trope for Easter from
Limoges; 10) "Of the Resurrection of the Lord"
from St. Gall; 11) "The Visit to the Sepulchre"
from the *Regularis Concordia*; 12) "The Visit to
the Sepulchre" from Winchester; 13) "The Visit to
the Sepulchre" from Aquileia (?); 14) "The Visit
to the Sepulchre" from St. Lambrecht; 15) [The
Service] for Representing the Scene at The Lord's
Sepulchre from Fleury; 16) The Service [for
Representing] the Pilgrim, at Vespers of the
Second Holy Day of Easter [Easter Monday] from
Beauvais; 17) "For the Mass of Our Lord" from
Limoges; 18) The Service for Representing Herod
from Fleury; 19) [The Service for Representing]
the Slaughter of the Innocents from Fleury; 20)
The Service for Representing Adam; 21) "The Holy
Resurrection" 22) "The Play of Daniel" from
Beauvais; 23) "The Raising of Lazarus" of
Hilarius; 24) [The Service] for Representing the
Conversion of the Blessed Apostle Paul from
Fleury; 25) [The Service] for Representing How
Saint Nicholas Freed the Son of Getron from
Fleury; 26) The Christmas Play from
Benediktbeuern; and 27) The Passion Play from
Benediktbeuern.

Presents the following Corpus Christi and morality
plays: 1) The Banns (N Town); 2) The Creation and
the Fall of the Angels (Wakefield); 3) The Fall of
Man (York); 4) The Killing of Abel (Wakefield); 5)
Noah (Wakefield); 6) The Sacrifice of Isaac
(Brome); 7) Pharaoh (Wakefield); 8) The Ten
Commandments, Balaam and Balak, and the Prophets
(Chester); 9) The Annunciation (Wakefield); 10)
The Salutation of Elizabeth (Wakefield); 11) The
Birth of Jesus (York); 12) The Shepherds (York);
13) The Second Shepherds' Pageant (Wakefield); 14)

The Offering of the Magi (Wakefield); 15) The
Flight into Egypt (York); 16) Herod the Great
(Wakefield); 17) The Death of Herod (N Town); 18)
The Woman Taken in Adultery (N Town); 19) The
Raising of Lazarus (Wakefield); 20) The Passion
Play (N Town); 21) The Buffeting (Wakefield); 22)
The Scourging (Wakefield); 23) The Crucifixion of
Christ (York); 24) Christ's Death and Burial
(York); 25) The Harrowing of Hell (Wakefield); 26)
The Resurrection of the Lord (Wakefield); 27)
Christ Appears to the Disciples (Chester); 28) The
Last Judgment (Wakefield); 29) The Conversion of
St. Paul (Digby); 30) Mary Magdalene (Digby); 31)
The Play of the Sacrament (Croxton); 32) The
Castle of Perseverance; 33) Mankind; 34) Everyman.

Also offers Johan Johan (Heywood?); The Play of
the Weather (Heywood); and Wit and Science
(Redford).

15.   Blackstone, Mary A., ed.   *Robin Hood and the Friar.*
      Toronto: *Poculi Ludique Societas*, 1981.   PLS
      Performance Text: No. 3.   61 pp.

      Introduction discusses the text (from the earliest
      [1560] edition), English sources and the Robin
      Hood tradition, staging, acting, music, costumes,
      and Friar Tuck and Robin Hood in early drama.
      Presents the text of the play, with bibliography,
      notes, and appendixes (on May games, music and
      dance [by David Parry], stage fighting, and
      information on the *PLS* production).   With
      illustrations.

16.   Bowen, John.   *The Fall and Redemption of Mary,*
      Selected, Arranged and Rendered into Modern
      English from the Chester, Coventry, Lincoln,
      Norwich, Wakefield and York Mystery Plays.
      London: Faber, 1968.   112 pp.

      Contains a Modern English composite acting text
      for 12 players, with a brief introduction and no
      apparatus.

16a. Brock, Alice J., and David G. Byrd.   *The Digby Plays:*
      Rendered into Modern English.   Dallas: Paon Press,
      1973.   144 pp.

      Presents a Modern English version in prose, aimed
      at students.   Contains brief preface covering the
      Bodleian Digby MS. 133, which "consists of four
      complete late fifteenth-century plays and a
      fragment of a morality play [*Wisdom*], which is to
      be found complete in the Macro MS" (5).   Presents

6

modernized texts of "Herod's Killing of the
Children," "The Conversion of St. Paul," "Mary
Magdalene" (in two parts), "A Morality of Wisdom,
Who is Christ," and "Christ's Burial and
Resurrection" (in two parts). With no apparatus.

17. Brown, John Russell. *The Complete Plays of the
Wakefield Master. In a New Version for Reading
and Performance.* London: Heinemann, 1983. 140
pp.

Presents the six plays in a modernized version,
with introduction, glossary, and notes. Retains
the original meter and rhyme scheme. Refers to
the fourth play as "The Second Shepherds' Play
(with the adventures of Mak, the Sheep-Stealer)."
"Glossary and Notes" (pp. [138]-140) contains
primarily glossary; the few notes are only very
brief explanations of the vocabulary (i.e. they
are not textual notes).

Rev. *EDAMN* 6.2 (Spring 1984): 49.

18. ---, Jack Shepherd, and Tony Harrison. "Creation to
Nativity" and "Baptism to Judgment." Cottesloe
Theatre performances, 1980. Texts published by
Rex Collings Ltd., London, 1977. See entry for
Nicholas R. Jones, "Medieval Plays . . ." (entry #
864 below).

19. Cawley, A.C., and Martin Stevens, intro. *The Towneley
Cycle: A Facsimile of Huntington MS HM I.* San
Marino, California: The Huntington Library, 1976.
xix, 264 facsimile pages, 1 color plate.

Issued jointly by the Huntington Library and by
Leeds Studies in English, University of Leeds.
Same volume as Leeds Texts and Monographs
Medieval Drama Facsimiles II, Gen. eds
Cawley and Stanley Ellis.

Contains introduction with information on earlier
ownership, binding and pressmark, number and size
of leaves, number of lines per page, signatures,
lacunae, order of the plays, condition, titles,
initial letters at the beginning of plays, date of
text, stage directions, metrical indications,
speakers' names, speech-separating rules,
explicit, scribal errors and corrections, later
alterations, marginalia, names of crafts, persons,
and places, rubrication, the problem of the blank
leaf, and the problem of the distinctive
handwriting at the beginning of plays 23-29 and
12. Gives full facsimile with color frontispiece.

Rev. Richard Beadle, *TLS* (Feb. 25, 1977): 225.
G.C. Britton, *N&Q* 24 (Aug. 1977): 372-73.
Norman Davis, *RES*, n.s. 29.113 (Feb. 1978):
83-84.

20. ---, ---, eds. "The Towneley *Processus Talentorum:*
Text and Commentary." *LSE*, n.s. 17 (1986): 105-
30.

Offers an edition of the play with commentary.
Introduction discusses details from the play,
stanza forms, the ms, editorial problems. With a
facsimile of the opening leaf of the play. (See
A.C. Cawley, "The Towneley *Processus Talentorum:* A
Survey and Interpretation." *LSE*, n.s. 17 [1986]:
131-39, entry # 288 below).

xx. Chaundler, Thomas. *Liber Apologeticus* . . . .

See Doris Enright-Clark, ed. and trans. (# 35
below).

21. *The Chester Play of the Deluge.* London: Clover Hill
Editions, Rampant Lions Press, 1977. With a note
on the illustrations, the text, and the
performances by Douglas Cleverdon, and with ten
wood engravings by David Jones.

Contains an edition of the text, with glossary and
translation of the Latin stage directions.
Limited to 337 copies: 7 on vellum (lettered A-G);
80 on Barcham Green handmade paper (numbered I-
LXXX); 250 on Barcham Green mouldmade paper
(numbered 1-250).

22. Clark, James D., ed. *The Bugbears: A Modernized
Edition.* New York and London: Garland, 1979. ix,
271 pp.

Offers complete text with music. Introduction
covers the ms, the present text, date, authorship,
staging, prosody, sources. With appendixes
containing textual notes, a list of
reconstructions, historical collation, remnants of
leaf 61, and the ending planned by reviser 1.
With bibliography and index of glossed words.

23. Clarke, Annette C. *"The Castell of Perseverance."*
Ph.D. diss., U. of South Carolina, 1970.

Diplomatic edition of the play.

24. Coleman, Roger, ed. *John Rastell: "The Four Elements"
as Performed at the University Printing House,*

Cambridge, in the Summer of this year, Now Printed for Friends at Christmas. Cambridge: University Printing House, 1971. 79 pp.

Contains a modern text with introduction on style, sources, etc.

25. Conley, John, Guido deBaere, H.J.C. Schaap, and W.H. Toppen, trans. The Mirror of Everyman's Salvation: *A Prose Translation of the Original Everyman.* Amsterdam: Rodopi; Atlantic Highlands, NJ: Humanities Press, 1985. 110 pp.

Presents a literal translation of the Dutch *Elckerlijc* with parallel original. With brief (7-page) preface and a few notes.

Rev. Robert Potter, *CompD* 20.2 (Summer 1986): 177-80.

26. Cooper, Geoffrey, and Christopher Wortham, eds. *The Summoning of Everyman.* Nedlands: U. of Western Australia, 1980. 67 pp.; intro. ix-l; bibliog. li-lvi.

Introduction contains sections on "*Everyman* and Medieval Drama"; "The Plot . . ."; "Sources and Analogues"; "Religion in *Everyman*"; "Interpretative Approaches"; "Language, Style, and Versification"; "Staging"; "Stage History"; and "Early Texts . . . and Editorial Policy." With bibliography, notes, and appendix of textual variants. Text printed on rectos with glosses and notes on facing versos.

Rev. J.M. Maguin, *CahE* 20 (Oct. 1981): 145-46.

27. *The Corpus Christi Mass According to the Use of York.* Kalamazoo, Michigan: The Medieval Institute, Western Michigan University, 1976. 32 pp.

Contains brief introductory essay--pp. 5-10--by Clifford Davidson plus full text of the Latin mass with English translation.

28. Davies, R.T., ed. *The Corpus Christi Play of the English Middle Ages.* Totowa, NJ: Rowman and Littlefield; London: Faber, 1972. 458 pp.

Contains an edition of the Ludus Coventriae and five different Abraham and Isaac plays (Brome, Chester, Dublin, Towneley, and York). Omits from the cycle "the episodes of the Baptism and Temptation of Christ, the episode of Mary's

Assumption, and those episodes involving Mary
which are not found in the other cycles" (15).
Introduction (15-70) covers the audience,
performances of the play, the controversy over the
playing of the drama, the liturgical drama,
saints' plays, secular entertainment, the origin
of the Corpus Christi plays, the selection and
organization of the plays, variations in the
cycles, the cultural importance of the plays,
staging, props, scenery, costumes, the plays'
didactic function, scripts and mss, the changing
of the plays over the years, the provenance of the
Ludus Coventriae and the process and nature of its
composition, the language of the cycle and its
prosody, and the relationship among the Abraham
and Isaac plays. Gives footnote glosses, chart
comparing plays in the cycles, notes, and brief
bibliography.

29. Davis, Norman, ed. *Non-Cycle Plays and Fragments*.
     London: EETS, s.s. 1, 1970. cxxxii, 168 pp.

     Includes edited texts of Shrewsbury Fragments, the
     Norwich Grocers' Play, the Newcastle Play, the
     Northampton and the Brome Plays of Abraham, the
     Croxton *Play of the Sacrament, Pride of Life, Dux
     Moraud, The Cambridge Prologue,* the Rickinghall
     (Bury St. Edmunds) Fragment, The Durham Prologue,
     The Ashmole Fragment, and the Reynes Extracts,
     with introductions for each, along with an
     appendix on "The Music in the Shrewsbury
     Liturgical Plays," a glossary, Anglo-Norman
     glossary, and index of proper names. With three
     plates and musical notations of Shrewsbury music,
     edited by Frank Ll. Harrison.

     Rev. Donald C. Baker, *ELN* 9.4 (June 1972): 293-95.

30. ---, intro. and transcript of the Dialogues. *Non-Cycle
     Plays and The Winchester Dialogues: Facsimiles of
     Plays and Dramatic Fragments in Various
     Manuscripts and the Dialogues in Winchester
     College MS 33.* [Leeds]: The University of Leeds
     School of English, 1979. Leeds Texts and
     Monographs, *Medieval Drama Facsimiles V,* gen. eds.
     A.C. Cawley and Stanley Ellis. 208 pp. including
     114 in facsimile.

     Contains facsimiles of all the texts printed in
     Non-Cycle Plays and Fragments (item 29, above)
     except the Shrewsbury Fragments. Also contains
     facsimiles of the *Interludium de Clerico et Puella*
     and *Robin Hood and the Sheriff of Nottingham,* and
     (with transcripts) of *Lucidus and Dubius* and

Occupation and Idleness (both printed for the first time).

> Rev. David Bevington, *Specu* 46.4 (Oct. 1981): 733-36.
> G.C. Britton, *N&Q,* n.s. 29.3 (227) (June 1982): 241-43.

31. ---, ed. *Paston Letters and Papers of the Fifteenth Century.* 2 vols. Pt. I, Oxford: Clarendon Press, 1971; Pt. II, Oxford: Clarendon Press, 1976. lxxxvii, 671; xxxiii, 664 pp.

> Contains transcripts of 930 documents, with notes, introduction, chronological table, biographical summaries, table of authors and clerks, and index. Not on drama, but offers a great deal of information about the times. Chronological table helps relate the text of the letters to contemporary literary events (e.g. *Castle of Perseverance*, 1425; mss of York plays, 1440; etc.). Contains letter of Sir John Paston II to Sir John Paston III about W. Woode (I. 461-62), apparently an actor who was in John Paston II's employ "to pleye Seynt Jorge *and* Robynhod *and* the shryff off Notyngham . . ." (461).

> Rev. Pt.I. *RES*, n.s. 23 (1972): 468-70.
> Conrad Lindberg, *SN* 44.2 (1972): 438-39.
> Donald C. Baker, *ELN* 11.2 (Dec. 1973): 128-31.
> Pt. II. A.I. Doyle, *RES*, n.s. 29 (Nov. 1978): 472-73.

32. Davis, R.T., ed. *The Corpus Christi Play of the English Middle Ages.* Totowa, NJ: Rowman & Littlefield, 1972. 458 pp.

> Presents modern English versions of 1) a Corpus Christi play and 2) "texts of all the extant versions of one episode found in all the known cycles, that of Abraham and Isaac" (15). Introduction covers audience, aim of the playwrights, liturgical plays, etc. (pp. 15-70). With glosses, notes, bibliography, chart comparing the "Episodes before the Passion" (446-47) in the cycles.

32a. Denny, Neville, ed. *Medieval Interludes.* London: Ginn, 1972. 95 pp.

> Contains a brief introduction (5-8) explaining the *raison d'etre* of the collection: a group of plays performed at the Drama Department of Bristol

University "which sought to capture something of
the feeling of the popular, open-air theatre of
the late Middle Ages" (4). Discusses "Popular
street theatre of the fifteenth and early
sixteenth centuries" (5), the presentation of the
plays, the audience, staging methods, acting, and
so on. Offers modern English acting texts for
"The Pie and the Tart" (from the French), "The
Wandering Scholar" (German), "John John, Tyb and
Father John" (by John Heywood), "The Troublesome
Olives" (Spanish), and "The Blessed Apple Tree"
(Dutch). With no bibliography, notes, or index.

33. Donovan, Robert Barry, ed. "The MS. Digby 133 *Mary
Magdalene*: A Critical Edition." Ph.D. diss.,
Arizona State U., 1978.

34. Dutka, JoAnna. "The Fall of Man: *The Norwich Grocers'
Play*." *REEDN* 9.1 (1984): 1-11.

Facsimile of transcript by John Kirkpatrick. (See
entry # 491 below.)

35. Enright-Clark, Doris, ed. and trans. *Liber
Apologeticus de Omni Statu Humanae Naturae: A
Defence of Human Nature in Every State. (c. 1460)*.
A Moral Play by Thomas Chaundler. London and New
York: The Modern Humanities Research Center in
Conjunction with Renaissance Society of America,
1974. 208 pp.

This is the earliest extant English academic play
(c. 1460). Offers a critical examination and dual
language edition. Introduction discusses
Chaundler's life and times and his work, along
with many bibliographic details of the *Liber
Apologeticus* (date, genre, staging, theme,
sources, literary and dramatic qualities, ms,
illustrations . . .). With fifteen illustrations,
notes, bibliography. In Latin (with an English
translation *en face*), but related to the mystery
and morality plays in context, scope, genre, etc.

Rev. J.H.P. Pafford, *N&Q* 23 (Jan. 1976): 25-6.
B.B. Adams, *RenQ* 29 (Spring 1976): 126-28.
R.S. Sylvester, *MLR* 72 (Oct. 1977): 888-89.

36. *Facsimile of the [Chester] Shepherds' Play*. Leeds,
University of Leeds School of English, 1983.

37. Fattic, Grosvenor R., ed. "*Mankind:* An Edition of the
Fifteenth-Century Morality Play." Ph.D. diss.,
Michigan State U., 1973. 974pp.

12

38. Garbáty, Thomas J., ed. *Medieval English Literature.*
    Lexington, Mass.: D.C. Heath, 1984. 974 pp.

    Contains *Noah* and *Crucifixion* plays from York
    Cycle, the Wakefield *Second Shepherds' Play*, and
    Everyman; with brief introduction and footnote
    glosses.

39. Hallwas, John Edward, ed. "'The Shearmen and Taylors'
    Pageant': A Critical Edition." Ph.D. diss., U. of
    Florida, 1972.

40. Happé, Peter, ed. *The Complete Plays of John Bale.*
    Cambridge: D.S. Brewer, 1985. 2 vols. x, 167;
    xii, 193 pp.

    Vol. I contains introduction, *King Johan,* four
    appendixes [1) cancelled lines from the play, 2)
    autobiography from *Catalogus,* 3) discussion of
    sources, 4) Doubling Schemes], and glossary. Vol.
    II has *God's Promises, Johan Baptystes Preachynge,
    The Temtation of Our Lord,* and *Three Laws*--with
    notes and glossary.

    Rev. John Wasson, *CompD* 20.3 (Fall 1986): 283-85.

41. ---, ed. *English Mystery Plays: A Selection.*
    Harmondsworth: Penguin Books, 1975. 713 pp.

    Contains introduction (9-35), bibliography, notes,
    glossary, the Pre-Reformation Banns of the *Chester
    Cycle,* and 38 plays in updated orthography--with
    footnote glosses. The plays are 1) The Fall of
    Lucifer (Chester), 2) The Creation of Adam and Eve
    (Chester), 3) The Killing of Abel (Towneley), 4)
    Noah (Towneley), 5) Noah (Chester), 6) Abraham and
    Isaac (Chester), 7) Abraham and Isaac (Brome), 8)
    Moses (York), 9) Balaam, Balak and the Prophets
    (Chester), 10) The Parliament of Heaven, the
    Salutation and Conception (Ludus Coventriae), 11)
    Joseph (Ludus Coventriae), 12) The Nativity (Ludus
    Coventriae), 13) The First Shepherds' Play
    (Towneley), 14) The Second Shepherds' Play
    (Towneley), 15) Introduction to the Three Kings
    (York), 16) The Adoration (York), 17) The Flight
    into Egypt (Towneley), 18) The Purification, and
    Christ with the Doctors (Chester), 19) The Death
    of Herod (Ludus Coventriae), 20) The Shearmen and
    Tailors' Play (Coventry), 21) John the Baptist
    (York), 22) The Temptation of Christ, and the
    Woman Taken in Adultery (Chester), 23) Lazarus
    (Towneley), 24) The Council of the Jews (Ludus
    Coventriae), 25) The Last Supper (Ludus
    Coventriae), 26) The Betrayal (Ludus Coventriae),

27) The Buffeting (Towneley), 28) The Dream of
Pilate's Wife (York), 29) The Scourging
(Towneley), 30) The Crucifixion (York), 31) The
Death and Burial (York), 32) The Harrowing of Hell
(York), 33) The Resurrection (Towneley), 34)
Christ's Appearances to the Disciples (Ludus
Coventriae), 35) The Ascension (York), 36)
Pentacost (York), 37) The Assumption and
Consecration of the Virgin (York), 38) Judgment
Day (York).

42.   ---, ed. *Four Morality Plays.* Harmondsworth: Penguin
Books, 1979. 709 pp.

Contains *The Castle of Perseverance, Magnyfycence*
(by Skelton), *King Johan* (by Bale), and *Ane Satire
of the Thrie Estatis* (by Lindsay). With
introduction, "A Note on the Books" (67), notes,
and glossary. Also with two appendixes: 1)
"Doubling in *Magnyfycence* and *King Johan*" (677);
and 2) "Bale's Revision of 11. 1666-1803 in *King
Johan*" (684).

Rev. A.C. Cawley, *N&Q*, n.s. 28.2 (226) (Apr.
1981): 181.

43.   ---, ed. *Tudor Interludes.* Harmondsworth: Penguin
Books, 1972. 434 pp.

Contains texts of *Pride of Life; Mankind*; *Fulgens
and Lucres** (Medwall); *Youth; The Play of the
Wether* (Heywood); *Wit and Science* (Redford);
*Respublica** (Udall); *Apius and Virginia (R.B.);
Like Will to Like* (Fulwell); *Sir Thomas More**
(Munday). [Plays marked with an asterisk are
extracts only.] With introduction, editorial
note, a note on the books, notes on the plays, and
glossary.

xx.   Harrison, Frank Ll., ed. See edition of the Shrewsbury
music in Norman Davis, *Non-Cycle Plays and
Fragments* (entry # 29 above).

44.   Harrison, Tony. *The Mysteries.* London and Boston:
Faber and Faber, 1985. 229 pp.

A performance edition of three plays ("The
Nativity," "The Passion," and "Doomsday"), done
for the National Theatre production; the trilogy
was first performed in the Cottesloe Theatre,
January 19, 1985. Contains no introduction,
notes, or textual apparatus.

45. [---.] *The Passion: Selected from the 15th Century Cycle of York Mystery Plays, in a Version by the Company with Tony Harrison.* London: Rex Collings, 1978. 64 pp.

Contains a modernized version of the play first performed by the National Theatre Company, April 21, 1977. Contains a plan of the stage ([4]) and a list of scenes and songs ([5]).

46. Helm, Alex, ed. *Eight Mummers' Plays.* London: Ginn, 1971. 72 pp. With illustrations.

Contains texts of the Cheshire Souling Play "Alderley"; "Greens Norton"; "Chadlington"; "West Woodbay"; "Kirkby Lonsdale"; "Howick"; "Baronscourt"; and "The Four Champions of Christendom." Not on medieval English drama, but offers "persistent traditional ceremonies" ([5]).

Rev. *Drama* (Autumn 1972): 84.

47. Hill, Francis A., ed. "The Marian Pageants in the Towneley Cycle: A Critical Edition." Ph.D. diss., Southern Mississippi U., 1970.

48. Lancashire, Dauphin Ian, ed. "*Hycke Scorner:* A Critical Edition." Ph.D. diss., U. of Toronto, 1969.

49. Lancashire, Ian, ed. *Two Tudor Interludes: The Interlude of Youth, Hick Scorner.* Manchester: Manchester U. Press, The Johns Hopkins U. Press, 1980.

Contains editions of both plays, introduction, appendixes. Introduction deals with editorial principles, date, staging, auspices, authorship, sources. Appendixes on historical background of and Tudor allusions to *Hick Scorner*, source and analogue material; late revivals of *Youth*. With glossarial index to annotations.

Rev. *EDAMN* 3.2 (Apr. 1981): 12.
John Scott Colley, *CompD* 16.2 (Summer 1982): 193-96.
Paul Werstine, *M&RD* 1 (1984): 243-62, [esp. 255-62].

50. LaRosa, Frank E., ed. *A Critical Edition of John Heywood's A Play of Love.* New York and London: Garland, 1979. cxxxi, 163 pp.

Originally a thesis, U. of Illinois, 1968.

Contains textual and critical introductions, list
of emendations of accidentals, textual notes,
glossary, and bibliography. With facsimiles.

51. Lennam, Trevor N.S., ed. *The Marriage Between Wit and
      Wisdom*. Oxford: Printed for the Malone Society by
      Oxford U. Press, 1966 (1971). 59 pp.

      Contains a reprint of the play based on the unique
      ms (British Museum Additional MS. 26782).
      Introduction describes the ms, speculates that it
      may have been copied from a printed source,
      discusses the date (c. 1579), discusses the BM
      acquisition of the ms, gives information about the
      author (Francis Merbury), and considers sources
      and other editions. With four facsimiles of pages
      of the ms and with textual footnotes.

52. ---, ed. *The Play of the Weather, 1533*. Oxford:
      Printed for the Malone Society at Oxford U. Press,
      1971 (1977). Malone Society Reprints. x, 41 pp.

      Gives a brief introduction, facsimiles of selected
      pages of early printed editions, and full text of
      the 1533 edition.

53. ---, ed. *Sebastian Wescott, The Children of St. Paul's,
      and* The Marriage of Wit and Science. Toronto and
      Buffalo: U. of Toronto Press, 1975. xviii, 220
      pp.

      Contains much on the play (its composition,
      influence, date, staging, etc.), as well as
      comments on other plays covered in this
      bibliography (e.g. *Nature, Jack Juggler*, and many
      others). Contains full edition of the play, with
      explanatory notes, bibliography, and index. Looks
      at Wescott, director of the Children of St.
      Paul's, who produced many plays in the era,
      including this one.

      Rev. *MLR* 72 (Apr. 1977): 389.
          RES, n.s. 28 (May 1977): 206.

54. Lester, G.A., ed. *Three Late Medieval Morality Plays:
      Mankind, Everyman, Mundus et Infans*. London:
      Ernest Benn; New York: W.W. Norton, 1981. xliii,
      157 pp.

      Introduction contains sections on morality plays,
      authors, dates, sources and analogues, staging,
      and discussions about each play. Glosses and
      notes at the foot of pages.

Rev. A.C. Cawley, *N&Q*, n.s. 30.5 (228) (Oct. 1983): 450.

xx.   Lozar, Paula, trans. "The 'Prologue' to the Ordinances of the York Corpus Christi Guild." (See entry # 1011 below.)

55.   Lumianski, R.M., and David Mills, eds. *The Chester Mystery Cycle,* vol. I: Text. London: Oxford University Press, 1974. EETS, s.s. 3. xliv, 624 pp. [The designation "Vol. I: Text" is on the half title, not on the title page.]

Contains an edition of the full text of the cycle's 24 plays with appendixes of variant scenes from several plays. With introduction, textual notes, bibliography, and two plates (facsimiles of pages from two mss). Introduction covers the mss, the selection and treatment of a copy-text for the present edition, and the rationale for emendation and textual notes. [See entry # 1160 below.]

56.   ---, ---. *The Chester Mystery Cycle,* [vol. II]: Commentary and Glossary. London: Oxford University Press, 1986. EETS, s.s. 9. xx, 465 pp. [The designation "Vol. II: Commentary and Glossary" is on the half title, not on the title page.]

Contains the full apparatus for vol. I (see previous entry), including corrigenda to vol. I, short title index, bibliography, commentary (play by play--considering internal evidence relating to production, analogous material, explanatory notes), appendixes (relating to the appendixes in vol. I), a list of Latin errors, and an English glossary.

57.   ---, ---, Intro. *The Chester Mystery Cycle: A Facsimile of MS Bodley 175.* [Leeds]: The University of Leeds School of English, 1973. Leeds Texts and Monographs, *Medieval Drama Facsimiles I,* gen. ed. A.C. Cawley. xv, 352 facs. pp.

Contains introduction covering information on other mss containing Chester plays, description of the Bodley 175 ms, history of the ms, scribal practice, and bibliography. Gives full facsimile.

58.   ---, ---, Intro. *The Chester Mystery Cycle: A Reduced Facsimile of Huntington Library MS 2.* [Leeds]: The University of Leeds School of English, 1980. Leeds Texts and Monographs, *Medieval Drama*

Facsimiles VI, gen. eds. A.C. Cawley and Stanley Ellis. xvi, 300 facs. pp.

Contains introduction with information on contents, size of pages, binding, ownership, supposed disappearance of the ms, the nineteenth-century addition, the lost folios, the sixteenth-century folios. Gives full facsimile.

Rev. Lawrence M. Clopper, *CompD* 15.4 (Winter 1981-82): 384.
    Norman Davis, *N&Q*, n.s. 29.1 (227) (Feb. 1982): 68-69.
    Cecily Clark, *EngStud* 64.1 (Feb. 1983): 93.

59. McKinnell, John, ed. *The Chester* Moses, Balaak and Balaam. Lancaster: Medieval English Theatre, 1983. Medieval English Theatre Modern Spelling Texts No. 2. Gen. ed. Meg Twycross and Peter Meredith. 16 pp. [See note to Twycross, entry # 82 below.]

Contains brief introduction (2-3) covering the performance of the play and the guild which performed it, the history of the play's performance, the surviving versions, and the text presented here. Gives full modernized text with side notes and brief bibliography.

60. ---, ed. *Three Mary Plays from the York Cycle.* Lancaster: Medieval English Theatre, 1988. Medieval English Theatre Modern Spelling Texts No. 7. Gen. eds. Meg Twycross and Peter Meredith. 60 pp. [See note to Twycross, # 82 below.]

Contains brief introduction and full modernized, annotated text with side notes and bibliography. Introduction covers history, sources and conventions, staging, versification. With music for the Assumption play, and a later Coronation play fragment in an appendix.

61. Meredith, Peter, ed. *The Mary Play from the N. town Manuscript.* London and New York: Longman, 1987. 185 pp.

Contains introduction which discusses the cycle, the evidence that a Marian group was incorporated into an already extant group of plays, sources, analogues, style, language, meter. Presents an edition of the text, with notes, commentary, and glossary.

Rev. *Choice* 25 (Mar. 1988): 1094.
Stephen Spector, *CompD* 22.2 (Summer 1988):
192.
Stephen K. Wright, *EDAMN* 11.1 (Fall 1988): 9-
13.

62. ---, and Stanley J. Kahrl, Intro. *The N-Town Plays: A
Facsimile of British Library MS Cotton Vespasian D
VIII.* [Leeds]: The University of Leeds School of
English, 1977. Leeds Texts and Monographs,
Medieval Drama Facsimiles IV, gen. eds. A.C.
Cawley and Stanley Ellis. xxix, 450 facs. pp., 1
color plate.

Contains introduction covering numbering and size
of leaves, number of lines per page, binding,
contents, numbering and titling of plays,
handwriting and date, collation, watermarks,
physical condition of leaves, rubrication, stage
directions, speakers' names, metrical indications,
alterations and additions, and history. With full
facsimile.

63. Mills, David, Intro. *The Chester Mystery Cycle: A
Facsimile of British Library MS Harley 2124.*
[Leeds]: The University of Leeds School of
English, 1984. Leeds Texts and Monographs,
Medieval Drama Facsimiles VIII, gen. eds. Stanley
Ellis and Peter Meredith. xxii, 286 facs. pp.

Contains introduction presenting notes on binding,
covers, number and size of pages, contents, date,
scribes and production, format of ms, practices of
individual scribes, folio numbering and lacuna,
scribal errors and corrections, non-scribal
material, ownership and history of ms, and
significance of ms. Gives full facsimile;
contains a version of the 24 plays which make up
the Chester Cycle.

64. Moeslein, M.E., ed. *The Plays of Henry Medwall: A
Critical Edition.* New York and London: Garland,
1981. Renaissance Drama: A Collection of Critical
Editions. vi, 481 pp.

Revision of 1968 dissertation (U. of North
Carolina at Chapel Hill), with comments on
Medwall's life, sources, style, and fame.
Contains texts of *Fulgens and Lucres* and *Nature*,
with tables of emendations, histories of the
texts, lists of press variants, and commentaries
on each. Includes appendixes of Medwall's life
records, the text of the "Installation Banquet at
Ely" (468), and a note on the woodcut on the title

19

page of the original edition (c. 1495). With
illustrations.

Rev. *BBN* (Nov. 1980): 690.
CompD 15 (Summer 1981): 176.
Specu 57 (Oct. 1982): 918.
RES 34 (May 1983): 208.
MLR 78 (July 1983): 672.

65. Nelson, Alan H., ed. *The Plays of Henry Medwall*.
Cambridge and Woodbridge, Suffolk: D.S. Brewer;
Totowa, NJ: Rowman and Littlefield, 1980. Tudor
Interludes, vol. 2. General eds. Marie Axton and
Richard Axton. 237 pp.

Contains texts of *Fulgens and Lucres* and *Nature*,
with general editorial notes and editorial notes
for each play, and a glossary and bibliography.
Also with an appendix: "Medwall Life Records."
With illustrations.

Rev. Paula Neuss, *TLS* (Sept. 5, 1980): 973.
R. Morse, *BBN* (Nov. 1980): 690.
EDAMN 3.2 (Apr. 1981): 11-12.
David Bevington, *CompD* 15.2 (Summer 1981):
176-78.

66. Neuss, Paula, ed. and trans. *The Creacion of the
World: A Critical Edition and Translation*. New
York and London: Garland, 1983. 344 pp.

Gives full text and translation of this Cornish
play of 1611, written by William Jordan of
Wendron, Helston. Shows that the play was
performed in a plan-an-gwary staging.

Rev. EDAMN 6.1 (Fall 1983): 18-20.
Robert T. Meyer, *CompD* 18.1 (Spring 1984):
95-96.
Theresa Coletti, *ThSur* 25.2 (Nov. 1984): 253-
55.

67. ---, ed. *Magnificence*. Manchester: Manchester U.
Press; Baltimore: Johns Hopkins U. Press, 1980.
xvi, 229 pp.

Contains full edition of the text with notes,
glossarial index, and introduction. Introduction
discusses author (John Skelton), text, date,
satire, staging, language, productions, etc.

Rev. Norman Davis, *N&Q*, n.s. 28.5 (226) (Oct.
1981): 437-38.

John Scott Colley, *CompD* 16.2 (Summer 1982): 193-96.

68. Nosworthy, J.M., ed. *Lusty Juventus*. London: Printed for the Malone Society by Oxford U. Press, (1966) 1971. Malone Society Reprints. xxxi, [48] pp.

Contains a reprint of Abraham Vele's sixteenth-century printing (c. 1550-1566). [See item no. 6416 in Stratman.] Has a new introduction (v-xxxi), covering other editions, historical and textual matters, collations of other editions, dating of the play and of the printed editions, and bibliographical information. With a facsimile of Vele's edition and extracts from Copeland's edition.

69. *The Pardoner and the Friar, 1533; The Four Ps, ?1544*. Oxford: Malone Society, 1984. The Malone Society Reprints. xi, 16; xiv, 40 pp.

Reprints the texts with no apparatus. Essentially an unedited text.

Rev. Peter Meredith, *CompD* 21.4 (Winter 1987-88): 387-88.

69a. Parry, David Mackenzie. "*The Castle of Perseverance:* A Critical Edition." Ph.D. diss., U. of Toronto, 1983.

69b. ---, and Kathy Pearl, eds. *Nice Wanton*. Toronto: Poculi Ludique Societas, forthcoming. PLS Performance Text, No. 1.

xx. *The Passion*. London: Rex Collings Ltd., 1977.

See entries for 1) John Russell Brown, Jack Shepherd, and Tony Harrison (# 18 above); and 2) Nicholas R. Jones (# 864 below).

70. Peek, George S. "Four English Morality Plays: An Anthology for the Modern Reader." Ph.D. diss., Case Western Reserve U., 1972.

Includes *The Castle of Perseverance, Wisdom Who is Christ, Mankind*, and *Everyman*.

70a. Proudfoot, G.R., ed. "Five Dramatic Fragments." In *Collections, Volume IX*, 52-75. Oxford: Printed for the Malone Society by Oxford U. Press, 1971 (1977).

Contains the text of five fragments of plays, four
from the Folger Library, one from the Huntington,
dating c. 1550, 1620, 1630, 1580s to 1590s, and
1625.

71. ---, ed. *Johan Johan the Husband*. Oxford: Oxford U.
Press, 1967 (1972). Malone Society Reprints. ix,
[19] pp.

Presents a reprint of the play, supposedly by John
Heywood. Contains a brief introduction and
facsimiles of two of the pages of the Bodleian
Library copy of the first printing.

72. ---, ed. *The Pardoner and the Friar, 1533; The Four
Ps, ?1544*. Oxford: Oxford U. Press, 1984. Malone
Society Reprints. ix, [18]; vii, [46] pp.

Presents reprints of the two John Heywood plays.
With a brief introduction for each, and facsimiles
of some of the pages of the first two printings.

73. ---, ed. *A Play of Love, 1534*. Oxford: Oxford U.
Press, 1977 (1978). Malone Society Reprints.

Presents a reprint of John Heywood's play. With
brief introduction, a list of irregular and
doubtful readings, and facsimiles of title pages
and some text pages of early editions.

Rev. *RES* 31 (May 1980): 207.

74. Rastall, Richard, ed. *Six Songs from the York Mystery
Play "The Assumption of the Virgin."* North
Harton, Lustleigh, Newton Abbot, Devon, England:
Antico Edition, 1985. 8 pp.

Presents texts with score and musical notation.
With editorial note, a note on the performance,
Latin lyrics, translations, commentary, and notes.

75. ---, ed. *Two Coventry Carols for 3 Voices (S/ATB) with
Optional Instruments*. Newton Abbot, Devon: Antico
Edition, 1973. 5 pp.

A five-page pamphlet with three inserted
broadsides, presenting the text with musical
notation of songs "found in the play of the
Nativity and the Killing of the Innocents
performed by the Tailors and Shearmen of Coventry"
(i).

76. Robertson, D.W., ed. *The Literature of Medieval
England*. New York: McGraw-Hill, 1970.

See entry in criticism (entry # 1393 below).
Chapter 12, "Middle English Literature: Early
Drama in England," presents *Mactacio Abel, Secunda
Pastorum,* and *Everyman,* with brief introduction
(571-72) and glossary.

77. Schell, Edgar T., and J.D. Shuchter, eds. *English
Morality Plays and Moral Interludes.* New York:
Holt, Rinehart and Winston, 1969. 554 pp.

Contains introduction (v-xxv) defining the genre,
discussing the sequence of action in the plays;
considers the plays' humor and didactic elements
and their relation to sermon, the conditions of
the plays' performance, their theatricality, the
history of the genre, the genre's relation to
other, later plays, its characterization, and its
demise. Gives modernized texts of the following
plays (with brief headnotes for each: *The Castle
of Perseverance, Everyman, The Interlude of Youth,
The World and the Child (Mundus et Infans), Wit
and Science, Respublica, The Tide Tarrieth No Man,
Enough Is as Good as a Feast, All for Money,* and
The Conflict of Conscience. With side- and
footnotes and a bibliography.

xx. Shoukri, Doris Enright-Clark. See entry under Enright-
Clark (# 35 above).

78. Somerset, J.A.B., ed. *Four Tudor Interludes.* London:
U. of London, Athlone Press, 1974. 184 pp.

Offers texts of *Mankind, A Play of Love, Lusty
Juventus,* and *Like Will to Like.* With
introduction, bibliography, and notes.

Rev. *Choice* 12 (Apr. 1975): 224.
H.P. Pafford, *N&Q* 22 (June 1975): 271.

79. Stevens, Martin, and Margaret Dorrell, eds. "The *Ordo
Paginarium* [sic] Gathering of the York *A/Y
Memorandum Book." MP* 72 (1974): 45-59.

Contains a full transcription of the *Ordo,*
compiled in 1415 by Roger Burton, with "a list of
torches and a set of instructions for the order of
crafts in the Corpus Christi procession, the
proclamation of the play, a second list of
pageants, and . . . a second list of torches"
(45). Describes the ms and the gathering under
scrutiny, and discusses its importance to scholars
of drama.

79a.   Taylor, Betsy S. *Selections from the Castle of Perseverance*. Sydney: U. of Sydney, Drama Studies Unit, Department of English, 1977. Sydney English Texts 3. x, 185 pp.

Introduction offers background on the play, ms, date, dialect, critical history, stanza forms, music, staging, and with a note on the edited text. With bibliography, notes, glossary, and appendix discussing staging. Text with modernized orthography on rectos with facing glosses on versos.

80.   Tennenhouse, Leonard, ed. *The Tudor Interludes:* Nice Wanton *and* Impatient Poverty. New York: Garland, 1984. The Renaissance Imagination; Important Literary and Theatrical Texts from the Late Middle Ages through the Seventeenth Century, 10. Ed. by Stephen Orgel. ix, 217 pp.

Contains introduction (1-61) which deals with "the occasion for a typical Tudor interlude" (1); the historical context of the plays; a definition of the Tudor interlude; plot; performance and legal control of the plays; prodigal son plays; and the two plays in this volume with respect to many ideas, motifs, historical documents, etc. Presents texts, followed by Textual Notes and Historical Collation. Contains no glossary or index.

Rev. John Wasson, *CompD* 19.2 (Summer 1985): 183-84.

81.   Thomas, Helen Scarborough, ed. *An Enterlude Called Lusty Iuuentus. Liuely describyng the frailtie of youth: of nature, prone to vyce: by grace and good councell traynable to vertue.* By R. Wever. An old-spelling critical edition. New York and London: Garland, 1982. The Renaissance Imagination, vol. 2. lxvii, 89 pp.

Introduction covers texts and authors, dating, dramatic and literary qualities, dramatic context. With notes, glosses, and bibliography.

82.   Twycross, Meg, ed. *The Chester Antichrist.* Lancaster: Medieval English Theatre, 1983. Medieval English Theatre Modern Spelling Texts No. 4. Gen. eds. Meg Twycross and Peter Meredith. 24 pp. [N.B. The title pages of this and the following entries (along with entries # 58 and 59 above) say "Modern Spelling Texts"; the blurb inside the cover and on

the last leaf of each says "Modern-Spelling
Texts."]

Contains brief introduction (2-3) placing the play
in the tradition, mentioning its theatricality,
discussing its "Blasphemy, black magic, and
violence" (2), pointing out its ms survival, and
explaining the modernization which follows. Gives
full modernized text of the play with side notes
and brief bibliography.

83. ---, ed. *The Chester Noah's Flood*. Lancaster:
     Medieval English Theatre, 1983. Medieval English
     Theatre Modern Spelling Texts No. 3. Gen. eds.
     Meg Twycross and Peter Meredith. 13 pp.

     Contains brief introduction (2-3); discusses the
     play in the cycle, the possible means of
     performance, the stage properties and
     characterization, Noah's wife, the text of the
     script of the present edition, the stage
     directions, and the Harley ms which is the only
     one including the raven/dove episode. Gives full
     modernized text of the play with side notes and
     brief bibliography.

84. ---, ed. *The Chester Purification and Doctors*.
     Lancaster: Medieval English Theatre, 1983.
     Medieval English Theatre Modern Spelling Texts No.
     1. Gen. eds. Meg Twycross and Peter Meredith. 16
     pp.

     Contains introduction (2-4) covering the
     production of the play, the players and their
     compensation, costuming, the presentation in
     separate episodes, the language of the play, the
     biblical sources, the ceremony of Purification,
     the liturgy, and so on, along with the text of the
     script for the present edition. Gives full
     modernized text with side notes, along with
     musical notation for the *Nunc Dimittis*, and with
     brief bibliography.

85. ---, ed. *Virtuous and Godly Susanna*, by Thomas Garter.
     Lancaster: Medieval English Theatre,
     (forthcoming). Medieval English Theatre Modern
     Spelling Texts No. 5.

86. Wickham, Glynne, ed. *English Moral Interludes*.
     Totowa, NJ: Rowman and Littlefield; London: Dent,
     1976. xvi, 213 pp.

     Contains general introduction and texts of
     Mankind, Fulgens and Lucres (by Medwall), *The*

Conversion of Saint Paul, The Temptation of Our
Lord (by Bale), *Nice Wanton, The Marriage Between*
Wit and Wisdom (by Francis Merbury), *The Interlude*
of the Student and the Girl, Mumming at Hertford
(by Lydgate), and *Mumming at Bishopswood* (by
Lydgate), each with its own introduction.

Rev. R.T. Davies, *N&Q*, n.s. 23.5-6 (221) (May-June
        1976): 252-53.
    Choice 13 (June 1976): 516.
    Drama (Autumn 1976): 73.
    Charles Whitworth, *CahE* 17 (Apr. 1980): 109.

87.   Wilson, Edward, ed. "A Poem Presented to William
      Waynflete as Bishop of Winchester." In *Middle*
      English Studies Presented to Norman Davis in
      Honour of his Seventieth Birthday, 127-51. Ed. by
      Douglas Gray and E.G. Stanley. Oxford: Clarendon
      Press, 1983.

      Presents a critical edition of a quasi-mumming
      text of 1451.

Criticism

88. Abrahams, Roger D. "Folk Drama." In *Folklore and Folklife: An Introduction*, 351-62. Ed. by Richard M. Dorson. Chicago and London: The U. of Chicago Press, 1972.

    Presents a general overview, definition of "folk drama," the distinction from games, the assumption of masks, its public nature, various techniques and styles, mobile audiences, association with festivals, and so on.

89. "A.C. Cawley: Published Work." *LSE*, n.s. 12 (1981 for 1980 and 1981): 299-301.

    Lists about 48 works for which Cawley was wholly or partly responsible.

90. Adams, George R. "Comedy and Theology in the 'Second Shepherds' Play.'" In *Medieval Drama: A Collection of Festival Papers*, 63-68. Edited by William A. Selz (see entry # 1454 below).

    Examines the play "as a well-structured representative of the comic tradition and as a typical late medieval art work" (63). Shows how the "secular form" reveals the "religious theme" (63). Calls the play "a great comedy" (67).

91. Adams, Robert. "The Egregious Feasts of the Chester and Towneley Shepherds." *ChauR* 21.2 (1986): 96-107.

    Analyzes the origins and significance of the menus of the feasts in the *First Shepherds' Play* (Towneley cycle) and *De pastoribus* (Chester cycle). Points up the literal and symbolic levels of these feasts, and the unusual parallel elements in the two plays (needless clashes between shepherds "who are obsessed with sheep diseases and cures" [97], and who would rather eat than tend sheep . . .). Also notes the gluttonous attitudes of the shepherds, what they eat, their corrupt natures, etc.

92. Adams, Victor J. "When the Players Came to Poole." *The Dorset Year Book* (1978): 129-36.

    Discusses accounts from the town which mention the players of the Marquis of Dorset who performed in 1551 and the players of Lord Mountjoy and Leicester who played in 1569-1570. [The rest of

this item covers performances postdating the
middle ages.]

93. Adler, Thomas Peter. "The Concept of Providence in
Cain and Abel Plays: From the Chester 'Creation'
to Van Itallie's *The Serpent*." Ph.D. diss., U. of
Illinois, 1970.

94. Agha-Jaffar, Tamar Abdul Latif. "English Melodrama:
From the Beginnings to 1642." Ph.D. diss.,
Washington State U., 1981.

95. Aichele, Klaus Erwin. "Das Antichristdrama des
Mittelalters, der Reformation und
Gegenreformation." Ph.D. diss., Columbia U.,
1972. (Text in German.)

96. ---. *Das Antichristdrama des Mittelalaters, der
Reformation und Gegenreformation*. The Hague:
Nijhoff, 1974. 248 pp.

Considers the use of the Antichrist in plays from
1150 to 1650, with special emphasis on his social,
political, and exegetical use.

97. Alexander, Robert. "Corrections of Bath Dramatic
Records 1568-1620 in Printed Lists." *REEDN* 10.1
(1985): 2-7.

Gives "corrections of John Tucker Murray's list of
payments to players in Bath published in *English
Dramatic Companies 1558-1642* (London, 1910), 2,
200-5" (2). Corrects omissions,
mistranscriptions, and additions to the various
mss.

98. Ames, Ruth M. *The Fulfillment of the Scriptures:
Abraham, Moses, and Piers*. Evanston, IL:
Northwestern U. Press, 1970. 215 pp.

Focuses mostly on *Piers Plowman*, but contains many
references to English drama. Looks at the cycles
in general (39-40; 66-69) and at several
individual plays.

Rev. *Choice* 8 (July 1971): 662.
LJ 96 (Jan. 15, 1971): 193.

99. Anderson, Harry Sheldon. "The Vice: The Structure of
Evil in the English Morality Play." Ph.D. diss.,
Temple U., 1972.

99a. ---, and Leanore Lieblein. "Staging Symbolic Action in
      the Medieval Cycle Drama: The York Towneley [sic]
      Harrowing of Hell." *FCS* 13 (1988): 211-20.

100. Anderson, J.J. "The Durham Corpus Christi Play."
      REEDN 6.2 (1981): 1-3.

      Discusses the often overlooked Durham Corpus
      Christi procession. Mentions the guilds known to
      have participated (butchers, weavers, cordwainers,
      barbers, goldsmiths, plumbers, pewterers, potters,
      glaziers, and painters). Cites sources for
      primary information on these. Prints for the
      first time a transcription (of the weavers'
      ordinary of 1450) of the play.

101. ---. "The Newcastle Pageant 'Care.'" *MET* 1.2 (Dec.
      1979): 60-61.

      Discusses a pageant of the dyers, slaters, and
      fullers. Says that the pageant required a
      wheelless vehicle. Examines evidence for portable
      stages among the documents of the Fullers' and
      Dyers' Company and the Slaters' Company; concludes
      that the Newcastle "care" (i.e. portable stage)
      seems to have been carried, not pushed or pulled
      on wheels.

102. ---, ed. *Records of Early English Drama, Newcastle
      upon Tyne.* Toronto and Buffalo: U. of Toronto
      Press, 1982. 216 pp.

      Gives excerpts of various kinds from thirty mss
      and two printed books: account books, enrolment
      books, records of many guilds, books of acts, and
      so on. Records cover several drama-related
      topics: the performances of the Corpus Christi
      plays, processions, acting companies, financial
      data, dancing and music, baitings, etc. Describes
      Newcastle and its early drama, civic officers,
      guilds, cycle plays and procession, non-Corpus
      Christi festivals, musicians, players, and other
      entertainment, foods, royal visits. With notes,
      glossary, and index.

      Rev. *Choice* 20 (June 1983): 1456.
            Donna Smith Vinter, *CompD* 18.1(Spring 1984):
                  87-89.
            Richard C. Kohler, *ShakS* 18.1 (1986): 279-84.

103. Anderson, John. "John Skelton's *Magnificence.*" *MET*
      6.2 (Dec. 1984): 162-63.

Reports on performances at Edinburgh, August 13-23, 1984, by the Salford Players.

104. ---. "The Newcastle Dragon." *MET* 3.2 (Dec. 1981): 67-68.

Records several payments for dragons from the 1508-11 volume of the Chambarlains' accounts of Newcastle-upon-Tyne. Describes one of the dragons: "evidently a framework covered by painted canvas, held together by nails . . ." (68). Says the "costume" was probably worn by a man like a hobby horse.

105. ---, and A.C. Cawley. "The Newcastle Play of *Noah's Ark*." *REEDN* 2.1 (1977): 11-17.

Discusses the scant knowledge of the Newcastle Corpus Christi plays. Offers a facsimile of Henry Bourne's printing (1736) of the play, apparently performed by The Shipwrights Company.

106. Ando, Shinsuke. "More and the English Drama." In *Thomas More and His Age*, 277-88. Ed. by Akio Samada, Hideo Tamura, and P. Milword. Tokyo: Kenkyusha, 1978.

In Japanese with abstract in English. Discusses the drama of Medwall, Rastell, and Heywood, but focusing mostly on Medwall. Considers the transition from medieval religious plays to the secular plays of the early Tudor period. Points up the change in focus from eternal to temporal worlds. Hence, the main characters in *Fulgens and Lucres* are real people living in this secular world. Looks at the role of Rastell (Thomas More's brother-in-law) in the dissemination of the plays as producer, stage director, costume designer, etc. Sees the play, though somewhat dull, as a kind of propaganda for Rastell's interests as a humanist, and as a record of the philosophical and mental atmosphere and environment of the period. Also sees the roots of the drama in contemporary morals, not necessarily in the Bible. Comments on the dramatic nature of the writings of More, stemming from his contact with the playwrights of the period.

107. Anglo, Sydney. *Spectacle Pageantry, and Early Tudor Policy*. Oxford: Clarendon Press, 1969. viii, 375 pp.

Contains sections on "Court Festivals: Their Form and Purpose" (Chap. III, 98-123); and "The

Reformation and the Decline of Court Festivals"
(Chap. VII, 238-80). Offers much discussion on
pageants and disguisings. ". . . concerned with
. . . courtly and public spectacle--festivals,
disguisings, masks, plays, tournaments, and royal
entries . . ." (3). Not exclusively on English
works. With notes and index.

Rev. *Choice* 7 (April 1970): 283.
AHR 75 (Dec. 1970): 2045.
RES, n.s. 22 (Aug. 1971): 333.
EHR 86 (Oct. 1971): 837.

108. Anttila, Raimo. "Loanwords and Statistical Measures
of Style in the Towneley Plays." *Statistical
Methods in Linguistics* (Stockholm) 2 (1963): 73-
93.

Outlines investigation of words of foreign origin:
words with French, Scandinavian, Latin, Low
German, and Celtic influences. Investigates
"three clearly individual groups" of plays (73)--
the earliest stage (*Processus Prophetarum, Caesar
Augustus, Annunciation,* the *Salutation of
Elizabeth*); the two fragments (*Isaac and Jacob--*
"which may be the earliest English miracles"
[73]); and the six Wakefield Master plays.
Screens words for native or foreign origin.
Discusses the 974 foreign words (French = 682;
Scandinavian = 228; Latin = 50; Low German = 13;
Celtic = 1). Presents, compares, and plots the
frequency distributions. Looks at a "measure of
concentration" (83) of the loanwords. Considers
synonyms, the date of adoption of the romance
words. Concludes "that the vocabulary of the
plays should not be considered as a random sample
from the total language of the time . . ." (89),
and "that the results obtained through stylo-
statistical methods do not conflict with those of
philology in general" (90). Shows the use of data
in dating the plays.

109. Aoki, Nobuyoshi. "Love and Women in Some Interludes."
MFLAE 25 (Feb. 1974): 13-19.

In Japanese. Looks at Lucrece (especially in
Medwall's play) as one of the first English
dramatic heroines.

110. Arner, Robert D. "Hemingway's 'Miracle' Play: 'Today
is Friday' and the York Play of the Crucifixion."
Markham Review 4.1 (Oct. 1973): 8-11.

Shows that Hemingway may have used the York
Crucifixion play as a model for his "Today is
Friday." Discusses the language, metrics, and
plot of the play and shows parallels in
Hemingway's play. Acknowledges the speculative
and inconclusive nature of this investigation.

111.   Arnold, John Willis.   "Time and the Religious Drama:
        An Investigation into the Formal Dramatic
        Structure of Twelve Passion Plays of the Middle
        Ages." Ph.D. diss., Michigan State U., 1977.

111a.   Arnott, James Fullarton, and John Williamson Robinson.
        *English Theatrical Literature, 1559-1900. A
        Bibliography, Incorporating Robert W. Lowe's A
        Bibliographical Account of English Theatrical
        Literature, published in 1888.* London: Society
        for Theatrical Research, 1970. xxii, 486 pp.

        An update of Lowe's work. Lists works that
        comment on the theatre in one way or another (e.g.
        a 1559 note on interludes [20]; "An Acte for the
        punishment of vacabondes and for relief of the
        poor . . ." of 1572 proclaiming as vagabonds
        "Comon Players in Enterludes & Minstrels . . ."
        [20]). Has sections on "Government and Regulation
        of the Theatre," "The Morality of the Theatre,"
        "The Arts of the Theatre" (i.e. acting, costume,
        scenery and machines, etc.), "General History,"
        and so on.

111b.   Ashley, Kathleen M.   "An Anthropological Approach to
        the Cycle Drama: The Shepherds as Sacred Clowns."
        FCS 13 (1988): 123-36.

112.   ---. "Chester Cycle and Nominalist Thought." *JHI*
        40.3 (July-Sept. 1979): 477.

        Answers James R. Royse's "Nominalism and Divine
        Power in the Chester Cycle" (see entry # 1420
        below), which was a response to Ashley's "Divine
        Power in Chester Cycle and Late Medieval Thought"
        (see next entry). Shows that Royse's idea (that
        the playwrights of the cycle took their texts
        directly from the Bible) is not accurate:
        "Traditions of exegesis . . . were another example
        of a screen between the simple Bible verse and the
        medieval understanding of it" (477). Claims that
        her earlier study aimed at showing the wider
        historical, philosophical, and theological context
        of the cycle.

113.   ---. "Divine Power in Chester Cycle and Late Medieval
        Thought." *JHI* 39.3 (July-Sept. 1978): 387-404.

Aims to show how "the effect of overpowering
divinity" (388) in the cycle is achieved. Shows
how nominalism was prevalent in society and how
the conservatism of the cycle is explainable as "a
trait to be expected in the cycle which is closest
to the philosophical and theological
preoccupations of its day" (389). Studies the
vocabulary of power ("might," "majesty," "power,"
"potesty," "mastery"), the selection and
interpretation of events, "The theme of God's
omnipotence" (392), and contemporary influences in
philosophical doctrines. Claims that the cycle is
"a paean to an all-powerful God" (403). Calls for
more scholarship into *English* theology for more
elucidation.

See response by James R. Royse, "Nominalism and
Divine Power in the Chester Cycle," (entry # 1420
below). See also preceding entry.

114. Ashley, Kathleen M. "The Guiler Beguiled: Christ and
Satan as Theological Tricksters in Medieval
Religious Literature." *Crit* 24.2 (Spring 1982):
126-37.

Points out the importance of "distinguishing folk
from establishment culture" (126); uses this
distinction to explain the long popularity of the
Christ-and-Satan-as-tricksters tradition, and to
show why this tradition "has been patronized if
not disdained by modern scholars" (127). Examines
the trickster figure historically and in various
literary works. Looks at the cycle plays, with
special reference to *Secunda Pastorum* of the
Wakefield cycle (134-36).

115. Ashley, Kathleen May. "The Idea of Order in the
Towneley Cycle." Ph.D. diss., Duke U., 1973.

116. ---. "Report of the 1985 MLA Medieval Drama Session."
RORD 29 (1986-87): 73-75.

See the entries under Sheila Lindenbaum, "Informal
Minutes . . .," "Informal Report . . .," and
"Report . . ." (entries # 992-1000 below).

117. ---. "The Resurrection of Lazarus in the Late
Medieval English and French Cycle Drama." *PLL*
22.3 (Summer 1986): 227-44.

Considers the ministry plays, with special note of
the Lazarus play. Reviews scholarship. Mentions
the prefigurative nature of this play. Looks at
other possible functions of the play. Discusses

sources, the focus on bereavement and consolation, the different English versions, the wealth of dialogue it allows and "its variety of action and motif" (243), and the adaptations possible to each dramatist.

118.   ---.   "The Specter of Bernard's Noonday Demon in Medieval Drama." *ABR* 30.2 (June 1979): 205-21.

Compares the relatively humorous or foolish devil of most plays to the "noonday demon" (205) whose presence "lurks in the background of numerous scenes in the English cycle plays" (205). Examines the history of this demon. Shows Bernard of Clairvaux to be the most influential writer in the middle ages concerned with this devil. Shows its use in the Towneley "Annunciation," in other plays, and in other literature.

119.   ---.   "Titivillus and the Battle of Words in *Mankind.*" *AnM* 16 (1975): 128-50.

Examines the great popularity of Titivillus in the mid-fifteenth century and his thematic coherence in *Mankind* in which he counterpoints God. Explains how dialogue, action, and allusion "contribute to a central theme of words as vehicles of salvation or damnation" (129). Shows how the play creates "a convincing portrait of the human condition--the transitory state of misery, obscurity, and confusion with regard to spiritual matters" (150).

120.   ---.   [Untitled review.] *RORD* 20 (1977): 110-12.

Reviews a performance of The York Cycle at Toronto, 1-2 October 1977.

121.   ---.   "'Wyt' and 'Wysdam' in N-Town Cycle." *PQ* 58.2 (Spring 1979): 121-35.

Points out the difficulty of finding a pattern through all of the cycle plays since the plays "vary among and within themselves in scribal hand, meter, verse form, diction, tone, and supposed source" (121), and since the cycles were probably written by more than one author. Raises the issues of using modern criticism on medieval plays and of understanding individual plays only as part of cycles. Aims to examine the notion that the N-Town Cycle is "more learned than the other three cycles" (122). Claims that this view comes from the cycle's characterization, theme, and concern with learning. Claims also that the cycle's

Christology sets it apart, as does its emphasis on
wisdom and wit, money and reward. Supports the
idea of a "'learned' tone" (133).

122. Astington, John H. "Comment." *Records of Early
English Drama: Proceedings of the First Colloquium
. . .*, 93-97. Edited by JoAnna Dutka. Toronto:
REED, 1979. (See entry # 497 below.)

Comments on the papers of Peter Meredith ("'Item
for a grone . . .," entry # 1094 below) and
Reginald Ingram ("'Pleyng geire . . . .," entry #
790 below) with respect to the way to read
theatrical records in order to develop a sense of
English theatrical history.

122a. Aston, Margaret. "Iconoclasm in England: Official and
Clandestine." In *Iconoclasm vs. Art and Drama*,
47-91. Ed. by Davidson and Nichols (see entry #
410a below).

Discusses the "iconoclasm of the English
Reformation" (47) with respect to many arts and in
terms of the political climate of the age. Looks
at many kinds of "image-breaking" (62), including
that related to the drama (see esp. pp. 60 ff.,
76-77).

123. Axton, Marie, and Raymond Williams, eds. *English
Drama: Forms and Development; Essays in Honour of
Muriel Clara Bradbrook*. Cambridge: Cambridge U.
Press, 1977. 263 pp.

Contains only one essay appropriate to the present
bibliography: Richard Axton, "Folk Play in Tudor
Interludes" (# 126 below).

Rev. *Drama* (Winter 1977-78): 80.
Choice 15 (Mar. 1978): 68.
K. Muir, *TLS* (July 28, 1978): 858.
B. Ruddick, *CritQ* 20 (Summer 1978): 81-86.
Rolf Soellner, *CompD* 13.2 (Summer 1979): 168-
71.
MP 77 (May 1980): 453.
M. Draudt, *EngStud* 61 (Oct. 1980): 475-78.

124. Axton, Richard. "Church Drama and Popular Drama." In
Medieval Literature: The European Inheritance,
150-66. Vol. I, pt. 2 of *The New Pelican Guide to
English Literature*. Edited by Boris Ford.
Harmondsworth, Middlesex: Penguin, 1983.

Offers a brief overview, not focusing specifically on English drama, but giving background information.

125.   ---. *European Drama of the Early Middle Ages.*   N.p.: U. of Pittsburgh; London: Hutchinson, 1974.

Attempts to present a new synthesis of various traditions and shows the ubiquity and strength of folk drama. Considers the non-ecclesiastical drama, which has fewer documents than does the church drama. Aims to reconstruct the three traditions of secular drama (mimicry, combat, the dancing-game), each of which contained a distinct idea of the genre. Looks also at church drama, then discusses particular plays of the eleventh to thirteenth centuries. Concentrates on the earlier texts. Chap. 8 ("The Earliest English Drama") and Chap. 9 ("The Cycle Plays") are the only ones focusing directly on English plays. Chap. 8 tries to reconstruct the lost popular drama. Looks at the importance of sermons in helping to shape the drama. Discusses *Pride of Life.* Shows that the plays before the Corpus Christi cycles were "quite free of liturgical influence" (168)--and were clearly of a popular tradition. Chap 9 concentrates on the cycle plays' debt to liturgical drama, folk elements in the cycle plays, Chester plays and Midsummer Watch, and the shepherds' plays. The Epilogue (Chap. 10) deals with mystery and morality plays. With bibliography and index.

Rev. *TLS* (Nov. 1, 1974): 1232.
     Drama (Winter 1974): 82.
     E. Catherine Dunn, *CompD* 9.4 (Winter 1975-76): 365-67.
     Malcolm Brennan, *MAe* 45.1 (1976): 126-28.
     Choice 13 (March 1976): 61.
     VQR 52 (Spring 1976): 40.
     WHR 30 (Winter 1976): 76.
     E. Catherine Dunn, "Recent Medieval Theater Research . . ." (entry # 487 below).

126.   ---. "Folk Play in Tudor Interludes." In *English Drama: Forms and Development; Essays in Honour of Muriel Clara Bradbrook*, 1-23, 225-27. Edited by Marie Axton and Raymond Williams. Cambridge: Cambridge U. Press, 1977 (# 123 above).

Begins with a discussion of "The Historical Problems of Folk Play" (1); discusses the difficulty in defining "folk drama," then defines the term with respect to its features: disguise, boisterous activity, impersonation, dances, disruption of normal order, audience involvement, etc. Traces development of the form. Discusses pre-Reformation drama and its transformation in the interludes. Mentions how traditional themes or motifs are transformed for special occasions. Treats briefly some of the works of Rastell and Bale and some other plays.

127. ---. "Popular Modes in the Earliest Plays." In *Medieval Drama*, 12-39. Edited by Neville Denny. London: Edward Arnold; New York: Crane, Russak, 1973. (See entry # 442 below.)

Discusses popular elements in early English drama, including the actors' conventions and their relationship with the audience, costumes, song, mime, dance, the presentation of diabolic figures, elements of stagecraft, masks, audience participation, the use of expository prologue. Says that the cycle plays are not the end result of secularization, but are a reaction to miracle plays of worldly clerks and friars, acting before popular audiences.

128. Bacquet, Paul. "*Everyman* et l'orthodoxie catholique médiévale." *EtAng* 35.3 (July-Sept. 1982): 296-310.

Claims that Cooper and Wortham, in their edition of *Everyman*, are wrong in seeing a proto-protestantism in the play. Says that statements alluding to the availability of Heaven to all (54), to the need for good works (431-33; 625-32), and the value of Confession, as well as reference to Mary (597-600), refute the assertion. Shows also that the use of Extreme Unction (last anointing) and emphasis on a Good Death are Catholic phenomena. Additionally demonstrates that the importance of the priest and reference to the real presence in the Eucharist support Catholic doctrine. Lists the names and achievements of many Catholic thinkers of the middle ages.

129. Bailey, Terence. "Processions, Liturgical." In *Dictionary of the Middle Ages* 10: 130-33. Edited by Joseph R. Strayer (see entry # 1553 below).

Looks at classical sources, Christian adaptation, use "in times of public calamity" (131), use in the reception of dignitaries, and for other purposes.

130. Baird, Joseph L., and Lorrayne Y. Baird. "Fabliau
     Form and the Hegge Joseph's Return." *ChR* 8.2
     (Fall 1973): 159-69.

     Shows how Joseph is closer to the fabliau's *senex
     amans* than he is to a saint. States that all
     Joseph plays depict him as the "cuckolded," comic
     old man. Points out the relationship between the
     Hegge version of the play and French fabliaux.
     Compares these in terms of their overlapping
     elements: "the husband's unexpected return"
     (161), "the blinding of the husband" (162), "the
     stratagem" (163), and the "Apology and great joy"
     (164).

131. ---, and Amy Cassidy. "Humility and the Towneley
     Annunciation." *PQ* 52.2 (Apr. 1973): 301-06.

     Claims that the theme of the play is humility,
     both for Mary and for Joseph, who "represents a
     strikingly new treatment of inherited material"
     (301), because the traditional Joseph "is
     irascible, harsh, wrong-headed" (301). Says that
     the Towneley Joseph is the most sympathetic of the
     medieval dramatic Josephs. Concludes by
     asserting, "The Towneley *Annunciation* might almost
     indeed be called a dramatic sermon on the proper
     uses of humility" (306).

132. Baird, Lorrayne Y. "'Cockes face' and the Problem of
     poydrace in the Chester *Passion*." *CompD* 16.3
     (Fall 1982): 227-37.

     Tries to define "poydrace"--some kind of sexual
     insult. Argues for the lateness of the Huntington
     ms in that it contains fewer vulgarities than the
     other mss of the plays since it is unlikely that
     such "stereocoraceous effects and obscenities"
     (228) would be added "to a version originally free
     of them" (228). Examines the many meanings and
     usages of "cock"; explains its usage with
     reference to Christ. Reveals the "shocking
     suggestion of the phallic face common in medieval
     devil iconography" (233). Suggests that *poydrace*
     may be a corruption of *"pewter-arse"* (pewter being
     an inferior metal), *"powder-arse"* (with reference
     to the slang term for "powder puff" and "powder
     box"--female and male genetalia, respectively), or
     "pudor-arse" (related to *pudendum*).

133. ---, Alice Crosetto, and Mary Sandra, comps. Ed. by
     Jim Villani. *"Musical Texts, Recordings, Films
     and Filmstrips for Medieval Drama." SMART 10.1
     (Spring 1983): 3-8.*

Lists 119 audio and videotapes, filmstrips, texts
and musical scores, and recordings of a general
nature, on series and collections, on liturgical
drama, on mystery, miracle, and cycle plays, on
moralities, and on folk drama. Also, contains a
short list of publishers, producers, and
distributors.

134.   Baker, Donald C. "The Drama: Learning and
        Unlearning." In *Fifteenth Century Studies: Recent
        Essays,* 189-214. Ed. by Robert F. Yeager.
        Hamden, CT: Archon, 1984.

        Summarizes scholarship from E.K. Chambers (1903),
        Karl Young (1933), and Hardin Craig (1955) through
        contemporary criticism. Gives a brief survey,
        also, of the extant mss of the cycles and non-
        cycle plays and their productions.

135.   ---. "Is *Wisdom* a 'Professional' Play?" Paper
        delivered at the *Wisdom* Symposium, Trinity
        College, Hartford, CT, 14 Apr. 1984. Rpt. in *The*
        Wisdom *Symposium: Papers from the Trinity College
        Medieval Festival,* 67-68. Ed. by Milla Cozart
        Riggio. New York: AMS Press, 1986 (see entry #
        1390 below).

        Aims to define "popular" and "professional" in
        terms of moral drama, using *Wisdom* as his model.
        Says that the play is not "popular" in its
        learnedness. Intends to answer the play's
        negative critics (that it is boring, too full of
        Latin and aureate language, stagey, lacking in
        action . . .). Concludes discussing the criticism
        by saying that the play is quite intellectual--but
        shows this to be associated with its strength in
        the subtlety of its presentations. Claims "it is
        the dramatization of the ancient liturgical
        quarrel about the meaning of the Song of Songs"
        (79). Says that its other strengths are its
        powerful sense of morality and clear grappling
        with legal and ecclesiastical issues. Looks
        briefly at the play's origin, the ms, and the
        method of acting the play. Concludes that the
        author, the actors, and the place of performance
        are still a mystery.

136.   ---. "When is a Text a Play? Reflections upon What
        Certain Late Medieval Dramatic Texts Can Tell Us."
        In *Contexts for Early English Drama,* 20-40. Ed.
        by Marianne G. Briscoe and John C. Coldewey. (See
        # 228 below.)

Discusses "What the surviving texts tell us about the plays, their history of performance, the people who created and altered them." Draws upon his work (with Murphy and Hall) on the Bodleian mss Digby 133 and E Museo 160 (see entry # 7 above).

137. Bakere, Jane A. *The Cornish Ordinalia: A Critical Study*. Cardiff: U. of Wales Press, 1980. 191 pp. Revised from Ph.D. thesis done under the name Jane Earthy, U. of Exeter School of English, 1968.

Surveys history and criticism. Chap. I--"The Ordinalia and Ordinalia Studies"--describes the trilogy, the ms (Bodley MS 791), the stage directions, vocabulary, editions and translations, scholarship, English influences. Chap. II discusses "The Historical and Topographical Setting." Chap III covers "Biblical and Liturgical Sources." Chap. IV examines "Apocryphal and Legendary Sources." Chap V is on "Theme and Structure"; calls the *Ordinalia* "a powerful and closely unified celebration of the Passion" (109). Shows the focus to be on the redemptive act of Calvary, the theme to be Redemption. Chap VI discusses the "plen-an-gwary" [sic] staging (151), which "emphasizes doctrinal and thematic significance" (151). Says, "the *Ordinalia* was performed in a circular amphitheatre 126 to 130 feet wide" (151). Claims there was a 7' to 8' high outer bank with steps on its inner slope for seats. Postscript speculates briefly on the playwright. With notes, bibliography, and index.

Rev. *TLS* (Aug. 1, 1980): 880.
BBN (Oct. 1980): 633.
Choice 18 (Mar. 1981): 942.
Specu 56 (Oct. 1981): 847.
EHR 98 (Apr. 1983): 409.

138. Ball, David Allen. "Selected Wakefield Master Plays: Verbal Clues to Non-Verbal Production Elements." Ph.D. diss., U. of Minnesota, 1970.

139. Barber, Joan. [Review.] *Daily Telegraph*, June 9, 1980.

Review of The York Cycle, performances of June 6-30, 1980, York Festival, at St. Mary's Abbey, York.

140. Barber, Vivian Ann Greene. "Medieval Drama and Romance: The Native Roots of Shakespearean

Tragicomedy." Ph.D. diss., U. of Texas at Austin,
1981.

141. Barish, Jonas. *The Antitheatrical Prejudice.*
Berkeley, Los Angeles, and London: U. of
California Press, 1981.

Chap III, "Antitheatrical Lollardy" (66-79),
covers medieval drama. Points out that
antitheatrical sentiment often accompanies a
flourishing theater: "The stage provokes the most
active and sustained hostility when it becomes a
vital force in the life of a community" (66).
Says this does not hold true in the middle ages;
"occasional reprimands . . . seem aimed mainly at
specific abuses" (66). Explains this, then looks
at the "chief surviving antitheatrical document
from the Middle Ages . . . *A tretise of miraclis
pleyinge*" (67). Summarizes and examines this
treatise at length. Claims that the treatise
refers to liturgical as well as to cycle drama.
Shows where it fails.

Rev. *LJ* 106 (Feb. 15, 1981): 453.
VV 26 (Sep. 9, 1981): 46.
Choice 19 (Oct. 1981): 249.
Nicholas Davis, *CompD* 15.4 (Winter 1981-82):
381-83.
PAJ 6.3 (1982): 119.
NewRep 186 (Jan. 27, 1982): 27.
NYRB 29 (Feb. 18, 1982): 35.
ThJ 34 (Mar. 1982): 130.
WHR 36 (Spring 1982): 85.
Enc 58 (May 1982): 70.
JAAC 41 (Fall 1982): 101.
Crit 24 (Winter 1982): 73.
RenQ 35 (Winter 1982): 669.
SevCN 40 (Winter 1982): 72.
MP 81 (Feb. 1984): 329.
CompL 36 (Summer 1984): 260.

142. Barker, Kathleen. *Bristol at Play: Five Centuries of
Live Entertainment.* Bradford-on-Avon, Wilts:
Moonraker Press, 1976.

Chap. 1 covers "Pageants and Players, 1461-1729."
Says there is no evidence for cycle plays in
Bristol, though there were "Seynt Kateryns" plays
(1), minstrels, and "bearers of the 'pageant'" (2)
in the sixteenth century, along with
entertainments at fairs: "jugglers, minstrels,
puppeteers, strolling players" (2), and private
theatrical companies connected to royal
households.

143. Barker, Kathleen M.D. "An Early Seventeenth Century
      Provincial Playhouse." *ThN* 29.2 (1975): 81-85.
      With a postscript by S[ybil] R[osenfeld].

      Discusses "a privately-owned playhouse in Wine
      Street . . . only the second 'working' indoor
      theatre known in the provinces" (81). Claims that
      this Bristol playhouse was erected between 1598
      and 1602. (See David Galloway's response, "The
      'Game Place' and 'House' at Great Yarmouth, 1493-
      1595"; no. 596 below. See also Pilkinton's
      response, # 1312.)

144. Barroll, J. Leeds, III, ed. *Medieval and Renaissance
      Drama in England*, I. New York: AMS Press, 1984.
      290 pp.

      Contains articles by John Wasson ("Professional
      Actors . . .," entry # 1653 below) and W.R.
      Streitberger ("Henry VIII's Entertainment . . .,"
      # 1554).

      Rev. Sandra Billington, *ThRI* 10.2 (Summer 1985):
          161-62.
          Michael E. Mooney, *CompD* 20.1 (Spring 1986):
          85-87.

145. Baugh, Albert C. "A Fifteenth-Century Dramatic
      Performance at the Inns of Court." *TennSL* 11
      (1966): 71-74.

      Documents a performance called a "disguising" of
      1490. Explains the term; shows that there were
      other Inner Temple dramatic performances, that
      they were related to the cycle plays, that they
      contained "elements of gentility and refinement"
      (74).

146. Beadle, Richard. "Dramatic Records of Mettingham
      College, Suffolk, 1403-1527." *ThN* 33.3 (1979):
      125-31.

      Quotes these records (126-128) from British
      Library Additional MSS 33985-33990, which are
      registers of accompt from the college. Reveals
      references to actors, frequent dramatic
      entertainment, and the use of puppets.

147. ---. "The East Anglian 'Game Place': A Possibility
      for Further Research." *REEDN* 3.1 (1978): 2-4.

      Looks at John Capgrave's *Solace of Pilgrimes* which
      distinguishes theaters from amphitheaters, the
      latter apparently a theater in the round. Cites

records of Yarmouth which mention game-places
which were also apparently round. Calls for
research to substantiate that such plays as *The
Play of the Sacrament, Mary Magdalene,* and the two
N-Town Passion plays (along with the *Castle of
Perseverance*) were also played in the round.

148.   ---.   "Entertainments at Hickling Priory, Norfolk,
        1510-1520." *REEDN* 5.2 (1980): 17-19.

        Recounts some dramatic records (notably Christmas
        ludi) from this northeast Norfolk priory, focusing
        on expenditures to players, minstrels, and other
        entertainers.

148a.   ---.   "The Medieval Drama of East Anglia: Studies in
        Dialect, Documentary Records and Stagecraft."
        Ph.D. diss., York U., United Kingdom, 1977.   2
        vols.

149.   ---.   "Mystery Plays." In *Dictionary of the Middle
        Ages,* vol. 8, 657-63. Ed. by Joseph R. Strayer
        (see entry # 1553 below).

        Discusses history, origins, scope, background,
        relation to the Corpus Christi feast, organization
        of the cycles, performance, and decline.   With
        bibliography.

150.   ---.   "The Origins of Abraham's Preamble in the York
        Play of *Abraham and Isaac.*" *YES* 11 (1981): 178-
        87.

        Reviews the scholarship which examines the
        relationship between some parallel passages in the
        *Middle English Metrical Paraphrase of the Old
        Testament* and parts of the York Cycle. Dates the
        Paraphrase to "some time between the middle and
        the end of the fourteenth century" (179).   Claims
        the York *Abraham and Isaac* could well have
        antedated the *Metrical Paraphrase*; but the
        evidence is inconclusive. Compares the two in
        terms of verbal parallels, their relationship to
        the Bible, and the Anglo-Norman verse paraphrase.
        Concludes that Herbert Kalén (who first edited
        part of the *Metrical Paraphrase,* 1923) is wrong in
        assuming that it borrowed from the York play; the
        author of the *Paraphrase* was working from a
        thirteenth-century Anglo-Norman metrical
        paraphrase of the Old Testament.   Says that the
        York playwright is the borrower.

151.   ---.   "Plays and Playing at Thetford and Nearby 1498-
        1540." *TN* 32.1 (1978): 4-11.

Quotes records of dramatic activity from Cambridge
University Library Additional MS 6969, a register
from the Cluniac Priory of St. Mary at Thetford.
Records payments to groups of players visiting the
monastery, payments in connection with parish
plays, and payments towards plays at villages in
nearby areas; some records show a "collaboration
between the house itself and the visiting players"
(8).

152.   ---.   "The Scribal Problem in the *Macro Manuscript*."
ELN 21.4 (June 1984): 1-13.

Explains the "problem": "whether or not the
scribe who copied the play *Wisdom* (fols. 98-121)
also copied the bulk of the play *Mankind* (fols.
122-32)" (1). Approaches the ms paleographically,
with respect to its "scribal milieu" (4) and date,
linguistically, and in terms of its possible
scribe (trying to identify Hyngham).

153.   ---.   "The Shipwrights' Craft." In *Aspects of Early
English Drama*, 50-61, 144-45. Ed. by Paula Neuss.
(See # 1213 below.)

Considers play 8 (Noah) from the York Cycle--how
the ark is "built" on stage, what the audience
saw, the ark's symbolism and craftsmanship, the
depiction of "God's redemptive scheme, and . . .
the guildsmen's skills" (50). Mentions the
"sacral significance" taken on by the Shipwrights'
craft "through its ancient role in the divine
order of things" (50). Points up the cycle's
unique separation of "The Building of the Ark"
from the Fishers' and Mariners' "Flood" play.
Briefly looks at the plain verse, "well-adapted to
its purpose" (52), and the carefully chosen
technical vocabulary--with special reference to
words concerning "work" and "make." Describes
"clinker-built" ships. Concludes by revealing the
playwright's pun on the word "craft" (skill,
trade; vessel) and its implications. With one
illustration.

154.   ---.   "The Textual Basis." In *A Concordance to* The
York Plays, xix-xxiii. By Gerald Byron Kinneavy.
(See entry # 907 below.)

Explains the textual basis for this concordance.

155.   ---.   "An Unnoticed Lacuna in the York Chandlers'
Pageant." In *So meny people longages and tonges:
Philological Essays in Scots and Mediaeval English
Presented to Angus McIntosh*, 229-35, 398. Ed. by

Michael Benskin and M.L. Samuels. Edinburgh: Michael Benskin and M.L. Samuels, 1981.

Discusses "a single leaf . . . deliberately removed or accidentally lost, [which] was originally interpolated between the extant sixth and seventh leaves" (229) of quire G--in the Adoration of the Shepherds play. Speculates on the lost matter, which seems to consist of an "appearance of an angel to sing 'Gloria in excelsis deo' etc." (232) and to converse with the shepherds. Says that possibly as many as sixty lines have been lost. Proposes a newly edited version.

156.   ---. "The York Hosiers' Play of *Moses and Pharaoh:* A Middle English Dramatist at Work." *Poetica* 19 (1984): 3-26.

Looks at some of the vernacular sources used by medieval playwrights, with special reference to the York *Moses* play, which contains much symbolism and typology. Examines the play's pace, characterization, spectacular elements (the burning bush, . . .), compression of time, thematic concerns, use of a source (the *Middle English Metrical Paraphrase of the Old Testament*), the play's staging, and the special effects.

157.   ---, and Peter Meredith. "Further External Evidence for Dating the York Register (BL Additional MS 35290)." *LSE,* n.s. 11 (1980 for 1979): 51-58.

Examines Rogerson's dating of the ms of the York Corpus Christi play (see entry # 1408 below). Uses data in the *Ordo Paginarum* in the A/Y Memorandum Book to suggest that the main compilation of the ms was done between 1463 and 1477.

158.   Beal, Peter, comp. *Index of Literary Manuscripts.* Vol. I, pts. I-II. London: Mansell; New York: Bowker, 1980. [Vol. I is in two parts, I and II.]

Lists mss from many authors, 1450-1625. Bale's dramatic works are numbered BaJ 31-2 (Vol. I, pt. I, p. 60: *King Johan* and *The Resurrection of Our Lord.*)

Rev. *BBN* (Jan. 1981): 14.
     TLS (Jan 23, 1981): 95.
     LJ 106 (Feb. 15, 1981): 439.
     ANQ 19 (May 1981): 161.
     LQ 51 (Oct. 1981): 437.

ARBA 13 (1982): 666.
C&RL 42 (July 1981): 351.
Lib 4 (Dec. 1982): 435.

158a. Beck, Ervin, Jr. "Prodigal Son Comedy: The Continuity of a Paradigm in English Drama, 1500-1642." Ph.D. diss., Indiana U., 1973.

Considers morality plays and the *Interlude of Youth*.

159. Beene, LynneDianne. "Language Patterns in *Mankind*." *USFLQ* 21.3-4 (Spring-Summer 1983): 25-29.

Claims that "the characters' speech patterns parallel the dramatic structure" (25). Comments on "the frequent references to language throughout the play" (25) which are thematic. Shows the two kinds of language—that of salvation and that of perdition. Looks at the rhythm (or lack of it) in the language of several characters.

159a. Bell, A. Robert. "The Harrowing of Hell: A Study of Its Reception and Artistic Interpretation in Early Mediaeval European Literature." Ph.D. diss., U. of Maryland, 1971.

160. Bellamy, John. *Robin Hood: An Historical Enquiry*. Bloomington, Indiana: Indiana U. Press, 1985. 150 pp.

Contains a general treatment. Does not concentrate on dramatizations, but offers background for a study of the character.

Rev. *TLS* (Feb. 22, 1985): 191.
TES (Mar. 8, 1985): 25.
NYRB 32 (May 8, 1985): 27.
Come-All-Ye 6 (Summer 1985): 4.
Choice 23 (Nov. 1985): 438.
Historian 49 (Nov. 1986): 89.

161. Belsey, Catherine. "The Stage Plan of *The Castle of Perseverance*." ThN 28.3 (1974): 124-32.

Recounts various views about staging, asserting that "the stage plan itself embodies the spiritual cosmos which the play presents" (124) and that "The stage . . . becomes an icon, an essential part of the allegory" (124). Discusses and challenges the views of Natalie Crohn Schmitt ("Was There a Medieval Theatre in the Round?"—see # 1447 below). Claims that "the circular stage . . . is an allegorical representation of the

world" (127). Examines allegory, symbolism,
action.

161a. Belton, Ellen Rothenberg. "The Figure of the Steward:
Some Aspects of Master-Servant Relations in
Elizabethan and Early Stuart Drama." Ph.D. diss.,
Columbia U., 1972.

Looks at morality plays.

162. Beltrán, Luis. "Los sentidos del caos: El 'Eya velar'
de Berceo y la Crucifixión de York." *RABM* 81.3
(July-Sept. 1978): 553-64.

Counters assertions by Leo Spitzer and others that
the structure of the Spanish poem "Eya velar"
(about the soldiers guarding Christ in the tomb)
is in disarray by comparing the "chaos" in the
order of its elements with that of the
conversation of the four soldiers in the
"Crucifixion" of York. Comments on the regular
metrical pattern of the York play, its orderly
alteration among the four speakers--each speaking
six times in the first four strophes (with a
seventh line added for the first soldier to close
the fourth strophe). Notes that between lines 101
and 265 (i.e. from the first blow of the hammer
nailing Christ to the cross to the completion of
the soldiers' work), chaos sets in: for thirteen
strophes (a number of evil omen and the same
number of strophes in the "Eya velar") there seems
to be no ordering principle to the soldiers'
exchange. Points out that as the order of
creation is reversed (the Son of God reduced from
Heaven to death and entombment), there is a period
of time, the crucifixion, in which Christ is
suspended between Heaven and earth. Claims that
during this period of crucifixion (vv. 81-88 ff.)
the soldiers again speak in order, 2-3-4-1,
nailing the right and left hands, the feet, and
holding the head. Both poems seem to follow the
same tradition, that of religious theater of
liturgical origin.

163. Benbow, R. Mark. "Dutton and Goffe versus Broughton:
A Disputed Contract for Plays in the 1570s."
REEDN 6.2 (1981): 3-9.

Recounts details of litigation against Rowland
Broughton and George Keavall concerning a breech
of contract: eighteen plays were to have been
composed, presumably by Broughton. Prints a
Modern English transcription of the bill. Claims
that the bill suggests "that a company sought a

playwright who was seemingly unconnected to the
theatre" (9). Points out that Broughton was to
pay 1/6 of the play's cost and receive 1/6 of its
profit. Sheds light on dramatic activity in the
1570s.

163a. Benedukt, Mathilde. *Bild und Bedeutung in der
englischen Tragödie zwischen 1550 und 1600*. Wien:
W. Baumüller, 1974. Studien zur Anglistik und
Amerikanistik. viii, 223 pp.

Primarily on Elizabethan drama, but with sections
on morality, with glances at the *Castle of
Perseverance* and at Medwall's *Nature* (62), on
pageantry (101-09), and on *Pride of Life* (183-
213). Also with a discussion of conventional
scenes and their origins (12-37). Discusses the
visual in the plays: Chap. II, "Bilder als
Material der Invention."

164. Bennett, J.A.W. *Poetry of the Passion: Studies in
Twelve Centuries of English Verse*. Oxford:
Clarendon Press, 1982.

Chap II, "The Meditative Movement," briefly treats
the Wakefield *Coliphizacio* (55). Gives much
background information, though not focusing
specifically on drama.

Rev. *RS* 18 (Dec. 1982): 547.
     Enc 61 (July 1983): 84.
     CSM 77 (Apr. 3, 1985): 23.

165. Bennett, Jacob. "The Language and the Home of the
'*Ludus Coventriae*.'" *Orb* 22.1 (1973): 43-63.

Claims that the language is probably the only way
one may ascertain the "home" of these plays. Says
the home is Norfolk, probably Norwich; "proves"
this by showing how the language there in
contemporary documents is the same as that in the
ms. Gives extensive analysis of phonology,
morphology, orthographic features. Concludes,
"Cotton Vespasian D. VIII, then, is from Norfolk"
(63)--most probably in the cathedral city of
Norwich.

166. ---. "The *Mary Magdalene* of Bishop's Lynn." *SP* 75.1
(Late Winter 1978): 1-9.

Shows that the language of the Digby play is from
Bishop's Lynn, a rich area of Norfolk; the
language proves a knowledge of the sea. Calls the
play "an original, well-structured, and unified

dramatic creation" (2). Shows the play's richness
in its elements: medieval religious lore, legends
of Mary Magdalene and Lazarus, a Passion story
with Herod and Pilate, etc. Mentions "the
playwright's constant striving for structural
unity" (8).

167. Bennett, Robert B. "Homiletic Design in the Towneley
Abraham." *MLS* 7.1 (Spring 1977): 5-15.

Summarizes recent scholarship on the "contextual
influences and formal principles that shape the
great English cycles" (5). Aims to demonstrate
the originality of the Towneley *Abraham.* Examines
the play in depth to reveal the play's original
features: realistic (not spiritual) characters, a
moral (not a doctrinal) theme, and the alteration
of the biblical account.

168. Bentzinger, Susan Elaine. "Comic Structure and
Perspective in Middle English Treatments of
Christ's Passion." Ph.D. diss., U. of Missouri,
Columbia, 1979.

169. Berger, Thomas L., and William C. Bradford, Jr. *An
Index of Characters in English Printed Drama to
the Restoration.* Englewood, Colorado: Microcard
Editions, 1975. 222 pp.

Contains an alphabetical list of characters'
names, nationalities, occupations, religious
preferences, and psychological states for c. 840
printed plays, beginning with Medwall's *Fulgens
and Lucrece.*

Rev. *LJ* 100 (Nov. 15, 1975): 2126.
RenQ 15 (Winter 1975): 169.
Choice 13 (Mar. 1976): 41.
Lib, 5th ser. 31 (Mar. 1976): 90.
Christopher Spencer, *CompD* 10.3 (Fall 1976):
270-72.

170. Bergeron, David M. "Actors in English Civic
Pageants." *RenP 1972*, 17-28. Ed. by Dennis G.
Donovan and A. Leigh Deneef. Durham, North
Carolina: Southeastern Renaissance Conference,
1973.

Aims "to bring together all the evidence we have
about who performed in the pageants of Tudor-
Stuart England" (17). Shows a high level of
professionalism overlooked thus far by other
scholars. Discusses guild and city records which
are sources for research.

171. ---. "The Bible in English Renaissance Civic
          Pageants." *CompD* 20.2 (Summer 1986): 160-70.

          Refers to Corpus Christi dramatic practices, the
          Corpus Christi festivities, other civic pageants,
          royal entries, Lord Mayor's Shows, and the
          biblical content of the Renaissance plays.

172. ---. "Civic Pageants and Historical Drama." *JMRS* 5.1
          (Spring 1975): 89-105.

          Shows that "the spirit of medieval cycle drama
          . . . survived . . . to inform Tudor-Stuart civic
          entertaiments" (89). Shows also how street
          entertainments, which presented historical themes
          and characters, were the offspring of the cycle
          plays. Claims there is "a broad area of common
          ground between medieval cycle drama, Elizabethan
          history plays, and . . . civic entertainments"
          (105).

173. ---. *English Civic Pageantry 1558-1642*. Columbia,
          South Carolina; London: Edward Arnold, 1971. 325
          pp.

          Very briefly traces the pageantry to medieval
          influences (see esp. pp. 7-8, 42, 44 . . .).

          Rev. *TLS* (Nov. 12, 1971): 1414.
               AB 49 (Mar. 27, 1972): 1180.
               George R. Kernodle, *ThN* 27.2 (Winter
                  1972-73): 78-79.
               History 58 (1973): 100.
               RES, n.s. 24 (May 1973): 205.
               EHR 88 (July 1973): 627.
               J.A. VanDorsten, *Neoph* 58.1 (Jan. 1974):
                  147-48.
               David L. Stevenson, *ELN* 13.1 (Sep. 1975):
                  52-54.

174. ---. "Medieval Drama and Tudor-Stuart Civic
          Pageantry." *JMRS* 2.2 (Fall 1972): 279-93.

          Looks at the continuity of English drama from the
          cycle plays to the early Renaissance street
          pageants. Sees continuity in "The involvement of
          the guilds and the community in the production of
          civic drama, certain aspects of stagecraft, and
          vestiges of the medieval mystery and morality
          traditions" (293). Considers such influences as
          the guild associated with the particular play,
          stagecraft, costume, iconography, and moral
          allegory.

175. ---. *Twentieth-Century Criticism of English Masques, Pageants and Civic Entertainments: 1558-1642.* San Antonio: Trinity U. Press, 1972.

   Contains 416 citations on General Works (# 1-31); Ben Johnson (32-100); Milton's *Comus* (102-245); other writers (246-416); and a supplement on the folk play and related forms (# s1-s103).

176. ---. "Urban Pastoralism in English Civic Pageants." In *The Elizabethan Theatre VIII: Papers Given at the Eighth International Conference on Elizabethan Theatre . . . University of Waterloo, Ontario, in July 1979*, 129-43. Ed. by G.R. Hibbard. Port Credit, Ontario: P.D. Meany, 1982.

   Generally discusses the urban links and sources of pastoralism. Briefly mentions the cycle plays (136).

177. Berkowitz, Gerald M. [Untitled review.] *ETJ* 29.1 (March 1977): 108.

   Reviews a performance of *The Second Shepherds' Play* at The Theatre of London, 1976.

178. ---. [Untitled review.] *RORD* 25 (1982): 149.

   Reviews performances of *Everyman*, August 25- September 4, 1982, at The Place, Edinburgh, by Dublin University Players.

179. ---. [Untitled review.] *RORD* 25 (1982): 148-49.

   Reviews performances of several plays, including *Mankind*, August 17-29, 1982, at Circuit Supertent, Edinburgh, by The Medieval Players.

180. Besserman, Lawrence L. "The Wakefield *Noah*, Lines 55-56." *PLL* 15.1 (Winter 1979): 82-84.

   Explains the difficult 56th line by offering a new etymology (and meanings) for "alod." Suggests meaning "freebold" which gives a "more poetically striking" (84) meaning than is suggested by Onions in the traditional reading of "wasted, dissipated."

181. Bettey, J.H. *Church & Community: The Parish Church in English Life.* Bradford-on-Avon, Wilts.: Moonraker Press; New York: Barnes and Noble, 1979.

   Offers much ecclesiastical and social background to the drama. Looks at plays in churches and churchyards; minstrel performances; Robin Hood, Hocktide, and May Day celebrations; secular and religious drama . . . .

Rev. *BBN* (Feb. 1980): 82.
　　Choice 17 (June 1980): 553.
　　CHR 68 (Jan. 1982): 70.

182. Bevington, David. "'Blake and wyght, fowll and fayer': Stage Picture in *Wisdom Who Is Christ.*" *CompD* 19.2 (Summer 1985): 136-50.

[Paper delivered at the *Wisdom* Symposium, Trinity College, Hartford, Connecticut, Apr. 13-14, 1984. Rpt. with slightly abbreviated title and one additional fn. in *The* Wisdom *Symposium: Papers from the Trinity College Medieval Festival*, 18-38. Ed. by Milla Cozart Riggio. New York: AMS Press, 1986. See entry # 1390 below.]

Mentions Walter Hilton's *Scale of Perfection* (before 1396) as a major source for *Wisdom*, especially for lines 103-170, in which Christ and Anima appear. Compares their oxymoronic language, their depictions of the soul, their stress on sensuality. Discusses the depiction of these two characters (Christ and Anima); claims that *Wisdom* gets "its theatrical form from the visualizing of metaphor, from the concretizing of homiletic and scriptural proposition" (137). Examines other sources/influences. Looks at "the metaphor . . . of inner purity and outward corruption" (149) which effects costuming and groupings of characters. Also looks at language, costume, characterization, staging, allegory, visual and verbal contrasts.

183. ---. "*Castles* in the Air: The Morality Plays." In *Medieval Drama* . . . . Edited by Eckehard Simon (forthcoming). (See entry # 1469 below.)

184. ---. "Discontinuity in Medieval Acting Traditions." In *The Elizabethan Theatre V: Papers Given at the Fifth International Conference on Elizabethan Theatre . . . University of Waterloo, Ontario, in July 1973*, 1-16. Ed. by G.R. Hibbard. Hamden, Connecticut: Archon, 1975. (See entry # 745 below.)

Reviews scholarship on the development of the drama. Examines the discontinuities between church and cycle drama and between cycle drama and morality drama, with a focus on the actors and their traditions. Summarizes other scholarship.

Discusses who the actors were, what their social
backgrounds were and their sources of income,
whether they were amateurs or professionals,
whether boys or women were among them, and how
staging and theme are effected.

185.   ---. "Drama Editing and Its Relation to Recent Trends
in Literary Criticism." In *Editing Early English
Drama* . . ., 17-32. Ed. by A.F. Johnson. New
York: AMF Press, 1987. (See # 828 below.)

Recounts the older critical approaches (especially
the evolutionary concept) fostered by Karl Young
and his followers and the follow-up study by O.B.
Hardison; also looks at the philological
approaches taken by editors and the use of
collections or anthologies of plays. Focuses on
the distortions a reader can perceive because of
the selection and arrangement of plays in an
anthology. Looks at several collections of plays,
including his own (*Medieval Drama*; see entry # 14
above). Concludes with some comments on stage
directions.

186.   ---, ed. Homo, Memento Finis: *The Iconography of
Just Judgment in Medieval Art and Drama.*
Kalamazoo: Medieval Institute Publications,
Western Michigan University, 1985. Early Drama,
Art and Music Monograph Series, 6. 219 pp.

Contains Essays by Ronald B. Herzman ("Let Us
. . .," # 741 below); Emmerson ("'Nowe Ys . . .,"
539 below); Sheingorn and Bevington ("Alle This
. . .," # 1466 below); Bevington ("'Man . . .," #
187 below); and Huston Diehl ("'To Put . . .," #
457 below). With preface and an introduction with
notes on medieval drama by the editor. Also
contains an Envoy by Bevington (209-212), 27
illustrations, and an index.

Rev. *Specu* 61 (Oct. 1986): 1025.

187.   ---. "'Man, Thinke on Thine Endinge Day': Stage
Pictures of Just Judgment in *The Castle of
Perseverance.*" In Bevington, Homo . . . (see
previous entry), 147-77.

Sees throughout the seemingly diverse elements of
the play the unifying function of the "emphasis on
judgment and on Last Things" (148). Considers the
play's imagery (especially that of the fall), and
its "spatial metaphors of salvation and damnation"
(172)--with respect also to the visual arts.

53

187a. ---. "The Nature of the Moral Play." Foreword to
        Everyman & Company . . . . Ed. by Donald Gilman.
        (See entry # 628a below.)

188. ---. "Popular and Courtly Traditions on the Early
        Tudor Stage." In *Medieval Drama*, 90-107. Ed. by
        Neville Denny. London: Edward Arnold, 1973. (See
        # 442 below.)

        Considers such things as the locus of the play's
        performances, the audiences, and the difference
        between popular and courtly traditions--showing
        how they were separate. Looks at the backgrounds
        of the actors and choristers, the relation of the
        Tudor plays to Medieval forms of drama, and the
        staging of the plays and positioning of the
        audience.

189. ---. [Untitled review.] *RORD* 20 (1977): 107-10.

        Reviews a performance of The York Cycle at
        Toronto, October 1-2, 1977.

190. Bezdek, Marice Cecile. "Medieval Literary Concepts of
        Tragedy and Comedy." Ph.D. diss., U. of
        Pennsylvania, 1973.

191. Billington, Sandra. "Routs and Reyes." *Folklore* 89.2
        (1978): 184-200.

        Looks at origins of the sixteenth-century Morris
        dance with respect to other dances of the same
        period and earlier. Discusses "dance and game"
        activities (185).

192. ---. "Sixteenth-Century Drama in St. John's College,
        Cambridge." *RES*, n.s. 29 (113) (Feb. 1978): 1-10.

        Uses a recently rediscovered account book and
        single loose-leaf folio to add to our knowledge
        about academic drama at St. John's. Recounts the
        important entries, which reveal costumes ("players
        apparrill"--3) and the plays they were made for.
        Speculates about the plays--probably those of
        Terence (*Adelphi, Phormio, The Eunuch*) and
        possibly *Mankind*.

193. ---. "'Suffer Fools Gladly': The Fool in Medieval
        England and the Play *Mankind*." In *The Fool and the
        Trickster: Studies in Honor of Enid Welsford*, 36-
        54, 125-33. Ed. by Paul V.A. Williams.
        Cambridge: D.S. Brewer; Totowa, N.J.: Rowman &
        Littlefield, 1979.

An essay in two parts. First part concentrates on the figure of the fool in Renaissance drama (36-46). Second part deals with folk game elements in *Mankind*, "authorial intention" (47), characterization, comic behavior and a grave subject matter, and the idea of *play*. Concludes with a comparison between French and English fool activity.

194. Billman, Carol. "Grotesque Humor in Medieval Biblical Comedy." *ABR* 31.4 (Dec. 1980): 406-17.

Looks not at the light humor of such characters as Mak and Gill or Noah's wife, but at the "grim humor" (407) in such plays as the "Slaughter of the Innocents" and the Passion dramas. Reviews scholarly explanations of this humor of "brutal violence" (406), which she compares to "modern 'dark comedy'" (408) and "black humor" (409). Points out that such comedy suggests "a cosmos out of control" (416) in modern drama, but in the middle ages it was "understood to be subsumed under a larger pattern of cosmological order" (416). Says that the aim of the bitter chaos was to persuade people to turn to "the wonderful Christian alternative to chaos" (416).

195. Bills, Bing Duane. "The Demise of the English Corpus Christi Cycle Play: A Re-Examination of Attitudes and Perceptions of the Tudor Age in the Sixteenth Century." Ph.D. diss., U. of Iowa, 1974.

196. ---. "The 'Suppression Theory' and the English Corpus Christi Play: A Re-Examination." *ThJ* 32 (1980): 157-68.

Agrees minimally with the prevailing idea that anti-Catholic sentiment in England led to the plays' demise, but says that that was only a subsidiary cause. Calls this view "problematical and oversimplified" (158). Finds an economic basis for the plays' disappearance, especially with respect to "municipal projects, craft poverty, loss of industry" (159). Says that these causes of the plays' demise are "unconnected with dramatic content or even with how the plays were perceived by the citizenry or those in power" (159).

197. Bjork, David A. "On the Dissemination of *Quem quaeritis* and the *Visitatio sepulchri* and the Chronology of Their Early Sources." *CompD* 14.1 (Spring 1980): 46-69. Rpt. in Davidson,

Gianakaris, and Stroupe, eds., *The Drama* . . ., 1-
24 (see # 409 below).

Discusses the trope-to-drama theory. Outlines the
scholarship. Examines the *Quem* with respect to
"how it corresponds to other chants in the Easter
liturgy" (49). Looks at its history, style, use,
dissemination, placement in the Mass. Looks also
at the relationship between the *Quem* and the
Visitatio. Traces their history and the
relationship between them and other chants in the
Easter liturgy. Argues for geographical, not
chronological, consideration of the *Quem*. Posits
a ninth-century origin.

198.   Blackburn, Ruth H. *Biblical Drama under the Tudors*.
        The Hague and Paris: Mouton, 1971. Studies in
        English Literature 65. An updating of her Ph.D.
        dissertation, "Tudor Biblical Drama," Columbia U.,
        1957.

        Aims to "discern the phases of development through
        which Biblical Drama passed" (7). Chap. I deals
        with "Backgrounds," including discussions of the
        mystery plays, morality plays and allied forms,
        and "The Reformers and the Drama" (23); in chapter
        II examines at length the work of John Bale.
        Contains other chapters which deal with post-
        medieval dramaturgy.

199.   Blackstone, Mary A. "Notes Towards a Patrons
        Calendar." *REEDN* 6.1 (1981): 1-11.

        Claims to be a beginning in assembling data on the
        movements of performers, the identity of their
        patrons, and analysis of the relationship between
        the two. Surveys such information in the
        currently available REED and Malone Society
        Collections volumes. Examines the many types of
        data published. Gives samples of patrons
        calendars.

200.   Blake, N.F. "The English Language in Medieval
        Literature." *SN* 48 (1976): 59-75.

        Discusses "the characteristic features of the
        English language in the medieval period" (59).
        Looks at "the absence of a standard language"
        (59), syntax, vocabulary, the literature of the
        period, verse and prose, alliteration and rhyme,
        etc. Looks briefly at Medwall's *Fulgens and
        Lucrece* (71). Not specifically on the drama, but
        offers suggestions on how to understand the

"relationship between literature and language" (75).

201. Blake, Norman. *The English Language in Medieval Literature.* London, Melbourne, and Toronto: Dent; Totowa, N.J.: Rowman and Littlefield, 1977.

    Gives a general treatment of language. Draws some examples from the plays. See previous entry.

    Rev. *TLS* (Jan. 20, 1978): 68.
        Choice 14 (Feb. 1978): 1642.
        TES (Feb. 10, 1978): 24.
        RES, n.s. 29 (Aug. 1978): 330.
        Specu 53 (Oct. 1978): 788.

202. Blanch, Robert J. "The Gifts of the Shepherds in *Prima Pastorum:* A Symbolic Interpretation." *Cithara* 13.2 (May 1974): 69-75.

    Gives a symbolic reading of the gifts showing that they are linked to "that rich repository of symbolic lore, the Epiphany" (69). Shows how these gifts are associated with those of the Magi. Also shows how the rustics parallel the Wise Men. Discusses the Mary tradition, and shows the spruce coffin to be associated with death, regeneration, and resurrection, as well as with "the divine majesty of Christ and the sweetness of a holy life" (70). Discusses also the significance of the ball: "the Creator's omnipotence, perfection, and eternal nature" (71); also symbolic of the world and "Christ's imperial dignity and sovereignty" (71). Says the "botell" or "gowrde" represents "fides baptismi" (72), salvation, Christ's Resurrection, Eucharistic wine, and Christ's sacrifice.

203. ---. "The Symbolic Gifts of the Shepherds in the *Secunda Pastorum.*" *TennSL* 17 (1972): 25-36.

    Claims that the shepherds' gifts reveal a symbolism "rooted in the lore of the Epiphany" (25) as expressed in Matthew ii.1-12. Sees parallels in music, art, patristic commentary, and English social customs.

204. Blau, Eleanor. [Review of performance.] *NYT* (29 Jan. 1982).

    Reviews performances of *Everyman*, January 29 to February 20, 1982, by Classical Theatre Ensemble at the Cathedral of St. John the Divine.

205. Blewitt, David W. "Records of Drama at Winchester and Eton, 1397-1576." *ThN* 38.2 (1984): 88-95.

Discusses drama performed in schools, recounting findings in school accounts. Studies Winchester's Bursarial Rolls and Hall Books and Eton's Audit Rolls and Books, focusing on entries which reveal dramatic activities. Shows the connection between the colleges and the town, the use of itinerant troupes, the benefit to the community. Points out that "dramatic entertainment was seasonal" (91), that "troupes carried drama into the provinces and that a local school might provide a performance venue for the whole community" (91). Looks at the troupes' remuneration and some of the plays they performed. Concludes by showing how "Drama and education allied in public affirmation of the mystery of the Incarnation" (94). Suggests that the college boys were not the players.

206. ---. "Records of Drama at Winchester and Eton, 1397-1576 (Continued)." *ThN* 38.3 (1984): 135-44.

Continuation of previous entry. Quotes Eton College records (135-40). Discusses payments, costumes, travelling troupes, the fact that the Eton boys were actors, and the plays they performed.

207. Bohringer, Kenneth C. "A Comparative Biographical Dictionary of Historical Characters in Ten Non-Shakespearean English History Plays of the Renaissance." Ph.D. diss., U. of Tennessee, 1973.

208. Bonfield, June Phelps McKenna. "The Penitence of the Medieval Magdalen: A Study in the Meanings of Her Appellation 'Penitent' as Reflected in Vernacular Literature of the British Isles c. 1250-c. 1500." Ph.D. diss., U. of Texas, Austin, 1969.

209. Boone, Blair W. "The Skill of Cain in the English Mystery Cycles." *CompD* 16.2 (Summer 1982): 112-29.

Points out--with respect to typological criticism --that "it is often . . . impossible to distinguish between necessary recapitulation of sacred history and conscious artistic manipulation" (112). Claims that a typological approach "teaches us more about the structure of the cycles than about the internal structure of particular plays within the cycles" (112). Looks at the Cain and Abel plays in the cycles, focusing on Cain's sin. Also observes the use and abuse of language which "Constitute(s) the theme of those plays" and "unites the structural ambivalence with the moral theme of the plays" (113). Shows how the word "skill" is a "key for a comparison of this structural and thematic unity" (113).

210. Bourgeault, Cynthia Warren. "The Jongleur Art: A Study in Medieval Role-Playing and Its Significance for the Cycle Drama." Ph.D. diss., U. of Pennsylvania, 1972.

211. ---. "Liturgical Dramaturgy." *CompD* 17.2 (Summer 1983): 124-40.

Contains useful observations, with emphasis on performance, though draws from French drama for examples.

211a. Bourgy, V[ictor]. *Le Buffon sur la Scène anglaise au XVIe siècle (c. 1495-1594).* Paris: O.C.D.L., 1969. Collection Synthèses. x, 544 pp.

Contains a lengthy discussion of the fool (jester, buffoon, . . .) on the English stage in the sixteenth century. Chap. I covers the types of fools in their diverse manifestations (classical types, the parasite, the rascally servant or page, the braggart soldier, the pedant; a discussion about the fool; English contemporary types: the hawker/peddler, artisans, executioner, murderer, representatives of the law, the parish priest, the shrew or vixen, the boor or lout; clowns) and the proliferation of these comic figures with respect to Vice.

Chap. II is on the repertoire of the fool, focusing on Vice and clowns; looks at the repertoire independent of types, chronologically considered with respect to the effects the figure has on stage, disguising, plays or games on the stage, etc.

Chap. III deals with the psychological picture of the buffoon: structure, rigidity, and fixations of the types; the awkwardness of the character's portrait (as rogue or simpleton, etc.), and the figure's language.

Chap. IV covers the dramatic and comic justification of the character's use and the place of the comic in the theater in its many manifestations. Speaks of comic juxtapositions and the clown's liberty and growth. Explains the

dramaturgy of the buffoon and the marginal status
of the comic in the morality.

Chap. V discusses the freedoms of the comic actors
with respect to scene, text, and improvisational
forms, and also discusses the nature and function
of improvisation. Adds to the discussion of the
origin of the figure, his common portraits and
typical predicaments.

Chap. VI is on the quality of laughter in the
character. Portrays Vice as Comedy, morality as
theater, the comic as amusement, the social and
literary face of the clown, and the moral face and
themes of the fool.

Draws upon a wide variety of English dramatic
sources (*Fulgens and Lucres, Respublica, Apius and
Virginia, The Castle of Perseverance, Everyman,
Nature, The Four Elements, Cambises, Horestes,
Hyckescorner, Lusty Juventus, Magnificence,
Mankind*, etc., etc.). With notes, bibliography,
and index.

212.   Bourquin, Guy. "The Dynamics of the Signans in the
        Spiritual Quest." In *The Medieval Mystical
        Tradition in England: Papers Read at Dartington
        Hall, July 1982*, 182-98. Ed. by Marion Glasscoe.
        Exeter: U. of Exeter, 1982.

        Explains the word *signans* in relation to *sign* and
        signatum. Shows the *sign* to be in relation to an
        agent, a referent, and a recipient. Briefly
        discusses this in terms of the cycle plays (esp.
        pp. 193 ff.).

213.   Bowers, R.H. "The Comic in Late Medieval Sensibility
        (*Piers Plowman* B.v.)." *ABR* 22.3 (Sept. 1971):
        353-63.

        Discusses the relationship of the sacred and the
        profane. Looks briefly at some Corpus Christi
        cycles which "abound in juxtapositions of clowning
        and adoration, of reverence and apparent
        blasphemy" (354). Mentions also "how a medieval
        audience attending a Corpus Christi performance at
        Chester responded to the impersonation of Noah's
        wife as a tipsy, raucous shrew . . ." (362), or to
        the depictions of Joseph and Mary.

214.   Braeger, Peter. "Typology as Contrast in the Middle
        English *Abraham and Isaac* Plays." *PIMA* 2 (1985):
        131-53.

Discusses which character is the central figure of
the play. Shows Abraham's centrality and looks at
"the typological relationship between Abraham and
God" (132). Looks at the typology of the Abraham
and Isaac plays. Concludes that there is a
figural contrast between Abraham and God and that
Abraham thus comes off as "a human, dynamic
character" (144).

215. Braet, Herman, Johan Nowé, and Gilbert Tournoy, eds.
      The Theatre in the Middle Ages. Leuven: Leuven U.
      Press, 1985. Medievalia Lovaniensia, Series I,
      Study XIII.

      Contains seventeen essays on the drama. Only that
      by Alexandra F. Johnston ("The York Corpus Christi
      Play . . .," see # 843 below) is on English drama.

      Rev. *Specu* 61 (July 1986): 727.
      Edelgard E. DuBruck, *FCS* 12 (1987): 227-32.

216. Brawer, Robert A. "The Characterization of Pilate in
      the York Cycle Play." *SP* 69.3 (July 1972): 289-
      303.

      Looks at the complex and seemingly contradictory
      characterization. Claims that a careful,
      systematic reading should produce a consistent
      vision of Pilate as being of the "good" tradition.
      Examines Pilate as the administrator of a pagan
      court. Says that he has a dual function, "as both
      the object of satire and the agent of satire
      directed against those whose worldly arguments
      against Christ rebound on them and reveal their
      folly" (296). Relates Pilate's actions to those
      of other secular rulers in the Corpus Christi
      plays. Shows how Pilate is a solid administrator
      and judge, hard of heart, exemplary of earthly
      kingship, and oblivious to divine law.

217. ---. "The Dramatic Function of the Ministry Group in
      the Towneley Cycle." *CompD* 4.3 (Fall 1970): 166-
      76.

      Looks at the plays of Christ's ministry and their
      varying order and number in the different cycles.
      Explains the dramatic function of these plays.
      Examines the similarity in selection and function
      in the Benediktbeuern Passion Play. Claims they
      are chosen and arranged for their "figural,
      prophetic, exemplary, and sequential" (174)
      elements, which "illuminate and advance the
      central conflict and its resolution in the cycle"
      (174).

218.   ---.   "Dramatic Technique in the Corpus Christi
            Creation and Fall." MLQ 32.4 (Dec. 1971): 347-64.

            Talks of the simplicity of the dramaturgy in the
            cycles, and "the figural interpretation of history
            as the primary principle of selection in the cycle
            plays" (348). Looks at how "diction, thought,
            character, and incident were used to make
            traditional narrative materials dramatically
            viable" (349). Shows how the simple language
            emphasized the typology. Urges that individual
            plays be analyzed not in isolation, but within the
            contexts of the whole cycle.

219.   ---.   "The Form and Function of the Prophetic
            Procession in the Middle English Cycle Play." AnM
            13 (1972): 88-124.

            Shows that the aim of the procession of prophets
            is "to expose future events . . . and, in one
            instance, to exhort the play's audience to repent"
            (88); most of the other plays in the cycle imitate
            events, and "create and develop characters who
            communicate with each other" (88), not just with
            the audience. Also points out that "each
            prophetic procession in some sense illustrates
            what is distinctive about each cycle's
            representation of salvation history" (88).
            Considers the narrative and the dramatic
            antecedents of prophetic materials in the cycles.
            Tries "to establish the origin and nature of the
            tradition" (88). Looks at each cycle's
            presentation of the prophets. Says that the
            Towneley version is the most dynamic presentation.

220.   ---.   "Medieval Theater-in-the-Round: Winchester,
            1974." RORD 17 (1974): 131-33.

            Reviews a performance of "the Hegge N-town cycle"
            [sic] (131) at the Bishop's Palace.

221.   ---.   "The Middle English Resurrection Play and its
            Dramatic Antecedents." In Studies in Medieval
            Drama in Honor of William L. Smolden on His 82nd
            Birthday, 77-100. Ed. by Clifford Davidson, et
            al. (see entry # 410 below).

            Looks at antecedents to and at Latin and
            vernacular plays. Assesses the function of the
            "resurrection play as a dramatic action" (78).
            Considers the different scales of action in
            vernacular and Latin performances (i.e. "how much
            is to be represented over what period of time"--
            79), and "the dramatic principle which gives form

and emotional power to the play" (79). Compares various versions.

222.   ---.   "St. Augustine's Two Cities as Medieval Dramatic Exempla." *Medi* 4 (1978): 225-44.

Examines the extent to which one ought to employ exegesis in interpreting cycle plays. Points up the similarity "between exegesis and religious drama" (225), both of which, like Augustine's *City of God*, "offer . . . a theological view of history, systematically presented" (225). Compares Augustine's work to exegesis and the play cycles. Analyzes the texts in terms of discord and accord. Looks specifically at the Towneley *Thomas of India* and *The Second Shepherds' Play* as well as the dramatization of Pilate and the Passion plays.

222a. Breitenberg, Mark.   "Reading Elizabethan Iconicity: *Gorboduc* and the Semiotics of Reform." *ELR* 18 (1988): 194-217.

223.   Brent, Harold Patrick.   "Authority and Heresy in the Towneley Cycle--Structure as Reflection of Theme." Ph.D. diss., U. of Wisconsin, Madison, 1973.

223a. Briscoe, Marianne G.   "Deserts of Desire: Reading Across the Midlands." *FCS* 13 (1988): 263-74.

224.   ---.   "Preaching and Medieval English Drama."   In *Contexts for Early English Drama*, 150-172.   Edited by Marianne G. Briscoe and John C. Coldewey (see entry # 228 below).

Looks at scholarship which reviews the relationship between preaching and dramaturgy. Mentions the extant weakness in the scholarship on medieval English preaching. Discusses the connections between the two genres with respect to matter, manner, and technique. Also considers auspices, authors, production. Cautions that the relationship between the two genres is often tenuous and is based on circumstanstial evidence. Calls for a wider study of the relationship between the two genres.

225.   Briscoe, Marianne Grier.   "The Relation of Medieval Preaching Manuals to the Medieval English Morality Plays."   Ph.D. diss., Catholic U. of America, 1975.

226.   ---.   "Resources at the Newberry Library."   *EDAMN* 2.1 (Nov. 1979): 2-3.

Lists and briefly discusses this library's holdings for the study of medieval drama.

227.   ---. "Some Clerical Notions of Dramatic Decorum in Late Medieval England." *CompD* 19.1 (Spring 1985): 1-13.

Considers the church's opposition to dramatic performances. Tries "to reconcile . . . anti-dramatic legislation and polemic" with the plays' "enthusiastic and frequent performance" (2). Warns that diatribes against certain kinds of public entertainment may not be against drama. Explains the church's prohibitions: "Church leaders were not outlawing all drama, merely particular plays or certain sorts of playing for clergy" (10). Follows V.A. Kolve in explaining "play" and "game." Examines Alexander Carpenter's preachers' aid, *Destructorium Viciovum*, and the sources of his views, and puts the prohibitions to dramatic performance into the proper context. Mentions "the rather genial overall view that prevailed" (10).

228.   ---, and John C. Coldewey, eds. *Contexts for Early English Drama*. Bloomington and Indianapolis: Indiana U. Press, 1989. 252 pp., + index.

Contains twelve essays on various aspects of the drama. Essays by 1) Alexandra F. Johnston ("What If . . ."; # 841 below); 2) Donald C. Baker ("When is . . ."; # 136 above); 3) Robert Potter ("The Unity . . ."; # 1328); 4) Lynette Muir ("Medieval English Drama . . ."; # 1176); 5) John C. Coldewey ("Some Economic . . ."; # 319); 6) Lawrence M. Clopper ("Lay and Clerical . . ."; # 303); 7) Alan H. Nelson ("Contexts . . ."; # 1194); 8) Marianne G. Briscoe ("Preaching . . ."; # 224); 9) Pamela Sheingorn ("The Visual . . ."; # 1465); 10) Richard Rastall ("Music in the Cycle Plays"; # 1363); 11) Stanley J. Kahrl ("Medieval Staging and Performance"; # 881); 12) John R. Elliott ("Medieval Acting"; # 525). With introduction. Each article has its own bibliography of works cited and suggested readings.

229.   Brittain, R.L. "A Catalogue of Comic and Satiric Scenes in English Drama--1375-1550." Ph.D. diss., Auburn U., 1970.

230.   Britton, G.C. "Language and Character in Some Late Medieval Plays." *E&S*, n.s. 33 (1980): 1-15.

Points up the distinction between "character
function" and "character portrayal" (2). Looks at
how language and character change or remain static
in *World and Child*; also looks at the Towneley
Pharaoh, the Chester *Annunciation and Nativity*,
Mankind, the Towneley *Noah*, *Salutation*, and *Second
Shepherds' Play*, and *The Castle of Perseverance*.
Concludes that the playwright of *World and Child*
was skillful in adapting language to a growing
character, and that character portrayal in the
play was moving away from medieval and toward
Elizabethan practices and ideas.

230a. Brockett, Clyde W. "Reconstructing an Ascension Drama
from Aural and Visual Art: A Methodological
Approach." *FCS* 13 (1988): 195-210.

231. Brockett, Oscar G. *History of the Theatre*. 4th ed.
Boston, London, Sydney, Toronto: Allyn and Bacon,
1982. x, 768 pp.

Has chapters on origins of the theater, Greek and
Roman drama, plays from the Byzantine Empire,
India, and elsewhere in the East, etc. Chap. 4
includes sections on liturgical drama and its
staging and the Feast of Fools. Chap. 5--"Theatre
and Drama in the Late Middle Ages" (118-52)--
examines plays throughout western Europe.
Presents the "church-to-secular-drama" theory and
the newer views of Kolve et al. Looks closely at
the development of the drama. Summarizes
scholarship. Discusses "Production Arrangements,"
"The Director," "Actors and Acting," "Costumes,"
"The Stages," "Scenery," "Special Effects,"
"Music," "Audiences and Auditoriums," "Secular
Dramatic Forms," "Farce," "The Morality Play,"
"Chambers of Rhetoric," "Interludes,"
"Tournaments, Mummings, and Disguisings" (144),
"Royal Entries and Street Pageants," and "The
Decline and Transformation of Medieval Drama."
Ignores the cycle plays except for a single
mention of them generically (120). With
illustrations, bibliography, and index.

232. Brockman, Bennett A. "Cain and Abel in the Chester
Creation: Narrative Tradition and Dramatic
Potential." *M&H*, n.s. 5 (1974): 169-82.

Looks at the play in terms of its genre as
tragedy. Comments on the appropriateness of the
structure of the story for tragic interpretation
and performance and the playwright's uniting of
"the basic human meaning of the plot with
doctrinal implications and emotional overtones"

(169). Claims that the Chester play "exposes more clearly than its counterparts [in other cycles] the essential dramatic quest of the cycle playwright" (169). Examines characterization, plot, structure, the play's movement, doctrine. Concludes that the play is "skillfully constructed and dramatically effective" (179).

233. Brockman, Bennett Albert. "Christian Tradition in a Critical Analysis of the English Medieval Plays of Cain." Ph.D. diss., Vanderbilt U., 1970.

234. ---. "Comic and Tragic Counterpoint in the Medieval Drama: The Wakefield *Mactacio Abel*." *MedS* 39 (1977): 331-49.

Says that the humor helps the play establish a deep "human and theological meaning" (331) and gives it "resonance, scope, and impact" (331). Shows the fusion of comic and somber "timebound and . . . timeless" elements (333-34). Offers a typological reading.

235. ---. "The Law of Man and the Peace of God: Judicial Process as Satiric Theme in the Wakefield *Mactacio Abel*." *Specu* 49.4 (Oct. 1974): 699-707.

Examines the play's seemingly purposeless foolery to show how it is satire about legal processes. Compares Cain's words to those in legal documents--a "royal letter patent of protection" (700) and a "royal letter patent of pardon" (701)--and to his references to sanctuary, documents and theological and judicial processes that would have been familiar to the audience.

236. Brodnax, Mary Margaret O'Bryan. "Medieval Analogues of *Paradise Lost*." Ph.D. diss., Texas Christian U., 1968.

237. Brody, Alan. *The English Mummers and Their Plays: Traces of Ancient Mystery*. London and Philadelphia: U. of Pennsylvania Press, 1970.

Examines many kinds of folk drama and offers several texts. "Attempt[s] to deal most explicitly with the possible relationship between myth, ritual, and the mummers' play" (viii). Aims to analyze the ties between English plays and classical analogues and to show that drama can emerge from ritual. Works by analogy to Greek drama and ritual. Surveys scholarship; discusses the action, players, stage and circle, costumes, acting style, the hero combat, the sword play, the wooing ceremony, and "Traces of Ancient Mystery" (117). Offers texts of several plays and other documents (e.g. An Account of the Mummers, 1793, p. 168). With notes, bibliography, and indexes.

Rev. *ANQ* 9 (Mar. 1971): 109.
   Booklist 67 (May 1, 1971): 719.
   TLS (Aug. 27, 1971): 1033.
   JAF 84 (Oct. 1971): 452.
   Choice 8 (Dec. 1971): 1338.
   J.H.P. Pafford, *N&Q* 19.4 (217) (Apr. 1972): 141-42.
   RES, n.s. 23 (Nov. 1972): 470.

238. ---. "Three Mumming Plays." *ELR* 3.1 (Winter 1973): 105-30.

Looks at the Wooing Ceremony in these late plays.

239. ---. "Traces of Ancient Mystery: The Form and Development of the Men's Dramatic Ceremonial in England." Ph.D. diss., Columbia U., 1968.

240. Brown, Arthur. "The Study of English Medieval Drama." In *Franciplegius: Medieval and Linguistic Studies in Honor of Francis Peabody Magoun, Jr.*, 265-73. Ed. by Jess B. Bessinger, Jr. and Robert P. Creed. New York: NYU Press, 1965.

Contains an overview of the problems facing students of the drama. Discusses what has been lost, the origin, religious content, and didactic purpose of the plays, their language, the available texts, the careless treatment of the surviving material.

240a. Brown, Cheri A. "The *Susanna* Drama and the German Reformation." In *Everyman & Company* . . . . Ed. by Donald Gilman. (See entry # 628a below.)

241. Browne, E. Martin. "The Medieval Play Revival." *ContempRev* 219 (Sept. 1971): 132-37.

Comments on the renewed interest in performances of the cycles, with special reference to the York plays. Claims that the plays "merit the same kind of serious study and imaginative treatment" (137) that we give to plays "from Shakespeare onwards" (137).

242. Brownstein, O.L. "The Saracen's Head, Islington: A Pre-Elizabethan Inn Playhouse." *ThN* 25.2 (Winter 1970/71): 68-72.

Calls for a "renewed investigation of the inn-
playhouses" (68) by showing that inns were sites
of dramatic performances in the sixteenth century.

242a. Brubaker, David. *Court and Commedia: Medieval and
Renaissance Theatre.* New York: Richards Rosen
Press, 1975. The Theatre Student Series.

243. Bryan, George B. *Ethelwold and Medieval Music-Drama
at Winchester: The Easter Play, Its Author, and
Its Milieu.* Berne, Frankfurt am Main, and Las
Vegas: Peter Lang, 1981. European University
Studies, ser. 30, vol. 10. 150 pp.

Looks at the original environment which produced
the tropes and the drama. Concludes that
Ethelwold, Bishop of Winchester, was the author of
the "Visitatio Sepulchri" of the "Regularis
Concordia," c. 950-970. Says Ethelwold drew from
secular theatrical conditions and adapted them to
liturgical requirements. Not on the English
drama, but offers background for its study. With
bibliography and index.

244. Bryan, George Barton. "The Monastic Community at
Winchester and the Origin of English Liturgical
Drama." Ph.D. diss., Indiana U., 1971.

245. Bucknell, Peter A. *Entertainment and Ritual, 600 to
1600.* London: Stainer and Bell, 1979.

Offers a history of the performing arts.
Introduction (11-18) gives historical context.
Chap 1, "In the Church: The Mysteries" (25-41),
covers the Christian contexts of drama. Chap. 2,
"In the Church: Play-making becomes Ambitious"
(61-72), discusses the rise of the drama, oriental
and western. Chap. 3, "In the Streets and the
Town Square: Commercial Theatre" (83-98), begins
with the old theory of the development of drama:
"Some time between 1200 and 1300 the plays left
the Church to be performed in the town square"
(83); covers the development of the mystery plays.
Says that "mystery" may serve for both mystery and
miracle plays. Treats the cycles superficially.
Chap. 4, "In the Schools, in the Home, and in the
Streets: Instruction Versus Entertainment" (115-
28), discusses professional actors, scholars,
morality plays, interludes. Chap. 5, "In the
Home: Courtly Pleasures and Pageantry" (147-58),
is on drama at court. Chap. 6, "In the
Countryside: Underground Theatre, Secret Worship,
and Dancing" (185-94), covers other kinds of
entertainment. [Intervening pages between

chapters are illustrations by the author.] A
fairly superficial treatment.

Rev. *Drama* (Jan. 1980): 71.
Choice 17 (May 1980): 384.

246. Bullock-Davies, Constance. *Menestrellorum Multitudo:
Minstrels at a Royal Feast.* Cardiff: U. of Wales
Press, 1978.

Examines documents which reveal much about
minstrelsy in England in the early fourteenth
century. Looks specifically at a Whitsunday (May
22) knighting of 1306 in honor of the knighting of
Edward of Carnarvon. Does not focus on the drama,
but does reveal data about medieval
entertainments.

Rev. *AJ* 59.102 (1979): 461.
Specu 54 (Apr. 1979): 349.
EHR 94 (July 1979): 625.

247. Burke, Peter. *Popular Culture in Early Modern Europe.*
New York: NYU Press, 1978. 365 pp.

Not specifically on English drama, but contains
many observations about earlier European culture,
with references to various kinds of public
entertainment, ritual, and recreations.

Rev. *Obs* (May 7, 1978): 34.
JPC 12 (Fall 1978): 372.
Socio 5 (Sept. 1978): 166.
TLS (Sept. 1, 1978): 968.
TES (Sept. 15, 1978): 25.
Choice 15 (Dec. 1978): 1354.
EHR 94 (Apr. 1979): 387.
JHI 40 (July 1979): 481.
AHR 84 (Oct. 1979): 1037.
CHR 67 (Jan. 1981): 154.

247a. Burns, Edward. "Seeing is Believing: The Chester Play
of the Nativity at Chester Cathedral, Summer
1987." *CahE* 34 (Oct. 1988): 1-9.

248. Burrow, J.A. *Medieval Writers and Their Work: Middle
English Literature and its Background 1100-1500.*
Oxford and New York: Oxford U. Press, 1982. 148
pp.

Looks briefly at English drama (esp. pp. 58-60,
93-94, 131). Offers some background information
on the historical setting. With notes,
bibliography, and index.

Rev. *B&B* (Sept. 1982): 31.
  LRB 4 (Sept. 2, 1982): 10.
  BBN (Oct. 1982): 635.
  TES (Oct. 1, 1982): 52.
  Choice 20 (Nov. 1982): 424.
  TLS (Dec. 24, 1982): 1425.
  RES 36 (Feb. 1985): 142.
  MLR 81 (Jan. 1986): 164.

249. Butterworth, Philip. "Gunnepowdyr, fyre and thondyr."
  MET 7.2 (1985): 68-76.

  Tries to determine how the burning gunpowder in
  Belial's anus (as specified in the stage
  directions) might have been carried out on stage
  in a performance of *The Castle of Perseverance.*
  Considers "the discovery and early development of
  gunpowder" (68). Suggests that Gluttony or other
  sins could have carried burning faggots to "'set
  off' Belial" (72). Considers the actor's
  protective clothing and the "Pipes or tubes of
  parchment or wood" (72-3) that would have held the
  powder.

250. ---. "Stage Directions of the Towneley Cycle." M.A.
  diss., U. of Leeds, 1977.

251. ---. "The York Mercers' Pageant Vehicle, 1433-1467:
  Wheels, Steering, and Control." *MET* 1.2 (Dec.
  1979): 72-81.

  Looks at primary documents (including the 1433
  York Mercers' indenture) to examine the
  technology, construction, and movement of this
  wagon.

252. Caldwell, Harry B., and David L. Middleton, comps.
  *English Tragedy, 1376-1600: Fifty Years of
  Criticism.* San Antonio, Texas: Trinity U. Press,
  1971. 89 pp.

  Contains bibliographical citations for dramatic
  and non-dramatic texts. Has entries for Skelton,
  Bale, William Wager, Sackville and Norton, George
  Gascoigne, etc. With indexes.

  Rev. *Choice* 9 (Jan. 1973): 1429.

252a. Calvert, Hugh. *A History of Kingston upon Hull from
  the Earliest Times to the Present Day.* London and
  Chichester: Phillimore, 1978. xii, 349 pp.

  Contains a section on "Drama and theatres" (269-
  77). Mentions "Corpus Christi processional cycle

performed by the trade guilds" (269) in Beverley
(1372) and York (1378), but no such phenomenon in
Hull. Says it is unlikely that there were
mystery, miracle, or morality plays there, "other
than certain brief entries in an account book of
the Guild of the Blessed Virgin Mary implying a
simple type of religious play . . . and the well-
authenticated Noah Play of the Guild of Holy
Trinity performed on Plough Monday in the 15th and
16th centuries" (269). Also mentions other
dramatic activity of the late sixteenth century,
with much discussion of the social background and
popular amusements of the city. Mentions
information about payments of the Guild of the
Blessed Virgin to minstrels along with money spent
for an angel and garlands (in 1642).

253. Campbell, Gordon, and N.M. Davis. "*Paradise Lost* and
the Norwich Grocers' Play." *MiltQ* 14.4 (Dec.
1980): 113-16.

Shows how Milton was influenced--in writing *PL*--
by, not the play itself, but the tradition of
drama represented by the Norwich play. Says that
"the play is a manifestation of a popular
tradition" (113) that Milton may have had access
to. Displays the parallels between the two works.

254. Campbell, Josie P. "English Cycle Drama: 'Thou Art a
pilgreme . . . .'" In *Popular Culture in the
Middle Ages*, 128-43. Ed. by Josie P. Campbell.
Bowling Green, Ohio: Popular, 1986.

Offers a general statement as to the nature of the
drama, "performed every year [from 1335-1600] in
virtually every major English town" (128). Claims
the plays were "written by the local clergy"
(128), "prepared over many months by an entire
town and performed by hundreds of actors and walk-
ons" (128). Reviews critical approaches. Looks
at the "entrepreneurial voices of the text" (129),
the use of conventions and formulas, the structure
of the cycles, characterization, and several
individual plays.

255. ---. "Farce as Function in Medieval and Shakespearean
Drama." *The Upstart Crow* 3 (Fall 1980): 11-18.

Looks at the use of farce as illuminating crucial
passages and as furthering action. Aims "to
present a theory of the functional use of farce as
method in medieval drama" (11), focusing on *The
Second Shepherds' Play*. Also looks at *1 Henry IV*
and *A Midsummer Night's Dream*. Considers the

"integrative use of farce as a structural device
or 'method' that not only illuminates the dramatic
action that precedes it but also prepares for what
follows" (11).

256. ---. "Farce as Function in the Wakefield Shepherds'
      Plays." *ChauR* 14.4 (Spring 1980): 336-43.

      Explains the Shepherds' plays in terms of the
      social function of farce, where farce
      "interpenetrates and illuminates the serious and
      official ideology presented by the drama" (336).
      Discusses "the integrative use of farce as a
      structural device or 'method' that illuminates the
      dramatic action" (336).

257. ---. "The Idea of Order in the Wakefield *Noah*."
      ChauR 10.1 (Summer 1975): 76-86.

      Discusses "confused, if not erroneous, readings"
      (76) of the play, which has for its theme one type
      of love, and which demonstrates that the dramatic
      involves "man's mistaken notion of 'mastre'" (76).
      Analyzes the criticism, the comic structure, and
      the failings of Noah and his wife.

258. Campbell, Josie Prescott. "The Polarization of
      Authority: A Study of the Towneley Cycle." Ph.D.
      diss., Pennsylvania State U., 1972.

259. Campbell, Thomas P. "Eschatology and the Nativity in
      the English Mystery Plays." *ABR* 27.3 (Sept.
      1976): 297-320.

      Shows that "eschatology occurs as a typological
      theme throughout the mystery cycles" (297)--even
      in the Nativity plays. Explores the notion of
      Advent, the penitential tone in these plays,
      Christmas and post-Christmas celebrations,
      elements of eschatology, the "Slaughter of the
      Innocents" plays, the Antichrist figure and Herod.
      Concludes that "to prepare for . . . Christ's
      birth was also to prepare for His return as Judge"
      (320).

260. ---. "The Liturgical Shepherds Play and the Origins
      of Christmas Drama." *Mosaic* 12.2 (Winter 1979):
      21-32.

      Says that it is wrong to believe that the
      Christmas plays "took their form and inspiration
      from the Easter *Visitatio* of the tenth century"
      (21). Aims to show the resemblances of the *Ordo
      Pastorum* and the *Visitatio*, the "liturgical

context for which the shepherds' play was
composed" (21); questions "the traditional
chronology of events through which the Christian
drama is assumed to have risen" (21). Calls for a
close "examination of the context in which this
dramatic activity took place" (32). Counters the
"gradual evolution" theory.

261. ---. "Liturgy and Drama: Recent Approaches to
Medieval Theatre." *ThJ* 33.3 (Oct. 1981): 289-301.

Recounts the liturgy-to-drama theory, and says
that the fundamental question behind the rise of
English vernacular drama is "what is the
relationship between the medieval Theatre and the
medieval Church?" (289). Shows how the drama
developed in accordance with medieval church
practices. Focuses on Christmas plays. Concludes
"that medieval drama as a whole is 'ritual drama'
in a surprisingly uniform and narrow way" (301).

262. Campbell, Thomas Patterson, III. "The Nativity in the
Medieval Liturgy and the Middle English Mystery
Cycles." Ph.D. diss., Indiana U., 1972.

263. ---. "The Prophets' Pageant in the English Mystery
Cycles: Its Origins and Function." *RORD* 17
(1974): 107-21.

Justifies the inclusion of these plays in the
cycles. Points out the erroneous origin of the
plays as "the list of prophetic testimonies
contained in a sixth-century sermon, the pseudo-
Augustinian *Contra Judeos, Paganos . . .*" (107).
Shows that the "prophetic testimonies . . . are
only a small part of the longer original sermon"
(107). Shows why a knowledge of the medieval
liturgy is important in studying the English
mystery plays--"because the liturgy itself can
explain the specific function of a particular"
play (116).

264. ---. "Why Do the Shepherds Prophesy?" *CompD* 12
(1978): 137-50. Rpt. in Davidson, Gianakaris, and
Stroupe, eds., *The Drama . . .*, 169-82 (entry #
409 below).

Considers the traditions behind the cycle plays'
shepherds' pageants and the moment of prophecy in
the *Secunda Pastorum*. Traces the prophecy to "the
very roots of the Christmas drama itself" (138).
Looks at the function and meaning of prophecy, the
English plays, liturgical drama, and the liturgy
itself. Identifies three inseparable aspects of

the Christian story: prophecy, spiritual
community, and shepherds.

265. Candido, Joseph. "Language and Gesture in the Chester
Sacrifice of Isaac." *Comitatus* 3 (1972): 11-18.

Shows how the play's focus on gesture and language
works thematically and visually. Concludes that
the integration of language and gesture produces a
"total dramatic effect" (18).

266. Cardullo, Bert. "The Chester *Sacrifice of Isaac.*"
Expl 43.3 (Spring 1985): 3-4.

Comments on Phillip McCaffrey's "The Didactic
Structure of the Chester *Sacrifice of Isaac*" (see
1021 below). Shows that where McCaffrey speaks
of only two parts to the Expositor's first two
speeches, there is really a third part to each.

267. Carlson, Marvin. *Theories of the Theatre: A
Historical and Critical Survey, from the Greeks to
the Present.* Ithaca and London: Cornell U. Press,
1984. 529 pp.

Chap. 3--"The Medieval Period" (31-36)--looks at
drama criticism with respect to scriptural
allegory and other approaches contemporary with
the drama. Surveys medieval attitudes toward and
commentaries on the drama; not on the plays of the
era. Shows how contemporary views of drama "were
clearly reflected in the development of the cycle
dramas" (36). Also points out that "medieval
drama essentially came into harmony with the
Horatian goal 'to delight and to instruct'" (36).

268. ---. [Untitled review.] *RORD* 28 (1985): 201-03.

Reviews performances of the National Theatre's
production of *The Mysteries* of January 21-23,
1985, in London's Cottesloe Theatre.

269. Carnahan, Shirley Eileen. "Past in the Present: The
Staging of 'The Killing of the Children.'" Ph.D.
diss., U. of Colorado, Boulder, 1983.

270. Carpenter, Nan Cooke. "Music in the English Mystery
Plays." In *Music in English Renaissance Drama*, 1-
31, 161-70. Ed. by John H. Long. Lexington: U.
of Kentucky Press, 1968.

Traces the history of the use of music in drama
from the Mass and its tropes; recounts the old
religious-to-secular theory of the origins of

drama. Points out the association of music with angelic beings in many of the cycles' episodes, along with its occurrence in other characters (Mary, David, other people in the Noah play [Chester and Hegge], shepherds, etc.). Looks also at instrumental music, the musicians' guild at York (1561-), discussion among characters about music, various instruments used, and the music's "deeper significance" (25), which was generally "to strengthen the faith of the viewers" (29), to add realism or symbolism, and to serve a "didactic and moral purpose" (31).

271. Carpenter, Sarah. "Ane Satyre of the Thrie Estaits." *MET* 6.2 (Dec. 1984): 163-68.

Reports on a performance at the Edinburgh Festival, 1984.

272. ---. "John Bale's *Kynge Johan*: The Dramatisation of Allegorical and Non-Allegorical Figures." In *Le Théâtre au Moyen Age* . . ., 263-69. [Discussion on 270-76.] Ed. by Gari R. Muller (see entry # 1181 below).

Discusses the difference in presentation of naturalistic and allegorical characters and the characteristics of each. Focuses on Bale's play to show how "Johan shows the two different kinds of relationship with the audience" (269) that are required by the two modes.

273. ---. "Morality-Play Characters." *MET* 5.1 (July 1983): 18-28.

Treats special problems of characterization presented by morality plays (problems such as allegory, "self-presentation" [18], "self-revelation" [19], personification, the "sense of distance between speaker and character" [22], evil personified, the "demonstrative mode of presentation" [26]).

274. ---. "Reports on Productions: Summer 1980: Towneley Plays at Wakefield." *MET* 2.1 (July 1980): 49-52.

Covers a July 28-29, 1980, performance of the full cycle.

275. ---. "Reports on Productions: The Chester Cycle at Leeds." *MET* 5.1 (July 1983): 29-35.

Discusses a performance of the complete cycle, April 30 to May 2, 1983.

xxx.   ---.   See Peter Happé et al. "Thoughts on
          'Transvestitism' by Divers Hands" (# 689 below).

276.   Carr, Sherwyn T.   "The Middle English Nativity Cherry
          Tree: The Dissemination of a Popular Motif." *MLQ*
          36.2 (June 1975): 133-47.

          Looks at the "remarkably similar miracles" (133)
          of a Middle English ballad ("The Cherry-Tree
          Carol"), in *Sir Cleges*, and that in the fifteenth
          century play of the *Ludus Coventriae* (The
          Adoration of the Shepherds)--the miracle of the
          fruitful cherry tree which bows down to Mary.
          Traces the history of the motif from the Pseudo-
          Matthew. Shows the similarities and differences
          in the occurrences of the motif.

277.   Carroll, Virginia Schaeffer.   "The 'Noble Gyn' of
          Comedy in the Middle English Cycle Plays." Ph.D.
          diss., Kent State U., 1984.

277a. ---.   *The 'Noble Gyn' of Comedy in the Middle English
          Cycle Plays.* New York, Bern, Frankfurt, Paris:
          Peter Lang, 1989. American University Studies.
          Series IV. English Language and Literature, vol.
          79.

278.   Carruthers, Mary J., and Elizabeth D. Kirks, eds.
          *Acts of Interpretation: The Text in Its Contexts,
          700-1600: Essays on Medieval and Renaissance
          Literature in Honor of E. Talbot Donaldson.*
          Norman, Oklahoma: Pilgrim, 1982.

          Contains the essay by Van Dyke on *Everyman* (see #
          1624 below).

          Rev. William F. Pollard, *StudAC* 6 (1984): 181-86.

278a. Carson, Ada Lou, and Herbert L. Carson. *Domestic
          Tragedy in English: Brief Survey.* 2 vols.
          Salzburg: Institut für Anglistik und
          Amerikanistik, U. of Salzburg, 1982. Salzburg
          Studies in English Literature under the direction
          of Professor Erwin A. Stürzl. Poetic Drama and
          Poetic Theory, 67. Ed. by James Hogg. 1-218,
          219-465 pp.

          Defines the term "Domestic Tragedy." Sect. I
          covers "Beginnings to 1731," with chapter on
          "English Domestic Tragedy to the Interregnum"
          focusing on "Pre-Elizabethan Drama" and "Early
          Domestic and Theological Tendencies." Touches on
          the mystery plays (26 f.), miracle plays (27), and
          moralities (27 f.)--especially *The Castle of*

Perseverance, Everyman, and *Mankind,* and how they
prepared audiences to receive plays which "coupled
a serious moral purpose with recognizable people
and situations" (28). Looks briefly also at
Udall's *Ralph Roister Doister* and *Gammer Gurton's
Needle,* Fulwell's *Like Will to Like,* and Wapull's
The Tide Tarrieth No Man. With bibliography and
index.

279. Cassee, Elly, and Kees Berserik. "The Iconography of
the Resurrection: A Re-Examination of the Risen
Christ Hovering Above the Tomb." *BurlM* 126.970
(Jan. 1984): 20-24.

Not on drama. But deals with pictorial
representation of the Resurrection and the
changing image of Christ, probably familiar to the
playwrights.

280. *The Castle of Perseverance.* [Toronto]: Poculi Ludique
Societas in Association with Records of Early
English Drama, 1979. 16 pp.

Program for performances at the University of
Toronto, August 4, 5, and 6, 1979. Contains
information on plot, text, "The Challenge" ([6])
of performance, the production at Toronto, the
costumes, masks, and music. With illustrations.

281. Cawley, A.C. "Everyman." In *Dictionary of the Middle
Ages* 4: 526-29. Ed. by Joseph R. Strayer. New
York: Charles Scribner's Sons, 1984. (See item #
1553 below.)

Summarizes history and scholarship, versions and
contents, doctrine and appeal. Considers the
play's popularity, sources, printed texts,
theology, staging, language, and meter. With
bibliography.

xxx. ---, foreword. Thomas Sharp's *A Dissertation on the
Pageants or Dramatic Mysteries anciently performed
at Coventry.* (See item # 1457 below.)

282. ---. "Medieval Drama and Didacticism." In *The Drama
of Medieval Europe,* 3-12 (plus discussion, 13-21).
Leeds Medieval Studies 1. Ed. by Richard Rastall
(see entry # 1359 below).

Deals with "the six things which provide the
groundwork of Christian faith and practice: the
Creed, the decalogue, . . . the seven sacraments,
the seven corporal works of mercy, the seven
principal virtues, and the seven deadly sins" (3).

Shows the didactic aim of the cycle plays as the
Church's effort to bring religious instruction to
lay people. Looks specifically at religious works
in the vernacular as influencing the drama. Shows
that in the cycles "the basic dramatic conflict
between good and evil is expressed in terms of the
commandments and of the cardinal sins that offend
against them" (12).

283. ---. "Middle English Metrical Versions of the
       Decalogue with Reference to the English Corpus
       Christi Cycles." *LSE*, n.s. 8 (1975): 129-45.

Deals "with the didactic background to vernacular
texts of the commandments and with the
christianizing of the Old Testament decalogue in
England during the later Middle Ages.
. . . identifies the Old and New Testament
versions of the commandments in the Prophets' and
Doctors' plays respectively of the Corpus Christi
cycles. . . . [E]xamines the different renderings
of the commandments in the Doctors' plays of the
Towneley and York cycles" (129). Shows and
explains the divergence between the Towneley and
York versions of the commandments.

284. ---. "Noah's Ark or, the Shipwrights' Ancient Play,
       or Dirge." In *A Medieval Miscellany in honour of
       Professor John Le Patourel*, 138-53. Ed. by R.L.
       Thomson. Leeds: Leeds Philosophical and Literary
       Society, April 1982. Proceedings of the Leeds
       Philosophical and Literary Society, Literary and
       Historical Section, 18.1.

Examines "the form of [Henry] Bourne's printed
play [of 1736] and offers . . . evidence that he
may have transcribed a late sixteenth-century copy
of the text" (138). Looks at the Noah story and
the non-biblical elements which add entertainment
and humor. Also considers how morality plays
influence the play; and looks at the play's
structure and its typological and dramatic
features. With four illustrations.

285. ---. "Pageant Wagon Versus Juggernaut Car." *RORD* 13-
       14 (1970-71): 204-08. Medieval Supplement of the
       Report of the Modern Language Association Seminar.

Pleads for additional study of pageant wagons and
productions. Mentions "the great variety of
production methods" (204). Calls for
investigation of written and pictorial sources.
Warns against speculation unsupported by
historical evidence. Mentions his own paper

circulated for discussion at the MLA Medieval
Drama Seminar, Denver, December 28, 1969:
"Presentation of the Wakefield Plays." [This
article is followed by "Informal Minutes of
Seminar 17," a seven-page transcription of the
discussion following Cawley's talk.]

xxx.   ---. "Presentation of the Wakefield Plays." (See
previous entry.)

286.   ---. "The Staging of Medieval Drama." In *The* Revels
History of Drama in English. Vol. I, 1-66. See
Cawley, et al., *The* Revels *History of Drama in
English*. Vol. I. (See # 289 below.)

Concentrates on religious and moral drama of
medieval England. Deals with different types of
staging and the organization of the Corpus Christi
plays. Looks at the production of the Chester and
Coventry *Purification of Mary* play and the
presentation of the Wakefield plays. Draws from
medieval documents and iconography. On "Different
types of staging" (8-35), considers "The church as
theatre," "Outside the church," "The 'round':
place-and-scaffold presentation," "The rectangular
acting area," "The 'houses' arranged in a straight
line or in a semicircle," "Scottish plays and N-
town plays," "The pageant-wagon processional
staging," "Tournaments and royal entries," "The
booth stage," "The indoor theatre: the acting of
interludes," and "The medieval heritage of the
Elizabethan public theatre." Also looks at stage
directions (Chester and Coventry plays), costumes,
make-up, properties, music, payment to actors, and
total expenditure on the play.

287.   ---. "Thoresby and Later Owners of the Manuscript of
the York Plays (BL Additional 35290)." *LSE*, n.s.
11 (1980 for 1979): 74-89.

Talks generally about the manuscript's various
owners and its increase in value.

288.   ---. "The Towneley *Processus Talentorum:* A Survey and
Interpretation." *LSE*, n.s. 17 (1986): 131-39.

Discusses themes, the play's unexpected elements,
criticism of the play, characterization, the
influence of Psalm 21 from the Vulgate, number
symbolism, staging. (See A.C. Cawley and Martin
Stevens. "The Towneley *Processus Talentorum:* Text
and Commentary." *LSE*, n.s. 17 [1986]: 105-30;
item # 20 above.)

288a. ---. "*A Yorkshire Tragedy* Considered in Relation to
           Biblical and Moral Plays." In *Everyman & Company*
           . . . . Ed. by Donald Gilman. (See entry # 628a
           below.)

288b. ---, Jean Forrester, and John Goodchild. "References
           to the Corpus Christi Plays in the Wakefield
           Burgess Court Rolls: The Originals Rediscovered."
           LSE, n.s. 19 (1988): 85-104.

289.   Cawley, A.C., Marion Jones, Peter F. McDonald, and
           David Mills. *The* Revels *History of Drama in
           English*. Vol. I, *Medieval Drama*. Ed. by Lois
           Potter. London and New York: Methuen, 1983.
           xlviii, 348 pp.

           Contains three essays: Cawley, "The Staging of
           Medieval Drama" (# 286 above); Mills and McDonald,
           "The Drama of Religious Ceremonial" (# 1163
           below); and Jones, "Early Moral Plays . . ." (#
           860 below). Also contains appendix: "Manuscripts
           and contents of the extant English cycles" (Mills,
           292-302; see # 1151 below). Gives a chronological
           table showing reigns, public events, drama and
           dramatic records, other literature, and art and
           architecture (xvii-xlv).

           Rev. T.P. Dolan, A.J. Fletcher, and S. Powell,
                   YWES 64 (1983): 138.
               BBN (Feb. 1984): 114.
               TES (Feb. 10, 1984): 27.
               Drama (Winter 1984): 52.
               BBN (Feb. 1985): 74.
               William Tydeman, *ThRI* 10.1 (Spring 1985): 72-
                   73.
               Alexandra F. Johnston, *N&Q* 32.1 (230) (Mar.
                   1985): 89-92.
               Alasdair A. MacDonald, *EngStud* 66.4 (Aug.
                   1985): 365-66.
               Hans-Jürgen Diller, *Anglia* 104.3/4 (1986):
                   506-09.

290.   Cawte, E.C. "Even More About the Mummers' Play." *JAF*
           87.345 (July-Sept. 1974): 250-52.

           Reacts to Kirby's views against the life-cycle
           theory. (See E.T. Kirby, "Mummers' Plays and the
           Calendar," *JAF* 84 (1971): 275-88; see # 914 and
           915 below. Also see next entry.)

291.   ---. "More on the 'Mummers' Play.'" *JAF* 85.338
           (Oct.-Dec. 1972): 375-76.

Asserts the life-cycle theory and responds to
Kirby's objections to it. (See Kirby, "Origin of
the Mummers' Play," *JAF* 84 (1971): 275-88; # 915
below.) Says that Kirby may be correct in seeing
shamanism as an origin; but claims that the life-
cycle ritual may also be. Refutes several of
Kirby's claims.

292. ---. "The Revesby Sword Play." *JAF* 87.345 (July-
Sept. 1974): 250.

Adds a few points to Michael J. Preston's account
("The Revesby Sword Play," *JAF* 85.335 [Jan.-Mar.
1972]: 51-57; see entry # 1334 below) concerning
the provenance of the ms and its occasion. Not
directly on medieval drama, but deals with early
folk origins.

292a. ---. *Ritual Animal Disguise: A Historical and*
Geographical Study of Animal Costume in the
British Isles. Cambridge: D.S. Brewer; Totowa,
NJ: Rowman and Littlefield, 1978. The Folklore
Society, Mistletoe Series 8. xv, 293 pp.

Covers "seasonal rituals in the British Isles"
([xiii]) from early days to the twentieth century.
Deals with a great number of phenomena, disguises,
and events, including many relating to early
drama. Considers, e.g., Hero-Combat, Sword
Dances, Wooing Plays, Plough Monday, etc. A rich
source of information. With 24 illustrations,
thirteen maps, an appendix on "A Geographical
Index of Animal Disguise Customs in the British
Isles" (228-49), notes, bibliography (255-86), and
index.

293. Chaillet, Ned. [Review.] *The Times* (London), June 13,
1980.

Review of The York Cycle, performances of June 6-
30, 1980, York Festival, at St. Mary's Abbey,
York. (Cited by Sheila Lindenbaum, *RORD* 23
[1980]: 84.)

294. Chambers, Albert F. "The Vicars Choral of York
Minster and the Tilemakers' Corpus Christi
Pageant." *REEDN* 2.1 (1977): 2-9.

Discusses the "involvement of corporations and
individuals other than the occupational crafts or
guilds in the events of Corpus Christi day" (2).
Claims that the tilemakers "appear to have
strongly associated themselves in the tilemakers'

pageant to the extent that they considered it their own" (7).

295. Chandler, Arthur Bayard. "The Concept of Justice in Early English Drama." Ph.D. diss., U. of Illinois, Urbana-Champaign, 1974.

296. Christ, John Peter. "The Achievement of Form: A Rhetorical Study of Henry Medwall's 'Fulgens and Lucres.'" Ph.D. diss., Fordham U., 1970.

297. Church, Jo Hall. "Discourse Theory and Deconstruction: The Rhetoric of the York Cycle Passion Plays." Ph.D. diss., Texas Woman's U., 1985.

298. Clein, Wendy. "The Towneley *Magnus Herodes* and the Comedy of Redemption." *Renascence* 38.1 (Autumn 1985): 54-63.

Comments on the playwright's having to deal with the dual nature of the Slaughter of the Innocents episode--as a "cause for exultation" (54) and as a horrible scene. Looks at the Wakefield Master's treatment in human and cosmic terms. Compares the Wakefield treatment with that in the other versions. Points out the use of "grim humor" (59), the comic effects, the women's roles, the use of Christian history, the "triumph of divine justice" (60), the use of foreshadowing, and the many theological allusions.

298a. Cleland, John H.. "*Second Shepherd's* [sic] and *Homecoming:* Two Dramatic Imitations of Life." *F&R* 3.2 (1977): 46-64.

" . . . examines the dramatic realism of two plays . . . to show something of the different value systems by which men may govern their activities" (abstract preceding article, p. 46). Aims "to consider the metaphysics of what is 'real' in life" (46). Bases argument partly on Erich Auerbach's discussion (in his *Mimesis*) of reality in Western literature. Defines reality--for the middle ages with a tendency to look to the next world. Also considers the views of Heraclitus, Plato, and Aristotle. Mentions how the Wakefield Master "demolished the medieval convention . . . that exalted subjects are to be exclusively presented in elevated diction and syntax" (48), and also mentions how the play violates the three unities. Focuses on the realistic characterization of the shepherds (see esp. pp. 50-54). Has similar discussion for Harold

Pinter's *Homecoming*. Concludes that the world of the *Second Shepherds' Play* "is an intensely real world" (54) and is therefore convincingly realistic.

298b. Clifford, G. *The Transformations of Allegory.* London and Boston: 1974.

299. Clopper, Lawrence M. "Arnewaye, Higden and the Origin of the Chester Plays." *REEDN* 8.2 (1983): 4-11.

Shows how an entry in an antiquarian's list is inaccurate in associating certain dates and names with the Chester plays. Looks at other documents concerned with the plays' origins, author(s), and dates. Examines Higden's and Arneway's possible contributions (which are nil); points out the possibility that "the plays were not written by Higden but [were] based on some version of his *Poly chronicon*" (7). Notes the "potential for confusing author and authority" (7). Says that "Sir Henry Francis may have been the author" (7); points out that Francis lived too early, but may have composed an early version based on Higden. Speculates on Higden's and Francis's hands in the development of the cycle.

300. ---. "The Chester Plays at Toronto." *RORD* 26 (1983): 109-16.

Reviews a performance of 21-23 May 1983, with reference to how scholars and actors worked together. Considers props, costumes, wagons, the use of music, sets, and so on, with mention of many specific plays and how they were staged. Concludes with comments on the feasibility of wagon performances, the use of the ground before the wagon for some of the action, period style, the sense of pageantry, and a striving for authenticity.

301. ---. "*The Chester Plays:* Frequency of Performance." *ThSur* 14.2 (Nov. 1973): 46-58.

Analyzes primary sources (account books, proclamations, the David Rogers *Brevarye*, legal documents, assembly meeting minutes, Mayor's book) to discover performances in 1532, 1546, 1561, 1567, 1568, 1572, 1575, and possibly 1550 and 1554. Claims that performances were probably not held regularly even before the Reformation. (See response by John Marshall, "The Chester Whitsun Plays . . .," entry # 1065 below.)

301a. ---. "Florescence in the North: Traditions of Drama
and Ceremony." *FCS* 13 (1988): 249-56.

302. ---. "The History and Development of the Chester
Cycle." *MP* 75.3 (Feb. 1978): 219-46.

Says that--contrary to popular criticism--the play
in the fifteenth century "was more a Passion play
than a cycle" (219) and that the full cycle
emerged in Tudor times. Examines the documents to
demonstrate how the cycle grew. Offers a chart
(243-44) to depict this growth.

303. ---. "Lay and Clerical Impact on Civic Religious
Drama and Ceremony." In *Contexts for Early
English Drama*, 102-36. Ed. by Marianne G. Briscoe
and John C. Coldewey (see # 228 above).

Reviews scholarship about the relationship between
religious and secular drama and looks at "the
social and cultural contexts of the civic drama."
Focuses on the Chester cycle for his example.
Looks at the didactic, spiritual, practical, and
economic sources of the plays. Remarks on the
fact that it was not spiritual leaders but
guildsmen who were given the task of teaching
through the plays.

304. ---. "*Mankind* and Its Audience." *CompD* 8.4 (Winter
1974-75): 347-55.

Looks at the learned (especially Latin) content of
the play to challenge the assertion that its
audience was "local yokels" (347). Assesses 1)
the evidence that it was performed indoors; 2) the
possibility that it was directed at a private, not
a public, audience; 3) the play's satiric
language.

305. ---. "The Principle of Selection of the Chester Old
Testament Plays." *ChauR* 13.3 (Winter 1979): 272-
83.

Claims that scholars should examine each cycle
separately with the idea that each selects plays
on different principles. Focuses on the Chester
cycle. Says "that figuration is not exclusive
enough to function as a principle of selection"
(272). Challenges Kolve's idea that the cycles
were aimed at depicting the Seven Ages of Man.
Says that the Chester plays were selected, it
seems, to display the Old Law in opposition to the
New Law, to show "the historical process of

salvation and to reveal the central beliefs,
rituals, and ethics of the Christian faith" (281).

306.   ---. *Records of Early English Drama: Chester.*
Toronto and Buffalo: U. of Toronto Press, 1979.
lxxii, 591 pp.

Gives excerpts from 132 mss and many printed
sources of civic and ecclesiastical records of
drama, minstrelsy, and ceremonial, 1268-1642.
Contains introduction covering the documents,
dramatic and ceremonial activity, editorial
procedures, and notes. Presents the records with
appendixes on undated entries and printed
documents. With translations, end-notes,
glossaries, map, and bibliography.

Rev. *EDAMN* 2.2 (Apr. 1980): 3-4.
    Peter W. Travis, *CompD* 14.3 (Fall 1980): 284-
        86.
    Paula Neuss, *ThN* 35.1 (1981): 33-36.

307.   ---. "The Rogers' Description of the Chester Plays."
LSE, n.s. 7 (1974 for 1973 and 1974): 63-94.

Discusses the Rogers' *Brevaryes,* "early
seventeenth-century histories of . . . Chester
[which] include the earliest and most extensive
descriptions of that city's medieval plays" (63).
Describes the *Brevaryes* and points out why they
seem to contradict other documentary evidence
about the performance of the plays. Looks at
stage directions and guild accounts. Considers
the accuracy of the *Brevaryes* and their sources,
their attacks on the plays, their descriptions of
the plays (their authorship, performance, dates,
days, and place of performance, the structure of
the pageant carts, the roles of the actors, and
the use of stages). Warns not to ignore or
repudiate the Rogers' documents "until they have
been fully examined side by side with the stage
directions in the texts" (83). Appendix contains
transcriptions of some of the primary documents
(Rogers' *Brevary,* Cheshire Record Office MS, B.M.
Harley 1948, and The Lysons copy).

308.   ---. "The Staging of the Medieval Plays of Chester: A
Response." *ThN* 28.2 (1974): 65-70.

Responds to several scholars who speculate on the
accuracy of the Rogers description of processional
performance. Specifically answers Ruth B. Davis'
"The Scheduling of the Chester Cycle Plays" (*ThN*
27.2 [Winter 1972/73]: 49-67; see # 425 below).

Questions whether there were four or five stops of
the wagons. Refutes Harry N. Langdon's "Staging
of the Ascension" article (# 961 below); concludes
that processional staging is the most likely way
the plays were performed.

309.   Clopper, Lawrence Mason, Jr.   "The Structure of the
Chester Cycle: Text, Theme and Theatre."   Ph.D.
diss., Ohio State U., 1969.

310.   ---.   "Tyrants and Villains: Characterization in the
Passion Sequences of the English Cycle Plays."
MLQ 41.1 (Mar. 1980): 3-20.

Focuses on "the medieval dramatists' materials and
sources and their playwriting techniques" (4) to
show how tyrants and villains have been
oversimplified and also how they are treated in
three distinct ways in their sources.   Claims
there is a simple "ultimate source" (5) of
individual villains.   Looks at exegetical
interpretations, social commentary in the plays,
Herod, Annas, Cayphas, Pilate, the nature of
Christ with respect to the villains, staging
conditions, and emphases in the various plays.

311.   Cochran, Carol M.   "Flyting in the Mystery Plays."
ThJ 31.2 (May 1979): 186-97.

Relates the verbal abuse of the plays to flytings,
"which were popular in medieval life and
literature and which ultimately derive from the
insult contests of ritual and festivity" (186).
Examines this phenomenon in the plays
historically, with respect to language, content,
and characters, and looks at the dramatic aspects
of the flyting.   Concludes that "the mystery plays
are celebratory rather than didactic" (197).

312.   Cohen, Walter.   *Drama of a Nation: Public Theater in
Renaissance England and Spain*.   Ithaca and London:
Cornell U. Press, 1985.

Chap. 1--"Medieval Theater and the Structure of
Feudalism" (33-81)--covers social, political, and
religious conditions.   Shows how Spain and England
had "a uniquely similar cast" (15) in their drama,
even though the countries developed in isolation
from one another.   Does not consider "court
masques, mythological spectacles, civic
pageants . . . and closet drama" (17).   Examines
liturgical drama, twelfth-century plays, urban
theater, the plays of Arras, and fourteenth- and
fifteenth-century theater (religious and secular).

Mostly theoretical, with little focus on specific plays.

Rev. *TLS* (July 18, 1986): 790.
RenQ 39 (Winter 1986): 812.
ShakQ 37 (Winter 1986): 512.
RES 38 (Feb. 1987): 70.
ThJ 39 (May 1987): 266.

313. Coldewey, John C. "Comment." *Records of Early English Drama: Proceedings of the First Colloquium . . . ,* 118-25. Ed. by JoAnna Dutka. Toronto: Records of Early English Drama, 1979. (See # 497 below.)

Comments on the paper of Stanley J. Kahrl ("Learning about Local Control"; see # 879 below) with respect to a scholar's thinking with a medieval English frame of mind in looking at dramatic records and historic places. [Comment is pp. 118-25; discussion is pp. 126-27.]

314. ---. "The Digby Plays and the Chelmsford Records." *RORD* 18 (1975): 103-21.

Suggests that the "productions may have included the plays in Bodleian MS. Digby 133" (103). Compares internal evidence from the ms with external evidence of stages and props provided for in the 1562 Chelmsford performances.

315. Coldewey, John Christopher. "Early Essex Drama: A History of Its Rise and Fall, and a Theory Concerning the Digby Plays." Ph.D. diss., U. of Colorado, Boulder, 1972.

316. ---. "The Last Rise and Final Demise of Essex Town Drama." *MLQ* 36.3 (Sept. 1975): 239-60.

Gives several reasons for the fall of the drama: it was the result of political and religious harrassment, financial problems brought on by the vicissitudes experienced by protestant and romanist sects, a lack of play-texts and playwrights, the Vestiarian Controversy (255-57-- having to do with the use of vestments as costumes), and the spread of "preaching and prophesyings" (257) as public entertainment. Concludes that the demise of the drama in Essex was not because "of any discernible 'plot' by ecclesiastical or governmental authorities . . . [but] hinged on events and issues quite removed from such rational considerations" (260).

317.   ---.   "Playing Companies at Alderburgh, 1556-1635."
       In *Collections, Volume IX*, 16-23.   Oxford: Printed
       for the Malone Society by Oxford U. Press, 1971
       (1977).

       Presents extracts mostly from Chamberlains'
       Accounts (1566-1567 to 1634-1645).

318.   ---.   "Plays and 'Play' in Early English Drama."   *RORD*
       28 (1985): 181-88.

       Aims at drawing a picture of medieval life in
       which the plays were performed; shows "that the
       ordinary life of an ordinary townsman had much to
       commend it" (181), including holidays, feasts,
       celebrations, games, sports, and plays. ". . .
       there was much to occupy people of all ages and in
       every station of life by way of play" (181).
       Focuses on elements of "play"--not theatrical
       performances. Examines contemporary documents for
       references to "plays" and game, sport, music, card
       playing and dicing, bullbaiting, cockfighting,
       etc.

319.   ---.   "Some Economic Aspects of the Late Medieval
       Drama."   In *Contexts for Early English Drama*, 77-
       101.   Ed. by Marianne G. Briscoe and John C.
       Coldewey (see # 228 above).

       Shows how the "historical fortunes" of the plays
       were linked with the economics of nations,
       religions, towns, and people, thus explaining why
       our present knowledge coming primarily from non-
       dramatic documents is from economic records
       (Churchwardens' accounts, Chamberlains' accounts,
       etc.). Reviews the sources and shows how
       economics affected the drama.

320.   ---.   "Some Nottinghamshire Waits: Their History and
       Habits."   *REEDN* 7.1 (1982): 40-49.

       Discusses the importance of the study of music by
       those interested in medieval drama. Looks at
       musical activities in Nottinghamshire; focuses on
       waits (visiting town musicians). Suggests that
       the "players" there could often have been
       musicians, not actors.

321.   ---.   "That Enterprising Property Player: Semi-
       Professional Drama in Sixteenth-Century England."
       ThN 31.1 (1977): 5-12.

       Defines "professional" and "amateur" player and
       suggests that there was a parallel tradition of

"semi-professional" actors in counties near
London; they were amateur in their supplying
costumes, materials, and performers, and they were
professional in importing directors from London
and in being paid. Discusses the evidence of
their activities and the implications these
"property players" (5) have for English dramatic
history. Examines documents to learn of when and
where they played, the nature of their stages and
props, and their expenditures and financing.

321a. ---. "Watersheds: Thames Valley Traditions." *FCS* 13
(1988): 257-62.

322. Cole, Howard C. *A Quest of Inquirie: Some Contexts of
Tudor Literature.* Indianapolis and New York:
Pegasus/Bobbs-Merrill, 1973.

Contains much discussion on Entertainments, Lord
Mayors' Shows, Masks and Devisings at Court,
Miracle and Morality Plays, and Interludes.

Rev. *LJ* 98 (June 15, 1973): 1920.
JEGP 73 (Jan. 1974): 116.

323. Coleman, Janet. *Medieval Readers and Writers, 1350-
1400.* London: Hutchinson; New York: Columbia U.
Press, 1981. *English Literature in History*
series, ed. by Raymond Williams.

Contains material on minstrels. Does not focus on
visual, dramatic performances, but has much
background on the times.

Rev. *Choice* 19 (July 1982): 1552.
VQR 58 (Autumn 1982): 116.
Historian 44 (Aug. 1982): 546.
SewR 90 (Oct. 1982): 608.
AHR 87 (Dec. 1982): 1375.
ContempRev 243 (Aug. 1983): 109.
SoAQ 82 (Winter 1983): 109.
CHR 70 (Apr. 1984): 310.

324. Coletti, Theresa. "The Design of the Digby Play of
Mary Magdalene." *SP* 76.4 (Oct. 1979): 313-33.

Comments on the great diversity of dramatic
elements and devices in the play, and its thematic
unity and "theological pattern of fall,
forgiveness, and salvation" (314). Looks further
at its "thematic intricacy" (314), its recurring
motifs, and its religious and dramatic design.
Mentions images of eating, banqueting, and
nourishment, and of clothing to suggest how these

would have effected performance. Says that these
images reflect Mary's roles of sinner, penitent,
apostle, and saint.

325.   ---.   "Devotional Iconography in the N-Town Marian
Plays." *CompD* 11 (1977): 22-44. Rpt. in
Davidson, Gianakaris, and Stroupe, eds., *The Drama
. . .*, 249-71 (see entry # 409 below).

Notes the preoccupation with Mary in the cycles;
examines the "iconographic and devotional
richness" (22) of the Mary plays. Looks at the
relationship between devotion and drama.
Considers the plays as devotional art and shows
how "stage iconography could have embodied the
spiritual concerns of the dramatic audience" (22).
Considers staging, the plays as microcosm, the
apocryphal tradition and scripture, theological
motifs, and contemporary art. Concludes that
"Drama and devotion are one" (41).

326.   ---.   "Sacrament and Sacrifice in the N-Town Passion."
Medi 7 (1984 for 1981): 239-64.

Points out the Eucharistic elements ("the
sacramental meaning of Christ's body"--[239]) in
the cycle plays. Shows that they are especially
strong in the N-Town Passion where they are used
figuratively and thematically. Shows the
iconographic link of "the sacrament of *corpus
christi* with the sacrifice of Christ's human
flesh" (239). Relies on the visual arts to
suggest "the degree to which the play movingly
incarnates its sacramental and sacrificial theme
in its visual effects" (239). With seven
illustrations.

327.   Coletti, Theresa Margaret. "Spirituality and
Devotional Images: The Staging of the Hegge
Cycle." Ph.D. diss., U. of Rochester, 1975.

328.   ---.   "Theology and Politics in the Towneley *Play of
the Talents*." *M&H*, n.s. 9 (1979): 111-26.

Discusses the problems of the play (provenance,
title, mixed tone, redundancy in treating for a
second time in the cycle the Crucifixion, its
inclusion in the cycle, the role of Pilate).
Claims that the play "is . . . thematically
appropriate to its position in the . . . cycle and
integrally related to the religious and dramatic
significance of the Corpus Christi play" (111).
Deals with the problematic issues. Concludes that
the play is "not the anomaly that some of its

readers have judged it to be" (123). Calls it "tightly constructed" (123), with skilled characterization and use of language, fitting in appropriately with the theological design of Corpus Christi plays.

329. ---, and Kathleen M. Ashley. "The N-Town Passion at Toronto and Late Medieval Passion Iconography." *RORD* 24 (1981): 181-92. With an appendix-- bibliography of iconographic sources--by Theodore De Welles (188-92). (See item # 453 below.)

Recounts a performance designed for production partly based on representations of the Passion taken from the visual arts--appropriate for a cycle with a strong emphasis on iconography, which is examined along with costume.

330. ---, and Pamela Sheingorn. "Playing *Wisdom* at Trinity College." *RORD* 27 (1984): 179-84.

Reviews the April 12-14, 1984, performances. Comments on what one learns from such a performance in terms of the play's abstractness and concreteness, its concept of deity, characterization, costumes, stage directions, pageantry, "actability," audience involvement, and so on.

331. Colley, John Scott. "*Fulgens and Lucres:* Politics and Aesthetics." *ZAA* 23.4 (1975): 322-30.

Sees the play as a presentation of "true and false nobility, or plebeian ingenuity and aristocratic decay" (322). Looks at Medwall's political motives and the verisimilitude in the play. Concludes that the play allows the playwright to look "in upon the nature of art and . . . out at the responses of his audience" (330).

332. Collier, Richard J. "The Action of Fulfillment in the York Corpus Christi Play." *PCP* 11 (1976): 30-38.

Claims that the cycle coheres because of the action of fulfillment, which is crucial historically and doctrinally. Points to the internal transition from promise to fulfillment, which is the basis of the plot and characterization. Shows how the fulfillment is realized in the drama, and serves as a goal for human endeavor.

333.   ---.   *Poetry and Drama in the York Corpus Christi
       Play*. Hamden, Conn.: Shoe String, Archon Books,
       1978. 303 pp.

       Chap. I--"The Poetry of the Play"--considers
       "Poetry on the Stage," "The Verse Forms," and "The
       Language." Chap. II--"Poetry and Instruction: The
       Homiletic Modes"--looks at "Teaching and
       Understanding," "Following Christ in Word and
       Deed," and "The Play of the Baptism of Christ
       (Play XXI)". Chap. III--"Poetry and Communion:
       The Lyric Modes"--deals with "Grieving and
       Rejoicing," "From Sorrow to Joy," and "The Play of
       the Death and Burial of Christ (Play XXXVI)."
       Chap. IV--"Poetry and Fulfillment: The Narrative
       Modes"--discusses "The Congruence of Events,"
       "From Promise to Fulfillment," and "The Play of
       the Last Judgment (Play XLVIII)." Concludes by
       discussing the "Vastness and variety" (258) of the
       cycle, its playing time and scope, the coherence
       of the plays, the interaction between audience and
       actors physically and temporally, the
       appropriateness and functions of the verse, and
       the dramatic and rhetorical elements. With notes,
       bibliography, and index.

       Rev. Clifford Davidson, *CompD* 12.3 (Fall 1978):
            273-77.
            Choice 15 (Oct. 1978): 1046.
            Specu 54 (Oct. 1979): 789.

334.   Collier, Richard James. "A Re-evaluation of the
       Poetry of the York Corpus Christi Plays, with
       Special Reference to Plays I (Creation); XLI
       (Purification); XXI (Baptism); XXXVI (Mortificacio
       Cristi); XLIII (Ascension)." Ph.D. diss.,
       Washington U., 1969.

335.   Collins, Fletecher, Jr., ed. and transcr. *Medieval
       Church Music-Dramas: A Repertory of Complete
       Plays*. Charlottesville, VA: U. Press of Virginia,
       1976. xiii, 497 pp.

       Companion volume to his *The Production of Medieval
       Church Music-Drama* (see next entry). Gives
       introduction, dramatis personae, text, and musical
       notation for sixteen plays and for the *Te Deum
       Laudamus*. (For a list of the plays, see next
       entry.)

       Rev. *Choice* 13 (Nov. 1976): 1148.
            TLS (Feb. 11, 1977): 165.

336.   ---.   *The Production of Medieval Church Music-Drama.*
       Charlottesville, VA: U. Press of Virginia, 1972.
       xiii, 356 pp.   (See previous entry.)

       Concentrates on liturgical drama. Offers
       introduction and several illustrations for sixteen
       plays and the *Te Deum Laudamus*. Valuable for
       general discussions on dramatic applications of
       music and for the iconography presented in the 71
       illustrations. Also useful for various comments
       on staging, costuming, make-up, properties and
       furnishings, movement and gesture,
       characterization, sound effects, lighting, and
       determination of major episodes. With appendix
       ("The Practical Repertory of Medieval Church
       Music-Drama, with Manuscript Locations") and
       index. The plays presented are: 1) Visit to the
       Sepulchre; 2) Lament of Mary; 3) Pilgrim; 4)
       Shepherds; 5) Play of Herod with the Slaughter of
       the Innocents; 6) Procession of Prophets; 7)
       Raising of Lazarus; 8) Conversion of St. Paul; 9)
       Wise and Foolish Maidens; 10) Three Daughters; 11)
       Three Clerks; 12) Image of St. Nicholas; 13) Son
       of Getron; 14) Play of Daniel; 15) Play of the
       Annunciation; 16) Purification; [17]) *Te Deum
       Laudamus*.

       Rev. *AB* 49 (Mar. 27, 1972): 1180.
            TLS (July 28, 1972): 884.
            Choice 9 (Sept. 1972): 796.
            QJS 58 (Dec. 1972): 482.
            Notes 29 (Mar. 1973): 465.
            Grace Frank, *Specu* 48.4 (Oct. 1973): 738-40.
            Barbara Raw, *N&Q*, n.s. 20.11 (218) (Nov.
                 1973):437-39.
            David Bevington, *MP* 72.3 (Feb. 1975): 287-90.

337.   Collins, Patrick James. "Medieval Drama and the
       Pictorial Tradition." Ph.D. diss., U. California,
       Berkeley, 1974.

338.   ---.   "Narrative Bible Cycles in Medieval Art and
       Drama." *CompD* 9 (Summer 1975): 125-46. Rpt. in
       Davidson, Gianakaris, and Stroupe, eds., *The Drama
       of the Middle Ages*, 118-39 (entry # 409 below).

       Claims that common medieval pictorial
       representations of biblical episodes account for
       the selection and ordering of the plays in the
       cycles. Looks at ms art and wall paintings.

339.   ---.   *The N-Town Plays and Medieval Picture Cycles.*
       Kalamazoo: Medieval Institute Publications,

Western Michigan University, 1979. Early Drama,
Art, and Music Monograph Series, 2.

Looks at the plays in their wider artistic
contexts, with respect to the motifs of symbolic
fruit, fraud and disguise, worldly chaos and
heavenly calm, and a coalescence of these; with
special emphasis on the plays of Herod and the
Magi. Examines arts such as paintings,
sculptures, and tapestries to discover
iconographic connections between these and the
plays. Focuses on the iconography of medieval
bible picture cycles and the verse of the N-Town
plays. Claims the playwrights employed the same
iconography as did the artists, and used it to
link plays thematically. Discovers "significant
thematic pattern[s] within" the cycle (2).

340.   ---.   "Typology, Criticism, and Medieval Drama: Some
Observations on Method."   *CompD* 10.4 (Winter 1976-
77): 298-313.

Shows how "systems of doctrinal concordances
appear in the pictorial programs of biblical art"
(298), and how a clear view of religious art will
make one aware "of when and how typology was used
in the depiction of the bible story" (298).

341.   Collins, Suzanne Reider.   "Conventional Speeches in
the Towneley Mystery Plays."   Ph.D. diss., U. of
Iowa, 1969.

342.   Colthorpe, Marion.   "Pageants Before Queen Elizabeth I
at Coventry in 1566."   *N&Q* 32.4 (230) (Dec. 1985):
458-60.

Discusses the description by John Nichols and
others of the visit of the queen at Kenilworth
Castle, where she saw pageants by the Tanners,
Drapers, Smiths, and Weavers. Locates another
description in the De L'Isle ms in Kent, which
"gives the exact site of four pageants, and the
subject matter of three of them" (459). Quotes
from this description.

343.   Conley, John.   "Aural Error in 'Everyman'?"   *N&Q*, n.s.
22.6 (220) (June 1975): 244-45.

Points out guesses which the English translator
made based on the sound of the original Dutch.
Surveys scholarship. Uses "hertly" to demonstrate
the aural error and to substantiate the claim that
the Dutch text was the original.

344.   ---.   "*Everyman* 504: *Ase, Beholde,* or 'Ah, See'?"   *N&Q*
       29.5 (227) (Oct. 1982): 399-400.

       Examines how editors have handled *Ase* and *Beholde*.
       Says *Ase* is suspect, "as *Beholde* suggests" (400).

345.   ---.   "*Everyman* 29: 'Lawe' or 'Love'?"   *N&Q* 27.4 (225)
       (Aug. 1980): 298-99.

       Discusses the debate over which reading is
       correct. Claims that "the emendation of *love* for
       lawe is rash" (299). Cites *Elckerlijc* for
       confirmation.

346.   ---.   "The Identity of Discretion in *Everyman*."   *N&Q*,
       n.s. 30.5 (228): (Oct. 1983): 394-96.

       Reviews scholarship. Seeks the identity of
       Discretion in the Dutch source in the character of
       Wijsheit, later called Vroetscap (Wisdom and
       Prudence). Concludes that Discretion, as the
       source and the Christian tradition show, is
       prudence.

347.   ---.   "The Phrase 'The oyle of forgyuenes' in
       'Everyman': A Reference to Extreme Unction?"   *N&Q*,
       n.s. 22.3 (220) (Mar. 1975): 105-06.

       Examines Confession's last line in his speech to
       Everyman. Doubts Cawley's reading of "oyle" as
       "oil" [of extreme unction]; offers instead the
       more literal olive oil, "a traditional metaphor
       for mercy" (105).

348.   ---.   "'Reson' in 'Mankind,' 173."   *N&Q*, n.s. 23.10
       (221) (Oct. 1976): 447-48.

       Looks at the synonymy of "reson" and "acownte."
       Sees two parallel uses, one in "Earl Rivers's
       translation of Gerard van der Vlyderhoven's
       Cordiale" (447) and one in Matthew 12.36.

348b. Conrad, Peter.   *The History of English Literature: One
       Indivisible, Unending Book*.   Philadelphia: U. of
       Pennsylvania Press, 1985.   x, 740 pp.

       Chap. 9--"Miracles, Moralities and Marlowe" (126-
       44)--discusses the plays as "emerg[ing] from the
       daily celebration of the mass" (126). Looks
       mostly at the *Second Shepherds' Play* and *Everyman*
       as exemplars of the two main types of drama in the
       era. Chap. 39--"The Stages of Drama" (636-54)--
       also touches on these genres (esp. pp. 645 f.).

Has brief discussions on typology. Contains
index, but no notes or bibliography.

349. Cook, Philip S. "*Crown of Thorns*--Compiled from the
English Mystery Plays." *MET* 3.1 (July 1981): 57-
58.

Reports on performances March-April 1981 at
Victoria Theatre, Stoke-on-Trent.

350. Cooke, William G. "*The Tournament of Tottenham:* An
Alliterative Poem and an Exeter Performance."
REEDN 11.2 (1986): 1-3.

Mentions the "dramatic potential" (2) of this
narrative piece and evidence from the Exeter
Receiver's Account Rolls for 1432-3 that the work
was given some "dramatic" performance.

351. Cooper, Helen. "A Note on the Wakefield 'Prima
Pastorum.'" *N&Q* 20.9 (218) (Sept. 1973): 326.

Agrees with A.C. Cawley's view that Garcio is the
third shepherd. Claims that "Consistency of
speech order, role and dramatic technique
. . . indicate that Iak Garcio is indeed the Third
Shepherd and . . . the youngest of the three"
(326). Cites other views (especially England and
Pollard's ed., E.E.T.S., e.s. 71).

352. Cope, Jackson I. *The Theatre and the Dream: From
Metaphor to Form in Renaissance Drama*. Baltimore
and London: Johns Hopkins U. Press, 1973.

Looks at Medwall's *Fulgens and Lucrece*.

Rev. *LJ* 98 (Mar. 15, 1973): 870.
Choice 10 (Oct. 1973): 1184.
CompL 27 (Spring 1975): 166.
Raymond B. Waddington, *ELN* 12.3 (Mar. 1975):
200-02.
MP 74 (Aug. 1976): 94.
A.D. Nutall, *ShakS* 11 (1978): 292-96.
MLR 73 (July 1978): 578.

353. Corder, Jim W. "*Everyman:* The Way to Life." In
*Studies in Medieval, Renaissance, American
Literature: A Festschrift Honoring Troy C.
Crenshaw, Lorraine Sherley, and Ruth Speer Angell*,
53-56. Ed. by Betsy F. Colquitt. Fort Worth:
Texas Christian U. Press, 1971. Revised version
of article originally published in *Drama Critique*.

Argues "that the play's theme is not the hero's discovery of the way to Christian death, but his discovery of the Christian way to life" (53). Summarizes and comments on the plot with respect to the summoning "as the dramatic metaphor for human mortality" (55).

354. Cosman, Madeleine Pelner. "Feasts and Festivals, European." In *Dictionary of the Middle Ages* 5, 33-37. Ed. by Joseph R. Strayer (see entry # 1553 below).

Offers background information on the festive characteristics of the society. Mentions many dramatic celebrations or play-like social events.

355. Cotton, Nancy. "Katherine of Sutton: The First English Woman Playwright." *ETJ* 30.4 (Dec. 1978): 475-81.

Mentions the women who "belonged to religious guilds responsible for plays" (475) and the plays they performed. Identifies Lady Katherine "who wrote, or rewrote, the Easter dramatic offices for Barking nunnery while she was abbess there from 1363 to 1376" (475).

356. ---. *Women Playwrights in England c. 1363-1750*. Lewisburg: Bucknell U. Press; London and Toronto: Associated U. Presses, 1980.

Mentions only "The first recorded playwright in England . . . Katherine of Sutton, abbess of Barking" (27), writing in Latin between 1363 and 1376. Shows that the liturgical plays were acted by nuns. Also deals with Jane Lumley, translator/author of "Iphigenia in Aulis" (see Appendix B).

Rev. M. Havener, *LJ* 105 (Nov. 15, 1980): 2403.
Choice (June 1981): 1412.
SevCN 40 (Fall 1982): 46.

357. Courtney, Richard. *Outline History of British Drama*. Totowa, NJ: Littlefield, Adams & Co., 1982. ix, 336 pp.

Chap. 2--"Mysteries, Miracles, and Moralities" (15-35)--presents the "liturgy-to-drama" theory; ignores Kolve and later criticism. Has sections on the cycles, miracle plays, moralities. With "selected date list" (296), bibliography, and index.

Rev. *KPBG* 17 (Winter 1983): 24.

358. Cowan, Ian B. "Church and Society." In *Scottish Society in the Fifteenth Century,* 112-35. Ed. by Jennifer M. Brown. New York: St. Martin's; London: Edward Arnold, 1977.

Contains general information about "the religious processions and other celebrations" held by the craft guilds (118), and "the plays and pageants" (119) on "scriptural subjects . . . first acted in churches and afterwards in the streets on a moveable stage" (119).

359. Cowen, Janet. "'Heven and erthe in lytel space.'" In *Aspects of Early English Drama,* 62-77. Ed. by Paula Neuss. Cambridge: D.S. Brewer; Totowa, NJ: Barnes & Noble, 1983. (See entry # 1213 below.)

Treats the space allotted in staging, drawing data from the texts and the records. Looks at specific plays for evidence.

360. ---, and Richard Proudfoot. "*Tom Tiler and His Wife.*" *MET* 3.1 (July 1987): 61-63.

Reports on a performance of May 7, 1981, at Bedford College, London.

360a. Cowling, Douglas. "The Angels' Song in *Everyman.*" *N&Q* 233 (1988): 301-03.

361. ---. "The Liturgical Celebration of Corpus Christi in Medieval York." *REEDN* 1.2 (1976): 5-9.

Discusses the two York processions (ecclesiastical and dramatic). Claims that they were not connected in any way. Shows similarities between Palm Sunday and Corpus Christi processionals. Examines "the nature of the civic procession" (7). Notes that the religious procession passed through the streets, and there "is no indication that the procession stopped at any point, and it certainly did not halt at the various play stations in order to display the sacrament" (8). Emphasizes "that the liturgical procession and the pageant procession were separate entities" (8), that the pageants followed the procession, took their own pace, and eventually took different routes, and that "neither was dependent on the other" (9).

362. Cox, John D. "The Medieval Background of *Measure for Measure.*" *MP* 81.1 (Aug. 1983): 1-13.

Looks at morality play traits and analogues in the cycle drama. Finds many overlapping features.

363. Craik, T.W. "The Companies and the Repertory." In
     The Revels *History of Drama in English, Vol. II:
     1500-1576*, 101-39. Ed. by T.W. Craik. London and
     New York: Methuen, 1980. (See entry for Norman
     Sanders, et al., # 1432 below.)

     Discusses "Varieties of performers" (103-07);
     "Men's Companies" (108-16); "Boys' Companies: the
     Chapel Children" (117-23); "Boys' Companies:
     Paul's Boys and others" (124-29); "University and
     Inns of Court Performers" (130-32); "The
     Unattached plays" (13-39).

xxx. ---, ed. *The* Revels *History of Drama in English, Vol.
     II: 1500-1576*. (See entry for Norman Sanders, et
     al, # 1432 below.)

364. ---. "Tudor and Early Elizabethan Drama." In *English
     Drama (Excluding Shakespeare): Select
     Bibliographical Guides*, 29-41. Ed. by Stanley
     Wells. (See entry # 1672 below.)

     Briefly examines the period, dramatic types, and
     special themes. Offers a short bibliography of
     criticism (36-41).

365. ---. "Violence in the English Miracle Plays." In
     Medieval Drama, 172-95. Ed. by Neville Denny.
     London: Edward Arnold, 1973. (See # 442 below.)

     Shows that violence in the plays helps the cycles
     achieve a sense of inclusiveness. Looks at the
     origins of the violence, its relation to
     "tradition, selection, originality, and the
     development of pathos and of comedy" (175). Also
     considers violence "in relation to medieval stage
     practice" (175). Considers violence in several
     plays (e.g. the Murder of Abel, the Massacre of
     the Innocents, and the Sufferings and Death of
     Christ).

366. Cramer, James Douglas. "Theophany in the English
     Corpus Christi Play." Ph.D. diss., U. of
     Michigan, 1986.

366a. Crawford, Anne. *A History of the Vintners' Company*.
     London: Constable, 1977. 319 pp.

     Cites many instances of entertainments. Mentions
     "the early sixteenth century . . . chief civic
     procession [which] was held for the Midsummer
     Watch . . . a great torch-light procession" (100),
     with "pageants, dancers and entertainments" (100).
     Points out, too, that "In 1538 . . . the Midsummer

Watch . . . and its pageants were transferred to
the Lord Mayor's day in November" (99). Also
describes an early seventeenth-century Triumph put
on during "the festivities surrounding the
marriage of James I's daughter, Elizabeth" (103),
along with a pageant called "Troja nova
triumphans" by Thomas Dekker" (103). With notes,
appendixes, maps, bibliography, and index.

367. Creeth, Edmund. *Mankynde in Shakespeare*. Athens, GA:
U. of Georgia Press, 1976. 192 pp.

Gives a general historical account of the
development of the morality play, with references
throughout to all the English moralities.

Rev. R. Berman, *SewR* 84 (Oct. 1976): 657-58.
Choice 13 (Nov. 1976): 1132.
S. Sternlicht, *LJ* 101 (Dec. 1, 1976): 2490.
René E. Fortin, *CompD* 11.4 (Winter 1977-78):
345-47.
Alan C. Dessen, "Homilies and Anomalies: The
Legacy of the Morality Play." *ShakS* 11
(1978): 243-58. (See entry # 447 below.)
L. Walker, *VQR* 54 (Winter 1978): 185-91.
R. Battenhouse, *ShakQ* 30 (Summer 1979): 433-
35.
L. Barkan, *MP* 77 (May 1980): 420-24.

368. Cross, Sally Joyce. "Torturers as Tricksters in the
Cornish *Ordinalia*." *Neoph* 84.4 (1983): 448-55.

Sees the torturers in the Passion scenes "as
modulations of the trickster archetype that
anthropologists . . . see as mediators" (448).
Explains their actions in the play. Says they are
"preoccupied with scatology, act amorally and
antisocially, boast narcissistically" (448), and
show they do not understand the difference between
reality and reflection. Claims that they "mediate
the paradox inherent in the Christian framework of
man's redemption" (448).

369. Crow, Brian. "Lydgate's 1445 Pageant for Margaret of
Anjou." *ELN* 18.3 (Mar. 1981): 170-74.

Mentions Lydgate's exploiting "the allegorical
potential of street pageantry" (170), his
concentration on "[t]opical political concerns"
(171), and the "remarkably unified manipulation of
allegorical pageant conventions" (173).

370. Crowther, J.D.W. "The Wakefield Cain and the 'Curs' of the Bad Tither." *Parergon* 24 (Aug. 1979): 19-24.

Presents an argument about the articles of excommunication as listed in *Jacob's Well* "to point to the connection between them and the arguments between Cain and Abel about tithing" (19). Shows the lesson for the play's audience.

371. Crupi, Charles W. "Christian Doctrine in Henry Medwall's *Nature*." *Renascence* 34.2 (Winter 1982): 100-12.

Looks doctrinally at the use of personifications of figures of evil. Claims that "the analysis of morality drama must not begin with a Manichaean struggle between good and evil but with orthodox Christian ideas about the role of free will in human life" (100-01). Analyzes *Nature* in these terms.

371a. Cunningham, John. "Comedic and Liturgical Restoration in *Everyman*." *CompD* 22 (1988): 162-73.

372. Cutts, John P. "The Shepherds' Gifts in *the Second Shepherds' Play* and Bosch's 'Adoration of the Magi.'" *CompD* 4.2 (Summer 1970): 120-24.

Sees parallels between the gifts and the painting with respect to the use of a bird, a ball, and cherries. Points out a single pictorial source containing all three of the shepherds' gifts: Bosch's painting. Supports Lawrence J. Ross's views about the meaning of the symbolic gifts (the ball is symbolic of Christ's kingship, the bird of His divinity, the cherry of His sacrificial manhood). (Cites Ross, "Symbol and Structure in *The Secunda Pastorum*," *CompD* 1.2 [Spring 1967]: 122-43.) Supports the notion that the playwright was familiar with iconographic conventions.

373. ---. "'Wee happy heardsmen here': A Newly Discovered Shepherds' Carol Possibly Belonging to a Medieval Pageant." *CompD* 18.3 (Fall 1984): 265-73.

Discusses the recently discovered part-song ms books (compiled c. 1637) of Bishop Thomas Smith of Carlisle. Traces the history of the books. Looks at the "Wee happy heardsmen" carol, presenting the text with music. Speculates on the relationship of the carol to the *Officium Pastorum*, to the shepherds' song in *The Second*

Shepherds' Play, to *The First Shepherds' Play*, and
to the Shrewsbury Fragments.

374. Dahl, Liisa. *Nominal Style in the Shakespearean
Soliloquy. With Reference to the Early English
Drama, Shakespeare's Immediate Predecessors and
His Contemporaries*. Turku: Turun Yliopisto, 1969.
Turun Yliopiston julkaisuja, ser. B. 112.

Chap. II covers "The Early English Drama,"
"Miracle Plays and Moralities," and "Other Pre-
Shakespearean Plays" (138-51). Focuses on the use
of the soliloquy in several plays from a
linguistic perspective.

375. Daniels, Richard Jacob. "A Study of the Formal and
Literary Unity of the N-Town Mystery Cycle."
Ph.D. diss., Ohio State U., 1972.

376. ---. "*Uxor* Noah: A Raven or a Dove?" *ChauR* 14.1
(Summer 1979): 23-32.

Concerns the different treatment of Noah's wife in
all the cycle plays. Looks at the first speech of
each play, the shrewish-wife sections, and the
scene of the release of the raven and the dove to
determine if the wife is on the side of the dove
or the raven. Concludes that she does not wish to
believe Noah (though "[s]he does not doubt him"--
29), and that she is "a spokesman for fallen
humanity, for those who are excluded from the ark"
(29). Hence "she is never really on the raven's
side" (29).

377. Danner, Constance S. "The Staging and Significance of
Selected Wakefield New Testament Mystery Plays."
Ph.D. diss., U. Nebraska, Lincoln, 1987.

378. Davenport, Tony. "'Lusty fresche galaunts.'" In
Aspects of Early English Drama, 110-28, 147-48.
Ed. by Paula Neuss. Cambridge: D.S. Brewer;
Totowa, NJ: Barnes & Noble, 1983. (See entry #
1213 below.)

Deals with "the heedless folly of young men" (111)
as it is reflected in their clothing. Examines
clothing in several dramatic and non-dramatic
texts. Shows how attire reflects "youth and
education [which] are central themes for late
medieval plays . . ." (127). With one illus.

379. Davenport, W.A. *Fifteenth-Century English Drama. The
Early Moral Plays and their Literary Relations*.

Cambridge: D.S. Brewer; Totowa, NJ: Rowman & Littlefield, 1982. vii, 152 pp.

Aims "to write a simple account of the different types of drama being written in fifteenth-century England" ([iii]) with special emphasis on morality plays. Says that the plays are "early versions of familiar theatrical genres" (v). Looks at links between plays and among other writings of the era. Chap. I discusses the various dramatic genres, the subject matter, characters, and form of the cycles and moralities, and shows the commonality between the drama and other literary genres. Chap. II deals with pride, death, and tragedy, with special reference to *The Pride of Life* and *Everyman;* analyzes the medieval notion of tragedy. Chap. III considers *Mankind* in the context of exemplum books and exemplum plays, medieval satire, and comedy. Chap. IV looks at "*Wisdom* and the Drama of Ideas" (79), treating also closet-drama and debate, and salon pageants, mummings, and masques. Chap. V is on "*The Castle of Perseverance* and the Long Play" (106), showing the breadth of inclusiveness suggested by the play ("all human life is here!"--114), and dealing with "Medley, panorama and chronicle" (120). Chap. VI is on "Scope and Style: Lydgate and East Anglian Drama" (130). With notes, bibliography, and index. The main controversy in this book is the author's suggestion that scholars drop the traditional and imprecise genre designations and replace them with other traditional designations such as "comedy" and "tragedy."

Rev. *Choice* 20 (Feb. 1983): 828.
　　　Meg Twycross, *English* 32.144 (Autumn 1983): 251-57.
　　　Sarah Carpenter, *MedAe* 53.2 (1984): 321-22.
　　　Stanley J. Kahrl, *StudAC* 6 (1984): 186-89.
　　　Pamela Gradon, *N&Q,* n.s. 31.2 (229) (June 1984): 258-59.
　　　RES 35 (Nov. 1984): 524.
　　　Alasdair A. MacDonald, *EngStud* 66.2 (Apr. 1985): 162-66. (See entry # 1025 below.)
　　　Specu 60 (July 1985): 738.

380. ---. "Peter Idley and the Devil in *Mankind.*" *EngStud* 64.2 (Apr. 1983): 106-12.

Explains the figure Tutivillus. Summarizes scholarship. Points to a parallel in Peter Idley's *Instructions to his Son* for a treatment similar to that of Tutivillus, and claims the Idley text may have been a source.

381.   Davidson, Clifford.   "After the Fall: Design in the
        Old Testament Plays in the York Cycle."   *Medi* 1.1
        (Spring 1975): 1-24.

        Shows how an understanding of medieval visual arts
        may help to explain the selection of episodes from
        the Old Testament in the York Cycle. Discusses
        each play--plot, characters, themes, etc.

381.1 ---.   "The Anti-Visual Prejudice."   In *Iconoclasm vs.
        Art and Drama*, 33-46.   Ed. by Davidson and Nichols
        (see entry # 410a below).

        Discusses the anti-theatrical and anti-artistic
        prejudice of the early period which eventuated in
        the iconoclasm of the renaissance focused on the
        presentation of sacred images. Points out many
        instances of this prejudice.

381a.   ---.   "An Apocalypse Manuscript from York."   *EDAMN* 6.1
        (Fall 1983): 3-5.

        Comments on an Apocalypse ms from c. 1270
        displaying a good deal of biblical iconography,
        especially with respect to musical instruments
        (harp, fidel, and trumpet), but also noting other
        iconographic details: toads, snakes, Tree of
        Virtues, and Tree of Vices. Useful in recognizing
        iconographic features common in the plays.

382.   ---.   "Civic Concern and Iconography in the York
        Passion."   *AnM* 15 (1974): 125-49.

        Looks at the plays of the York Realist with
        respect to the indigenous arts and iconography of
        the era. Claims the playwright's work was aimed
        at a popular audience. Examines the plays
        individually to reveal the "immense dramatic
        skill" (148) of the playwright in his use of
        realistic detail in the iconographic features.

383.   D[avidson], C[lifford].   "The Concept of *Purpose* and
        Early Drama."   *EDAMN* 2.2 (Apr. 1980): 9-16.

        Argues that an understanding of the *purpose* of
        early drama is crucial to its interpretation.
        Claims that "Drama . . . reveals itself in ways
        which are often subtly subversive of attempts to
        objectify its experiences" (9). Explores the
        purposes of drama not with respect to the artist's
        intent (which is irrelevant), but in terms of what
        knowledge one must bring to the study of the play
        in order to interpret it properly. Points to the
        inaccurate notion that medieval art and drama are

crude or primitively naive. Considers acting
styles and traditions and conditions of
production. Dispells the notion that medieval
drama developed and evolved "along a linear path
toward the high point of Elizabethan drama . . . .
it is no longer acceptable to view drama as going
through development from simple to complex, from
sacred to secular modes" (12). Separates medieval
drama from the modern notions of comedy and
tragedy; medieval drama is less tied to form, more
related "to the function of the devotional image
in the visual arts" (13).

383a. ---. "The Contribution of W.L. Hildburgh." *EDAMN*
11.2 (Spring 1989): 30-37.

On Hildburgh's collection of alabaster sculptures
(now at the Victoria and Albert Museum), which
show many visual elements related to the drama.
Also discusses Hildburgh's scholarship on the
subject, its strengths and weaknesses.

383b. ---. "'The Devil's Guts': Allegations of Superstition
and Fraud in Religious Drama and Art during the
Reformation." In *Iconoclasm vs. Art and Drama*,
92-144. Ed. by Davidson and Nichols (see entry #
410a below).

Considers iconoclastic behavior against drama and
art. With respect to the plays, mentions the
liturgical drama (104 f.), Wager's *Life and
Repentaunce of Marie Magdalene* (105 f.), the Digby
Mary Magdalene (107 f.), and many other plays.

384. D[avidson], C[lifford]. "The Devotional Impulse and
Drama at York." *EDAMN* 1.2 (Apr. 1979): 2-4.

Looks at York records to examine what they reveal
about "late Medieval devotional life--aspects
which depend heavily on imaginative visual
display" (2). Says that devotion was a motive for
presenting plays. Shows the reason for the
inaccurate stereotyped notion that the late Middle
Ages was religiously corrupt. Says that
understanding the devotion of the age helps one to
understand the plays and that medieval attitudes
supported drama as good and praiseworthy.

385. Davidson, Clifford. "The Digby *Mary Magdalene* and the
Magdalene Cult of the Middle Ages." *AnM* 13
(1972): 70-87.

Mentions the facts that this is one of the few
surviving saints' plays in English, that it uses

an elaborately staged playing area, and that its
structure and characterizations are complex.
Looks at the theology and artistry of the play,
which depicts a pilgrim's spiritual *peregrinatio*.
Treats the central figure in traditional terms
with respect to the cult of Magdalene followers.
Concludes that the play "was designed to inspire
intense religious devotion" (87). With two
illustrations.

386. ---. *Drama and Art: An Introduction to the Use of
Evidence from the Visual Arts for the Study of
Early Drama.* Kalamazoo, Michigan: The Medieval
Institute, Western Michigan U., 1977. Early Drama,
Art, and Music Monograph Series 1. iv, 169 pp.

Deals with many, mostly pre-Reformation, British
arts: carvings, Easter sepulchres, embroideries,
jewelry, ms art, etc. Explains how to prepare
bibliographical entries, photographs, subject
cards, flow charts for on-line retrieval, etc. for
dramatic records. Represents a prolegomenon for
other volumes in a reference series which will
present subject lists and bibliographies. Has
chapters on "Subject Headings and Abbreviations"
(33); "The Card Files" (42); "The Computer" (71);
"Dating, Authenticity, Provenance" (80); "Costume"
(90); "Interdisciplinary Criticism and Medieval
Drama" (100). With appendix: "Art and
Renaissance Drama: The Example of Shakespeare"
(126). With illustrations, notes, and
bibliography.

387. ---. "Early Drama, Art, and Music: A New Project."
RORD 20 (1977): 91-94.

Announces the *EDAM* project.

388. ---. "The End of the World in Medieval Art and
Drama." *MichAc* 5.2 (Fall 1972): 257-63.

Discusses medieval ideas about "the end of
collective human life in this fallen world" (257).
Looks at the drama's use of Matthew, Chap. 15, and
"additional features borrowed from the Apocalypse"
(257), along with the "well-known Fifteen Signs of
Doomsday" (257). Considers these images in
stained glass and other arts and their
implications for scholars of the drama. With two
illustrations.

388a. [---.] "Enlightenment vs. Antiquarianism: What We
Always Wanted to Know But Others Didn't." *EDAMN*
8.1 (Fall 1985): 4-5.

Comments on the annotated copy of Thomas Sharp's
Dissertation on the Pageants . . .--along with the
1825 review in the *Gentleman's Magazine* and the
1826 review in *The Monthly Review*. Shows the low
regard the reviewers had for the mystery plays,
indicating "the indifference of the Enlightenment
[which] followed hard upon Protestant iconoclasm"
(5). Explains the plays' disrepute in the
nineteenth century.

389. ---. [Foreword.] See Patrick J. Collins, *The N-Town
Plays and Medieval Picture Cycles* (entry # 339
above).

390. ---. *From Creation to Doom: The York Cycle of Mystery
Plays*. New York: AMS Press, 1984. ix, 256 pp.

Presents a full-scale study of the York plays.
Chap. 1--"The Visual Arts and Medieval Drama at
York"--examines what the visual arts can suggest
about dramatic performances since "The artists and
dramatists were . . . in the business of
visualizing the same sacred history" (3). Talks
about the "new style" of art in York brought about
by new--more realistic--aesthetic values and
"altered theology" (5), and discusses the
literalizing of biblical metaphors. Shows the
similarity in purpose of drama and art. Warns
against drawing too many conclusions from the
similarities.

Chap. 2--"The Creation: Iconography, Staging, and
Costume"--examines the opening play of the cycle
in terms of the "splendidly elaborate" (22)
costuming and pageantry.

Chap. 3--"After the Fall"--looks at Old Testament
plays with special reference to "the marked
alteration in the human condition" after the fall
(39) and "the moral and physical disaster" it
brought (41).

Chap. 4--"The Early Life of Christ"--considers
some textual matters (e.g. revision, erasures) and
some of the plays in this part of the cycle in
relation to the visual arts and music.

Chap. 5--"The Ministry Plays"--looks at the
limited and perhaps disappointingly brief plays
from Christ's ministry--similar to the treatment
in the other cycles. Explains them as preparation
for the Passion and thus "very important" (80).

Chap. 6--"Civic Patronage of the York Passion"--
looks at the revisions of the York Realist as
raising the literary quality, while his
contemporaries would have seen his contribution in
religious and practical terms. Points to the
realism in the iconographic features of the plays.
Examines the plays from the Agony and Betrayal to
the condemnation of Christ.

Chap. 7--"The Realism of the York Realist"--
examines the term "realism" and discusses how it
applies to the work of the York Realist--
especially in terms of "the relationship between
detail and meaning" (119).

Chap. 8--"From *Tristia* to *Gaudium*"--examines the
Harrowing of Hell play, with its mime and music.

Chap. 9--"Pilgrimage and Transcendence"--looks at
the continued movement from *tristia* to *gaudium*
(sadness to joy). Explains the thematic unity in
the seemingly fragmented vision of the crucial
events of human history in the cycle. Shows that
"the structure of the drama is fixed by
iconographic and exegetical traditions" (155).
Examines the pilgrimage motif in relation to
transcendence.

Chap. 10--"The Virgin Mary"--looks at the
veneration of Mary both in relation to Christ and
as a model of womanhood, depicted in drama and
non-dramatic arts.

Chap. 11--"The Last Judgment"--looks at the
absence of Mary from this play and examines its
various relationships to the arts. "The drama and
the art are . . . expressions of the civic piety
that informed communities such as York . . ."
(191). Focuses throughout on the relationship
between drama and the arts. With sixteen plates
reproducing stained-glass windows and ms arts.

Rev. *Choice* 22 (Nov. 1984): 422.
    Specu 60 (Oct. 1985): 964.
    J.W. Robinson, *CompD* 19.4 (Winter 1985-86):
        365-67.
    Alexandra F. Johnston, *M&RD* 3 (1986): 305-07.

391. ---. "From *Tristia* to *Gaudium:* Iconography and the
York-Towneley *Harrowing of Hell.*" *ABR* 28.3
(Sept. 1977): 260-75.

Examines the movement in the play from sorrow to
joy. Considers the play in its context, the

imagery of light, the element of anticlimax in the
York and Towneley presentations, the
characterizations of Christ, the use of the gates
of Hell, the staging of the play, the use of
Michael in York (and his lack of appearance in the
Towneley play), and the final movement to joy,
"for the sorrowful sight of Christ crucified is
transformed . . . into the spectacle of the
victorious Lord" (275) who invites all men to
partake of the supreme joy of Paradise.

392. ---. "Gesture in Medieval Drama with Special
Reference to the Doomsday Plays in the Middle
English Cycles." *EDAMN* 6.1 (Fall 1983): 8-17.

Tries to determine what gestures would have been
appropriate for actors. Looks at stage
directions, dialogue, analogous scenes in the
visual arts. Examines only one subject to
demonstrate the value of such a pursuit. Also
considers biblical sources. Analyzes each
character separately.

392a. ---. *The Guild Chapel Wall Paintings at Stratford-
upon-Avon.* New York: AMS Press, 1988. AMS
Studies in the Renaissance, No. 22. x, 60 pp., 20
leaves of plates.

Points up the Dance of Death and Seven Deadly Sins
wall painting from the middle of the sixteenth
century in the chapel, probably known by
Shakespeare but stemming from the arts of the
middle ages. Mentions the painting of St. George
and the "dragon and an actor impersonating St.
George" (5) associated with the riding of 1541-47,
and later in the 1550s.

392b. ---. "Interdisciplinary Drama Research at Western
Michigan University." *Tréteaux* 2 (1980): 17-20.

393. ---. "Jest and Earnest: Comedy in the Work of the
Wakefield Master." *AnM* 22 (1982): 65-83.

Claims that the plays must be visualized--seen--
for their comedy and the plays themselves to be
understood. Compares the iconography of the
visual arts to the actions in the plays. Does not
deny the serious sacred intent of the drama.
Looks at "comic," "comedy," and the structures
they appear in. Concludes that the laughter in
these plays is no proof of "increasing
secularization" (83) or aimless "comic relief"
(83).

394.   ---.   "The Lost Coventry Drapers' Play of Doomsday and
its Iconographic Context." *LSE*, n.s. 17 (1986):
141-58.

Sees the plays as expressions of "civic pride and
devotion that helped to bind together the various
units of the community" (141); emphasizes the
visual aspects of the drama. Looks at "the
documents and other evidence that illuminate the
lost Coventry Drapers' play" (141). Uses an
iconographic approach, considering visual arts of
the time. With illustrations.

395.   ---.   "Medieval Drama: Diversity and Theatricality."
In *Studies in Medieval Drama in Honor of William
L. Smoldon on His 82nd Birthday*, 5-12. Ed. by
Clifford Davidson, et al. Kalamazoo, Michigan:
Western Michigan U. Press, 1974. Special issue of
CompD, 8.1 (Spring 1974).

An introductory essay to this collection. Offers
a general overview of approaches, points of
interest in the scholarship, and brief comments on
the essays in this volume.

396.   ---.   "Medieval Puppet Drama at Witney, Oxfordshire,
and Pentecost Ceremony at St. Paul's, London."
EDAMN 9.1 (Fall 1986): 15-16. [N.B. The table of
contents to this issue has the title, "Medieval
Puppet Theater . . . ."]

Comments on William Lambarde's description of an
annual Resurrection puppet show, specifically
referring to the use of a "'white Pigion'" (16)
let down on a string.

397.   ---.   "The Middle English Saint Play and Its
Iconography." In *The Saint Play in Medieval
Europe*, 31-122. Ed. by Clifford Davidson.
Kalamazoo, Michigan: Medieval Institute
Publications, Western Michigan U., 1986. Early
Drama, Art, and Music Monograph Series, 8. (See
entry # 404 below.)

Comments on how few plays of this genre survive,
which plays once existed, the plays' devotional
intent, their fund-raising possibilities, recorded
instances of specific plays and their contents,
and the iconography of these dramas. Examines
stained glass, paintings, and other related arts.
Discusses "Franciscan involvement in the medieval
drama" (44), the figures of Catherine, Thomas
Becket, St. George, and the plays related to them;
also, discusses other lost British saint plays and

the two extant ones from Digby MS. 133 (*Mary Magdalene* and the *Conversion of St. Paul*).

398.   ---, ed. *A Middle English Treatise on the Playing of Miracles*. Washington, D.C.: U. Press of America, 1981. 87 pp.

This is the text of the Lollard *Tretise of Miraclis Pleyinge*, with introduction, textual notes, critical notes, and glossary. Introduction covers historical data and milieu of the treatise, its religious background and hostility to drama, mimesis in religious plays, the ms, etc. With selected bibliography.

Rev. *EDAMN* 3.2 (Apr. 1981): 9-10.
    Theresa Coletti, *CompD* 16.2 (Summer 1982): 184-88.
    Nicholas Davis, "Another View of the *Tretise of Miraclis Pleyinge*." *MET* 4.1 (July 1982): 48-55. (See entry # 417 below.)
    RES 35 (May 1984): 280.
    MLR 80 (Jan. 1985): 115.

399.   ---. "Northern Spirituality and the Late Medieval Drama of York." In *The Spirituality of Western Christendom*, 125-51, 205-08. Ed. by E. Rozanne Elder. Kalamazoo: Cistercian Publications, 1976.

Looks at the plays and the art of York with respect to fifteenth- and sixteenth-century spirituality, which an examination of the art will reveal. Has sections on "Early and Late Medieval Spirituality" (130), "The Humanity of Christ" (133), "The York Cycle" (136), "Creation to Judgment" (141), "Good Works" (146), and "Iconography" (147). With illustrations from stained glass windows of York.

400.   D[avidson], C[lifford]. "Of Woodcut and Play." *EDAMN* 3.2 (Apr. 1981): 14-17.

Examines the woodcuts on the title pages of John Skot's undated editions of *Everyman*. Points out the inappropriateness of the depiction of Death as not matching the character in the play. Shows how "the printer drew directly on traditional scenes in the visual arts" (16). Considers the play and the Dance of Death theme.

401.   Davidson, Clifford. "On the Uses of Iconographic Study: The Example of the *Sponsus* From St. Martial of Limoges." *CompD* 13.4 (Winter 1979-80): 300-19.

Says that the notion of the unity of early drama
is an "inaccurate conception" (300). Urges the
study of iconography to put the plays in their
proper context. Shows that art and drama should
be "bracketed" to one another for each to
illuminate the other. Demonstrates this with the
story of the wise and foolish virgins from the
Sponsus.

402.   ---. "La phénoménologie de la souffrance, le drame
       médiéval, et 'King Lear.'" *RHT* 37.4 (1985): 343-
       57.

Responds to critical view of Elizabethan drama as
evolving from medieval morality plays. Compares
medieval portrayal of world history and
Shakespearean tragedy (with respect to *King Lear*).
Attempts to base the phenomenological concept of
suffering on the uniquely human sense of moral
loss in a world torn between good and evil
choices. Claims that an audience can feel
suffering/sadness even without sharing a
character's physical pain. Points up the medieval
notion that suffering resulted from natural human
estrangement from God. Also points out that
depictions of Eden provoked a feeling of nostalgia
for original perfection, and that external,
satanic forces could tempt one further from God.
Shows that medieval drama contrasts the fallen
angels, without any choice or regret, and Adam and
Eve, who feel deeply the consequences of their
chosen response to external persuasion. Shows
also that the Noah story illustrates human
stubbornness even when salvation is offered, and
that the ark becomes the new Eden when Noah's wife
calms herself to accept her role as the new Eve.
Says that women became symbols of suffering due to
the pain of childbirth and the sadness experienced
by Mary, mother of Jesus. Compares the medieval
plays to *Lear*.

403.   ---. "The Realism of the York Realist and the York
       Passion." *Specu* 50.2 (Apr. 1975): 270-83. Rpt.
       in *Medieval English Drama: A Casebook*, 101-17.
       Ed. by Peter Happé. London: Macmillan, 1984 (see
       entry # 684 below).

Reviews scholarship. Claims that this playwright
"believed primarily that he was giving new life to
the symbolic pictorial narrative of the Passion"
(270-71). Looks at the minute details of the
works with respect to the visual arts, showing how
these details carry meaning and give

verisimilitude to plot and character, "producing a desired emotional response" (274).

404.   ---, ed. *The Saint Play in Medieval Europe.* Kalamazoo, Michigan: Medieval Institute Publications, Western Michigan U., 1986. Early Drama, Art, and Music Monograph Series, 8. x, 269 pp.

Contains six essays, only one of which is on English drama: Clifford Davidson, "The Middle English Saint Play and Its Iconography," 31-122 (see entry # 397 above).

Rev. *Choice* 24 (Apr. 1987): 1227.
    Darryll Grantley, *CompD* 21.3 (Fall 1987): 295-97.
    Helen Phillips, *MedAe* 57.1 (1988): 87-88.

405.   ---. "Space and Time in Medieval Drama: Meditations on Orientation in the Early Theater." In *Word, Picture, and Spectacle*, 39-93. Ed. by Clifford Davidson. Kalamazoo: Medieval Institute Publications, Western Michigan U., 1984. Early Drama, Art, and Music Monograph Series, 5. (See entry # 408 below.)

Claims that since drama is a visual art, it should be studied "in terms of its spatial elements" (39). Also shows that medieval--not contemporary--views must be taken into account. Aims "to sketch the foundations for a phenomenology of early drama" (39), which drama is rooted in space and time. Emphasizes *"perceived experience* and *observable structures"* (39). Writes on Space (part I); Time (part II); and Rising, Falling, Levitation, Ecstasy (part III).

405.1 ---. "Stage Gesture in Medieval Drama." In *Atti del IV Colloquio della Société Internationale pour l'Etude Théâtre Médiéval*, 465-78. Ed. by M. Chiabo, F. Doglio, and M. Maymone. Viterbo, Italy: Centro Studi sul Teatro Medioevale e Rinascimentale, 1984.

405a. ---. "Thomas Aquinas, the Feast of Corpus Christi, and the English Cycle Plays." *MichAc* 7.1 (Summer 1974): 103-10.

Comments on the similarity between the drama and other arts in terms of their "philosophical thinking and aesthetic developments" (103). Examines "specific doctrinal points" (103) in the plays, and broader matters as well. Shows the influence of Aquinas, especially with respect to the part he played "in the establishment of the Feast of Corpus Christi" (104) and his notions about play and recreation, pleasure and enjoyment.

406. D[avidson], C[lifford]. "Thomas Sharp and the Stratford Hell Mouth." *EDAMN* 1.1 (Dec. 1978): 6-8.

Discusses plate 6 of Sharp's *A Dissertation on the Pageants or Dramatic Mysteries Anciently Performed at Coventry* (1825), which shows a Hell mouth scene (illustration reproduced on p. 6). Relates this to the Drapers' accounts of dramatic performances--specifically a performance of Doomsday.

406a. ---. "Toward a Sociology of Visual Forms in the English Medieval Theater." *FCS* 13 (1988): 221-35.

407. ---. "The Visual Arts and Drama, with Special Emphasis on the Lazarus Plays." In *Le Théâtre au Moyen Age*, 45-59, discussion 59-64. Ed. by Gari R. Muller. Quebec: Aurore-Univers; Montreal: Les Editions Universe, 1981. (See entry # 1181 below.)

Looks at design and iconography to show the theater's use of the visual arts for dramatic purposes. Deals with setting, gesture, relationship of drama to the visual arts. Glances briefly at English drama.

407a. ---. *Visualizing the Moral Life: Medieval Iconography and the Macro Moralities*. New York: AMS Press, 1989.

Contains chapters on *Mankind, The Castle of Perseverance, Wisdom*, and "Life's Terminus and the Morality Drama." Looks at the "visualizing dimensions" of the Macro plays. Considers the iconography of the era and the relationship of the plays to the visual arts.

407b. ---. "Women and Medieval Drama." *WS* 11 (1984): 99-113.

408. ---, ed. *Word, Picture, and Spectacle*. Kalamazoo, Michigan: Medieval Institute Publications, Western Michigan U., 1984. Early Drama, Art, and Music Monograph Series, 5.

Contains essays on pictorial representations of iconography. Includes Davidson's "Space and Time in Medieval Drama" (# 405 above), and Roger

Ellis's "The Word in Religious Art . . . ." (# 536
below).

408a. ---, and Jennifer Alexander. *The Early Art of
Coventry, Stratford-upon-Avon, Warwick, and Lesser
Sites in Warwickshire: A Subject List of Extant
and Lost Art, Including Items Relevant to Early
Drama.* Kalamazoo, Michigan: Medieval Institute,
Western Michigan U., 1985. Early Drama, Art and
Music Reference Series, 4. xii, 216 pp.

Considers what drama historians and critics can
learn from various arts: tapestries, ivory
panels, stained glass windows, wall paintings,
architecture, tombs, other carvings, metalwork,
seals, stonework, musical instruments, etc.
Discusses the iconographic value of the arts.
Lists the arts by subject (e.g. Representations of
God, Angels, and Devils; Old Testament; Parents of
the Virgin and Her Life; etc.) in more than a
dozen specific and various miscellaneous
categories. With appendixes on relics and
iconography. With bibliography (179-95), 71
illustrations, index, and map.

409. ---, C.J. Gianakaris, and John H. Stroupe, eds. *The
Drama in the Middle Ages: Comparative and Critical
Essays.* New York: AMS Press, 1982. AMS Studies
in the Middle Ages 4. xxi, 378 pp.

Contains introduction by Davidson and reprints of
21 essays. Those pertinent to this bibliography
are as follows: 1) Bjork (# 197 above); 2) Muir
("The Trinity . . .," # 1179); 3) Edwards (# 510);
4) Collins (# 338); 5) Hanning (# 681); 6) Thomas
P. Campbell (# 264); 7) Munson (# 1182); 8)
Staines (# 1514); 9) Poteet (# 1321); 10) Coletti
(# 325); 11) Squires (# 1510); 12) Fifield (#
552); 13) Schmitt (# 1445); 14) Wasson (# 1652);
15) Spector (# 1498); 16) Preston (# 1335).

Rev. Alasdair A. MacDonald, "Some Recent Work
. . .," *EngStud* 66.2 (Apr. 1985): 162-66
(see entry # 1025 below).

410. ---, ---, ---, eds. *Studies in Medieval Drama in
Honor of William L. Smoldon on His 82nd Birthday.*
Kalamazoo, Michigan: Western Michigan U., 1974.
Special issue of *CompD* 8.1 (Spring 1974).

Contains essays on English drama by Davidson
("Medieval Drama: Diversity . . .," # 395 above);
Robert A. Brawer ("The Middle English Resurrection
Play . . .," # 221); Cynthia Haldenby Tyson

("Noah's Flood, the River Jordan . . .," # 1614);
JoAnna Dutka ("Mysteries, Minstrels, and Music," #
495); and Alan H. Nelson ("'Of the seuen ages'
. . .," # 1201). Also contains essays by C.
Clifford Flanigan ("The Liturgical Context of the
Quem Queritis Trope," # 562), Sandro Sticca ("The
Christos Paschon and the Byzantine Theater," #
1539), and Dunbar H. Ogden ("The Use of
Architectural Space . . .," # 1241).

Rev. Alasdair A. MacDonald, *EngStud* 66.2 (Apr.
1985): 162-66.

410a. ---, and Ann Eljenholm Nichols, eds. *Iconoclasm vs.
Art and Drama*. Kalamazoo, Michigan: Medieval
Institute, Western Michigan University, 1989.
Early Drama, Art, and Music Monograph Series, 11.
xxv, 210 pp.

Contains essays by Davidson, "The Anti-Visual
Prejudice" (entry # 381.1 above); Aston,
"Iconoclasm . . ." (# 122a); Davidson "'The
Devil's Guts' . . ." (# 383b); and Sheingorn, "'No
Sepulchre . . ." (# 1462a). Also contains essay
by Nichols not focusing on drama. With preface by
the editors, 34 illusts., and index.

411. ---, and David E. O'Connor. *York Art: A Subject List
of Extant and Lost Art, Including Items Relevant
to Early Drama*. Kalamazoo: Medieval Institute
Publications, Western Michigan U., 1978. Early
Drama, Art, and Music Reference Series, 1.

Lists c. 1245 pieces of art from York from 53
buildings and repositories. Offers items under
the following subject headings: 1) Old Testament;
2) Parents of Virgin and Her Life (to Nativity);
3) Infancy of Christ; 4) Christ's Ministry; 5) The
Passion; 6) The Risen Christ; 7) Conclusion of
Life of the Virgin; 8) The Last Judgment; 9) The
Creed; 10) The Apostles; 11) Saints; 12) Seven
Sacraments; 13) Allegorical Subjects; 14)
Miscellaneous Subjects. With a note on Relics in
York Minster, and appendix on musical iconography,
bibliography, and 48 illustrations. Also contains
a small pamphlet (pp. 211-34) in a pocket in back
cover of book) with an index, compiled by Joan
Rossi and Michael Rossi: *Index to York Art*.

412. ---, and Nona Mason. "Staging the York *Creation, and
Fall of Lucifer*." *ThSur* 17.2 (November 1976):
162-78.

Examines the conditions of production as a way to
prepare audiences for the plays which follow.
Looks at theories of dramatic historical
development (e.g. from *tableaux vivants*) and the
plays' relationship to the visual arts (stained
glass, sculpture, wall paintings). Tries to
reconstruct the spectacle of the play. Discusses
the pageant wagon stage, the characters' movement,
costumes, props, the creation of the angels, the
possible use of a ramp, slide, or trap door to
facilitate Satan's fall, masks, and so on.
Concludes by observing that traditional
iconography is used to encourage spectator
participation, and that the *tableaux* of the drama
come from artistic works familiar to the audience.

413.   Davis, Marian. "Nicholas Love and the N-Town Cycle."
        Ph.D. diss., Auburn U., 1979.

414.   Davis, Michael T. "Passion Cycle." In *Dictionary of
        the Middle Ages*, 9: 446-47. Ed. by Joseph R.
        Strayer (see entry # 1553 below).

        Describes the cycle in the arts--its use of
        imagery and its components.

415.   Davis, Nicholas, ed. "Allusions to Medieval Drama in
        Britain: A Finding List (1)." *MET* 4.2 (Dec.
        1982): 75-76.

        The first of a series designed "to locate and
        indicate something of the content of surviving
        contemporary or near-contemporary allusions to
        medieval drama in the British Isles" (75). Refers
        to "allusions" and not to "records." Offers three
        such allusions. (See Jocelyn Price, "Theatrical
        Vocabulary . . ." and "Allusions to Medieval Drama
        in Britaian: A Finding List (2)," entries # 1337-
        1339 below. See also entry # 421 below.)

416.   ---, ed. "Allusions to Medieval Drama in Britain: A
        Finding List (3)." *MET* 5.2 (Dec. 1983): 83-86.

        Presents five allusions from different
        contributors (including Liz Urquhart and Eileen
        White, the only two named).

417.   ---. "Another View of the *Tretise of Miraclis
        Pleyinge*." *MET* 4.1 (July 1982): 48-55.

        Review article of Clifford Davidson's edition of *A
        Middle English Treatise on the Playing of Miracles*
        (see entry # 398 above). Calls Davidson's
        approach to the Treatise "oblique" (48). Analyzes

the Treatise and discusses it in its historical
context. Critiques Davidson's edition. Prepares
for the appearance of his own edition.

418.   ---.   "The Art of Memory and Medieval Dramatic
Theory." *EDAMN* 6.1 (Fall 1983): 1-3.

Summarizes paper presented at The Fourth
International Colloquium on Medieval Drama (July
10-15, Viterbo, Italy). Claims "that formal
mnemonic theory contributed to medieval
conceptions of drama and, perhaps, influenced the
drama itself" (1). Mentions the esteem of memory
and its facilitation by dramatic means. Considers
such matters in the light of evidence in the
Tretise of myraclis pleyinge and the *Ad Herennium*.
Concludes that the *Ad Herennium*'s discussion of
mnemonics could be a valuable source of
information "as a previously unrecognized
'blueprint' for medieval dramatic performances"
(3).

419.   ---.   "The Meaning of the Word 'Interlude': A
Discussion." *MET* 6.1 (July 1984): 5-15.

Points out that the modern usage stems from J.P.
Collier in 1831. Gives historical analysis of the
word from c. 1300. Discusses the almost
exclusively British use of the term. Suggests
that the term is applied sometimes to "small or
even solo performances" (8) which were "simple,
homely affairs" (9); sometimes the term was used
synonymously for "miracles." Looks at modern
connotations of the word.

420.   Davis, Nicholas M.   "The Playing of Miracles, c. 1350
to the Reformation." Ph.D. diss., Cambridge U.,
1978.

420a.   ---.   "Spectacula Christiana: A Roman Christian
Template for Medieval Drama." *MET* 9 (1987): 125-
52.

421.   Davis, Nick.   "Allusions to Medieval Drama in Britain
(4): Interludes." *MET* 6.1 (July 1984): 61-91.
(See entries # 415 and 416 above.)

Gives 159 allusions from many different sources.
Aims at completeness up to 1560; is selective
after 1560.

422.   Davis, Norman.   "The Brome Hall Commonplace Book."
ThN 24.2 (Winter 1969/70): 84-86.

Responds to Stanley J. Kahrl's "The Brome Hall
Commonplace Book," *ThN* 22.4 (Summer 1968), 157-61.
Contradicts Kahrl's translation of the front cover
Latin inscription. Shows that the inscription is
"the common form of an indenture of receipt" (84),
not a statement by the scribe that he had copied
for a sum. ". . . the inscription appears to be
not an actual receipt but a model or draft of a
form of receipt" (85). This inscription "cannot
be taken as evidence of the date of completion of
the book" (85). Also criticizes as "sadly
slipshod" (85) Kahrl's attack on Lucy Toulmin
Smith's 1886 edition of the mss.

xxx.   ---, ed. *Paston Letters and Papers of the Fifteenth
Century*. See this item in Editions . . ., entry #
31 above.

423.   ---. "Provenance of the N-Town Cycle." *Lib*, ser. 6:
2.3 (Sept. 1980): 333-34.

Reply to Stephen Spector, "The Provenance of the
N-Town Codex" (see entry # 1502 below). Claims
that Spector--in discussing the date of
acquisition of the ms--misreads "Hath demised" as
"has died." Points out that *demise* means "'to
give, grant, convey, or transfer (an estate) by
will or by lease'" (333). Concludes that the
inscription used by Spector "cannot be regarded as
evidence that the manuscript remained with the
Hegge family after Kinge's death" (334).

424.   ---. "Two Unprinted Dialogues in Late Middle English,
and Their Language." *Revue des Langues Vivantes*
35.5 (1969): 461-72.

Looks at Winchester quasi-dramatic dialogues
(Winchester College MS. no. 33): 1) between
Lucidus and Dubius; 2) between Occupation,
Idleness, and Doctrine. Shows their relationship
to early morality plays. Primarily discusses the
language of the texts. Describes the ms.

425.   Davis, Ruth Brant. "The Scheduling of the Chester
Cycle Plays." *ThN* 27.2 (Winter 1972/73): 49-67.

Answers F.M. Salter (*Medieval Drama in Chester*,
1955) and others that the *Chester Breviary* does
record eye-witnesses of dramatic performances.
Claims that new probing into the stop-to-stop
method of performance would show this a smooth and
feasible method--as effective as theater in the
round. (See Lawrence M. Clopper, "The Staging of

the Medieval Plays of Chester: A Response" [# 308 above] for a response to this article.)

426. Davison, Nigel. "So Which Way Round Did They Go? The Palm Sunday Procession at Salisbury." *M&L* 61.1 (Jan. 1980): 1-14.

Concerns the Rite of Sarum and its processions. Describes the processions: "The Early Route" (3) and "The Later Route" (7). On liturgical drama.

427. Davison, Peter. *Popular Appeal in English Drama to 1850*. London: Macmillan, 1983.

Chap 2--"The Medieval Tradition" (12-33)--looks at cultural traditions (of the "great tradition"--the educated few; and the "little tradition"--the unlettered many [citing Robert Redfield, *Peasant Society and Culture*, Chicago, 1956]). Shows that the drama was part of the little tradition, but that the elite participated; in this respect the plays were between both classes, with their "fusing of learning and low wit" (14). Mentions the relationship between sermon and drama with their narrative method. Considers mysteries, moralities, and interludes, and Medwall's *Fulgens and Lucres*.

Rev. *Choice* 19 (July 1982): 1569.
    BBN (Oct. 1982): 637.
    ThJ 35 (May 1983): 272.
    BBN (Feb. 1985): 73.

428. Dean, William Kenneth Hall. "The Concept of the Comic in English Drama, ca. 1400-1612." Ph.D. diss., U. of Toronto, 1970.

429. ---. "The Towneley Cycle as Religious Comedy." *AULLA* 45 (May 1976): 5-26.

Discusses the comic in the drama. Proposes "that the comic in the cycles . . . is more complex than might be suggested by limiting consideration to farce, or to the dramatic effects of rant, rage, and buffoonery" (5). Claims that the comic reveals "an awareness of a contradiction between the capacity of man to fulfill his nature in the image of God and the actuality of life as lived in the fallen order of creation" (5). Examines the diversity of humor; looks at many Towneley plays.

430. Dean-Smith, Margaret. "Folk-Play Origins of the English Masque." *Folklore* 65 (1954): 74-86.

Defines "masque" and "folk play"; summarizes
scholarship. Points up the amount of invention
possible in the later genre.

431. Debax, Jean-Paul. "The Divinity of the Morality
      Plays." *CahE* 28 (Oct. 1985): 3-15.

      Discusses the definition of "morality play."
      Briefly reviews the definitions of others. Claims
      that the morality play is more than the appearance
      of allegorical characters, the presence of Vice,
      or the non-historic time and non-referential space
      of the framework. Shows that even when these
      characteristics are present, they appear in quite
      diverse ways, and in varying "quantities" in the
      plays.

432. ---. "*Militia est vita hominis super terram:* Guerre
      au théâtre et guerre du théâtre." *Caliban* 19
      (1982): 3-21.

      Discusses representations of war/battle in
      theater, from medieval drama to the seventeenth
      century--English, German, and French. On English
      drama: says that war is a metaphor for the
      struggle between good and evil, both within the
      soul and in the world at large. Looks at the use
      of war in the mystery plays (e.g. God vs. Lucifer,
      God vs. Adam and Eve, Satan, Abel and Cain, etc.).
      Also looks at the Slaughter of the Innocents,
      Herod, Belial in *The Castle of Perseverance.* Says
      that because of physical restraints, medieval
      drama hints at battle scenes using parades (as in
      the *Castle*), duels, pursuit scenes, messengers or
      wounded announcing the results of battle, the
      presence of a castle on stage, the jaws of Hell,
      and so on.

433. de Bruyn, Lucy. *Woman and the Devil in Sixteenth-
      Century Literature.* Tisbury, Wiltshire,
      [England]: A Bear Book, 1979. 180 pp.

      Considers Noah's wife in the plays. Looks briefly
      at her depiction in York, Towneley, Newcastle
      plays (133-36).

      Rev. *TLS* (Sept. 26, 1980): 1074.
           RenQ 34 (Winter 1981): 609.
           Ren&Ref 6 (Aug. 1982): 210.

434. DeCoo, Jozef. "A Medieval Look at the Merode
      Annunciation." *ZeitK* 44.2 (1981): 114-32.

Examines some of the iconographic details of this
triptych (in the Cloisters, New York). Compares
the work to other contemporary art. Useful in the
study of the drama in its attention to details
also found in the plays.

435. Degroote, Gilbert. "*Everyman* en *Murder in the
Cathedral.*" *HandZ* 23 (1969): 41-46. In Dutch.

Shows how Eliot echoes *Everyman* in verse form and
allusions to Death's sudden appearance. Cites
Eliot's own writing to show his awareness of the
Everyman materials. Claims that *Elckerlijc* may
also have been an influence on Eliot.

436. del Villar, Mary. "The Medieval Theatre in the
Streets: A Rejoinder." *ThSur* 14.2 (Nov. 1973): 76-
81.

Responds to Pentzell's article "The Medieval
Theatre in the Streets" (see the two Pentzell
articles, # 1285 and 1286 below), in which
Pentzell calls into question del Villar's views.
Claims "that Pentzell is not familiar with recent
scholarship" (78), and is "irresponsible" (78) and
misleading (80). (See also entry # 439 below.)

437. del Villar, Mary Harmon. "The Saints Play in Medieval
England." Ph.D. diss., U. of Arizona, 1970.

438. ---. "Some Approaches to the Medieval English Saint's
Play." *RORD* 15-16 (1972-73): 83-91.

Tries to define the terminology of the genre,
offer information about continental predecessors,
and survey the types of such plays. Offers a list
of six types, dramatizing the whole life: 1)
based on legend; 2) based on historical sources;
3) dramatizing part of a saint's life--usually "a
crucial or emblematic episode" (87); 4) presenting
a miracle; 5) focusing on a martyrdom; 6)
"Romantic plays using the conventions of the
saint's drama . . . to dramatize legends" (87).
Mentions other areas of research open.

439. ---. "The Staging of *The Conversion of Saint Paul.*"
ThN 25.2 (Winter 1970-71): 64-68.

Claims that the play was performed in a place-and-
scaffold theater, in the round, and "that the
misunderstandings that have arisen about a
'procession' result from a misreading of the
language" (64). Surveys other scholarship and
internal evidence. (See Raymond J. Pentzell's

commentary on this article: "The Medieval Theatre
in the Streets," entries # 1285 and 1286 below,
and del Villar's article # 436 above.)

440.   Denny, Neville. "Arena Staging and Dramatic Quality
       in the Cornish Passion Play." In *Medieval Drama*,
       124-53. Ed. by Neville Denny. London: Edward
       Arnold, 1973 (see entry # 442 below).

       Shows that the Cornish passion play is a form of
       folk or popular art, not sophisticated and
       courtly, ritual, or didactic and ecclesiastical.
       Speaks of the "primitive realism of unusually
       compelling dramatic power" (128) of the play.
       Describes the arena staging and the audience's
       placement in the *plan-an-gwarry* set-up.

441.   ---. "Aspects of the Staging of *Mankind*." *MedAe* 43.3
       (1974): 252-63.

       Considers "the significance of its occasion and
       the relation of this to the subtlety and
       complexity of its staging" (252). Reveals the
       homiletic pattern of exordium, exemplum, and
       application. Reviews other scholarship.
       Speculates on the actors and the original
       presentation. Relates the play to other types of
       dramatic presentation. Looks at costume and
       disguise. Examines individual characters. Says,
       "a cleared acting area would be all that was
       required to present the play" (261). Concludes
       that the play was put on by six to ten local
       performers (who acted in other plays) at floor
       level, in an ebullient, "vulgar" (262) style.

442.   ---, ed. *Medieval Drama*. London: Edward Arnold; New
       York: Crane, Russak, 1973. Stratford-upon-Avon
       Studies 16; gen. eds. Malcolm Bradbury and David
       Palmer.

       Contains ten essays on various aspects of Medieval
       English drama. See entries as follows: Axton (#
       127 above); Neuss (# 1212); Jeffrey (# 817);
       Bevington (# 188); Williams (# 1702); Denny (#
       440); Roddy (# 1404); Craik (# 365); Rose (#
       1414); and Elliott (# 526).

       Rev. *B&B* 19 (Nov. 1973): 132.
           Choice 11 (June 1974): 598.
           Marjory Rigby, *RES* 26.101 (Feb. 1975): 64-66.

443.   ---. "The Staging of Medieval Drama." In *The Drama
       of Medieval Europe*, 67-80, discussion 81-85. Ed.
       by Richard Rastall (entry # 1359 below).

Tries to explain how the plays were produced--"to
recreate the original staging procedures" in order
to suggest "something of the original theatrical
experience" (67). Looks at indoor and outdoor
performances, historically and theoretically.
Describes at length the plan-an-gwarry [sic]
staging of the Cornish Cycle. Mentions ground-
level presentation, plays in halls and taverns,
platform staging, arena, and--briefly--
processional staging.

444.   Dent, Robert William. *Proverbial Language in English
Drama Exclusive of Shakespeare, 1495-1616: An
Index.* Berkeley, Los Angeles, and London: U. of
California Press, 1984. 797 pp.

Serves as a companion volume to his *Shakespeare's
Proverbial Language: An Index* (Berkeley, Los
Angeles, and London: U. of California Press,
1981). Deals with drama from Medwall on. Lists
proverbs and cites sources for them.

Rev. *Choice* 22 (June 1985): 1469.
ARBA 17 (1986): 467.

445.   De Smet, Imogene L. "A Study of the Roles of Mercy
and Justice in the Morality Plays, *Everyman, The
Castle of Perseverance,* and *Mankind.*" Ph.D.
diss., U. of Toronto, 1969.

446.   Dessen, Alan C. *Elizabethan Drama and the Viewer's
Eye.* Chapel Hill: U. of North Carolina Press,
1977. xi, 176 pp.

Chapter 2 is on "Staging and Structure in the Late
Morality Play" (32-49). Considers the visual
aspects of the action and their relationship to
plot, theme, audience reaction. Chap 6 (126-56)
--"The Stage Psychomachia"--considers morality
plays such as *The Interlude of Youth* and *The
Castle of Perseverance.*

447.   Dessen, Alan C. "Homilies and Anomalies: The Legacy
of the Morality Play to the Age of Shakespeare."
ShakS 11 (1978): 243-58.

Review article. Surveys scholarship. Reviews
Robert Potter's *The English Morality Play* (London:
Routledge and Kegan Paul, 1975; see # 1324 below)
and Edmund Creeth's *Mankynde in Shakespeare*
(Athens, GA: U. of Georgia Press, 1976; see # 367
above).

448. ---. "The Intemperate Knight and the Politic Prince: Late Morality Structure in 1 Henry IV." *ShakS* 7 (1974): 147-71.

Explains what a morality play is; looks at the genre with respect to history plays. Shows the debt Shakespeare has to the morality tradition. [This article incorporated into chap. 4 of his book *Shakespeare and the Late Moral Plays*, entry # 451 below.]

449. ---. "The Logic of Elizabethan Stage Violence: Some Alarms and Excursions for Modern Critics, Editors, and Directors." *RenD* 9 (1978): 39-69.

Traces the violence on the stage back to its allegorical sources in medieval morality plays.

450. ---. "The Morall as an Elizabethan Dramatic Kind: An Exploratory Essay." *CompD* 5.2 (Summer 1971): 138-59.

Examines the morality play tradition and the meaning of the term "morality"/"moralité." Not specifically on medieval drama, but contains many insights useful to medieval drama criticism. [This article incorporated into chap. 1 of his book *Shakespeare and the Late Moral Plays*; see next entry.]

451. ---. *Shakespeare and the Late Moral Plays.* Lincoln and London: U. of Nebraska Press, 1986.

Reviews scholarship. Chap. 1--"The Problem and the Evidence" (1)--focuses on "an inherited sense of how a certain kind of play could be constructed" (9). Aims to deal with the moral plays themselves and with how they were viewed in the Renaissance (see previous entry). Chap. 2--"The Public Vice and the Two Phase Moral Play" (17)--looks at what Renaissance playwrights viewed, from historical evidence and literary allusions. Chaps. 3-6 deal with specific Shakespearean plays (see entry # 448 above). Chap. 7 deals with the components of the moral play. With notes, list of plays and editions, and index.

Rev. *Choice* 23 (July 1986): 1673.
ShakQ 37 (Winter 1986): 520.
RenQ 40 (Spring 1987): 168.

452. Devereux, E.J. "John Rastell's Utopian Voyage." *Moreana* 13.51 (Sept. 1976): 119-23.

Examines the author's unsuccessful exploration to the American coast--begun as a commercial voyage-- and how it appears in "The Four Elements."

453. De Welles, Theodore. "A Bibliography of Iconographic Sources." Appendix to Theresa Colletti and Kathleen M. Ashley, "The N-Town Passion . . ." (see # 329 above).

Contains sixty items on iconography and costume.

454. De Welles, Theodore Richard. "The Social and Political Context of the Towneley Cycle." Ph.D. diss., U. of Toronto, 1980.

455. ---, et al. *The Chester Mystery Cycle of Plays.* [Toronto]: *Poculi Ludique Societas* in Association with the Graduate Centre for Study of Drama, Victoria U. and Records of Early English Drama, 1983. 12 pp.

Program for performance, May 21-23, 1983, at the U. of Toronto. Contains introductory section by De Welles; section on music by Geoff Gaherty; historical background and notes on the present performance by David Parry; and notes on the performance by Alexandra Johnston. With illustrations.

456. Dickman, Susan Joy. "Late Medieval Tragedy from Chaucer to Cavendish." Ph.D. diss., U. of California, Berkeley, 1979.

457. Diehl, Huston. "'To Put Us in Remembrance': The Protestant Transformation of Images of Judgment." In Homo, Memento Finis: *The Iconography of Just Judgment in Medieval Art and Drama*, 179-208. Ed. by David Bevington. Kalamazoo: Medieval Institute Publications, Western Michigan U., 1985. (See entry # 186 above.)

Examines the iconographic/iconoclastic attitudes to the Judgment in early art from the Middle Ages to the Reformation in England.

458. Dietrich, Julia C. "Doctrine and the Aesthetic of the Morality Drama." Ph.D. diss., U. of Cincinnati, 1976.

459. ---. "*Everyman*, Lines 346-7." *Expl* 40.3 (Spring 1982): 5.

Sees in Cousin's proverbial statement about abstaining from all food except bread and water an

allusion to penitential canons (from the 1215
Lateran Council and later) which prescribed five-
year fasts for habitual serious crimes committed
by laymen. Suggests that cousin's lines mean, "I
would rather repent . . . than die."

460. ---. "Folk Drama Scholarship: The State of the Art."
RORD 19 (1976): 15-32.

Lists 218 items, some with notes, on English folk
drama.

461. ---. "Justice in this World: The Background of the
Revenger in the English Morality Drama." *JMRS*
12.1 (Spring 1982): 99-111.

Reviews scholarship. Discusses the theological
and philosophical traditions of justice and
punishment, and exhortations to virtue in the
plays.

462. Diller, Hans-Jürgen. "The Composition of the Chester
Adoration of the Shepherds." *Anglia* 89.2 (1971):
178-98.

Takes issue with Hardin Craig's notion that
earlier forms of the play are more religious,
later--edited/redacted--forms are more secular and
humorous. Claims that such a distinction should
be modified and that "*some* comic action has been
part of the original structure" of the play (178).
Uses a detailed metrical analysis to "establish a
relative chronology" (179); seeks "to distinguish
the tones and moods which characterize" the stanza
forms (179). Looks at the short tail-rhyme
stanza, the Chester stanza, quatrains, and
unidentified stanza-forms. Shows that the play
"did not develop from didacticism to realism"
(198), but contained some of the humor in its
early form.

462a. ---. "Erste und Zweite Welt im geistlichen Spiel des
Mittelalters." In *Meaning and Beyond: Ernst Leisi
zum 70. Geburtstag*, 3-19. Ed. Udo Fries and
Martin Heusser. Günter Narr Verlag, n.d.

463. ---. *Redenformen des englischen Misterienspiels*.
Munich: Wilhelm Fink, 1973.

Opens with an overview of liturgical drama,
omitting questions of music and costume, and
focusing on those aspects that are comparable with
mystery plays. Discusses mystery plays in order
to define the technique of their playwrights.

Analyzes the concepts of stage-space and stage-
time, and the addresses of the actors to the
audience. Treats aspects of emotional expression
and partner relationships among the actors. Asks
whether the scenic potential of the medieval stage
was exploited or whether forms of expression
borrowed from school rhetoric were used. Looks at
specific geographical variations of the plays
(Chester, York, Towneley plays) and at specific
characters (Mary, the Devil, Cain and Abel, etc.).

463a. ---. "The Verbal Representation of Space in the
English Mystery Plays." *FCS* 13 (1988): 177-94.

464. Divett, Anthony W. "An Early Reference to Devil's-
Masks in the Nottingham Records." *MET* 6.1 (July
1984): 28-30.

Refers to legal matters of July 28 and August 11
and 25, 1372, pertaining to a mask used in the
drama.

465. Djwa, Sandra. "Early Explorations: New Founde Landys
(1496-1729)." StudCL 4.2 (Summer 1979): 7-21.

Sees the utopian and "providential view" (7) of
the New World in *The Interlude of the Four
Elements* and relates it to Rastell's focus on
education, his "moral passion for learning and his
somewhat Utopian plans for the 'new found landys'
[as] an extension of his concern for the health of
the 'common-weal'" (10).

466. Dobson, R.B. "Admissions to the Freedom of the City
of York in the Later Middle Ages." *EconHR*, 2nd
ser. 26.1 (Feb. 1973): 1-22.

Examines the Freeman's Register (kept from 1272 to
1671). Focuses on 1272-1500. Discusses data on
the number of Freemen in York, where they lived,
the accuracy of the documents, their occupations,
their living conditions, the financial reasons for
their admission into the city, and other
background information. Possibly useful for the
study of the social conditions extant when the
drama was flourishing.

467. ---, ed. *York City Chamberlains Account Rolls, 1396-
1500*. Gateshead: Northumberland Press, 1980 (for
1978 and 1979). Surtees Society, 192. xlii, 236
pp.

Contains many references to Corpus Christi plays
(mentioned in the Subject Index, p. 233). Also

Analyzes the concepts of stage-space and stage-
time, and the addresses of the actors to the
audience. Treats aspects of emotional expression
and partner relationships among the actors. Asks
whether the scenic potential of the medieval stage
was exploited or whether forms of expression
borrowed from school rhetoric were used. Looks at
specific geographical variations of the plays
(Chester, York, Towneley plays) and at specific
characters (Mary, the Devil, Cain and Abel, etc.).

463a. ---. "The Verbal Representation of Space in the
English Mystery Plays." *FCS* 13 (1988): 177-94.

464. Divett, Anthony W. "An Early Reference to Devil's-
Masks in the Nottingham Records." *MET* 6.1 (July
1984): 28-30.

Refers to legal matters of July 28 and August 11
and 25, 1372, pertaining to a mask used in the
drama.

464a. Dixon, Mimi: Skll "Tragicomic Recognition ... ; in *Ren Tragi-Comedy* (1987)

465. Djwa, Sandra. "Early Explorations: New Founde Landys
(1496-1729)." StudCL 4.2 (Summer 1979): 7-21.

Sees the utopian and "providential view" (7) of
the New World in *The Interlude of the Four
Elements* and relates it to Rastell's focus on
education, his "moral passion for learning and his
somewhat Utopian plans for the 'new found landys'
[as] an extension of his concern for the health of
the 'common-weal'" (10).

466. Dobson, R.B. "Admissions to the Freedom of the City
of York in the Later Middle Ages." *EconHR*, 2nd
ser. 26.1 (Feb. 1973): 1-22.

Examines the Freeman's Register (kept from 1272 to
1671). Focuses on 1272-1500. Discusses data on
the number of Freemen in York, where they lived,
the accuracy of the documents, their occupations,
their living conditions, the financial reasons for
their admission into the city, and other
background information. Possibly useful for the
study of the social conditions extant when the
drama was flourishing.

467. ---, ed. *York City Chamberlains Account Rolls, 1396-
1500*. Gateshead: Northumberland Press, 1980 (for
1978 and 1979). Surtees Society, 192. xlii, 236
pp.

Contains many references to Corpus Christi plays
(mentioned in the Subject Index, p. 233). Also

A.V.C. Schmidt, *RES*, n.s. 27 (May 1976): 198-200.

A.B. Friedman, *Specu* 52 (Jan. 1977): 135-36.

G.C. Britton, *N&Q* 24 (Feb. 1977): 86-87.

R.W. Ackerman, *CompL* 29 (Spring 1977): 183-85.

D.R. Howard, *MP* 76 (Aug. 1978): 63-66.

471. Dorrell, Margaret. "The Butchers', Saddlers', and Carpenters' Pageants: Misreadings of the York *Ordo*." *ELN* 13.1 (Sept. 1975): 1-4.

Points out misreadings in the *Ordo Paginarum* in Lucy Toulmin Smith's edition of the *York Plays* (Oxford, 1885). Shows how the errors in the early edition could lead to confusion.

472. ---. "The Corpus Christi Play at York: Discussions and Documents." Ph.D. diss., U. of Leeds, 1973.

473. ---. "The Mayor of York and the Coronation Pageant." *LSE*, n.s. 5 (1971): 35-45.

Explains that ms readings of the *Ordo paginarum ludi Corporis Cristi*, which were damaged in a flood, can still be deciphered and reveal that not the Taverners but the governing body of the city (represented by the mayor) was responsible for the Coronation pageant. Shows that this is supported by other documents, especially the accounts of the Chamberlains, which the author quotes.

xxx. ---. "Performance in Procession: A Medieval Stage for the York Corpus Christi Play." See Dorrell, "Two Studies . . ." (# 474 below).

xxx. ---. "Procession and Play: Corpus Christi Day in York before 1427." See Dorrell, "Two Studies . . ." (# 474 below).

474. ---. "Two Studies of the York Corpus Christi Play." *LSE*, n.s. 6 (1972): 63-111. (This is followed by "Postscript" by Martin Stevens, 113-15, # 1533 below).

Study 1: "Procession and Play: Corpus Christi Day in York before 1427" (pp. 63-77, 108-09). Looks at various historical documents pertaining to the religious procession and the dramatic procession of York on Corpus Christi day before 1427. Suggests that the two "were separate entities and that the [religious] procession preceded the play along the route through the streets" (63). With a

map of the procession and a drawing of the York
Mercers' wagon, 1433.

Study 2: "Performance in Procession: A Medieval
Stage for the York Corpus Christi Play" (pp. 77-
107, 109-11). Reconsiders Alan Nelson's
"Principles of Processional Staging" (see entry #
1204 below) in light of medieval city records
which claim that processional performance was
possible (contradicting Nelson's argument).
Claims "that processional performance was the rule
at York and that Nelson's calculations are
inaccurate because they do not allow for the
topography of the pageant route or the variation
in distances between the stations" (77). Also
suggests that plays were acted after dark. Looks
at the mode of performance and the stations, and
reconstructs a performance in procession.
Concludes that "the whole play could be performed
within a reasonable time-limit" (98); it could run
between 4:30 a.m. and about "twenty-nine minutes
past midnight" (98); "the performance was a spoken
one" (101), and "each pageant was performed at
each station" (101). Tabulates the 48 plays, the
performing time of each, and the time of day of
each performance (102-07).

475. Douglas, Audrey W. [Research in Progress.] *REEDN* 4.1
(1979): 13-16.

Discusses work in progress and planned on the
papers in the record offices in Cumbria (at
Carlisle, Kendal, and Barrow). Briefly treats her
findings.

476. ---, and Peter Greenfield, eds. *Records of Early
English Drama, Cumberland, Westmorland,
Gloucestershire.* Toronto, Buffalo, and London: U.
of Toronto Press, 1986. xi, 547 pp.

Offers hundreds of dramatic records through 1642.
Introduction covers "Historical Background" for
the counties, towns, and households, "Drama,
Music, Ceremony, and Custom" (plays, waits,
drummers, etc.), a discussion about the documents
and editorial procedures, and notes. Examines
guild, chamberlain, and churchwarden accounts,
household books, records of dioceses and Star
Chambers. With translations, bibliography, notes,
and appendixes. N.B. Cumberland and Westmorland
ed. by Douglas; Gloucestershire ed. by Greenfield.

Rev. Carol Chillington Rutter, *ThN* 42.2 (1988):
83-84.

477. Driver, J.T. *Cheshire in the Later Middle Ages: 1399-1540.* A History of Cheshire, vol. 6. Chester: The Cheshire Community Council, 1971. 168 pp.

Chap. VI covers "Religious Life, The Mystery Plays, Literacy and Education" (134-50). Shows "the close bonds between medieval society and the Church" (139) as being reflected in the plays and the Corpus Christi processions. Ascribes to the old idea "that the medieval drama grew out of the Church" (139). Discusses performances, audiences, plays in the cycles, the plays' "lack [of] sophistication" (141), and their importance "in the development of the English theatre" (141). With bibliography, index, and illustrations (illustrations not on the drama).

Rev. *NorH* 8 (1973): 165.

478. Dronke, Peter. "Narrative and Dialogue in Medieval Secular Drama." In *Literature in Fourteenth-Century England: The J.A.W. Bennett Memorial Lectures, Perugia, 1981-1982*, 99-120. Ed. by Piero Boitani and Anna Torti. Tübingen: Gunter Narr Verlag; Cambridge: D.S. Brewer, 1983. Tübinger Beiträge zur Anglistik, 5.

Raises the possibility that the narrative elements and dialogue could indicate that the secular drama was recited or mimed by a single performer. Does not concentrate on English drama. Mentions *Dame Sirith* and *Interlude of the Clerk and the Girl*.

479. Duclow, Donald F. "*Everyman* and the *Ars Moriendi:* Fifteenth-Century Ceremonies of Dying." *FCS* 6 (1983): 93-113.

Recounts Johan Huizinga's theories about death (from his *Herfsttij der middeleeuwen/The Waning of the Middle Ages*). Shows that "the picture of death in the fifteenth century appears more complex than Huizinga allows" (94). Looks at *Everyman* and the *Ars moriendi* tradition.

480. Duffy, R.A. "*Wit and Science* and Early Tudor Pageantry: A Note on Influence." *MP* 76.2 (Nov. 1978): 184-89.

Points out the similarities between this play and the pageants. Examines characters (like savage giants or "woodwos" [184]) and motifs and pageant influences (e.g. setting, dramatic content, mask imagery, dancing and music, mock combat).

481.   Duncan, Robert L.   "Comedy in the English Mysteries."
        IIQ 35.4 (1973): 5-14.

        Opens with the assertion "that medieval drama
        began in connection with the ceremonies of the
        Catholic Church" (5).   Ascribes the existence of
        "raucous comedy . . . in later versions of this
        religious drama" (5) to the fact that the later
        plays were written to please not the church but
        the people.   Says, "in order to cultivate the
        highest interest, the dialogue had to be
        understood and a few laughs provided" (6).   Looks
        at the Noah plays in the York, Chester, and
        Coventry versions.   Concludes with a statement of
        how a modern audience can learn from the
        significance of the humor.

482.   Dunn, Anne.   "The Boundaries of Art: A Theoretical
        Study of English Drama from the Medieval
        Beginnings to the Renaissance."   Ph.D. diss., U.
        of Texas, Austin, 1978.

483.   Dunn, E. Catherine.   "French Medievalists and the
        Saint's Play: A Problem for American Scholarship."
        M&H, n.s. 6 (1975): 51-62.

        Addresses the paucity of American scholarship on
        saints' plays.   Discusses drama from French
        critical emphases on origins, the knowledge of the
        Gallican liturgy, the use of chanting and music in
        the presentation of the saint's life, their
        stanzaic patterns of composition, and religious
        dance.

484.   ---.   "The Origin of the Middle English Saints'
        Plays."   In *The Medieval Drama and Its Claudelian
        Revival*, 1-15.   Ed. by E. Catherine Dunn, et al.
        Washington, D.C.: The Catholic U. of America
        Press, 1970 (see # 488 below).

        Discusses the rise, extent, and disappearance of
        English miracle plays.   Looks at past and current
        theories.   Considers the "farced epistle" theory,
        and the relation of the plays to liturgy and to
        mystery plays.   Examines at length the "farced
        epistle" origin of saints' plays.   Explains term
        to mean a spoken gloss "stuffed" into the spoken
        Mass in a second lector's voice; the added voice
        shows "the partial or total assumption of a role
        in a fictive impersonation that trembles on the
        verge of genuine drama" (9).   [This is a version
        of Dunn's earlier "The Origin of the Saints'
        Plays: The Question Reopened."   See next entry.]

485.   ---.   "The Origin of the Saints' Plays: The Question
       Reopened." In *Medieval Drama. A Collection of
       Festival Papers*, 46-54. Ed. by William A. Selz.
       Vermillion, SD: 1968. [See previous entry, and #
       1454 below.]

486.   ---.   "Popular Devotion in the Vernacular Drama of
       Medieval England." *M&H*, n.s. 4 (1973): 55-68.

       Defends the liturgical, spiritual elements in the
       cycle plays. Discusses the Gallican and Roman
       forms the liturgy took. Says Kolve's claim that
       the plays are divorced from the liturgy are not
       completely accurate. Defines mysteries as a
       "paraliturgical form of spirituality" and "the
       people's Bible'" (57). Focuses on three aspects
       of the drama: "the Biblical texture, the
       liturgical mode of expression, and the thematic
       joy that prevails in the developing pattern of
       narrative line and dramatic conflict" (67).

487.   ---.   "Recent Medieval Theater Research: A Problem for
       Literary Scholars." *Allegorica* 2.1 (Spring 1977):
       183-93.

       Reviews critical approaches with respect to
       "theater research" and "literary criticism" (183).
       Offers a critique of current studies from a
       literary--not an iconographic--viewpoint. Looks
       especially at the work of Kahrl (*Traditions of
       Medieval Drama*, # 886 below), Nelson (*The Medieval
       English Stage,* # 1199), and Axton (*European Drama
       of the Early Middle Ages*, # 125 above).

488.   ---, Tatiana Fotitch, and Bernard M. Peebles, eds.
       *The Medieval Drama and Its Claudelian Revival:
       Papers Presented at the Third Symposium in
       Comparative Literature Held at The Catholic
       University of America, April 3 and 4, 1968.*
       Washington, D.C.: The Catholic U. of America
       Press, 1970. (Foreword by Helmut A. Hatzfield.)

       Contains five essays, only one of which is on
       English drama: E. Catherine Dunn, "The Origin of
       the Middle English Saints' Plays"--# 484 above.

       Rev. *Specu* 46.4 (Oct. 1971): 754.

489.   Dunn, F.I. "The Norwich Grocers' Play and the
       Kirkpatrick Papers at Norwich." *N&Q*, n.s. 19.6
       (217) (June 1972): 202-03.

       Discusses "the two versions of . . . 'The Creation
       of Eve and the Fall'" (202) play. Sheds light on

the play based on an examination of the papers of
John Kirkpatrick. Looks at the words *cokelys* and
whelys and at "stage directions concerning music"
(203). [See essay by Dutka, "The Fall of Man
. . .," # 491 below.]

490. Durkan, John, and James Kirk. *The University of
Glasgow 1451-1577*. Edinburgh: U. of Glasgow
Press, 1977.

Cites annual faculty feasts (held from 1462) which
included a procession of masters and students, who
performed "a short play" (an *interludium*--190).

Rev. G. Donaldson, *TLS* (Sept. 9, 1977): 1086.
W.S. Reid, *CanJH* 13 (Aug. 1978): 269-71.
C.I. Hammer, Jr., *EHR* 93 (Oct. 1978): 905.
W.S. Reid, *ChHist* 48 (Mar. 1979): 103-04.
V.L. Bullough, *RenQ* 32 (Spring 1979): 83-
85.
C. Burns, *CHR* 67 (Jan. 1981): 79-80.

491. Dutka, JoAnna. "The Fall of Man: The Norwich Grocers'
Play." *REEDN* 9.1 (1984): 1-11.

Offers a facsimile of a transcript of the Norwich
Grocers' Play of "The Fall of Man" done by John
Kirkpatrick. [See essay by F.I. Dunn, "The
Norwich Grocers' Play . . .," # 489 above.]

492. ---. "The Lost Dramatic Cycle of Norwich and the
Grocers' Play of the Fall of Man." *RES*, n.s. 35.
137 (Feb. 1984): 1-13.

Examines the extant versions of the play. Looks
at the social context in which the play was
written. Suggests "that Norwich probably had a
religious drama equal in its treatment of
materials to the better-known plays of York,
Chester, and Coventry" (2). Talks about the
coherence and integrity of the "Fall" play.

493. ---. "Music and the English Mystery Plays." *CompD*
7.2 (Summer 1973): 135-49.

Says that music "is essential to the production"
(135), is there "for its dramatic utility as well
as its beauty" (135), and helps in
characterization and setting and in advancing the
action. Concludes that "music cannot be regarded
. . . as subsidiary to the other elements" (145)
of the plays.

494.   ---.   *Music in the English Mystery Plays*. Kalamazoo:
         Medieval Institute Publications, Western Michigan
         U., 1980. Early Drama, Art, and Music Reference
         Series, 2. viii, 171pp., 6 plates.

         Uses references in the texts of the plays and in
         the documents which are concerned with the
         production of the drama. Offers "lists of songs,
         with texts and transcriptions of music . . ., and
         of instruments . . . a glossary of musical terms
         . . . an introduction to the material and
         commentaries on it" (iii.). With notes,
         bibliography, and illustrations.

         Rev. Beverly Boyd, *CompD* 15.1 (Spring 1981): 80-
               81.
               Richard Rastall, *UTQ* 50 (Summer 1981): 105-
               06.

495.   ---.   "Mysteries, Minstrels, and Music." In *Studies
         in Medieval Drama* . . ., 112-24; see # 410 above.

         Shows that "the writers and revisers of the cycle
         plays utilized instrumental music with marked
         skill for dramatic effect, internal consistency,
         and realism" and exhibited "a lively awareness of
         the religious symbolism of musical instruments"
         (112). Examines plays from all cycles.

496.   ---.   "Mystery Plays at Norwich: Their Formation and
         Development." *LSE*, n.s. 10 (1978): 107-20.

         Discusses the growth and decline of the plays as
         deduced from historical documents, with special
         reference to the petition of St. Luke's Guild to
         the Assembly "that they be released from bearing
         sole burden of 'disgisinges and pageauntes' on
         Whit Monday" (107). Examines the ambiguous words
         "disgisinges" and "pageauntes," as well as other
         unclear words and phrases in the petition.
         Questions whether the presentation on Whit Monday
         is related to Corpus Christi drama. Discusses the
         obscure beginning of Corpus Christi drama in
         Norwich and its clear decline; quotes Grocers'
         Accounts.

497.   ---, ed.   *Records of Early English Drama. Proceedings
         of the First Colloquium at Erindale College,
         University of Toronto, 31 August-3 September 1978*.
         Toronto: Records of Early English Drama, 1979.
         191 pp.

         Contains essays by Richard Rastall ("Minstrels and
         Minstrelsy . . .," # 1360 below); Peter Meredith

("'Item for a grone . . .," # 1094); Reginald W.
Ingram ("'Pleyng geire . . .," # 790); Stanley J.
Kahrl ("Learning about Local Control," # 879);
John Wasson ("Records of Early English Drama:
Where they are . . .," # 1657); Neil Carson (too
late for this bibliography); Martin Stevens ("The
Johnston-Rogerson . . .," # 1528); and Trevor H.
Howard-Hill ("REED's Bibliographical Imperative,"
776). With a list of members of the colloquium.

498. ---. "The Use of Music in the English Mystery Plays."
      Ph.D. diss., U. of Toronto, 1972.

499. Dutschke, D.W., Richard Rouse, et al. *Guide to
      Medieval and Renaissance Manuscripts at the
      Huntington Library*. San Marino, CA: Huntington
      Library, forthcoming.

      Incorporates the Schulz *Catalogue of The Towneley
      Plays*. (See entry # 1450 below.)

500. Dutton, Richard. [Review.] *Fulcrum* (Mar. 24, 1971).
      Cited by Sheila Lindenbaum, *RORD* 20 (1977): 99.

      Reviews performances of *The Resurrection of
      Christ*, March 9-11, 1977, at Nuffield Theatre
      Studio, Lancaster U., Lancaster, England.

501. Earl, James W. "The Shape of Old Testament History in
      the Towneley Plays." *SP* 69.4 (Oct. 1972): 434-52.

      Discusses the selection and sequence of Old
      Testament plays with particular attention to the
      Processus Prophetarum and *Pharaoh* plays. Follows
      Craig and Hardison in seeing the Septuagesima
      season as a clue to the origin of the Old
      Testament plays. Asserts that "Septuagesima
      season, which is Scripturally represented by the
      books of Genesis and Exodus, is a figure for all
      salvation history, as well as for the exile of
      each soul's life . . ., and is also a review of
      Old Testament history leading up to the moment of
      redemption at Easter" (442). Hence, the
      Septuagesima "would be a natural place to turn,
      for a cleric who was designing, writing, or adding
      to a dramatic cycle like the Towneley plays"
      (442). Explains "the apparent transposition of
      the *Processus Prophetarum* and the *Pharaoh*" (442),
      the former having no theological relationship to
      other Old Testament plays. Looks briefly at the
      Lazarus play.

502. Ebihara, Hiroshi. "The English Political Morality
      from *Magnyfycence* to *Wealth and Health*, with

Special Attention to Bale's Treatment in *King
Johan* of the Doctrine of Absolutism." *SEL*,
English Number 47.2 (Mar. 1971): 141-64.

Looks at the secularization of the old morality
themes, especially "the wealth and health of the
state with particular emphasis upon the lesson of
prudence for the royal ruler who is directly
responsible for the welfare and good government of
the country" (141). Says that the later
moralities "were mainly concerned with the wealth
and health of the state" (141), emphasizing the
wisdom a royal ruler needs for the welfare of the
country. Defines political morality; discusses
the place and nature of such plays "in the
development of the English history play with
special reference to . . . *King Johan* . . . a
transitional drama from moralities to histories"
(141). Shows how the moralities served a function
of uniting a country and making it safe.

503.   ---. "Theme and Structure in John Bale's *King Johan.*"
SELL 19 (Mar. 1969): 1-13.

In Japanese with abstract in English. Looks at
the history-play elements of the play, the use of
allegory, and the use of contemporary references.

504.   Ebin, Lois A.   *John Lydgate.*   Boston: Twayne, 1985.
163 pp.

Has chapters on Lydgate's life, poetry, politics,
and works. With notes, bibliography, and index.

Rev. *Choice* 23 (Dec. 1985): 602.
Specu 62 (Oct. 1987): 933.

505.   Eccles, Mark.   "'Halfe a yard of Red Sea.'"   *N&Q*, n.s.
31.2 (June 1984): 164-65.

Points out many editors' errors in interpreting
"say" as "sea"; shows that it should be rendered
as "cloth."

506.   ---. "*Ludus Coventriae:* Lincoln or Norfolk?"   *MedAe*
40.2 (1971): 135-41.

Discusses the Cotton MS. Vespasian D.viii,
containing the *Ludus Coventriae* plays, looking at
the different names given to the cycle: *Ludus
Coventriae*, the Hegge Plays (after a former owner
of the ms), the N-Town Plays (from a note in the
Banns). Considers linguistic and orthographic
evidence (e.g. sal/suld/xal/xuld/schal(l)/

schuld(e), etc.) and other plays in the same
dialect to try to determine where the plays of the
Cotton ms were written and performed. Concludes
that though the plays are traditionally called
Ludus Coventriae, they almost certainly have
nothing to do with Coventry, the inclusion of the
city name in the title indicating that they "are
the kind of plays acted at Coventry" (135).
Proves that they "cannot have been acted at
Lincoln" (140), and that they "all were either
written or revised in the dialect of East Anglia
and were copied by an East Anglian scribe,
probably in Norfolk" (140). They "may have been
acted in Norwich or in Lynn, or only on tour in
more than one 'N. town'" (140)--the *N* standing for
the name of any town the banner bearer needed to
announce when proclaiming the name of the town in
which they were to be acted.

507.   ---. "The Macro Plays." *N&Q*, n.s. 31.1 (229) (Mar.
        1984): 27-29.

        Discusses editions, performances, the ms, and
        specific readings of a number of cruxes.

507a.   Edmond, Mary. "Pembroke's Men." *RES*, n.s. 25
        (1974): 129-36.

        Considers Simon Jewell, an actor from Pembroke's
        Men, discovered in his "unnoticed registered will
        of 1592" (129). Reveals information about the
        acting company. (See article by McMillan, entry #
        1045 below.)

508.   Edwards, Francis. *Ritual and Drama: The Mediaeval
        Theatre*. Guildford and London: Lutterworth Press,
        1976. (Line drawings by George Tuckwell.)

        Traces and discusses "in non-academic terms the
        emergence of the mediaeval play from Christian
        ritual" (7). Aimed at "young students and general
        readers" (7). Has chapters on "Ritual and
        Theatre" (9); "The Theatre of the Early Church"
        (20): "The Growth of the Dramatic Idea" (32); "The
        Spirit of Irreverance" (55); "The Theatre of the
        People" ["The Transition from Latin to the Common
        Tongue" (64) and "The Miracle Plays" (79)]; and
        "Religion and the Stage" (97). With glossary,
        bibliography, index, and illustrations.

508a.   Edwards, John. "The Mural and the Morality Play: A Suggested

509.   Edwards, Robert. *The Montecassino Passion and the* Source for
        Poetics of Medieval Drama. Berkeley and Los   a Wall-Painting
        Angeles: U. of California Press, 1977.   at Oddington."

                                Trans of the Bristol &
                                Glos. Arch Soc., 1986

                        139

Focuses on church drama, with special reference to art, iconography, music, etc. Not specifically on English drama. Refers briefly to English plays in passing (e.g. to the York Crucifixion, 166-67).

510.   ---.   "Techniques of Transcendence in Medieval Drama." *CompD* 8.2 (Summer 1974): 157-71.   Rpt. Davidson, Gianakaris, and Stroupe, eds., *The Drama . . .*, 103-117 (# 409 above).

Looks at drama and its evolution from Aristotle's perspective on spectacle, and "along the lines suggested by both phenomenology and structuralism" (158).   Explains Aristotle's views.   Points out that "Aristotelian categories maintain a separation between the internal and external elements of drama, and the confounding of these elements by medieval drama makes necessary the search for a different basis of unity" (169). Uses John Dewey's *Art as Experience* to explain the unity of elements in medieval drama, resulting "from various fusions, including those of 'fringe' elements outside the art work" (170).

511.   Einstein, Frank H.   "Didactic Artistry in Corpus Christi Drama."   Ph.D. diss., U. of Chicago, 1974.

512.   Eldredge, Laurence.   "A Note on the Attribution of Line 746 of the Coventry *Weavers' Pageant*."   *ASNSL* 215.130.1 (1978): 84-86.

Examines the marginal additions to the text in the original ms, written in a different hand from that of Robert Croo, the original scribe.   Tries to decide to which character one line should be ascribed.

513.   El Itreby, Elizabeth J.   "The *N-Town* Play of 'The Woman Taken in Adultery'--Central to a Recapitulative 'Redemption Trilogy.'"   *BSUF* 26.3 (Summer 1985): 3-13.

Relates the "Woman" play to the ones before and after it.   Calls these three "A 'redemption trilogy'" (3) which prepares the audience for the following Passion sequences.   Examines specifically "the abuse-of-power redemption theory and the doctrine of the recapitulated fall" (4). Calls the play "the first . . . in man's 'comic' movement upward" (11).

514.   El Itreby, Elizabeth Jeanne.   "Re-Creation, Ritual Process and the N-Town Cycle." Ph.D. diss., Loyola U. of Chicago, 1985.

515. Elliott, John MacKay. "An Historical Study and
      Reconstruction of the Fifteenth-Century Play *The
      Castle of Perseverance*." Ph.D. diss., City U. of
      New York, 1977.

516. Elliott, John R., Jr., comp. "Census of Medieval
      Drama Productions." *RORD* 20 (1977): 97-106.

      Offers seven passages reviewing performances of
      English plays.

517. ---, comp. "Census of Medieval Drama Productions."
      RORD 21 (1978): 95-102.

      Gives four reviews of English plays.

518. ---, comp. "Census of Medieval Drama Productions."
      RORD 22 (1979): 137-45.

      Presents eight brief passages from various
      contributors and several sources recounting
      performances.

519. ---, comp. "Census of Medieval Drama Productions."
      RORD 23 (1980): 81-91.

      Offers several passages reviewing performances.

520. ---, comp. "Census of Medieval Drama Productions."
      RORD 24 (1981): 193-200.

      Has six passages reviewing performances.

521. ---, comp. "Census of Medieval Drama Productions."
      RORD 25 (1982): 145-50.

      Presents six passages from three contributors
      recounting performances.

522. ---, comp. "Census of Medieval Drama Productions."
      RORD 26 (1983): 117-23.

      Offers passages from six various contributors
      about performances, four of which are of English
      drama.

523. ---, comp. "Census of Medieval Drama Productions."
      RORD 27 (1984): 185-91.

      Offers eight passages recounting performances.

524. ---, comp. "A Checklist of Modern Productions of the
      Medieval Mystery Cycles in England." *RORD* 13-14
      (1970-71): 259-66.

Discusses modern (post-1951) performances in
England--"complete cycles or reasonable facsimiles
thereof" (260). Intends to be complete through
1969. Breaks list down into cycles. Does list
several pre-1950 performances. More than 40
performances recorded.

525. ---. "Medieval Acting." *In Contexts for Early
English Drama*, 237-50. Ed. by Marianne G. Briscoe
and John C. Coldewey (see # 228 above).

Discusses the problems faced by those wishing to
do research on acting in the middle ages. Asks
many questions, discusses different kinds of
evidence, and compares the scholarship to that
done for Elizabethan acting. Points out the
difference between professional and amateur
actors. Cautions in the use of eye-witness
accounts. Talks about the style and quality of
the acting.

526. ---. "Medieval Rounds and Wooden O's: The Medieval
Heritage of the Elizabethan Theatre." In *Medieval
Drama*, 222-46. Ed. by Neville Denny. London:
Edward Arnold, 1973. (See # 442 above.)

Stresses theatrical continuity from medieval to
Renaissance times, especially with respect to
staging. ". . . the Elizabethan public theatre,
in its design and its stagecraft, shows a clear
ancestry reaching back to the medieval rounds and
playing-places" (224). Uses what we know "about
the medieval stage . . . to illuminate what is
obscure about the stage practices of Shakespeare
and Marlowe" (224). Looks at props, siege scenes,
theater shapes, and scenery.

526a. ---. *Playing God: Medieval Mysteries on the Modern
Stage*. Toronto: U. of Tornoto Press, forthcoming
(1989). c. 224 pp.

". . . studies the modern context of this
important medieval genre." Describes "general
attitudes towards religious drama from the time of
the Reformation . . . [and] traces the history of
the major modern productions of the mystery
cycles." Also, "provides information about the
careers of the two leading pioneers of modern
mystery-play production, Nugent Monck and E.
Martin Browne." Concludes by discussing "the
chief practical and aesthetic problems involved in
staging mystery plays for modern audiences, and
assesses the . . . importance of their revival in
the larger context of British theatre today."

With illustrations. (All information taken from flier, "Medieval Studies, University of Toronto Press 1989," p. [3].)

527. ---. "Playing the Godspell: Revivals of the Mystery Cycles in England, 1973." *RORD* 15-16 (1972-73): 125-30.

Reviews performances of plays of 1973 in York, Chester, Ely, Cornwall, and Exeter.

528. E[lliott], J[ohn] R., [Jr.]. [Untitled review.] *RORD* 20 (1977): 97-98.

Reviews performance of the *York Mystery Cycle of Plays*, June 11 to July 3, 1976, York Festival, York, England.

529. ---. [Untitled review.] *RORD* 20 (1977): 102-03.

Reviews performance of *Mankind*, December 5, 1976, May Memorial Unitarian Church, Syracuse, New York, by The Seventh Heaven Players.

530. ---. [Untitled review.] *RORD* 20 (1977): 103-06.

Reviews performances of *The Merry Play of Johan Johan the Husband, Tyb his Wife, and Sir John Priest* (by Heywood), and of *The Creation of Adam and Eve, The Fall of Man*, and *The Temptation of Jesus in the Wilderness* (York Cycle), Spring and Summer 1977, various locations in New York.

531. ---. [Untitled review.] *RORD* 28 (1985): 203-05.

Briefly reviews a performance of the National Theatre's production of *The Mysteries* of May 18, 1985, in London's Lyceum Theatre.

532. ---, and Sheila Lindenbaum, comps. "Census of Medieval Drama Productions." *RORD* 28 (1985): 201-09.

Contains entries for about five productions, submitted by various scholars.

533. Elliott, R.W.V. *Chaucer's English*. London: Andre Deutsch, 1974. Language Library.

A general examination of late Middle English, focusing primarliy on Chaucer; with brief passing mention of English dramatic works (e.g. The Towneley Herod, p. 98). Useful for a discussion of one of the dialects contemporary to some of the drama.

534. Elliott, Ralph W.V. "The Topography of *Wynnere and Wastoure.*" *EngStud* 48.2 (Apr. 1967): 134-40.

(Response to Richard Southern's *Medieval Theatre in the Round*, London: Faber, 1957; see entry # 1493 below.)

Looks at the poem's vivid language, eloquence, pageantry, and--especially--settings (in waking experience and in dream) which, with their theme and presentation, provide "an interesting link with the medieval theatre" (140).

535. Ellis, Robert P. "'Godspell' as Medieval Drama." *America* 127.21 (Dec. 23, 1972): 542-44.

Discusses medieval drama as popular entertainment and briefly describes the cycle plays. Shows how "Godspell" conforms in several respects to medieval dramatic performance styles and content. Claims that "Godspell" is "the closest approximation our times have made to the medieval religious drama" (544).

536. Ellis, Roger. "The Word in Religious Art of the Middle Ages and the Renaissance." In *Word, Picture, and Spectacle*, 21-38. Ed. by Clifford Davidson. Kalamazoo: Medieval Institute Publications, Western Michigan U., 1984 (See # 408 above.)

Claims that the *word*, other than the halo, is "the commonest iconographic feature of religious art" (21). Shows how it focuses on the intrinsic and extrinsic meanings of a work of art. Uses dramatic texts for examples.

537. Elton, Geoffrey Rudolph. *England, 1200-1640.* Ithaca and London: Cornell U. Press, 1969. The Sources of History: Studies in the Uses of Historical Evidence.

Not specifically on drama; but discusses the documents and non-documentary sources which historians may use to reconstruct history. Anticipates the *REED* project.

538. Emmerson, Richard Kenneth. *Antichrist in the Middle Ages: A Study of Medieval Apocalypticism, Art, and Literature.* Seattle: U. of Washington Press, 1981. 366 pp.

Chap. 5 is on "Antichrist in Medieval Literature" (146-203). Covers the drama (163-87), with references to English plays in the Chester cycle (180-87). With notes, bibliography, and index.

Rev. B.D. Hill, *LJ* 106 (Sept. 15, 1981): 1730.
   D.P. Walker, *THES* 465 (Oct. 2, 1981): 18.
   Choice 19 (Dec. 1981): 517.
   ChrCnt 98 (Dec. 23, 1981): 1348.
   D.J. Osheim, *HRNB* 10 (Mar. 1982): 118.
   C.T. Davis, *AHR* 87 (June 1982): 760.
   RSR 8 (July 1982): 275.
   Specu 57 (July 1982): 601.
   Peter W. Travis, *EDAMN* 5.1 (Fall 1982): 12-14.
   E.D. Craun, *History* 67 (Oct. 1982): 461.
   TheolT 39 (Oct. 1982): 357.
   Ronald B. Herzman, *StudAC* 5 (1983): 164-66.
   ChHist 52 (Sept. 1983): 355.
   CHR (Jan. 1984): 123.
   JRel 64 (Jan. 1984): 119.

539.   ---.   "'Nowe Ys Common This Daye': Enoch and Elias, Antichrist, and the Structure of the Chester Cycle." In Homo, Memento Finis: *The Iconography of Just Judgment in Medieval Art and Drama*, 89-120. Ed. by David Bevington. Kalamazoo: Medieval Institute Publications, Western Michigan University, 1985. Early Drama, Art and Music Monograph Series 6. (See # 186 above.)

Looks at human and supernatural characters and the play's moment of decision in which Antichrist is taken to hell and Enoch and Elias are taken to heaven. Also deals with the Antichrist tradition --its iconographic and exegetical features and the prominence of Enoch and Elias.

540.   Epp, Garrett.   "The Semiotics of Flatness: Characterization in Medieval Cycle Drama." *Scintilla* 2-3 (1985-86): 132-40.

Treats "round" and "flat" characters, the latter being the rule in the cycle plays. Combines this notion with that of medieval realism, which states that "Ideas constitute the eternal, immutable reality of things" (133). Examines characters in these terms, concluding that "these characters are signes, or *semes* . . . suited to the popular didactic purpose of the cycle" (139). (See review of this article by Reynolds, entry # 1381 below.)

541.   Epstein, Steven.   "Guilds and Métiers." In *Dictionary of the Middle Ages* 6: 13-20. Ed. by Joseph R.

Strayer. New York: Charles Scribner's Sons, 1982. (See # 1553 below.)

Discusses the types and activities of the guilds (early guilds; their use; late guilds; their legacy). With bibliography.

542. Evett, David. [Untitled review.] *RORD* 24 (1981): 197-98.

Reviews performances of The Cornish Passion, June 5-7, 1981, at Cleveland State University, Cleveland, Ohio.

543. Evett, Marianne. [Untitled review.] *RORD* 21 (1978): 96-99.

Reviews performances of *The Passion* from the York Mystery Plays, April 21, 1977; Fall 1977; Spring and Fall 1978; National Theatre, London.

543a. Evitt, Regula Meyer. "Musical Structure in the *Second Shepherd's* [sic] *Play*." *CompD* 22 (1988-89): 304-22.

544. Faber, M.D. "The Summoning of Desdemona: *Othello*, V.ii.1-82." *ANQ* 9.3 (Nov. 1970): 35-37.

Points up "the similarity between the posture of Othello and Desdemona . . . and the posture of Death and his victims" (35) in late medieval literature. Deals mostly with *Everyman* as an analogue.

545. Fairfield, Leslie P. *John Bale: Mythmaker for the English Reformation*. West Lafayette, Indiana: Purdue U. Press, 1976.

Contains new information on Bale. Mentions four depositions from the Chapter Library of Canterbury which reveal that a John Okeden berated two tailors for offering to make a friar's outfit for a play of Bale's. Okeden insulted Bale by refusing to go to his play and Bale tried to charge Okeden with slander. Says that the play may have been *King Johan* or *The Three Laws*.

545a. Falk, Heinrich Richard. "Text-Free Methodology for Medieval Theatre." *FCS* 13 (1988): 23-30.

546. Feldman, Sylvia D. *The Morality-Patterned Comedy of the Renaissance*. The Hague and Paris: Mouton, 1970.

Chap. II discusses "The Morality Pattern, A
Definition" (40-64). Looks at *Pride of Life,
Castle of Perseverance, Everyman, Wisdom,* and
Mankind.

Rev. Joel H. Kaplan, "The Medieval Origins of
Elizabethan Comedy." *RenD*, n.s. 5
(1972): 225-36 (entry # 891 below).
RenQ 25.3 (1972): 362.
TLS (Feb. 4, 1972): 134.
MLR 67 (Apr. 1972): 401.

546a. Fengler, Christine K., and William A. Stephany.
"Medieval Art and Drama: An Interdisciplinary
Approach." In *Teaching the Middle Ages II*, 113-
20. Ed. by Robert V. Graybill, John Hallwas, Judy
Hample, Robert L. Kindrick, and Robert E. Lovell.
Warrensburg, Missouri: Central Missouri State U.,
1985. *Studies in Medieval and Renaissance
Teaching*, vol. 2.

547. Fichte, Jörg O. *Expository Voices in Medieval Drama:
Essays on the Mode and Function of Dramatic
Exposition.* Nürnberg: Hans Carl, 1975. Erlanger
Beiträge zur Sprach- und Kunstwissenschaft 53.
168 pp.

(An updated version of this writer's dissertation,
"The Role of the Expositor in Medieval Drama.")
Contains five essays, I. on Latin drama from the
ninth and tenth centuries; II. on Liturgical
drama; III. on "The Use of Exposition as
Compositional Technique in the Vernacular Drama"
(44 ff.--looking at French plays); IV. on German
Easter and Passion plays; V. on "The Role of
Expositor and Contemplacio in the *Chester Cycle*
and the *Ludus Coventriae*" (98 ff.). Comments on
the rarity of expository figures in English
medieval drama, on the didactic nature of the
cycles, on the religious feast related to the
plays. Looks at the origins and functions of the
expositors who "help to reveal the divine plan for
man's redemption, and thus . . . serve as
spiritual guides for the audience" (117). With
notes, appendixes, bibliography, and index.

548. ---. "The Presentation of Sin as Verbal Action in the
Moral Interludes." *Anglia* 103.1-2 (1985): 26-47.

Identifies "certain recurrent speech acts" (26)--
using Stanley Fish's notions of Speech Act Theory
--in the morality plays, with special focus on
sin. Concludes that "the main contingent of sins
enacted in the moral interludes were sins of the

tongue, because they could be presented easily by means of verbal action" (47).

549.   Fifield, Merle.   "The Arena Theatres in Vienna Codices 2535 and 2536." *CompD* 2.4 (Winter 1968-69): 259-82.

With repsect to Richard Southern's *The Medieval Theatre in the Round* (see entry # 1493 below), discusses "the six extant plans for late medieval arena stages" (259). Looks carefully at the *Castle of Perseverance* and at the illustrations in the Vienna codices, which "realize the imagined richness of theatrical presentations in the fifteenth-century simultaneous arena theatre--a castle, a place, a place barrier, and an outer ring . . ." (280).

549a.   ---.   "Applications of Genre Theory to Description of Moral Plays and Their Dramatic Modes." In *Everyman & Company* . . . . Ed. by Donald Gilman. (See entry # 628a below.)

550.   ---.   "The Assault on the *Castle of Perseverance*--The Tradition and the Figure." *BSUF* 16.4 (Autumn 1975): 16-26.

Looks for but finds no antecedents to the place of battle--"a moral castle under vicious attack . . . [with] ladies defending themselves with roses and being defeated" (17). Compares street pageantry, *château d'amour, entremés, pas d'armes* to the setting/staging of the *Castle of Perseverance*. Concludes that the "staging of the Battle of Vices and Virtues . . . was most probably based . . . upon the secular renditions" of the figures represented in the *château d'amour* and *entremés*.

551.   ---.   "'The Castle of Perseverance': A Moral Trilogy." In *Medieval Drama: A Collection of Festival Papers*, 55-62. Ed. by William A. Selz. (See entry # 1454 below.)

Examines the length of the play and sees in it three plays: 1) The Debate of Body and Soul; 2) the section from "the rousing of the armies of Vice and Virtue" to "the forsaking of Heaven from worldly goods" (56); 3) The Coming of Death. Points out that each play is c. 1065 lines long. Posits a five-act structure for each and analyzes each in terms of the traditional conflict, climax, and resolution.

552. ---. "The Community of Moral Plays." *CompD* 9.4
(Winter 1975-76): 332-49. Rpt. in Davidson,
Gianakaris, and Stroupe, eds., *The Drama* . . .,
286-303 (# 409 above).

Looks at the internationality of the tradition of
plays called *moralities, moralités, histoires,
zinnespelen,* and *abele spelen.* Claims that there
is "a communality of source materials" (332).
Defines the genre. Says that all such plays "meet
a single definition of the genre and develop their
morals by identifiable and parallel techniques"
(333). Looks at dialogue, narrative events,
characterization, allegory, rhetorical
organization, dramatic conflict, five-action
structure. Argues for "the presence of a body of
commonly known moralizing literature" (347) and a
five-part structure requiring only three actions:
"exposition, catastrophe, and resolution" (348).

553. ---. "Medwell's [sic] Play and No-Play." *StudMedCul*
6 (1974): 531-36.

Discusses the transitionary nature of Medwall's
Interlude of Nature and *Fulgens and Lucres*--
between medieval and Renaissance plays. Points
out "the absence of a clear boundary" (532)
between the middle ages and the Renaissance.
Looks at dramatic structure and plot to comment on
the plays' transitional elements.

554. ---. "The Miraculous Morality." *FCS* 5 (1982): 67-97.

Offers a general discussion about moralities;
refers to the content, description of the genre,
characterization, use of allegory, origins,
"participation of historical, religious
personages" (76), the use of miracles, etc.
Compares plays with similar characteristics in
other languages.

555. ---. "Quod quaeritis, o discipuli." *CompD* 5.1
(Spring 1971): 53-69.

Defines the historical approach to the drama.
Examines the method of Karl Young, E.K. Chambers,
Bertholt Brecht, O.B. Hardison. Looks at *rite* and
jeu through a Brechtian aesthetic. Calls medieval
drama *jeu.* Looks also at staging. Does not focus
specifically on English drama.

556. ---. *The Rhetoric of Free Will: The Five-Action
Structure of the English Morality Play.* Leeds:

University of Leeds, School of English, 1974.
Leeds Texts and Monographs, New Series 5. 52 pp.

Examines the plays in terms of structure rather
than in terms of their "materials" (iii). Defines
Man as "the true protagonist" (iv). Looks at
analogues, "Present Critical Approaches" (7 f.),
and the supposed five-part structure of the plays,
including the exposition, the "second and third
actions" (18 ff.), and the "fourth and fifth
actions" (26 ff.). Uses the standard vocabulary
(catastrophe, reversal, climax, resolution . . .).
Discusses the rhetorical effects. Concludes with
a discussion of "The Renaissance: Decay and
Invention" (35 ff.). With notes and bibliography.

557.   ---. "The Sacrifice of Isaac: Tradition and
         Innovation in Fifteenth-Century Dramatizations."
         FCS 8 (1983): 67-88.

         Looks at the "narrative and thematic tradition"
         (67) and the themes of obedience, "faith, hope,
         good works, and praise of the Lord" (67). Focuses
         mostly on non-English plays which depart from
         traditional presentations.

557a. Finkelstein, Richard. "Formation of the Christian
         Self in *The Four P.P.*" In *Early Drama to 1600*.
         Ed by Albert H. Tricomi. (See # 1589b below.)

558.   Finnegan, Robert E. "Research in Progress:
         Gloucestershire and Bristol." *REEDN* 2.1 (1977):
         9-10.

         Claims that civic and parish records and a manor
         court book show that Gloucester "had a flourishing
         drama in the sixteenth and early seventeenth
         century, and that Tewksbury and probably also
         Cheltenham had active amateur dramatists" (9).

558a. Fiondella, Maris G. "Augustine's Concept of the
         'Letter' and the Viewer as Subject in Selected
         Plays from the Towneley Cycle." In *Early Drama to
         1600*. Ed. by Albert H. Tricomi. (See entry #
         1589b below.)

559.   Fisher, Anne Adele. "A Reading of *Macbeth* in the
         Light of Earlier Native Drama." Ph.D. diss., U.
         of Toronto, 1978.

560.   Fitz-Simon, Christopher. *The Irish Theatre*. London:
         Thames and Hudson, 1983.

Chap. 1 contains brief treatment of religious
drama and John Bale (9-10). Mentions the Dublin
guilds which "were deputed to enact stories which
had some relevance to their own members' craft or
trade" (10).

561. Flanigan, C. Clifford. "Karl Young and the Drama of
the Medieval Church [sic]: An Anniversary
Appraisal." *RORD* 27 (1984): 157-66. (N.b. Book
title not italicized.)

Celebrates Young's book on its 50th anniversary.
Summarizes some of Young's theories and critical
commentators on those theories. Looks at the
treatment or ignoring of tropes, music, and ms
tradition.

562. ---. "The Liturgical Context of the *Quem Queritis*
Trope." In *Studies in Medieval Drama in Honor of
William L. Smoldon on His 82nd Birthday*, 45-62.
Ed. by Clifford Davidson, et al. (see # 410
above).

Reviews scholarship on tropes and their relation
to drama. Aims to show the way tropes functioned
in order to elucidate medieval drama. Points up
the importance of studying the relationship
between music and tropes, the meaning of the word
trope, its connection with introit texts, the
development of dialogue; examines the *Quem
queritis* closely.

563. ---. "The Liturgical Drama and Its Tradition: A
Review of Scholarship 1965-1975. [Part I.]" *RORD*
18 (1975): 81-102.

Deals with newly discovered texts and a new
anthology. (See next entry.)

564. ---. "The Liturgical Drama and Its Tradition: A
Review of Scholarship 1965-1975. (Part II.)" *RORD*
19 (1976): 109-36.

Deals with texts and studies of individual plays
and examinations of performances. (See previous
entry.)

565. Flanigan, Charles Clifford. "Liturgical Drama and
Dramatic Liturgy: A Study of the *Quem Queritis*
Easter Dialogue and Its Cultic Context." Ph.D.
diss., Washington U., 1973.

566. ---. "Medieval Latin Music-Drama." In *Medieval Theatre* . . . (forthcoming). Ed. by Eckehard Simon. (See entry # 1469 below.)

567. ---. "The Roman Rite and the Origins of the Liturgical Drama." *UTQ* 43.3 (Spring 1974): 263-84.

Shows that liturgical drama was influenced by the dramatic elements of the emotive Gallic Rite when it was replaced by the more solemn Roman Rite. Says that the church drama "needs to be viewed in terms of both the human religious experience and the great cultural achievement which we call the medieval liturgy" (282).

568. Fleenor, Terry Richard. "The Martyr Figure in the Dramatic Literature of the West, Preceded by an Essay on the Evolution of the Word *Martyr*." Ph.D. diss., U. of California, Riverside, 1972.

569. Fleischer, Martha Hester. *The Iconography of the English History Play*. Salzburg: Institut für Englische Sprache und Literatur, Universität Salzburg, 1974. Salzburg Studies in English Literature under the Direction of Professor Erwin A. Stürzl; Elizabethan & Renaissance Studies, No. 10. Ed. by James Hogg. 363 pp.

Contains many passages on mystery and morality plays, as well as discussions on themes, motifs, characters.

569a. Fletcher, Alan. The Civic Drama of Old Kilkenny." *REEDN* 13.1 (1988): 12-30.

570. Fletcher, Alan J. "The 'Contemplacio' Prologue to the N-Town Play of the Parliament of Heaven." *N&Q* 27.2 (225) (Apr. 1980): 111-12.

Examines the prologue to show that W.W. Greg was in error in ascribing it to two particular speakers. Reviews Greg's theories and shows that the speeches in question were spoken "not by the angels and archangels, but by representatives of the patriarchs and prophets" (111). Points out the vernacular tradition of patriarchs and prophets who speak imploringly (as in the passage in question); they are speaking for Isaiah and Jeremiah.

570a. ___. "Coventry Cupbord ..." *English Studies* 1982.

571. ---. "The Design of the N-Town Play of Mary's Conception." *MP* 79.2 (Nov. 1981): 166-73.

Discusses the "patchwork compilation" (166) nature
of the play, the raw materials of which it is
composed, its theological elements, its
didacticism, and its effect.

572. ---. "*Everyman:* An Unrecorded Sermon Analogue."
EngStud 66.4 (Aug. 1985): 296-99.

Relates the play to sermon literature. Sees the
analogue in Bodley Library MS Lat. th. d. 1, which
has "the Faithful Friend *exemplum* on fol. 135r-v"
(297). Says that "certain themes and
preoccupations are shared both by the morality
stage and by the pulpit" (296). Looks at
narrative structure, the use of exempla, setting,
and the Faithful Friend motif.

573. ---. "'Farte Prycke in Cule': A Late-Elizabethan
Analogue from Ireland." *MET* 8.2 (Dec. 1986): 134-
39.

Finds another example of this "jousting" game
(also called "Skiver the goose"--134) in the
writings of Josias Bodley. Finds an Ulster
analogue which may shed light on Medwall's use of
the game. (See article by Peter Meredith, "'Farte
Pryke in Cule' and Cock-fighting." # 1093 below.)

574. ---. "Layers of Revision in the N-Town Marian Cycle."
Neoph (July 1982): 469-78.

Discusses revision and accretion in these plays.
Tabulates "the first Marian group" plays (475-76).

575. ---. "The Marginal Glosses in the N-Town Manuscript,
British Library, MS Cotton Vespasian D.VIII."
[Submitted to *Manuscripta*; cited in *MET* 1.2 (Dec.
1979): 83.]

Claims that the glosses were entered by the
scribe-compiler. Says they may show what text(s)
the scribe was working from.

576. ---. "The Meaning of 'Gostly to Owr Purpos' in
Mankind." *N&Q* 31.3 (229) (Sept. 1984): 301-02.

Points out the formulaic nature, "borrowed from
contemporary vernacular preaching" (301), of the
phrase. Shows the phrase's use in sermons,
signalling some form of exegesis. Also shows the
scandalous use of the phrase in the play.

577. ---. [Untitled review.] *RORD* 28 (1985): 207-09.
Reviews performances of the Lincoln Mystery Plays

of July 8-20, 1985, at Lincoln Cathedral
Cloisters.

578. Forrester, Jean. *Wakefield Mystery Plays and the
Burgess Court Records: A New Discovery*. Ossett,
Yorkshire: Harold Speak and Jean Forrester, 1974.
42 leaves.

Reproduces the ms and printed court records, with
brief introduction. Shows "that the Burgesses of
Wakefield had their own court" (1). Also
discusses A.C. Cawley's comment that certain rolls
are untraced. Locates a ms "copy of the record of
the Court for 1556" (2). Prints different sets of
documents relating to the drama.

579. ---, and A.C. Cawley. "The Corpus Christi Play of
Wakefield: A New Look at the Wakefield Burgess
Court Records." *LSE*, n.s. 7 (1974, for 1973 and
1974): 108-115.

Examines the Wakefield Burgess Court Records
(which contain the "only known references to the
Corpus Christi play of Wakefield" [108]) in light
of the newly discovered documents referred to in
Jean Forrester's *Wakefield Mystery Plays* . . .
(see previous entry). Briefly discusses J.W.
Walker's ms copy of the Burgess Court records, and
the records for 1556 and 1554 [1559/60].

580. Forstater, Arthur, and Joseph L. Baird. "'Walking and
Wending': Mankind's Opening Speech." *ThN* 26.2
(Winter 1971/72): 60-64.

Focuses on Mankind's probably moving slowly around
the playing area, "from point to point, as he
makes his four-part speech" (60). Claims that the
speech before the four scaffolds forms a microcosm
of the whole play, "with Mankind moving through
each of the cardinal points and ending with a plea
for mercy before *Deus skaffold*" (61). Calls the
opening words a "progressional speech" (61), and
claims that the speech itself indicates which
scaffold Mankind is before for each part of the
monologue. Concludes that "the first stanza is
delivered in the south . . .; the direction of
walking and wending is clockwise, moving from
south to west to north to east" (64), and that all
scaffolds are open to view.

580a. Fowler, Alastair. *A History of English Literature*.
Cambridge, Massachusetts: Harvard U. Press, 1987.
xi, 395 pp.

Chap I--"The Middle Ages: From Oral to Written
Literature"--contains brief mentions of the
cycles' use of Old Testament narrative, typology,
development with relation to the Corpus Christi
festival, use of comic elements, use of religious
art, and "the shift towards late gothic realism"
(18). Also looks briefly at moralities and
interludes (66-69). Contains no notes or
bibliography. With index.

581.   Fowler, David C. *The Bible in Middle English
Literature.* Seattle and London: U. of Washington
Press, 1984. 326 pp.

Chap. 1 is on Medieval Drama (3-52). Has sections
on "Biblical Drama in Cornwall" (3 ff.), "The Rise
of Vernacular Drama" (23 ff.), "Cycle Plays" (28
ff.), "The Chester Cycle" (30 ff.), "The Wakefield
Master" (36 ff.), Morality plays (44 ff.), and
"The Castle of Perseverance" (47 ff.).

Rev. L.B. Hall, *Choice* 22 (May 1985): 1331.
ChHist 54 (Summer 1985): 397.
A.J. Minnis, *TLS* (Aug. 9, 1985): 884.
TheoStud 46 (Dec. 1985): 718.
RSR 12 (Jan. 1986): 58.
David L. Jeffrey, *EngStudC* 12.4 (Dec. 1986):
452-54.

582.   Franks, Alan. "Unravelling the Old Mysteries of
Heaven and Hell in a Day." *The Times* (London),
January 18, 1985.

Briefly reviews a performance of the National
Theatre's production of *The Mysteries* of January
17, 1985, in London's Cottesloe Theatre.

583.   Freier, Mary P. "Woman as Termagant in the Towneley
Cycle." In *PIMA* 2 (1985): 154-67.

Claims that in the cycle "women are neither more
nor less negatively presented than are men" (154).
Looks at many characters--beyond Noah's wife and
Gill--and at misogyny in general in the middle
ages.

584.   Fridén, Ann. "Nyare forskning kring det medeltida
religiösa dramat i England." *Samlaren* 103 (1982):
112-19. (In Swedish.)

Summarizes recent research on medieval religious
drama in English. Presents the "liturgy/ritual-
to-secular-drama" theory of Chambers, Young, etc.
Gives Hardison's critique of this theory. Talks

of "Det medeltida dramats slutfas" ["The demise of medieval drama"--114]. Claims that to suppress the plays, authorities would demand copies of the mss that the guilds proposed to perform, then the authorities would simply not return the mss. Cites the work of F.M. Salter, Glynne Wickham, Eleanor Prosser, V.A. Kolve.

585.   Friedenreich, Kenneth. "'You Talks Brave and Bold': The Origins of an Elizabethan Stage Device." *CompD* 8.3 (Fall 1974): 239-53.

Examines medieval drama--specifically the treatment of devils and Herod, the popular mummers' plays, and the tournament--for antecedents to the "public confrontation scene" (239) of Renaissance drama.

586.   Fries, Maureen. "*Femina Populi:* Popular Images of Women in Medieval Literature." *JPC* 14.1 (Summer 1980): 79-86.

Not specifically on the drama. Looks at courtly images, popular conceptions, the misogynistic tradition, fabliaux women, the notion of chastity, and the struggle between the sexes (with a glance at the Noah plays, 83-84).

587.   Fries, Udo. "Zur Syntax der Chester Plays." Diss., U. of Vienna; Vienna: Notring, 1968. 208 pp.

Rev. Broder Carstensen, *Anglia* 89.4 (1971): 538-40.

588.   Frost, Cheryl. "*Everyman* in Performance." *LitNQ* 6.1 (1978): 39-48.

Discusses the effect and the effectiveness of the play on stage. Aims "to analyse the dramatic excellence" (39) of the play from the perspectives of the director, the actors, and the audience. Examines staging, audiences, actors (the cast), the "heavy cueing of entrances" (42), blocking, and so on.

589.   Fuhrich-Leisler, Edda, Gisela Prossnitz, and Fritz Furich. *Jedermann in Europa, Vom Mittelalter bis zur Gegenwart:* Eine Ausstellung der Max Reinhardt-Forschungs- und Gedenkstätte. Salzburg: Reischl-Druck, 1979. 112 pp.

Presents a catalogue of an exhibition which traces the appearance of the Everyman motif in art and drama, covering its several manifestations: ars-moriendi, Totentanz, Hecastus, Elckerlijc, Homulus, etc. From medieval to modern times, presents the theme of human beings confronted with death, both with religious and artistic purposes. Includes illustrations and photographs of stage productions keyed to catalogue entries. Text, 1-62; illustrations, 63-104. With table of imprints.

590. Furnish, Shearle. "The Reflexivity of the Plays of the Wakefield Master." Ph.D. diss., U. of Kentucky, 1984.

591. ---. "Technique *versus* Feeling in the Wakefield *Magnus Herodes.*" *KPAB* (1984): 36-43.

Claims that the play is "a self-conscious reflection on the art of drama" (36) and "an experiment with a novelty" (36)--the novelty of the dramatic experience to a medieval audience. Deals with reality and illusion, and with the character of Herod and the playwright's treatment of him.

592. Gaede, Ruth B. "The Theatre of the English Pageant Wagons, with Particular Attention to the Cycle Plays of Chester and York." Ph.D. diss., Brandeis U., 1970.

593. Gailey, Alan. *Irish Folk Drama.* Cork: Mercier Press, 1969. 104 pp.

Contains chapters on "Mummers and Christmas Rhymers," mummers and rhymers in various countries, sources of the texts, "Origins of the Action," "Folk Drama in Irish Seasonal Festivals," "Weddings and Wakes," and "The Life-Cycle Drama." Looks at the possibly pre-Christian ritual origins of folk drama. Presents five play texts from different parts of Ireland. Observes costumes, disguises, modern uses of mummers' folk plays, the spread of mumming in Ireland, mostly post-medieval.

Rev. *ScotStud* 15 (1971): 83.

594. Gair, Reavley. *The Children of Paul's: The Story of a Theatre Company 1553-1608.* Cambridge: Cambridge U. Press, 1982. ix, 213 pp.

". . . seeks to challenge some of the orthodoxies about the theatre of the children" (1). Briefly touches on morality plays.

Rev. *Choice* 20 (May 1983): 1300.
Brean S. Hammond, *ThRI* 8.3 (Autumn 1983):
253-55.
Richard Foulkes, *ThN* 38.3 (1984): 148-49.
Ejner J. Jensen, *CompD* 18.1 (Spring 1984):
82-84.
RenQ 37 (Spring 1984): 138.
BBN (Feb. 1985): 73.
RES 36 (Feb. 1985): 80.

595. Galloway, David. "Comment: The East Anglian 'Game-
Place': Some Facts and Fictions." *REEDN* 4.1
(1979): 24-26.

Records a Wymondham game-place from c. 1583-4.
Points out that "[m]ost of the towns and villages
of Norfolk and Suffolk seem to have had their
games" (25). Claims that "game-places" were not
permanent structures or areas with scaffolds.

596. ---. "The 'Game Place' and 'House' at Great Yarmouth,
1493-1595." *ThN* 31.2 (1977): 6-9.

Cites Kathleen M.D. Barker's "An Early Seventeenth
Century Playhouse" (entry # 143 above). Quotes
from the Great Yarmouth Assembly Minutes of March
15, 1538. Claims that the structure used for
interludes, plays, and possibly athletic contests
was probably "not a theater" (8) but some kind of
refectory used for eating, drinking, and lodging.

597. ---. "Records of Early English Drama in the Provinces
and What They May Tell Us about the Elizabethan
Theatre." In *The Elizabethan Theatre VII: Papers
Given at the Seventh International Conference on
Elizabethan Theatre . . . University of Waterloo,
Ontario, in July 1977*, 82-110. Ed. by G.R.
Hibbard. Hamden, Connecticut: Archon Books and
University of Waterloo, 1980.

Discusses the REED project. Shows how the REED
volumes will be useful.

598. ---, ed. *Records of Early English Drama: Norwich,
1540-1642*. Toronto, Buffalo, London: U. of
Toronto Press, 1984. xcvi, 501 pp.

"Documents the dramatic, musical, and ceremonial
activities in Norwich from the Reformation to
. . . 1642" (from the flier). Surveys conditions
and events, government, dramatic entertainments,
acting companies, and musical activity in Norwich.
Introduction contains information on "Norwich
History and Character" (xv); "The Government of

the City" (xx); "The Guild of St. George" (xxvi);
"Plays, Players, and Other Entertainments" (xxx);
"The Music Makers" (with Carole Janssen--xxxvii);
"The Documents" (xliv); and "Editorial Procedures"
(lxxv). With maps, the records, seven appendixes,
translations, endnotes, Latin and English
glossaries, and index.

Rev. *Choice* (Dec. 1984): 559.
William Tydeman, *ThRI* 11.2 (Summer 1986):
154-57.

599. ---. "'The Seven Deadly Sins': Some Verses from an
Archdeacon's Visitation Book (1533-51)." *REEDN*
4.1 (1979): 9-13.

Speculates on a fragment of a poem on the Seven
Deadly Sins as possibly a piece of drama.

600. ---, and John Wasson, eds. *Records of Plays and
Players in Norfolk and Suffolk, 1330-1642*.
Oxford: For the Malone Society, Oxford U. Press,
1980/1. *Collections XI*.

Contains extracts of civic documents from eighteen
towns in Norfolk and 23 in Suffolk. (For an
extensive list of contents, see Ian Lancashire,
"Annotated Bibliography . . .," *REEDN* 7.1 [1982]:
29-30; see entry # 944 below.)

Rev. Alan H. Nelson, *CompD* 17.1 (Spring 1983):
82-84.
Choice 22 (Dec. 1984): 559.

601. Gardiner, F.C. *The Pilgrimage of Desire: A Study of
Theme and Genre in Medieval Literature*. Leiden:
Brill, 1971. 161 pp.

Deals with the Medieval peregrinatio theme. Seeks
"a context for understanding the pilgrim-plays"
(7). Contains chapters on "Commentaries" (11) and
"Letters" (52). Then examines Latin plays (86).
Chap. 4 covers the English plays (129-56): Hegge
plays (130 ff.), Chester (141 ff.), York (144
ff.), and Towneley (148 ff.). With bibliography.

Rev. *Specu* 48 (Apr. 1973): 359.

602. Gardner, John. *The Construction of the Wakefield
Cycle*. Carbondale and Edwardsville: Southern
Illinois U. Press; London and Amsterdam: Feffner
and Simons, 1974. xii, 162 pp.

Brings together several already published and a
few new essays on various topics. Chap. 1--
"Decorum and Satanic Parody in the Wakefield
Creation." Chap. 2--"Theme and Irony in the
Mactacio Abel." Chap. 3--"Christology in the
Noah." Chap. 4--"Idea and Emotion in the
Abraham." Chap. 5--"'Insipid' Pageants: The
Limits of Improvisation." Chap. 6--"Light Dawns
on Clowns: *Prima Pastorum*." Chap. 7--"Structure
and Tone in the *Secunda Pastorum*." Chap. 8--
"Christian Black Comedy: The *Magnus Herodes*."
Chap. 9--"The Tragicomedy of Devil Worship: From
the Conspiracy to the Play of the Talents." Chap.
10--"The Comic Triumph: From the Deliverance to
the Judgment." With an epilogue on the Wakefield
Master, notes, and index.

Rev. *TLS* (Nov. 22, 1974): 1324.
　　　LJ 99 (Dec. 1, 1974): 3133.
　　　AmS 44 (Winter 1974-75): 151.
　　　Choice 11 (Jan. 1975): 1630.
　　　D.P. Poteet, *JEGP* 74 (Oct. 1975): 572-74.
　　　Robert J. Blanch, *CompD* 11.2 (Summer 1977):
　　　　177-79.

xxx.　---, foreword. See Michael R. Kelley, *Flamboyant
　　　Drama* (entry # 898 below).

603.　---.　"Idea and Emotion in the Towneley Abraham."　*PLL*
　　　7.3 (Summer 1971): 227-41.

Looks at "the handling of language in the Towneley
version" (227) and claims that it is superior to
the language in the other Abraham plays. Compares
the different versions. Says that the Chester
play "cannot be called an artistic success" (230)
and that the Hegge version is "sparer and more
intellectual" (230). Points out the importance of
doctrine and symbolism in the York version.
Points up the superiority of the Towneley play.
Says that the Brome play "is fundamentally a play
of emotion" (233) and it "looks forward to later
sentimental drama" (233). Says the Brome play is
basically an adaptation of the Chester play.

604.　---.　"Structure and Tone in the *Second Shepherds'
　　　Play*."　*ETJ* 19 (Mar. 1967): 1-8.

Examines the symbolic three-part structure of the
play and enumerates and comments on all the
threes--e.g. shepherds, soliloquies, Trinity,
motifs, gifts, etc.

604a . Garner, Stanton. "Theatricality in *Mankind* & *EV*,"
SP 1987

605.   Gascoigne, Bamber. *World Theatre: An Illustrated
       History*. London: George Rainbird Ltd.; Boston and
       Toronto: Little, Brown & Co., 1968. 335 pp.

       Chap. 4, on "The Middle Ages" (67-95), discusses
       liturgical drama, the mystery cycles, pageantry.
       Looks briefly at performance methods, characters,
       etc.

       Rev. T.E. Luddy, *LJ* 94 (Jan. 15, 1969): 213.
           TLS (Jan. 23, 1969): 82.
           NatOb 8 (Feb. 3, 1969): 21.
           Booklist 65 (Mar. 15, 1969): 795.
           Choice 6 (Summer 1969): 838.
           LibR 22 (Fall 1969): 166.

606.   Gash, Anthony. "Carnival against Lent: Ambivalence of
       Medieval Drama." In *Medieval Literature:
       Criticism, Ideology & History*, 74-98. Ed. by
       David Aers. New York: St. Martin's; Brighton:
       Harvester Press, 1986.

       Argues with John R. Elliott's view ("The Sacrifice
       of Isaac as Comedy and Tragedy," in Jerome Taylor
       and Alan H. Nelson's *Medieval English Drama*, 157-
       76; see entry # 1573 below) that the English drama
       was basically religious at all times. Agrees with
       A.P. Rossiter (*English Drama from Early Times to
       the Elizabethans*. London: Hutchinson, 1950) that
       some drama is "ambivalent" (74). Aims to redefine
       the plays "in the light of recent historical
       research into medieval popular culture and belief"
       (74). Considers authorship, reception, parody,
       audiences, popular festivals, "popular social and
       religious scepticism" (81). Examines *Mankind*
       closely.

607.   Gatch, Milton McC. "Mysticism and Satire in the
       Morality of *Wisdom.*" *PQ* 53 (1974): 342-62.

       Suggests that "certain aspects of the background
       and context of the play have been overlooked or
       confused so as to obscure its dramatic strategies"
       (342) and to bring severe criticism against the
       play. Looks at the play's shape and structure,
       sources, intended audience, satire, and
       provenance. Concludes that the play is "based on
       mystical writings . . . is clearly directed to a
       lay audience" (362), and contains satire "directed
       to legal practitioners in London" (362). Claims
       the play deserves a better reputation.

608.   Gates, Joanne. [Untitled review.] *RORD* 26 (1983):
       120-21.

161

Reviews performances of *The Digby Mary Magdalene* on May 15 and 18, 1983, at the U. of Massachusetts, Amherst.

609. Gauvin, Claude. *Un Cycle du Théâtre Réligieux Anglais du Moyen Age: Le jeu de la ville de "N."* Paris: Éditions du Centre National de la Recherche Scientifique, 1973. 409 pp.

Aims to show that the N-Town Cycle conforms most closely to the laws of the genre and benefits from a higher level of development because of its lateness (1468). Analysis of dialect forms leads to location of the play at or near Lincoln. Shows how its context conforms to that of the Corpus Christi cycles. Says that the cycle contributes to our understanding of the medieval point of view, based on its treatment of historical events and characters. Points out that certain of the cycle's "problems," such as the didactic nature of the contents, can be resolved in the recognition that the union of the dramatic with the religious is complete and constitutive. Proposes a new theory of medieval English theater: that the episodes portrayed were consciously chosen to entertain and benefit spectators and actors alike with the drama of Christian Redemption. Points out how this is not the same as the re-enactment of the Mass. Examines the ms, the text, the structure and composition of the cycle, its localization, pageant elements, tradition and innovation, its place in the contemporary world, and its theology and dramaturgy. With plates, appendixes, bibliography, and index.

Rev. E.M. Kelly, *JEGP* 74 (Oct. 1975): 570-72.
Daniel P. Poteet, II, *ThN* 30.1 (1976): 36-37.
Peter Meredith, *MLR* (July 1976): 622-24.
Stanley J. Kahrl, *Specu* 51 (Oct. 1976): 746-50.

610. ---. "Regards neufs sur le théâtre religieux anglais du moyen âge." *EtAng* 25.1 (Jan.-Mar. 1972): 3-16. [Followed by "Note sur les représentations modernes des cycles anglais" in collaboration with A. Lascombes, 17-18.]

Recounts the evolutionist view of English drama (the liturgy-to-secular-drama theory). Cites the appropriate scholarship. Claims that this theory does not explain the absence of certain key biblical events from the cycles. Recounts other scholarship and its weaknesses (e.g. the plays were often judged with modern standards; the

protestant/puritan training of many critics made
them too wary of things Catholic to appreciate the
didactic/catechismic intention of the drama).
Cites more recent criticism (Southern, Wickham,
iconographic research, Prosser, Kolve, Hardison).
Explains the absence of certain biblical episodes
(as being typologically redundant of themes
already present); thus, certain key events which
would duplicate reference to a particular age were
never included (e.g. Joseph in Egypt, Judith's
victory over Holofernes). Looks at the grouping
of characters and their doctrinal purposes.
Concludes that the drama did not intend to replace
or supplant religious practices, but was meant as
a suggestion, not a re-creation, of reality. Says
the concept of theater as rite is a misrepresenta-
tion. Sees the drama as worthy art in itself, not
just a precursor to comedy or later drama.

The "Note sur les représentations . . ." is a list
of modern performances, giving dates, places,
play/cycle performed, director, notes.

611. ---. "La Fête-Dieu et le théâtre en Angleterre au XVe
siècle." In Les Fêtes de la Renaissance, III,
439-49. Paris: Éditions du Centre National de la
Recherche Scientifique, 1975. Fifteenth
international colloquy on humanist studies, Tours,
10-22 July 1972.

Discusses the doctrinal background and
ecclesiastical history of the feast of Corpus
Christi, leading to a description of its
celebration with a procession of the Blessed
Sacrament and a dramatic performance dating back
in England to 1325 and 1375, respectively.
Disagrees with the scholarship which links the
drama with "tableaux vivants"; opts instead for an
association with the procession and the feast day
(except in York, Chester, Wakefield, or Lincoln).
Shows that the 1548 suppression of the feast did
not stop the performances. Says that the length
of the cycles made it probably impossible to
perform them in a single day, especially when
preceded by a procession. Recounts staging
methods and approximate times for performances.
Examines the contents of the cycles for relevance
to the themes of the Fall, the Incarnation, and
the Passion/Redemption. Discusses the Old
Testament episodes as prefigurement; the
coinciding of liturgy and drama, with an emphasis
on their connection with Redemption; the structure
of the whole cycle and particular local versions,
which fit into the local urban milieu as

demonstrations of guild skill and wealth. Says
the plays were not liturgy/rite, but were
imitative *play*, thus allowing the cycles to remain
after political and doctrinal climates had
changed. Relates the earlier plays to those of
the Renaissance.

612.   ---.   "Rite et jeu dans le théâtre anglais religieux
du Moyen-Age." *RHT* 29.2 (1977): 128-40.

Addresses the debate of whether medieval religious
drama constituted a rite/worship in itself, or
whether it was removed from the reality of worship
as mere image/representation. Cites historical
disapproval (from church fathers) of religious
drama and reason for such disapproval. Shows that
even as play/game, the drama presented models for
good behavior and encouraged attention to
salvation history. Says that like the cult of
images (statues, pictures), drama did not claim to
be the event depicted. Points out and explains
the doctrinal approval of such images. Says also
that ultimately the church approved of the plays,
not as a substitute for the Mass or catechism, but
as a supplement--serving the same function as the
images used for devotional purposes.

613.   ---.   "Sur quelques problèmes du théâtre médiéval
anglais." In *Arts du spectacle et histoire des
idées: recueil offert en hommage à Jean Jacquot*,
117-26. Preface by Jean-Michel Vaccaro. Tours:
Centre d'Etudes Supérieures de la Renaissance,
1984.

Describes stages in the criticism of medieval
theater as reflections of critics' own interests;
e.g. nineteenth-century antiquarians who were
occupied with text and language; scientists
(Chambers to Craig) who analyzed theater on
literary grounds alone, considering the religious
content to be a "handicap." Recent critics' work
on text reconstruction and the formation of a
theory of the genre *in context*, especially as part
of medieval *religious* culture. Looks at the more
recent attempts at reconstructing accurate
performances, with "original" sets and staging,
costumes, processions or pageants, and so on.
Deals with other issues like ms problems (e.g. the
locations of sections of the Digby or Macro mss).
Has three sections on 1) Processional
representation--myth or reality; the Toronto
processional performance of 1977 described at
length. 2) The Sherborne Corpus-Christi Play;
relies on Malone Society Collections publication

revealing two stages of dramatic activity--1500-
1543 (Corpus Christi processional) and 1543-1549
and 1572-1576 (plays, costumes, characters, and
tents--for outside stage sets and dressing
rooms?). 3) Another look at the city "N"; shows
the problems with attributing the plays to
Norwich/Norfolk; looks at extant records, the
Norfolk and Lincolnshire boundary and the language
in these locales, and the likelihood that the
plays were from Lincolnshire, not from Norfolk.

614.   ---.   "Le théâtre et son public en Angleterre au
Moyen-Age et à la Renaissance." In *La relation
théâtrale*, 55-65. Ed. by Régis Durand. Lille:
Presses Universitaires de Lille, [1980].

Says that English medieval stages blended into the
audience. Claims that no fee was charged, so all
classes, limited only by geographical proximity
and the constraints of fixed buildings surrounding
the open area, could attend. Points out that
money for actors and costumes was contributed by
guild members. Discusses religious, symbolic,
thematic issues (e.g. the relation between the
religious content and the audience's lives, the
time frame of eternity which yields a symbolic,
not historical, presentation), and the
relationship between audience and actors. Looks
at the Renaissance developments of medieval drama.

615.   ---, and A. Lascombes. "Note sur les représentations
modernes des Cycles anglais." See Gauvin,
"Regards neuf . . .," entry # 610 above.

616.   George, David.   "The Walmesley of Dunkenhalgh
Accounts." *REEDN* 10.2 (1985): 6-15.

Concerns the accounts of Dunkenhalgh Manor, which
record "a wide variety of entertainers" (7),
including 23 companies of players, mostly
performing early Renaissance drama.

617.   Geritz, Albert J.   "*Calisto and Melebea* (ca. 1530)."
Celestinesca 4 (May 1980): 17-29.

Sees Fernando de Rojas's *La Celestina* as a source
for Rastell. Looks at characterization, moral
views, genre, rhetoric, and allusions.

618.   ---.   "The Dramas and Prose Works of John Rastell."
Ph.D. diss., U. of Missouri, Columbia, 1976.

619.   ---.   "Recent Studies in John Rastell." *ELR* 8.3
(Autumn 1978): 341-50.

Offers a bibliographical study under the three
categories: I. General; II. Studies of Individual
Works; III. Canon and Texts.

620.   Gibson, Gail McMurray. "Bury St. Edmunds, Lydgate,
       and the *N-Town Cycle*." *Specu* 56.1 (January 1981):
       56-90.

       Claims that the cycle came from Bury St. Edmunds
       and that Lydgate thus had some influence on the
       cycle, directly or indirectly.

621.   ---. "East Anglian Drama and the Dance of Death: Some
       Second Thoughts on the 'Dance of Paul's.'" *EDAMN*
       5.1 (Fall 1982): 1-9.

       Studies Dance of Death banners in Long Melford
       Church for clues to East Anglian dramatic
       traditions. Supports arguments with references to
       literary treatment (Lydgate, More) and to
       historical figures. Claims that the banners are
       associated with a possible dance of Paul's
       ceremony at St. Edmunds, Salisbury in 1490 and
       with the N-Town plays, among others.

622.   ---. "The Images of Doubt and Belief: Visual
       Symbolism in the Middle English Plays of Joseph's
       Troubles about Mary." Ph.D. diss., U. of
       Virginia, 1975.

623.   ---. "Long Melford Church, Suffolk: Some Suggestions
       for the Study of Visual Artifacts and Medieval
       Drama." *RORD* 21 (1978): 103-15.

       Looks to church "artifacts as primary sources of
       information about English drama" (103). Examines
       stained glass, architecture, a churchwarden's
       account, and an alabaster relief. With two
       illustrations.

624.   ---. "The Play of *Wisdom* and the Abbey of St.
       Edmund." *CompD* 19.2 (Summer 1985): 117-35. Paper
       delivered at the *Wisdom* Symposium, Trinity
       College, Hartford, Connecticut, 13-14 April 1984.
       Rpt. with slight emendations in *The* Wisdom
       *Symposium: Papers from Trinity College Medieval
       Festival*, 39-66. Ed. by Milla Cozart Riggio.
       (See entry # 1390 below.)

       Studies date and provenance of *Wisdom*. Points out
       that the Macro ms is linked to Bury St. Edmunds--
       possibly linked with a free grammar school there,
       or it may have been in private hands--and suggests
       that the play comes from there by associating the

Hyngham whose name is in the ms with a monk of
Bury, Richard Hyngham. Says that the ms was in
the monastery from the late fifteenth century
until the dissolution of the monastery in 1539.
Points out that the ms contains an acting text or
a record of a performance. Looks through archival
evidence for records of performances. Gives
historical account of Bury St. Edmunds. Says that
Wisdom dates almost certainly to the 1460s; cites
historical and internal justification for this
dating.

625.   ---. "'Porta haec clausa erit': Comedy, Conception,
and Ezekiel's Closed Door in the *Ludus Coventriae*
Play of 'Joseph's Return.'" *JMRS* 8.1 (Spring
1978): 137-56.

Explains the "Joseph's Doubt" feature of the
plays. Suggests fabliaux origins. Examines the
humor, parody, symbolism, characterization, etc.

626.   ---. [Untitled review.] *RORD* 20 (1977): 114-17.

Reviews performance of The York Cycle at Toronto,
October 1-2, 1977.

627.   Gibson, James M. "*Quem queritis in presepe:* Christmas
Drama or Christmas Liturgy?" *CompD* 15.4 (Winter
1981-82): 343-65.

Tries to decide whether the trope was "a
liturgical act, a ritual re-enactment of the
Nativity" (343), or a miniature play with
dialogue, characters, and setting. Claims that it
was more liturgy than drama. Reviews extant
scholarship. Concludes that "The purpose was
neither to dramatize nor to impersonate, but . . .
to re-create the historical event for the benefit
of the participants" (363). Says that the trope
and the extended ritual were not meant to be
dramatic. Does not cover English drama, but
offers much background to the study of the later
plays.

628.   Gillespie, Patti P., and Kenneth M. Cameron. *Western
Theatre: Revolution and Revival.* New York:
Macmillan; London: Collier Macmillan, 1984.

Chap. 8 focuses on "Vernacular Religious Theatre
of the Middle Ages, ca. 1250-1600" (177-203).
Offers sketchy comments on medieval institutions,
language, the church's influence, technology,
religious and vernacular performances, the cycle
plays, saints' plays, moralities, staging,

processions, costs of productions, actors,
machinery and special effects, costumes,
audiences.

Rev. *PAJ* 10.1 (1986): 116.

628a. Gilman, Donald, ed. *Everyman & Company: Essays on the
Theme and Structure of the European Moral Play.*
New York: AMS Press, 1988. AMS Studies in the
Middle Ages, No. 15.

Contains nine essays, the following five of which
are germane to the present bibliography: 1)
Bevington, "The Nature . . ." (entry # 187a
above); 2) Fifield, "Applications of Genre . . ."
(# 549a); 3) Cheri A. Brown, "The *Susanna* Drama
. . ." (# 240a); 4) Cawley, "A *Yorkshire Tragedy*
. . ." (# 288a); 5) Donald Gilman, "Selected
Bibliography . . ." (# 628b). With preface by
Gilman, an afterword by Robert Potter, and an
index.

628b. ---. "Selected Bibliography of Texts and Criticism of
Biblical Drama and Moral Plays." In *Everyman &
Company* (see previous entry).

629. Glaap, Albert-Reiner. Das englische Drama bis
Shakespeare: Gattungen und Formen in der
unterrichtlichen Präsentation." In *William
Shakespeare: Didaktisches Handbuch*, vol. 1, 199-
217. Ed. by Rüdiger Ahrens. Munich: Wilhelm
Fink, 1982.

Directs comments to teachers at the secondary
level (Gymnasium) in Germany. Argues that English
classes using Shakespeare as a study text need a
unit on earlier drama because of the influences
the earlier plays had and also because of the
allusions to earlier drama in the later plays.
Describes mystery, miracle, and morality plays.
Looks at themes, particular influential scenes,
specific characters.

630. Glage, Liselotte. "Wer lacht über wen? Henry Medwalls
Interlude von *Fulgens und Lucres*." *ZAA* 25.3
(1977): 254-63.

Analyzes the societal changes of Medwall's time--
the rise of the bourgeoisie and the fading of
"virtue" from the noble class. Shows how this
early English secular drama involved all classes,
including the audience, in the laughter. Shows
also how Medwall portrays a spiritually bankrupt
nobility unwilling to give alms and also appearing

foolish. Dissects the play in these social and
political terms.

631. Glasheen, Adaline. "*Everyman.*" *AWN*, n.s. 13.1 (Feb.
1976): 16.

Refers to Richard Axton's review of Robert
Potter's *The English Morality Play* (entry # 1324
below). Mentions the possible influence of
Everyman on James Joyce. (See Archie K. Loss,
"Everyman Blooms as Everybody," entry # 1009
below.)

632. Glassie, Henry. *All Silver and No Brass: An Irish
Christmas Mumming.* Bloomington and London:
Indiana U. Press, 1975.

Contains an ethnological study, not focusing
specifically on medieval English drama, but
looking at folk traditions of the mummers.

Rev. *KR* 44 (Mar. 1, 1976): 312.
      LJ 101 (Mar. 15, 1976): 826.
      DramRev 20 (June 1976): 124.
      BkW (June 20, 1976): L1.
      Choice 13 (July 1976): 649.
      SewR 84 (Winter 1976): R21.
      AmAnth 79 (Mar. 1977): 185.
      ContempSoc 6 (July 1977): 437.
      AmJSoc 84 (July 1978): 191.

633. Göllner, Theodor. "The Three-Part Gospel Reading and
the Medieval Magi Play." *JAMS* 24.1 (Spring 1971):
51-62.

Concerns the polyphonic rendition of scriptural
reading. Says that biblical passages often
alternated between monophonic and polyphonic
textures to relieve the monotony of the passages.
Describes the mono- and polyphonic pattern in the
Magi play. Says that in some versions the kings
are realistically impersonated and there is a
synchronization of text, music, and action. But
says also that at various stages in its
development, the play's staging and music, which
convey the drama of the play, are radically
transformed.

634. Goldhamer, Allen D. "*Everyman:* A Dramatization of
Death." *C&M* 30 (1969): 595-616. Also published
in *QJS* 59.1 (Feb. 1973): 87-98.

Reviews scholarship. Treats the theological
aspect of death in the play, especially with

respect to the *ars moriendi* theme. Looks at the
"unusual" (596) presentation of death, medieval
death literature, the psychological state of the
main character. Uses Elisabeth Kübler-Ross's
analysis of the human psychological reaction to
death.

635. Goldman, Michael. *The Actor's Freedom: Toward a*
     Theory of Drama. New York: Viking Press, 1975.
     180 pp.

     Contains several references to medieval English
     drama. See, e.g., passages on medieval drama (24-
     26), *Everyman* (35, 123), Towneley Cycle (79-81),
     York Cycle (77).

     Rev. *KR* 43 (Apr. 1, 1975): 419.
          LJ 100 (May 1, 1975): 875.
          KR 43 (July 1, 1975): 747.
          PW 208 (July 14, 1975): 56.
          NewRep 173 (Oct. 4, 1975): 25.
          VV 20 (Oct. 20, 1975): 56.
          Nation 221 (Nov. 8, 1975): 470.
          Booklist 72 (Dec. 15, 1975): 538-39.
          Choice 12 (Dec. 1975): 1318.
          T. Herstand, *ETJ* 28 (May 1976): 278.
          S. Rusinko, *BksA* 50 (Spring 1976): 483.
          J. Taft, *ComQ* 24 (Spring 1976): 43-44.
          P. Johnson, *YaleR* 66 (Dec. 1976): 306.
          R.L. Smith, *CompD* 10 (Winter 1976-77): 352-
               54.

636. Goldstein, Leonard. "On the Origin of Medieval
     Drama." *ZAA* 29.2 (1981): 101-15.

     Reviews scholarship. Tries to explain "Why the
     dramatic dialogue became metrical" in hopes of
     "solving the problem of the genesis of the new
     type of verse" (101). Offers a sociological view.
     Concludes that the source of the drama is in "the
     social process by which private property emerges
     from the Ninth and Tenth Centuries" (112-13).
     Does not discuss the drama of any country
     specifically.

637. Gottfried, Robert S. *Bury St. Edmunds and the Urban*
     Crisis: 1290-1539. Princeton, NJ: Princeton U.
     Press, 1982.

     Not specifically on drama. Has sections on the
     guilds (107-15) and on "The Wealth of the Town and
     the Townsmen" (116-30). Offers background
     information on conditions which produced the
     drama.

Rev. *Choice* 19 (July 1982): 1629.
RenQ 36 (Autumn 1983): 425.
Specu 58 (Oct. 1983): 1039.
Historian 46 (Nov. 1983): 92.
CHR 70 (Apr. 1984): 294.
ChHist 53 (June 1984): 241.
EHR 99 (Oct. 1984): 868.

638. Gowda, H.H. Anniah. *Dramatic Poetry from Mediaeval to Modern Times: A Philosophic Enquiry into the Nature of Poetic Drama in England, Ireland and the United States of America.* Madras, Bombay, Calcutta, Delhi: The Macmillan Company of India, 1972.

Chap. I (1-34) considers "Medieval Drama and Poetry." Looks at the poetry in the plays, at the influence that poetry had in their writing, and at many passages in the plays as poetry.

Rev. *TLS* (Mar. 2, 1973): 246.

639. Graham, Colin. "Staging First Productions, 3." In *The Operas of Benjamin Britten*, 44-58. Ed. by David Herbert. New York: Columbia U. Press, 1979.

Concerns Britten's use of the Noah's Flood play, an adaptation from the Chester Cycle. Prints a modernized text of the play (249-54).

640. Grantley, Darryll. "The National Theatre's Production of *The Mysteries:* Some Observations." *ThN* 40.2 (1986): 70-73.

Reviews performances and reflects on the plays. With illustrations.

641. ---. "Producing Miracles." In *Aspects of Early English Drama*, 78-91, 146-47. Ed. by Paula Neuss. Cambridge: A.S. Brewer; Totowa, NJ: Barnes & Noble, 1983. (See entry # 1213 below.)

Concerns the staging of miracles in plays. Describes the saints' legends and plays, the "forms and functions of miracles in these plays" (79), the devices the plays used (e.g. scaffolds, trap doors), ascents and descents, Hell's mouth, the bleeding of the Host (of the Croxton play), the appearance of fire and light, and other features.

642. ---. "The source of the Digby *Mary Magdalen*." *N&Q*, n.s. 31.4 (229) (Dec. 1984): 457-59.

Shows the sources to be the New Testament and apocryphal legend. Discusses parallels in the *South English Legendary*, patristic writings, and the *Legenda Aurea* (but primarily the *South English Legendary*).

643.   ---. "*The Winter's Tale* and Early Religious Drama."
        CompD 20 (1986): 17-37.

        Looks at early dramatic influences in the figures
        of the Virgin Mary and Herod from the cycle plays.
        Points out Shakespeare's use of "themes central to
        the religious drama of his youth" (36) and his use
        of traditional images.

643a.   Gray, Douglas, ed.   *The Oxford Book of Late Medieval*
        Verse and Prose.   Oxford: Clarendon Press, 1985.
        586 pp.

        Contains sections on Skelton (382-91), More (407-
        14), *Everyman* (332-55), *Mankind* (236-64), and
        Lydgate (59-70), each with brief introduction.
        The plays have textual notes (*Mankind*, pp. 466-69;
        Everyman, pp. 479-81). With "Notes on Grammar and
        Spelling in the Fifteenth Century" by Norman
        Davis, and a glossary and index.

644.   Green, Barbara, and Rachel M.R. Young.   *Norwich: The*
        Growth of a City.   [Norwich]: City of Norwich
        Museums, 1968; rpt. Hunstanton, Norfolk: 1981.   42
        pp.

        Considers the history of the city from prehistoric
        times to the present.   Has a section on "The Black
        Death and After--1348-1485" (16 ff.) discussing
        the city's prosperity and its guilds, its
        government, mercantilism, and industry.   Points
        out that "all craft guilds took a corporate part
        in the religious life of the time and later, in
        the early 16th century, there was an elaborate
        procession of all the guilds on Corpus Christi
        day" (18).   Not specifically on drama, but paints
        a picture of the city in which the drama was
        performed.   With maps and bibliography.

645.   Green, Maureen Flanagan.   "Verbal and Structural
        Repetition as Devices of Representation in the
        York Cycle."   Ph.D. diss., U. of Wisconsin,
        Madison, 1973.

646.   Green, Richard Firth.   "Three Fifteenth-Century
        Notes."   *ELN* 14.1 (Sept. 1976): 14-17.

Note II is on Lydgate's *Mumming at Hertford*.
Dates the piece to 1426 or 1427, and not to the
generally accepted 1430.

647. Green, Thomas A. "Folk Drama." Intro. to special
edition of *JAF* 94.374 (Oct.-Dec. 1981): 421-32.

Reviews current trends in research. This issue
devoted to traditional drama.

648. Greene, Richard Leighton. "Carols in Tudor Drama."
In *Chaucer and Middle English Studies in Honour of
Rossell Hope Robbins*, 357-65. Ed. by Beryl
Rowland. London: George Allen and Unwin; Kent,
Ohio: Kent State U. Press, 1974.

Looks at carols in *Tom Tyler and His Wife, Jacob
and Esau, Apius and Virginia*, and *Damon and
Pythias*.

649. Greenfield, Peter H. "'All for your delight/We are
not here': Amateur Players and the Nobility."
RORD 28 (1985): 173-80.

Comments on amateur players' performances and
rewards (like the one referred to in the title of
this article from *Midsummer Night's Dream*).
Claims that amateur performances "gave birth to a
somewhat different kind of performing situation
. . . connected with some of the references to
noblemen's players in civic and household records"
(174). Calls them "semi-professional"
performances (174). Correlates records of one
patron's players with the patron's biography to
show a connection between amateur performances
before their patron and performances elsewhere by
players bearing that patron's name. Looks at one
such case (from household book of Edward Stafford,
3rd Duke of Buckingham) and at Gloucestershire
patrons.

650. Greenfield, Peter Henry. "Medieval and Renaissance
Drama in Gloucestershire." Ph.D. diss., U. of
Washington, 1981.

651. Grennen, Joseph E. "Tudd, Tibbys Sonne, and Trowle
the Trewe: Dramatic Complexities in the Chester
Shepherds' Pageant." *SN* 57.2 (1985): 165-73.

Addresses "the question of artistic intention and
practice" (165) to elucidate the play's structure
and meaning, especially with respect to the sacred
and profane elements in the play. Examines the
playwright's dramatic strategy, his use of the

names Tudd (traditionally the name of a priest's
bastard) and Tibb (the name of a loose woman), and
the "farcical counterpoint" (168) suggested here.
Also observes passages concerning Trowle, echoing
the consecration in the mass, yielding paradox and
ambiguity, and revealing linguistic richness.
Associates the name Trowle with "troll," which
relates him to the devil. Looks also at the use
of music in the play.

652.   Griffin, John R.   "The Hegge Pilate: A Tragic Hero?"
       EngStud 51.3 (June 1970): 234-44.

       Offers a character study of Pilate, one of the
       best delineated characters in the cycles, and
       "perhaps the first character of artistic depth in
       the cycles" (244). Says that Pilate lacks moral
       nobility but is nonetheless human and sympathetic.
       Looks at sources, audience, and characterization.

653.   Griffith, Benjamin W.   "Faulkner's Archaic Titles and
       the *Second Shepherds' Play*."   *NMW* 4 (1971): 62-63.

       Briefly explains the use of the words *reiver* (or
       reaver), meaning robber or plunderer, and *light*,
       meaning delivered of a baby, both of which appear
       in the *Second Shepherds' Play*. Claims "that
       Faulkner read such early plays as the *Second
       Shepherds' Play*" (62) and that he had a "great
       capacity for remembering words" (63).

654.   Griffiths, Ralph A.   *The Reign of King Henry VI: The
       Exercise of Royal Authority, 1422-1461*.   London:
       Ernest Benn; Berkeley and Los Angeles: U. of
       California Press, 1981.

       Not specifically on drama, but mentions minstrels
       (297), playing companies (64, n. 17), pageants
       (220-21, 488-89), and masques (257, 271, n. 134).

       Rev. R.C. Hoffmann, *LJ* 106 (June 15, 1981): 1301.
            B. Wolffe, *Spectator* 247 (Sep. 19, 1981): 20.
            Obs (Oct. 4, 1981): 29.
            R. Virgoe, *THES* 472 (Nov. 20, 1981): 20.
            P. Horden, *BBN* (Dec. 1981): 765.
            Choice 19 (Jan. 1982): 675.
            AHR 87 (June 1982): 762.
            HistT 32 (June 1982): 52.
            AAPSS 463 (Sept. 1982): 176.
            EHR 98 (Jan. 1983): 138.

655.   Grose, B. Donald, and O. Franklin Kenworthy.   *A Mirror
       to Life: A History of Western Theatre*. New York:
       Holt, Rinehart and Winston, 1985.

Part IV--"Reflections of Heaven and Earth: The
Medieval Period" (87-119)--contains sections on
vernacular plays, staging, and production. Deals
with York Plays, morality plays, characteristics
of medieval stage forms (church staging, outdoor
staging [pageant wagons and *mansion* stages],
indoor staging [banquet halls, university stages,
and mummings], tournaments, royal entries, street
fairs, pageants), scenery, production machines and
devices, production aids for the actor, acting
styles, actor organization, festival organization,
festival finances, and the audience.

656. Grove, Thomas N. "Light in Darkness: The Comedy of
the York 'Harrowing of Hell' as Seen Against the
Backdrop of the Chester 'Harrowing of Hell.'" *NM*
75 (1974): 115-25.

Calls the York play "the first true comedy in the
cycles" (115) and possibly "the first positive,
visual assurance to the medieval audience that God
can and will control" fate (115). Shows how the
York version uses comedy and focuses on the
confrontation between Satan and Christ, while the
Chester version is quite different.

657. Grudin, Michaela Paasche. "Pathos in English Medieval
Literature: The Religious Lyric, The Corpus
Christi Drama and the Canterbury Tales." Ph.D.
diss., U. of California, Berkeley, 1974.

658. Gruhn, Shari Janet. "The Noah Plays in Medieval
English Drama." Masters thesis, Brown U., 1968.

659. Guerrant, Mary Thorington. "*The Shepherds:* The
Chester Mystery Play Set to Music." Ph.D. diss.,
Texas Tech U., 1976.

660. Guilfoyle, Cherrell. "*Mactacio Desdemonae:* Medieval
Scenic Form in the Last Scene of *Othello.*" *CompD*
19.4 (Winter 1985-86): 305-20.

Examines the religious imagery in the last scene.
Shows the three sets of images and their
prototypes in the Abraham, Cain, and Judas figures
of medieval drama. Concludes that the "scenic
forms, in parallel to those of the eucharistic
plays in the mystery cycles, are deployed in a
series of variations on the theme of the sacrifice
of the innocent" (318).

661. ---. "'The Riddle Song' and the Shepherds' Gifts in
Secunda Pastorum with a Note on the 'Tre callyd
Persidis.'" *YES* 8 (1978): 208-19.

Shows the link between "The Riddle Song" ("I gave
my love a cherry that has no stone . . .") and the
shepherds' gifts. Looks at pagan customs and
festivities, rings, birds, cherries, and balls.
Then shows how elements from the legend of Perseus
"bear on the present enquiry" (218)--especially in
the playwright's use of the pagan magic tree.

662. Gussenhoven, Frances Helen. "Corpus Christi Drama as
Medieval Comedy." Ph.D. diss., Stanford U., 1977.

663. Guthrie, William Bruce. "New Materials in Dramatic
Research in Oxfordshire in the Fifteenth and
Sixteenth Centuries with Some Additional Notes."
Ph.D. diss., U. of Colorado, Boulder, 1980.

664. Habicht, Werner. "Das Drama in England." In
Europäisches Spätmittelalter, 713-32. Ed. by
Willi Erzgraber. Wiesbaden: Athenaion, 1978.
Neues Handbuch der Literaturwiss, 8.

Mentions the preliterary, pre-Christian, mythical,
and magical rites which were common in agrarian
societies (such rites as spring fest, games, sword
dances, seasonal festivals, etc.), which contained
dramatic elements. E.g. the mummers' play with
the death and resurrection of the hero, and the
circular arrangement of the actors both prefigured
theater in the round. Says that other popular
dramatic representations in the thirteenth through
the fifteenth centuries became more and more
common; they merged mythological and historical
elements with those of the mummers' play.
Mentions the parallel tradition of religious drama
and says that every class of society had its own
dramatic practices. Considers the growth of
English drama, the hypothetical origins of the
genre, the nature of the various source materials
that the drama is composed of, the historical
conditions (social, commercial, financial,
religious, etc.) which prompted the assignment of
specific plays to particular guilds, the religious
substance of the plays, the lack of identifiable
sources or authors, the malleability of the plays'
form and the evolving nature of the plays from one
year's performance to another, their performance-
oriented nature and the specific audiences they
were intended for, the didactic elements and aims,
the realistic elements which demonstrate human
weakness, the juxtapositions of the saintly
characters with their unholy parodies. Also looks
at morality plays, grounded in common experience,
didactic about the way to live, the actors and
their commercial efforts, staging, themes. Claims

that *interlude* is a general term for any theater
piece and is not a genre distinction. Talks about
two types: professional and elite (migrant and
literary), their performances, and their content
and nature.

665. ---. *Studien zur Dramenformen vor Shakespeare:
      Moralität, Interlude, romaneskes Drama.*
      Heidelberg: Carl Winter Verlag, 1968.
      Anglistische Forschungen 96. 259 pp.

For moralities, discusses heroes, characters, and
settings, the openings of the plays which were
designed to put the audience into a specific mood
and to address and engage the audience, the
process of seeking and the fall into sin,
personifications of the vices, confession and
absolution, the impulse toward penitence,
righteousness and grace, the morality of
contrasted characters (good and evil, just and
lust . . .). Considers interludes as mirror and
satire, and discusses king and tyrant, the vices,
world satire, the world of fools. Looks at folk
figures, worldly disgust, and comic or satiric
disclosure of worldly weaknesses and vices. Sees
morality as a structural principle. Examines
drama and exempla, native and classical drama,
conditions for mixture of the forms, moral
thematics, and rhetorical adaptations. Also
considers Christian school dramas and native
adaptations, Roman comedy and native interlude,
and interludes and Senecan tragedies. Defines the
term *Romanesque* in storytelling and in drama.
With bibliography, index, and summary in English.

Rev. *MLR* 67 (Jan. 1972): 165.

666. Hacker, Hans-Jürgen. *Zur Poetologie des
      mittelalterlichen Dramas in England.* Heidelberg:
      Carl Winter Universitätsverlag, 1985. 279 pp.
      Originally presented as a Ph.D. diss., Mannheim,
      1980.

Looks for an appropriate perspective from which to
study the drama: literary, theological . . . .
Summarizes and analyzes earlier critical
approaches, the religious elements in the cycles,
the different *times* of the plays (depicted time
and performance time), and anachronistic elements.
Presents "the thesis that the plays generated a
consistently high homogenous illusionary
potential, which completely involved the audience"
(278). Also looks at the reasons for putting on
the plays from a "hermeneutic perspective" (179).

Concludes that critical judgment must take into
account what the plays "reflect of the fears and
the needs of their producers" (279). In German,
with English summary (277-79).

667. Haden, Roger Lee. "'Ilike a Creature, Takes Entente':
      A Re-Investigation of the Purpose and
      Effectiveness of Medieval Corpus Christi Drama."
      ESRS 27.1 (Summer 1978): 5-33.

      Examines the didactic and entertainment values of
      the plays, focusing primarily on the drama's
      public appeal. Looks at dramatic conventions,
      medieval concepts (aesthetics, universal order,
      community, realism, personification, allegory,
      symbolism), characterization, the growth of the
      church, "naturalistic influences" (19), the
      relevance of the plays to the lives of the
      audience, "theatrical illusion" (24), "topical
      allusions" (25), and audience involvement.
      Contains bibliography (28-33).

668. Hahn, Thomas. [Untitled review.] *RORD* 20 (1977):
      117-21.

      Reviews a performance of The York Cycle at
      Toronto, Oct. 1-2, 1977.

669. Hailes, Roger Paulson. "The Influence of Morality
      Plays on Drama of the English Renaissance." Ph.D.
      diss., U. of South Carolina, 1973.

670. Halevy, Miriam. *The Evolution of Medieval Drama: From
      The Life to Come to Recorded Time.* London: A
      Jewish Quarterly Publication, 1974. 131 pp.

      Part I discusses "The English Old Testament Play
      in relation to its sources" (plays about creation,
      Cain, the flood, Abraham and Isaac, the prophets,
      Herod). Part II deals with German drama. Part
      III treats Lucifer and the Harrowing of Hell.
      Part IV is on "Medieval Drama in the light of
      Literary Criticism." With an appendix on three
      medieval Welsh plays, notes, and bibliography.
      This is a "shortened and edited version of her
      doctoral thesis presented at Ruhr Universitaet,
      Buchum, Germany" (4).

671. Halevy, Miriam. "The Secular Element in English and
      German Medieval Drama." Inaugural Dissertation,
      Bochum, 1971.

672. Haman, Mark Stefan. "The Introspective and Egocentric
      Quests of Character and Audience: Modes of Self-

Definition in the York Corpus Christi Cycle and in Chaucer's *Merchant's Tale*." Ph.D. diss., U. of Rochester, 1982.

673.   Hamilton, Alice B.   [Research in Progress.]   *REEDN* 4.1 (1979): 17-19.

Discusses work in progress on the records of Leicester at the University of Leicester, the Leicestershire Record Office, the city's Public Reference Library, churchwardens' accounts at St. Martin's Cathedral. Treats findings concerned with drama and music, especially Whitsun processions and figures from pageants.

674.   Hanawalt, Barbara A.   "Keepers of the Lights: Late Medieval English Parish Gilds." *JMRS* 14.1 (Spring 1984): 21-37.

Looks at the role of the guilds in "keeping alive the traditional religious ceremonials" (21) in the middle ages. Treats their plays (27 ff.) and processions (28 ff.) and overall religious functions in light of the economic and emotional benefit they offered.

675.   Hanchin, John Milan.   "The Sermons of the British Museum Royal MS. 18 B. XXIII and the Seven Deadly Sins in the Medieval Morality Plays *The Castle of Perseverance*, Digby *Mary Magdalene*, and Henry Medwall's *Nature*." Ph.D. diss., Indiana U. of Pennsylvania, 1979.

676.   Hanks, Dorrel T., Jr.   "The *Mactacio Abel* and the Wakefield Cycle: A Study in Context." *SoQ* 16.1 (Oct. 1977): 47-57.

Opens with general statements about English cycle plays. Aims to discuss "the sophistication and craftsmanship" (49) of the Wakefield Master. Looks at "characterization, theme, and time-scheme in the context of the entire cycle" (49). Aims also to show that plays must be seen within the context of their cycles. Concludes that the Abel play is "a highly sophisticated, carefully unified work of dramatic art" (56).

677.   ---.   "New Sources for York Play XLV, 'The Death of Mary': *Legenda Aurea* and Vincent's *Speculum Historiale*." *ELN* 14.1 (Sept. 1976): 5-7.

Reviews scholarship of sources. Points out three of the play's incidents "modeled solely upon *Legenda Aurea*" (6) and shows the play's relationship also to Vincent's work. Claims that earlier scholarship attesting to Italian sources was in error.

678. Hanks, D. Thomas, Jr. "Not for Adults Only: The English Corpus Christi Plays." *CLAQ* 10.1 (Spring 1985): 21-22.

Claims that the plays would have been enjoyed by children, who clearly attended the performances. Says that the plays attracted children in their portrayal of children, villains, and children's games. Also discusses the role of children as actors and as characters.

679. ---. "'Quike Bookis': The Corpus Christi Drama and English Children in the Middle Ages." In *Popular Culture in the Middle Ages*, 118-27. Ed. by Josie P. Campbell. Bowling Green, Ohio: Popular, 1986.

Sees the plays as "quick books"--convenient sources of knowledge about the tenets of the audience's religion. Claims that one function of the plays was to pass along to succeeding generations the religious and secular preoccupations of the society. Focuses on the role of children in the audience and on stage and also on the appeals to children in the plays themselves. Claims that medieval children would have been captivated by "the stage-children, villains and familiar games" (126) and that the plays transmitted social and religious values.

680. Hanks, Dorrell Thomas, Jr. "Social Satire in the Medieval English Cycles." Ph.D. diss., U. of Minnesota, 1976.

680a. Hanning, Robert W. *The Wakefield Master and Other Dramatists*. Leiden, Brill, forthcoming.

(Announced in Brill's 1985 catalogue "The Middle Ages and The Renaissance," p. 16.)

681. Hanning, R.W. "'You Have Begun a Parlous Pleye': The Nature and Limits of Dramatic Mimesis as a Theme in Four Middle English 'Fall of Lucifer' Cycle Plays." *CompD* 7.1 (Spring 1973): 22-50. Rpt. in *The Drama* . . ., 140-68. Ed. by Davidson, Gianakaris, and Stroupe (see entry # 409 above).

Examines the N-Town, Wakefield Master, Chester, and York versions in terms of their elements of play and game such that the mimesis of God would be acceptable to the medieval church. Claims that

medieval playwrights saw the similarity between
Lucifer's attempt to mimic God and their own, and
that they understood their own attempt--in their
mimesis--to glorify God while Lucifer's aim was to
subvert Him. Examines each play individually.
Points out their didacticism. Says that all four
plays, from the beginning of the cycles, focus the
audience's attention on what each cycle aims to do
and not to do.

682.   Happé, Peter.   "Aspects of Dramatic Technique in
        Thomas Garter's 'Susanna.'"   *MET* 8.1 (July 1986):
        61-63.

        Looks at verse form, structure (the use of
        "repeated assurance that things would turn out
        right" [61], the "sense of an interpretative
        intention" [62]), and the function of the comic.

683.   ---.   "*The Comedy of Virtuous and Godly Susanna.*"
        RORD 29 (1986-87): 110-11.

        Reviews performances of April 29-May 1, 1986,
        Nuffield Theatre Studio, Lancaster; May 10, 1986,
        Rufford Old Hall; July 10, 1986, Promenade des
        Platanes, Prepignan.

684.   ---, ed.   *Medieval English Drama: A Casebook*.   London:
        Macmillan, 1984.   222 pp.

        Offers a selection of modern critical statements
        about the drama taken from published works.
        Introduction summarizes critical concerns for the
        last few centuries.   Part I prints excerpts from *A
        Tretise of Miraclis Pleyinge*, Robert Mannynge of
        Brune, The Mercers' Pageant Waggon at York, and
        David Rogers.   Presents criticism in four areas:
        Introductory, The Corpus Christi Plays, Morality
        Plays and Interludes, and Aspects of Performance.
        Part II contains an introduction by David Mills
        ("Approaches to Medieval Drama"--see entry # 1131
        below), and fifteen other pieces.   Those not in
        Stratman (and which are reviewed in this
        bibliography) are: 1) Vinter ("Didactic
        Characterization . . .," # 1635); 2) Rosemary
        Woolf ("The Wakefield Shepherds' Plays," from *The
        English Mystery Plays*, entry # 1714 below); 3)
        Davidson ("The Realism . . .," # 403 above); 4)
        Kahrl ("Of History . . .," from *Traditions of
        Medieval English Drama*, entry # 886); 5) Potter
        ("Forgiveness as Theatre," from *The English
        Morality Play*, entry # 1324); 6) Kantrowitz
        ("Allegory," from *Dramatic Allegory*, entry # 888);
        7) Twycross and Carpenter ("Purposes and Effects

. . .," from "Masks in Medieval English Theatre:
The Mystery Plays," entry # 1606); 8) Tydeman
("Costumes and Actors," from *The Theatre of the
Middle Ages*, entry # 1613); 9) Neuss ("The Staging
of the 'Creacion . . .," entry # 1218); 10)
Lindenbaum ("The York Cycle at Toronto," entry #
1003). With bibliography, notes, and index.

Rev. *BBN* (Dec. 1984): 755.
    BBN (Feb. 1985): 73.
    TES (Feb. 22, 1985): 25.
    Peter Meredith, *CompD* 21.1 (Spring 1987):
      9598.

685. ---. "Mystery Plays and the Modern Audience." *MET*
2.2 (Dec. 1980): 98–[101].

Discusses "what directors are revealing about
their attitudes to audiences" (98) in modern
productions of mystery plays in terms of
modernizing the plays. Looks at recent
performances.

686. ---. "Properties and Costumes in the Plays of John
Bale." *MET* 2.2 (Dec. 1980): 55-65.

Shows how Bale made careful use of props and
costumes, but unsystematically. Considers
dialogue and stage directions. Looks at "the
state of each as it has come down to us, and the
dramatic conventions which Bale inherited or
developed in each play" (55). Contains a
"Checklist of References to Costumes and
Properties" (60-64). Relates costume to symbolic
action, state of life, doubling.

686a — · "Recent Studies in Bale," *ELR*, 17 (1987)

687. ---. "*The Second Shepherds* [sic] *Play*." *RORD* 29
(1986-87): 111-12.

Reviews performance of July 8, 1986, Cathédrale
St. Jean, Prepignan.

688. ---. "Sedition in *King Johan:* Bale's Development of a
'Vice.'" *MET* 3.1 (July 1981): 3-6.

Discusses Bale's autograph version in the ms,
which can be followed somewhat chronologically to
a point. Claims the work probably dates to c.
1536, with later interpolations. Analyzes the
revisions (some add ridicule and satire, some
replace lost lines, some add historical materials,
some effect characterization). Also says that the
enlargements of Sedition's role are related to the
depiction of Vice.

689.   ---, et al.   "Thoughts on 'Transvestism' by Divers
       Hands."   *MET* 5.2 (Dec. 1983): 110-11.

       Explores the practicability of using men in
       women's roles in medieval English drama.   Other
       commentators are Sarah Carpenter (111-12);
       Henrietta Twycross-Martin (112-14); Diana Wyatt
       (114-18); and Carl Heap (119-22).   Precedes
       article by Twycross, "'Transvestism' In the
       Mystery Plays" (entry # 1604 below).

690.   ---.   [Untitled review.]   *RORD* 21 (1978): 102.

       Reviews performances of *The Castle of Perseverance*
       at St. Albans Cathedral between June 3 and 24,
       1978.

691.   ---.   [Untitled review.]   *RORD* 23 (1980): 81-82.

       Reviews performances of The York Cycle, June 6-30,
       1980, at the York Festival, St. Mary's Abbey,
       York, and of The Wakefield Cycle, June 28-29,
       1980, at the Wakefield Festival, Wakefield
       Cathedral Precinct.

692.   ---.   [Untitled review.]   *RORD* 23 (1980): 85-86.

       Reviews performance of *Mankind*, July 10, 1980, at
       University College, Dublin, by *Poculi Ludique
       Societas*, Toronto.

693.   ---.   [Untitled review.]   *RORD* 24 (1981): 198-99.

       Reviews performances of *The "Lincoln" Cycle of
       Mystery Plays*, June 22 to July 4, 1981, at Lincoln
       Cathedral Precinct.

694.   ---.   [Untitled review.]   *RORD* 24 (1981): 195-96.

       Reviews performance of *Mactacio Abel*, April 23,
       1981, at Hall of Magdalene College, Cambridge, by
       Poculi Ludique Societas.

695.   ---.   [Untitled review.]   *RORD* 24 (1981): 196-97.

       Reviews performances of *Wisdom*, May 21-23, 1981,
       at Winchester Cathedral by King Alfred's College
       Drama Department.

696.   ---.   [Untitled review.]   *RORD* 25 (1982): 145-46.

       Reviews performances of *The Conversion of St.
       Paul*, May 27-29, 1982, at Winchester Cathedral by
       King Alfred's College Drama Department.

697.   ---.   [Untitled review.]   *RORD* 26 (1983): 119-20.

Reviews performances of *The Killing of the
Children*, May 26-29, 1983, at Winchester Cathedral
by King Alfred's College Drama Department.

698.   ---.   [Untitled review.]   *RORD* 26 (1983): 117-19.

Reviews performances of The Playes [sic] of
Chester, April 30-May 2, 1983, at The Renaissance
Festival, University of Leeds.

699.   ---.   [Untitled review.]   *RORD* 27 (1984): 185-86.

Reviews performances of Medwall's *Fulgens and
Lucres*, March 27-29, 1984, at Lancaster and March
30, 1984, at Christ's [sic] College, Cambridge,
performed by Joculatores Lancastrienses.

700.   ---.   "The Vice: A Checklist and an Annotated
Bibliography."   *RORD* 22 (1979): 17-35.

Offers a list of appearances with bibliography of
criticism, with 98 entries. Contains entries on
the Machiavel, the parasite, the braggart, the
clown. Entries look at the forerunners, the
mature Vice figure, and "characters who are
influenced by the Vice, or who are significantly
reminiscent of him" (17).

701.   ---.   "'The Vice' and the Popular Theatre, 1547-80."
In *Poetry and Drama 1570-1700: Essays in Honour of
Harold F. Brooks*, 13-31. Ed. by Antony Coleman
and Antony Hammond. London and New York: Methuen,
1981.

Deals with "the actual theatrical experience"
(13), especially with respect to "the dramatic
figure called 'the Vice'" (13). Defines and
considers "popular theatre" (15). Defines "the
Vice" within certain limits and shows his
expository function.

702.   Harding, Alan.   *The Law Courts of Medieval England*.
London: George Allen and Unwin; New York: Barnes
and Noble, 1973.

Not specifically on drama. Offers information on
the legal background of the times during the
growth and popularity of the plays.

Rev. *TLS* (June 15, 1973): 668.
     Choice 10 (Dec. 1973): 1615.
     TLS (Jan 25, 1974): 88.

AHR 79 (Apr. 1974): 494.
D.W. Sutherland, Specu 50 (Oct. 1975): 728-
30.

703. Hargreaves, H.A. "'Christ and the Doctors': Sir
      Walter Greg's Work with the Chester Cycle Plays."
      Lib, 6th ser., 1.3 (Sept. 1979): 236-46.

      Comments on Greg's own ms of his collation of the
      play. Discusses Greg's editing practices, why he
      chose a particular ms (H) as his base text, why
      his collation preceded by about 22 years his
      publication of his edition. Shows the
      complexities of the text that Greg was dealing
      with.

704. Hark, Ina Rae. "*Stop the World--I Want to Get Off:*
      The Vice as Everyman." *CompD* 12 (Summer 1978):
      99-112.

      Shows how the modern play draws upon medieval
      morality tradition.

705. Harper, James Farrell. "Style in Medieval Art and
      Literature: Three Essays in Criticism." Ph.D.
      diss., State U. of New York, Stony Brook, 1974.

706. Harris, B.E., ed. Assisted by A.T. Thacker. *A
      History of the County of Chester.* 3 vols.
      London: Published for the *Institute of Historical
      Research*, Oxford U. Press. The Victoria History
      of the Counties of England. Ed. by C.R.
      Elrington. The U. of London Institute of
      Historical Research. Vol. I, 1987; Vol. II, 1979;
      Vol. III, 1980.

      Vol. I covers the county through the Anglo-Saxon
      period (391 pp.). Vol. II covers documents in the
      Public Record Office and elsewhere, administrative
      history, Parliamentary representation, forests,
      etc. (266 pp.). Vol. III covers the Diocese of
      Chester, religion, hospitals, education and
      schools, etc. (276 pp.). Much background
      information on Chester during the period of the
      presentation of the plays.

707. Harris, Max. "Flesh and Spirit: The Battle Between
      Virtues and Vices in Mediaeval Drama Reassessed."
      MedAe 57.1 (1988): 56-64.

      Reviews scholarship that looks at virtues and
      vices in psychological terms. Says that "the
      vices represent both human sin and supernatural
      demons in the service of Satan" (56). Looks at

the dual references for and the "'double' reading"
(57) of the morality plays.

707a. Harrison, Alan. "Disguised Entertainers in the Gaelic
Tradition." *FCS* 13 (1988): 51-66.

708. Hartigan, Karelisa V., ed. *Legacy of Thespis: Drama
Past and Present*, Vol. IV. Lanham, Maryland, New
York, and London: U. Press of America, 1984. U.
of Florida Department of Classics Comparative
Drama Conference Papers.

Contains essay by Kenneth E. Johnson ("The
Rhetoric of Apocalypse . . .," entry # 823 below).

709. Hartnett, Edith. "Cain in the Medieval *Towneley*
Play." *AnM* 12 (1971): 21-29.

Says that Cain is an example of Augustine's belief
of "sin as a progressive alienation from God and
man" (29); sin leads to sin and leads one to
disobedience, murder, and despair. Recounts the
treatment of the character in the other cycles and
claims that the Towneley play "provides the most
naturalistic development" (23). Analyzes Cain's
actions and words in the Towneley play, which play
is the "most effective" (29) of all the Cain and
Abel plays "because Cain's humanity is thoroughly
convincing" (29).

710. Hartnoll, Phyllis. *The Concise History of the
Theatre*. New York: Harry N. Abrams, n.d. 288 pp.

Chap. 2 is on "The Medieval Theatre" (32-50). Not
specifically on English drama. Covers the plays
of western Europe, liturgical and secular.
Mentions different staging practices, characters,
and methods of production. With many
illustrations.

Rev. *Booklist* 65 (Feb. 15, 1969): 626.
LJ 94 (Mar. 1, 1969): 1018.

711. ---, ed. *The Concise Oxford Companion to the Theatre.*
London, Oxford, and New York: Oxford U. Press,
1972. 640 pp.

A shorter version of *The Oxford Companion to the
Theatre* (see next entry). Contains many brief
entries on medieval English theater (e.g. Cornish
Rounds--115; Mystery Play--375 f.).

Rev. *Choice* 10 (Mar. 1973): 60.

712. ---, ed. *The Oxford Companion to the Theatre.* 4th
      ed. Oxford and New York: Oxford U. Press, 1983.
      934 pp.

      Contains many brief entries on medieval English
      theater (e.g. Cornish Rounds--183; Mystery Plays--
      580; Moral Interlude--560; Morality Play--560;
      Mummers' Play--567; Miracle Play--550; Medwall--
      537; etc.).

713. ---. *The Theatre: A Concise History.* Rev. ed. N.p.:
      Thames and Hudson, 1985.

      Contains a brief and superficial treatment of
      medieval English drama (37-50), with many
      illustrations.

      Rev. *TES* (June 6, 1986): 25.

714. Hartung, Albert E., gen. ed. *A Manual of the Writings
      in Middle English: 1050-1500.* Vol. 5. [Based on *A
      Manual of the Writings in Middle English, 1050-
      1400*, ed. by John Edwin Wells; New Haven: 1916,
      and Supplements 1-9, 1919-1951.] New Haven: The
      Connecticut Academy of Arts and Sciences; Hamden,
      Connecticut: Shoe String (Archon), 1975. 10,
      1315-1742 pp.

      Contains three essays on medieval English drama:
      1) Mill ("The Miracle Plays and Mysteries," entry
      # 1128 below); 2) Lindenbaum ("The Morality
      Plays," entry # 1001); and 3) Utley and Ward ("The
      Folk Drama," entry # 1621). Also contains
      extensive unannotated bibliography for each of
      these essays.

      Rev. *ARBA* 8 (1977): 593.
           Choice 14 (Sept. 1977): 834.

715. Harty, Kevin J. "Adam's Dream and the First Three
      Chester Plays." *CahÉ* 21 (Apr. 1982): 1-11.

      Mentions the two groups into which the plays fall:
      those dealing with salvation history up to the
      Deluge; and those which offer "types and
      prophecies of the Incarnation and the Redemption"
      (1). Says that the first three Chester plays "are
      carefully interrelated and give evidence of
      greater dramatic skill . . . than has previously
      been admitted" (1). Also shows that Adam's dream
      in Play II "is consistent with the principles of
      medieval historiography" (1). Discusses the
      thematic and dramatic function of Adam's dream.

716. ---. "'And sheepe will I keepe no more': Birth and
      Rebirth in the Chester *Adoration of the
      Shepherds.*" *ABR* 29.4 (Dec. 1978): 348-57.

      Looks at the "curious ending" (348) of this play.
      Reviews scholarship and offers a reading to
      explain the choices of professions of the
      shepherds and the boy, Trowle. Shows historical
      data about the cycle's origin to explain the
      ending, and shows that the professions the
      shepherds choose were available to the play's
      audience.

717. Harty, Kevin John. "The Apocalyptic Unity of *The
      Chester Mystery Cycle.*" Ph.D. diss., U. of
      Pennsylvania, 1974.

718. ---. "The Chester *Fall of Lucifer.*" *McNR* 22 (1975-
      76): 70-79.

      Considers this fall in all the cycles, in
      tradition, and superficially in the Chester cycle.
      Presents the fall doctrinally. Concludes that the
      Chester version is "dramatically effective and
      dogmatically sound" (79).

719. ---. "The Identity of "Freere Bartholemewe' (Chester
      Play VI.565): A Suggestion." *ANQ* 16.2 (Oct.
      1977): 18-19.

      Explains the Expositor's reference in the Salome
      story to Bartholemewe as coming from the *Stanzaic
      Life of Christ* (and ultimately from Higden's
      Polychronicon and the *Legenda aurea* [sic]).
      Claims that the Bartholomew in question was the
      one supposedly the author of the apocryphal gospel
      of Pseudo-Matthew.

720. ---. "'Unbeleeffe is a Fowle Sinne': The Chester
      Nativity Play." *SUS* 11.1 (1979): 35-41.

      Looks at sources of the play (chiefly the *Stanzaic
      Life of Christ*) and the equivalent--less compact
      and less efficient--presentations of the nativity
      in the other cycles, to demonstrate the Chester
      playwright's greater artistry and his achieving
      greater unity. Concludes that "The Chester
      Nativity is purposefully didactic" (40).

721. ---. "The Norwich Grocers' Play and Its Three Cyclic
      Counterparts: Four English Mystery Plays on the
      Fall of Man." *SN* 53.1 (1981): 77-89.

Aims to show the importance of the Creation and
Fall in "the subsequent events of salvation
history" (77) by analyzing the four plays, with
particular attention to "the Norwich play's unique
features in terms of the Protestant temperment of
late sixteenth-century England" (77).

722.   ---.   "The Unity and Structure of *The Chester Mystery
       Cycle.*" *Medi* 2 (1976): 137-58.

       Examines "the monastic influence on the Chester
       Plays . . . to show how the pervasive influence of
       monasticism on the cycle contributed to its unity
       and structure" (137). Claims that the cycle has
       more unity than previously acknowledged--a unity
       deriving from the monastic concerns for "prophecy,
       Christian perfection, and the end-times" (153).

723.   Hartzell, K.D.   "Diagrams for Liturgical Ceremonies,
       Late 14th Century."   In *Local Maps and Plans from
       Medieval England*, 339-41.   Ed. by R.A. Skelton and
       P.D.A. Harvey.   Oxford: Clarendon Press, 1986.

       Refers to a series of eleven woodcuts in British
       Library Add. MS 57534, depicting "the positions of
       the participants in ceremonies of more than
       average importance in the church year" (339). Not
       on English drama, but offers background into the
       depiction of dramatic performances.

724.   Harvey, Nancy Lenz, and Julia C. Dietrich.   "Recent
       Studies in the Corpus Christi Mystery Plays."   *ELR*
       5.3 (Autumn 1975): 396-415.

       Offers brief précis of articles and books through
       1974 along with a more extensive unannotated
       bibliography.

725.   Harward, Vernon.   "*Ane Satyre of the Thrie Estaitis*
       Again."   *SSL* 7 (1970): 139-46.

       Considers the "differences of opinion about the
       development of the play" (139). Opts for a later
       date (c. 1540) rather than for the proposed
       earlier one (c. 1530). Uses his own and Anna
       Mill's arguments (see Mill, "The Original Version
       of Lindsay's *Satyre* . . .," *SSL* 6 [Oct. 1968]: 67-
       75) to refute the ideas of John MacQueen ("*Ane
       Satyre of the Thrie Estaitis,*" *SSL* 3 [1965-66]:
       129-43).

726.   Harwood, Ronald.   *All the World's a Stage.*   London:
       Secker & Warburg, British Broadcasting
       Corporation, 1984.   321 pp.

Offers a history of the theater for a television
audience, with a chapter on "Mysteries" (77),
including also a discussion on Latin origins and
morality plays. For a general audience. With
many illustrations.

Rev. *BBN* (Feb. 1985): 73.
PW 228 (Aug. 2, 1985): 55.
Booklist (Jan. 1, 1986): 652.
LJ 111 (Jan. 1986): 98.

727. Hawkins, Harriet. "'Merrie England': Contradictory
Interpretations of the Corpus Christi Plays."
Engl 29.135 (Autumn 1980): 189-200.

Explains variant readings of the era and of the
plays, from literary, social, and economic
perspectives. Looks at the standard critical
views of the cycles. Claims that the "plays . . .
cannot be discussed purely as drama" (194), but
must be seen in their historical, theological
context.

728. Hawkins, Richard H. "Some Effects of Technique
Developed in the Native English Drama on the
Structure of Shakespeare's Plays." Ph.D. diss.,
Washington State U., 1971.

729. Heap, Carl. "On Peforming *Mankind*." *MET* 4.2 (Dec.
1982): 93-103.

Reviews a performance of *Mankind* including such
considerations as stage dressings, effects, text,
characters, the progress of evil, working with the
audience, and business and running gags.

xxx. ---. See Peter Happé, et al. "Thoughts on
'Transvestitism' by Divers Hands" (entry # 689
above).

730. Helm, Alex. *The Chapbook of Mummers' Plays: A Study
of the Printed Versions of the North-West of
England.* Leicester, England: Guizer Press, 1969.
54 pp.

Establishes relationship between contemporary
versions of this "traditional revitalisation
ceremony" (5) and nineteenth-century chapbook
versions. Though not on medieval drama, article
looks at plays with roots in the middle ages.
Offers texts (40-54). With illustrations.

Rev. *JAF* 84 (Apr. 1971): 256.

731.   ---. *The English Mummers' Play*. Foreword by N.
        Peacock and E.C. Cawte. Woodbridge, Suffolk: D.S.
        Brewer; Totowa, New Jersey: Rowman and
        Littlefield, for the Folklore Society, 1981. The
        Folklore Society, Mistletoe Series 14. 116 pp.

        Contains much information about the various
        manifestations of mummers' plays: wooing
        ceremonies, sword dance and hero combat
        ceremonies, "abnormal" texts, and disguises. With
        illustrations, notes, bibliography, and index, and
        with examples of texts, some with musical
        notation.

        Rev. *BBN* (Oct. 1981): 606.
             TES (Dec. 4, 1981): 18.
             Brian Hayward, *ThRI* 7.2 (Spring 1982): 142.
             Michael Preston, *ELN* 20.1 (Sept. 1982): 21-
             23.
             Come-All-Ye 4 (Winter 1983): 4.
             RES 35 (Aug. 1984): 420.
             B.D.H. Miller, *N&Q*, n.s. 33.2 (231) (June
             1986): 218-19.

731a.   ---. *Staffordshire Folk Drama*. Ibstock: Guizer,
        1984.

732.   Helterman, Jeffrey. "Satan as Everyshepherd: Comic
        Metamorphosis in *The Second Shepherds' Play*."
        TxSLL 12.4 (Winter 1971): 515-30.

        Looks at allegorical and folk elements and the
        development of the characters, as well as the use
        of the comic plot. Says that "the sense of
        process and change operates constantly" (516).

733.   Helterman, Jeffrey Alec. "Symbolic Action in the
        Plays of the Wakefield Master." Ph.D. diss., U.
        of Rochester, 1969. (See next entry.)

734.   Helterman, Jeffrey. *Symbolic Action in the Plays of
        the Wakefield Master*. Athens, Georgia: U. of
        Georgia Press, 1981. 202 pp.

        Contains chapters on the Wakefield Master, the six
        plays, and "Symbolic Action: Some Analogues in Art
        and Drama." Chap. I conjectures about the
        playwright and the construction of the cycle.
        Surveys scholarship. Discusses realism, comedy,
        morality, parody, symbolism, and typology. Chap.
        II--"Cain's Foul Wrath"--discusses madness and
        isolation in the *Mactacio Abel*; analyzes
        characterization, charity, typology, and imagery.
        Chap. III, on the Noah play, looks at "Henpecked

Man in the Image of His Maker" (47). Discusses "the contrast in style between the dignified opening and the boisterous struggle between Noah and his wife" (47), the integrity of the play symbolism, the three-scene division of the play, marital conflict and human sovereignty, and disobedience. Chap. IV, on the First Shepherds' Play, "Folly Hungers after the New Wisdom" (73 ff.), "examines the growth of the imagination as it learns how to read symbolic meanings" (73). Looks at allusions, symbolism, and folklore elements. Chap. V, on "Second Shepherds' Play," concentrates on character development, allegory, comic effects, and symbolic gifts. Chap. VI, on the Herod play, speaks of dramatic tension, characterization, the play's emotional impact, parody. Chap. VII, on "Coliphizacio," examines "the progressive stages of spiritual blindness" (139), symbolism, transferred imagery, characterization, and character confrontations. Chap. VIII is on analogues of symbolic action in art and drama. Discusses realistic elements in the plays, the interaction between the temporal and the eternal worlds. Compares drama with Bosch, Bruegel. Analyzes typology, pageants, stage design. Concludes that the "playwright, through symbolic action, gives value to man's individual acts as a means of relating to the divine. . . . thus the actor becomes a symbol of man, created in the image of his maker, who in this fallen world remains at an infinite distance from him" (167).

Rev. Barbara D. Palmer, *CompD* 16.2 (1982): 182-84.

735. Hengstebeck, Irmlind. "*The Pride of Life*, Vers 444." *NM* 72 (1971): 739-41.

Argues that v. 444 of the work reads "thi mete is ffeyt & moide"--based on evidence from the *Oxford English Dictionary* and other verses in the work. "Mete" means "goal or boundary," in contrast to "outrage," "passing beyond reasonable bounds" in v. 438 ff. Intreprets "Ffeyt & moide" as "filth and mold" to rhyme with "gold" in v. 446. Essentially, vv. 443-46, spoken by the Bishop to the King of Life, point out that, after death, when one is destined for decay, the crown (gold) is of little use.

736. Henry, Avril. "Wisdom at Winchester Cathedral." *MET* 3.1 (July 1981): 52-55.

Reports on performances of May 21-23, 1981, by
King Alfred's College Drama Department.
Illustration on p. 52.

737. Henson, Gail Clark Ritchie. "A Holy Desperation: The
Literary Quest for Grace in the Reformed English
Tradition from John Bale to John Bunyan." Ph.D.
diss., U. of Louisville, 1981.

738. Hentschel, H.J. "Die Gestalt des Vice und seine
Redekonventionen im Wandel und Niedergang
Moralität. Ein Beitrag zur Dramaturgie des
Moralitäten Theatres." Diss., Munich, 1974.
(Abstract in *English and American Studies in
German*, 1976 [for 1975], 59-61.)

739. Herbert, Catherine A. "Udall's *Ralph Roister
Doister.*" *Expl* 37.2 (Winter 1979): 20.

Explains Merrygreek as coming from "merry grig," a
cheerful cricket or grasshopper.

740. Hertzbach, Janet Stavropoulos. "From Congregation to
Polity: The English Moral Drama to Shakespeare."
Ph.D. diss., Indiana U., 1978.

741. Herzman, Ronald B. "'Let Us Seek Him Also':
Tropological Judgment in Twelfth-Century Art and
Drama." In Homo, Memento Finis: . . ., 59-88.
Ed. by David Bevington. (See entry # 186 above.)

Useful for its methodology and its treatment of
the medieval use of biblical material. Deals with
non-English drama in terms of sermon, sculpture,
iconography, and pilgrimage.

742. Heslop, T.A. "Brief in Words but Heavy in the Weight
of Its Mysteries." *ArtH* 9.1 (Mar. 1986): 1-11.

Explains the serious use of symbol in the medieval
arts. Not specifically on drama; but offers a way
of interpreting visual images, "fundamental
truths, allegorically expressed" (10).

743. ---. "A Walrus Ivory Pyx and the *Visitatio
Sepulchri.*" *JWCI* 44 (1981): 157-60.

Concerns "the influence of liturgical drama and
mystery plays on medieval art" (157). Sees an
actual dramatic performance on an eleventh- or
twelfth-century oval box in the Victoria and
Albert Museum. Suggests that it depicts the
Miracle of St. Lawrence possibly explainable with
reference to the Barking Ordinale from Barking

Abbey--a text which closely resembles the
iconography of the pyx. With four illustrations
(plate 19 at end of volume).

744. Heyworth, P.L., ed. *Medieval Studies for J.A.W.
Bennett. Aetatis Suae LXX.* Oxford: Clarendon
Press, 1981.

Contains article by Twycross, "Playing 'The
Resurrection'" (entry # 1600 below).

Rev. Piero Boitani, *StudAC* 5 (1983): 166-73.

745. Hibbard, George Richard, ed. *The Elizabethan Theatre,
V.* Papers Given at the Fifth International
Conference on Elizabethan Theatre held at the
University of Waterloo, Ontario, in July 1973.
Toronto: Macmillan; Hamden, Connecticut: Archon,
1975.

Contains essays by Bevington ("Discontinuity
. . .," # 184 above); Ingram ("'To Find . . .," #
792); Southern ("Methods . . .," # 1494); Somerset
("'Fair is foul . . .," # 1488); also other essays
on Renaissance plays.

746. Hieatt, A. Kent. "Eve as Reason in a Tradition of
Allegorical Interpretation of the Fall." *JWCI* 43
(1980): 221-26.

Not specifically on English drama, but offers
background for the study of the plays.

747. Hieatt, Constance B. "A Case for *Duk Moraud* as a Play
of the Miracles of the Virgin." *MedS* 32 (1970):
345-51.

Takes up the idea that this fragment is from a
miracle play. Reviews scholarship. Sees two
elements which suggest that this is a play about
the miracle of the Virgin: 1) the focus of action
on sensational sinners whose redemption stems from
hearing a sermon; 2) that the play "is clearly a
version of the 'Tale of the Adulterous Daughter'"
(351).

748. Higgins, Anne Thorn. "Time and the English Corpus
Christi Drama." Ph.D. diss., Yale U., 1985.

749. Hildahl, Frances Erdey. "Dramaturgy and Philosophy in
The Castle of Perseverance: The Issues of
Authority, Power, and Influence." Ph.D. diss., U.
of Rochester, 1985.

749a. ---. "Penitence and Parody in *The Castle of Perseverance.*" In *Early Drama to 1600.* Ed. by Albert H. Tricomi. (See entry # 1589b below.)

750. Hill, Eugene D. "The Trinitarian Allegory of the Moral Play of *Wisdom.*" *MP* 73.2 (Nov. 1975): 121-35.

Considers "the absence of a central figure" (121) of the Everyman type, and looks at the "'psychological' personifications in the play" (121), which can be found in Augustine. Examines "the context of thought, Augustinian or Scholastic, within which the play is properly to be interpreted" (121). Reviews criticism and offers "a basic account of the author's 'psychological' allegory, of the way in which he shows the soul to be the image and likeness of a trinitarian God" (122). Shows that one of the play's strengths is its focus on the human soul in its religious development, and that criticism should take into account "the Augustinian and Bernardian framework of the allegory" (135).

751. Hill, R.F., with F.P. Wilson. *Dramatic Records in the Declared Accounts of the Office of Works, 1560-1640.* Oxford: The Malone Society, 1975 (1977). Collections X.

Presents dramatic records, with introduction covering the nature of the document, principles of extraction, banqueting houses, masquing rooms, the cockpit-in-court, and drama at court (staging).

751a. Hill, Malcolm Kendall. "The Development of the Magician Character in English Drama through Shakespeare." Honors thesis, Harvard U., 1971.

752. Hillman, Richard. "*Everyman* and the Energies of Stasis." *Flor* 7 (1985): 206-26.

Suggests that the play's main "strategies of representation are active ones, best described in terms of resistance, subversion, and disruption" (206). Analyzes the dramatic techniques of the play, its versification and language, its characterization and plot, and so on. Shows the audience's involvement in the plot.

753. Hirata, Mitsuo. "The Dramatic Structure of the Early Tudor Interlude." *BCGE* 32 (Dec. 1979): 1-20. (In Japanese with abstract in English.)

Looks at the reputation of morality plays in criticism and surveys how researchers now show greater enlightenment in their approach to the genre. Discusses "Hickscorner," "Mankind," and "The Interlude of Youth." Treats the didactic purpose of the plays--especially with respect to the realistic depiction of vice in order to show the audience the nature of their own sins. Says that later playwrights used the genre to spread their own ideology. Looks also at Rastell's "Four Elements" and why it fails to reach its goals. Relates the vicissitudes of the genre to the social conditions in which it exists. Says that the formats of the morality plays were inadequate to support the new themes that the Humanists were trying to present in their works, though there was a successful resurrection of the form later in the Renaissance.

754. Hirsh, John C. "Mak Tossed in a Blanket." *N&Q* 28.2 (226) (Apr. 1981): 117-18.

Associates Mak's punishment with cowardice and contempt for an unworthy adversary. Relates the episode to an analogous one in the late seventeenth century--a duelling challenge.

755. Hirshberg, Jeffrey Alan. "Noah's Wife on the Medieval English Stage: Iconographic and Dramatic Values of Her Distaff and Choice of the Raven." *StudIcon* 2 (1976): 25-40.

Explores the iconographic tradition in the Wakefield Noah play, with emphasis on the distaff and the raven, which icons function as conventions. Relates Noah's wife to her depictions in medieval art; looks at her recalcitrance, her typological relation to Eve. Says that the distaff "suggests the primary significance . . . of a radical alteration of the human condition" (30) and the "renewed necessity of man's humility" (30). Claims that the raven has more than one meaning: the darkness of the mind (hence, its casting out is education), procrastination, Satan. With illustrations.

756. Hogan, Jerome William. "The Rod and the Candle: Conscience in the English Morality Plays, Shakespeare's *Macbeth* and Tourneur's *The Atheist's Tragedy*." Ph.D. diss., City U. of New York, 1974.

756a. Holbrook, S.E. "Covetousness, Contrition, and the Town in the *Castle of Perseverance*." *FCS* 13 (1988): 275-90.

757. Holding, Peter. "Stagecraft in the York Cycle." *ThN* 34.2 (1980): 51-60.

Looks at internal evidence to suggest ways the cycle was staged. Concludes "that the York audience was immediately involved with its drama to an extent never surpassed in theatrical history" (59); and asserts that the dramatists and actors used "every possible device . . . to present an impressively wide ranging spectacle" (59).

758. Hole, Christina. *A Dictionary of British Folk Customs.* London: Hutchinson & Co., 1976; Paladin, Granada Publishing, 1978. 349 pp.

Lists scores of customs, many of which relate in one way or another to dramatic performances or practices. See e.g. Hocktide festivals (144 ff.).

759. Holloway, Julia Bolton. "Medieval Liturgical Drama, the *Commedia*, *Piers Plowman* and *The Canterbury Tales*." *ABR* 32.2 (June 1981): 114-21.

Explains how performances of liturgical dramas help one to understand the texts in a way that reading them does not permit. Claims that these sung Latin plays had more influence on medieval and modern literature than did the vernacular Corpus Christi plays.

760. ---. "Monks and Plays." SMART 10.1 (Spring 1983): 10-12.

Talks about how monastic drama presented information on the Gospels and saints' legends, Latin and musical chants, iconography, the representation of holy scenes, and medieval monasteries. Recounts her specific experiences in putting on several plays. Not specifically on English drama, but offers useful background material.

761. Holmes, Jerry Donald. "An Ancient Structure: A Study of the Influence of Medieval Drama on Selected Contemporary English and American Plays." Ph.D. diss., U. of Mississippi, 1969.

762. Holt, J.C. "The Origins and Audience of the Ballads of Robin Hood." *P&P* 18 (Nov. 1960): 89-110.

Not specifically on drama, but covers the Robin Hood legend: literary and possible historical sources. Concludes that the Robin Hood figure

seems to "be derived from a combination of fact
and fiction" (107).

763.   ---.   *Robin Hood*.   London: Thames and Hudson, 1982.
        208 pp.

        Gives an overview of the tradition, with several
        references to minstrels and players (12-13, 111-
        13, 128, 137-41).   With notes, bibliography,
        index, and illustrations.

        Rev. E. Christiansen, *Spectator* 248 (June 5,
            1982): 26.
            Listener 107 (June 10, 1982): 21.
            TLS (June 11, 1982): 631.
            GW 126 (June 13, 1982): 21.
            D.K. Fry, *LJ* 107 (June 15, 1982): 1221.
            TES (June 18, 1982): 24.
            Obs (June 20, 1982): 30.
            Economist (June 26, 1982): 103.
            BestS 42 (Aug. 1982): 192.
            BBN (Sept. 1982): 583.
            HistT 32 (Sept. 1982): 56.
            Choice 20 (Nov. 1982): 486.
            AJ 63.2 (1983): 466.
            D.M. Palliser, *NotMS* 27 (1983): 102-07.
            LRB 5 (May 5, 1983): 22.
            Obs (Aug. 21, 1983): 25.
            HistT 33 (Oct. 1983): 64.
            EHR 99 (Oct. 1984): 858.

764.   Homan, Richard L.   "Devotional Themes in the Violence
        and Humor of the *Play of the Sacrament*."   *CompD*
        20.4 (Winter 1986-87): 327-40.

        Reviews scholarship, especially that which points
        out that the comedy of the play "is not integral"
        (327).   Explains the relevance of the play's
        violence and comedy and shows how they are used
        thematically.   Shows also how the play's
        dramaturgy "is consistent with fifteenth-century
        stage practice, while its contents are consistent
        with devotional art" (339).   Concentrates on the
        three main comic scenes of the play.   Suggests
        "that the scenes with the Jews could have been
        taken quite seriously by the original audience"
        (328) and that the comic interlude offers a
        serious message.   Discusses the *Arma Christi*
        theme, contemporary stage techniques and anti-
        Semitism, and devotional art.

765.   ---.   "Ritual Aspects of the York Cycle."   *ThJ* 33.3
        (Oct. 1981): 302-15.

Aims to examine "performances documented by
theatre historians and to ask whether they are
ritualistic in some aspects" (303). Uses an
anthropological approach to distinguish ritual
from theater and to show where they converge.
Looks at a good deal of criticism. Shows how one
function of the Corpus Christi cycle is "as an
arena in which actual conflicts could be ritually
resolved" (313). Focuses discussion on the York
cycle.

766. ---. "Two *Exempla:* Analogues to the *Play of the
Sacrament* and *Dux Moraud.*" *CompD* 18.3 (Fall
1984): 241-51.

Points out the relationship between English
vernacular drama and sermons, especially with
reference to the sermons' *exempla*. Shows two
exempla from one sermon collection to be analogues
to the drama. Reveals similarities and
differences. Quotes the two sermons.

767. Hoppin, Richard H. *Medieval Music*. New York: W.W.
Norton & Co., 1978. The Norton Introduction to
Music History.

Offers twenty chapters on backgrounds and all
aspects of music--secular and religious--in many
countries in the middle ages, with passages on
liturgical and vernacular drama. Briefly
discusses miracle and mystery plays (186).

Rev. *Booklist* 75 (Sept. 1, 1978): 13.
    J.M. Borders, *LJ* 103 (Nov. 15, 1978): 2336.
    H.J. Stauffenberg, *BestS* 38 (Dec. 1978):
        269-70.
    Choice 15 (Dec. 1978): 1381.
    E.A. Keitel, *MEJ* 65 (May 1979): 79-81.
    R.A. Baltzer, *Notes* 35 (June 1979): 869-70.
    C. Roederer, *MQ* 65 (July 1979): 447-51.
    J. Caldwell, *M&L* 61 (Jan. 1980): 89-92.
    A. Hughes, *Specu* 55 (July 1980): 539-42.

768. Horall, Sally. "The Secularization of the Middle
English Morality Plays." *RUO* 40 (1970): 149-62.

Points out that morality plays can suffer the loss
of such figures as Virtues and Vices and can still
remain viable dramas with the new figures of "two
political factions struggling for control of a
state substituted" (149). Discusses the
transition from morality to secular interlude,
which is occasioned by the spread of humanist
thought and a growth of realism and social satire

on stage. Also shows "how religious the later plays are" (162), though with different emphases than there were in the earlier plays.

769. Horner, Olga. "Susanna's Double Life." *MET* 8.2 (Dec. 1986): 76-102.

Discusses Thomas Garter's play with respect to legal matters, especially ones contemporary to Garter. Considers "the exposition, application, and judicial process of biblical law" (76), "Hebrew court procedure" (77), the use of witnesses, defamation, slander, and so on. Relates the character Ill Report to the contemporary preoccupation with slander and sedition.

770. Hosley, Richard. "The Interpretation of Pictorial Evidence for Theatrical Design." *RORD* 13-14 (1970-1971): 123-25.

Summarizes the content of a paper presented at the Modern Language Seminar. Points out that pictorial representations may distort scale, point of view, and shape. With an illustration.

771. ---. "The Playhouses and the Stage." In *A New Companion to Shakespeare Studies*, 15-34. Ed. by Kenneth Muir. Cambridge: University Press, 1971.

Looks at pre-Shakespearean staging, mostly following the medieval practices of using wagons or scaffolding. Glances back at medieval practices. With illustrations.

772. ---. "Shape of the Early Theatres." *ShakN* 36.3 (142) (May 1976): 27. In section entitled "Abstracts of Papers at The International Shakespeare Association Congress. The First Public Playhouse: The Theatre 1576-1976."

This is a one-paragraph abstract of a paper on a polygonal playhouse in Calais in 1520 known to Henry VIII. Says that the theater "was probably about 122' in diameter and 32' high at the outside edges" (27).

773. ---. "Three Kinds of Outdoor Theatre before Shakespeare." *ThSur* 12.1 (May 1971): 1-33.

Examines the "circular *platea* or Place surrounded by 'scaffolds'" (1); pageant-wagon performances; and booth stages in marketplaces or on village greens. Offers new evidence and reinterprets old

evidence to sum up present state of knowledge.
Focuses on physical form of staging backed up with
pictorial evidence, not origins or use. With
fifteen illustrations.

774. Houle, Peter Joseph. "A Comparative Study of the
English and French Full-Scope Morality Drama."
Ph.D. diss., U. of Massachusetts, 1972.

775. Houle, Peter J. *The English Morality and Related
Drama: A Bibliographical Survey.* Hamden,
Connecticut: Archon, Shoe String, 1972.

Part I gives an alphabetical list of 59 morality
plays, occasional historical data, information on
editions, dramatis personae, play length, plot
summary, comments, and brief bibliography. Part
II contains appendixes: "Coming of Death"
(describes plays with the Summons of Death motif),
"Debate of the Body and Soul" (on this theme),
"Debate of the Heavenly Graces or the Parliament
in Heaven," "The Devil in the Morality," "The
Psychomachia," and "Staging of Morality Plays."
Part III is a general bibliography. With an index
of characters.

Rev. *LJ* 98 (Jan. 15, 1973): 152.
Choice 10 (June 1973): 600.

775a. ---. "A Reconstruction of the English Morality
Fragment *Somebody and Others.*" *PBSA* 71.3 (1977):
259-77.

776. Howard-Hill, Trevor H. "REED's Bibliographical
Imperative." *Records of Early English Drama:
Proceedings of the First Colloquium . . .*, 178-90.
Ed. by JoAnna Dutka (see entry 497 above).

Considers REED's plan "to produce a comprehensive
set of bibliographies and indexes to its own
volumes and related works published elsewhere"
(178). Comments on the value of these proposed
bibliographies and indexes and on "the
effectiveness of the methods proposed to construct
the indexes and checklists" (189).

777. Howe, Kenneth Arthur. "Commercialism in the Fifteenth
Century English Cycle Plays." Ph.D. diss.,
Michigan State U., 1979.

778. Hoy, James F. "On the Relationhship of the Corpus
Christi Plays to the Corpus Christi Procession at
York." *MP* 71.2 (Nov. 1973): 166-68.

Examines the controversy that the plays evolved
from the procession. Says that civic records seem
to prove that the plays were an independent
development. Shows that the plays and the
procession took different routes "from the very
beginnings" (168).

779. ---. "Records of Dramatic Activity in Medieval York:
A Translated Collection." Ph.D. diss., U. of
Missouri (Columbia), 1970.

780. ---. *The Staging Time of the York Cycle of Corpus
Christi Plays.* *ESRS* 21.3 (Winter 1973). [A
separate monograph.] 22 pp.

Reviews scholarship on the time it took to perform
the cycle. Deals with the number of stations, the
elapsed time for the playing of each play, the
problems of a processional presentation, the
audience, lighting, contemporary records.
Suggests production on more than one day; plays
performed in groups, "with several plays being
performed continuously on one wagon before it was
moved on to the next stop" (15); plays performed
several times in one place while the audience
moved (essentially a "fixed staging" [16]). Gives
tables for "Length of Route and Travel Time" (18);
"Playing Time for First Three Plays at 12
Stations" (19); "Times at Which Each Play Will
Begin Playing at the First Station and Finish
Playing at the Last Station" (20). With
bibliography.

781. Hsin, Fang. "*Macbeth* as a Morality Play: A
Comparative Study of the Play with Reference to
Everyman and *Doctor Faustus*." *FJS* 7 (1974): 1-24.

Analyzes theme, structure, and techniques of
morality plays to shed light on *Macbeth*. Looks at
the messages that morality plays present, the
summoning theme, characterization, the "theme of
the undependable, deceiving nature of the values,
powers and pleasures of the evil and the earthly"
(20), the themes of death and judgment, the three-
part structure, and so on.

782. Hudson, Anne, ed. "'Here bigynnis a tretise of
miraclis pleyinge.'" In *Selections from English
Wycliffite Writings*, 97-104 (text); 187-89
(notes). Cambridge: Cambridge U. Press, 1978.

Offers the text of this often cited treatise.
With textual variants at the foot of the pages,
notes, brief glossary, and index.

Text abridged — Part I only.

783. Hughes, Andrew. "Liturgical Drama: Falling Between the Disciplines." In *Medieval Drama* . . . (forthcoming). Ed. by Eckehard Simon. (See entry # 1469 below.)

784. ---. *Medieval Music: The Sixth Liberal Art.* Rev. ed. Toronto, Buffalo, London: Toronto U. Press, 1980. 360 pp.

A bibliography with brief annotations. Contains sections on General Reference Works; General Histories; Texts; Collections and Editions; Philosophy and Speculative Music Literature; Notation; and nearly three dozen other topics. Includes sections on Iconography, Plainsong, Tropes, Liturgical Drama, The Lauda, The British Isles. With indexes.

Rev. M. Wood, *BkF* 5.2 (1980): 196.
Choice 18 (Nov. 1980): 406.
J.E. Druesedow, Jr., *ARBA* 12 (1981): 450.
PBSA 76 (Jan. 1982): 104.

784a. Hummelen, William M.H. "Late-Medieval Drama and the Theory of Segmentation." *FCS* 13 (1988): 91-104.

785. Hunter, Frederick James. *Drama Bibliography: A Short-Title Guide to Extended Reading in Dramatic Art for the English-Speaking Audience and Students in Theatre.* Boston: G.K. Hall, 1971.

Lists only a few works on medieval drama with no annotations.

785a. Hyland, Peter. "Disguise and the Drama of Evil." *AULLA* 60 (Nov. 1983): 184-96.

Discusses the theatrical tradition of the use of disguise and its associations with evil. Covers "the growth of disguise conventions within the development of the morality play" (184). Looks at Vice, appearance changing, the *Castle of Perseverance*, *Pride of Life*, *Wisdom*, *Nature*, *Magnyfycence*, *Ane Satyre of the Thrie Estaitis*, and other plays.

786. Ikegami, Tadahiro. "Corpus Christi Cycle Plays and
      Morality Plays." In *Igirisu-bunga Kushi-josetsu*
      or *A History of English Literature*, 178-80. Ed.
      by Bishu Saito. Tokyo: Chukyo Shujipan, 1978.
      (In Japanese.)

787. ---. "Medieval Religious Plays to Elizabethan Plays."
      In *Igirisu-engeki* or *English Drama*, 9-22. Tokyo:
      Keio Tsushiri, 1979. (In Japanese.)

788. Ingram, Reg. "The Coventry Pageant Waggon." *MET* 2.1
      (July 1980): 3-14.

      Presents an entry in a 1581 Survey of Rentals that
      mentions a "house" (i.e. something like a garage),
      which was possibly a storage area for a pageant
      wagon. Discusses such "garages," their cost and
      use. Also looks at data about pageant wagons
      (number of wheels, "manhandled," curtains,
      machinery, "Extra Pageants/Stages," number of
      actors, decorations, floats, and route). Points
      out the need for accurate interpretation of
      vocabulary used in early play productions, with
      particular focus on the wagon's size, housing,
      mobility, cost, etc.

789. Ingram, R.W. "Fifteen Seventy-nine and the Decline of
      Civic Religious Drama in Coventry." In *The
      Elizabethan Theatre VIII: Papers Given at the
      Eighth International Conference on Elizabethan
      Theatre . . . University of Waterloo, Ontario, in
      July 1979*, 114-28. Ed. by G. R. Hibbard. Port
      Credit, Ontario: P.D. Meany, 1982.

      Traces the drama's decline generally to the late
      1560s with the rise of a puritan ethic and
      specifically to 1568 with the suppression of the
      joyful Hocktide play, "the result of the pressure
      exerted by certain narrow-minded preachers" (118).

790. Ingram, Reginald W. "'Pleyng geire accustumed
      belongyng & necessarie': Guild Records and Pageant
      Production in Coventry." In *Records of Early
      English Drama: Proceedings of the First Colloquium
      . . .*, 60-92. Ed. by JoAnna Dutka (see entry #
      497 above).

      Discusses his work on the pageants of Coventry
      with respect to his basic sources, "the accounts
      of the Weavers' and Drapers' Companies" (60).
      Mentions others who have used civic records to
      shed light on the plays. Comments on the records,
      on actors' wages, the financing of the pageants
      and other "economics of play production" (69), the

guilds' relations with the city, and the city's
profit. (Comment and discussion on this paper are
on pp. 93-97 and 98-100. See John H. Astington,
"Comment," entry # 122 above.)

791.   Ingram, R.W., ed. *Records of Early English Drama:
       Coventry.* Toronto and Buffalo, New York: U. of
       Toronto Press, 1981. 712 pp.

       Records hundreds of dramatic records from 1392-
       1642. Introduction covers "Drama, Music, and
       Public Ceremonial" (xiv); "Coventry Antiquarians"
       (xxiv); "The Documents" (xxx); "Editorial
       Procedures" (li); "Notes" (lxi). With
       bibliography, notes, maps, the documents, ten
       appendixes, translations, endnotes, English and
       Latin glossaries, and index.

       Rev. *BBN* (Aug. 1982): 502.
            Choice 20 (Sept. 1982): 82.
            Paula Neuss, *TLS* (Nov. 26, 1982): 1314.
            ARBA 14 (1983): 456.
            J.M. Cowen, *ThN* 37.2 (1983): 87-88.
            Derek Pearsall, *EngStud* 64.1 (Feb. 1983): 81-
                 82.
            EDAMN 5.2 (Spring 1983): 86.
            RES 35 (Nov. 1984): 522.
            RSR 12 (Jan. 1986): 73.

792.   ---.   "'To find the players and all that longeth
       therto': Notes on the Production of Medieval Drama
       in Coventry." In *The Elizabethan Theatre V:
       Papers Given at the Fifth International Conference
       on Elizabethan Theatre . . . University of
       Waterloo, Ontario, in July 1973*, 17-44. Ed. by
       G.R. Hibbard. (See entry # 745 above.)

       Gives many extracts from account books of the
       Coventry Cappers (1534-1591), and some from
       Drapers, Smiths, and Weavers. All extracts
       pertain to the drama. Discusses the *Resurrection,
       Harrowing of Hell,* and *Meeting with the Maries*
       play (lost), and "Robert Crow, Capper, playwright,
       actor and property-man" (17). Speculates on the
       number of performances the pageant had, its
       revisions, some other actors, props, costumes,
       staging, and the cost of production.

793.   ---.   [Untitled; in "Research in Progress."] *REEDN*
       2.2 (1977): 28-30.

       Discusses the author's attempts to gather
       documentary evidence on the drama of Coventry.
       Points up lost and available materials for

publication in *The Dramatic Records of Coventry 1392-1642* (see entry # 791, with a different published title).

794.   Ingram, William.   "The Theatre and Curtain Contracts."
       See "Abstracts and Papers at The International
       Shakespeare Association Congress. The First Public
       Playhouse: The Theatre 1576-1976." *ShakN* 36.3
       (142) (May 1976): 27.

       A one-paragraph note about a 1585 contract between
       James Burbage and John Brayne concerning profits
       made in the Curtain.

795.   Institute of Cornish Studies.   *The Medieval Cornish
       Drama*.   Special Bibliography No. 2.   Cornwall:
       Trevenson House, 1973.   Introductory note by
       Charles Thomas.   [6] pp., booklet.

       An expansion of the 1969 bibliography (issued by
       the Cornwall Archaeological Society).   Aims to
       present a list of works on Cornish drama with an
       emphasis on the open-air, "*plain-an-gwary* [sic],
       or earthwork amphitheatre, and also on the part
       played by the Cornish texts within the wider
       development of European liturgical drama" [1].
       Contains references to the *Ordinalia*, the *Charter
       Fragment, Bewnans Meryasek* (The Life of Meriasek),
       and *Gwreans an Bys* (The Creation of the World),
       along with sections on general works on Cornish
       drama, the Plain-an-Gwary theater, archeological
       excavations, and articles and references of
       general interest.   Also has an appendix on early
       references to plays and players.

796.   Ishii, Mikiko.   "Joseph's Proverbs in the Coventry
       Plays."   *Folklore* 93.1 (1982): 47-60.

       Reviews interpretations and scholarship.   Focuses
       on Joseph's use of proverbial language in its
       historic and literary contexts.   Shows how the
       figure, with his use of proverbs, "achieve[s] the
       fusion of the popular, secular figure of Joseph,
       and Joseph, the servant of God" (47).   Defines
       "proverb."   Examines particular statements in the
       play which have "both serious and comic
       intentions" (58) in Joseph's language.

797.   Isono, Morihiko, Tadanobu Torii, and Koshi Yamada.   "A
       Comprehensive Study of *Everyman* (1)."   *BFE* 30.2
       (Feb. 1979): 77-97.   (See next three entries.) (In
       Japanese.)

       Offers a translation of the play into Japanese.

798. ---, ---, ---. "A Comprehensive Study of *Everyman*
      (2)." *BFE* 31.2 (Feb. 1980): 15-59. (See previous
      and following entries.) (In Japanese.)

      Examines the play's textual problems. Offers an
      introduction to the play, discussing its history,
      editions, and textual variants, with a table of
      the variants in the different editions. The table
      (in English) is pp. 22-59. With five
      illustrations from early printed editions.

799. ---, ---, ---. "A Comprehensive Study of *Everyman*
      (3)." *BFE* 32.2 (Feb. 1981): 13-44. (See previous
      and following entries.) (In English.)

      Contains textual notes for their Japanese
      translation of the play. This part contains notes
      through line 100, drawing from many scholars.

800. ---, ---, ---. "A Comprehensive Study of *Everyman*
      (4)." *BFE* 33.2 (Feb. 1982): 43-66. (See previous
      entries.) (In English.)

      Contains additional textual notes, in English, for
      lines 101-200. Draws from many sources. [These
      are the only fascicles of this study available to
      or known of by this editor.]

801. Iverson, Gunilla. "Aspects of the Transmission of the
      Quem Quaeritis." *TEXT* 3: 155-82. Ed. by D.C.
      Greetham and W. Speed Hill. New York: AMS Press,
      1987.

      Describes the trope; looks at critical history and
      approaches, chronology, geographical distribution,
      ms occurrences, "The textual basis for the central
      dialogue" (163), and the different uses of the
      trope.

802. Jack, R. Ian. *Medieval Wales*. Ithaca, New York:
      Cornell U. Press, 1972. The Sources of History:
      Studies in the Uses of Historical Evidence. 255
      pp.

      Demonstrates the uses of primary evidence. Has
      chapters on literary sources, official records,
      English governmental records, public and private
      archives, ecclesiastical records, antiquaries,
      archaeology and numismatics, and place names. Not
      specifically on drama, but details the kinds of
      records and their use being considered by scholars
      of medieval English drama (especially in the REED
      volumes). With index.

Rev. *LJ* 98 (June 15, 1973): 1915.
AHR 78 (Oct. 1973): 1032.
Choice 10 (Nov. 1973): 1358.
EHR 89 (July 1974): 652.
Specu 50 (Jan. 1975): 129.

803. Jambeck, Thomas J. "The 'Ayll of Hely' Allusion in the *Prima Pastorum.*" *ELN* 17.1 (Sept. 1979): 1-7.

Explains the phrase as meaning the ale of Elias, an exegetical use of "penitential discipline which fills man with the 'spirit of wisdom' . . . [and] signifies the sacrifice incumbent upon man under the new dispensation" (7).

804. ---. "The Canvas-Tossing Allusion in the *Secunda Pastorum.*" *MP* 76.1 (Aug. 1978): 49-54.

Looks at the traditional associations of the tossing, which "clarify the point of the rustic comedy" and "link it typologically" to the Nativity (48). Links the act to the exegetical themes of Advent. Shows the ridicule and the symbolic theological association of man as Anti-Christ in the tossing.

805. ---. "The Dramatic Implications of Anselmian Affective Piety in the Towneley Play of the Crucifixion." *AnM* 16 (1975): 110-27.

Views Christ's suffering in "the larger context of the religious sensibility that gave it shape" (111): the eleventh-century Anselmian devotional impetus and its focus on the Passion and on Christ's compassion for mankind. Looks at the fourteenth- and fifteenth-century handling of these elements, with a focus on piety--evidenced in the Wakefield play. Examines the play in terms of Anselm's views. Explains how the torturers' evil shows them to embody "all human culpability" (127).

806. ---. "The Elements of Grotesque Humor in the Passion Sequences of the English Medieval Cycle Drama." Ph.D. diss., U. of Colorado, 1969.

807. ---. "*Everyman* and the Implications of Bernardine Humanism in the Character 'Knowledge.'" *M&H*, n.s. 8 (1977): 103-23.

Points up two possible interpretations of the character Knowledge: 1) like our modern sense of "scientia, intelligentia" (103), or 2) the archaic sense of "acknowledge." Another possible meaning is Bernard's which "describes a penitential ascesis" (104), the central character's personal growth.

808. ---, and Reuben R. Lee. "'Pope Pokett' and the Date of *Mankind*." *MedS* 39 (1977): 511-13.

Identifies a historical person--John Poket, prior of Barnwell Abbey from 1444 to 1464--as the one referred to in line 144 of the play. Speculates (on the basis of this identification) on the date of the play: 1464, the year Poket died.

809. James, Mervyn. "Ritual, Drama and Social Body in the Late Medieval English Town." *P&P* 98 (Feb. 1983): 3-29.

Discusses "the cult of Corpus Christi" (3). Looks at various rites, dramatic and theatrical manifestations, and the mythology associated with these. Looks also at "the late medieval social background against which the cult was practised and the plays performed" (3-4), as well as the "social needs and pressures to which [they] responded" (4). Aims to show that the theme of the ritual is "society seen in terms of body" (4); also that this notion yields a mythology and ritual which allow the affirmation of "social wholeness and social differentiation" (4). Claims that the aim of the cult was to express social integration in a society in which "symbols and ties of lordship, lineage and faithfulness, available in countrysides, were lacking" (4). Says that the cult's expression of a social need for bonding into one body was paralleled by the individual craft's drive for differentiation; hence the procession could stand for social order while the play cycle stood for a means of changing social status.

810. Janecek, Thomas John. "The Literary History of the Parliament of Heaven Allegory from Origination in Christianity to Culmination in the Renaissance Drama of England." Ph.D. diss., U. of Illinois, Urbana/Champaign, 1975.

811. Janssen, Carole A. "The Waytes of Norwich and an Early Lord Mayor's Show." *RORD* 22 (1979): 57-64.

Considers the opening pageant of the Lord Mayor's show, "a *tableau vivant* of the popular emblem, *Veritas Filia Temporis*, or Truth the Daughter of Time" (57). Looks at other contemporary documents for additional information on the Lord Mayor's show, the staging, the cast, and the emblem.

812.   ---.   "The Waytes of Norwich in Medieval and Renaissance Civic Pageantry." Ph.D. thesis, U. of New Brunswick, 1978.

813.   Jaques, Sister Bernarda.   "Ancient Magic Distilled: The Twentieth Century Productions of the York Mystery Plays." Ph.D. diss., Tufts U., 1971.

814.   Jaye, Barbara H.   "A Study of the *Castle of Perseverance*." Ph.D. diss., Rutgers U., 1970.

814a. ---, and William P. Mitchell.   "The Only Game in Town: The Latin-American Fiesta System and the York Feast of Corpus Christi." *FCS* 13 (1988): 485-504.

815.   Jeffrey, David L.   "Bosch's 'Haywain': Communion, Community, and the Theater of the World." *Viator* 4 (1973): 311-331, 2 pp. of plates.

Sees in the triptych not the commonly attributed references to Dutch proverbs concerning the symbolic interpretations of hay, but a picture of "all three time zones of our *historia salvationis*" (330), including all the elements one finds in the Corpus Christi cycle of plays.

816.   ---, ed. *By Things Seen: Reference and Recognition in Medieval Thought*. Ottawa, Canada: U. of Ottawa Press, 1979.   270 pp.

Not specifically on drama, but contains some dozen articles by different scholars on "the principle of referral for understanding." Mentions the York Cycle (158), mystery plays (67, 157-58), Digby ms (157), drama (157), Corpus Christi cycles (157), and much background material. With bibliography and indexes.

Rev. *Specu* 55 (Apr. 1980): 408.
      Ren&Ref 5.2 (1981): 110.

817.   ---.   "English Saints' Plays." In *Medieval Drama*, 68-89. Ed. by Neville Denny (see Entry # 442 above).

Discusses the homiletic elements in English Saints' plays, in which popular elements unite with homiletic and romantic ones. Explains why so many saints' plays are lost. Deals with saints' plays as "a kind of history . . . as much as a romance" (73). Examines the *Mary Magdalene* play extensively, as well as the play *The Conversion of*

St. Paul. Considers the staging and subject
matter of the plays.

818. ---. "Franciscan Spirituality and the Rise of Early
English Drama." *Mosaic* 8.4 (Summer 1975): 17-46.

Examines "English drama in the light of Italian
models" (19), especially appropriate since there
is a strong parallel and demonstrable connection
between English and Italian literary history.
Substantiates this view with reference to the
vernacular lyric, "which so often lent itself to
dramatic performance in the Middle Ages" (19).
Considers "Vernacular Pedagogy" (19), "Sermone
Semidrammatico" (25), "Friars and Players" (34),
"Structure and Motif" (40). Calls for greater
attention in scholarship to "the influence of
Franciscan spirituality on the early English
cycle, morality, and saint's play" (46). Sees a
continuum from verse to dialogue lyrics to semi-
dramatic passages in Middle English sermons.

819. Jeffrey, David Lyle. "Pastoral Care in the Wakefield
Shepherd Plays." *ABR* 22.2 (June 1971): 208-21.

Claims that the plays are aimed at the clergy.
Says that the shepherds in the first play fail
because of sloth until they seek grace; the
shepherds in the second play represent the
"prelatical, married and contemplative" (215)
states of the Christian service, and as good
shepherds they seek and find their sheep. In both
plays the shepherds exhibit a tendency toward
sloth, but in the second play they exhibit also
fortitudo (214). Concludes that the playwright
provides "a pageant of the gospel harmonized with
a gloss interwoven . . . . the gloss speaks . . .
of stewardship and salvation" (221) and their
interrelationship.

820. ---. "Stewardship in the Wakefield *Mactacio Abel* and
Noe Plays." *ABR* 22.1 (Mar. 1971): 64-76.

Says that both plays "demonstrate the theme of
harmonious Christian service, or stewardship"
(64). Also says that good stewardship triumphs
over bad and shows that grace is always available.
Looks at characterizations (Noah, his wife, Cain)
and at the figure of the plow (and vineyard
imagery, husbandmen, and plowmen).

821. Jennings, Margaret. "Tutivillus: The Literary Career
of the Recording Demon." *SP* 74.5 (Dec. 1977):
Texts and Studies, 95 pp.

Studies manifestations of the Devil and his use in
medieval literature and liturgy. Says that demons
"assumed a definite place in the economy of
salvation" (10); they might instill any of the
seven deadly sins. Examines sources and the
expansion of the character; refers to the
character in the Wakefield *Judicium* play and in
Mankind. Chap. IV, "Tutivillus in the Drama,"
points out that the stage was the ideal forum for
the figure in his entertaining, absorbing, and
enlightening nature, and in the opportunity for
satire he offers. Examines the figure in other
dramas, then concentrates on Wakefield (58-64) and
Mankind (64-68). Concludes by looking at later
treatments.

822. Johnson, B.P. "The Gilds of York." In *The Noble City
of York*, 447-610. Ed. by Alberic Stacpoole, et
al. York: Cerialis Press, 1972.

Contains much information on the guilds including
origin, The Gild Merchant, Socio-Religious Gilds,
Merchant Companies, and Craft Gilds. Contains
sections on "The Corpus Christi Procession and
Gild" (469 f.); "The Corpus Christi Cycle of
Mystery Plays" (470 ff.); "The Morality Plays and
Connected Gilds" (475 ff.). Tries to distinguish
some plays from others generically (see especially
502 ff.). Has a chart: "List of Crafts and
Corpus Christi Mystery Plays Allotted to Them"
(574-75).

823. Johnson, Kenneth E. "The Rhetoric of Apocalypse in
Van Eyck's 'Last Judgment' and the Wakefield
Secunda Pastorum." In *Legacy of Thespis*, 31-41.
Ed. by Karelisa V. Hartigan (entry # 708 above).

Points out similarities in the two works. Claims
that the artists probably never saw one another's
work, but shared an aesthetic which manifested
itself in "similar structures and rhetorical
intentions" (31). Adds that the works "share
. . . a structure influenced by the book of
Revelation and a rhetorical intention achieved
through this apocalyptic structure" (31). With
two illustrations.

824. Johnson, Robert Carl. "Audience Involvement in the
Tudor Interlude." *ThN* 24.3 (Spring 1970): 101-11.

Discusses the closeness of the audience to the
action and claims that a modern reader should
realize how an audience even participated in the
action. Brings in examples from *Fulgens and*

Lucrece; Heywood's *The Weather, Love, The Pardoner and the Friar*, and *Johan Johan*; Medwall's *Nature*; and several other plays. Draws parallels to medieval cycle plays. Discusses the different kinds of responses a participating audience exhibits when the illusion of the stage is broken.

825. ---. *John Heywood*. New York: Twayne, 1970. 159 pp.

Aims "to re-evaluate the position of John Heywood in the development of English drama and to demonstrate his importance as a minor adherent to and propagandist for Christian Humanism" ([7]). Contains chapters on historical background, non-dramatic works, dramatic works, sources, and Heywood's position as a Tudor dramatist. With notes, bibliography, and index.

Rev. *RenQ* 24.4 (1971): 555.

826. ---. "Stage Directions in the Tudor Interlude." *ThN* 26.1 (Autumn 1971): 36-42.

Analyzes the importance of stage directions. Categorizes them into four types: 1) plays that have "no apparent interplay suggested by the dramatist through specific directions" (37); 2) stage directions that indicate only entrances and exits, but no control over action; 3) stage directions that "exert control over the action of the play" (38); 4) stage directions which exert extensive control.

827. Johnston, Alexandra F. "*All the World Was a Stage*: Records of Early English Drama." In *Medieval Drama* . . . (forthcoming). Ed. by Eckehard Simon (see entry # 1469 below).

827a. ---. "The Audience of the English Moral Play." *FCS* 13 (1988): 291-98.

827b. ---. "Chaucer's Records of Early English Drama." *REEDN* 13.2 (1988): 13-20.

827c. ---. "Cycle Drama in the Sixteenth Century: Texts and Contexts." In *English Drama to 1600*. Ed. by Albert H. Tricomi. (See entry # 1589b below.)

828. Johnston, A.F., ed. *Editing Early English Drama: Special Problems and New Directions. Papers Given at the Nineteenth Annual Conference on Editorial Problems, University of Toronto, 4-5 November 1983*. New York: AMS Press, 1987. 143 pp.

Contains an Introduction by Johnston and five essays: Bevington ("Drama Editing . . .," entry # 185 above); Parry ("A Margin of Error . . .," # 1266); Meredith ("Stage Directions . . .," # 1108); Somerset ("'this hawthorn-brake . . .," # 1492); and Johnston ("The *York Cycle* and the *Chester Cycle* . . .," # 844).

Rev. Clifford Davidson, *CompD* 22.1 (Spring 1988): 82-84.

829. ---. "*Errata* in *York*." *REEDN* 5.1 (1980): 35-38.

Offers a list of corrections of typesetting and typographical errors and misreadings in the REED York volumes. (See entry # 852 below.)

830. ---. "Folk-drama in Berkshire." *Études D'Histoire du Théâtre Medieval* I (forthcoming). Cited by Johnston in "What If No Texts Survived? . . .," entry # 841 below.

831. ---. "The Guild of Corpus Christi and the Procession of Corpus Christi in York." *MedS* 38 (1976): 372-84.

Sketches the history of the guild over its 139 years of existence (1408-1547). Claims that the guild "never at any time had anything to do with the Corpus Christi Play" (373). Points out that the play was in the hands of the craft guilds. Looks at this guild's contribution to and participation in the procession of Corpus Christi, though it never controlled the procession.

832. ---. "A Medieval and Renaissance Dramatic Records Project." *RORD* 17 (1974): 105-06.

Outlines the project which eventuated in the REED publications.

833. ---. "Medieval English Drama: The York Cycle." Videotape. Scarborough, Ontario: Software Distribution, 1973.

Reconstructs a play procession.

834. ---. "The Medieval English Stage." *UTQ* 44 (1975): 238-48.

Review article. Deals primarily with Alan H. Nelson's *The Medieval English Stage* (entry # 1199 below).

835.   ---. *The N-Town Pageants: A Medieval History of the
       World.* [Toronto]: *Poculi Ludique Societas,* the
       Presidents' Players of the University of Toronto,
       1988. 16 pp.

       Program for performance, May 28-29, 1988, at the
       Univerisity of Toronto. Lists the 21 plays; has
       sections on the ms, "The Challenge" of such a
       performance, the modernized text, the music, and
       the design of the production.

836.   ---. "Parish Entertainments in Berkshire." In
       Pathways to Medieval Peasants, 335-38. Ed. by
       J.A. Raftis. Toronto: Pontifical Institute of
       Mediaeval Studies, 1981. Papers in Mediaeval
       Studies, 2.

       Examines old customs of fund raising, Robin Hood
       plays, morris dancers, and other folk
       entertainments. Concedes that "The exact nature
       of the plays . . . must remain obscure" (337), but
       adds that "They were not the consciously didactic
       Christian drama of the cycle and morality plays"
       (337).

837.   ---. "The Plays of the Religious Guilds of York: The
       Creed Play and the Pater Noster Play." *Specu* 50.1
       (Jan. 1975): 55-90.

       Speculates on the contents of the plays; cites
       historical records which are sources of her
       speculations (39 documents dating from 1388/9 to
       1575). Explains that the "Corpus Christi Guild
       was responsible for the Creed Play and the Pater
       Noster Guild . . . was responsible for the Pater
       Noster Play" (55).

838.   ---. "The Procession and Play of Corpus Christi in
       York after 1426." *LSE,* n.s. 7 (1974 [for 1973 and
       1974]): 55-62.

       Brings together evidence from extant documents to
       discuss the division onto two days of the
       procession and the play of Corpus Christi.
       Mentions the William Melton 1426 sermon urging
       this division, and refers to several other
       records. Concludes that "until 1468 at the
       earliest the procession of Corpus Christi and the
       play of Corpus Christi were probably two separate
       events taking place in . . . York on the day of
       the feast" (59).

839.   ---. "Research in Progress." *REEDN* 1.2 (1976): 16.

Warns that when money is mentioned with regard to
a play, it is not necessarily an indication that
the actors were professionals; in fact, it seems
"to have been a common practice in some parishes
to perform plays . . . to make money for the use
of the parish."

840. ---. [Research in Progress.] *REEDN* 4.1 (1979): 19-
20.

Discusses her position as executive editor of *REED*
and her work on Berkshire records.

841. ---. "What If No Texts Survived?: External Evidence
for Early English Drama." In *Contexts for Early
English Drama*, 1-19. Ed. by Marianne G. Briscoe
and John C. Coldewey (see entry # 228 above).

Reviews scholarship and points to the recent work
with primary documents of the REED project. Cites
the many documents scholars are now using to seek
information on the drama. Discusses the various
forms the drama took. With a Bibliographical
Footnote reviewing scholarship.

842. ---. "*Wisdom* and the Records: Is There a Moral?"
Paper delivered at the *Wisdom* Symposium, Trinity
College, Hartford, Connecticut, April 14, 1984.
In *The* Wisdom *Symposium: Papers from the Trinity
College Medieval Festival*, 87-102. Ed. by Milla
Cozart Riggio. (See entry # 1390 below.)

Discusses provenance and why it is important to
envision a particular scene and occasion of
performance when presenting the play. Shows that
there is a paucity of contemporary records on
morality plays and explains why this paucity
exists. Explains the homiletic nature of the
genre, as well as its cerebral and abstract form
and its ephemerality, the last of which accounts
for its not surviving in records. Exposes Eton
College records which suggest the existence of
dramatic performances without naming any play.
Looks for internal and external evidence for
information about the plays. Claims that *Wisdom*
was designed to be performed indoors. Posits that
"*Wisdom* was commissioned from the abbey by some
local magnate" (99). Discusses the difficulty of
performing the play and says that it is a play to
be performed "by seasoned professionals" (100),
"for a learned and powerful audience of mixed
secular and clerical magnates" (101).

843.   ---.   "The York Corpus Christi Play: A Dramatic
        Structure Based on Performance Practice." In *The
        Theatre in the Middle Ages*, 362-73. Ed. by Herman
        Braet, Johan Nowé, and Gilbert Tournoy (entry #
        215 above).

        Examines the processional mode of performance.
        Reviews scholarship on the subject. Looks at
        "evidence from actual performance and . . . from
        the text of the cycle itself" (365). Concludes,
        despite contradictory criticism, that all evidence
        supports the theory that the plays were performed
        processionally.

844.   ---.   "The *York Cycle* and the *Chester Cycle:* What do
        the Records Tell Us?" In *Editing Early English
        Drama* . . ., 121-43. Ed. by A.F. Johnston (entry
        # 828 above; see also entry # 1736 below).

        Reviews old notions about the plays and the
        advances made in scholarship by the REED project.
        Reviews recent criticism and the use of original
        records. Looks at "the nature of the manuscripts
        themselves" (124). Summarizes the views of
        Lawrence Clopper, R.M. Lumiansky, and David Mills
        with respect to the Chester documents, and the
        views of Richard Beadle with respect to York.
        Discusses the good and bad points of some recent
        editions.

845.   ---.   "The York Cycle: 1977." *UTQ* 48.1 (Fall 1978):
        1-9.

        Reviews a performance of the cycle, October 1-2,
        1977, at the University of Toronto campus.
        Answers critics of the performance. With eight
        illustrations. Mentions the availability of a
        videotape of the performance. (See Johnston and
        Margaret Dorrell Rogerson, "Medieval Drama . . .,"
        entry # 851 below; see also # 1736.))

846.   ---.   "York Notes." *REEDN* 1.2 (1976): 9-11.

        Mentions items observed in her editing of the
        REED, York volumes (entry # 852 below)--items
        concerning Yule, "New early play references from
        York" (10), and "Ministralli and histriones" (10).

847.   ---.   "York Pageant House: New Evidence." *REEDN* 7.2
        (1982): 24-25.

        Shows that a royal inquisition of York (14 May
        1388) proves that certain unnamed guilds kept

their plays' pageant wagons in the Archbishop of
York's palace.

848.   ---.   "Yule in York."   *REEDN* 1.1 (1976): 3-10.

Demonstrates that the word "Yule" is "associated
with ancient ceremonies in York reaching back into
the mythical past" (3).   Substantiates this by
citing several texts (e.g. Hector Boece's *Scotorum
Historial* [1527], George Buchanan's *Rerum
Scoticarum Historia* [1582], the *Itinerary of John
Leland*, and so on).   Mentions the "frivolous" or
"licentious" nature of this feast (5).   Reproduces
a broadside of c. 1570 describing and defending
the Yule riding in York.   Relates the feast to the
drama in terms of its music and other features
(e.g. "the mercers' pageant wagon with its twenty
artificial angels" [9] and the processional nature
of the feast).

849.   ---, and Margaret Dorrell.   "The Doomsday Pageant of
the York Mercers, 1433."   *LSE*, n.s. 5 (1971): 29-
34.   (See also, the same authors, "The York
Mercers . . .," entry # 853 below.)

Examines a 1433 "indenture made between the master
and the constables of the Mercers" of York (29)
which contains an inventory of the props of the
pageant.   Discusses also costumes, the number of
characters, the angels, and the endorsement of the
document.

850.   ---, and S.B. MacLean, comps.   With contributions from
M. Blackstone and C. Louis.   Records of Early
English Drama.   *Handbook for Editors*.   Toronto:
REED, 1980.

Aimed at the REED editors; explains principles of
selection, transcription rules, bibliography,
dating, subject indexing, etc.

851.   ---, and Margaret Dorrell Rogerson.   "Medieval Drama:
The York Cycle in the Fifteenth Century."
Videotape, sponsored by the Centre for Medieval
Studies, 1972.   (See Johnston, "The York Cycle:
1977," entry # 845 above.)

852.   ---, and ---, eds.   *Records of Early English Drama,
York*.   2 vols.   Toronto and Buffalo, New York: U.
of Toronto Press, 1979.   668, 356 pp.

Vol. I is Introduction and The Records; Vol. II is
Appendixes, Translations, End-Notes, Glossaries,
Indexes.

Vol. I covers York and National Events, Civic
Government, Craft and Religious Guilds, Principles
of Selection (of the present records), and a
discussion of the documents and editorial
procedures. Vol. II contains appendixes, notes,
abbreviations, glossaries, and indexes. (See
entry # 829 above.)

Rev. *LJ* 104 (June 1, 1979): 1259.
Choice 16 (Sept. 1979): 841.
V.J. Scattergood, *BBN* (Nov. 1979): 949.
Martin Stevens, "The Johnston-Rogerson
Edition . . .," (entry # 1528 below).
G.B. Shand, *UTQ* (1980).
Clifford Davidson, *CompD* 14.1 (Spring 1980):
79-81.
RenQ 33 (Summer 1980): 278.
D.E. Litt, *ARBA* 12 (1981): 473.
Ren&Ref 6 (Feb. 1982): 47.
Sheila Lindenbaum, *MP* 80.1 (Aug. 1982): 80-
83.
MLR (Oct. 1983): 892.

853. ---, and ---. "The York Mercers and Their Pageant of
Doomsday, 1433-1526." *LSE*, n.s. 6 (1972): 10-35.
(See also, by the same authors, "The Doomsday
Pageant of the York Mercers, 1433," entry # 849
above.)

Shows the control the Mercers (local shopkeepers)
had over the production of the Corpus Christi
plays. Demonstrates through reference to records
of the Mercers' Guild the political power they had
in York. Explains how the Mercers' wealth allowed
them to produce lavish plays on expensive wagons.
Describes the documents they observed (account
rolls, a Chartulary and Minute Book, and other
papers). Discusses the pageant masters, the
preparation for performances, the clerks who
helped select a cast and direct the play, the
expenses, the proclamation of the play, the
arrangement for the props, the moving of the heavy
wagon, the payments involved, the wagons, the
props, and the costumes. Details the physical
appearance of the pageant wagon (e.g. wheels,
hanging angels, banners, Hell mouth . . .).
Appendix I lists documents studied; Appendix II
discusses dates of the documents; Appendix III
discusses the Pageant Masters' Ordinance, 1433;
Appendix IV considers one further document, "a
formal agreement confirming forfeit" (34) that
three men would have to pay to the Mercers if they
failed to fulfill the terms laid down in "certain

indentures" (34) concerning the production of the
Doomsday pageant.

854.   ---, David Parry, Geoff Gaherty, and Ralph Blasting.
        *The Towneley Cycle: In a New Modernization by
        David Parry.* [Toronto]: *Poculi Ludique Societas*
        in Association with Victoria University and
        Records of Early English Drama, 1985. 16 pp.

        Program for performance, May 25-26, 1985, at the
        University of Toronto by The Presidents' Players
        of the University of Toronto. Has sections on
        "The Challenge" of such a performance, "The
        Hypothesis" concerning the method of production,
        the text and its modernized version, music, the
        design of the production. With illustrations.

855.   ---, ---, Steven Putzel, and Reed Needles. *The York
        Cycle.* [Toronto]: *Poculi Ludique Societas* in
        Association with Records of Early English Drama
        and the Graduate Centre for Study of Drama, 1977.
        12 pp.

        Program for performances at the University of
        Toronto, October 1-2, 1977. Contains essays by
        Johnston ("The York Cycle"); Parry ("The Toronto
        Production"); and Putzel and Needles ("The Pageant
        Wagons"). With illustrations.

856.   Johnston, Paul William. "From Mime to Marlowe: An
        Introduction to Savage Farce." Ph.D. diss., New
        York U, 1977.

857.   Jonassen, Frederick B. "Elements from the Traditional
        Drama of England in *Sir Gawain and the Green
        Knight.*" *Viator* 17 (1986): 221-54.

        Looks at mummings and other folkloric material in
        Gawain (e.g. sword dances, the Rapper Dance, use
        of the pentangle/knot, sun symbolism, seasons).

858.   Jones, Emrys. *The Origins of Shakespeare.* Oxford:
        Clarendon Press, 1977.

        Chap. 2 discusses "Shakespeare and the Mystery
        Cycles" (31-84). Considers "The Mysteries in
        Protestant England" (31); "The Passion Sequence:
        The Fall of Duke Humphrey" (35); "Judas and Herod"
        (74); "From Mystery to Tragedy" (83). With many
        references to specific cycles.

        Rev. *Obs* (Jan. 30, 1977): 31.
            S. Sternlicht, *LJ* 102 (Apr. 15, 1977): 926.
            T. Weiss, *TLS* 3919 (Apr. 22, 1977): 482.

        Choice 14 (July 1977): 682.
        J. Harvey, *EssCrit* 27 (July 1977): 248-70.
        E.A.J. Honigmann, *N&Q* 25 (Apr. 1978): 172-73.
        V.K. Whitaker, *JEGP* 77 (Apr. 1978): 272-74.
        T.W. Craik, *RES*, n.s. 29 (May 1978): 203-04.
        J.A. Bryant, Jr. *SewR* 86 (July 1978): 406.
        F.D. Hoeniger, *RenQ* 31 (Autumn 1978): 412-15.
        E.M. Waith, *ShakQ* 29 (Winter 1978): 96-100.
        L.S. Champion, *EngStud* 61 (Apr. 1980): 177-
          80.
        G.K. Hunter, *MLR* 75 (Apr. 1980): 359-60.
        BBN (Oct. 1981): 584.

859. Jones, M.L. [Untitled review.] *RORD* 21 (1978): 96.

    Reviews performance of the Digby *Mary Magdalen*,
    July 23-25, 31, and August 1, 1976, at the
    University of Colorado, Boulder, by Whitsun
    Productions.

860. Jones, Marion. "Early Moral Plays and the Earliest
    Secular Drama." In Cawley, et al., *Medieval
    Drama.* Vol. I, *The* Revels *History* . . ., 211-91.
    (See entry # 289 above.)

    Pt. 1, "Introduction" (213-24), discusses morality
    play tradition as distinct and independent from
    the plays of the biblical tradition, and reviews
    the "nine allegorical plays with English
    affiliations . . . before 1500" (220): *Pride of
    Life, Castle of Perseverance, Lucidus and Dubius,
    Occupation and Idleness, Mankind, Wisdom, Liber
    Apologeticus de Omni Statu Humanum Naturae* (the
    only one in Latin), *Everyman*, and *Nature*--the nine
    plays which "are the main source of our
    information about the morality tradition in
    England" (224).

    Pt. 2 deals with "The Earliest Secular Drama:
    Mirth and Solace" (225-46). Discusses the
    entertainment function of drama, medieval views of
    the genre, the meanings of the word "ludus," the
    use of French in the court, popular minstrelsy,
    "the prejudice against professional players and
    the very limited toleration for amateur
    theatricals which were freely expressed by . . .
    the clergy" (223), the meanings of the word
    "interludium," patrons, mummings and disguisings,
    and the plays of Lydgate, Medwall, and Rastell.

    Pt. 3, "Allegory into drama: Souls in jeopardy"
    (247-62), discusses the didactic nature of
    allegory and the notion of *psychomachia* in the
    morality tradition. Shows how the themes of

Hildegard of Bingen's *Ordo Virtutem* reappear "in vernacular plays throughout the Middle Ages" (251). Examines *Wisdom* at length, explaining "why so much is said and so little happens" in this play (256): because of the urgency and compelling interest of the doctrinal material. Briefly looks at *The Castle of Perseverance, Mankind, The Pride of Life,* and *Everyman* in terms of their allegorical presentation of doctrine.

Pt. 4, "Sermon into drama: borrowed gear" (263-73), discusses the guild-play called the Paternoster play as the link between early continental allegorical pieces and the well-developed fifteenth-century English allegorical plays, but then discredits this old view. Examines the records pertaining to and the content of the Paternoster plays. Pieces together information from fragmentary records to show how the play was performed (on pageant wagons used by the guilds in their performances of the cycle plays), and that its content was based on the separate clauses of the Lord's Prayer as defenses against the seven deadly sins. Examines the Beverley Paternoster play at length, showing that it "dealt with the Lord's Prayer in a dramatic manner" (272) and that "in 1469 it made use of at least seven allegorical personages" (272). Concludes that "the late fourteenth century and the fifteenth century brought forth some special examples of dramatized sermon in English" (272-73).

Pt. 5, "Sermon into allegory: shared concepts" (274-91), shows that the allegorical moralities present materials common to other religious drama, and that the "mode of presentation is based on the Bible, apocryphal tradition, and church ritual" (274). Examines the *Liber Apologeticus* for its use of stock "characters and themes most frequent in allegorical drama" (280). Looks at themes and stock figures in morality plays.

861. Jones, Mary Loubris. "How the Seven Deadly Sins 'Dewoyde from the Woman' in the Digby *Mary Magdalen.*" *ANQ* 16.8 (Apr. 1978): 118-19.

Considers the terminology in the play's stage directions for "exits [and] moves within and about the *platea*" (118). Looks specifically at *voyd, avoyd,* and *devoyd,* meaning "to leave the acting area completely or to be completely hidden from the audience's view within a single mansion" (118). Also shows that *devoyd* could mean "*to come*

out of rather than to exit" (118). Discusses this
and lighting in terms of actual performance
practices.

862.   Jones, Mary K. Loubris. "Pilgrimage from Text to
Theater: A Study of the Staging of the Digby *Mary
Magdalen*." Ph.D. diss., U. of Colorado, Boulder,
1977.

863.   ---. "Sunlight and Sleight-of-Hand in Medieval
Drama." *ThN* 32.3 (1978): 118-26.

Notes the need of "stage trickery . . . to achieve
the miraculous rather than the blackout or the
spotlight" (118). Looks at Digby *Mary Magdalene*
play's stage directions for special effects or
spectacular devices through sudden concealment or
appearance, ascensions and descents.

864.   Jones, Nicholas R. "Medieval Plays for Modern
Audiences." *Gamut* 4 (Fall 1981): 47-58.

Subheading to article: "A production by the
British National Theatre uses contemporary
techniques to engage audiences whose beliefs are
different from those assumed by the original
author" (47). Describes a production of selected
medieval mystery plays by the Cottesloe Theatre in
London. Shows how new meanings can be wrought
from an outdated ethos. Covers the history and
form of the cycles, their growth and social
milieu. Suggests how "techniques of 'avant-garde'
theater can be used to bridge the gaps of
language, custom, and belief" (57). Presents
historical data about the cycles and offers a
modern perspective. Refers to performances of
part 1 (Creation to Nativity) and part 2 (Baptism
to Judgment) at the Edinburgh Festival of 1980 and
at the Cottesloe Theatre in the same year. (Part
2 also performed at Cottesloe in 1977.) Cites
texts of these published by Rex Collings Ltd. in
London (see entry # 18 above). Texts were
"adapted by the company of the Cottesloe, with
John Russell Brown and Jack Shepherd (Part One)
and with Tony Harrison (Part Two)" (58). With
photographs of the production.

865.   Jones, Robert C. "Dangerous Sport: The Audience's
Engagement with Vice in the Moral Interludes."
RenD, n.s. 6 (1975, for 1973): 45-64.

Shows that Vice creates entertainment, but also
alienates the audience; makes the audience wonder
which side it should be on. Deals with the ways

playwrights "worked to resolve that conflict, and
to reinforce . . . the doctrine of their plays
through the theatrically engaging antics of their
sportive vices" (45-46). Says that "though the
vices may have the last laugh, they never have the
last word" (47).

866. ---. "The Stage World and the 'Real' World in
Medwall's *Fulgens and Lucres.*" *MLQ* 32.2 (June
1971): 131-42.

Mentions the audience's reaction to the play in a
hall-banquet setting in 1964 at Bristol
University. Argues that "Medwall's use of A and B
both as audience for and characters in the play
gives it its essential satirical point" (131) by
showing the relationship between the Roman and
Tudor audiences. Shows how the play calls upon
the audience's laughter as well as its "serious
reflection" (141). Discusses "the audience's
sense of its relationship to the play" (142).

867. Joseph, Stephen. *Theatre in the Round.* New York:
Taplinger Publishing Co., 1968. 179 pp.

Responds to Richard Southern's *The Medieval
Theatre in the Round* (London: Faber & Faber, 1957;
see entry # 1493 below for a later edition of this
work). Offers a historical study through the
twentieth century. Chap. 2, "The Early Story"
(11-33), glances at medieval English drama (17-
26). Provides theoretical information about this
structure. With illustrations, bibliography, and
index.

Rev. *Choice* 6 (Apr. 1969): 240.

868. Jungman, Robert E. "An Analogue in Fortescue to the
Wakefield *Magnus Herodes.*" *ANQ* 14.1 (Sept. 1975):
2-3.

Comments on Sir John Fortescue's treatment of
kingship in *The Governance of England* (c. 1471-
1476). Claims that Fortescue's views on the
tyrant are an analogue to the Wakefield treatment
of Herod.

869. ---. "Mak and the Seven Names of God." *L&L* 3.6A
(Jan. 1982): 24-28.

Explains Mak's reference to the Lord's seven names
(line 190). Reviews scholarship. Cites James G.
Frazer's idea and suggests that the reference may
be related to magic. Also cites the *Lemegeton* (or

Lesser Key of Solomon), a treatise on magic, which
expounds on God's seven names. Concludes that
Mak's reference shows him to be "an inept magician
or warlock" (26).

870.   ---.   "'Christicolae,' Prudentius, and the *Quem
       Quaeritis* Easter Dialogue."   *CompD* 12.4 (Winter
       1978-79): 300-08.

       Examines the trope in terms of its being a
       "bridge" (300) between ritual and drama. Shows
       that part of the text of the dialogue may come
       from Prudentius.

871.   Jungman, Robert Emery.   "Irony in the Plays of the
       Wakefield Master."   Ph.D. diss., Florida State U.,
       1972.

872.   Justice, Alan David.   "The English Corpus Christi Play
       in Its Social Setting: The York Cycle."   Ph.D.
       diss., U. of California, Santa Barbara, 1977.

873.   ---.   "Trade Symbolism in the York Cycle."   *ThJ* 31.1
       (Mar. 1979): 47-58.

       Deals with the appropriateness of the craft to the
       play assigned to it: "the connection between
       guild and subject was not entirely arbitrary"
       (47).   Points out two avenues of connection: the
       association of the guild with a particular
       character in a given play (as with a patron
       saint), or a detail of the pageant which makes use
       of the "work tools, or products of the producing
       craft" (47).   Substantiates some readings from
       internal and external sources for several plays
       from York.

874.   Justice, Nan.   [Untitled review.]   *RORD* 20 (1977): 98.

       Reviews performance of *John the Baptist*, play 19
       of The Wakefield Cycle, June 1976, Chester,
       England, by the Christleton Players.

875.   Kahrl, Stanley J.   "The Civic Religious Drama of
       Medieval England: A Review of Recent Scholarship."
       RenD, n.s. 6 (1975, for 1973): 237-48.

       "Buries" the term "pre-Shakespearean drama" (237)
       to reveal a new re-assessment of medieval drama.
       Looks at several works from the 1940s to the
       1970s. Stresses the importance of understanding
       English drama as a continuum.

876. ---. "Editing Texts for Dramatic Performance." In
The Drama of Medieval Europe, 39-52 (plus
discussion, 53-65). Ed. by Richard Rastall (see
entry # 1359 below).

Discusses early (nineteenth-century) editing aims
and practices, including those of the Early
English Text Society (EETS) editions with a focus
on their introductions. Critiques most of the
EETS editions on their omissions. Points out the
difference in aim of EETS editions (with their
emphasis on language) from the aim of editions of
Renaissance plays (with their wider scope--on
language, literary qualities, etc.). Urges
editors of medieval drama to make their editions
useful to the reader--"to assist the reader . . .
to visualize the scene . . . on the imaginary
stage" (46); this requires a discussion by the
editor of the shape of a performance (including
stage directions, explanatory notes, etc.).
Discusses normalization, punctuation,
capitalization, ms contractions, treatment of
certain letters, cited emendations, and the
apparatus. Shows how a well-edited edtion for a
critic may be used by a director for a
performance.

877. ---. "Informal Minutes of Conference 53." *RORD* 12
(1969): 85-92.

Offers minutes to seminar 53 of the Modern
Language Association (MLA) meeting on Medieval
Drama, December 29, 1968, in New York. Discusses
staging (processional, etc.), length of
performance, and so on. Reviews comments of
participants at the seminar.

878. ---. (John Elliott, discussion leader.) "Informal
Minutes of Seminar 22" (from The Report of the
Modern Language Association Seminar: "The Idea of
a Morality Play"). *RORD* 13-14 (1970-71): 235-38.

Lists names of people present at the MLA seminar,
December 29, 1970, in New York. Discussion
followed by paper by Robert A. Potter, "The Idea
of a Morality Play" (see entry # 1325 below).
Discusses a recent performance of *Jedermann*
(Salzburg). Shows that *Jedermann* is closer to
Hans Sachs's *Ein comedi von dem reichen sterbenden
menschen, der Hecastus gennant* than it is to
Everyman. Also discusses morality plays in which
man does not fall or is not redeemed. Concludes
that "evidence of dramatic form in the morality

genre should be adduced from a variety of locales in medieval Europe" (237).

879.   ---.   "Learning about Local Control."   In *Records of Early English Drama: Proceedings of the First Colloquium* . . ., 101-18.   Ed. by JoAnna Dutka. (See entry # 497 above.)

Offers "a view . . . to suggest how one ought to think about the life behind the records" (101). Proposes that researchers looking for county documents get to know one town very well--the town and region, not just the documents.   Recounts his own experiences.   (Comment and discussion on this paper on pp. 118-25 and 126-27.)   See John C. Coldewey, "Comment" (entry # 313 above).

880.   ---.   "Medieval Drama in England, 1973: Chester and Ely."   *RORD* 15-16 (1972-73): 117-23.

Discusses the approaches taken to several performances, the use of modern dress, the use of a chorus which shifted roles, theatrical movement, and other modern features, along with pacing and other elements of drama.

881.   ---.   "Medieval Staging and Performance."   In *Contexts for Early English Drama*, 218-36.   Ed. by Marianne G. Briscoe and John C. Coldewey (see entry # 228 above).

Points out that the dramatists had specific staging realities in mind when they wrote.   Talks of the necessity of looking at primary documents to determine the kind of staging each play used. Surveys old .and recent criticism and the other documents scholars resort to, and stresses the importance of the REED volumes.

882.   ---, ed.   *Records of Plays and Players in Lincolnshire, 1300-1585.   Collections VIII.* Oxford: Printed for the Malone Society by Oxford U. Press, 1969 (1974).   108 pp.

Presents dramatic records from fourteen towns. Introduction discusses the records, towns, plays, "Mysteries End," and editorial methods.

Rev. Clifford Davidson, *CompD* 9.3 (Fall 1975): 269-72.

883.   ---.   "Secular Life and Popular Piety in Medieval English Drama."   In *The Popular Literature of Medieval England*, 85-107.   Ed. by Thomas J.

Heffernan. Knoxville: U. of Tennessee Press,
1985. Tennessee Studies in Literature, 28.

Examines the notion (for medieval and modern
audiences) of *literature* and its relation to
drama. Looks at the oral nature of the genre and
how the plays related to a popular audience and to
authorship; also considers other elements of the
plays relating to audience, performance, origin.
Concludes that "the plays . . . are one of the
most assuredly popular forms of literataure to
survive from the Middle Ages" (104).

884. ---. "The Staging of Medieval English Plays." In
Medieval Drama . . . (forthcoming). Ed. by
Eckehard Simon (see entry # 1469 below).

885. ---. "Teaching Medieval Drama as Theatre." In *The
Learned and the Lewed: Studies in Chaucer and
Medieval Literature*, 305-18. Ed. by Larry D.
Benson. Cambridge: Harvard U. Press, 1974.

Uses the N-Town "Assumption of the Virgin" as "a
model approach to the teaching of all medieval
drama" (318).

885a. ---. "The Texts of Religious Drama: Collections of
Anthologies." In *Early Drama to 1600*. Ed. by
Albert H. Tricomi. (See entry # 1589b below.)

886. ---. *Traditions of Medieval English Drama*. London:
Hutchinson U. Library; Pittsburgh: U. of
Pittsburgh Press, 1974.

Presents "a set of model approaches to the drama
of England in the fifteenth and sixteenth
centuries" (10). Chap. 1, "Locating the Plays in
Space and Time," looks at the social conditions in
England which spawned and supported the plays;
establishes "the texts of the surviving plays as
firmly as possible in their appropriate locales,
and determin[es] as accurately as possible at what
point in time they came into being" (19).
Establishes the dates of the plays in the four
extant complete cycles. Examines the "geological
school of criticism" which sees the cycles as
being composed over a long period of time, the
earlier plays being inferior dramatically to the
later. Looks at the geographical locations of the
plays.

Chap. 2, "The Major Theatrical Traditions,"
considers the "two well-developed theatrical
traditions" (27) available to the fifteenth-

century playwrights: the continental Latin
cathedral plays of the High Middle Ages, and the
vernacular plays like the *Jeu d'Adam* and the
Seinte Resurreccion. Considers stage directions,
costumes, staging, actors, sizes of the stages,
the repertoire of the liturgical celebration and
its relation to the Corpus Christi plays, the "new
dramatic impulse" (41) created by the institution
of the Corpus Christi feast in 1311, the
establishment of English celebrations of this
feast, the statutes regulating the procession, the
frequency of performance, the parallel tradition
in Barcelona, Spain, and the two basic types of
presentation (station-to-station and place-and-
scaffold).

Chap. 3, "Dramatic Possibilities," examines the
quality of the plays as drama. Aims at
"establishing standards by which we may judge the
effectiveness of the cycle plays written for
pageant wagon stages" (57) and for place-and-
scaffold plays. Shows how the place-and-scaffold
staging allows for "certain theological
connections" (67); examines at length the N-Town
Passion play in this regard. Concludes that
"Determining the relative excellence of a
particular medieval play requires, then,
consideration of the adaptation made to the
theatre for which the play was written" (70).

Chap. 4, "Character and Verisimilitude," treats
the realistic detail of medieval English drama,
pointing out that the term "realistic" is not
generally used "to describe the physical settings
for the plays . . . . Rather the term 'realism'
is most often used to describe the comic or
violent elements" (72). Examines the notions of
realism and verisimilitude. Assesses the
strengths and weaknesses of character portrayal in
the plays against the background of the
dramatists' ends with respect to realistic
details. Deals with "the conflict between deep
religious feeling and the verisimilitude of
satire" (75) in the plays; examines the N-Town
Trial of Joseph and Mary in this regard, finding
that in this play there is no such conflict, but
rather a wide range of comic and serious
characters, all realistically portrayed. "The
reality consists of the eternal verities of human
existence" (82). Shows that the portrayal of
brutality "is necessary to the theme and structure
of the plays" (84). Examines the Wakefield
Buffeting and the York *Crucifixion* in this regard.
Points out that the verisimilitude in the plays is

"typical of the cultural life of the late Middle
Ages" (97). Concludes with a focus on the
specifics of this world, consonant with the
artistic movement of the fifteenth and sixteenth
centuries; hence, "The appearance of
verisimilitude . . . in the cycle drama cannot
. . . be noted as a particular virtue" of the
plays, "nor is the presence or absence of
verisimilitude an index of the playwright's skill.
Rather . . . it is the use to which the playwright
puts that verisimilitude . . . that should be of
interest" (97-98).

Chap. 5, "Morality and Farce," turns from civic
religious drama to other major forms of medieval
English drama. Distinguishes between civic
(amateur) and travelling (professional) troupes
and their plays. Draws heavily on Glynne
Wickham's discussion (in *Early English Stages*, I,
262-73; see entry # 1688 below) of the rise of
professional acting companies. Deals with
terminology (*mimi, ministralli, histriones,
lusores, ludatores*), interludes, repertory,
morality plays, allegory, costumes, the tradition
of penitential literature, the plays which
"universalize the patterns of moral choice in
man's life" (110), stage conventions in these
plays, language, the scatology of the plays, and
humor.

Chap. 6, "Of History and Time," points out that
medieval drama did not die of its own senescence,
but "was systematically put down by Elizabeth's
reforming bishops" (152, n. 1), and was "still
part of [the] normal experience" (121) of the new
dramatists in the sixteenth century. Treats John
Rastell as a case in point. Treats also the shift
away from medieval to Renaissance drama, which
still retains its focus on history. (Chap. 6 rpt.
in *Medieval English Drama: A Casebook*, 117-29.
Ed. by Peter Happé. See entry # 684 above.)

Rev. W. Temple, *Drama* 115 (Winter 1974): 82-84.
    TLS (Nov. 1, 1974): 1232.
    Clifford Davidson, *CompD* 9.3 (Fall 1975):
        269-72.
    Choice 12 (Dec. 1975): 1308.
    E. Catherine Dunn, *ELN* 13.4 (June 1976): 294-
        96.
    ChHist 45 (Sept. 1976): 378.
    Bills, Bing D., *ETJ* 28 (Dec. 1976): 568-70.
    E. Catherine Dunn, "Recent Medieval Theater
        Research . . .," *Allegorica* 2.1 (Spring
        1977): 183-93 (entry # 487 above).

887. ---. "What We Do Not Find in Chambers." *SoTh* 22
       (1979): 11-16.

       Challenges the universal applicability suggested
       in Chambers's chapters 21 and 22, in which
       Chambers suggests that there is "a norm with
       exceptions" (Kahrl's words, 11). Points out that
       no single description of the plays will hold for
       all cycles or all other dramatic performances.
       Shows how some of Chambers's notions were
       misleading. Calls for assistance in the editing
       of dramatic records--describing the efforts of the
       REED project.

888. Kantrowitz, Joanne Spencer. *Dramatic Allegory:*
       Lindsay's 'Ane Satyre of the Thrie Estaitis.'
       Lincoln, Nebraska: U. of Nebraska Press, 1975.
       166 pp.

       Contains chapters on Date, History, Theme,
       Allegory, Drama, and "The Morality Reconsidered."
       With appendix of letter by Sir William Eure (147-
       51) containing "notes on an interlude presented at
       the royal court in Linlithgow . . . 1540." With
       bibliography and index. (Part of one chapter on
       "Allegory" rpt. in *Medieval English Drama: A*
       Casebook, 144-51. Ed. by Peter Happé (see entry #
       684 above).

       Rev. Matthew P. McDiarmid, *ThRI* 2.2 (Feb. 1977):
             145-47.
       Derek Pearsall, *RenQ* 31 (Spring 1978): 90-92.

889. ---. "Dramatic Allegory, or, Exploring the Moral
       Play." *CompD* 7.1 (Spring 1973): 68-82.

       A general examination of the morality genre as
       dramatic allegory; looks at the plays as basically
       not mimetic but didactic.

890. ---. "Encore: Lindsay's *Thrie Estaitis*, Date and New
       Evidence." *SSL* 10 (1972): 18-32.

       Shows how an accurate dating will affect the
       interpretation of the play. Reviews scholarship.
       Concludes that it is likely that the first
       performance of the play was June 7, 1552.

891. Kaplan, Joel H. "The Medieval Origins of Elizabethan
       Comedy: Review Article." *RenD*, n.s. 5 (1974, for
       1972): 225.

       Reviews three books: Willard Farnham's *The*
       Shakespearean Grotesque (Oxford: Clarendon Press,

1971); Sylvia D. Feldman's *The Morality-Patterned Comedy of the Renaissance* (see entry # 546 above); and Alan C. Dessen's *Jonson's Moral Comedy* (Evanston, IL: Northwestern U. Press, 1971). Discusses medieval origins.

892. Keane, Ruth M.   "Kingship in the Chester Nativity Play." *LSE* 13 (1982): 74-84.

Compares the Chester version of the Nativity with the brief one in York and the Mary-centered one in *Ludus Coventriae*. Aims to show "Chester's unique dramatic principles and themes, especially that of kingship" (75), and to point out how the nativity "is only one element in a complex dramatic structure" (75). Assesses the role of the principal character: Octavian. Looks at thematic links among the four sections of the play, especially the themes of faith, humility, and kingship. Shows how the playwright opposes and parallels the Jewish and Gentile worlds in the Judean and Roman scenes.

893. ---. "The Theme of Kingship in the Chester Cycle." M.A. thesis, U. of Liverpool, 1977.

894. Keen, Maurice H. *The Outlaws of Medieval Legend*. London: Routledge and Kegan Paul; Toronto: U. of Toronto Press, 1961. xi, 235 pp.

Contains much information on Robin Hood: in literature, his historicity, the legends.

Rev. *History* 47 (1962): 299.
  SocSR 46 (1962): 362.
  Specu 37 (1962): 442.
  EHR 78 (1963): 155.

895. Keilstrup, Lorraine Margaret. "The Myth of Cain in the Early English Drama." Ph.D. diss., U. of Nebraska, Lincoln, 1974.

896. Kelley, Michael Robert. "*The Castle of Perseverance:* A Critical Reassessment." Ph.D. diss., Catholic U. of America, 1970.

897. ---. "Fifteenth-Century Flamboyant Style and *The Castle of Perseverance*." *CompD* 6.1 (Spring 1972): 14-27.

Traces the style and examines *The Castle* in light of the style's features. Claims "that the

morality play genre . . . is a result of the
flamboyant stylistic process" (14). Outlines the
style, pointing up its amalgamation of "ornamental
use of the plain style of direct realistic
description" and "those rhetorical devices
appropriate to the ornate grand or high style"
(17). Calls the morality play "a totally natural
extension and culmination of flamboyant dualism"
(17). Emphasizes the popular appeal elicited by
this style.

898.   ---.   *Flamboyant Drama: A Study of* The Castle of
Perseverance, Mankind, *and* Wisdom.   Foreword by
John Gardner.   Carbondale: Southern Illinois U.
Press; London and Amsterdam: Feffer and Simons,
1979.   xiv, 162 pp.

Points out the "controlling aesthetic" (ix) of the
Macro plays and explains their contemporary
popularity.   Explains their entertainment value.
Aims not to do literary scholarship (i.e. to
reveal facts about the plays), but to do literary
criticism (i.e. to evaluate the plays as art).
Chap. 1 discusses the innocence/fall/redemption
elements of the plays.   Places the ms in its
historical context.   Chap. 2 examines *The Castle*;
looks at the play's stylistic flamboyance (32
ff.); treats costumes, realism, stage plan, music,
props, verse, symmetrical pattern, appeal to its
audience, plot, and its overall "ornate theatrical
spectacle" (62).

Chap. 3 is on *Mankind*'s seemingly disorganized
texture--"characterization, comedy, stage
business, bawdy language, social commentary" (64).
Points out its organized design, diction, realism,
action, sermon elements, "allegorical and
semifictional characters" (76), fiction and
doctrine, production requirements (sets, costume,
props . . .), organizing principle (the sermon)--
and the aesthetic pleasure all these afford.
Concludes that the play is "a flamboyantly
illustrated sermon" with a "consistency of design"
(93).   Chap. 4 is on *Wisdom*--calls the play
"neither a drama nor a dramatization" (94).
Considers characterization, "flamboyant spectacle"
(95), diction, rhetoric, verse, "perceptual
realism" (101) and "concrete immediacy" (103),
symbolism, genre ("a particularized masque"--105),
number symbolism, and the play's design and
"mathematical symmetry" (118).   Concludes that the

play "may fail as drama in the usual sense" but it "succeeds as flamboyant celebration" (118).

Chap. 5--"Art as Design" (119)--discusses the artistic elements in the plays: music, song, poetry, costumes, props, stage action. Calls the three plays "admittedly minor works" (119) since "each falls short of greatness . . . because its characters are presentational rather than representational, the actions they perform are schematic rather than exploratory," and the characters' "message is narrowly doctrinal rather than humanly universal" (120). Concludes that the plays present many "surfaces for contemplation" (128) and are pleasing as dramatic spectacles.

Rev. *Choice* 16 (Feb. 1980): 1581.
   D.C. Baker, *ELN* 17.3 (Mar. 1980): 208-09.
   EDAMN 3.1 (Nov. 1980): 11-12.
   David Staines, *CompD* 15.1 (Spring 1981): 82-84.
   Theresa Coletti, *CompD* 16.2 (Summer 1982): 184-88.

899.   Kelly, Ellin M. "The 'Days of Creation' in Medieval English Mystery Cycles: Hints for Staging from Bible Manuscript Illuminations." *ABR* 30.3 (Sept. 1979): 264-80.

Speculates on staging practices by observing pictorial representations in Bible illuminations. Looks at works of creation, the creation of man, and the use of "Disks" (278). Claims that the Bible depictions "may well be an instance of the illuminators' art influencing the plays" inasmuch as the playwrights "had ready access to the miniatures in the illuminated Bibles" (280).

900.   Kelly, Ellin Margaret. "The *Ludus Coventriae* Old Testament Plays: Their Structure and Function." Ph.D. diss., U. of Wisconsin, 1970.

901.   ---. "'Ludus Coventriae' Play 4 and the Egerton 'Genesis.'" *N&Q* 19.12 (217) (Dec. 1972): 443-44.

Looks at the placement of the death of Cain episode in the Noah play. Claims that the scene is so placed to permit "the Noah family to leave the acting area and to return in the boat for the second part" (443) of the play; the placement also "suggests the time lapse between God's command to build the ark and the flood; and places the cause, Cain's death, immediately before the effect, the

flood" (443). Looks at sources and analogues.
Sees an analogue in the Egerton Genesis (BM MS
Egerton 1894), which "provides an interesting
visual parallel" (444) for the *Ludus Coventriae*
play.

902. Kelly, Henry Ansgar. *The Devil at Baptism: Ritual,
Theology, and Drama.* Ithaca and London: Cornell
U. Press, 1985. 301 pp.

Does not cover English drama specifically, but
talks about these phenomena in dramatic history,
ritual, and theology. Offers thus a broad
background with which to look at English medieval
plays. With bibliography and index.

Rev. *ChrCnt* 103 (May 21, 1986): 525.
ChHist 55 (June 1986): 219.
TheoStud 47 (Dec. 1986): 711.
RSR 13 (Jan. 1987): 52.
CHR 73 (Apr. 1987): 268.
JRel 67 (Oct. 1987): 601.
C.W. Marx, *MedAe* 57.1 (1988): 82-83.

903. Keyishian, Harry, comp. "A Checklist of Medieval and
Renaissasnce Plays (Excluding Shakespeare) on
Film, Tape, and Recording." *RORD* 17 (1974): 45-
58.

Lists plays and cycles alphabetically by author,
when known, or by title. With many entries for
medieval English drama.

904. Kikata, Yosuke. *Eikoku-geki no naedoko--Iago no
Sosen.* Kyoto: Aporonsha, 1968. (The Nursery
[Seed Bed] of English Drama--Iago's Ancestors.)

Chap. 1 covers ethnic customs and folkloric
festivals and plays by seasons; spring plays
(mummers' plays; St. George plays; Plough Monday
plays; Sword Dances; Hock Tuesday plays; drama as
entertainment or spring play); winter and new year
festivals (campfire festivals; festivals to avoid
demons; events to bring good luck; feast of fools;
boy bishop; Société Joyeuse; Christmas in court).
Chap. 2 deals with masques and pageants,
entertainments, welcomings of noble guests, St.
George Riding, midsummer shows, Lord Mayor's
shows. Chap. 3 covers the life of medieval actors
and their dramatic art. Summarizes different
kinds of plays. Looks at dialogue, "Harrowing of
Hell," farce, "Interludium de Clerico et Puella,"
Robin Hood plays, puppet plays, Commedia dell'arte
of Italy, and Punch and Judy plays. Gives

excerpts and specimens from several plays.
Discusses medieval sources of Iago--works which
influenced Iago's dialogue.

905. King, Pamela, and Jackie Wright. "Rex Vivus at
Southwark Cathedral." MET 4.1 (July 1982): 61-63.

Review of a performance of Dec. 12, 1981.

906. ---, and Jacqueline Wright. "*Mankind* at York." *MET*
3.1 (July 1981): 58-60.

Reports on a performance in England of May 4,
1981, by the *Poculi Ludique Societas* of Toronto.

907. Kinneavy, Gerald Byron. *A Concordance to* The York
Plays. New York: Garland, 1986. xxxviii, 936 pp.

Contains a complete line concordance, with a
textual introduction by Richard Beadle (entry #
154 above). Also contains the text of *The
Creation of Adam and Eve*, the play duplicated in
the ms (designated IIIB; IIIA is concorded),
corrections to the Beadle edition of the York
plays (see item # 9 above), and several other
sections: ranking frequency list, reverse index
of forms, index of hyphenated forms, a KWIK
concordance to the York play 30 (*Christ Before
Pilate*), ranking frequency list for play 30, and
reverse index of forms for the same play.

Rev. *Choice* 24 (Feb. 1987): 864.
ABRA 19 (1988): 483.
Specu 63 (Apr. 1988): 493.

908. Kipling, Gordon. "'Grace in this Lyf and Aftirwarde
Glorie': Margaret of Anjou's Royal Entry into
London." *RORD* 29 (1986-87): 77-84.

Discusses the use of "the liturgical imagery of
Advent" (77) in the civic triumph, and shows how
the pageant for a queen differed from that of a
king. Examines Margaret's entry in detail.

909. ---. "The London Pageants for Margaret of Anjou: A
Medieval Script Restored." *MET* 4.1 (1982): 5-27.

Discusses royal entry pageantry in England and
their differences from continental approaches in
performance. Claims that the English emphasis on
acting--as opposed to the continental one on the
pageants as related to the static arts (especially
painting)--"played a decisive role in the
development of the English civic triumph" (6).

Analyzes the 1445 performance for the reception of
Margaret of Anjou, showing how the devisers of the
performance "provided their actors for the first
time with a complete series of mimed speeches. In
doing so, they established a fashion for scripted
civic triumphs in England which endured . . .
throughout the next two centuries" (6). Considers
sources; denies Lydgate's authorship, thus
restoring these verses to "their proper context in
the history of the medieval English theatre" (13).
Points out that the verses are "a successful
experimental script . . . the journeyman work of
one or more civic pageant devisers" (13).
Restores some of the script by explaining scribal
errors. Explains the nature of the transcription
of the ms and establishes the text of the original
script. Offers an edited text (19-23) with
textual notes (23-24).

910.   ---.   "Richard II's 'Sumptuous Pageants' and the Idea
of Civic Triumph." In *Pageantry in the
Shakespearean Theatre*, 83-103. Ed. by David M.
Bergeron. Athens: U. of Georgia Press, 1985.

Discusses the pageantry in Richard's day with
respect to drama and ritual.

911.   ---.   *The Triumph of Honour: Burgundian Origins of the
Elizabethan Renaissance*. The Hague: Leiden U.
Press, 1977. Published for the Sir Thomas Browne
Institute. 188 pp.

Discusses "England's adoption of Burgundian
culture" (3). Glances at the effect on drama (see
reference to Medwall, 21-22) and at civic
pageantry (see especially Chap. 4, "The Triumph of
Honour," 72-95). Focuses on "Burgundian Pageants
and Tudor Disguisings" (Chap. 5, 96-115) and on
"Burgundian Pageants and Tudor Chivalry" (Chap. 6,
116-36). Also looks at other courtly writers.
With an appendix on "William Cornish, John
English, and the Disguisings of 1501" (175-77) and
an index.

Rev. F. Yates, *TLS* (June 23, 1978): 696.
     H. Smith, *JEGP* 78 (Jan. 1979): 114.
     E. Jones, *N&Q* 26 (Apr. 1979): 185-87.
     J. Grundy, *RES*, n.s. 30 (May 1979): 211-13.
     R. Strong, *RenQ* 32 (Summer 1979): 211-14.
     R.R. Griffith, *JLH* 15 (Winter 1980): 101.
     D. Norbrook, *EHR* 96 (Jan. 1981): 210.
     MLR 76 (Oct. 1981): 925.

912. ---. "Triumphal Drama: Form in English Civic
Pageantry." In *Renaissance Drama. New Series
VIII: The Celebratory Mode*, 37-56. Ed. by Leonard
Barkin. Evanston: Northwestern U. Press, 1977.

Shows how London produced civic triumphs while
York, Chester, and Coventry expanded their
traditional religious pageants. Examines these
triumphs of different kinds--their characters,
form, themes, arrangements, aims, etc.

913. Kirby, E.T. "Malin's 'Doubled Figures' and Free's
'Greek/Kutiyattam.'" *ThJ* 33.3 (Oct. 1981): 386-
87.

Response to Stephen D. Malin's "Four Doubled
Figures in the Origins of English Folk Theatre"
(*ThJ* 33.1 [Mar. 1981]: 18-33). (See entry # 1052
below.)

914. ---. "Mummers' Plays and the Calendar." *JAF* 86 (341)
(July-Sept. 1973): 282-85. [See Cawte, "Even
More," entry # 290 above, which comments on
Kirby's "The Origin . . .," see next entry.]

Answers Cawte's comments about Kirby's "theory of
the origin of the mummers' play" (282). Claims
that "the performances are meaningfully related to
the seasonal calendar" (282).

915. ---. "The Origin of the Mummers' Play." *JAF* 84
(July-Sept. 1971): 275-88. [See Cawte, "More,"
entry # 291 above.]

Reviews criticism of the play. Focuses on
mummers' plays with respect to hobby-horse dances
and enactments. Shows their origin in shamanism
which aims at trances or curing. Aims to prove
that "these performances were not . . . seasonal"
(276), that their combat "was not a Combat of the
Seasons nor any variant thereof" (276), and that
they are not connected with Death/Resurrection or
fertility rites.

916. Klausner, David. [Reseach in Progress.] *REEDN* 4.1
(1979): 20-24.

Discusses work on documents of Hereford that seem
to show "a limited tradition of drama which . . .
ceased to be a living force in the community in
the mid-sixteenth century" (20).

917. Klawitter, George. "Dramatic Elements in Early
     Monastic Induction Ceremonies." *CompD* 15.3 (Fall
     1981): 213-30.

     Valuable insofar as it sheds light on the
     religious precursors to the *Quem quaeritis* trope
     and the introduction of dramatic elements into
     Christian service. Concentrates on early medieval
     continental dramatic elements.

918. Klein, David. *Milestones to Shakespeare: A Study of
     the Dramatic Forms and Pageantry that Were the
     Prelude to Shakespeare.* New York: Twayne, 1970.
     126 pp.

     Contains chapters on Bible plays and School Drama.
     Very briefly discusses mystery, morality, and
     miracle plays and liturgical drama.

     Rev. *Choice* 8 (July 1971): 676.

919. Knaub, R.K. [Review.] *Lancaster Comment*, 17 March
     1977. Cited by Sheila Lindenbaum, *RORD* 20 (1977):
     99.

     Reviews performances of *The Resurrection of
     Christ*, March 9-11, 1977, at Nuffield Theatre
     Studio, Lancaster University, Lancaster, England.

920. Knight, Alan E. "From the Sacred to the Profane."
     Tréteaux 1 (1978): 41-49.

     Discusses sacred and profane elements in the cycle
     plays--e.g. the use of farce, the mythical past,
     heaven versus hell. Points out that in the middle
     ages the sacred and the profane were not
     necessarily "two distinct and opposing realms"
     (44). Does not focus on specific English plays.

921. Knight, W. Nicholas. "Equity and Mercy in English Law
     and Drama (1405-1641)." *CompD* 6.1 (Spring 1972):
     51-67.

     Looks at legal development of equity ("that which
     legally recognizes the exception to the law in the
     name of higher or natural justice"--51). Examines
     The Castle of Perseverance as "the archetype of
     the English play that concludes with civil law
     proceedings" (53-54). Also looks briefly at
     Mankind (56) and at Renaissance plays. Concludes
     that "the theatre borrowed the legal concept of
     equity to structurally resolve plot situations by
     introducing a higher, but more arbitrary, system
     of law" (66).

922. Knowles, Richard Paul. [Untitled review.] *RORD* 24
          (1981): 193-94.

          Reviews performances of *Mankind*, February 19-21,
          1981, at Windsor Theatre, Mount Allison
          University, Sackville, New Brunswick.

923. ---. [Untitled review.] *RORD* 25 (1982): 149-50.

          Reviews performance of the N-Town *The Woman Taken
          in Adultery*, December 6-8, 1982, at Windsor
          Theatre, Mount Allison University, Sackville, New
          Brunswick.

924. Könneker, Barbara. "Die Moralität 'The Somonynge of
          Every-man' und das Münchner Spiel vom Sterbenden
          Menschen." In *Virtus et Fortuna: zur deutschen
          Literatur zwischen 1400 und 1720. Festschrift für
          Hans-Gert Roloff zu seinem 50. Geburtstag*, 91-105.
          Ed. by Joseph P. Strelka and Jörg Jungmayr. Bern,
          Frankfurt/M. and New York: Peter Lang, 1983.

          Mentions English drama only as a contrast to the
          German for which it serves as an *apologia*.
          Compares *Everyman* with the Munich play "The
          Dying/Mortal Man/Human"; aims to show that the
          morality play was not the only type of drama in
          the middle ages. Says that other types had
          greater influence on the sixteenth-century
          Protestant theater. Looks at the characters in
          Everyman as generic types whose clothing and
          demeanor carry primary meaning while the words
          they speak are only secondary (in contrast to the
          practices in the Renaissance drama). Claims that
          the morality play's aim was to support the
          medieval church's theological position on the
          activity of God in human life via the sacraments.
          Shows how the German and the English plays differ,
          and examines the plays at length.

925. Kolin, Philip C. "A Bibliography of Scholarship on
          Henry Medwall." *RORD* 22 (1979): 65-72.

          Contains 105 citations, including editions and
          criticism.

926. ---. "The Elizabethan Stage Doctor as a Dramatic
          Convention." Ph.D. diss., Northwestern U., 1973.

          [Considers folk, cycle, and morality plays.]

927. Kolve, V.A. "*Everyman* and the Parable of the
          Talents." In *The Medieval Drama*, 69-98. Ed. by
          Sandro Sticca (see entry # 1541 below). Rpt. in

Jerome Taylor and Alan H. Nelson, eds. *Medieval English Drama . . .*, 316-40 (see entry # 1573 below).

Focuses on sources of *Everyman* with special reference to the play's account-book vocabulary (lending, reckoning, account-making, spending). Explains the play as being influenced by the Parable of the Talents and other biblical references to talents which were loaned or placed in trust. Considers betrayals and desertions, the pilgrimage elements, the play's dual time scheme, the character and function of Good Deeds--all with relation to the Parable of the Talents. Demonstrates that the subject matter of *Everyman* "was elsewhere and in important places conceived in terms of the parable of the talents" (88).

928. Konigson, Elie. *L'Espace Théâtral Médiéval*. Paris: Éditions du Centre National de la Recherche Scientifique, 1975.

Focuses on French medieval dramatic stages and sets, as they evolved from parts of the (Catholic) church building into independent entities. Not on English drama, but may serve as a parallel study.

Rev. L.R. Muir, *MLR* 72 (Oct. 1977): 938-39.
      A.M. Nagler, *ThRI* 3.1 (Oct. 1977): 67-69.
      A.H. Nelson, *Specu* 53 (Apr. 1978): 393-95.

929. Koontz, Christian, R.S.M. "The Duality of Styles in the Morality Play *Wisdom Who Is Christ*: A Classical-Rhetorical Analysis." *Style* 73 (Fall 1973): 251-70.

Analyzes two sections of the play (ll. 1-165; 793-892) to show that the play belongs to the flamboyant tradition of literature "inherited from the French through Chaucer" (251). Shows that the comparison "reveals that aureation is part of the static style of the Gothic tradition and alien to the dynamic style of the bourgeois" (251). Also shows how the spiritual message is revealed through this style. Concludes by explaining how the play "unites the comic and the serious" (267), resulting "in total meaning" (268).

930. ---. "A Stylistic Analysis of the Morality Play *Wisdom Who is Christ*." Ph.D. diss., Catholic U., 1971.

931. Kossick, Shirley. "The Morality Play: *Everyman*." *Comm* 5.1 (1980): 32-39.

Looks briefly at the origins of the genre ("roots in medieval pulpit literature and the religious interlude"--32), along with influences from the fabliau, the folk play, and the miracle and mystery plays. Summarizes the play with brief commentary.

932. Kroll, Norma. "Christ: Center and Circumference of the Corpus Christi Cycles." Ph.D. diss., Brown U., 1971.

933. ---. "Cosmic Characters and Human Form: Dramatic Interaction and Conflict in the Chester Cycle 'Fall of Lucifer.'" *M&RD* 2 (1985): 33-50.

Addresses "the ways in which the dramatists transform Christian doctrine and history from sets of principles and sequences of acts into networks of interaction" (33). Shows how the Chester God's body images are manipulated so that He is humanized (along with the angels) "so that they can engage in . . . moral and emotional interactions essential to . . . dramatic conflicts" (33). Examines the play's language and unusual handling of conventional material.

934. Kroupa, Susan. "Middle English Doesn't Obscure Meanings of Plays." Bloomington, Indiana, *Herald Telephone* [sic], May 20, 1985.

Reviews performances of the Towneley *Annunciation* and *Salutation* of May 19, 1985, at Indiana University at Bloomington.

935. Laine, Amos Lee. "John Rastell: An Active Citizen of the English Commonwealth." Ph.D. diss., Duke U., 1972.

936. Laird, Shirley Dale. "Scenes of Judgment in the Chester Cycle." Ph.D. diss., Auburn U., 1976.

937. Lake, James Hammond, Jr. "The Influence of the Old Testament Upon the Early Drama of the English Renaissance." Ph.D. diss., U. of Delaware, 1969.

937a. Lampes, David. "The Magi and Modes of Meaning: *The Second Shepherds' Play* as an Index of the Criticism of Medieval Drama." In *Early Drama to 1600*. Ed. by Albert H. Tricomi. (See entry # 1589b below.)

938. Lancashire, Anne. "Chaucer and the Sacrifice of Isaac." *ChauR* 9.4 (Spring 1975): 320-26.

Claims that the medieval cycle play influenced
Chaucer in his story of child-sacrifice in the
Physician's Tale.

939.   ---.   "Correction."   *REEDN* 6.2 (1981): 13.

Corrects an earlier entry cited in her report (in
REEDN 3.2 [1978]: 1-7; 7-9; see next entry) of the
London craft guild records. Clarifies one
reading.

940.   ---.   "Research in Progress: London Craft Guild
Records"; with "Other London Records."   *REEDN* 3.2
(1978): 1-7; 7-9.

Discusses editing of pre-1642 records of 92 London
craft guilds--getting to the records, getting
permission to study and/or photocopy them, the
extent of the material, weeding through it all.
Lists the kinds of records available (court minute
books, account books, ordinances, charters, etc.--
over forty types). Mentions the great research
potential of these records. Recounts her own
efforts and some of her findings. (See previous
entry.)

941.   ---.   "Players for the London Cutlers' Company."
REEDN 6.2 (1981): 10-11.

Points out that the 36 surviving London Cutlers'
company rolls all mention payment to players at a
"cony feast." (See next entry.)

942.   ---.   "Plays for the London Blacksmiths' Company."
REEDN 6.1 (1981): 12-14.

Analyzes London Blacksmith Guild records which
seem to indicate a long tradition of annual and
then biennial drama in which the players are
compensated partly from "gate receipts." Points
out that the blacksmiths in these plays at the
cony feast "may have provided both a regular
audience and a regular source of income for
working actors" (13). (See previous entry.)

943.   Lancashire, Ian.   "Annotated Bibliography of Printed
Records of Early British Drama and Minstrelsy for
1978-9."   *REEDN* 5.1 (1980): 1-34.

Contains 257 items with brief annotations; some
entries not on medieval drama. Focuses on records
of performers and performance. [This and the
following four entries are rich sources of
bibliographical information.]

944.   ---.   "Annotated Bibliography of Printed Records of
       Early British Drama and Minstrelsy for 1980-81."
       REEDN 7.1 (1982): 1-40.

       Contains 259 items with brief annotations; some
       items not on medieval drama. Focuses mostly on
       "documentation or material records of performers
       and performance" (1).

945.   ---.   "Annotated Bibliography of Printed Records of
       Early British Drama and Minstrelsy for 1982-83."
       REEDN 9.2 (1984): 1-56.

       Lists 316 items--most annotated--with a brief
       introduction discussing five areas of scholarship:
       London theaters, general theater history,
       provincial drama, court revels from Edward IV to
       Charles I, and biography of players and patrons.
       Contains many items beyond the scope of the
       present bibliography.

946.   ---.   "Bibliographer's Report."   *REEDN* 1.2 (1976): 11-
       15.

       Explains that a Location and Patron List "with
       known dramatic, minstrel, and ceremonial records
       to 1642 is in progress" (11). Discusses
       bibliographical aids to scholarship on dramatic
       records. Gives an annotated list of recent
       records and articles of special interest (some of
       Renaissance interest). Also mentions work in
       progress. Contains many Renaissance entries.

947.   ---.   "Bibliography of Printed Records of Early
       British Drama and Minstrelsy for 1976-7."   *REEDN*
       3.1 (1978): 5-17.

       Lists 111 items "published after 1975 [concerning]
       records of performers and performance" (5), mostly
       annotated. Contains many Renaissance items.

948.   ---.   "The Corpus Christi Play of Tamworth."   *N&Q* 26.6
       (224) (Dec. 1979): 508-12.

       Describes the play from contemporary records.
       Says it "may have been a Doomsday play, perhaps
       from a longer cycle" (510). Shows how the play is
       appropriate to Tamworth. Transcribes three
       excerpts from the source documents.

949.   ---.   *Dramatic Texts and Records of Britain: A
       Chronological Topography to 1558*. Toronto and
       Buffalo: U. of Toronto Press, 1984. Studies in

244

Early English Drama, 1. Gen. ed. J.A.B. Somerset.
lxvi, 633 pp.

Contains 1,810 entries for the British Isles,
offering dates or chronological limits, names of
texts or records of "a dramatic representation or
show, a playing place, a playwright, visits of
acting troupes, an official act of control over
playing, or other evidence relating to plays and
their production" (ix). Gives bibliographical
citations to reliable published editions or
records to ms sources. Contains illustrations and
maps, appendixes, index of playing companies,
index of playwrights, index of playing places and
buildings, a chronological list of "Salient Dates
and Entry Numbers" (461), and a general subject
and name index. Introduction (ix-xlii) explains
form and scope of volume and offers much
historical data; suggests "areas for further
research" (xxxi-xxxiii); discusses dating
(xxxiii). Aims to "gather scattered materials
together from our best sources . . . about theatre
history . . . from government publications . . .
and from . . . the most useful product of British
historical scholarship" (xxxvii).

Rev. *Choice* 22 (Sept. 1984): 65.
   ARBA 16 (1985): 459.
   BBN (Feb. 1985): 73.
   Gail McMurray Gibson, *StudAC* 8 (1986): 215-
      19.
   JEGP 85 (Jan. 1986): 106.
   RES 37 (May 1986): 238.
   William Tydeman, *ThRI* 11.2 (Summer 1986):
      154-57.
   David Bevington, *CompD* 21.1 (Spring 1987):
      84-86.

950. ---. "History of a Transition: Review Article." *M&RD*
      3 (1986): 277-88.

      Reviews *The* Revels *History of Drama in English.
      Vol. II: 1500-1576.* (See entry # 1432 below.)

951. ---. "'Ioly Walte and Malkyng': A Grimsby Puppet Play
      in 1431." *REEDN* 4.2 (1979): 6-8.

      Discusses the puppet play which seems to be
      related to *Interludium de Clerico et Puella* and to
      other works briefly mentioned. Speculates, on the
      basis of analogues, that the puppet play "was a
      straightforward comedy of seduction and clerical
      incontinence" (7).

952.   ---.   "Medieval Drama."   In *Editing Medieval Texts: English, French, and Latin Written in England*, 58-85.   Ed. by A.G. Rigg.   New York and London: Garland, 1977.   Papers Given at the 12th Annual Conference on Editorial Problems, University of Toronto, 5-6 November 1976.

Offers a brief history of scholarship, performance, and editions of the Corpus Christi plays.   Discusses the evolution of editorial practice on the plays.   Points out the three kinds of editions: facsimile editions, critical editions of full cycles or of whole mss, and clusters of plays.   Outlines what needs to be done, the tools that editors need (e.g. concordances, external records), some editorial policies to consider, some areas of expertise that editors need ("Philology, textual criticism, diplomatics, history, palaeography, literary explication, source studies . . . the techniques of book production" [77]).

953.   ---.   "N-Town Plays."   In *Dictionary of the Middle Ages* 9: 49-51.   Ed. by Joseph R. Strayer (see entry # 1553 below).

Gives brief overview; discusses background, banns, performance, composition of the cycle, etc.   With brief bibliography.

954.   ---.   "Orders for Twelfth Day and Night circa 1515 in the Second Northumberland Household Book."   *ELR* 10.1 (Winter 1980): 6-45.

Looks at a ms compiled between 1519 and 1527, with focus on entries concerning the drama--specifically Christmas revels in three parts: "a play followed by a masked dance during which a pageant and a morris dance revealed themselves" (19).   With a transcription of the pertinent entries with facsimiles and extensive notes (23-44).

955.   ---.   "Records of Drama and Minstrelsy in Nottinghamshire to 1642."   *REEDN* 2.2 (1977): 15-28.

Discusses the location of Nottinghamshire and says that it "appears not to have staged Corpus Christi plays" (16).   Claims, however, that it did have "dramatic activities" (16) similar to those in Lincolnshire.   Talks about these activities: "Spectacula," "ludi" (16), "itinerant companies" (21), and "local minstrels" (22), for example.

956.　---.　"Records of Early English Drama and the
　　　　　Computer."　*C&H* 12.1/2 (1978): 183-88.

　　　　　Discusses the computer system now used by REED;
　　　　　describes the data base for dramatic, minstrel,
　　　　　and ceremonial records of performance up to 1642.
　　　　　Shows that bibliography and indexes may be derived
　　　　　from this work.　Hopes to "stimulate editorial
　　　　　work" (188).

957.　---.　"REED Research Guide."　*REEDN* 1.1 (1976): 10-23.

　　　　　Presents a guide to those wishing to edit "records
　　　　　of dramatic, ceremonial, and minstrel activity in
　　　　　Great Britain" (10).　Lists the "activities" to be
　　　　　edited, including, among many others, the mystery
　　　　　cycles; the Creed, Pater Noster, and saints'
　　　　　plays; miracles; moralities; liturgical plays;
　　　　　mummings; etc.　Lists also the kinds of records to
　　　　　peruse:　legal instruments, administrative or
　　　　　ministerial proceedings, judicial proceedings, and
　　　　　miscellaneous records (with types of each
　　　　　detailed).　Points out the need for observing
　　　　　bibliography of printed materials; histories of
　　　　　drama and ceremonial; minstrel histories;
　　　　　publications on historical or antiquarian
　　　　　scholarship or records.　Gives advice about
　　　　　locating mss, visiting local record offices and
　　　　　private libraries, transcription, document
　　　　　description, dating, and editorial format.
　　　　　Contains a bibliography (18-23).

958.　---.　"The Sources of *Hyckescorner*."　*RES*, n.s. 22.87
　　　　　(Aug. 1971): 257-73.

　　　　　Discusses the priority of *Youth* over *Hyckescorner*,
　　　　　the latter influenced by "the pseudo-Lydgatean
　　　　　fifteenth-century allegorical poem, *The Assembly
　　　　　of Gods*" (259) and Chaucer's *Pardoner's Tale*, and
　　　　　not by *Youth*.

959.　Lane, Harry.　[Untitled review.]　*ETJ* 30.1 (Mar.
　　　　　1978): 102-06.

　　　　　Reviews performance of The York Cycle of Mystery
　　　　　Plays (a complete version by J.S. Purvis),
　　　　　performed by *Poculi Ludique Societas*, Oct. 1-2,
　　　　　1977, at the University of Toronto.

960.　Lane, Richard.　*Snap the Norwich Dragon*.　Norwich:
　　　　　Trend Litho Limited, 1976.　32 pp.

　　　　　Describes a dragon from a pageant:　"'the Mayor's
　　　　　dragon,' last of a pure line stretching back over

four hundred years" (5). Explains that the dragon
"was the central feature of a procession which
evolved from a religious pageant in honour of St.
George to a grand civic occasion on Guild Day
during which the new Mayor was sworn into office"
(5). Discusses the history of St. George's Guild
and the procession. With many illustrations.

961. Langdon, Harry N. "Staging of the Ascension in the
Chester Cycle." *ThN* 26.2 (Winter 1971/72): 53-60.

Discusses whether the ascension was accomplished
on stage by mechanical or by symbolic means. Says
the actors may have relied on "the audience's
acceptance of a symbolical representation of the
event" (53). Says also that the techniques for
staging may well have varied from play to play and
over time in any cycle. Looks at internal and
external evidence. Speculates on the use of
machines to raise the actors. Claims that in
England by the end of the fourteenth century there
were "machines to fly people" (56). (See response
by Clopper, "The Staging . . .," entry # 308
above.)

962. Lasater, Alice E. *Spain to England: A Comparative
Study of Arabic, European, and English Literature
of the Middle Ages.* Jackson, Mississippi: U.
Press of Mississippi, 1974. 230 pp.

Glances at English drama's metrics as an
"adaptation of Provençal poetic forms and devices"
(53) in the cycle plays. Looks mostly at stanza
forms. Also notes briefly the use of alliteration
and rhyme in the York plays (74-75).

Rev. *LJ* 100 (Feb. 1, 1975): 297.
   Choice 12 (Sept. 1975): 834.
   T.J. Garbáty, *Specu* 52 (Apr. 1977): 390-94.

963. Lascombes, André. "Rôle, type, masque: Structures et
fonctions du personnage populaire dans le théâtre
anglais du moyen age." In *Figures théâtrales du
peuple*, 15-27. Ed. by Elie Konigson. Paris:
Centre National de la Recherche Scientifique,
1985.

Sees in pre-1500 English drama the beginnings of
"popular culture"--i.e. a theater performed by and
for the greatest number of people, and judged
agreeable by the people. Says that the
"personnage populaire"--character with popular
appeal--is the key component in this theater.
Considers the typology, realization, and

relationship to the audience of the "personnage populaire."

964. Latz, Dorothy L. "L'expression corporelle dans
      quelques mystères anglais et français." In *Le
      Théâtre au Moyen Age,* Actes du deuxième colloque
      de la Société Internationale pour l'Étude du
      Théâtre Médiéval, Alençon, 11-14 juillet 1977, 19-
      44. Ed. by Gari R. Muller. Paris, Quebec:
      L'Aurore Univers, 1981.

      Looks at Chester, York, Wakefield, and Digby
      plays. Comments that the plays are "amplified" in
      the fifteenth and sixteenth centuries: more
      characters appear, and roles expand until the
      closing of theaters (1576) and final disappearance
      of the genre (1579-1604). Traces the process of
      amplification, especially with respect to the
      appearance of devils and angels, human traits
      attributed to Mary and to Christ, longer plays,
      and elaborate sets, costumes, music, and effects.
      Points out how the mystery plays became less
      dependent on biblical texts, more inventive.
      Elaborates on these areas of expansion. Concludes
      by mentioning the increasing emphasis on
      characterization, decreasing manifestations of
      divine power, and diminished emphasis on concepts
      or great ideas. Compares all this to French
      drama.

965. Laver, James. *Costume in the Theatre.* London: George
      G. Harrap, 1964. 223 pp.

      Chap. 3 "Mysteries, Miracles, and Moralities" (39-
      57) briefly discusses early costuming from
      liturgical performances through to morality plays.
      With illustrations.

966. ---. *Isabella's Triumph: May 31st, 1615.* London:
      Faber & Faber, 1947. 24 pp.

      Has color reproductions of pageant cars which are
      used in the Brussels "Triumph" for Archduchess
      Isabella, 1615, as painted by Denis van Alsloot,
      useful as a visual source of the presentation of
      pageants. With 12 plates.

967. Lawlor, John. "Problems of Adaptation from Middle
      English: The *Chester Plays* and *Piers Plowman.*" In
      *Expression, Communication and Experience in
      Literature and Language,* 280-82. Ed. by Ronald G.
      Popperwell. Proceedings of the XII Congress of
      the International Federation for Modern Languages
      and Literatures Held at Cambridge University, 20

to 26 August 1972. [London]: Modern Humanities
Research Association, 1973.

An abstract only of a paper presented at the
congress. Examines--for English drama--"adapting
a work already in dramatic form" (280). Considers
the problems such an adaptation presents, with
special focus on language, audience comprehension,
and boredom. Says that "the language of the
original is to be trusted" (282) and all the
resources of a modern theater are to be employed.

968. Lawrence, Natalie Grimes. "Quem Quaeritis." In *A
Chaucerian Puzzle and Other Medieval Essays*, 47-
61. Ed. by Natalie Grimes Lawrence and Jack A.
Reynolds. Coral Gables, Florida: U. of Miami
Press, 1961. U. of Miami Publications in English
and American Literature, No. V, Oct. 1961.

Sees the trope as at the root of medieval
liturgical drama. Offers a simple discussion of
the trope.

969. Leacroft, Richard. *The Development of the English
Playhouse: With Comparative Reconstructions*.
London: Eyre, Methuen, 1973. xiii, 354 pp.

Chap. 1--"Medieval Origins and Renaissance
Influences"--considers origins in church
performances, pageants, performances in mansions,
halls, the use of screens, staging, interludes and
masks, banqueting houses, and so on. Looks
briefly at pageants and Corpus Christi drama.

Rev. *B&B* 18 (Sept. 1973): 136.
Drama (Autumn 1973): 71.
Booklist 70 (Dec. 1, 1973): 362.
Booklist 70 (Dec. 1, 1973): 382.
Richard Southern, *ThN* 28.2 (1974): 92-94.
Choice 11 (Sept. 1974): 958.

970. ---, and Helen Leacroft. *Theatre and Playhouse: An
Illustrated Survey of Theatre Building from
Ancient Greece to the Present Day*. London and New
York: Methuen, 1984. 246 pp.

Examines pageants, processions, rounds, circles,
churches, scaffolds, mysteries. Not much
specifically on medieval English drama, but
contains much general information.

Rev. *Booklist* 81 (Jan. 1, 1985): 610.
BBN (Mar. 1985): 174.

　　　　　　　　Drama (Fall 1985): 53.
　　　　　　　　TLS (Sept. 6, 1985): 978.

971.　Lee, B.S.　"*Lucidus and Dubius:* A Fifteenth-Century
　　　　Theological Debate and Its Sources."　*MedAe* 45.1
　　　　(1976): 79-96.

　　　　Examines the *Elucidarium* as a source, from which
　　　　"Lucidus and Dubius is a free adaptation in verse
　　　　dialogue" (79).　Looks also at the *Cursor Mundi.*
　　　　Discusses the play in terms of its being a
　　　　morality.

972.　Lehrman, Walter David.　"Courtly Ritual: A Study of
　　　　the English Masque."　Ph.D. diss., Case Western
　　　　Reserve U., 1972.

973.　Leigh, David J.　"The Doomsday Mystery Play: An
　　　　Eschatological Morality."　*MP* 67 (1970): 211-23.
　　　　Rpt. in *Medieval English Drama*, 260-78.　Ed. by
　　　　Jerome Taylor and Alan H. Nelson (entry # 1573
　　　　below).

　　　　Considers the distinct features of the Last
　　　　Judgment play in the four English mystery cycles
　　　　that "mark the play off from all the others" (260)
　　　　in the cycles.　Looks at five distinctive
　　　　features:　nonhistorical setting, types of actions
　　　　that cannot be "taken in a literal representative
　　　　sense" (262), nonhistorical representation of
　　　　character, the relation of these plays to their
　　　　audience, and their "explicit narration of the
　　　　history of salvation" which makes them "relevant
　　　　to the present time" (266).　Shows how these five
　　　　features make the Doomsday plays different from
　　　　other plays in the cycle in subject matter,
　　　　structure, and dramatic techniques; also shows the
　　　　relation between these plays and early morality
　　　　plays, of which the Doomsday play may be a source.
　　　　Concludes with a summary of "The General Judgment
　　　　in Medieval Theology" (274-78).

xxx.　Lennam, Trevor, ed.　*Sebastian Westcott, The Children
　　　　of St. Pauls, and* the Marriage of Wit and Science.
　　　　(See entry # 53 above.)

974.　Leonard, Frances M.　"The School for Transformation: A
　　　　Theory of Middle English Comedy."　*Genre* 9.3 (Fall
　　　　1976): 179-91.

　　　　Discusses the generic notion of comedy with a
　　　　glance at the *First* and *Second Shepherds' Plays*
　　　　(189-90).

975. Leonard, Robert Joseph. "Patterns of Dramatic Unity
     in the N-Town Cycle." Ph.D. diss., State U. of
     New York, Stony Brook, 1984.

976. Lepow, Lauren. "Daw's Tennis Ball: A Topical Allusion
     in the *Secunda Pastorum*." *ELN* 22.2 (Dec. 1984):
     5-8.

     Claims that Daw's gift may be an allusion to "the
     dauphin's sending [Henry V] a tun of tennis balls,
     a sneering comment on Henry's youth and inability
     to enforce his claims" (7). Points out the
     popularity and appropriateness of the allusion
     (though the incident itself may be apocryphal).

977. ---. "Drama of Communion: The Life of Christ in the
     Towneley Cycle." *PQ* 62.3 (Summer 1983): 403-13.

     Claims that the eleven plays in the cycle dealing
     with Christ's life aim "to maximize the audience's
     sense of communion with Christ" (403), and to
     point up "Christ's eternally contemporary
     sacramental existence" (403). Shows how the plays
     draw on the audience's familiarity with the
     liturgy.

978. Lepow, Lauren Ethyl. "Eucharistic Reference in the
     Towneley Cycle: A Reconsideration of Corpus
     Christi Theology and Drama." Ph.D. diss., U. of
     Connecticut, 1980.

979. ---. "Middle English Elevation Prayers and the Corpus
     Christi Cycles." *ELN* 17.2 (Dec. 1979): 85-88.

     Shows that the "'Hail' lyrics are modeled upon
     versified prayers, written for the laity, intended
     for address to the Real Presence in the Sacrament
     of the Altar at the moment of its elevation" (85).

980. ---. "'What God Has Cleansed': The Shepherds' Feast
     in the *Prima Pastorum*." *MP* 80.3 (Feb. 1983): 280-
     83.

     Reviews interpretations of the feast. Shows its
     eucharistic significance. Claims that the feast's
     components were chosen "to define the universality
     of the New Covenant sealed by the sacrament"
     (280). Employs biblical law to show that what the
     shepherds find in their feast, "the spectators
     find upon the altar at Mass: the feast shared
     universally under the New Law" (283).

981. Lester, G.A. "The Wakefield Master." In *Great
     Writers of the English Language: Dramatists*, 592-

93. Ed. by James Vinson and D.L. Kirkpatrick.
London: Macmillan, 1979.

Offers a brief overview of the plays attributed to
this writer. Looks at plot, character, criticism,
and so on.

982. Levenson, Geraldine Bonnie. "'That Reverend Vice': A
Study of the Comic-Demonic Figure in English Drama
and Fiction." Ph.D. diss., U. of British
Columbia, 1977.

983. Levey, D. "'Nowe is Fulfillid all my For-thoght': A
Study of Comedy, Satire and Didacticism in the
York Cycle." *EngStudA* 24.2 (Sept. 1981): 83-94.

Shows that the notion "that theology is
necessarily boring and that comedy or satire" (83)
is used to allow the audience a rest from doctrine
is a modern idea, "not necessarily consonant with
medieval practice" (83). Interprets the
vocabulary (humor, comedy, satire, laughter,
irony, farce, . . .), especially with respect to
medieval ideas. Shows "that satiric and comic
elements in the York cycle are usually fully
justified" (91) because they are didactic.

984. Levin, Carole. "A Good Prince: King John and Early
Tudor Propaganda." *SCJ* 11.4 (Winter 1980): 23-32.

Considers the bad reputation that John had for
centuries: "as a coward, a bully, and a
voluptuary" (23). Discusses John as something of
a hero, "a kind of anticipant Protestant, a lonely
pioneer in resisting the tyrannies of Rome" (23).
Looks at Bale's use of John as a precursor to
Henry VIII (see especially 29-32).

985. Levin, Harry. "From Play to Plays: The Folklore of
Comedy." *CompD* 16.2 (Summer 1982): 130-47.

Offers a wide-ranging interpretation of "play,"
"*jeu*," "*ludus*," "game." Though not specifically
on medieval English drama, touches on many issues
useful in interpretation. Looks briefly at Robin
Hood plays, mummers' plays.

986. Levin, Richard. "The Acting Style of the Children's
Companies." *ANQ* 22.3 and 4 (Nov./Dec. 1983): 34-
35.

Looks at some precedents of acting styles, with
casual reference to Medwall's *Fulgens and Lucrece*.
Refers to the low social status of the characters

portrayed as influencing acting styles--as opposed
to the influence of the shortness of the young
actors. [Note followed by a rejoinder by Kenneth
Tucker--p. 35--whose article Levin was
questioning.]

987. ---. *The Multiple Plot in English Renaissance Drama*.
Chicago and London: U. of Chicago Press, 1971.
277 pp.

Looks briefly at mystery cycles and morality
plays.

Rev. *Choice* 8 (Jan. 1971): 568.
Booklist 68 (Sept. 1, 1971): 26.
JEGP 70 (Oct. 1971): 663.
TLS (Nov. 19, 1971): 1461.
RES, n.s. 24 (Feb. 1973): 65.

988. Lewis, Leon E. "The Complexion of Medieval English
Drama." In *Medieval Drama: A Collection of
Festival Papers*, 38-45. Ed. by William A. Selz
(see entry # 1454 below).

Discusses origins and development of the plays,
the terminology "mystery play," "cycle play,"
"miracle play." Focuses on the last and discusses
their disappearance.

989. Lewis, William. "Playing with Fire and Brimstone:
Auctor Ludens, Diabolus Ludicrus." In *Auctor
Ludens: Essays on Play in Literature*, 47-61.
Philadelphia and Amsterdam: John Benjamins
Publishing Co., 1986. Cultura Ludens: Imitation
and Play in Western Culture. Gen. eds. Giuseppe
Mazzotta and Mihai Spariosu.

Looks at "the theatrical treatment of devils" and
"the sufficiency of 'play' as motive and motif in
literary creation" (47). Looks briefly at the
cycle plays. Analyzes the notion of "play,"
drawing heavily from V.A. Kolve.

990. Leyerle, John. "Medieval Drama." In *English Drama
(Excluding Shakespeare): Select Bibliographical
Guides*, 19-28. Ed. by Stanley Wells. London:
Oxford U. Press, 1975. (See entry # 1672 below.)

Offers a very brief overview and a short,
selective bibliography (27-28). With a short
discussion of authorship and the performance-
orientation of the plays ("to read them instead of
experiencing them as theatre is a serious
distortion because a reader unfamiliar with their

dramatic power may think them childish, even crude"--26).

991.   Lindenbaum, Sheila, comp.   "Census of Medieval Drama Productions."   *RORD* 29 (1986-87): 109-12.

Contains three reviews, one on a French play and two on English drama (Happé on *The Comedy of Virtuous and Godly Susanna*; Happé on *The Second Shepherds* [sic] *Play*).

991a. ---.   "Entertainment in English Monasteries."   *FCS* 13 (1988): 411-22.

992.   ---.   "Informal Minutes of Seminar 20."   *RORD* 15-16 (1972-73): 79-81.

These and the following eight entries recount proceedings of Modern Language Association Conference sessions.   This entry is for the MLA 1971 conference.   Seminars discuss medieval drama. Each report summarizes the papers of various speakers and the subsequent discussions.   [N.B. Not every volume of *RORD* contains such an article.]   See also Kathleen Ashley, "Report of the 1985 Medieval Drama Session," entry # 116 above.

993.   ---.   "Informal Minutes of Seminar 35."   *RORD* 15-16 (1972-73): 93-96.

For the 1972 MLA meeting.

994.   ---.   "Informal Report of the 1973 Medieval Drama Seminar."   *RORD* 17 (1974): 97-103.

For the MLA meeting of 1973.

995.   ---.   "Informal Report on the 1974 MLA Seminar on Medieval Drama."   *RORD* 18 (1975): 77-80.

For the meeting of 1974.

996.   ---.   "Informal Report of the 1975 MLA Medieval Drama Seminar."   *RORD* 20 (1977): 83-86.

For the meeting of 1975.

997.   ---.   "Informal Report of the 1976 MLA Medieval Drama Seminar."   *RORD* 20 (1977): 87-90.

For the meeting of 1976.

998. ---. "Report of the 1978 MLA Special Session on
      Medieval Drama." *RORD* 22 (1979): 95-99.

      Details the MLA meeting of Dec. 30, 1978, "Current
      Approaches to the Drama of Medieval England and
      Europe."

999. ---. "Report of the 1980 MLA Session on Medieval
      Drama." *RORD* 24 (1981): 177-79.

      For the 1980 meeting.

1000. ---. "Report of the 1983 MLA Programs." *RORD* 27
      (1984): 149-50.

      For the 1983 meeting.

1001. ---. "The Morality Plays." In *A Manual of the
      Writings in Middle English, 1050-1500*, 1357-1381,
      1599-1621. Ed. by Albert E. Hartung (see entry #
      714 above).

      Gives an overview of critical concerns including
      history of the genre, literary sources, didactic
      elements and aims, relation to the Elizabethan
      drama, appreciation of the plays as drama, and
      staging. Deals with The Pater Noster Play, The
      Creed Play, The Pride of Life, The Macro Plays
      (The Castle of Perseverance, Wisdom, and Mankind),
      Everyman, Nature (by Medwall), A Speech of Delight
      (Reynes Extract), and Processus Satanae. With a
      bibliography (1599-1621).

1002. L[indenbaum], S[heila]. [Untitled review.] *RORD* 28
      (1985): 207.

      Briefly reviews a performance of The Towneley
      Annunciation and *Salutation* of May 19, 1985, at
      Indiana University in Bloomington.

1003. ---. "The York Cycle at Toronto: Staging and
      Performance Style." *ThRI*, n.s. 4.1 (Oct. 1978):
      31-41. Rpt. in *Medieval English Drama: A
      Casebook*, 200-11. Ed. by Peter Happé (entry # 684
      above).

      Shows how a twentieth-century performance was put
      on, incorporating "the results of recent scholarly
      research" (32).

1004. Lombardo, Agostino. "English Medieval Drama." In
      *Literature in Fourteenth-Century England: The
      J.A.W. Bennett Memorial Lectures, Perugia, 1981-2*,
      121-36. Trans. by Christopher Whyte. Ed. by

Piero Boitani and Anna Torti. Tübingen and
Cambridge: Gunter Narr Verlag, and D.S. Brewer,
1983. Tübinger Beiträge zur Anglistik, 5.

Opens with the notion that English drama "has its
immediate origins in religious ritual and
liturgical drama" (121). Elaborates on this
theory. Discusses terminology, miracle plays,
cycle drama, popular plays, morality plays.

1005. Long, P.R. "New Light on the Mystery Plays of
Cornwall." *OldC* 7.10 (1972): 458-59.

Considers the *Ordinalia* and theater in the round.
Offers a brief overview of the *Ordinalia:* raison
d'être, its use of realism, Cornish place names,
and its means of performance. Aims to show "how
mediaeval life can be illuminated by study of a
contemporary text" (459). Comments on the
suitability of the round as a "place for serious
study of common matters" (459), and on the recent
Piran Round performances.

1006. Longley, Clifford. "Religious Triumph in the
Theatre." *The Times* (London) (July 8, 1985): 14.

Briefly reviews a performance of the National
Theatre's production of *The Mysteries* of May 18,
1985, in London's Lyceum Theatre.

1007. Longsworth, Robert M. "Art and Exegesis in Medieval
English Dramatizations of the Sacrifice of Isaac."
ETJ 24.2 (May 1972): 118-24.

Considers the play's inclusion in the cycle, its
typology, its relation to the liturgy, the
dramatist's necessary change from the biblical
emphasis and "a major rearrangement of its
narrative elements" (120), the "allure of pathos"
(123) the play contains, and the freedom of the
playwrights to experiment with the
characterization of Isaac.

1008. ---. "Two Medieval Cornish Versions of the Creation
of the World." *CompD* 21.3 (Fall 1987): 249-58.

Looks at "similarity of subject matter . . . [and]
some identical text" (249) in the two plays: the
Origo Mundi and the *Creation of the World*
(sometimes called *Gwryans an Bys*, the Cornish
title). Sees the latter as a shaping of earlier
materials, "a work with its own theatrical
coherence and intellectual interest" (256).
Comments on the shifting interests--dramaturgical

and intellectual--between the writing of the two plays.

1009. Loss, Archie K. "Everyman Blooms as Everybody." *AWN*, n.s. 13.5 (Oct. 1976): 96-98.

Responds to Adaline Glasheen's "*Everyman*" (see entry # 631 above) with respect to "the revival of *Everyman* in London" (96) in 1901. Points out other influences on Joyce than *Everyman*.

1010. Lovelace, Martin J. "Christmas Mumming in England: The House Visit." In *Folklore Studies in Honour of Herbert Halpert, A Festschrift*, 271-81. Ed. by Kenneth S. Goldstein and Neil V. Rosenberg. St. John's, Newfoundland: Memorial U. of Newfoundland, 1980.

Hypothesizes that the modern Newfoundland house-visit custom stems from early Renaissance mumming tradition. Says the custom theoretically can be traced to the "ancient mystery plays" (278).

1011. Lozar, Paula, trans. "The 'Prologue' to the Ordinances of the York Corpus Christi Guild." *Allegorica* 1.1 (1976): 94-113.

Presents a transcription with facing translation and notes. Introduction discusses the guild and its almost nonexistent connection with the plays. Points out that though the two were distinct, the "guild officials who were responsible for producing the Corpus Christi Plays would be essentially the same group . . . who contributed 2d. yearly to the Corpus Christi Guild and participated in its observances" (94-95). Emphasizes the commonality in religious beliefs between the two groups.

1012. ---. "Time in the Corpus Christi Cycles: 'Aesthetic' and 'Realistic' Models." *PLL* 14.4 (Fall 1978): 385-93.

Mentions the two main approaches with respect to time: "as a cultural construct and . . . as a factor in staging" (385). Aims to combine these views in her reading. Considers audience reaction and "Medieval theories of time perception" (386). Focuses on the York and N-Town Passion plays. Shows that the two cycles require a different audience perception with respect to time: the York plays prolong "events through detailed sequential presentation detached from real time" while the N-Town plays "present actions simultaneously" (393).

1013. Lozar, Paula Marie. "The Virgin Mary in the Medieval Drama of England: A Psychological Study." Ph.D. diss., U. of California, Berkeley, 1974.

1014. Lucarelli, John Anthony. "Figural Typology and Medieval History in the English Mystery Cycles." Ph.D. diss., U. of Pittsburgh, 1971.

1015. Lucas, Elona Kay. "The Attitude toward Death in the Corpus Christi Plays." Ph.D. diss., Ohio U., 1981.

1016. Lumianski, R.M., and David Mills. *The Chester Mystery Cycle: Essays and Documents.* Chapel Hill and London: U. of North Carolina Press, 1983. [Contains an essay on "Music in the Cycle" by Richard Rastell, entry # 1362 below.]

Contains "four essays about various aspects of the cycle" (vii). Chap. 1--"The Texts of the Chester Cycle"--evaluates evidence for establishing a text, based on distribution of variants and the demonstrable errors in the mss. Looks also at various types of errors and extant alternative passages.

Chap. 2--"Sources, Analogues, and Authorities"-- deals with "immediate sources" and "the wider issue of evocation of authorities within the cycle" (87). Considers French and English influences, a *Stanzaic Life of Christ*, the *Legenda Aurea*, and biblical sources.

Chap. 3, by Rastall--"Music in the Cycle"--looks at the meager evidence for music in the mss themselves and the abundance of external evidence. Assesses "the representational and practical functions of music, and . . . the evidence for music in the Chester cycle . . ., the Banns, and the accounts" (113). Lists musical items and musical texts. Speculates on the type of music that may have been used.

Chap. 4--"Development of the Cycle"--evaluates "the external evidence for the cycle in order to suggest a context for the extant texts of the cycle" (165). Looks at traditions of Origins and Authorship, the cycle in Chester, the Whitsun Plays, the final performance of 1575, and the cyclic texts.

Chap. 5--"Documents Providing External Evidence"--
lists evidence from twenty documents. Appendix
contains play-by-play list of five stanza forms in
the cycle. With bibliography and index.

Rev. Darryll Grantley, *ThN* 38.3 (1984): 146-47.
RES 35 (Feb. 1984): 79.
EDAMN 6.2 (Spring 1984): 43-46.
SewR 92 (Apr. 1984): 669.
Specu 59 (July 1984): 669.
D.C. Baker, *ELN* 22.1 (Sept. 1984): 67-68.
Lawrence M. Clopper, *M&RD* 2 (1985): 283-91.
MLR 80 (Jan. 1985): 115.
RES 36 (Aug. 1985): 412.
J.M. Cowen, *N&Q*, n.s. 32-3 (230) (Sept.
1985): 390-91.

1017.   ---, ---.   "The Five Cyclic Manuscripts of the
Chester Cycle of Mystery Plays: A Statistical
Survey of Variant Readings." *LSE* 7 (1974 [for
1973-74]): 95-107.

Gives a selection of "separate table[s] for each
variation-pattern showing the distribution of the
pattern play by play throughout the cycle" (95).
Briefly discusses their choice of a base text for
their edition (see entries # 54 and 55 above), the
ms relationships, and "Cycle or Play-collection"
(98).

1018.   Luxton, Imogen.   "The Reformation and Popular
Culture."   In *Church and Society in England: Henry
VIII to James I*, 57-77, 182.   Ed. by Felicity Heal
and Rosemary O'Day.   London: Macmillan; Hamden,
Connecticut: Archon, 1977.

Considers popular customs and beliefs, traditions
and practices. Focuses on religious activity,
specifically on the mystery plays (60 f.), and
how "they exemplify the main features of late
medieval religious culture" (60). Comments as
well on mummings, saints' lives (61-62), the
"Corpus Christi gild" (70), and the cycle plays
(70-71).

1019.   Lyall, Roderick.   [Untitled review.]   *TLS* (Aug. 24,
1984).

Reviews a performance of Lindsay's *Ane Satyre of
the Thrie Estates*, Aug. 1984, at the Assembly
Hall, Edinburgh, at the Edinburgh Festival.

1020. McCaffrey, Phillip. "Chester's 'Balaam and Balak':
An Example of Responsible Revision." *BSUF* 24.4
(Autumn 1983): 55-60.

Examines the revision of the Chester play, of
which two versions exist, neither of which clearly
predates the other. Says "the reviser . . .
changed one pageant while accommodating himself to
the requirements of the cycle as a whole" (55).
Adds that the substitution of one for the other
did not affect the "thematic and structural
functions of the pageant" (55). Looks closely at
the differences.

1021. ---. "The Didactic Structure of the Chester
'Sacrifice of Isaac.'" *Comitatus* 2 (1971): 16-
26.

Considers the structure "to document a subtlety in
the play" (17) in the inclusion of Melchizedek.
Discusses the three-part structure of the pageant
and its unity. Looks at how the three parts "are
linked in a strict chain of historical causality"
(22), at the symbolic and historical elements, and
at the role of the Expositor. (See comment by
Bert Cardullo, entry # 266 above.)

1022. McCaffrey, Phillip C. "Historical Structure in the
Chester Old Testament Pageants: The Literary and
Religious Components of a Medieval Aesthetic."
Ph.D. diss., U. of Pennsylvania, 1972.

1023. McClure, Donald S. "Commercialism in the York
Mystery Cycle." *StudHum* 2.1 (1970): 32-34.

Looks at the appropriateness of the guild which
performed individual plays. Says that "the guilds
seized the opportunity to display their
workmanship or to emphasize the dignity of their
callings within the dramatic context of their
plays" (32). Also says they often "indulged their
commercial instincts [to] promote their products"
(32). Cites examples of guilds' taking the
opportunity to display their wares. Comments on
the relationship between the playwrights and the
guilds.

1024. McCracken, Natalie Jacobson. "Medieval Mysteries for
Modern Production." Ph.D. diss., U. of Wisconsin,
1969.

1025. MacDonald, Alasdair A. "Some Recent Work on the
Early English Drama." *EngStud* 66.2 (Apr. 1985):
162-66.

Review article. Discusses 1) Marie Axton's *Three Tudor Classical Interludes* (entry # 4 above); 2) Peter W. Travis's *Dramatic Design . . .* (# 1588); 3) W.A. Davenport's *Fifteenth-Century English Drama* (# 379); and Davidson, Gianakaris, and Stroupe's *Drama in the Middle Ages* (# 409).

1026. McDonald, Marcia Ann. "A Two-World Condition: The Carnival Idiom and Its Function in Four Morality Plays." Ph.D. diss., Vanderbilt U., 1984.

1026a. McDonald, Peter F. "Drama Criticism and the Value of Productions." *FCS* 13 (1988): 13-22.

1027. ---. "Drama in the Church." In *The* Revels *History of Drama in English*, Vol. I, *Medieval Drama*, Part II, 3, 92-121. Discussed at entry for David Mills and Peter F. McDonald, "The Drama of Religious Ceremonial" (entry # 1163 below).

1028. ---. "The Towneley Cycle at Toronto." *MET* 8.1 (July 1986): 51-60.

Reviews the performance at Victoria College Quadrangle, Toronto, in 1985.

1029. MacFarlane, Jean Elizabeth. "Antichrist in English Literature, 1380-1680." Ph.D. diss., U. of Florida, 1980.

1030. McGavin, John J. "Sign and Related Didactic Techniques in the Chester Cycle of Mystery Plays." Ph.D. diss., U. of Edinburgh, 1981.

1031. ---. "Sign and Transition: The *Purification* Play in Chester." *LSE* 11 (1980 for 1979): 90-104.

Claims that "critics should reconsider the importance of individual authorship in any discussion of the structural integrity of the text" (90). Discusses the relationship between the "Purification" and the "Doctors" episodes, the latter apparently a later addition to the play; looks at the textual "instability" (91) of the play over the years, the source of the "Doctors" episode, and the "rationale for the extant shape of the play" (91). Discusses biblical, stylistic, and structural links between the two parts of the play, and the use of signs which "mark the fulfilment [sic] by the first and second persons of the Trinity of prophecies inspired by the third person" (97). Shows how the supposed different authors of the two parts of the play deal with signs differently. Points out the play's "complex

history of revision" (101) and explains the unity
of the play despite its "clearly discontinuous
composition" (101).

1032. McGee, Edward. "A Reception for Queen Elizabeth in
Greenwich." *REEDN* 2 (1980): 1-8.

Cites an entry in Egerton MS 2877 illustrating
"dramatic activity of the Children of the Chapel
Royal" (1). Describes the pageant and transcribes
the speech of Goodwill (60 lines). With textual
notes and footnotes.

1033. ---. "Drama, Liturgical." In *Dictionary of the
Middle Ages*, 4: 272-77. Ed. by Joseph R. Strayer
(see entry # 1553 below).

Offers a brief historical survey with musical
notations, some theory, and bibliography. Reviews
scholarship and defines key terms.

1034. ---. "The Liturgical Placements of the *Quem
quaeritis* Dialogue." *JAMS* 29 (1976): 1-29.

Presents arguments on "the traditional theories
concerning [the dialogue's] origin and early
history" (1). Reviews scholarship. Posits the
theory that the trope was not related to dialogue.
Not specifically on English drama, but offers
much information on the predecessors of English
plays.

1035. ---. *Medieval and Renaissance Music: A Performer's
Guide*. Toronto: U. of Toronto Press, 1985. 273
pp.

Not on English drama, but presents information on
dramatic music and iconography. Part 2, Chap. 6
is "Music for Large Ensembles and Dramatic
Productions" (131-45).

Rev. *Choice* 23 (Dec. 1985): 614.

1036. ---. "The Role of the *Quem Quaeritis* Dialogue in the
History of Western Drama." *RenD*, n.s. 7 (1977,
for 1976): 177-91.

Attacks the traditional notion that the trope
"originated in the early tenth century [as part
of] . . . the Easter Mass Introit" (177). Offers
a more circumspect view of its origin and
development. Reexamines the data to present "a
more comprehensive theory" (177). Looks at the
placement of the tropes, mimes, liturgical drama,

etc. Explains that the trope helped "to establish
a legitimate, Church-recognized form of drama
within the liturgy" (191).

1037. McGinn, Bernard. "Awaiting an End: Research in
Medieval Apocalypticism 1974-81." *M&H*, n.s. 11
(1982): 263-89.

A bibliographic essay surveying works on the
Apocalypse. Defines terminology and explains
parameters. Not specifically on drama, but
contains many insights into current views familiar
to playwrights and audiences.

1038. McIntosh, Angus. "Towards an Inventory of Middle
English Scribes." *NM* 75 (1974): 602-24.

Aims to make detailed suggestions on how to
catalogue scribal practices and traits in order to
be able to identify scribes. Not specifically on
drama, but possibly useful in drama criticism when
inventory is completed.

1039. Mack, Maynard, Jr. "The *Second Shepherds' Play:* A
Reconsideration." *PMLA* 93.1 (Jan. 1978): 78-85.

Claims that the play is one "of rare
sophistication and even artistic daring" (78).
Considers the "uninterrupted movement" (78)
between the two sections of the play. Looks at
the play's move from *planctu* to farce to
celebration.

1040. McKinnell, John. "Staging the Digby *Mary Magdalen.*"
MET 6.2 (Dec. 1984): 126-52.

Recounts his own experience in producing the play
with respect to appropriate staging. Considers
the four types of staging proposed, dismissing the
three-level-wagon theory and the theory which has
a straight line of scaffolds facing the audience.
Prefers a semi-circular stage or a theater in the
round. Adopts a half-round stage. Looks at
staging structures and practical considerations
(e.g. location of the Heathen temple, the "old
lodge," the stage procession of Satan and Flesh,
etc.).

1041. McLachlan, Elizabeth Parker. "Possible Evidence for
Liturgical Drama at Bury St Edmunds in the Twelfth
Century." *PSIAH* 34.4 (1980): 255-61.

Looks for concrete evidence of performances.
Finds "an illuminated initial which may . . .

reflect the enactment of the basic liturgical
Epiphany drama, the *Officium Stellae*, at Bury St
Edmunds in the 12th century" (225). Not on
English drama, but indicates early dramatic
activity in England.

1042. MacLean, Sally-Beth. *Chester Art: A Subject List of
Extant and Lost Art Including Items Relevant to
Early Drama*. Kalamazoo, Michigan: Medieval
Institute Publications, Western Michigan
University, 1982. Early Drama, Art, and Music
Reference Series, 3. viii, 115 pp.

Examines all arts in Chester and surveys them in
various subject areas: Old Testament; Parents of
the Virgin and Her Life; Christ's Infancy,
Ministry, and Passion; The Risen Christ;
Conclusion of the Life of the Virgin; Christ in
Majesty and Trinity; The Apostles; Saints; and
miscellaneous subjects. Contains appendixes on
Cult and Shrine of St. Werburgh; Musical
Instruments in Chester Art; Chester Cathedral
Misericords. With bibliography, index,
illustrations, etc. Points out how a familiarity
with the visual arts complements our knowledge of
the drama.

1043. ---. "King Games and Robin Hood: Play and Profit at
Kingston upon Thames." *RORD* 29 (1986-87): 85-93
(and map, 94). Rpt. in *FCS* 13 (1988): 309-20.

Recounts the details of Robin Hood and other
entertainment celebration of 1509. Speculates on
the nature of the performance, the audience, the
sponsors, and so on. Presents the "Chart of
Receipts and Expenses for Kingston Robin Hood and
King Game 1504-1538" (89-91).

1044. ---. "Records of Early English Drama and the
Travelling Player." *RORD* 26 (1983): 65-71.

Discusses the REED project: what the editors must
do, where they must seek records, which records to
examine, etc.

1045. McMillan, Scott. "Simon Jewell and the Queen's Men."
RES, n.s. 27.106 (May 1976): 174-77.

Comments on Mary Edmonds' discovery of the Will of
Simon Jewell, actor (see entry # 507a above).
Discusses this actor's will with respect to the
personnel of the acting companies.

1046. McMunn, Meradith T. "Children as Actors and Audience for Early Scottish Drama and Ceremony." *CLAQ* 10.1 (Spring 1985): 22-24.

Looks at primary documents to find records of dramatic activities of children in Scotland. Focuses on non-cycle plays and dramatized ceremonies. Discusses sacred and secular drama: folk plays, May plays, Robin Hood plays, comedies and tragedies, interludes, classical plays (e.g. by Terence), civic pageants for royal audiences. Analyzes staging, symbolism of the children ("innocence or its opposite, satire" [23]), etc.

1047. MacQueen, John. "The Literature of Fifteenth-Century Scotland." In *Scottish Society in the Fifteenth Century*, 184-208. Ed. by Jennifer M. Brown. New York: St. Martin's; London: Edward Arnold, 1977.

Contains a brief discussion of Scottish "dramatic performances" (198).

1048. McRae, Murdo William. "Everyman's Last Rites and the Digression on Priesthood." *CL* 13.3 (Fall 1986): 305-09.

Reviews scholarship. Asks the often ignored question, "why does Everyman visit Presthode offstage for the last rites?" (305). Sees the answer in more than "dramatic economy" (305). Claims that the offstage scene "cannot be dramatized because there are implications to what Knowledge and V. Wyttes say about the priesthood that prevent such a visit from being staged" (305-06). Examines the digression in these terms. Shows how "the conversation between V. Wyttes and Knowledge paradoxically occupies the center of the play's vision" (308).

1049. McRoberts, David. "The Edinburgh Hammermen's Corpus Christi Herod Pageant." *IR* 21 (1970): 77-81.

Offers a transcript "of the entries relating specifically to the Hammermen's group of Herod and his associates" (77), the transcript revealing the existence of a cast of characters which generally corresponds to those found in the Slaughter of the Innocents plays in the cycles. Suggests that this indicates that there was a Herod play or "as seems more likely from the records, merely processional dumbshow" (78). Considers historical data and also the possibility that the Hammermen also were responsible for a St. Katherine play.

1050. McRoberts, J. Paul. "Shakespeare and the Medieval
       Tradition: An Annotated Bibliography." Ph.D.
       diss., Kent State U., 1972.

1050a. ---. *Shakespeare and the Medieval Tradition: An
       Annotated Bibliography*. New York and London:
       Garland, 1985. Garland Reference Library of the
       Humanities, Vol. 603. (See previous entry.)
       xxix, 256 pp.

       Contains citations for 933 entries, each with a
       brief annotation. Cites many articles and books
       which mention or discuss various medieval English
       plays or genres. Chap. One is on "General Works";
       Chap. Two covers "Medieval Influence Upon
       Particular Play Groups"; Chap. Three is on
       "Medieval Influence Upon Particular Plays." With
       author, Shakespearean play, medieval, and subject
       indexes.

1051. Maguin, Jean-Marie. "*Everyman* ou la mesure du
       concept de héros." In *Le Mythe du héros: Actes du
       colloque interdisciplinaire, Centre Aixois de
       Recherches Anglaises, 12-13-14 mars 1982*, 7-21.
       Intro. by N.J. Rigaud. Aix-en-Provence: Pubs.
       Univ. de Provence, 1982. C[entre] A[ixois] de
       R[echerches] A[nglaises] 3.

       Examines the concept of the hero, the term
       originally referring to mortals who, because of
       super-human deeds or virtues, had been deified
       after death and thus had become immortalized in
       human cultural memory. Considers the related
       concept of Worthie of the early fifteenth century,
       and looks at the narrowing of the term with
       respect to military feats or the central character
       of a literary work. Shows the development of the
       term into the twentieth century, and points out
       that the use of the term *hero* for the main
       character of a medieval morality play is
       anachronistic and conceptually imprecise.
       Explains why the term is inappropriate, and offers
       as better terms *protagonist* or *principal
       character*.

1052. Malin, Stephen D. "Four Doubled Figures in the
       Origins of English Folk Theatre." *ThJ* 33.1 (Mar.
       1981): 18-33.

       Looks at the origins of English folk drama in "an
       indigenous, widespread fertility-based religion"
       (18), the religion being a witch cult. Examines
       the beliefs of the cult's adherents to show where
       the drama came from and "to illuminate otherwise

obscure traditions of that theatre" (18). Looks
at the stage customs of skin-blackening, the
horse, the man-woman, and the doctor. Points out
"the similarities between witch cult and folk
theatre" (31). (See response to this article by
E.T. Kirby, "Malin's 'Doubled Figures' . . .,"
entry # 913 above.)

1053. Maltman, Sister Nicholas, O.P. "Light in and on the
Digby *Mary Magdalene.*" In *Saints, Scholars, and
Heroes: Studies in Medieval Culture in Honour of
Charles W. Jones.* 2 vols. Vol. I: 257-80. Ed.
by Margaret H. King and Wesley M. Stevens.
Collegeville, Minnesota: Hill Monastic
Manuscript Library, Saint John's Abbey and U.,
1979.

Reviews criticism of the play. Aims "to look at
the larger action [in the play], to observe the
literal fall and rise of characters and events"
(258) and how the "playwright has amplified that
meaning" (258). Looks at the use of beds, the
unity of action, the theme of God's grace and its
power, and the "use of light as an analogy to
God's presence and grace" (259). Concludes that
the play is based on a sermon.

1054. ---. "Meaning and Art in the Croxton *Play of the
Sacrament.*" *ELH* 41.2 (Summer 1974): 149-64.

Reviews critical approaches to the play. Points
up the play's didactic nature. Aims "to identify
the liturgical elements within the play and to
consider their import in relation to dramatic
structure and meaning" (150). Concludes that the
play's impulse was didactic, its message
doctrinal, "its matrix liturgical, and its tone
serious" (162).

1055. Malvern, Marjorie M. "The Magdalen: An Exploration
of the Shaping of Myths Around the Mary Magdalene
of the New Testament Canonical Gospels and an
Examination of the Effects of the Myths on the
Literary Figure, Particularly on the Heroine of
the Fifteenth-Century Digby Play *Mary Magdalene.*"
Ph.D. diss., Michigan State U., 1969.

1056. Manabe, Kazumi. "On the Prose of the Katherine
Group." *SELL* 30 (1980): 95-106. In Japanese with
English abstract, 133.

Discusses early Katherine group works--in the
style of Aelfric. Points out the dramatic and
fable elements of *Sawles Warde*, and looks at

268

language (especially alliteration, rhythm, and sentence length).

1057. Mandach, André de. "English 'Dramatic' Performances at the Council of Constance, 1417." *REEDN* 7.2 (1982): 26-28.

Discusses the performances at the lavish feasts held in the house of Walter Burkart during the Council of Constance. Offers extracts and paraphrases of those parts of Ulrich von Richenthal's account dealing with the performances. Says that the nature of these performances is indeterminable.

1058. Manion, F.P., S.J. "A Reinterpretation of *The Second Shepherds' Play*." *ABR* 30.1 (Mar. 1979): 44-68.

Reviews scholarship on the function of the two parts of the play and its unity. Looks for unity in the widely varying criticism. Claims that a full understanding of the play can be had only through "a comprehensive understanding of the Christian doctrine of the redemption" (46). Says that the play is as much about redemption as it is about nativity. Considers the Mak episode, Mak's character, and "the biblical concept of the Mystical Body of Christ . . . as a key to a more thorough understanding of the introductory lamentations . . . and of the characters of the drama in their relationship to Christ" (47-48). Deals with the theological background of the play.

1059. Marienstras, Richard. "Les termes du contrat dans *Everyman* et *Doctor Faustus*." In *De Shakespeare à T.S. Eliot: Mélanges offerts à Henri Fluchère*, 19-29. Ed. by Marie-Jeanne Durry, Robert Ellrodt, and Marie-Thérèse Jones-Davies. Paris: Didier, 1976. Etudes anglaises 63.

Says that a pre-established contract between God and humanity is assumed of which the terms are: for God--die (as Jesus) in order to offer salvation to all. And for human beings--repay the debt owed to God by a "good life" (specific good works as popularized by contemporary preachers). Details the way to salvation and alludes to the ways to perdition. Examines these notions in detail with respect to Everyman and Faustus.

1060. Marrocco, W. Thomas, and Nicholas Sandon. *The Oxford Anthology of Music: Medieval Music*. London: Oxford U. Press, 1977. 239 pp.

Contains sections on Sacred and Secular Monophony, The Ars Antiqua, The Ars Nova, and The Fifteenth Century. Not specifically on drama, but offers a broad view of music possibly familiar to the playwrights and their audience. With 106 selections of music with notation and texts.

1061. Marrow, James. *"Circumdederunt me canes multi:* Christ's Tormentors in Northern European Art of the Late Middle Ages and Early Renaissance." *ArtB* 59.2 (June 1977): 167-81.

Relates the art to plays of the Passion. Discusses the visual depictions of the Passion and shows their connection to the narrative arts. Analyzes many iconographic features of the depiction. With illustrations.

1062. Marrow, James H. *Passion Iconography in Northern European Art of the Late Middle Ages and Early Renaissance: A Study of the Transformation of Sacred Metaphor into Descriptive Narrative*. Kortrijk: Van Ghemmert, 1979. Ars Neerlandica series, Vol. I. 369 pp., 144 illus., 15 color plates.

Depicts and discusses the iconography of Christ's suffering. Not specifically on the drama, but offers a visual complement to literary and critical texts. Covers such topics as Christ's Tormentors, Suffering, Torments; The Secret Passion (Christ's Arrest, Night of Captivity, Judges, Mocking, Flagellation, Crown of Thorns, Bearing of the Cross, and Crucifixion); The Spikeblock. With appendixes, notes, bibliography, and indexes.

Rev. *BurlM* 124 (Jan. 1982): 35.
Specu 57 (Apr. 1982): 395.

1063. Marshall, John. "The Chester Coopers' Pageant: 'Selles' and 'Cathedra.'" *LSE* 8 (1975): 120-28.

Defines the word "selles"--as found in the 1572 Whitsun play accounts of the Chester Coopers' Company--as "seat, a low stool; a seat of dignity" (120). Shows from the play account that two seats were used in the stage setting. Explains the Latin "cathedra" in the stage directions also as "chair" (121). Says that both glosses help one

understand the staging of the play, whereas other
scholars' translations of these two words make no
sense.

1064.   ---.   "The Chester Pageant Carriage--How Right Was
         Rogers?" *MET* 1.2 (Dec. 1979): 49-55.

         Refers to David Rogers' early seventeenth century
         descriptions of the Chester pageant carriage.
         Looks at primary records (guild accounts) to
         demonstrate the possibility of four- and six-
         wheeled vehicles, a lower dressing room, and a
         covered higher room--tentatively substantiating
         Rogers' description.

1065.   ---.   "The Chester Whitsun Plays: Dating of Post-
         Reformation Performances from the Smiths'
         Accounts." *LSE*, n.s. 9 (1976-77): 51-61.

         Responds to Clopper's article *"The Chester Plays:*
         Frequency of Performance" (see entry # 301 above),
         pointing out evidence for specific performances of
         the Chester Whitsun plays--evidence drawn from
         contemporary documents. Claims that the Smiths'
         account books "provide evidence for post-
         Reformation performances of the Chester plays only
         in . . . 1546, 1561, 1567, 1568, 1572, and 1575"
         (57), though missing records "might reveal
         performances in 1550 and 1554" (57).

1066.   ---.   "'The manner of these plays': The Chester
         Pageant Carriages and the Places where They
         Played." In *Staging the Chester Cycle*, 17-48.
         Ed. by David Mills (see entry 1159 below).

         Examines the Rogers' descriptions for accuracy.
         Claims that he "was perpetuating an error" (17) in
         some--but not all--parts of his description.
         First looks at the description of the carriage,
         which is "tantalisingly ambiguous" (19), and
         considers the description's reliability and
         accuracy. Looks also at later artistic renditions
         of the carriages, Sharp's *Dissertation* (of 1825--
         see entry # 1457 below; see also Clopper, "The
         Rogers' Description," entry # 307 above), and
         other evidence. Claims that the "Chester pageant
         carriages possessed certainly four and possibly
         . . . six wheels attached to two or three fixed
         axles" (26). Gives many more details (e.g. about
         dismantling, construction, repair, accoutrements,
         size). Also works out a route that the wagons
         took. With six plates and two maps.

1067.   ---.   "Marginal Staging Marks in the Macro Manuscript
        of *Wisdom.*"   *MET* 7.2 (1985): 77-82.

        Considers the 27 crosses in the margins, "almost
        half coinciding with stage directions" (78).
        Relates them to different kinds of stage movement:
        exits, dancing, or some other "change in the stage
        picture as a consequence of movement or action"
        (80).   Says that "the manuscript bears evidence of
        having been a working text which takes account of
        such movements" (82).

1068.   ---.   "The Medieval English Stage: A Graffito of a
        Hell-Mouth Scaffold?"   *ThN* 24.3 (1980): 99-103.

        Cautiously offers a graffito in the church of St.
        Peter, Stetchworth, "which might conceivably
        represent a medieval stage" (99).   [The graffito
        is illustrated at plate 8, between pp. 114 and
        115.]   Claims that the graffito was probably
        created no later than the close of the fourteenth
        century.

1069.   ---.   "Players of the Coopers' Pageant from the
        Chester Plays in 1572 and 1575."   *ThN* 33.1 (1979):
        18-23.

        Notes the controversy over the amateur versus
        professional status of the players.   Examines
        guild accounts for payments to actors.   Discusses
        the distinction between amateur and professional.
        Names specific actors and speculates on the parts
        they played.   Warns of how unwise it is "to
        generalize about the players of Corpus Christi
        Cycles . . . from the evidence of the Coopers'
        cast list alone" (22).   Concludes by assessing the
        kind of "non-professionals" these well-paid actors
        were.

1070.   ---.   "The Staging of the Marian Group from the N-
        town Cycle."   M.A. thesis, U. of Leeds, 1973.

1071.   Marshall, Linda E.   "'Sacral Parody' in the *Secunda
        Pastorum.*"   *Specu* 47.4 (Oct. 1972): 720-36.

        Says that Mak represents a "humorous diabolism"
        (720) which links him to Antichrist, an
        understanding of which will emphasize the
        importance of the Nativity in relation to the
        cycle's beginning and end, and which will help one
        understand the staging.   Examines traditional
        views of Antichrist, with stress on parody and
        prophecy, the two main features of the Antichrist
        legend.   Looks at the play's typology and "anti-

typology" (734). Says that where Mak prefigures Antichrist, the Nativity prefigures the Second Coming.

1072. Marshall, Robert D. "The Development of Medieval Drama: A New Theology." *StudMedCul* 4 (1974): 407-17.

Reviews the growth of the doctrine of the Atonement in the middle ages. Traces the rise of the view of Christ as suffering and vulnerable, and as the victorious *Christus Victor*. Shows how the different tones of the cycles emerge from these different preoccupations.

1073. Marsicano, Vincent Anthony. "Medieval Old Testament Drama as Biblical Exegesis." Ph.D. diss., Indiana U., 1980.

1074. Martin, Jeanne S. "History and Paradigm in the Towneley Cycle." *M&H*, n.s. 8 (1977): 125-45.

Discusses "an internal principle of selection" (125) of the plays in the cycle in terms of the cycle's celebration of the feast. Reveals the possible Eusebian and Augustinean influences, and says that the former provided the playwright "with a structure which could encompass both conflict . . . and an affirmation of the unified nature of creation" (144).

1075. Martin, Jeanne Suzette. "History and Truth: Generic Transformations in Three Middle English Genres." Ph.D. diss., U. of Virginia, 1975.

Looks at hagiography, poetry, and drama.

1076. Martin, Leslie Howard. "Comic Eschatology in the Chester *Coming of Antichrist*." *CompD* 5.3 (Fall 1971): 163-76.

Shows the uniqueness of the play in medieval drama and in its comic elements. Looks at traditional treatments of Antichrist and the comic features of the play. Discusses the parallels between the lives of Christ and Antichrist, which suggested to the playwright a similar parallel in the formal structure of the cycle.

1077. Marx, C.W. "The Problem of the Doctrine of the Redemption in the ME [sic] Mystery Plays and the *Cornish Ordinalia*." *MedAe* 54.1 (1985): 20-32.

Examines the doctrine of the Redemption with
respect to the "abuse-of-power theory" (20),
quoting Timothy Fry that "'Satan was permitted to
inflict death on [Adam and Eve] and all of mankind
and hold them captive in hell [but was] deceived
by the human nature of Christ, and, in bringing
about His death, abused his power, and lost the
souls in hell'" (Fry, "The Unity of the *Ludus
Coventriae*," *SP* 48 [1951]: 527-70; Marx 20).
Modifies Fry's notions that the abuse-of-power
theory was a comprehensive theory of the
Redemption and that the devil's deception was an
integral part of the abuse-of-power theory.
Claims that "the plays employ the traditional
language of Redemption without . . . invoking any
sophisticated theories of ransom or sacrifice"
(29).

1078. ---, and Miriam Anne Skey.   "Aspects of the
Iconography of the Devil at the Crucifixion."
JWCI 42 (1979): 233-35.

Looks at art and non-dramatic texts. Useful for
study of the drama through its focus on
iconography.

1079. Mastriani, Ralph Louis.   "Wisdom, Who Is Christ and
Its Relationship to the Medieval Sermon." Ph.D.
diss., St. Louis U., 1977.

1080. Mattson, May. "Five Plays about King Johan." Ph.D.
diss., U. of Uppsala, 1977. (See next entry.)

1081. ---. *Five Plays about King Johan.* Uppsala and
Stockholm: Distributor, Almqvist & Wiksell, 1977.
185 pp.

Contains discussions of Bale's play with respect
to its historical and cultural backgrounds, royal
power, the church, the barons, and public and
private morality. Contains bibliography and
index.

1082. May, Stephen [sic; see next entry]. "Good Kings and
Tyrants: A Re-Assessment of the Regal Figure on
the Medieval Stage." *MET* 5.2 (Dec. 1983): 87-102.

Treats the tyrant stereotypes of rulers in
surviving medieval plays. Aims "to ascertain the
qualities of the good king in two genres closely
related to the regular drama, the romance and the
civic pageant" (87), and "to suggest a rather
different interpretation of the dramatic tyrant
than is commonly accepted" (87). Explains why a

"sympathetic portrayal of a splendid monarch is so
rare in the Corpus Christi cycles: . . . such
characters must appear guilty until proven
innocent" (98).

1083.   May, Steven [sic; see previous entry].   "A Medieval
        Stage Property: The Spade."   *MET* 4.2 (Dec. 1982):
        77-92.

        Discusses spades in medieval English drama as a
        tool for identifying characters (e.g. Adam), in
        its iconographic representation, and as a
        cultivating implement; it serves "to signify the
        bitter necessity of toil for Fallen Man" (85) and
        to show, on the other hand, an ideal, worthwhile
        occupation--opposed to Sloth.   Considers the
        medieval spectator's point of view.   Concludes
        that most spades in the drama serve "to divert
        attention away from individual identity and
        towards an apprehension of Man in general and his
        place in the universe" (90).

1084.   Meagher, John Henry, III.   "The Castle and the Virgin
        in Medieval and Early Renaissance Drama."   Ph.D.
        diss., Bowling Green State U., 1976.

1085.   Meier, Hans H.   "Middle English Styles in
        Translation: A Note on *Everyman* and Caxton's
        Reynard."   In *From Caxton to Beckett: Essays
        Presented to W.H. Toppen on the Occasion of His
        Seventieth Birthday*, 12-30.   Amsterdam: Rodopi,
        1979.   Costerus, new series 23, Essays in English
        and American Language and Literature.

        Discusses *Everyman* as a translation, which offers
        "an opportunity for the synchronic comparison of
        lexico-grammatical resources" (13).   Examines "the
        prosodic relations between Middle Dutch and Middle
        English" (15) and the vocabulary and language of
        the two plays.

1086.   Mellers, Wilfrid.   "Through *Noye's Fludde*."   In *The
        Britten Companion*, 153-60.   Ed. by Christopher
        Palmer.   Cambridge: Cambridge U. Press, 1984.

        Discusses the composer's piece for children, based
        on the Chester play.

1087.   Mellinkoff, Ruth.   *The Mark of Cain*.   Berkeley, Los
        Angeles, and London: U. of California Press, 1981.
        xiii, 151 pp.

        Examines historical and evolving views of the Mark
        of Cain.   Discusses medieval drama at various

points in the text. See, e.g., treatment in
Wakefield, N-Town, and York plays. With 22
illustrations, notes, bibliography, and index.

Rev. *Choice* 18 (June 1981): 1431.
    S.S. Prawer, *TLS* (Aug. 21, 1981): 950.
    RSR 8 (Jan. 1982): 67.
    Specu 57 (July 1982): 686.
    JAF 96 (Apr. 1983): 234.
    RS 20 (June 1984): 322.

1088. Merchant, W. Moelwyn. *Creed and Drama: An Essay in
       Religious Drama.* London: S.P.C.K., 1965. 119 pp.

       Contains a chapter on "Medieval Liturgical Drama"
       (Chap. 2, 19-36). Discusses the liturgical drama
       and the influence it had on the later English
       drama. Discusses also the two Wakefield
       Shepherds' plays, the four cycles in general, *The
       Castle of Perseverance*, and *Everyman*.

1089. Meredith, Peter. *"Alia eorundem."* *MET* 4.1 (July
       1982): 66-70.

       Review of performance of *Mary Magdalen* at Durham,
       June 27-28 and July 3-4, 1982. See Meg Twycross,
       "Mary Magdalen at Durham" (entry # 1597 below).

1090. ---. "The Chester Plays at Leeds, May Bank Holiday
       1983, Organized by the Centre for Medieval
       Studies." *ULR* 26 (1983): 137-45.

       Recounts the problems faced and how they were
       solved for the three-day performance of the
       Chester plays (using a Bank Holiday so as to put
       together the three days). With illustrations and
       photographs of the performance.

1091. ---. *"The Conversion of St. Paul* at Winchester
       Cathedral." *MET* 4.1 (July 1982): 71-72.

       Review of performances of May 27-29, 1982.

1092. ---. "The Development of the York Mercers' Pageant
       Waggon." *MET* 1.1 (Oct. 1979): 5-18. [An edited
       version of a talk at a meeting in Lancaster, April
       7, 1979.]

       Establishes "a general picture of the development
       of the Mercers' pageant waggon" (5). Uses a 1433
       indenture, 1463 Mercers' accounts of the soul's
       wagon, the 1501-07 Drawswerd wagon, and other
       primary evidence. Tentative reconstruction
       depicted in five illustrations. Shows the wagon

with a Hell-mouth, raising machinery, an iron
heaven (i.e. roof), etc. Claims to have "an iron-
frame heaven on the roof of the wooden box-frame
superstructure of the waggon, with the four ropes
from the 'brandreth' [God's seat] running over a
hub ('naffe'), and providing a simple raising
mechanism" (10). Discussion with Meg Twycross,
Meredith, John Anderson, Peter Happé, Jeremy
Maule, David Parry, John Marshall, and Richard
Beadle followed talk.

1093.   ---.   "'Farte Pryke in Cule' and Cock-fighting."   *MET*
6.1 (July 1984): 30-39.

Elucidates the reference in *Fulgens and Lucres*,
revealing the scatological nature of the phrase
and the game servants play which has this name.
Illustrates verbally, pictorially, and
photographically the "jousting" game.   (See
article by Alan J. Fletcher, "'Farte Prycke in
Cule . . .," entry # 573 above.)

1094.   ---.   "'Item for a grone--iij d'--Records and
Performance."   In *Records of Early English Drama:
Proceedings of the First Colloquium*, 26-60.   Ed.
by JoAnna Dutka (see entry # 497 above).

Stresses the importance of "accurate transcription
and painstaking interpretation" (26) in looking at
documents on the history and production of the
plays.   Warns of the kinds of errors that can be
made in transcription.   Points out some
problematical areas: the objects and people and
vocabulary of the documents, acting and actors,
the completeness of the documents, and so on.
Interprets the *Ordo Paginarum* and the other
documents in the same volume, guild ascriptions,
and some of Johnston and Dorrell's readings of
this data.   (Comment and discussion on this paper
are on pp. 93-97 and 98-100.   See John H.
Astington, "Comment," entry # 122 above.)

1095.   ---.   "John Clerke's Hand in the York Register."
LSE, n.s. 12 (1981, for 1980 and 1981): 245-71.

Offers biographical information about the
annotator, who accounts for c. 100 of c. 175
entries in the Register.   Shows what relationship
he had to the Register of the Corpus Christi play,
with particular attention paid to omissions and
organization.   Leads to an understanding of the
performance.   Concludes by showing how "Clerke's
work is . . . part of a continuing process of city

control and not the result of a sudden
ecclesiastical interest" (265).

1096.   ---.   "The Killing of the Children at Winchester
Cathedral."   *MET* 5.1 (July 1983): 51-52.

Review of performances of May 26-28, 1983.

1097.   ---.   *"The Leeds Descriptive Catalogue of Medieval
Drama."*   *RORD* 21 (1978): 91-93.

Reports work in progress on a projected two-volume
set--1) Biblical drama, 2) Other drama--on what
dramatic texts are extant from all over Europe.

1098.   ---.   "'Make the asse to speake' or Staging the
Chester Plays."   In *Staging the Chester Cycle*,
49-76.   Ed. by David Mills (see entry # 1159
below).

Looks broadly and narrowly at various kinds of
evidence to establish the kind of staging used in
Chester.   Examines acting, costume, carriages,
music, props, length of performance, date(s),
preparations for performances.   Also looks at
source documents and   "the context of the plays"
(51).   Concludes that the nature of the evidence
makes any final statements elusive, "that the
plays were wholly a product of the city of
Chester" (67), that the actors used skills which
were used in other kinds of dramatic performances,
and that we should try to visualize the kinds of
props they used (masks, crowns, swords, possibly
stilts, etc.).

1099.   ---.   "Medwall's *Fulgens and Lucres*."   *MET* 6.1 (July
1984): 44-48.

Reports on a performance at Christ's College,
Cambridge, March 30, 1984, by Joculatores
Lancastriensis.

1100.   ---.   "'Nolo Mortem' and the *Ludus Coventriae* Play of
the *Woman Taken in Adultery*."   *MedAe* 38.1 (1969):
38-54.

Considers whether the full Latin phrase is part of
the play.   Describes the ms to explain why there
is confusion.   Examines the "intimate connection"
(39) of the phrase with the play.   Sees the theme
of the play to be "mercy and the necessity of
repentance" (40).   Establishes "the sermon
structure of the play" (51).

1101.   ---.   "The *Ordo Paginarum* and the Development of the
         York Tilemakers' Pageant."   *LSE*, n.s. 11 (1980 for
         1979): 59-73.

         Looks at the scribal changes in the *Ordo* with
         special concentration on the Tilemakers' guild.
         Examines the different lists, with their various
         groupings of guilds. Notes that the extant
         evidence about earlier performances is suspect
         because of the changes in the *Ordo* entries.
         Explains the variations of combined versus
         separate pageants (i.e. individual pageants played
         by several guilds or by individual guilds). Tries
         to reconstruct the original form of *Ordo* entries.
         Says it is likely "that there was an amalgamated
         pageant which split up and then re-formed" (63).
         Cites over a dozen entries in York records to show
         the history of the development of the
         Millers'/Tilemakers' pageant. Generalizes that
         the documentary records need careful scrutiny.

1102.   ---.   "A Reconsideration of Some Textual Problems in
         the N-Town Manuscript (BL MS Cotton Vespasian D
         VIII)."   *LSE* 9 (1977, for 1976 and 1977): 35-50.

         First looks at a twenty-line passage in the N-Town
         play 13 (*The Visitation*); explains some of its
         obscurities, scribal errors, and uncertain
         punctuation. Relates his clarifications to the
         source of the passage. Then examines another
         passage from play 26 (*The Last Supper*) in which
         "calsydon" is explained, tentatively, as a scribal
         error for "cald syon." Finally looks at play 40
         (*The Assumption of the Virgin*), "the one play in
         the manuscript . . . which is written in a
         different hand" (42). Discusses the metrical
         arrangement of the play to explain the aims of the
         main scribe of the ms. Concludes that for this
         play the main scribe's aims were metrical, not
         substantive: "In no sense can the [scribe's]
         alterations . . . be considered of dramatic
         significance" (46).

1103.   ---.   "Reports on Productions."   *MET* 4.1 (July 1982):
         66-70.

         Discusses performances of June 27-28 and July 3-4,
         1982, of *Mary Magdalen* at Durham.

1104.   ---.   "Reports on Productions: *The Conversion of St.
         Paul* at Winchester Cathedral."   *MET* 4.1 (July
         1982): 66-70.

         Discusses performances of May 27-29, 1982.

1105.   ---. "Reports on Productions: The Killing of the
        Children at Winchester Cathedral." *MET* 5.1 (July
        1983): 51-52.

        Reports on performances of May 26-28, 1983.

1106.   M[eredith], P[eter]. "Reports on Two Mystery Play
        Productions in 1979: The Coventry Mystery Play,
        July-August 1979." *MET* 1.1 (Oct. 1979): 44.

        Reports on the performances of two Coventry plays
        "and a series of excerpts from the other cycles
        . . . up to the Resurrection" (44). (For the
        other production reported on here, see T[wycross],
        "Three Mystery Plays," entry # 1602 below.)

1107.   ---. "Scribes, Texts, and Performance." In *Aspects
        of Early English Drama*, 13-29, 142-43. Ed. by
        Paula Neuss (see entry # 1213 below).

        Examines ms evidence and shows how such evidence
        can "establish the kinds of basic question [sic]
        that need to be asked about the nature of the text
        and its relationship with performance" (13).
        Considers stage directions in the ms and other
        informative documents. Looks specifically at ms
        evidence for different cycles. With three
        facsimiles from mss.

1108.   ---. "Stage Directions and the Editing of Early
        English drama." In *Editing Early English Drama*
        . . ., 65-94. Ed. by A.F. Johnston (see entry #
        828 above).

        Stresses the importance of observing stage
        directions. Demonstrates this with several
        examples, some from medieval English drama. Looks
        primarily at those in the Chester mss and for the
        N-Town plays. Calls for a careful re-examination
        of the stage directions.

1109.   ---. "Stray Thoughts on Chester 1983." *MET* 5.1
        (July 1983): 42-44.

        Brief comment on the mini-cycle of eight plays,
        performed on June 26, 1983. With two photographs.

1110.   ---. [Untitled review.] *RORD* 20 (1977): 100.

        Reviews performance of the Towneley *Pharaoh*, July
        12, 1977, Graduate Centre for Medieval Studies,
        University of Leeds, at Place du Puits des Forges,
        Alençon.

1111.   ---.   [Untitled review.]   *RORD* 20 (1977): 101.

Reviews performance of the Croxton *Play of the Blyssyd Sacrament*, July 13, 1977, Cambridge Medieval Players, at Salle des Fêtes, Alençon.

1112.   ---.   [Untitled review.]   *RORD* 20 (1977): 112-14.

Reviews a performance of the York Cycle at Toronto, October 1-2, 1977.

1113.   ---.   [Untitled review.]   *RORD* 21 (1978): 100-01.

Reviews performances of *The Castle of Perseverance*, May 23-27, 1978, at St. Bartholomew the Great, Smithfield, London; and June 3-24, 1978, on tour.

1114.   ---.   "The York Cycle and the Beginning of Vernacular Religious Drama in England." In *Le Laudi Drammatiche Umbri delle Origini. Atti del V Convegno di Studio del Centro di Studi sul teatro medioevale e rinascimentale, Viterbo, 22-25 maggio 1980*, 311-333. Viterbo: Amministrazione Provinciale di Viterbo, Ente Provinciale del Turismo, 1983. (In Italian with translation.)

"[C]oncerned with evidence and with lack of it" about the rise of the drama (311). Recounts the older liturgy-to-secular-drama theory. Summarizes scholarship. Poses the question: "'If neither liturgical drama nor extra-liturgical drama is the source of the vernacular cycles, what is?'" (313); then suggests possible answers in the rest of the article, citing many primary civic documents, and speculating on the incremental growth of the cycles. Looks at the "gaps and problems" (324) in the documents. Focuses on York cycle. Contains two appendixes: 1) "1399 Petition of the Commons regarding the Play"; 2) "The 'Second List'"; both from the A/Y Memorandum Book.

1115.   ---.   "The York Millers' Pageant and the Towneley *Processus Talentorum*." *MET* 4.2 (Dec. 1982): 104-14.

Substantiates the existence of the lost York Millers' pageant. Supports the idea that the lost play was the basis for the Towneley *Processus Talentorum*. Brings in linguistic evidence (spelling, rhyme, verb forms, inflexions), the order of the plays, references to the lost play, references in other plays, and the subject matter of the Millers' play. Raises questions about the

relationship between the two (the dates of
performance, ms evidence, the dates of
composition, the source of copy for the Towneley
scribe/dramatist).

1116.   ---, and John Marshall. "The Wheeled Dragon in the
         Luttrell Psalter." *MET* 2.2 (Dec. 1980): 70-73.

         Looks at the marginal illustration of a "wheeled
         dragon"; claims it is a "pageant dragon" (71).

1117.   ---, and John E. Tailby, eds. *The Staging of
         Religious Drama in Europe in the Later Middle
         Ages: Texts and Documents in English Translation.*
         Trans. by Raffaella Ferrari, Peter Meredith,
         Lynette R. Muir, Margaret Sleeman, and John E.
         Tailby. Kalamazoo, Michigan: Medieval Institute
         Publications, Western Michigan U., 1983. EDAM
         Monograph Series, 4. 301 pp.

         Gives Modern English versions of descriptions,
         stage directions, and records of medieval
         religious plays; presents texts from works in
         English, Cornish, French, Latin, Italian, Spanish,
         and German. Offers texts on such topics as
         Arranging the Play, Organizing the Performance,
         the Audience, the Playing Area, Individual
         Locations and Sets, Machinery, Special Effects,
         Decor and Properties, Animals, Costumes, Stage
         Stuff, Music and Sound Effects, Movement, Dance,
         Mime and Gesture, After the Play, and Eye-Witness
         Accounts and Extended Descriptions.

         Rev. Raymond J. Pentzell, *CompD* 18.4 (Winter
              1984-85): 374-77.
              Paula Neuss, *ThN* 39.1 (1985): 43-44.
              Specu 60 (Oct. 1985): 998.
              Steven Urkowitz, *M&RD* 3 (1986): 335-37.

1118.   Merrix, Robert P. "The Function of the Comic Plot in
         Fulgens and Lucrece." *MLS* 7.1 (Spring 1977): 16-
         26.

         Examines the nature of the comic sub-plot.
         Defines the aesthetic basis for it and analyzes
         "the complex structural relationship of the comic
         plot to the rhetorical debate . . . to illustrate
         the mimetic function of the plot" (16). Concludes
         that the comic plot "accomplishes its purpose
         almost flawlessly" (23) since it is of equal
         significance to the serious plot.

1119.   Mervyn, James.   "Ritual, Drama and Social Body in the
        Late Medieval English Town."   *P&P* 98 (Feb. 1983):
        3-29.

        Discusses "the cult of Corpus Christi . . . the
        various rites which were celebrated on Corpus
        Christi Day, the various dramatic, theatrical
        manifestations . . ., and the mythology associated
        with both" (3).   Focuses on the "social background
        against which the cult was practised and the plays
        performed" (4).   Argues that the Corpus Christi
        theme "is society seen in terms of body; and that
        the concept of body provided urban societies with
        a mythology and ritual" (4) which allowed for
        senses of individualization and community.   Says
        that the cult's aim was "to express the social
        bond and to contribute to social integration" (4).
        Also explains the disappearance of the cycle
        plays.

1120.   Meyer, Robert T.   "The Liturgical Background of
        Mediaeval Cornish Drama."   *Trivium* 3 (1968): 48-
        58.

        Looks at the Breton and Cornish commonality of
        language and customs, especially the crossover of
        dramatic elements in the two countries.   Claims
        that Cornish drama "is more important to the
        linguist . . . than to the student of mediaeval
        literature" (48).   Considers the three-part
        Cornish *Ordinalia* (composed of the *Origo Mundi*,
        the *Passio Domini*, and the *Resurrecio Domini*),
        "the only mediaeval Cornish dramatic literature
        still extant" (49).   Examines the *Ordinalia* with
        respect to its connection with the liturgy.

1121.   Meyers, Walter E.   *A Figure Given: Typology in the
        Wakefield Plays*.   Pittsburgh, PA: Duquesne U.
        Press, [1970].   A Modern Humanities Research
        Association Monograph.   Duquesne Studies
        Philological Series, 14.   128 pp.

        Chap. I--Introduction--offers background to a
        typological study of the cycle.   Discusses unity
        of design and parallelism in individual plays,
        typology, the "'dogmatic' and 'realistic' parts"
        (13) of the plays, the cycle's use of time and
        anachronisms, and the audience.   Chap. II
        considers Old Testament plays.   Chap. III
        discusses "Diabolical Typology" (37).   Chap. IV is
        on "The Nativity and Childhood Plays" (57).   Chap.
        V covers "The Passion Plays" (79). And Chap. VI
        deals with "Resurrection and Last Judgment Plays"
        (93).   Chap. VII--"Some Conclusions" (111)--puts

the plays into historical perspective, with
respect to actors, dramatists, the religious
climate, and so on. With an appendix on the
Wakefield *Pharao* play, and an index.

1122. ---. "Typology and the Audience of the English Cycle
Plays." *SLI* 8.1 (Spring 1975): 145-58.

Warns of the misuse of typological criticism
applied to the drama. Reviews its use. Explains
what typology is with examples. Looks at the
Ludus Coventriae Prophets Play, the Chester Abel,
Abraham, and Melchisedech figures. Claims that
the audience would have understood the typological
references.

1123. Mezey, Nicole. "Creed and Prophets Series in the
Visual Arts, with a Note on Examples in York."
EDAMN 2.1 (Nov. 1979): 7-10.

Examines the iconography of the Creed from its
origins to the fifteenth century, with its pairing
of apostles and prophets. With fold-out tables
showing association of apostles and Creed scrolls
and "The Prophets, their texts and the Creed
clause to which they relate."

1124. Michael, W.F. "Humour and Comedy in Religious and
Secular Drama." In *The Drama of Medieval Europe,*
23-29 (plus discussion, 30-36). Ed. by Richard
Rastall (see entry # 1359 below.)

Surveys the "incursion of humor [sic] into the
tradition of the religious drama" (23). Considers
the characters, plots, motifs, and incidents from
the Bible which ultimately yield humor. Deals
primarily with continental sources.

1125. Michaels, Ronald. "The Judgment Day in Old and
Middle English Literature: A Study in Continuity
and Change." Ph.D. diss., St. John's U., 1980.

1125a. Miliaras, Barbara A. "The Politics of Religion and
the Heretical Left in Northern England:
Interaction between Theatre and Audience in the
Towneley Cycle." *FCS* 13 (1988): 435-46.

1126. Mill, Anna J. "The Edinburgh Hammermen's Corpus
Christi Herod Pageant." *IR* 21.1 (1970:) 77-80.

Looks at the records of the Hammermen's company
containing "a fine sequence of detailed accounts
running from 1494" (77), and revealing "the
provision of scriptural characters . . ." (77).

Presents transcript of the drama-related entries (1494-1516), with commentary. Corrects Hardin Craig's error about the supposed existence of a St. Katherine play, showing that "St. Katherine is not a play but a place" (79).

1127.   ---. "Medieval Stage Decoration: That Apple Tree Again." *ThN* 24.3 (Spring 1970): 122-24.

Discusses the orthographic similarity between *x* and *p*, leading to the confusion of "apeyll tre" for "axeyll tre" (the axle tree being one of the features of the pageant cars). Examines R.H. Morris' and Thomas Sharp's misreading and the implications this error has had on later readings of the apple tree.

1128.   ---. "The Miracle Plays and Mysteries." In *A Manual of the Writings in Middle English, 1050-1500.* Vol. V: 1315-1356; 1557-1598. Ed. by Albert E. Hartung (see entry # 714 above).

Contains an overview of the drama touching on such subjects as chronology, background materials, patterns of staging, liturgical and secular plays, processions, guilds, critical views, and recent editions. Deals with "Caiphas," Shrewsbury Fragments, Bodley Burial and Resurrection, Cambridge Fragment, Rickinghall (Bury St. Edmunds) Fragment, "Interludium de Clerico et Puella," Durham Prologue, "Dux Moraud," Chester Plays, York Plays, Towneley Plays, Ludus Coventriae, Coventry Plays, Newcastle Noah's Ark, Norwich Grocers' Play, Brome Abraham and Isaac, Dublin Abraham and Isaac, Croxton Sacrament, Digby Plays, Caesar Augustus (Ashmole) Fragment, Epilogue (Reynes Extract), The Resurrection of Our Lord, Stonyhurst Pageants. Has extensive bibliography (1557-1598).

1129.   ---. "The Perth Hammermen's Play: A Scottish Garden of Eden." *ScotHR* 49.2 (148) (Oct. 1970): 146-53.

Looks at "the ancient manuscript guild book" (146) which mentions "an annual religious play under ecclesiastical supervision" (146), performed in the late 1480s. Sees in the Hammermen's 1518 (and later) minutes a reference to a Corpus Christi play, probably a Creation and Fall of Man, and also possibly a St. Erasmus play. Also considers other plays that could have been performed as dumb shows as well as the participation of women in the play.

1130.   ---.   "The Records of Scots Medieval Plays:
        Interpretations and Misinterpretations."   In
        *Bards and Makars: Scottish Language and
        Literature: Medieval and Renaissance*, 136-42.   Ed.
        by Adam J. Aitken, Matthew P. McDiarmid, and
        Derick S. Thomson.   Glasgow: U. of Glasgow Press,
        1977.

        Discusses problems in interpreting Scottish
        records.   Speaks of "The tragic poverty of our
        pre-Reformation Scottish burgh records" (136) and
        the inexactitude and indeterminateness of
        terminology.   Mentions a Corpus Christi Day play
        at Haddington in 1543 and other performances.
        Also mentions problems with paleography, genre
        identification, dates of the mss (contemporary
        with plays or later), the confusions of medieval
        Latin, the politico-religious slant of the texts,
        the accuracy and completeness of extant court
        records, etc.

1131.   Mills, David.   "Approaches to Medieval Drama."   *LSE*,
        n.s. 3 (1969): 47-61.   Rpt. in Happé, *Medieval
        English Drama . . .*, 35-53 (entry # 684 above).

        Discusses historical, philosophical, and literary
        critical approaches to the drama.   Mentions the
        older view that drama developed from the liturgy,
        the newer view that it developed beside liturgy,
        and the idea that the latter view should be
        tempered by the former.   Examines terminology
        ('drama,' 'play,' 'dramatist,' 'actor,' etc.), and
        each approach ('Liturgical,' 'Literary,' and
        'Dramatic').   Warns against applying modern
        critical notions to medieval drama.

1132.   ---.   "A Corpus Christi Play and other Dramatic
        Activities in Sixteenth-century Sherborne,
        Dorset."   In *Collections, Volume IX*, 1-15.
        Oxford: Printed for the Malone Society by Oxford
        U. Press, 1971 (1977).   Gen. ed. G. R. Proudfoot.

        Presents extracts from Churchwardens' accounts
        (early sixteenth century to 1617) revealing Corpus
        Christi processions, a Corpus Christi play (c.
        1543-73), troupes of actors, and other dramatic
        activities.

1133.   ---.   "'Look at Me When I'm Speaking to You': The
        'Behold and See' Convention in Medieval Drama."
        MET 7.1 (July 1985): 4-12.

        Examines the nature of dialogue, with specific
        reference to the York *Crucifixion*, its individual

and group uses and effects. Also looks at its
relationship to action with respect to the
Wakefield *Noah* play. Claims that dialogue is more
central to medieval drama than is action.

1134. ---. "'Bushop Brian' and the Dramatic Entertainments
of Cheshire." *REEDN* 11.1 (1986): 1-7.

Discusses William Hinde's *A Faithfull Remonstrance
of the Holy Life and Happy Death of John Bruen of
Bruen Stapleford in the County of Chester Esquire*
(1641). Shows Bruen to be a strict reformer who
"epitomises the committed, skilful [sic] and
politically able opposition to drama and quasi-
dramatic entertainment in the north-west of
England in the later sixteenth and early
seventeenth centuries" (6).

1135. ---. "*The Castle of Perseverance* at Manchester."
MET 3.1 (July 1981): 55-56.

Reports on performances of April 29 to May 2,
1981.

1136. ---. "Characterisation in the English Mystery
Cycles: A Critical Prologue." *MET* 5.1 (July
1983): 5-17.

Discusses the meanings of the term
"characterisation" with respect to "internalised
and external characteristics" (6). Treats the
"medieval concern with the individual" (7) and the
"dramatist's contribution to characterisation" (8)
in terms of "the sources of meaning and action"
(9). Turns to the cycle plays to look at specific
characters (e.g. Abraham, Noah, Pilate, God, Cain,
Mak, etc.).

1137. ---. "Chester Plays." In *Dictionary of the Middle
Ages*, vol. 3, 298-99. Ed. by Joseph R. Strayer
(see entry # 1553 below).

Gives brief overview of the cycle: history,
performance, social basis, mss, influences on and
sources of the cycle. With bibliography.

1138. ---. "The Chester Cycle of Mystery Plays." *MET* 5.1
(July 1983): 44-51.

Reports on a performance by Poculi Ludique
Societas, Toronto, May 21-23, 1983. With four
photographs.

1139. ---. "The Comedy of Virtuous and Godly Susanna."
       MET 8.1 (July 1986): 67-71.

       Reviews a performance by Joculatores
       Lancastrienses at Rufford Old Hall, May 10, 1986.

1140. ---. "Concerning a Stage Direction in the *Ludus
       Coventriae.*" *ELN* 11.3 (Mar. 1974): 162-64.

       Examines "bemys" in stage direction after line 292
       of "The Salutation and Conception" play. Looks at
       others' suggestions for interpreting this word.
       Adds the possible rendering "the blast of a
       trumpet" (163).

1141. ---. "Coventry Plays." *MET* 3.2 (Dec. 1981): 134-36.

       Reports on performances of August 4-22, 1981.

1142. ---. "The *Creation and Fall.*" *MET* 6.1 (July 1984):
       59-60.

       Reports on a performance of this play from the
       Chester cycle, at Liverpool, June 27-28, 1984, by
       the Liverpool University Early Theatre Group.

1143. ---. "Diagrams for Staging Plays, Early or Middle
       15th Century." In *Local Maps and Plans From
       Medieval England*, 344-45. Ed. by R.A. Skelton and
       P.D.A. Harvey. Oxford: Clarendon Press, 1986.

       Discusses two mss (Folger, Washington, ms V.a.354,
       fo. 191^{v}; and Bodleian, MS Bodley 791, fos. 27^{r},
       56^{v}, and 83^{r}). The Folger (Macro) ms contains the
       Castle of Perseverance diagram (c. 1440). The
       Bodley ms contains three staging diagrams (first
       half of the fifteenth century), with diagrams
       following each of the three *Cornish Ordinalia*
       plays (Creation, Passion, Resurrection).

1144. ---. "The Doctor's Epilogue to the Brome *Abraham and
       Isaac:* A Possible Analogue." *LSE*, n.s. 11 (1980
       for 1979): 105-110.

       Looks at the traditional view of the epilogue as
       an occasional exemplum on the death of a child or
       perhaps a familiar, "traditional" moral (as found
       in Jerome, Vincent of Beauvais, and Origen)--an
       "exemplum for parents" (106). Concludes that the
       epilogue is probably not occasional but is a
       familiar moral.

1145. ---. "Drama and Folk-ritual." In *The* Revels *History
       of Drama in English*, Vol. I, Pt. II, 4, 122-51.

Ed. by. A.C. Cawley, et al. Discussed at entry
for David Mills and Peter F. McDonald, "The Drama
of Religious Ceremonial" (see entry # 1163 below).

1146. ---. "Drama, Western European." In *Dictionary of
the Middle Ages*, Vol 4., 277-89. Ed. by Joseph R.
Strayer (see entry # 1553 below).

Discusses terminology, Latin religious drama,
drama associated with scholarship, with civic
celebration, with religious instruction, and with
private entertainment. With bibliography.

1147. ---. "Edward Gregorie--A 'Bunbury Scholar.'" *REEDN*
7.1 (1982): 49-50.

Offers biographical information on Gregorie, the
scribe of the Huntington ms of the Chester Cycle,
who was churchwarden at St. Boniface Church,
Bunbury, in 1608. He died in 1628. Locates
historical records citing Gregorie, authenticating
his claim to have been the scribe (avowed in the
colophon to the Huntington ms).

1148. ---. "'In This Storye Consistethe Oure Chefe
Faithe': The Problems of Chester's Play(s) of the
Passion." *LSE*, n.s. 16 (1985): 326-36.

Addresses the question, "why does the latest
cyclic manuscript . . . present the events from
Christ's appearance before the High Priests to the
deposition and burial of His body after the
crucifixion as a single play" (326) where other
mss have two plays (*The Trial and Flagellation
. . . ,* and *The Crucifixion*)? Considers the
descriptions of the plays in the Banns and the
editorial decisions of the 1607 ms scribe, James
Miller. Looks at the two versions of the Banns,
the characterization, "The Ending of the
Crucifixion--action" (331). Claims that Miller
"was misled by the play--numbering, the colophon
and/or the description in the Banns" (334), and so
made the error of presenting the action as a
single play.

1149. ---. "James Miller: The Will of a Chester Scribe."
REEDN 9.1 (1984): 11-13.

Calls Miller "the first editor of the [Chester]
cycle" (11). Discusses Miller, one of the ms's
scribes, with respect to his will. Points out
"the antiquarian and scholarly tastes of those
working on the Chester exemplar and suggests the

kind of appeal that the plays may have had to educated Cestrians as history and divinity" (12).

1150.   ---. "The Language of Medieval Drama." In *The Revels History of Drama in English*, Vol. I, Pt. II, 69-78. Ed. by A.C. Cawley, et al. Discussed in entry for David Mills and Peter F. McDonald, "The Drama of Religious Ceremonial" (see entry # 1163 below).

1151.   ---. "Manuscripts and Contents of the Extant English Cycles." In *The* Revels *History of Drama in English*, Vol. I, appendix, 292-302. (See entry # 289 above.)

Lists the mss and contents (with the guilds responsible for putting on each play) for the Chester, Wakefield, N-Town, and York cycles, and the texts of fragments.

1152.   ---. "Medieval and Modern Views of Drama." In *The* Revels *History of Drama in English*, Vol. I, Pt. II, 2, 79-91. Discussed at entry for David Mills and Peter F. McDonald, "The Drama of Religious Ceremonial" (entry # 1163 below).

1153.   ---. "Modern Editions of Medieval English Plays." In *Medieval Drama* . . . (forthcoming). Ed. by Eckehard Simon (entry # 1469 below).

1154.   ---. "'None had the like nor the like darste set out': The City of Chester and its Mystery Cycle." In *Staging the Chester Cycle*, 1-16. Ed. by David Mills (entry # 1159 below).

Discusses the surviving mss, their scribes, and the local interest in the plays. Gives a history of the cycle; discusses "The Defence of the Cycle in the Late Banns" (5), the cycle's concern with authority, the plays as religious drama, and the danger of performing the cycle after Queen Elizabeth had voiced her disapproval and after the 1572 prohibition from the Archbishop of York. Points out that the 1572 and 1575 performances were thus dangerous ones.

1155.   ---. "Part Two of Medwall's *Nature*." *MET* 6.1 (July 1984): 40-42.

Reports on a performance at Ordsall Hall, Salford, February 3, 1984, by the University of Salford Arts Unit.

1156.   ---. "Religious Drama and Civic Ceremonial." In *The Revels History of Drama in English*, Vol. I, Pt. II, 5, 152-206. Discussed at entry for David Mills and Peter F. McDonald, "The Drama of Religious Ceremonial" (see entry # 1163 below).

1157.   ---. "Some Possible Implications of Herod's Speech, Chester Play VIII 153-204." *NM* 74.1 (1973): 131-43.

Examines Herod's language in the context of the play, with a look at its "possible range of meanings" (131). Suggests "that the literary structure of the best of medieval drama depends upon a relationship of 'actor' and 'rôle'" (131). Shows how the presentation of the role effects meaning. Uses Herod as a case in point, showing him to be both comic and tragic. Looks at "contemporary, personal, social and spiritual levels" (143).

1158.   ---. "The Stage Directions in the Manuscripts of the Chester Mystery Cycle." *MET* 3.1 (July 1981): 45-51.

Lists the mss, identifies the stage directions, discusses the textual evidence and the marginal material. Says that the abundant information is "the product of a practical and intelligent playwright" (51).

1159.   ---, ed. *Staging the Chester Cycle.* Leeds: The University of Leeds School of English, 1985. Leeds Texts and Monographs, New Series No. 9. Ed. by Stanley Ellis and Peter Meredith. 123 pp.

Contains five essays, "Lectures given on the Occasion of the Production of the Cycle at Leeds in 1983" (t.p.). The essays are by David Mills ("'None had the like . . .," # 1154 above); John Marshall ("'The manner of these playes' . . .," # 1066); Peter Meredith ("'Make the asse to speake' . . .," # 1098); Richard Rastall ("'Some myrth . . .," # 1366); and Meg Twycross ("The Chester Cycle Wardrobe," # 1593). Contains preface, brief bibliography, and "Some Dates" relevant to the cycle.

1160.   ---. "Theories and Practices in the Editing of the Chester Cycle Play-manuscripts." In *Manuscripts and Texts: Editorial Problems in Later Middle English Literature: Essays from the 1985 Conference at the University of York*, 110-21. Ed.

by Derek Pearsall. Wolfeboro, New Hampshire, and Cambridge: D.S. Brewer, 1987.

Briefly describes the mss and their history; discusses the editing problems he and R.M. Lumiansky had in doing their edition (see entry # 55 above). Also discusses other editions, "The Destabilising of the Cycle-text" (113) and the selection of an exemplar, and "The Books of the Scribes" (119).

1161.   ---.   "'The Towneley Plays' or 'The Towneley Cycle'?" *LSE*, n.s. 17 (1986): 95-104.

Considers the critical issue: "how far is it valid and helpful to regard 'cycle' as a term of generic definition?" (95). Looks at this in terms of the "dramatic diversity" (95) of the Towneley plays. [See Palmer, entry # 1259 below.]

1162.   ---.   "The Two Versions of Chester Play V: *Balaam and Balak.*" In *Chaucer and Middle English Studies in Honour of Rossell Hope Robbins*, 366-71. Ed. by Beryl Rowland. London: George Allen and Unwin; Kent, Ohio: Kent State U. Press, 1974.

Shows "how the writers of these two versions have adapted the subject matter to meet different dramatic and thematic requirements" (366). Discusses the order of composition, "local conditions" (366), the structure of the play with respect to its place in the cycle, and the differences between the two versions, especially with respect to "dramatic and thematic variations" (370).

1163.   ---, and Peter F. McDonald.   "The Drama of Religious Ceremonial." In *The* Revels *History of Drama in English*, Vol. I, 67-210. Ed. by A.C. Cawley, et al. (see entry # 289 above).

Part 1, by David Mills, "The Language of Medieval Drama" (69-78; # 1150 above), discusses the late Middle English and Early Modern English language of medieval drama. Shows the relation between French dialects and English, and how--by varying English vocabulary, rhetoric, syntax--the playwrights could create characterization. Talks about alliteration, the jargon of trades, dialect variety, and the editorial problems raised by the spelling/alphabet of the extant texts. Discusses the playwrights' concern for "high style" and "low style" for high and low themes.

Part 2, by David Mills, gives "Medieval and Modern Views of Drama" (79-91; # 1152 above), considers the history of the notion of "drama," and shows the social and cultural context for drama.

Part 3, by Peter F. McDonald, "Drama in the Church" (92-121; # 1027 above), relates drama to liturgy. Reviews the standard ideas about dramatization and the liturgy, devotional drama, religious drama, and liturgy as spectacle.

Part 4, by David Mills, "Drama and Folk-ritual" (122-51; # 1145 above), treats the "village and its rituals," "Rationalizations of ritual," "Robin Hood plays," "Plough plays and hero combats," "Christian myth in the village," and "Drama incorporating folk motifs."

Part 5, by David Mills, "Religious Drama and Civic Ceremonial" (152-206; # 1156 above), discusses "Mythology and the urban community," "Processional drama and cycle form," "Cycle structure and dramatic mode in Chester and Wakefield," "Character and structure: York, Coventry and the Digby *Mary Magdalen*," and "Ritual distancing: the N-town cycle."

Part 6, by David Mills and Peter McDonald, deals with "New Kinds of Drama" (207-10; see next entry)--the changing environment in England which allowed the plays to continue despite religious objection, and the replacement of the plays with different types of drama, no longer attached to its ritual origins. Point out that drama shifted from emphasis on God to emphasis on king; liturgical drama gave way to secular music-drama at court; the "view of history looking to Christ the King yielded to a view of national history looking to the King of England, the English chronicle play" (209), and victories of Christian heroes and deaths of martyrs gave way to "triumphs and tragedies of noble men" (209).

1164. ---, ---. "New Kinds of Drama." In *The* Revels *History of Drama in English*, Vol. I, 207-10. Ed. by A.C. Cawley, et al. (see # 289 above). Discussed at previous entry.

1165. Miyajima, Sumiko. *The Theatre of Man: Dramatic Technique and Stagecraft in the English Medieval Moral Plays*. Avon, England: Clevedon Printing Co., Ltd., 1977. [Originally written as a doctoral dissertation, U. of Paris, 1971.] vi, 193 pp.

Author makes no claim "to expertise in medieval
textual exegesis or to the discovery of new data
about them" [the plays], but tries "to see the
plays in a different light from that of the
professional scholars . . ." (vi). Chap. I
examines the genre, terminology, five plays in
general (*The Pride of Life, The Castle of
Perseverance, Wisdom, Mankind,* and *Everyman*), and
then looks closely at *Everyman,* "the beginning of
a new literary genre--the play for mass reading"
(17). Chap. II covers backgrounds and traditions,
including such issues as the times (in the
fifteenth century), the drama of the Mass,
costume, gesture, music, and staging. Chap. III
discusses dramatic techniques and stagecraft for
the five plays. Chap. IV looks at
characterization (of human beings, God, Death,
Good and Evil, and Vice). Chap. V considers idea
and form (space and time, dualism, relation to
sermons, plot, organization, structure). With
notes, bibliography, and index.

Rev. Leanore Lieblein, *ThJ* 31.1 (Mar. 1979): 134-
35.
Stanley J. Kahrl, *Specu* 55 (Jan. 1980): 160.
T.W. Craik, *ThRI* 5.2 (Spring 1980): 163-65.

1166. Molinari, Cesare. *Theatre Through the Ages.* New
York: McGraw Hill, 1974; London: Cassell, 1975.
Trans. by Colin Hamer. 324 pp.

Chap. 7--"Everyday Theatre in the Middle Ages:
Mimes and Minstrels" (75-84); Chap. 8--"Liturgical
Drama" (85-90); and Chap. 9--"The Mystery-Plays:
Religious Theatre for the People" (91-108) are
fairly brief surveys of stagecraft, costuming,
dramatic development, themes, topics of plays and
cycles, etc. Mostly a pictorial survey, with many
illustrations from mss and church art.

Rev. George Speaight, *ThN* 30.1 (1976): 39-40.
Peter Arnott, *CompD* 11.4 (Winter 1977-78):
358-59.

1166a. Moore, Bruce. "The Hobby Horse and the Court
Masque." *N&Q* 233 (1988): 25-26.

1167. ---. "The Narrator within the Performance: Problems
with Two Medieval 'Plays.'" *CompD* 22.1 (Spring
1988): 21-36.

Discusses *Interludium de Clerico et Puella* and
Dame Sirith as texts "intended for performance"

(21). Shows how they are similar in dramatic modes but different in their concerns.

1168. Moore, Charles Brown. "York Crafts and the Corpus Christi Pageants." Ph.D. diss., Princeton U., 1973.

1169. Moore, Marie Dolores. "The *Visitatio Sepulchri* of the Medieval Church: A Historical, Geographical, and Liturgical Survey." Ph.D. diss., U. of Rochester, 1971.

1170. Moran, Dennis V. "The Life of *Everyman.*" *Neoph* 56.3 (July 1972): 324-30.

Discusses the relation between the play and the Dance of Death. Calls the play "a profound celebration on the art of Christian dying" (324). Talks about the emphasis on the inevitability of dying and on God's mercy. Concludes that the play's appeal comes from its focus more on the nature of life than on the nature of doctrine.

1171. Moran, Joann H. *Education and Learning in the City of York 1300-1560.* N.p: n.p., 1979. Borthwick Papers No. 55.

Aims to delineate "the educational possibilities and the intellectual vitality" (4) of the city, drawing from primary sources (mostly wills). Not specifically on drama, but offers background information on the literacy of the populace. Discusses the intellectual activities of the city, including a "new Corpus Christi play as a means of purifying the city" (32). Looks at the plays (32-34).

1172. Morrison, George Peter. "Shakespeare's Lancastrian Tetralogy in the Light of the Medieval Mystery Cycles: A Theory for Unity." Ph.D. diss., State U. of New York, Stony Brook, 1977.

1173. Morrissey, L.J. "English Pageant-Wagons." *ECS* 9.3 (Spring 1976): 353-74.

Considers the debates over the size, structure, and other features of the wagons. Examines late seventeenth-century playbooks and guild records for Lord Mayor's Shows and Royal Entries. Claims that the medieval performers may have used "multiple stages, made up of several wagons that assembled, broke up, and reassembled in new combinations" (373). Suggests the possibility

that wagons were used for several plays, not just
for a single play.

1174. Muir, Lynette R. "Apocryphal Writings and the
Mystery Plays." In *Le Théâtre au Moyen Age*, 79-
83. Ed. by Gari R. Muller (see entry # 1181
below).

Calls for more modern editions of apocryphal texts
and for more reference materials. Defines
"apocryphal writings" (81). Does not focus on
English drama, but presents general suggestions
about approaching mystery plays. With one
illustration.

1175. ---. "The Fall of Man in the Drama of Medieval
Europe." *StudMedCul* 10 (1977): 121-31.

Looks at all "twenty extant medieval plays on the
Fall" with respect to "their teaching on the
atonement and the ways in which the authors varied
. . . the substance and the dramatic expression of
this doctrine" (121). Deals with the Chester,
Towneley, and York plays (124), the Cornish
Ordinalia and Norwich Grocers' plays (125), and
the N-Town cycle (129), showing the different
slants of doctrine presented by each.

1176. ---. "Medieval English Drama: The French
Connection." In *Contexts for Early English Drama*,
56-76. Ed. by Marianne Briscoe and John C.
Coldewey (see entry # 228 above).

Compares French and English vernacular biblical
plays. Discusses differences and similarities
under the headings of language, subject matter,
staging, and organization. With a "Descriptive
List of the Principal biblical plays of the 15th
and 16th Centuries (with English reference
names)."

1177. ---. "The *PLS* in Leeds." *MET* 3.1 (July 1981): 60-
61.

Reports of performances by the *Poculi Ludique
Societas* on May 3, 1981, of Hans Sachs' *The Stolen
Shrovetide Cock, Robin Hood and the Friar*, the
Wakefield *Murder of Abel*, and the Renaissance
musical of *Tom Tyler*.

1178. ---. "*Les Prophètes du Christ*, cent aus après." In
*Mélanges de Littérature du Moyen Age au xxe siècle
offert à Mademoiselle Jeanne Lods, Professeur
honoraire de Littérature médiévale à l'Ecole*

Normale Supérieure de Jeunes Filles par ses collègues, ses élèves et ses amis. 2 vols., I, 447-58. Paris: École Normale Supérieure de Jeunes Filles, 1978. Collection de l'École Normale Supérieure de Jeunes Filles, 10.

Cites the nineteenth-century work of Maurice Sepet on "Les Prophètes du Christ." Assesses the role of Old Testament prophets in medieval biblical drama of England, France, Italy, Germany, and Holland, focusing primarily on how the non-dramatic words spoken by the prophets become dramatic. Considers various techniques including 1) sermon/dialogue (in which another character asks the prophet to speak)--used in the York plays (in the introduction to the Annunciation scene); 2) the Ordo prophetarum and the tree of Jesse motif (which involve dialogue, or a prophet explaining a text, with or without a vocator [facilitator])--used in the Wakefield, Chester, and N-Town plays; 3) non-prophets, such as Nebuchadnezzar and the three young men in the fiery furnace (Shadrach, Meshach, and Abednigo), who were used as prophetic figures; 4) prophets shown in Limbo, discussing the impending birth of Christ or at the moment of His death; 5) classical figures and sibyls who foretell such events as the Virgin's giving birth to a son or discussing an emperor (like Herod) who plans either to destroy the infant (as in Wakefield) or do him homage (as in Chester). Looks at the ban from the stage of the prophets in the sixteenth and seventeenth centuries.

1179. ---. "The Trinity in Medieval Drama." *CompD* 10.2 (Summer 1976): 116-29. Rpt. in *The Drama in the Middle Ages* . . ., 75-88. Ed. by Davidson, et al. (see entry # 409 above).

Considers the Trinity in drama from "the earliest play based on the Gospels" (the Greek *Paschon Christi*, c. 4th century) to the English cycle plays. Looks at non-English texts as well. More descriptive than critical.

1180. Mullally, Robert. "The Source of the *Fulgens* Woodcut." *ThN* 30.2 (1976): 61-65.

Opens by recounting Richard Southern's views on the importance of the title-page illustration in the first edition of Medwalls *Fulgens and Lucres* (in Southern's *The Staging of Plays before Shakespeare*; see entry # 1495 below). Examines the printing history of the book. Discovers an

identical woodcut in Michael Toulouse's *L'Art et
instruction de bien dancer* (Paris, 1488?), and in
another volume, *Paris et Vienne* (Paris, 1489-91?).
Concludes that since the woodcut is a borrowing
from an older book, the costumes represented in it
are not contemporary with Medwall's play, but the
stylization of such costuming suggests "how two
characters in *Fulgens* might have been attired"
(64).

1181. Muller, Gari R., ed. *Le Théâtre au Moyen Age. Actes
du deuxième colloque de la Société Internationale
pour l'Etude du Théâtre Médiéval, Alençon, 11-14
juillet 1977.* Paris, Brussels, Quebec:
L'Aurore/Univers; Montreal: Les Éditions
Universe, 1981. Pref. by Jean-Charles Payen. 318
pp.

Contains essays on English drama by Dorothy L.
Latz ("L'expression corporelle . . .," entry # 964
above); Clifford Davidson ("The Visual Arts
. . .," # 407); Lynette Muir ("Apocryphal Writings
. . .," # 1174); Sarah Carpenter ("John Bale's
King Johan . . .," # 272).

1182. Munson, William F. "Audience and Meaning in Two
Medieval Dramatic Realisms." *CompD* 9.1 (Spring
1975): 44-67. Rpt. in *The Drama of the Middle
Ages*, 183-206. Ed. by Davidson, et al. (see entry
409 above).

Examines the Wakefield *First Shepherds' Play* and
the Chester *Adoration of the Shepherds* as low
comedies involving a realism which makes reference
to contemporary life and also makes "low jest of
high things" (44), characteristics making the
plays a transitional, not an extraordinary, type
of drama. Looks at the holiday life of the
community--the festive atmosphere of the plays--as
well as the character typology, plot episodes,
"comic deflation" (55), the "realization of
physical setting" (57), and language styles.

1183. ---. "Holiday, Audience Participation, and
Characterization in the Shepherds' Plays." *RORD*
15-16 (1972-73): 97-115.

Discusses "the holiday context of the
performances" (97), the social customs of the
times, "the reflexive relationship between
audience and 'representation' that is
characteristic of worship" (99), the various
feasts and levels of formality and how the actors
partook of them along with the audience, the

joining of the audience with the actors, the
seriousness and conviviality of the shepherds'
plays, the use of jest, and so on.

1184.   ---. "Knowing and Doing in *Everyman*." *ChauR* 19.3
(1985): 252-71.

Looks at the play in the light of "Bernardine
humanism, in which man is 'an active agent in the
work of his own redemption'" (252). Sees Good
Deeds "as an epitome of Everyman himself" (252).
Also considers how the play differs from others of
its genre.

1185.   Murphy, Maria Spaeth, Carole Ferguson, and James Hoy,
eds. "Bibliography of Medieval Drama, 1973-1976."
ESRS 35.1 (Summer 1986): 5-41.

Continues bibliography (see next entry). Contains
177 entries, as below. With brief index.

1186.   ---, ---, ---, eds. "Bibliography of Medieval Drama,
1969-1972." *ESRS* 34.4 (Spring 1986): 5-41.

Aims to update Stratman (see entry # 1551 below).
Contains chronological listing of 167 items:
books, articles, and dissertations. With brief
index. Continued in previous entry.

1187.   Murphy, Thomas Patrick. "The Characters Called
Corpus Christi: Dramatic Characterization in the
English Mystery Cycles." Ph.D. diss., Ohio State
U., 1975.

1188.   Mussetter, Sally. "The York Pilate and the Seven
Deadly Sins." *NM* 81.1 (1980): 57-64.

Analyzes Pilate's character with respect to the
play's structure to show "that his supposed
sympathy is a self-serving sham" (57). Calls him
"a hypocrite whose moral and psychological
tensions enhance the dramatic effectiveness of the
play" (57). Denies the notion that he is
sometimes sympathetic. Sees Pilate's
personification of the seven deadly sins, and sees
him as "an index of evil" (64).

1189.   Mycoff, David. "Two Sources of Osbern Bokenham's
'*Lyf of Marye Maudelyn*.'" *N&Q* 32.3 (230) (Sept.
1985): 310-12.

Shows sources in English literature. Not
specifically on the drama, but demonstrates the

widespread medieval interest in the Mary Magdalene
legend.

1190.   Nagler, A.M. [Alois Maria]. *The Medieval Religious
Stage: Shapes and Phantoms.* New Haven and London:
Yale U. Press, 1976. xii, 108 pp.

Bases his ideas on the premise that theater
historians must "reconstruct past styles of
performance" (xi). Speculates on methods of
performance, based in part on stage directions and
on topographical evidence. Chap. 3 considers
plays for which there are stage plans, including
"The Castle of Perseverance" (49 ff.) and the
Digby "Mary Magdalene" (52 ff.). Chap. 4 deals
with different methods of presentation--
"Processional or Stationary?" (55 ff.); looks at
the four cycles as well as at the Digby
"Conversion of St. Paul" and "The Pageant Wagon
Debate" (67) based on David Rogers's description.
Chap. 5 covers the use of pictorial evidence
(though not focusing on English drama). Chap. 6
deals with the question "Pictorial Art or
Theater?"; presents three views: 1) "pictorial
art borrows iconographic motifs from the religious
drama" (89); 2) art and drama have common sources;
3) "graphic art has temporal precedence and exerts
an influence on the mystery plays" (89).

Rev. R.J. Cormier, *LJ* 102 (Jan. 15, 1977): 216.
      Choice 14 (Mar. 1977): 76.
      TLS (Mar. 11, 1977): 263.
      David Bevington, *CompD* 11.1 (Spring 1977):
         95-98.
      VQR 53 (Spring 1977): 69.
      T.A. McVeigh, *Thought* 52 (June 1977): 221-22.
      R.T. Davies, *N&Q* 24 (Aug. 1977): 371-72.
      G.J. Brault, *FR* 51 (Oct. 1977): 112.
      Alan H. Nelson, *ETJ* 29.4 (Dec. 1977): 574-75.
      William A. Armstrong, *ThN* 32.3 (1978): 140-
         42.
      Dunbar H. Ogden, *ThSur* 19.1 (May 1978): 82-
         83.
      Stanley J. Kahrl, *Specu* 53 (July 1978): 604-
         06.
      M.M. McGowan, *SAHJ* 37 (Dec. 1978): 317-18.
      G.H.V. Bunt, *EngStud* 61 (Feb. 1980): 88-90.

1191.   Nakagawa, Tokio. "Chusei Dowa Geki *Bannin* to
Langland no *Nofu Piazu*." In *Eibungaku to no Deai*
[The Encounter of English and American
Literature], 244-51. Ed. by Naomi Matsuura.
Kyoto: Showado, 1983.

Offers the old liturgy-to-secular-drama theory
(drama began in the church with Latin dialogue
about Christ's Resurrection . . .). Says *Everyman*
developed from miracle plays. Describes the
morality genre. Summarizes the plot and says that
the play conjures up the atmosphere of medieval
England. Comments on the solemn religious
ceremonial nature of the play, the metrics, the
vocabulary, the uneducated audience, the didactic
elements, the play's popularity, its allegory
which is understandable to the common man, its
relevance to a modern audience, its theme which
focuses on real life and how best to lead it, and
how to prepare for death. Shows how the play
leads to the Puritan revolution and Puritan
literature (especially to *Paradise Lost* and
Pilgrim's Progress). Calls the latter a prose
version of *Everyman*. Mentions how the play
reflects current issues. Offers a similar
discussion for *Piers Plowman*.

1192. Needles, K. Reed, and Steven Putzel. "Toronto: The
Pageant Waggons." *MET* 1.1 (Oct. 1979): 32-33.
("Reprinted from the programme of the Toronto York
Cycle" [32].)

Describes the planning, locating, building, and
decorating the Toronto pageant wagons; with one
illustration. (See David Parry, "The York Mystery
Cycle at Toronto, 1977," entry # 1270 below.)

1193. Nelson, Alan H. "Castle of Perseverance." In
Dictionary of the Middle Ages, Vol. 3, 142-43.
Ed. by Joseph R. Strayer (see entry # 1553 below).

Contains a very brief account with a three-entry
bibliography.

1194. ---. "Contexts of Early English Drama: The
Universities." In *Contexts for Early English
Drama*, 137-49. Ed. by Marianne G. Briscoe and
John C. Coldewey (see entry # 228 above).

Considers the drama accepted by and produced in
the universities. Calls English university drama
"essentially a post-medieval phenomenon," part of
the humanist revival of the early sixteenth
century. Looks at current scholarship in the
field of academic drama.

1195. ---. "Early Pictorial Analogues of Medieval Theatre-
in-the-Round." *RORD* 12 (1969): 93-106.

Responds to Richard Southern's *The Medieval Theatre in the Round* (see entry # 1493 below). Aims mainly to record "a pictorial example of the circular disposition of witnesses to an action, a configuration which may . . . have connections with the drama" (93). Looks at a ms leaf from Victoria and Albert Museum MS. 661.

1196. ---. "Easter Week Pageants in Valladolid and Medina del Campo." *MET* 1.2 (Dec. 1979): 62-70.

Discusses (with twelve photographs) a pageant procession in Spain. Claims that the wagons are not "equivalents of medieval English pageant waggons" (69), but they "enable us to read the archival records of England from a fresh perspective" (70).

1197. ---. "Life Records of Henry Medwall, M.A., Notary Public and Playwright; and John Medwall, Legal Administrator and Summoner." *LSE* 11 (1980 for 1979): 111-55.

Offers a full transcription of several documents presenting data on the life of Henry and John Medwall; gives a brief biography of both Henry and his older brother John. Calls Henry possibly "the earliest English playwright whose name and career can be known with any certainty" (112).

1198. ---. "Mechanical Wheels of Fortune, 1100-1547." *JWCI* 43 (1980): 227-33.

Offers a ten-item checklist with discussions of ten wheels of fortune and medieval technology. Does not focus on English drama, but shows how such wheels were used in medieval plays in France and Bruges.

1199. ---. *The Medieval English Stage: Corpus Christi Pageants and Plays*. Chicago and London: U. of Chicago Press, 1974. xiv, 274 pp.

Presents chapters on 1) "Historical Inquiry and Formal Criticism"; 2) "Principles of Processional Staging: York Cycle." Then has chapters on individual towns: 3) York; 4) Wakefield; 5) Beverley; 6) Lincoln; 7) Norwich; 8) Coventry; 9) Chester; 10) London; 11) Miscellaneous Towns and Cities--includes more than two dozen places. Also contains appendixes on A) Formulas for True-Processional Productions; B) Doubling in True-Processional Productions; C) Ipswich Pageant

Lists. With illustrations, notes, bibliography, and index.

Rev. *LJ* 99 (May 1, 1974): 1304.
　Choice 11 (Nov. 1974): 1322.
　Stanley J. Kahrl, *CompD* 8.4 (Winter 1974-75): 386-90.
　Alexandra F. Johnston, *UTQ* 44 (1975): 238-48. (See entry # 834 above.)
　TLS (Jan. 17, 1975): 51.
　VQR 51 (Summer 1975): R105.
　G.C. Britton, *N&Q*, n.s. 22.9 (220) (Sept. 1975): 416-18.
　D.W. Robertson, Jr., *AHR* 80 (Dec. 1975): 1308.
　Richard Beadle, *MedAe* 45.3 (1976): 347-50.
　L.M. Clopper, Martin Stevens, and Stephen Spector, *JEGP* 75 (1976): 403-07.
　William Tydeman, *ThN* 30.2 (1976): 92-94.
　B.D. Bills, *ETJ* 28 (Mar. 1976): 127-31.
　R. Southern, *RenQ* 29 (Summer 1976): 274-75.
　David Mills, *RES*, n.s. 27.107 (Aug. 1976): 330-33.
　Donald C. Baker, *ELN* 14.1 (Sept. 1976): 57-61.
　Specu 52 (Apr. 1977): 414.
　G.H.V. Bunt, *EngStud* 58 (Aug. 1977): 353-55.
　Peter W. Travis, *MP* 75.4 (May 1978): 400-02.
　E.C. Dunn, *CHR* 64 (July 1978): 455-56.
　[See also E.C. Dunn, "Recent Medieval . . . .," entry # 487 above.]

1200. ---. "Morality Play." In *Dictionary of the Middle Ages*, Vol. 8, 484. Ed. by Joseph R. Strayer (see entry # 1553 below).

Offers brief overview, mentioning genre, themes, popularity, plays in English, French, German. With bibliography.

1201. ---. "'Of the seuen ages': An Unknown Analogue of *The Castle of Perseverance*." In *Studies in Medieval Drama in Honor of William L. Smoldon on His 82nd Birthday*, 125-38. Ed. by Clifford Davidson, et al. (see entry # 410 above).

Shows the correspondences between the poem and the play. With a transcription of the poem and illustrations from its ms of the two pages which contain the poem. Shows the poem to be an analogue "closer than any other discovered" (136).

1202. ---. "On Recovering the Lost Norwich Corpus Christi Cycle." *CompD* 4.4 (Winter 1970-71): 241-52.

Takes issue with the traditional idea that the
Norwich Corpus Christi plays should be called
Whitsun plays; claims that they were not performed
at Whitsun (Pentecost) before 1559 (and possibly
after). Says they may not have been performed in
the manner described in the petition of the
Norwich Guild of St. Luke of 1527. Shows why the
confusion exists. Says the production was of
"disguisings and pageants of the lives and
martyrdoms of the saints" (241), not "scenes from
sacred history" (241). Claims that it is possible
that the guilds "were expected to mount their
Corpus Christi pageants in the Whitmonday
procession" (242). Defines "pageant" as "wagon"
(242). Looks at contemporary documents about
costs, pageants, etc. Claims that the cycle plays
may have been moved from Corpus Christi to Whitsun
to avoid ecclesiastical censure after Elizabeth
took the throne and brought back Protestantism.
Says that the Corpus Christi plays "were regularly
performed on their proper festival day until at
least the 1540's" (246). Postulates that Norwich
is one possible place that the N-Town plays were
performed in. Posits reasons for this possibility
and objections to it. Mentions the "tantalizing
possibility that the N-Town cycle represents some
form of the lost Norwich plays" (250). With
illustrations.

1203.   ---.   "A Pilgrimage to Toledo: Corpus Christi Day
        1974."   RORD 17 (1974): 123-29.

        Reviews a performance in Spain, June 13, 1974.

1204.   ---.   "Principles of Processional Staging: 'York
        Cycle.'"   *MP* 67.4 (May 1970): 303-20.

        Claims that true processional performance is an
        impossibility. Questions the notion that
        processional performance was the norm. Defines
        processional staging: 1) the cycle has at least
        two plays; 2) the plays are shown to at least two
        audiences; 3) the plays have a serial arrangement;
        4) "The audiences are arranged in serial order"
        (303). Tabulates the length of the York Cycle,
        the time of performance, the beginning and ending
        times for the cycle, and so on. Claims that
        "true-processional staging seems utterly
        impractical, if not impossible" (315); examines
        possible alternative methods of presentation.
        [For an analysis and refutation of this article
        see Margaret Dorrell, "Two Studies of the York
        Corpus Christi Play: Study 2, 'Performance in
        Procession . . .,'" entry # 474 above.]

1204a. ---, ed. *Records of Early English Drama: Cambridge*.
2 vols. Toronto: U. of Toronto Press, 1988.
(Issued April 1989.) Records of Early English
Drama 8. 1100 pp.

Covers dramatic records at the college from the
fourteenth century to 1642, with an emphasis on
the renaissance. Includes university
administrative papers, diaries and letters of
school officials, information about performances,
royal visits, props, and costumes, and records of
payments to touring companies. With appendix,
bibliography, illustrations.

1205. ---. "Six-Wheeled Carts: An Underview." *T&C* 13
(1972): 391-416.

Discusses difficulties in steering six-wheeled
carts, with respect to pageant wagons.

1206. ---. "Some Configurations of Staging in Medieval
English Drama." In *Medieval English Drama: Essays
Critical and Contextual*, 116-47. Ed. by Jerome
Taylor and Alan H. Nelson (see entry # 1573
below).

Attempts to reconstruct the physical staging and
observe the symbolic reference in the
configurations he sees. Discusses stage clusters
in the Hegge Cycle. Looks at "staging" of divine
services in liturgical drama. Examines "localized
and unlocalized playing areas" (117)--the "*locus*"
and the "*platea*." Considers platforms, stages,
wagons, scaffolds, theater-in-the-round, and
processional dramatic production and its
relationship to the audience. Presents much
argument against the possibility of processional
production.

1207. ---. "Some Evidence of Staging Techniques Compiled
from the Text of the Towneley Plays." *RORD* 13-14
(1970-71): 215-19.

Lists lines from 26 of the Towneley plays which
suggest ways of staging performances. Contains no
commentary.

1208. ---. "The Temptation of Christ; or, The Temptation
of Satan." In *Medieval English Drama: Essays
Critical and Contextual*, 218-29. Ed. by Jerome
Taylor and Alan H. Nelson (see entry # 1573
below).

Deals with the symbolic projection of materials. Discusses the Temptation plays of York, N-Town, and Chester cycles as literal dramatizations of an allegedly historic event in the life of Christ. Sees the parable and allegory in this "historic" event. Sees also the "Temptation . . . [in] its place as a decisive episode in the sequential action which determines the essential dramatic structure of the cycles" (226). Concludes that "Christ rather than Satan is the real tempter" and that "the antagonist and the protagonist undergo a characteristic reversal of roles" (229).

1209. ---. "The Wakefield Corpus Christi Play: Pageant Procession and Dramatic Cycle." *RORD* 13-14 (1970-71): 221-33.

Warns against "using records from one city to effect an interpretation of Corpus Christi activities in another city" (221). Points out the similarities of civic records in Wakefield and York. Is convinced that the York Corpus Christi play consisted of two distinct events: a procession of pageants and then a presentation of the cycle "to the worthies of the town" (221) at a fixed site. Claims that similar events may have taken place at Wakefield. Substantiates views by referring to various primary documents. Claims that "the processional pageants and dramatic cycle apparently survived until the 1550's" (227), and that "the pageant procession [may have] outlived the cycle" (228). Concludes, "perhaps the wisest course is to confess how little is actually known or even knowable concerning the production of the Wakefield dramatic cycle" (230).

1210. Nelson, Malcolm A. *The Robin Hood Tradition in the English Renaissance.* Salzburg, Austria: Institut für englische Sprache und Literatur, 1973. Salzburg Studies in English Literature . . . ., Vol. 14. Ed. by James Hogg.

Chap. 1--"The Basis of the Tradition" (4-43)-- covers primary and secondary background material.

1211. Nelson, Sandra Robertson. "'Goddys Worde': Revelation and Its Transmission in the N-Town Cycle." Ph.D. diss., Duke U., 1976.

1212. Neuss, Paula. "Active and Idle Language: Dramatic Images in *Mankind.*" In *Medieval Drama*, 40-67. Ed. by Neville Denny (see entry # 442 above).

Analyzes the metaphorical strategy--in theatrical
terms--operating in *Mankind*, showing the play's
homiletic aims. Explains that the play's
unpopularity among readers is balanced by its
appeal to viewers, for the visual qualities--the
"use of concrete metaphor to convey an abstract
idea" (42)--render the play to its best effect.
Examines the characters' use of language and the
visual associations of Mankind with Job and Adam.
Shows how the play engages an audience by
personifying and externalizing the audience's own
feelings.

1213. ---, ed. *Aspects of Early English Drama*. Cambridge:
       D.S. Brewer; Totowa, NJ: Barnes and Noble, 1983.
       159 pp.

       Contains nine essays as follows: 1) Richard
       Rastall ("All hefne . . .," entry # 1358 below);
       2) Peter Meredith ("Scribes . . .," # 1107); 3)
       Meg Twycross ("'Apparell . . .," # 1592); 4)
       Richard Beadle ("The Shipwrights' Craft," # 153);
       5) Janet Cowen ("'Heven . . .," # 359); 6) Darryll
       Grantley ("Producing . . .," # 641); 7) Richard
       Proudfoot ("The Virtue . . .," # 1342); 8) Tony
       Davenport ("'Lusty . . .," # 378); 9) Robert
       Potter ("Divine . . .," # 1323).

       Rev. *BBN* (Apr. 1984): 244.
            Choice 22 (Sept. 1984): 112.
            John Wasson, *M&RD* 3 (1986): 337-38.
            RES 37 (Feb. 1986): 81.

1214. ---. "The Dyer's Hand in *Rex Diabole*." *ThN* 38.2
       (1984): 61-66.

       Discusses the reference in the Lisle letters to an
       interlude, *Rex Diabole*, and to players and
       costumes. Examines the role played by Felsted, a
       silk dyer, apparently "some sort of theatrical
       agent" (62), and one who could supply costumes.
       Speculates that "The matter of the play must have
       been similar to that of *Dr Faustus* or *Macbeth*"
       (65). Questions whether the play was ever
       written.

1215. ---. "Memorial Reconstruction in a Cornish Miracle
       Play." *CompD* 5.2 (Summer 1971): 129-37.

       Looks at the similarities between the Cornish
       Ordinalia and the c. 1611 miracle play known as
       Gwreans an Bys (The Creation of the Wrold), which
       is in Cornish, but with title and stage directions

in English. Some passages appear verbatim in both plays.

1216.   ---. [Review.] *TLS* (July 4, 1980): 755.

Review of performance of The Wakefield Cycle, June 28-29, 1980, Wakefield Festival, Wakefield Cathedral Precinct.

1217.   ---. "The Sixteenth-Century English 'Proverb' Play." *CompD* 18.1 (Spring 1984): 1-18.

Looks at educational plays which use proverbs as bases of plots; focuses on William Wager's *Enough is as Good as a Feast:* the playwright's rhetorical training, his use of proverbs, the hero and other characters, the abuse of language in the play, the plot, methods of amplification, the use of personification. Also treats Ulpian Fulwell's *Like Will to Like Quoth the Devil to the Collier* and Shakespeare's *All's Well that Ends Well* and *Measure for Measure.*

1218.   ---. "The Staging of the 'Creacion of the World.'" *ThN* 33.3 (1979): 116-25. Rpt. in *Medieval English Drama*, 189-200. Ed. by Peter Happé (entry # 684 above).

Considers the stage directions of this Cornish play, which are authorial instructions to actors and set designers or are prompt-copy instructions to a stage manager. Looks at a theater-in-the-round staging and at the structures for Heaven and Hell. Claims that, unlike other Cornish plays, this was not staged in the round, but in a "much more intimate kind of setting" (122). Mentions the elaborateness of the production.

1219.   Newall, Venetia. "The Turkish Knight in English Traditional Drama." *Folklore* 92.2 (1981): 196-202.

Discusses the hero-combat form of folk play (the other two forms being the sword dance ceremony and the wooing or plough play), with St. George the most common prototypical hero. Looks at sources, characterization, the plays' "lack of historical sense" (197), and their "mingling of racial traits, nationalities, and historical periods" (198).

1219a. Newlyn, Evelyn S. *Cornish Drama of the Middle Ages: A Bibliography.* Redruth: Institute of Cornish

Studies, 1987. Special Bibliography No. 6. 23
pp.

1220. Newton, Stella Mary. *Fashion in the Age of the Black
Prince: A Study of the Years 1340-1365.*
Woodbridge, Suffolk: Boydell Press; Totowa, NJ:
Rowman & Littlefield, 1980. 151 pp.

Contains chapters on "Tournaments and Orders of
Chivalry" (Chap. 6, 41-52) and "Actors, Minstrels
and Fools" (Chap. 9, 76-85. Draws from literary
and pictorial sources. With illustrations,
bibliography, and index.

Rev. *AJ* 61.2 (1981): 394.
C. Blair, *BBN* (Mar. 1981): 157-58.
Apollo 114 (July 1981): 65.
Connoisseur 207 (July 1981): 167.
Specu 57 (Apr. 1982): 398.
EHR 98 (Jan. 1983): 186.

1221. Nichols, Aidan. *The Art of God Incarnate: Theology
and Image in Christian Tradition.* London: Darton,
Longman, and Todd; New York: Paulist Press, 1980.
180 pp.

Contains a discussion of the depiction of Christ
in human form, with a chapter on iconographic
depictions (Chap. 4). Not on drama, but contains
observations useful to the study of medieval
plays.

Rev. A. Rowe, *BBN* (June 1980): 337.
Choice 19 (Sept. 1981): 102.
TheolT 38 (Oct. 1981): 442.
NatCR 225 (Nov. 1982): 287.

1222. Nichols, Ann Eljenholm. "Costume in the Moralities:
The Evidence of East Anglian Art." *CompD* 20.4
(Winter 1986-87): 305-14.

Aims "to describe one new art form that originated
in the second half of the fifteenth century and to
consider possible relationships between that form
and the costuming of contemporary drama" (305-6).
The "art form . . . is the seven-sacrament
baptismal font" (306), in which forms of dress are
carefully carved. Comments on literal and "non-
literal elements" (307), with special note about
the "literalism of the artisans" (312). Considers
several plays, including *Wisdom* and *The Castle of
Perseverance.*

1223.   ---.   "The Croxton *Play of the Sacrament:* A Re-
         Reading."   *CompD* 22.2 (Summer 1988): 117-37.

         Aims to read the play "not as a reaction to anti-
         Eucharistic piety, but . . . as a reflection of
         fifteenth-century piety" (117). Says the best way
         to understand the play is with respect to
         contemporary narrative and dramatic forms and not
         with respect to "anti-Lollard propaganda" (117).
         Looks at the play in its historical context.
         Shows the play to be a mixture of a number of
         genres.

1224.   Nichols, Jean R.   "The Origins of the Medieval
         Liturgical Drama: A Critical Guide."   [Part I].
         (See next entry.)   *Comitatus* 6 (1975): 45-80.

         Contains annotated bibliography of 67 items--
         "important studies of the origin of the liturgical
         drama, with special emphasis on those works which
         deal with the musical aspects of the plays" (45).
         [The Table of Contents of this volume gives the
         subtitle: "A Critical Guide to Secondary Source
         Materials, Part I."]

1225.   ---.   "The Origins of the Medieval Liturgical Drama:
         A Critical Guide, Part II."   *Comitatus* 7 (1976):
         27-78.   (See previous entry.)

         Continuation of previous article, listing 61 works
         from 1956 to 1976. With author, subject, and ms
         indexes. [The Table of Contents of this volume
         gives the subtitle: "A Critical Guide to
         Secondary Source Materials, Part II."]

1226.   Nicholson, R.H.   "The Trial of Christ the Sorcerer in
         the York Cycle."   *JMRS* 16.2 (Fall 1986): 125-69.

         Examines "the procedures by which Christ is
         condemned, especially in the York Cycle sequence
         of trial and passion plays" (125). Looks at the
         charges of witchcraft and sorcery against Christ
         and the legal problems these charges raise.

1227.   Nitecki, Alicia K.   "The N-Town Lamech and the
         Convention of Maximainus' [sic] First Elegy."   *ANQ*
         17.8 (Apr. 1979): 122-24.

         Explains the unusual entrance of Lamech into the
         N-Town play of the murder of Cain. Shows the
         influence on the play of "Maximianus' First Elegy
         and the convention of the old man's lament to
         which it gave rise" (122). Says that by using the
         popular portrayal of Lamech, the playwright shows

him as "vetus homo," unregenerate man. Points up
the connection to Cain.

1228. Nitecki, Alicia Korzeniowska. "The Presence of the
       Past: The Sense of Time in the York Cycle." Ph.D.
       diss., Kent State U., 1976.

1229. ---. "The Sacred Elements of the Secular Feast in
       Prima Pastorum." *Medi* 3 (1977): 229-37.

       Reviews scholarship on the feast. Challenges the
       notion that the feast be read as part of "a
       pastoral idyll in which the shepherds' complaints
       are satires of contemporary evil that define the
       world at its worst" (229). Claims the feast "is
       simultaneously a parody and type of the Eucharist"
       (229) and that the satire is aimed at the
       shepherds, not at society.

1230. ---. "The Dramatic Impact of the Didactic Voice in
       the York Cycle of Mystery Plays." *AnM* 21 (1981):
       61-76.

       Claims that "the didacticism contributes to the
       dramaturgy" (61). Points out that the theatrical
       effect of the plays comes primarily in the
       "reduction of aesthetic distance between on-stage
       action and spectator" (61). Aims to demonstrate
       that this reduction of distance renders the
       historical events as present and spiritual. Also
       claims that this reduction is most effectively
       displayed in the York Passion sequence. Shows the
       emotional impact and didacticism this reduction
       has on the audience.

1231. Noguchi, Rei R. "Conversational Interaction, Verbal
       Strategies, and Literary Response." *Lang&S* 18.2
       (Spring 1985): 192-204.

       Considers the interaction between playwright and
       audience and also between and among the characters
       in the play. Focuses on the language aspect of
       interaction in the Brome *Abraham and Isaac* play in
       order to prove that this approach "has
       considerable relevance to literary interpretation
       and other aspects of literary response" (192).
       Offers a linguistic analysis of dialogue, looking
       at solicitation and response and the biases of
       conversations.

1232. Nolden, Rainer. *Machtstrukturen und
       Erscheinungsformen der Insubordination in den
       mittelenglischen "Mystery Plays."* Frankfurt:

Lang, 1981. Anglo-American Forum, Vol. 14. 163
pp.

Says that the mystery plays reflected a view of
the world-order which placed God at the top as
King and Judge of all, and in which the world's
harmonious functioning depended on human beings'
fulfilling their God-given roles in a well-defined
power-structure. Considers hubris, the Fall of
Lucifer and of Adam and Eve, the Last Judgment,
and the hierarchy in which man and God exist.
Analyzes power relationships gone awry, as
depicted in the mystery plays. Looks at Herod's
cruelty, Pilate's tyranny (in the Towneley plays),
the manipulation of Pilate by Annas and Caiphas
(in York), the neglect of private/family power-
relations, Cain's killing of Abel and the notion
of disobedience in that play and in the Judgment
plays. Describes church and state rule, using the
seven deadly sins as the measure for evil. Treats
situations in which good and evil interact and the
literary *topoi* used for these instances. Looks
also at situations in which characters step beyond
the bounds of their God-ordained rank (such as
Eve's offering the apple to Adam, Noah's wife's
refusal to enter the ark, the murder of Abel,
etc.). Shows how the plays teach that only the
church offers a way out of damnation.

1232a. Norland, Howard B. "Folk Drama in Fifteenth- and
Sixteenth-Century England." *FCS* 13 (1988): 321-
34.

1233. ---. "Formalizing English Farce: *Johan Johan* and Its
French Connection." *CompD* 17.2 (Summer 1983):
141-52.

Claims that Rastell's play is the first "printed
in England to represent farce as a dramatic form"
(141). Reviews scholarship on authorship. Says
that the play is "a very careful adaptation of the
French farce [*Farce nouvelle très bonne et fort
joyeuse du Pasté*] to the English cultural and
dramatic context" (142). Compares the two.
Claims that the English play "extends the
relationship between actor and audience beyond its
source" (151), develops its characters, adapts the
clerical satire, and refines the conclusion of the
play.

1234. Norlin, Richard Floyd. "The Five Old Testament Plays
of the Chester Cycle: A Paradigm of Salvation
History." Ph.D. diss., U. of the Pacific, 1974.

1235.   Norton, Michael L. "Of 'Stages' and 'Types' in
        Visitatione Sepulchri (Part I)." *CompD* 21.1
        (Spring 1987): 34-61. (See next entry.)

        Examines how Carl Lange's "means for ordering the
        repertory of the medieval *Visitatio Sepulchri*"
        (34) in three developments or stages is flawed.
        Offers an alternative categorization. Questions
        whether this religious text can be considered
        drama. (Pp. 51-61 of this article contain musical
        notation.)

1236.   ---. "Of 'Stages' and 'Types' in *Visitatione
        Sepulchri* (Part II)." *CompD* 21.2 (Summer 1987):
        127-44. (See previous entry.)

        Looks at the contributions to scholarship of
        Chambers and Young, and the old liturgy-to-drama
        theory. Examines sources of the *Visitatio* and
        offers a new two-part classification. (Pp. 141-
        144 of this article contain musical notation.)

1237.   Oakshott, Jane. "The Dramatic Qualities of the
        Fabliaux." *PIBEC*, Galsgow, 1976.

1238.   ---. [Quoted in review.] *Yorkshire Post*, June 30,
        1980. Cited by Sheila Lindenbaum, *RORD* 23 (1980):
        84.

        Reviews The Wakefield Cycle, performance of June
        28-29, 1980, Wakefield Festival, Wakefield
        Cathedral Precinct.

1239.   O'Connell, Rosalie M. "Sovereignty through Speech in
        the Corpus Christi Mystery Plays." *Renascence*
        33.2 (Winter 1981): 117-28.

        Shows how the verbal act of God is the source of
        the creation and how the Corpus Christi
        playwrights emphasize this use of God's word in
        showing "the connection between language,
        sovereignty, and Godhead" (118). Mentions "The
        divine ability to make of the word a deed" (121).
        Concludes by showing how the cycle plays reinforce
        the "connection between sovereignty and inherently
        efficacious speech" (127).

1240.   O'Donaghue, Heather. "Arresting Anachronisms." *TLS*
        (Feb. 1, 1985): 121.

        Briefly reviews a performance of the National
        Theatre's production of *The Mysteries* of January
        19, 1985, in London's Cottesloe Theatre.

1241. Ogden, Dunbar H. "The Use of Architectural Space in
       Medieval Music-Drama." In *Studies in Medieval
       Drama in Honor of William L. Smoldon on His 82nd
       Birthday*, 63-76. Ed. by Clifford Davidson, et al.
       (see entry # 410 above).

       Examines the use of chancel and nave "as
       theatrical spaces" (63). Shows how particular
       texts were performed in known places. Looks at
       the *Visitatio Sepulchri* of the *Regularis
       Concordia*, a fifteenth-century *Visitatio*
       "identified with Magdeburg Cathedral" (63), and
       plays from the Church of St. John at Besançon.
       With illustrations of original floor plans. Not
       specifically on English drama, but useful in its
       observations of parallel traditions.

1242. Okuda, Hiroko Fukui. "The Old Testament Plays of the
       Middle English Cycle Drama: An Historical
       Approach." Ph.D. diss., Bryn Mawr College, 1980.

1243. Olmert, Michael. "'A Man May Seye Ful Sooth in Game
       and Pley': The Tradition of Sport in Middle
       English Literature." Ph.D. diss., U. of Maryland,
       1980.

1244. ---. "Towneley *Processus Talentorum:* Dicing toward
       Jerusalem." *Flor* 5 (1983): 157-77.

       Says the play "may be the most surprising work in
       literary history . . . because it depends so
       heavily on the use of game as a context for its
       narrative, its drama, its moral instruction, and
       ultimately its art" (157). Points up all the
       different kinds of gaming referred to in the play.
       Recounts critical views of laughter in the serious
       context of the play. Concludes that one of the
       play's messages is "that the way we 'play' and the
       way we live are inseparable" (172).

1245. Olson, Glending. *Literature as Recreation in the
       Later Middle Ages.* Ithaca, New York, and London:
       Cornell U. Press, 1982. 245 pp.

       Deals with the "vista of delight" (9), "literary
       pleasure" (10) in the works of the Middle Ages.
       Examines this notion with respect to the play
       ("*ludus*"). Not specifically on the drama, but
       contains a discussion of this background issue
       raised by Kolve, et al.

       Rev. Bennett D. Hill, *LJ* 107 (Sept. 1, 1982):
            1661.
       Choice 20 (Jan. 1983): 700.

AB 71 (Feb. 21, 1983): 1367.
J.A. Burrow, *TLS* (May 27, 1983): 537.
Historian 46 (Nov. 1983): 90.
Derek Pearsall, *N&Q*, n.s., 31.1 (229) (Mar. 1984): 89-90.
Specu 59 (Apr. 1984): 429.
QJS 70 (May 1984): 217.
JEGP 83 (July 1984): 432.
Clio 14 (Fall 1984): 114.
CompLS 21 (Fall 1984): 348.
GermanQ 58 (Fall 1985): 601.
RES 36 (Fall 1985): 69.

1245a. "On Six-Wheeled Pageant Wagons." *EDAMN* 11.2 (Spring 1989): 37-40. [Article unsigned; by the ed., Clifford Davidson (?)]

Examines the nineteenth-century engraving by David Jee (frontispiece to Sharp's *Dissertation on the Pageants* . . ., 1825), which depicts an "impossibly clumsy" (38) wagon--practically incapable of being steered. Shows that Sharp had relied on David Rogers' *Breviary*, which said six wheels in the early version, four wheels in the later text; Sharp and Jee relied on the earlier. Points out the later (twentieth-century) misuse of the drawing and the problems it has caused for scholarship.

1246. Oram, Alexandra. "Stylistic Ornament in Three Fifteenth-Century English Legends of Mary Magdalene: A Study in Flamboyant Styles." Ph.D. diss., Catholic U. of America, 1981.

Deals with the Digby *Mary Magdalene*.

1247. Ovitt, George, Jr. "Adam's Dream: Fortune and the Tragedy of the *Chester* 'Drapers Playe.'" *JRMMRA* 6 (Jan. 1985): 71-85.

Looks at the medieval concepts of Fortune and tragedy, especially in Chaucer and Boethius. Aims to show that tragedy is not dependent on Fortune but exists "within the context of freely chosen human actions" (72). Sees the Adam story as "an especially effective example of a tragedy of character" (72).

1248. ---. "Christian Eschatology and the *Chester* 'Judgment.'" *EssLit* 10.1 (Spring 1983): 3-16.

Claims that for the playwrights, "the End provides not only dramatic closure (of history, of the cycles themselves) but a destination that fills

the intervening time. The End gives meaning to
the process, and drama, of history" (3). Examines
the notion in the four extant cycles with a
discussion of the historically evolving notion of
the End. Looks at the plays in terms of their
expressing a "mimesis of the drama of salvation
history" (8). Shows the plays to present the End
in Augustinian terms: "a personal and
internalized judgment-by-conscience that aligns
living and dead alike with the bipolar post-
historical world of the two Cities" (13).

1249. Owen, Lucy DeGeer. "The Representation of
Forgiveness in Shakespeare and Medieval Drama."
Ph.D. diss., U. of Virginia, 1975.

1250. Oxtoby, Richard. [Quoted in review.] *York Evening
Press*, July 1, 1980. Cited by Sheila Lindenbaum,
RORD 23 (1980): 84.

Review of The York Cycle, performances of June 6-
30, 1980, St. Mary's Abbey, York.

1251. Ozawa, Hiroshi. "The Education Drama of the Early
Tudor Humanists." *Sylvan* 24-25 (Mar. 1982): 1-19.

(In Japanese.) Discusses *Nature, The Four
Elements,* and *Wit and Science.* See next entry.

1251a. ---. "The Play within the Play Structure of *Fulgens
and Lucres.*" *Shiron* 20 (Apr. 1981): 1-22.

In Japanese, with English abstract. Covers
materials similar to those in his "The Structural
Innovations . . ." (see # 1252 below).

1251b. ---. "Satire in *The Pardoner and the Friar.*" *Shiron*
22 (1983).

In Japanese, with English abstract. Covers
materials similar to those in his "The Structural
Innovations . . ." (see next entry).

1252. ---. "The Structural Innovations of the More Circle
Dramatists." *ShakStud* 19 (Feb. 1980-81): 1-23.

[A revised version, in English, of entry # 1251
and the two following articles.] Looks at the
plays of Medwall, Rastell, and Heywood with
respect to "dramatic form or structure" (1), their
areas of greatest innovation. Discusses these
innovations by examining Medwall's *Fulgens and
Lucres*, Rastell's *Four Elements*, and Heywood's *The
Pardoner and the Friar.*

1253. Pacholski, Richard Allen. "The Humanist Drama of the
       Sir Thomas More Circle." Ph.D. diss., U. of
       Wisconsin, 1969.

1254. Page, Susan Carolyn Ulichney. "The Emergence of the
       Humanist Tragic Hero: A Study of the Dramatization
       of the Psychomachia in the Morality Plays and in
       Selected Plays of Shakespeare (Volumes I-II)."
       Ph.D. diss., Purdue U., 1980.

1255. Palliser, D.M. "A Crisis in English Towns? The Case
       of York, 1460-1640." *NorH* 14 (1978): 108-25.

       Explains his use of the terms *crisis* and *decline*
       with respect to York and its "cycle of depression
       and recovery" (110). Looks at many phenomena,
       including immigration and population growth and
       decline, the trades of the city, its monetary
       inflation, etc. Mentions various kinds of
       entertainment, including "cockfighting and plays"
       (120) which marked the end of the city's crisis at
       the beginning of the 1560s.

1256. ---. "The Trade Gilds of Tudor York." In *Crisis and
       Order in English Towns 1500-1700*, 86-116. Ed. by
       Peter Clark and Paul Slack. Toronto and Buffalo:
       U. of Toronto Press, 1972.

       Defines the term "gild," and mentions dramatic
       activity and minstrelsy in York. Offers much
       background for the conditions in which plays
       flourished. Also mentions the Corpus Christi
       processions in the city (110).

1257. ---. *Tudor York*. Oxford and New York: Oxford U.
       Press, 1979. Oxford Historical Monographs. x,
       327 pp.

       Examines the political, ecclesiastical, economic,
       and social history of the city between 1485 and
       1603. Sees much evidence of drama and minstrelsy.
       Mentions Corpus Christi plays (105, 152, etc.),
       Creed, Midsummer, and Paternoster activities,
       Minstrels (waits), guilds, and so on.

       Rev. K. Sharpe, *THES* 391 (Apr. 18, 1980): 20.
           Valerie Pearl, *TLS* (May 23, 1980): 573.
           H.S. Reinmuth, Jr., *HRNB* 8 (Sept. 1980): 233.
           M.E. James, *EconHR*, ser. 2, 33 (Nov. 1980):
               623-24.
           R.M. Berger, *JEconS* 40 (Dec. 1980): 859-61.
           A.D. Dyer, *AHR* 85 (Dec. 1980): 1189-90.
           Alan Dyer, *History* 66 (Feb. 1981): 131.
           EHR 97 (Jan. 1982): 135.

D. Hibberd, *JHG* 8 (Jan. 1982): 79.
P. Slack, *SocH* 7 (Jan. 1982): 118.
JMH 54 (Mar. 1982): 103.

1257a. Palmer, Barbara. *The Early Art of the West Riding of Yorkshire.* Kalamazoo, Michigan: Medieval Institute, Western Michigan University, forthcoming.

1258. Palmer, Barbara D. "'To Speke of Wo that is in Mariage': The Marital Arts in Medieval Literature." In *Human Sexuality in the Middle Ages and Renaissance*, 3-14. Ed. by Douglas Radcliff-Umstead. Pittsburgh: Center for Medieval and Renaissance Studies, U. of Pittsburgh, 1978. University of Pittsburgh Publications on Middle Ages and Renaissance, 4.

Offers background information on marriage in the middle ages. Looks at several literary texts, including the Adam, Annunciation, Shepherds, and Noah plays. Speaks of the authors' "trying to transform an erotic and domestic reality . . . into literary allusion" (13) by focusing "almost exclusively on infidelity and shrewishness" (13), how this was for the purpose of creating a lively plot, interesting characters, and humor, and how this may not be an accurate picture of most marriages.

1259. ---. "'Towneley Plays' or 'Wakefield Cycle' Revisited." *CompD* 21.4 (Winter 1987-88): 318-48. [See entry for David Mills, # 1161 above.]

Distinguishes between cycle performances and other types of presentation. Focuses on the Towneley plays, the history and provenance of the document. States that "To assert that the Towneley manuscript is a Wakefield guild cycle also is to falsify or to ignore the documentary and demographic evidence" (322). Claims that Wakefield was too small to support such a production. Also discusses date/,and other historical evidence about the town, plays performed there, the ms, and scholarship on these. Examines contemporary documents. Calls into question the notion that Wakefield ever had a fully developed cycle play performance tradition.

1260. ---. "Ubi Sunt?" *EDAMN* 4.2 (Mar. 1982): 3-13.

Offers suggestions on compiling records of early drama, art, and music. Draws on her experiences in Leeds.

1261.   Parfitt, George. "Early Robin Hood Plays: Two
        Fragments and a Bibliography." *RenMS* 22 (Special
        number, Popular Theater) (1978): 5-12.

        Presents a fifteenth-century fragment of "Robin
        Hood and the Sheriff of Nottingham" and a
        sixteenth-century fragment of "Robin Hood and the
        Friar; Robin Hood and the Potter."

1262.   Parker, Elizabeth Crawford. "The Descent from the
        Cross: Its Relation to the Extra-Liturgical
        'Depositio' Drama." Ph.D. diss., New York U.,
        1975.

1263.   Parker, John T. *The Development of the Everyman
        Drama from "Elckerlijc" to Hofmannsthal's
        "Jedermann."* Doetinchem: 1970.

1264.   Parkes, M[alcolm] B. *English Cursive Book Hands
        1250-1500.* Berkeley, Los Angeles, and London: U.
        of California Press, 1969. xxxii, 26 pp., 24
        plates.

        Not on English drama, but contains selection of
        plates instructive of deciphering the handwriting
        of the period.

        Rev. *Archives* 9 (1970): 208.
             RenQ 24.3 (1971): 391.
             Specu 46 (Jan. 1971): 177.
             Lib, 5th ser. 26 (Mar. 1971): 67.
             EHR 87 (Jan. 1972): 166.
             MP 69 (Feb. 1972): 250.

1265.   Parry, Caroline Balderston. "'The Maypole is Up, Now
        Give Me the Cup . . . .'" *REEDN* 11.1 (1986): 7-9.

        Points out that the Maypole dancing at the 1983
        Chester Cycle and 1985 Towneley Cycle productions
        at the University of Toronto was anachronistic,
        the dancing tracing back only to the mid-
        eighteenth century, though Maypoles are
        "[u]ndoubtedly pre-Christian in origin" (8).

1266.   Parry, David. "A Margin of Error: The Problems of
        Marginalia in *The Castle of Perseverance*." In
        Editing Early English Drama . . ., 33-64. Ed. by
        A.F. Johnston (see entry # 828 above).

        Says that some of the audience would have
        understood the Latin tag lines in the play's ms--a
        notion emanating from one of his own marginal
        notes. Shows the importance of the correct
        interpretation of the ms's marginalia. Describes

his own work in producing the play and the problem
he had with the Latin lines, most of which were in
the margins, and may have been scribal commentary
and not text. Looks also at "stage directions and
staging annotations" (38). Stresses the need to
examine the text by means of performance as well
as through concomitant scholarly criticism.

1267.   ---.   "Masks and Faces: Reason, Sensuality, and the
        Actor in the Masque of *Wisdom*." Paper delivered
        at the *Wisdom* Symposium, Trinity College,
        Hartford, Connecticut, April 14, 1984. (Cited by
        Milla B. Riggio in "The Staging of *Wisdom*," *RORD*
        27 [1984] 175, n. 2; see entry # 1389 below. This
        essay not reproduced in Riggio's edition of the
        papers from the symposium; see entry # 1390
        below.)

1268.   ---.   "The Seasons Round: The Calendar and Folk
        Tradition." In *For What Time I am in this World*.
        Toronto: Peter Martin, 1977.

        Not on English drama, but explains folk tradition
        with respect to the calendar year and "the round
        of the seasons" (15). Discusses Easter, weather
        lore, "the traditional Cornish Hobby Horse
        ceremony" (18) of May Day, All Saints' Day, and so
        on. Volume also has a brief section by David
        Parry on Mumming (55-56).

1269.   ---.   "The York Cycle at the University of Toronto."
        REEDN 2.1 (1977): 18-19.

        Explains plans to perform the full 48-play York
        Cycle on the U. of Tornoto campus with the hope of
        offering "the closest possible modern equivalent
        to a medieval trade guild performance structure"
        (18). (Parry was artistic director of the
        production. See next entry; also see # 1736
        below.)

1270.   ---.   "The York Mystery Cycle at Toronto, 1977." *MET*
        1.1 (Oct. 1979): 19-31. (An edited version of a
        talk given at a meeting in Lancaster on April 7,
        1979.)

        Follows up previous article which explained plans
        to perform the cycle. Recounts the performance of
        a 47-play cycle at three stations with eleven
        wagons. Discusses the technical aspects of such a
        production; e.g. "Waggons are in fact remarkably
        easy to handle" (19). With fifteen photographs of
        the pageant and a discussion following the talk

among Parry, Meg Twycross, and Peter Meredith. (See entry # 1736 below.)

1271. Pasachoff, Naomi E. *Playwrights, Preachers, and Politicians: A Study of Four Tudor Old Testament Dramas*. Salzburg, Austria: Institut für englische Sprache und Literatur, Universität Salzburg, 1975. Salzburg Studies in English Literature under the Direction of Erwin A. Stürzl. Elizabethan And Renaissance Studies Series, ed. by Dr. James Hogg.

Chap. 1 covers backgrounds: "The Evolution of Old Testament Drama" (1), and contains a note about cycle plays (6).

1272. Pasch, William Allen. "Trinitarian Symbolism and Medieval English Drama." Ph.D. diss., U. of Massachusetts, 1977.

1273. Patrides, C.A. *The Grand Design of God: The Literary Form of the Christian View of History*. London: Routledge and Kegan Paul; Toronto: U. of Toronto Press, 1972. xvii, 157 pp.

Among much else, discusses "the place of the Mystery Plays in the mediaeval synthesis" (xiii). Looks at Patristic backgrounds. Deals briefly with Corpus Christi plays with respect to a "Christian view of history" (38).

Rev. *Choice* 10 (May 1973): 440.
MLR 68 (Oct. 1973): 883.
J. Carlsen, *EngStud* 56 (Apr. 1975): 173-74.
D. Hay, *N&Q* 22 (July 1975): 322-23.
C.H. Clough, *Apollo*, n.s. 103 (Jan. 1976): 70-72.

1274. Pattenden, Philip. "Robert Hegge, an Oxford Antiquary." *Oxon* 45 (1980): 284-99.

Offers biographical information on the early owner of the *Ludus Coventriae* ms, and reviews the corpus of his writing, dealing with several genres. Has a section on "Hegge's Library" (296), including the play ms. Discusses his possession of this ms, which was apparently "not possession but a loan" (297)--a translation of a Greek phrase on f. 164.

1275. Paull, Michael. "The Figure of Mahomet in the Towneley Cycle." *CompD* 6.3 (Fall 1972): 187-204.

Looks at historical interpretations of Mahomet to account for his use in the cycle as a type of Antichrist, "a type of the false prelates and

friars" (188) who were against Christianity.
Shows that Mahomet "ultimately serves Christ by
underscoring both His power and the absurdity of
those who would deny Him" (188). Concludes by
showing how "Mahomet represents all of those
aspects of material gratification and prideful
behavior which turn man against God" (201).

1276. Peach, L. DuGarde. *The Story of the Theatre: A
Ladybird Book*. Loughborough: Ladybird Books, 1970.

Basically a child's history. Contains a few pages
on the English drama (14-22). Illustrated.

1277. Pearsall, Derek. *John Lydgate*. Charlottesville: U.
Press of Virginia, 1970. 312 pp.

Has a discussion of Lydgate's mummings--at
Hertford (187-88) and Bishopswood (186), and other
mummings.

Rev. *NewS* 79 (Apr. 24, 1970): 587.
VQR 47 (Spring 1971): R66.
JEGP 70 (July 1971): 528.
MLR 67 (Jan. 1972): 163.
RES, n.s. 23 (Nov. 1972): 472.

1278. ---. *Old and Middle English Poetry*. London and
Boston: Routledge and Kegan Paul, 1977. The
Routledge History of English Poetry, Vol. 1. 352
pp.

Contains a section on drama (252-58). Points out
that with the exception of a few lines in *Nature*
by Henry Medwall, "The drama of the fifteenth
century is exclusively in verse" (252). Remarks
on the generally low level of verse in the mystery
cycles. Discusses the language of the plays.

Rev. H.T. Keenan, *LJ* 102 (May 15, 1977): 1189.
Choice 14 (July/Aug. 1977): 684.
A. Shippey, *TLS* (Sept. 2, 1977): 1048.
E.G. Stanley, *N&Q* (Dec. 1977): 558-61.
A. Hudson, *RES*, n.s. 29 (May 1978): 191-93.
Stanley B. Greenfield, *MP* 77 (Nov. 1979):
188-91.
P. Mroczkowski, *EngStud* 61 (Oct. 1980): 457-
62.

1279. Pederson, Steven Irvin. "The Staging of *The Castle
of Perseverance: A Re-Analysis*." Ph.D. diss., U.
of Iowa, 1983.

1280.   ---.   "The Staging of *The Castle of Perseverance:* A
        Re-Analysis."   *ThN* 39.2 (1985): 51-62.

        Reacts to Richard Southern's *The Medieval Theatre
        in the Round* (see entry # 1493 below).   Looks at
        parallel plays to claim that "the playwright
        intended his play to be staged within a tournament
        field . . . a 'list'" (52).   Claims that "the
        tournament tradition provides the only credible
        answers to the play's perplexing plan" (52).
        Shows how such staging works within the context of
        the play and within appropriate physical
        limitations delineated by the play's action.
        Focuses on dramatic elements such as disguise,
        allegory, impersonation; on the parallels between
        lists and the *Castle* plan; and on parallels
        between the "stytelerys" of the plan "and the
        heralds associated with tournament regulation"
        (52).   Defines "stytelerys" as those who arrange,
        set in order, umpire, or govern.   Claims that the
        lists were ready-made and acceptable arenas for
        dramatic performances.

1281.   ---.   "The Staging of *The Castle of Perseverance:*
        Testing the List Theory."   *ThN* 39.3 (1985): 104-
        13.

        Continues previous article "to analyse the script
        itself [to] focus on three issues: (1) textual
        evidence which dispels the moat theory, (2) the
        problem of audience placement, and (3) the
        difficulties inherent in list production" (104).
        Concludes that the moat theory is not tenable and
        that his own list theory is.

1282.   Peek, George S.   "Folklore Concepts and Popular
        Literature: A Strategy for Combining Folklore and
        Literary Studies."   *TFSB* 44.1 (Mar. 1978): 25-29.

        Illustrates the characteristics of folk narrative
        with respect to medieval English cycle plays.
        Looks at the Chester "Fall of Lucifer," "The
        Deluge" (i.e. Noah play), "The Oblation of the
        Magi."   Bases discussion on the work of Axel Olrik
        ("Epic Laws of Folk Narrative," in *The Study of
        Folklore*, 129-41.   Ed. by Alan Dundes.   Englewood
        Cliffs, NJ: Prentice Hall, 1965.)

1283.   ---.   "Sermon Themes and Sermon Structure in
        Everyman."   *SoCB* 40.4 (Winter 1980): 159-60.

        Looks at thematic and structural parallels between
        drama and sermons and the influence of sermons on
        the plays.   Says that an understanding of the

parallels "might help to explain the seemingly
digressive beginnings and endings of plays" (159)
and would explain the popularity of the
moralities. Analyzes sermon theory. Compares
Everyman to Wimbledon's sermon *Redde Rationem
Villacationis Tue.* Says that the play "is not
specifically an imitation of a sermon" (160), but
it draws on the sermon structure.

1284. Penninger, Frieda Elaine. *English Drama to 1660
(Excluding Shakespeare): A Guide to Information
Sources.* Detroit: Gale, 1976. American
Literature, English Literature, and World
Literature in English Information Guide Series,
Vol. 5.

Contains various resources under the categories of
Bibliographies, Editions, Availability [and]
Prices, Festschriften and Other Collections of
Essays, Including Some Serials, General Literary
Histories, and Individual Authors.

Rev. C.A. Bunge, *WLB* 51 (Dec. 1976): 361.
ARBA 8 (1977): 475.
Choice 14 (May 1977): 349.
Lib, 5th ser. 32 (June 1977): 189.
RQ 16 (Summer 1977): 358.

1285. Pentzell, Raymond J. "The Medieval Theatre in the
Streets." *ThSur* 14.1 (May 1973): 1-21.

Refutes Richard Southern's notions of a theater in
the round, and those of Mary del Villar (see her
"The Staging of *The Conversion of Saint Paul*,"
entry # 439 above; see also del Villar's "The
Medieval Theatre in the Streets . . .," # 436, and
also entry # 1286 below). Analyzes this play in
terms of its staging requirements. Looks at
internal evidence to call into question del
Villar's choice to stage the play in the round.
Posits a staging of "three separate *platae,* each
with its own requisite scenic units, set at enough
distance apart to make processions between them
meaningful" (12). Examines morality plays and
other processional festivity, and then looks at
"possible contemporary parallels with *The
Conversion of St. Paul*" (16): The Stations, The
Performers, and The Audience (16-17), an
understanding of which will help to elucidate the
unusual staging of this play.

1286. ---. "Reply to Mary del Villar." *ThSur* 14.2 (Nov.
1973): 82-90.

Replies to del Villar's "The Medieval Theatre in the Streets: A Rejoinder" (see entry # 436 above; see also entries # 439 and 1285). Claims that del Villar misread his arguments and misrepresented his readings.

1287. Percy, Joyce W., ed. *York Memorandum Book*, Vol III. Gateshead: Northumberland Press, 1973 [for 1969]. Surtees Society, 186. 320 pp.

Contains many entries dating from 1371-1596 pertaining to dramatic performances and performers. E.g. entries on Corpus Christi (mystery) plays, religious guilds, and pageant houses. [Vols. I and II were edited by Dr. Maud Sellers, Surtees Society # 120 and 125, 1912 and 1915 respectively.]

1288. Peter, John. "Magical Mystery Tour de Force." *The Sunday Times* (January 27, 1985).

Briefly reviews a performance of the National Theatre's production of *The Mysteries* of January 19, 1985, in London's Cottesloe Theatre.

1289. ---. [Review.] *The Sunday Times* (June 15, 1980).

Reviews performances of The York Cycle of June 6-30, 1980, York Festival, St. Mary's Abbey, York. [Cited by Sheila Lindenbaum, *RORD* 23 (1980: 84).]

1290. ---. [Untitled review.] *The Sunday Times* (August 19, 1984).

Reviews performance of Lindsay's *Ane Satyre of the Thrie Estates*, August 1984, at Assembly Hall, Edinburgh, during the Edinburgh Festival. [Cited by John Elliot, *RORD* 27 (1984): 191.]

1291. Pettit, Thomas. "Approaches to Medieval Folk Drama." *EDAMN* 7.2 (Spring 1985): 23-27.

Reviews recent progress in scholarship. Details approaches of modern researchers. Comments on the types of drama under scrutiny (primarily mummers' plays including the Hero Combat Play, but also summer plays for St. George's Day, Whitsun, Village Wakes, Robin Hood, etc.). Discusses the traditional criticism--its strengths and weaknesses. Calls for a "radical re-thinking and re-writing" (25) of the history of early folk drama in England. Indicates some new directions.

1292.   ---.   "Early English Traditional Drama: Approaches
        and Perspectives."   *RORD* 25 (1982): 1-30.

        Aims to provide an up-dating of bibliographical
        information on traditional drama scholarship.
        Uses "traditional" to mean "folk" and includes
        mummers' plays, "Life-Cycle" plays, ritual drama,
        etc.   Considers mostly pre-eighteenth-century
        drama of several kinds: institutional, summer
        events, outdoor.   Looks at summer and winter
        traditions and their influence on Renaissance
        drama.   Also looks at Hero Combat plays, Sword
        Dance plays, Wooing plays, and so on.   Summarizes
        much scholarship, not all of which focuses on
        medieval drama.

1293.   ---.   "English Folk Drama and the Early German
        Fastnachtspiele."   *RenD* 13 (1982): 1-34.

        Traces the tradition "back to the sixteenth or
        fifteenth centuries" (1-2).   Shows about 150
        parallels in the tradition and suggests that an
        examination of the German works could shed light
        on English plays for which no mss survive.

1294.   ---.   "'Here Comes I, Jack Straw:' [sic] English Folk
        Drama and Social Revolt."   *Folklore* 95.1 (1984):
        3-20.

        Looks at the relationship between drama and
        revolt, "the interaction of festival and
        rebellion" (4).   Essentially a prolegomenon to the
        study, drawing primarily from English materials.
        Looks at many customs, and at the Robin Hood plays
        (8).

1295.   ---.   "Ritual and Vaudeville: The Dramaturgy of the
        English Folk Plays."   In *Papers Presented at the
        Traditional Drama 1981 Conference* (forthcoming).
        A preliminary draft has been issued as *Pre-
        Publications of the English Institute of Odense
        University*, gen ed. Hans Hartvigson, No. 19
        (October 1981).   15 pp.

        Considers the folk plays as "traditional
        dramaturgy, a distinct mode of performance
        involving context, costume, action and interaction
        (both physical and verbal) between performers and
        between performers and audience" (1).   Aims to
        assess "the authenticity of idiosyncratic plays"
        (1), look at how folk drama interacts with other
        dramatic forms, and look for "atypical
        dramaturgical sequences in the folk plays which
        may be intrusions from an external source" (1).

Compares English plays with non-English sources.
Covers action, costuming, language in the plays,
etc.

1296. ---. "Tudor Interludes and the Winter Revels." *MET*
6.1 (July 1984): 16-27.

Deals with the "lost tradition" (16) of drama that
preceded Medwall's plays. Examines mummers' plays
and "the late medieval *Fastnachtspiele* . . . of
the cities of southern Germany" (16). Anatomizes
mummings (the presentation, the play proper, and
the concluding entertainment), their
characterization, seasonal nature, action, and
popular elements. Examines the *Fastnachtspiele*--
the meaning of the word, the elements of the
genre. Concludes with an examination of the
interlude in its relation to the other two genres.

1297. Pfaff, R.W. *New Liturgical Feasts in Later Medieval
England.* Oxford: Clarendon Press, 1970. xix 143
pp.

Not on drama, but has much information on the
Feasts of Corpus Christi, All Saints, the
Epiphany, and many more. With notes on
iconography, index of mss, and general index.

1298. Pfleiderer, Jean Diane. "The Community of Language
in the East Anglian Drama." Ph.D. diss., U. of
Colorado at Boulder, 1981.

1299. ---. "Middle English Drama and Text Archive." *EDAMN*
2.1 (Nov. 1979): 3-4.

Discusses holdings at the Archive at the Center
for Research in Early English Drama at the
University of Colorado, Boulder.

1300. ---, and Michael J. Preston. *A Complete Concordance
to* The Chester Mystery Plays. New York and
London: Garland: 1981. 513 pp.

Contains a verse-line concordance, a preface, and
tables (of abbreviations of names of plays and of
abbreviations and names of characters).

Rev. *ARBA* 13 (1982): 666.
     Choice 19 (Apr. 1982): 1071.
     Clifford Davidson, *CompD* 16.2 (Summer 1982):
     199-200.

1301. Phythian-Adams, Charles. "Ceremony and the Citizen:
The Communal Year at Coventry 1450-1550." In

Crisis and Order in English Towns, 1500-1700, 57-85. Ed. by Peter Clark and Paul Slack. Toronto and Buffalo: U. of Toronto Press, 1972.

Aims to show the connection between the city's social structure "and its ceremonial or ritualized expression" (57). Looks at various kinds of ceremonies, many of a dramatic nature (e.g. Hock Tuesday plays, Midsummer, St. Peter's Night, and May Day celebrations). Mentions the participation of women in some of the ceremonies and the activities of the Corpus Christi Guild.

1302. ---. *Desolation of a City: Coventry and the Urban Crisis of the Late Middle Ages.* Cambridge: Cambridge U. Press, 1979. Past and Present Publications.

Looks at the city's performances of the Corpus Christi pageants (pp. 44 f., 89 f., etc.) and their costs--and what light these shed on the city's history.

Rev. *Choice* 18 (Nov. 1980): 447.
EDAMN 3.1 (Nov. 1980): 16.
R.M. Berger, *JEconH* 40 (Dec. 1980): 859-61.
R.B. Dobson, *History* 66 (Feb. 1981): 123-25.
Valerie Pearl, *TLS* (Feb. 13, 1981): 174.
R.H. Hilton, *JHG* 7 (April 1981): 201.
D. Herlihy, *SocH* 6 (May 1981): 235-37.
Specu 56 (July 1981): 643.
A.F. Butcher, *EconHR*, ser. 2, 34 (Aug. 1981): 477-78.
JMH 54 (Mar. 1982): 103.
AHR 87 (Oct. 1982): 1070.
EHR 98 (Oct. 1983): 859.

1303. Pickering, F.P. *Literatur und darstellende Kunst im Mittelalter.* Berlin: Erich Schmidt Verlag, 1966. 229 pp.

Contains one chapter (Part II, ii, chap. 4) on drama: "Das religiöse Drama und die darstellende Kunst" (106-111). See next entry for discussion and other reviews.

Rev. *MLR* 64 (Jan. 1969): 202.

1304. ---. *Literature & Art in the Middle Ages.* Coral Gables, Florida: U. of Miami Press, 1970. 362 pp. An English translation of previous entry.

Part II, ii, chap. 4 is on "Religious Drama and Representational Art" (161-67). Though not

specifically on English drama, shows how elements
in the visual arts effect drama and *vice versa*.
Says, however, that the influence of the mystery
plays on art was slight. Says, "The artists did
not draw what they had seen enacted. They
followed the instructions of the Bible . . . "
(166).

Rev. *TLS* (Sept. 11, 1970): 997.
LJ 95 (Nov. 1, 1970): 3781.
Choice 8 (Apr. 1971): 210.
MLR 67 (Apr. 1972): 392.
HudR 25 (Winter 1972-73): 696.

1305.   Pickering, Jerry V.   "The English Plough Plays."   *WF*
32.4 (Oct. 1973): 237-48.

Says that the plays parody ritual of Christmas and
May games to produce comic relief. Looks at their
history and performance. Points out the ritual
aspects of fertility that the plays were to
produce.

1306.   ---.   "The Medieval English Folk Drama."   Ph.D.
diss., U. of California, Davis, 1971.

1307.   Pietropoli, Cecilia.   "Il dramma ciclico inglese come
teatro popolare: forme della consolazione e forma
della celebrazione."   *QFG* 2 (1982): 45-60.

Reviews scholarship of the word *popular*, with
respect to 1) ecclesiastical representations; 2)
the different treatment of medieval cycles as
literary works or as spectacles offered by a
"higher" culture to a "lower" culture (i.e. to an
illiterate audience); 3) the plays as an
instrument of the laity in the guilds, rather than
the clergy, to portray/analyze lay life; 4) the
product of guild members and peasants, who turned
Bible stories into comic reversals or caricatures
of the social order of their own time. Shows how
the plays contain elements of rural and urban life
and appeal to all classes. Mentions the theory
also that the plays were the small consolation and
entertainment offered by the ruling class to the
majority stuck in monotonous routine, but says
this is anachronistic. Explains that the plays
required abstract thought on the part of the
audience, unified their composers with their
audience, and helped the audience celebrate and be
educated. Points out that the audience's
participation in the action is part of the plays'
"popularity." Discusses also settings,
characters, and selected passages.

1308.   ---.   "La figurazione dell'immaginario: i mondi
         concentrici nel dramma ciclico inglese." *QFG* 1
         (1980): 23-40.

         Examines the quality "fantastic," which applies
         differently to medieval literature than to modern,
         especially as treated by Anglo-American critics.
         Defines the term *fantasy*. Points out that a
         profound distress at their lack of control over
         their world led medieval people to write about an
         ideal world where good always triumphed over evil
         and where harmony and order reigned. Discusses
         Lucifer as an example of the medieval treatment of
         fantasy in the cycles: stylized in the *Ludus
         Coventriae*, comic in York and Wakefield, symbolic
         of role-reversal in Chester. Looks at the
         incorporation in all the plays of punishment and
         the vertical heaven-hell structure. Explains the
         medieval divine/human hierarchy, and looks at a
         number of characters in the plays in terms of this
         hierarchy (Adam, Abraham, Satan, Cain, Herod,
         Pilate, Joseph, etc.). Mentions the didactic
         intent of the imaginary in the drama, and also the
         medieval audience's hope that the ideal world
         (i.e. the afterlife) was similar to their earthly
         experience.

1309.   ---.   "Realtà, illusione e sogno nella *Prima Pastorum*
         del ciclo di Wakefield." *LP* 43 (1980): 15-25.

         Analyzes the play as a precursor to the *Secunda
         Pastorum*. Sees evidence in the earlier play of
         experimentation with the portrayal of reality/
         dream/supernatural--a portrayal confined to a
         physical space by theoretical conventions, and
         thus presenting a challenge to the dramatist.
         Shows how the first play depicts both the fall and
         the ascent of humanity. Examines the play
         closely. Shows how the shepherds represent
         universal humanity and hence involve the audience
         in the action. Says that the playwright has used
         the theater's ambiguities and constraints to show
         tension between reality, illusion, and prophetic
         imagination.

1310.   Pilkinton, Mark C. "The Antagonists of English
         Drama, 1370-1576." Ph.D. thesis, U. of Bristol,
         1974.

1311.   ---.   "The Easter Sepulchre at St. Mary Redcliffe,
         Bristol, 1470." *EDAMN* 5.1 (Fall 1982): 10-12.

         Looks at a 1470 parish record memorandum of St.
         Mary Redcliffe which "discloses the delivery of a

new Easter sepulchre to the church, one which by
its very nature confirms the inherent
theatricality associated with the sepulchre
device" (10). Quotes the memorandum and points
out its importance to the theater historian.
Urges REED editors to consider inclusion of such
phenomena in their volumes.

1311a. ---. "Entertainment and the Free School of St.
Bartholomew, Bristol." *REEDN* 13.2 (1988): 9-13.

1311b. ---. "Pageants in Bristol." *REEDN* 13.2 (1988): 9-
13.

1312. ---. "The Playhouse in Wine Street, Bristol." *ThN*
37.1 (1983): 14-21.

Questions Kathleen M.D. Barker's dating of the
opening of the playhouse (entry # 143 above).
Also comments on the location of the theater.
Proves "that the playhouse in Wine Street operated
from Christmas 1614 to 5 March 1621," and that
"the playhouse ceased to operate on 5 March 1625"
(19). Other evidence could support a closing date
of 1621, 1625, or 1628. Mentions nothing on the
types of performances in the playhouse.

1313. ---. "The Raising of Lazarus: A Prefiguring Agent to
the Harrowing of Hell." *MedAe* 44.1-2 (1975): 51-
53.

Agrees with Kolve that the Lazarus plays prefigure
the Resurrection and the Last Judgment. Claims
they also prefigure the Harrowing of Hell in the
act by Anima Christi in all four cycles, and that
they also foreshadow "the approaching atonement--
the reconciliation between God and man brought
about by the death of Corpus Christi on the cross"
(53).

1314. Piltch, Ziva S. "From Cosmology to Psychology: The
Transformation of Acedia in the Medieval Morality
Play." *Cent* 1.1 (Spring 1974): 17-23.

Defines *Acedia* (sloth) in historic terms, both in
the mortal world and in the eternal realm. Looks
briefly at *Mankind* and then at *The Castle of
Perseverance*. Shows how, in the moralities, the
playwrights made of *Acedia* "a powerful
psychological force . . . that proves destructive,
and proves a potent counterforce in the commedia
of the early English morality" (22).

1315. Pival, Paul John, Jr. "Staging as Projection of
Imitated Action in the Chester Cycle." Ph.D.
diss., U. of Wisconsin, Madison, 1973.

1316. Pollack, Rhoda-Gale. "Angelic Imagery in the English
Mystery Cycles." *ThN* 29.3 (1975): 124-39.

Challenges stereotypic notions of winged, white-
clad figures. Describes the angelic hierarchy and
relates it to earthly hierarchy. Shows how angels
are used in the cycle plays. Discusses different
costuming for the various orders of angels,
including vestments of different kinds (albs,
chasubles, copes, dalmatics, surplices), armor,
wings, suits with "tunics and hose, made of
feathers" (134), long wavy hair, and diadem or
crown.

1317. ---. "Demonic Imagery in the English Mystery
Cycles." *ThN* 32.2 (1978): 52-62.

Looks at the different manifestations of the
Devil, sources, iconography, "hybrid imagery"
(53), zoological forms (basilisk, cockatrice,
dragon, fox, griffin, hog, leopard, owl, raven,
spider, wolf, woodpecker, whale, amphisbaena,
bear, blackbird, boar, cat, dog, falcon, etc.),
the various sins represented, and the physical
accoutrements and bodily parts as depicted in the
plays.

1318. Poteet, Daniel P., II. "Condition, Contrast, and
Division in the *Ludus Coventriae* 'Woman Taken in
Adultery.'" *Medi* 1.1 (Spring 1975): 78-92.

Mentions the comic, naturalistic, idealized, and
symbolic elements of the play. Looks at the
theological and aesthetic principles involved, the
"artistic integrity" (79) of the episode to
explain the conventions of the play "and their
relation to the world view they objectify" (78).
Concludes that the play imitates "an historical
moment and an enduring context, or . . . a
particular set of relationships and a general
state of being" (90).

1319. Poteet, Daniel Powell, II. "The *Hegge Plays:* An
Approach to the Aesthetics of Medieval Drama."
Ph.D. diss., U. of Illinois, 1969.

1320. ---. "Symbolic Character and Form in the *Ludus
Coventriae* 'Play of Noah.'" *ABR* 26.1 (Mar. 1975):
75-88.

Discusses the anachronistic placement of the play
in the cycle, "the meaningful structure and
symbolic form" (76) of many of the plays, the
dramatic qualities and aesthetic form of the play.
Says that this Noah play "does not fit comfortably
within categories for analysis" (79) as do three
other Noah plays, "because traditional drama
criticism cannot accommodate its relative
vagaries" (79). Looks at symbolism and
iconography, the characterization of Lamech,
charity, and cupidity.

1321.   ---. "Time, Eternity, and Dramatic Form in *Ludus
         Coventriae* 'Passion Play I.'" *CompD* 8.4 (Winter
         1974-75): 369-85. Rpt. in *The Drama of the Middle
         Ages*, 232-48. Ed. by Davidson, et al. (see entry
         # 409 above).

         Examines "timelessness in medieval thought . . .
         the distinction between time and timelessness"
         (369) with respect to action, theme, and
         structure. Considers "Time and the Conflation of
         History" (375 ff.), "Time and Sacramental
         Efficacy" (377 ff.), "Time and Plot" (380 ff.),
         and "Time and the Imitation of Reality" (382 ff.).

1322.   Potter, Lois. "The Plays and the Playwrights." In
         The Revels *History of Drama in English, Vol. II:
         1500-1576*, 141-257. Ed. by T.W. Craik (see entry
         for Norman Sanders, et al., # 1432 below).

         Breaks discussion down into four main parts, each
         with subdivisions: 1) "Pre-Reformation dramatic
         traditions" (143-76); 2) "The Reformation and the
         moral play" (177-206); 3) "Rival traditions" (207-
         32); and 4) "Elizabethan Experiments" (233-57).

xxxx.   ---, ed. *The* Revels *History of Drama in English,
         Vol. I: Medieval Drama*. (See entry for A.C.
         Cawley, Marion Jones, Peter F. McDonald, and David
         Mills, # 289 above).

1323.   Potter, Robert. "Divine and Human Justice." In
         Aspects of Early English Drama, 129-41, 147-48.
         Ed. by Paula Neuss (see entry # 1213 above).

         Looks at these "great themes of the early drama"
         (129) which are ubiquitous and timeless. Aims to
         deal with the question of justice in English
         medieval drama. Shows the drama's satirical view
         of worldly justice by examining several plays.
         Treats the "interconnectedness of drama and
         jurisprudence" (134), the evolution of the jury
         system, "[t]he fall of a morality hero into sin"

(135), "the theatrical possibilities of . . . a
trial scene" (136), and "the realization of heaven
on earth, of divine justice . . . in an earthly
context, [which] is the destination and chief end
of human history" (138).

1324.   ---.   *The English Morality Play: Origins, History,
and Influence of a Dramatic Tradition*. London and
Boston: Routledge and Kegan Paul, 1975. ix, 286
pp.

Covers morality plays from medieval to modern
times in Europe and England. Claims to offer a
prolegomenon to the study of the genre, to ask
questions and raise issues. Chap. I discusses the
genre: "The idea of a morality play" (6); focuses
on medieval dramatic unity, "Ritual and
Regeneration" (10), and "The forgiveness of sins"
(16). Chap. II talks about "the repentance drama
of early England" (30) with respect to conscience,
"Morality characterization and free will" (37),
and forgiveness. Chap. III touches on "Skelton,
Medwall, and the morality of state" (58). Chap.
IV mentions Lindsay, Bale, and Udall. Chaps. V–
VIII are on Elizabethan drama and the European
tradition. Chap. VIII also has a section on "The
recovery of *Everyman* and the Macro MS. 1760–1835"
(203) and a section on the sources of the plays.
Chap. IX--"*Everyman* in the Twentieth Century"
(222)--discusses the revivals and adaptations of
the story. With notes and index. [Part of Chap.
II rpt. in *Medieval English Drama: A Casebook*,
130-40. Ed. by Peter Happé (entry # 684 above).]

Rev. *LJ* 100 (July 1975): 1343.
        Sanford Sternlicht, *Economist* 256 (July
            12, 1975): 109.
        Richard Axton, *TLS* (Aug. 22, 1975): 934-35.
        Choice 12 (Oct. 1975): 1002.
        Alan H. Nelson, *MedAe* 45.3 (1976): 352-54.
        R.T. Davies, *N&Q*, n.s. 23.2 (221) (Feb.
            1976): 79-81.
        B.D. Bills, *ETJ* 28 (Mar. 1976): 127-31.
        C.J. Carlisle, *RenQ* (Summer 1976): 276-77.
        PQ 55 (Fall 1976): 479.
        A.C. Cawley, *RES*, n.s. 28 (May 1977): 248-49.
        Joanne Spencer Kantrowitz, *CompD* 11.2
            (Summer 1977): 183-87.
        E.M. Kelly, *JEGP* 76 (July 1977): 448-50.
        Stanley J. Kahrl, *ELN* 16.3 (Mar. 1979): 235-
            38.
        [See also review article by Alan C. Dessen,
            entry # 447 above.]

1325.   ---.   "The Idea of a Morality Play."   *RORD* 13-14
        (1970-71): 239-47.   [See entry # 878 above.]

        Begins with a general discussion of cycle and
        morality plays.   Looks at the terminology
        (*mystery, miracle, morality*), literary sources
        (sermons and penitential literature), and the
        "idea of the action" (240).   Shows the unity of
        purpose of the cycle and the mystery plays: "two
        manifestations of the same dramatic purpose"
        (241).   Considers the medieval technique of
        "illumination: to make visible the invisible
        truths of time and the universe" (241).   Calls the
        morality play "didactic drama" (242) about "the
        fall out of innocence into experience" (242).

1326.   ---.   "Images of the Human Predicament: Some Ancient
        and Modern Visualizations of the Morality Play."
        RORD 13-14 (1970-71): 249-58.

        Attempts to visualize morality plays to reveal
        their "human nature" (249).   (Using slides) looks
        at "*Mankind* as Process," "The Cyclical World
        Theater," and "The Morality Play as Popular
        Drama."   Considers the "notion that man is on
        trial" (250), the struggle between good and evil,
        the world as a place of danger, the "human
        predicament [which] . . . has a providential
        solution" (251), the play as entertainment, and
        recent morality plays.   Claims that the best way
        to understand a morality play is to visualize it.

1327.   ---.   "The *Ordo Virtutum:* Ancestor of the English
        Moralities."   *CompD* 20.3 (Fall 1986): 201-10.

        Considers Hildegard of Bingen's work (of c. 1151)
        as possibly "the first morality play" (201).
        Offers biographical information and comments on
        the theme and form of her work.   Shows parallels
        between her *Ordo* and the morality plays.
        Considers plot, characters, themes, and audience.

1328.   ---.   "The Unity of Medieval Drama: European Contexts
        of the English Traditions."   In *Contexts for Early
        English Drama*, 41-55.   Ed. by Marianne G. Briscoe
        and John C. Coldewey (entry # 228 above).

        Addresses the "literary bias" of scholarship which
        ignores continental influences.   Reviews
        publication history of English plays: 1)
        Anthologies; 2) Theatre Histories; 3) Genres of
        Drama.   Calls for more circumspect scholarship.

1329. Powlick, Leonard. "The Staging of the Chester Cycle:
An Alternate Theory." *ThSur* 12.2 (Nov. 1971):
119-50.

Uses the David Rogers description of a pageant
procession as a point of departure and looks at
other evidence to suggest alternative methods of
production. Concludes that scholars have too
readily accepted Rogers' description of the
performance, positing stationary performances.
With two illustrations.

1330. Preston, Michael J. "The British Folk Play: An
Elaborated Luck-Visit?" *WF* 30.1 (Jan. 1971): 45-
48.

Examines folk drama--its various forms, its
effects. Focuses on "the folk play and related
visits" (46). Emphasizes the importance of
seemingly unimportant portions and characters of
the plays. Concludes that the "'folk play' . . .
is not a play in origin at all . . . but . . . a
visit which brings luck, or at least wards off
evil" (48).

1331. Preston, Michael James, ed. *A Complete Concordance
to* The Wakefield Pageants in the Towneley Cycle.
Ann Arbor: University Microfilms, 1977. [No. LD
00098] 549 pp.

Based on A.C. Cawley's text (Manchester:
Manchester U. Press, 1958). A line concordance
with frequency lists for each of the six plays as
well as for all six plays combined, along with a
reverse index. With no cross references, no
separation of homographs, no gathering of variant
spellings under a single headword.

1332. ---. *A Concordance to Four "Moral" Plays:* The Castle
of Perseverance, Wisdom, Mankind, *and* Everyman.
N.p.: n.p., 1975. [A two-vol. bound printout from
Xerox University Microfilms, Ann Arbor, Michigan;
printed on rectos only.] vii, 802 pp.

With brief preface. Contains concordance of
English graphic forms, concordance for foreign
graphic forms, a frequency list for each play, and
a combined frequency list for foreign graphic
forms for all the plays. Offers no cross
references; does not group variant forms under a
single headword; does not distinguish among
homographs.

1333.   ---.   *A Concordance to "The Digby Plays."*   Ann Arbor:
        University Microfilms, 1977.   [No. LD 00095]
        [Also, a two-vol., bound printout.]   vi, 1-529;
        530-1080.

        Contains a concordance to the plays for English
        words along with a similar list for foreign words.
        Also has Ranking Lists of frequencies for each
        play, along with reverse indexes to English and
        foreign forms.   Excludes "stage directions and
        related verbal materials" (iii).   Does not
        distinguish homographs, bring variant spellings
        under a single headword, or present cross
        references.

1334.   ---.   "The Revesby Sword Play."   *JAF* 85.335 (Jan.-
        Mar. 1972): 51-57.

        Examines the play ("Morrice Dancers at Revesby")
        of October 20, 1779.   Looks at the ms, its
        provenance and date, analogues, and the folk
        tradition on which it is based.   [See Cawte, entry
        # 292 above, for additional remarks.]

1335.   ---.   "The Robin Hood Folk Plays of South-Central
        England."   *CompD* 10.2 (Summer 1976): 91-100.   Rpt.
        in *Drama in the Middle Ages*, 342-51.   Ed. by
        Clifford Davidson, et al. (entry # 409 above).

        Reviews scholarly views on the tradition, origins,
        and development of the plays.   Considers the plays
        from only one area: "parts of Gloucestershire,
        Oxfordshire, Somerset, and Wiltshire" (92).

1335a. ---, and Jean D. Pfleiderer.   *A Concordance to the
        Ludus Coventriae or N-Town Plays.*   New York:
        Garland, forthcoming.   c. 600 pp.

1335b. ---, ---.   *A Concordance to the Non-Cycle Plays and
        Fragments.*   Vol. I.   Plays from East Anglia.   New
        York: Garland, forthcoming.   [N.B.   Also in
        preparation is *A Concordance to the Non-Cycle
        Plays.*   Vol. II.   Non-East Anglia.   With an
        introduction by Donald Baker.   And also *A
        Concordance to "The Towneley Plays."*]

1336.   ---, and Jean D. Pfleiderer.   *A KWIC Concordance to
        the Plays of the Wakefield Master.*   New York:
        Garland, 1982.   472 pp.

        Contains an Extended KWIC Concordance, Mak's part
        and a KWILC [Key Word in Line Context] to his
        part, the Shepherds' parts (*Secunda Pastorum*) and
        a verse concordance to their parts, and five

experimental concordances: 1) a five-word KWIC
concordance for all six plays; 2) a three-word
KWILC concordance for the two shepherds' plays; 3)
a reverse extended KWIC concordance (sample pages
from the letter *E*); 4) an extended KLIC [Key
Letter in Context] concordance (sample page from
the letter *O*); and 5) a reverse extended KLILC
[Key Letter in Line Concordance] (sample page from
the letter *N*). Also contains ranking lists of
frequencies and reverse index forms for Wakefield
and Chester cycles.

Rev. Clifford Davidson, *CompD* 16.2 (Summer 1982):
     199-200.
     Choice 20 (Oct. 1982): 246.
     ARBA 14 (1983): 571.

1337. Price, Jocelyn. "Allusions to Medieval Drama in
      Britain (5): Additional Old English References."
      MET 6.2 (Dec. 1984): 159-60. (See entry # 415
      above, and also entries 1338-39.)

      Cites four new and one corrected entry.

1338. ---. "Theatrical Vocabulary in Old English: A
      Preliminary Survey (I)." *MET* 5.1 (July 1983): 58-
      71. (See entries # 415, 1337, and 1339.)

      Gives original contexts and translations of many
      Old English glosses or synonyms in sixty passages
      from Latin terms. ". . . the second instalment
      [sic] of 'Allusions to Medieval Drama in Britain:
      A Finding List' edited by Nick Davis" (58).
      Treats *Amphitheatrum, Comedia, Comicus, Histrio,
      Iocista, Ludi, Mima/Mimus, Orcestra, Pantomimus,
      Pulpitus, Saltator/Saltatrix, Scena, Scurra,
      Spectaculum, Temelici, Theatrum Tragicus,* and
      proper names.

1339. ---. "Theatrical Vocabulary in Old English (2)."
      MET 6.2 (Dec. 1984): 101-25.

      Continues previous study, concentrating on the
      legend of St. Genesius and "Actor," Orosius,
      Vitruvius, and "Theatre," Glossaries and glosses,
      and Plautus and Terence in Anglo-Saxon England.
      Reveals the Old English "knowledge of classical
      theatre traditions" (118).

1340. Priessnitz, Horst. "Bearbeitungen mittelalterlicher
      Dramentypen auf der englischen Gegenwartsbühne."
      In *Anglistentag 1980 Giessen: Tagungsbeiträge und
      Berichte im Auftrage des Vorstandes,* 75-99. Ed.
      by Herbert Grabes. Grossen-Linden: Hoffmann, 1981.

On the treatment of medieval dramatic genres on
the contemporary (i.e. primarily twentieth-
century) English stage. Covers cycle and morality
drama, focusing on problems with production,
translation, understanding of medieval religious
doctrine, characterization, and so on.

1341. Prindle, Dennis Joseph. "The Profane Moment: The
Deformation of Sacred History in the Late Medieval
English Cycle Drama." Ph.D. diss., Cornell U.,
1977.

1341a. Prior, Sandra Pierson. "Parodying Typology and the
Mystery Plays in the Miller's Tale." *JMRS* 16.1
(Spring 1986): 57-73.

Examines the use of episodes and stock characters
from the morality plays in Chaucer's work,
especially in terms of "fullness of detail . . .
hilarious ribaldry, and . . . sheer brilliance as
parody" (73).

1342. Proudfoot, Richard. "The Virtue of Perseverance."
In *Aspects of Early English Drama*, 92-110, 147.
Ed. by Paula Neuss (see entry # 1213 above).

Enumerates the extant (and no-longer-extant)
morality plays, with brief descriptions of each,
and a longer examination of the *Castle of
Perseverance*--its motifs (the Life of Man,
Psychomachia, perseverance), its moments of
surprise, presentation of mercy, debates,
patterns, length, staging, and revivals.

1343. Prudhomme, Danièle. "Métamorphoses du Juif au Moyen-
Age et à la Renaissance: réalité et fiction." In
Echanges: Actes du Congrès de Strasbourg, 75-88.
Société des Anglicistes de l'Enseignement
Supérieur. Foreword by G. Laprevotte. Paris:
Didier, [1982]. Etudes Anglaises 81.

Points out that originally Jews and Christians
were not distinguishable in England by dress until
the fourth Lateran Council (1215) which required
Jewish men to wear a white cloth or parchment
patch in the shape of the stone tablets of the
law; by 1275 this was the rule for both sexes, the
patches to be yellow. This prevented mixed
marriages and promoted segregation and degradation
of Jews. Discusses these developments in light of
medieval art, in which Jews were depicted in
caricature/costume as animals or as "satan." Says
that actual dress of both religions was
approximately the same, but in art Jews were

depicted by exaggerated beards or moustaches,
coin-like details on garments, pointed hats or
turbans. Discusses this with respect to the *Ludus
Coventriae* characters Annas and Caiaphas.
Mentions that some Old Testament Jews escaped such
characterization (Christ, Mary, the Apostles).
Discusses other exaggerations of depiction: long
or hooked noses, iconographic presentations as
usurers with sharp teeth, and with personality
traits in the caricature including comical
language, oaths, pomposity, and displays of anger
or rage. Says that they were even depicted as
animals. Points out that by the Renaissance, Jews
had assimilated so much into indigenous cultures
that they lost all evidence of their heritage, so
dramatists had to turn back to medieval
models/stereotypes, anachronistic clothing, and
the colors red, blue, and dark yellow.

1344. Psaty, Bruce Mark. "History and Ideology in the
Tudor Plays about King John." Ph.D. diss.,
Indiana U. 1979.

1345. Purvis, John S. *From Minster to Market Place*. York:
St. Anthony's Press, 1969. 81 pp.

Contains extensive notes on and observations about
the history and production of the cycle plays in
York, as well as the Paternoster and Creed plays.
Considers civic control and "particular features
of the Mystery cycle productions" (1). Looks at
liturgical origins, The Shrewsbury Fragments, and
"the Era of Civic Control" (Part II, 17-24); and
then has a section (Part III) of "Illustrations
and Extracts." Discusses more than two dozen
phenomena (e.g. The Cycles, particular mss,
pageant silver and pageant money, the plays'
Proclamation, the granting of new stations, the
interludes, etc.). With illustrations.

1346. ---. "The York Religious Plays." In *The Noble City
of York*, 841-54. Ed. by Alberic Stacpoole. York:
Ceralis Press, 1972.

Sees the religious sources of York's drama, which
"arose in the services of the Church" (841).
Looks at primary documents: Statutes of York
Minster, regulations for the Treasurer of the
Minster. Locates entries which prove "that in the
twelfth and early thirteenth centuries York
Minster had liturgical plays of a precise and
definite nature as parts of the Minster services,
and that these plays belonged to a Nativity and an
Epiphany series" (841). Quotes from the

Shrewsbury Fragments (842-44) and from the
textually related Chandlers' Play. Discusses the
Pater Noster Plays; and also the cycle plays,
which had their origins in a "now unknown . . .
Cycle of Plays" (845) of the fourteenth century.
Examines the long cycle--performance methods,
length of performance, route, performers, relation
to the Church, language of the plays, and so on.

1347. Quillian, William H. "'Composition of Place':
        Joyce's Notes on the English Drama." *JJQ* 13 (Fall
        1975): 4-26.

        Presents transcriptions and facsimiles of notes
        from Joyce's notebook. Contains several allusions
        to medieval English and liturgical drama.

1348. Quilligan, Maureen. "A Critique of 'The Allegory of
        Contradiction in *Everyman* and *The Faerie Queene*.'"
        In *Spenser and the Middle Ages*, 387-97. Ed. by
        David A. Richardson. Cleveland: Cleveland State
        U., 1976. (microfiche)

        Critiques John M. Webster's article (see entry #
        1667 below).

1349. Quint, Bernard Julius. "The *Quem Quaeritis:* Its
        Context as Liturgical Drama." Ph.D. diss.,
        Arizona State U., 1976.

1350. Ragusa, Isa. "The Princeton Index of Christian Art."
        MET 4.1 (July 1982): 56-60.

        Relates "pictorial representations" to medieval
        drama. Explains the value of the Princeton Index
        to students of drama.

1351. Ralston, Michael E. "The Four Daughters of God in
        The Castle of Perseverance." *Comitatus* 15 (1984):
        35-44.

        Traces the history of the Four Daughters story.
        Shows how the author of the *Castle* was familiar
        with this story, how he used it, and how he
        "extended his presentation" of it (36). Looks at
        the extensions. Shows that "Tradition and
        innovation come together . . . as the four
        heavenly virtues argue about the fate of man"
        (42).

1352. Ralston, Michael Earl. "A Typology of Guides in
        Medieval Literature." Ph.D. diss., Auburn U.,
        1984.

Looks at *Everyman*.

1353.   Rankin, Susan K.   "The Mary Magdalene Scene in the
        Visitatio Sepulchri Ceremonies."   In *Studies in
        Medieval and Early Modern Music*, 227-55.
        Cambridge, London, and New York: Cambridge U.
        Press, 1981.   Early Music History 1.

        Examines "the re-use of old material" (227) to
        show "how the melodies in any ceremony or group of
        ceremonies were composed" (227-28).   Discusses
        "methods of approach to the repertory of
        liturgical drama" (228) with respect to individual
        ceremonies and "traditions of the repertory"
        (228).   Focuses on a German Mary Magdalene scene.
        Not on English drama, but contains useful insights
        into medieval dramatic composition in antecedents
        to the English plays.

1354.   ---.   "A New English Source of the *Visitatio
        Sepulchri*."   *JPMMS* 4 (1981): 1-11.

        Notes "the presence of dramatic ceremonies . . .
        [including] an *Elevatio Crucis* and *Visitatio
        Sepulchri*" (1) in an English processional of
        between 1250 and 1320.   Presents the text with
        musical transcription and notes.   Not on English
        drama, but presents information about the
        background of the use of music in the drama.

1355.   ---.   "Shrewsbury School, Manuscript VI: A Medieval
        Part Book?"   *PRMA* 102 (1976): 129-44.

        Refers to an early fifteenth-century English ms
        containing "texts and music for processions,
        Passions and plays" (129).   Concentrates on the
        music of the ms.   Not on English drama
        specifically, but offers background to the plays
        in looking at other elements of public performance
        current with the drama, with possible reference to
        the York plays.

1356.   Rasmussen, Eric.   "Shakespeare's Use of *Everyman* in
        Timon of Athens."   *ANQ* 23.9 and 10 (May/June
        1985): 131-35.

        Shows many parallels between the two plays--
        structural, thematic, and verbal.   Shows also how
        Shakespeare used Everyman's "tragic movement into
        aloneness" (134).

1357.   Rastall, G.R.   "The Minstrel Court in Medieval
        England."   In *A Medieval Miscellany in Honour of
        Professor John Le Patourel*, 96-105.   Ed. by R.L.

Thomson. Leeds: Proceedings of the Leeds
Philosophical and Literary Society, Literature and
Historical Section 18.1 (April 1982).

Points out that some minstrels were static, some
were itinerant; some were independent, some were
attached to a court. Also shows that minstrels
were controlled with annual licensing and some,
"minstrel kings" (100), conducted visitations like
herald kings. Shows also that minstrels formed
their own guilds for self-government.

1358. Rastall, Richard. "'Alle hefne makyth melody.'" In
       Aspects of Early English Drama, 1-12, 142. Ed. by
       Paula Neuss (see entry # 1213 above).

       Considers music in English religious drama.
       Rejects "the nineteenth-century concept of
       'incidental music' directed at the emotions" and
       identifies "the philosophical traditions . . .
       that seem to inform the plays and their use of
       music" (1). Considers also music's functions, the
       music of the spheres, *musica humana*, and
       "representational" (4) music. Looks at
       performance, notation, and the "types of evidence
       to which we look for information" (10). Raises
       questions for further research.

1359. ---, ed. *The Drama of Medieval Europe*. Proceedings
       of the Colloquium held at the University of Leeds,
       10-13 September 1974. Leeds: Graduate Centre for
       Medieval Studies, University of Leeds, 1975. Rpt.
       1977. Leeds Medieval Studies 1. [With
       introducion by Lynette Muir.] ix, 101 pp.

       Presents summary and transcription of the
       proceedings. Gives the text of five talks, each
       followed by discussion. See Smoldon ("Music in
       Medieval Drama," entry # 1485 below); Cawley
       ("Medieval Drama and Didacticism," # 282); W.F.
       Michael ("Humour and Comedy . . .," # 1124); Kahrl
       ("Editing Texts . . .," # 876); and Denny ("The
       Staging of Medieval Drama," # 443).

1360. ---. "Minstrels and Minstrelsy in Household Account
       Books." In *Records of Early English Drama:
       Proceedings of the First Colloquium*, 3-25:
       [Essay, 3-21; discussion, 21-25.] Ed. by Joanna
       Dutka (see entry # 497 above).

       Discusses account books in various households,
       royal and non-royal, and shows many entries to be
       indicative of different types of entertainment.

343

Shows also how the examination of such records
could yield much information about drama.

1361. ---. "Music for a Royal Entry, 1474." *MT* 118.1612
       (June 1977): 463-66.

       Examines Coventry's welcome to Prince Edward in
       1474, one of the few instances of music's being
       specified in writing in medieval times. Shows how
       the information gleaned here is applicable to the
       late medieval dramas, specifically with respect to
       which instrument represents what on stage. E.g.
       trumpet and shawms equal royalty; organ music
       equals heaven.

1362. ---. "Music in the Cycle." In *The Chester Mystery
       Cycle: Essays and Documents*, 111-64. Ed. by R.M.
       Lumiansky and David Mills (see entry # 1016 above,
       Chap. 3).

1363. ---. "Music in the Cycle Plays." In *Contexts for
       Early English Drama*, 192-217. Ed. by Marianne G.
       Briscoe and John C. Coldewey (see entry # 228
       above).

       Discusses the scholarship on music in the plays
       and how this scholarship has been subsidiary to
       literary criticism. Looks at different critical
       approaches and issues, the various historical
       views and traditions, the notion of "musical
       'realism,'" the "ethics of musical performance"
       (both the social and the theological aspects),
       vocal and instrumental music, the music variations
       in the different cycles, the tradition of
       minstrelsy, etc.

1364. ---. "Music in the English Play-cycles." In *The New
       Oxford Companion to Music*, I, 386-87. Ed. by
       Denis Arnold. 2 vols. Oxford and New York:
       Oxford U. Press, 1983.

       Discusses the cycles in general and the
       speculative nature of the criticism on their
       music. Looks at "patterns of usage" (386) and the
       two principal functions of music in the plays:
       "representational" and "structural" (386).

1365. ---. "Some English Consort Groupings of the Late
       Middle Ages." *M&L* 55.2 (1974): 179-202.

       Deals with medieval musical iconography, which
       focuses on the celebration of special events
       rather than day-to-day minstrelsy. Says that
       scholarship is moving toward "a useful

understanding of medieval depictions of music and their relationship to reality" (179). Aims to show that isolated examples of iconography do not offer a good basis for theories. Considers different kinds of consort groupings. Not specifically on drama, but offers information about and criticism on one aspect of the drama.

1366. ---. "'Some myrth to his Majestee': Music in the Chester Cycle." In *Staging the Chester Cycle*, 77-99. Ed. by David Mills (see entry # 1159 above).

Considers all evidence to try to determine what kind of and how much music there was in the cycle. Points out that there are over thirty indications (in stage directions) that music was used. Focuses on functions, settings, instruments, voices, musical style, and performance. With an illustration and five appendixes of music notation.

1367. ---. "Vocal Range and Tessitura in Music from York Play 45." *MusAn* 3.2 (July 1984): 181-99.

Explains "tessitura" ("that part of the pitch-range in which the music tends to lie"--181). Shows "the need for precise, quantified information on the tessitura" (181), and shows how he found that information in the York *Assumption* play. Looks at angels' singing and at the musical notation which follows the play in the ms. Posits reasons for the existence of two settings (that they "are for a different type of voice, [or] that they are for more experienced or competent singers"--189). Uses a computer to analyze the PCG ("pitch centre of gravity"--190) of the music.

1368. ---. "Wait." In *The New Grove Dictionary of Music and Musicians*, Vol. 20, 154-55. Ed. by Stanley Sadie. London: Macmillan; Washington, D.C.: Grove's Dictionaries; Hong Kong: Peninsula, 1980.

Analyzes the word and its six various meanings. Meaning # 5 is "a civic minstrel, permanently employed by a town" (155). Discusses the activities of waits. With a brief bibliography.

1369. Reed, Anna Kremer. "The Tether and Pang of the Particular: A Study of the Function of Typology in the English Plays of Abraham and Isaac." Ph.D. diss., U. of Kentucky, 1973.

1369a.   ---.   "'A Thing Like a Love-Affair': A Study of the
         Passion of Obedience in the York Play of Abraham
         and Isaac."   *C&L* 29.2 (1980): 35-45.

         Claims that many contemporary scholars "fail to
         appreciate much that is in medieval drama because
         of our present tendency to assume that a good
         character is a dull character" (35). Says that
         modern readers "lack the medieval man's sense of
         the dramatic tension involved in obedience" (35).
         Looks at obedience and rebellion, primarily the
         former, in the York "Abraham and Isaac" play, with
         respect to the exegetical tradition. Talks of the
         play's supposed weaknesses, its stress on the
         father/son bond, the play's focus on the
         characters' striving to display perfect obedience
         to a father, the character development, Isaac's
         maturation, the play's "symbolic texture" (42),
         and the ultimate dramatic power that obedience
         yields in the play.

1370.   Reid, S.W.   "Two Emendations in 'Passion Play II' of
         the *Ludus Coventriae*."   *ELN* 11.2 (Dec. 1973): 86-
         87.

         Offers "un to" for "in to" (line 606, stage
         direction) which "enables us to make better sense
         of Pilate's actions" (86), and "ther skaffaldys"
         for "the skaffalde" (line 860, stage direction)
         which allows for more probable staging of Annas
         and Cayphas.

1371.   Reiss, Edmund.   "The Story of Lamech and Its Place in
         Medieval Drama."   *JMRS* 2.1 (Spring 1972): 35-48.

         Explains the appearance of the Lamech episode in
         the Noah plays, as well as the place of Noah's
         wife in the cycle plays. Comments on "the
         dramatic and symbolic function of Lamech" (48).

1372.   ---.   "The Symbolic Plow and Plowman and the
         Wakefield *Mactacio Abel*."   *StudIcon* 5 (1979): 3-
         30.

         Shows Cain to be "a man of wrath . . . a bad lord
         and vassal" (4) and the opening scene to be "a
         dramatic preparation for [Cain's] later defiance
         of parents, church, state, and God" (4). Explains
         the unexpected association of Cain with a plow.
         Examines the symbolism of the plow, "a reminder to
         the audience that after the Fall, man had to work
         for his food" (4), a symbol of peace and new life,
         of husbandry, man's rightful occupation,
         fertility, life forces, and so on. Looks at

source material for the plow symbolism, and at the
plow play source, "traditionally performed on Plow
Monday" (12). Shows that the plow was symbolic of
"a type of the cross" (15) with Christ as plowman
and plow.

1373.   ---. "The Tradition of Moses in 'the Underworld and
the York Plays of the Transfiguration and
Harrowing." *Medi* 5 (1979): 141-64.

Shows the connection between the two plays in
terms of theme and artistry. Explains the
connection as coming from the use of the Moses
figure. Discusses this figure--its sources and
symbolism, the traditions of Moses in the
underworld, Moses transfigured, and Moses
associated with the Harrowing. Points up the York
use of these traditions.

1374.   Reiter, Seymour. *World Theater: The Structure and
Meaning of Drama.* New York: Horizon Press, 1973.
259 pp.

Contains fifteen chapters on various plays or the
drama of various cultures. Chap. 12--"The
Medieval Achievement" (156-69)--discusses the
Second Shepherds' Pageant, The Brome *Sacrifice of
Isaac,* The Hegge *The Woman Taken in Adultery,* The
York *Creation* through *The Fall of Man,* "and
Others" (156). Considers "syllogistic plot-
structures" (156). Comments on the artistry and
sophisticated structures of much medieval English
drama.

1375.   Remly, Lynn. "*Deus Caritas:* The Christian Message of
the 'Secunda Pastorum.'" *NM* 72.4 (Dec. 1971):
742-48.

Discusses the unity of the two parts of the play.
Says that the humorous plot comments on and
prepares the audience for the Christian theme in
the Nativity plot.

1376.   Rendall, Thomas Ned. "Bondage and Freeing from
Bondage in the Corpus Christi Plays." Ph.D.
diss., Stanford U., 1971.

1377.   ---. "Liberation from Bondage in the Corpus Christi
Plays." *NM* 71.4 (Dec. 1970): 659-73.

Shows that the audience's understanding of the
plays is dependent on their understanding of
"certain medieval commonplaces" (659) and their
knowledge of Christian ceremony, ritual, and

practices, which include certain gestures.
Focuses on the acts of bonding and "loosing"
(661), the latter symbolic of the church's power
of forgiveness from sin. Shows the relationship
of this to Atonement. Looks at this phenomenon in
several Corpus Christi plays. Claims that the use
of binding and loosing is "part of the . . .
drama's conscious artistry" (672). Claims also
that the liberation from bondage in the plays is
the primary metaphor through which Christ's
offering of salvation to mankind is expressed.

1378.   ---.   "The Times of Mercy and Judgment in *Mankind*,
Everyman, and the *Castle of Perseverance*."
EngStudC 7.3 (Fall 1981): 255-69.

Examines justice and mercy in these plays and
shows that the plays were aimed primarily at
"large, unlearned, and for the most part, lay
audiences" (266-67).

1379.   ---.   "Visual Typology in the Abraham and Isaac
Plays."   *MP* 81.3 (Feb. 1984): 221-32.

Deals with the appropriateness of and varying
contexts for typological readings. Recounts
several critics on this problem and the related
one of staging. Analyzes the visual elements of
the play, especially gestures and props; claims
they were probably very extensively used on stage.

1380.   *The* Revels *History of Drama in English*.   Vols. I and
II cover the drama within the scope of this
bibliography. Since each volume has a different
editor and different authors, they are listed
separately here as follows:

Vol. I--see entry for A.C. Cawley, Marion Jones,
Peter F. McDonald, and David Mills (# 289 above).

Vol II--see entry for Norman Sanders, Richard
Southern, T.W. Craik, and Lois Potter (entry #
1432 below).

1381.   Reynolds, Philip Lyndon.   "Medieval Drama and the
Theory of Ideas." *Scintilla* 2-3 (1985-86): 141-43.

Review of Garrett Epp's "The Semiotics of
Flatness" (see entry # 540 above). Claims that
playwrights and audience "seem to have been much
more interested in the universal than in the
particular" (141).

1382.   Richards, Douglas William. "Preachers and Players:
         The Contest Between Agents of Sermon and Game in
         the Moral Drama from Mankind to Like Will to
         Like." Ph.D. diss., U. of Rochester, 1986.

1383.   Richardson, Christine. "Medieval into Modern. Can
         the Medieval Theatre Offer a Way Forward for
         Contemporary Theatre?" *QFG* 3 (1984): 217-34.

         Looks to the medieval drama for a "fruitful source
         of impetus of growth" (217) for modern drama
         productions. Considers some "characteristic forms
         of medieval theatre" (217). Aims to analyze
         "three modern productions to see how they related
         to the original form, purpose and spirit of
         medieval drama" (218), and to look at links
         between original and modern performances. Focuses
         on characteristics of mystery cycles and recent
         performances. Talks of "physical organisation and
         context of medieval drama" (220), the staging of
         the cycles, and the "spirit of the drama:
         Translations and Equivalents" (227).

1384.   Richardson, Janette. "Affective Artistry on the
         Medieval Stage." *QJS* 70.1 (Feb. 1984): 12-22.

         Shows how the Brome *Abraham and Isaac* is capable
         of moving an audience and disseminating knowledge.
         Gives a rhetorical exegetical analysis to
         illuminate the play and to explain the play's
         "apparent inconsistencies" (20).

1385.   Ricks, Christopher, ed. *English Drama to 1710*.
         London: Barrie & Jenkins, in association with
         Sphere Books, 1971. History of Literature in the
         English Language, Vol. III.

         Contains a chapter by Glynne Wickham, "Stage and
         Drama till 1669" (see entry # 1696 below).

         Rev. *TLS* (Dec. 3, 1971): 1526.

1386.   Riehle, Wolfgang. "English Mysticism and the
         Morality Play *Wisdom Who is Christ*." In *The
         Medieval Mystical Tradition in England: Papers
         Read at The Exeter Symposium, July 1980*, 202-15.
         Ed. by Marion Glasscoe. Exeter: U. of Exeter,
         1980. Exeter Medieval Texts and Studies.

         Surveys criticism. Examines the relationship
         between the play and medieval mystical works, the
         use of actors to portray Christ or to take "on a
         mystical attitude toward Christ's suffering in the
         passion" (203), the "affective and emotional

response on the part of the audience" (204).
Points out that *Wisdom* is an "adaptation of Suso's
Horologium Sapientiae, which deals with the
mystical union of Anima with her lover, Aeterna
Sapientia, i.e. Christ" (204). Considers medieval
psychology, the soul's path toward perfection, the
theological content of the play and its artistic
form. Concludes that the play "has no mystical
aspirations, but . . . confines itself . . . to
pastoral guidance and homiletic appeal" (211), and
that the play had a general, not a specialized,
audience.

1387. ---. "The Englishness of the English Corpus Christi
Plays." *FCS* 8 (1983): 179-94.

Discusses "the overall character or tone of the
[English] cycles" (179) in terms of the "various
forms and modes of didacticism" (179) and examines
"whether the didactic intention is maintained with
the same degree and intensity in different plays"
(179). Distinguishes the tone of the Chester
plays from that of the other cycles.

1387a. Riemer, Seth. "The Dramatic Significance of Christ's
Tears in a French and an English Version of the
Lazarus Play." In *Early Drama to 1600*. Ed. by
Albert H. Tricomi. (See entry # 1589b below.)

1388. Riggio, Milla Cozart. "The Allegory of Feudal
Acquisition in *The Castle of Perseverance*." In
Allegory, Myth, and Symbol, 187-208. Ed. by
Morton W. Bloomfield. Cambridge, Massachusetts,
and London: Harvard U. Press, 1981. Harvard
English Studies 9.

Shows that "allegorical drama could deal
simultaneously with political issues and spiritual
matters" (187), and that the *Castle* "contains a
consistent substructure of allusions that
associate economic and social abuse with feudal
patronage" (188). Claims that these allusions
reflect a political reality and economic fears of
the day, and reinforce the religious allegory of
the play. Also says that "the play utilizes two
different medieval concepts of kingship to
illustrate the irreparable corruption of the
world" (188). Shows how the play points up "the
acquisitive economic climate of the fifteenth
century" (208).

1388a. ---. *The Play of* Wisdom: *Its Texts and Contexts*.
New York: AMS Press, 1986. AMS Studies in the
Middle Ages, No. 14.

Contains introduction discussing the play in its
fifteenth-century contexts, theological
background, the genre of morality/masque. Also
looks at date. With modernized edited text,
glossary, production notes (from a 1984
performance at Trinity College), bibliography, and
index.

1389. ---. "The Staging of *Wisdom*." *RORD* 27 (1984): 167-
78. Rpt. in *The* Wisdom *Symposium* . . ., 1-17.
Ed. by Milla C. Riggio (see next entry).

Points out the explication and interpretation
involved in staging a medieval play for a modern
audience. Draws upon her experience with two
different kinds of performance, as a banquet
masque (April 12-14, 1984) and as an outdoor May
Day play (May 5, 1984). Reveals different
audience responses. Considers genre, time and
place, stage setting, costuming, etc.

1390. ---, ed. *The* Wisdom *Symposium: Papers from the
Trinity College Medieval Festival*. New York: AMS
Press, 1986. AMS Studies in the Middle Ages, No.
11. 110 pp.

Contains five essays: Riggio ("The Staging
. . .," previous entry); Bevington "'Blake and
wyght . . .," entry # 182 above); Gibson ("The
Play of *Wisdom* . . .," # 624); Baker ("Is *Wisdom*
. . .," # 135); and Johnston ("*Wisdom* and the
Records . . .," # 842). With index.

Rev. *Choice* 24 (June 1987): 1555.

1391. Righter, Anne. *Shakespeare and the Idea of the Play*.
London: Chatto & Windus, 1962. 224 pp. Rpt.
Harmondsworth, England: Penguin Books, 1967. 200
pp.

Preceeds an examination of Shakespearean theater
with a look at medieval drama and its
implications. Chap. I is "Mysteries and
Moralities: The Audience as Actor" (13-14).

1392. Roberts, R.J. "John Rastell's Inventory of 1538."
Lib, 6th ser. 1.1 (Mar. 1979): 34-42.

Comments on the recently discovered Public Record
Office document No. Prob. 2/692, containing
information on Rastell's holdings as a
printer/bookseller. Reprints and comments on the
inventory. Mentions a play by Rastell's son

William: *Good Order* (1533), and also Rastell's *Interlude of the Four Elements* (41).

1393. Robertson, D.W., Jr. *The Literature of Medieval England*. New York: McGraw-Hill, 1970.

Contains a general introduction covering such background matters as "Medieval Life and Ideals" (1-9); "Medieval Astronomy and Astrology" (10-23); "The Medieval Bible" (24-27); "The Character of Medieval Literature" (27-30); and "The Literature of Medieval England" (30-33). Chap. XII is on the drama. Includes editions of the Wakefield *Mactacio Abel* and *Secunda Pastorum* and of *Everyman*. With brief notes and glossary.

1394. ---. "The Question of 'Typology' and the Wakefield *Mactacio Abel*." *ABR* 25.1 (Mar. 1974): 157-73. Rpt. in *Essays on Medieval Culture*, 218-32, 371-72. Ed. D.W. Robertson, Jr. Princeton: Princeton U. Press, 1980.

Says that a typological approach is misleading because "it is a severely limited subject, theoretical rather than practical" (158). Claims that the plays were designed tropologically, with emphasis on dramatized events and parallels in the Christian lives of the spectators: "The plays must have had some bearing on their daily concerns" (158), and on their understanding of exegesis. Shows the importance of typology, tropology (which makes biblical events "immediately and practically relevant to the daily lives of the observer"--160), and anachronisms. Looks closely at the Wakefield *Mactacio Abel* to show how the playwright has made the actions practical to the lives of the audience.

1395. Robinson, J.W. "Ad Majorem Dei Gloriam." In *Medieval Drama: A Collection of Festival Papers*, 31-37. Ed. by William A. Selz (see entry # 1454 below).

Discusses medieval English drama "in its artistic, literary, religious, and social contexts" (31). Also considers the actors (the guilds), the relation of the plays to other arts, and the alignment of crafts with specific plays.

1396. ---. "A Commentary on the York Play of the Birth of Jesus." *JEGP* 70.2 (Apr. 1971): 241-54.

Claims that of the four English mystery plays which depict the birth of Jesus, only the York

play "can properly be called a true work of art"
(241). Describes the play; discusses the
playwright's use of sources and dramatic
tradition, the theological elements, the
characterization and symbolism, the dialogue and
tone, and the appropriateness of the players (the
"Tile Thackers"--i.e. Coverers of Roofs with
Tiles). Shows that part of the success of the
play comes from its focus on the meditative rather
than the legendary tradition, drawing from "the
dignified St. Birgitta" (254). Calls the play
"intelligent and shapely" (254).

1397.   ---. "Form in the Second Shepherds' Play." *PPMRC* 8
(1983): 71-78.

Aims to discuss "the formal and even numerical
quality of the dialogue, plot, stanza, and
diction" (71), with primary focus on the plot.
Considers the order of the speeches of the
characters, the play's numerology (especially the
significance of "the number of parts--4 or 6, 5 or
7, and 9--created by the positioning" [73] of the
speeches), etc. Concludes that the play "is
governed by patterns and numbers" (76) but still
displays a remarkable spontaneity. Comments on
the rigidity of patterns in plot, speeches, and
stanzas, and the concomitant naturalness of speech
and sense of "colloquial vigor" (77).

1398.   R[obinson], J[ohn] W. "Medieval Drama." In *The New
Cambridge Bibliography of English Literature.*
Vol. I, 600-1600. Sect. 5, cols. 719-42.
Cambridge: At the University Press, 1974.

Lists works in nine subgroups: 1) Bibliographies;
2) Histories; 3) Collections; 4) Liturgical drama;
5) Anglo-Norman Drama; 6) Cornish and Welsh Drama;
7) English Mystery and Miracle Plays; 8)
Spectacles and Minstrelsy to 1485; 9) Folk Drama.

1399.   ---. "Monuments to the Medieval Theatre." *ThN* 33.2
(1979): 86.

Points out two monuments, one on Farringdon Road--
a pump and an iron plaque which commemorates "in
remote Ages . . . sacred Plays" (86)--and the
other "on the left-hand side of the frieze which
runs along the front of what was . . . the Saville
Theatre (now a Cinema) in Shaftsbury Avenue" (86).

1400.   ---. "On the Evidence for Puppets in Late Medieval
England." *ThSur* 14.1 (May 1973): 112-17.

Uses recently published records from Kent (*Records
of Plays and Players in Kent 1450-1642*, ed. by
Giles Dawson; Malone Society Collections VII,
1965, pp. 26-27) to substantiate that puppets were
used. Cites George Speaight and Ann Haskell, who
believe that puppets were used in the production
of some plays. Quotes Speaight (whose authority
he questions) that it "'seems probable that
marionettes of some kind were occasionally
employed in the open-air miracle plays . . . and
these must have been manipulated from pageant
wagons'" (113). Explains, thus, the "God in
strings" (113) image of "the Chester plays, where
the Jews who capture Jesus treat him as if he were
an animal" (113), and the Lucifer and "spirits on
cords" image of the Cornish *Creation of the World*
play as having to do with their being bound, not
as having to do with any form of puppetry.
Concludes that it is likely that puppet shows were
part of the medieval repertoire, but "the
assumption that puppets took part with human
actors in performances of mystery plays . . .
should be discarded" (115).

1401.   ---.   "Regency Radicalism and Antiquarianism: William
Hone's *Ancient Mysteries Described* (1823)." *LSE*
10 (1978): 121-44.

Discusses this work, which he calls an "important
development in the literary and dramatic
historiography" (121). Evaluates Hone's
pronouncements on medieval drama.

1402.   Robertson, Nan.   [Review.]   *New York Times* (Apr. 11,
1980).   (Cited by Sheila Lindenbaum, *RORD* 23
[1980]: 91.)

Reviews performance of *The Woman Taken in
Adultery*, April-May 1980, by the Actors Guild, at
the Cloisters, New York City.

1403.   Rockey, Laurilyn Jay Harris.   "A Stylistic Analysis
of Three Plays of the Chester Cycle: *The Three
Kings, The Ablation of the Three Kings,* and *The
Slaughter of the Innocents.*"   Ph.D. diss., U. of
Iowa, 1972.

1404.   Roddy, Kevin P.   "Epic Qualities in the Cycle Plays."
In *Medieval Drama*, 154-71.   Ed. by Neville Denny
(see entry # 442 above).

Examines the epic character of the mystery cycles;
links these plays with Elizabethan chronicle
plays. Discusses the meaning of *epic*. Looks at

various cycles and plays using Tillyard's four
primary epic characteristics: "high seriousness,
amplitude and breadth, a sense of controlling
will, and a representation of the feelings of the
people" (156).

1405. ---. "The Ohio State University Videotape on Early
Medieval Drama: 'The Nest and the Egg.'" *Chronica*
23 (Fall 1978): 5-7.

Reviews the Ohio State series.

1406. ---. "Revival of the Cornish Mystery Plays in St.
Piran's 'Round' & of the York Cycle, 1969:
Experiments in Medieval Drama & Stagecraft."
NewTh 9 (1968-69): 16-21.

Calls for an understanding of medieval stagecraft
to add authenticity to modern performances. Draws
upon a performance of the York Cycle in 1969.
Complains about uninformed newspaper criticism of
the performances. Discusses the problems the
plays present to modern directors, actors, and
audiences. With photographs of the Cornish
mystery taken from a performance.

1407. Roddy, Kevin Padraic. "'Who Is This King of Glory?':
The Epic Element in English Cycle Drama." Ph.D.
diss., U. of California, Davis, 1972.

1408. Rogerson, Margaret. "External Evidence for Dating
the York Register." *REEDN* 1.2 (1976): 4-5.

Speculates that the York Corpus Christi Play (BL
Add. MS 35290) dates from "well into the last
quarter of the fifteenth century" (4). [See also
Beadle and Meredith, entry # 157 above.]

1409. ---. "The York Corpus Christi Play: Some Practical
Details." *LSE*, n.s. 10 (1978): 97-106.

Looks at contemporary documents to reveal
information about the financing of medieval Corpus
Christi play productions (including contributions
from guild members, from non-members, fines . . .)
and the storage of wagons. Aims to show that "the
city council and the crafts did all they could to
attend to practical matters and thus ensure the
efficient presentation of the Play" (103).

1410. Roney, Lois. "The Wakefield *First* and *Second*
Shepherds [sic] *Plays* as Complements in Psychology
and Parody." *Specu* 58.3 (July 1983): 696-723.

Examines the existence of two shepherds' plays in
the cycle. Surveys criticism. Looks at the two
in terms of "later medieval theories of
psychology" (697) and the debate of the greater
nobility of will or intellect. Notes a remarkable
similarity between the two plays in their
characterizations and in their use of comedy--a
"bold parody of the outward actions and inward
expectations of one of the two great Corpus
Christi mysteries, the Eucharist in the *First
Shepherds* [sic] *Play*, the Incarnation in the
Second . . ." (698). Points out, too, the
similarity in their conclusions, structure,
actions, subject matters, and style.

1411. Rood, Wayne R. "Mystery and Drama: A Lecture
       Supported by Two Actresses and Two Authors." In
       Medieval Drama: A Collection of Festival Papers,
       1-30. Ed. by William A. Selz (see entry # 1454
       below).

       Article written in the form of a play describing
       medieval English drama, with actors, actresses,
       and a Lecturer, in two acts (Act I, "Prehistoric
       Ritual and Drama"; Act II, "The Ancient Christian
       Mystery").

1412. Rorem, Paul. "Corpus Christi, Feast of." In
       Dictionary of the Middle Ages, vol. 3, 608. Ed.
       by Joseph R. Strayer (see entry # 1553 below).

       Offers a brief description and history of the
       celebration, with no special emphasis on the
       drama. Bibliography contains only one item
       (Kolve's *The Play Called Corpus Christi*).

1413. Rose, Martial. "The Magi: The Litter and the Wristed
       Crown." *MET* 5.1 (July 1983): 72-76.

       Treats the "relationship of medieval iconography
       to medieval drama" (72) with special reference to
       the Magi. Suggests that certain representations
       of the Magi in medieval art (e.g. stained glass,
       the Arundel Psalter) could be "the artists' recall
       of what had become a dramatic convention" (75).

1414. ---. "The Staging of the Hegge Plays." In *Medieval
       Drama*, 196-221. Ed. by Neville Denny (see entry #
       442 above).

       Explains why the information in the play's
       Proclamation may not be a reliable source as to
       the nature of the performance. Looks at stage
       directions, dialogue, and costumes, and compares

the words of the Proclamation to the action of the
plays to show how the Hegge plays were staged.
Considers which plays were performed with which
(on different days and in different years: "here
the evidence is that the plays in their entirety
were not performed within the same year" [211]).
Describes the "variety and flexibility of the
acting areas" (218) for the two Passion plays:
Heaven, Temple, council-house, sepulchre,
scaffolds, castle or mansion, Last Supper room,
and hills, and so on; "The emphasis seems
generally to be on drama in the round" (221).

1415. Rosenfeld, Sybil. *A Short History of Scene Design in
       Great Britain.* Totowa, NJ: Rowman and
       Littlefield, 1973. xviii, 214 pp.

       Chap. I covers "Medieval and Tudor Scenic
       Elements" (1-10). Discusses stationary and
       "perambulatory" (1) scenic units, extant ms plans,
       pageant wagons, mechanical effects, scenic
       elements, street theaters, artists, and so on.

       Rev. *B&B* 19 (Jan. 1974): 54.
            Choice 10 (Feb. 1974): 1880.

xxxx. Rossi, Joan, and Michael Rossi. *Index to York Art.*
       In *York Art* . . ., 211-34. Ed. by Clifford
       Davidson and David E. O'Connor (see entry # 411
       above).

1416. Rosso, Joan DePascal. "The Liturgical Basis of the
       Wakefield 'Secunda Pastorum': Redemption
       Redefined." Ph.D. diss., State U. of New York at
       Buffalo, 1981.

1417. Roston, Murray. *Biblical Drama in England: From the
       Middle Ages to the Present Day.* London: Faber and
       Faber, 1968.

       Chap. I considers "The Medieval Stage": Realism
       and Expressionism, The Sacred and the Profane, The
       Old Testament Plays, The Second Shepherd [sic]
       Play, and The Cain and Noah Plays. Shows that the
       mixture of realism and expressionism "by
       superimposing the spiritual significance of a
       scene upon its physical representation became a
       hallmark of martyrological art" (17). Discusses
       the relationship between the sacred and the
       humorous elements of the mystery plays. Suggests
       that the Old Testament plays, despite being
       subordinate to the New Testament plays in the
       cycles, still expressed the ultimately religious
       purpose of the drama. Considers the antecedent to

(or parallel of) the "Second Shepherds' Play" and
the realism and humor in the shepherds' plays.
Looks briefly at the sources of the
characterizations of Cain and Noah.

Rev. *Choice* 5 (Feb. 1969): 1596.
CompL 23 (Winter 1971): 71.

1418. ---. *Sixteenth-Century English Literature.* New
York: Schocken Books, 1982. History of Literature
Series.

Chap. 4--"The Growth of Secular Drama"--treats the
last years of the cycle plays, the inhibitions to
the growth of secular drama, the emergence of
interludes, the distinction between amateur and
professional actor. Examines plays of Bale,
Medwall, and Heywood, and school and university
plays.

Rev. *BBN* (Feb. 1983): 115.
LJ 108 (Mar. 1, 1983): 500.
Booklist 79 (Apr. 15, 1983): 1069.
Choice 20 (June 1983): 1458.
TES (Dec. 30, 1983): 22.
LibR 33 (Spring 1984): 63.

1419. Rowan, D.F. "'Inns, Inn-Yards, and Other Playing
Places.'" In *The Elizabethan Theatre IX: Papers
Given at the Ninth International Conference on
Elizabethan Theatre . . . University of Waterloo,
in July 1981*, 1-20. Ed. by G.R. Hibbard. Port
Credit, Ontario: P.D. Meany, n.d.

Reviews scholarship, mostly for Elizabethan
theater. Mentions medieval staging (see esp. pp.
15 ff.).

1420. Royce, James R. "Nominalism and Divine Power in the
Chester Cycle." *JHI* 40.3 (July-Sept. 1979): 475-
76.

Responds to Kathleen Ashley's "Divine Power in
Chester Cycle and Late Medieval Thought" (see
entry # 113 above). Points out that where Ashley
sees the cycle as being influenced by nominalism
and not by folk elements, the plays do have folk
origins in the New Testament. Claims that what
Ashley finds as examples of nominalist influence
"are in fact part of the common stock of Christian
motifs" (476). (See Ashley's response, "Chester
Cycle and Nominalist Thought," entry # 112 above.)

1421.   Rozett, Martha Tuck. *The Doctrine of Election and
        the Emergence of Elizabethan Tragedy.* Princeton,
        NJ: Princeton U. Press, 1984.

        Chap. 3--"Morality Play Protagonists" (74-107)--
        analyzes medieval dramatic influences. Discusses
        "The Fifteenth-Century Morality Plays" (77-82),
        "The Education-of-Youth Plays" (82-88), "The Dual-
        Protagonist Plays" (88-94), "The Ascendancy of the
        Vice" (94-100), and "Protestant Polemics and the
        Tragic Protagonist" (100-07).

        Rev. *Choice* 22 (Apr. 1985): 1161.
             TLS (Aug. 16, 1985): 906.
             AHR 91 (Feb. 1986): 104.

1422.   Ryan, Dennis Michael. "The Grotesque in the York
        Mystery Plays." Ph.D. diss., Loyola U. of
        Chicago, 1974.

1423.   Sachs, Arieh. "Ikonographia shel Tziporim be-Mister-
        'Yat Ha-Mabbul." *Bamah* 68 (1976): 37-46. In
        Hebrew.

        Examines the Wakefield flood play from his own
        experience in directing the play. Concludes that
        it is possible to use the paintings of the middle
        ages as a key to understanding the plays of the
        period as he uses the iconography of birds in the
        Wakefield flood play as painted in the Holkham
        Bible Picture Book. Believes one must see the
        play as a series of *tableaux vivants* of biblical
        appearances. The text links the pictures; the
        text is of two types: comic and "dramatic"
        (investigative) and both types link the pictures
        together. Says that the bird scene is an example
        of narrative visual drama.

1424.   St.-Jacques, Raymond. "The Hegge 'Mary in the
        Temple' and the Liturgy of the Consecration of
        Virgins." *N&Q* 27.4 (225) (Aug. 1980): 295-97.

        Reviews scholarship on sources of the play; posits
        an additional source, "the liturgy for the
        consecration of nuns" (295). Shows why the
        playwright would have used these liturgical rites:
        they offered an ideal model for the ritual
        demanded by the play.

1425.   ---. "Middle English Literature and the Liturgy:
        Recent Research and Future Possibilities." *Mosaic*
        12.2 (Winter 1979): 1-10.

Points up the importance of a knowledge of the
medieval liturgy in the interpretation of medieval
literature. Reviews available scholarship. Looks
briefly at such use in the interpretation of
English drama (3-5).

1425a.   Saito, Mamoru. "On John Bale's *King Johan*." In *The
         English Drama and Its Society before Shakespeare*,
         17-27. Tokyo, Tsuda College, 1981.

1426.   ---. "The Use of the Rhetorical Exordium in Middle
         English Drama." *Flor* 3 (1981): 268-82.

         Examines the medieval exordium, "meant to provide
         the audience with a brief, lucid, and interest-
         arousing summary" (268) of the forthcoming text.
         Considers classical and medieval definitions and
         its transformed use in several plays or cycles.

1427.   Salgado, Gamini. *English Drama: A Critical
         Introduction*. New York: St. Martin's Press, 1980.

         Chap. 1--"Medieval Drama" (1-24)--discusses the
         drama as "one of the great achievements of the
         European theatre" (1). Distinguishes the drama of
         church ritual with respect to Catholic Mass, the
         rise of miracle plays (drawing heavily on Kolve's
         scholarship), the English cycle plays, and
         morality plays. Shows that the selection of plays
         for the cycles is influenced "by a tradition of
         commentary and interpretation by the early fathers
         of the Church" (5), and the Old Testament
         materials are selected by a "well established
         tradition of figural interpretation" (6).
         Discusses the performances by the guilds and the
         "place-and-scaffold" and "pageant waggon" staging,
         costumes and props, competence of the actors,
         modern editions and problems with the cycles, and
         realism and the *play* or *game* aspects of the plays.
         Considers allegory and the ancestry of morality
         drama. Compares *The Castle of Perseverance* with
         Mankind and examines these as well as *Everyman*.

         Chap. 2--"The Emergence of the Secular Drama" (25-
         36)--discusses Medwall's *Fulgens and Lucrece*--its
         own treatment of the "gentilesse" theme and
         "debat" format, its original use as an interlude
         for John Morton (Archbishop of Canterbury), the
         play's shape in two parts, its having been written
         with Lambert Palace dining hall layout in mind,
         and its story. Discusses Medwall's *Nature* as a
         morality play also designed for Lambeth Palace
         ("the residence of the Archbishop of Canterbury"
         [27]), and Sir Thomas More's enthusiasm for the

drama (More was a page of John Morton). Shows
John Heywood's contributions to secular drama;
summarizes the plots of *A Play of Love, The Play
of the Weather, The Four Ps, The Pardoner and the
Friar*, and *Johan Johan*. Mentions Heywood's *Witty
and Witless*. Explains the emergence of an
emphasis on character, action, speech, and secular
concerns, and a movement away from scriptural or
predictably didactic material. Discusses "the
growth of professionalism" (30) among the actors
and "the conditions under which Tudor interludes
were performed [which] created a tradition of
acting in which improvisation, flexibility, a high
degree of conventionality in costume and gesture
and above all, a unique blend of familiarity and
formality between actors and audience were
essential features" (32). Shows that the secular
drama "was educational in intent or pretension"
(33), following classical models.

Rev. J.R. Mulryne, *THES* 429 (Jan. 14, 1981): 14.
    G. Bott, *SchLib* 29 (Mar. 1981): 79.
    Choice 18 (May 1981): 1265.
    SevCN 40 (Spring 1982): 6.
    Allan R. Botica, *N&Q*, n.s. 29.5 (227) (Oct.
      1982): 433-34.

1428.   Salingar, Leo. *Shakespeare and the Traditions of
Comedy*. London and New York: Cambridge U. Press,
1974. 356 pp.

Chap. 2--"Medieval Stage Romances"--looks at
medieval plays, "Medieval Stage Heroines" (39),
and "Survivals of Medieval Staging" (67).

Rev. *VQR* 51 (Spring 1975): R64.
    A.B. Kernan, *YaleR* 64 (Mar. 1975): 432.
    Choice 12 (Apr. 1975): 222.
    SewR 83 (Apr. 1975): 305.
    C.L. Barber, *TLS* (Aug. 8, 1975): 889.
    Alan C. Dessen, *CompD* 9.4 (Winter 1975-76):
      350-53.
    R.S. White, *N&Q* 23 (Apr. 1976): 176-78.
    J. Wilders, *RES*, n.s. 27 (May 1976): 207-09.
    H. Levin, *CompL* 28 (Fall 1976): 364-65.
    E. Jones, *EssCrit* 26 (Oct. 1976).
    D. Bain, *CR*, n.s. 1 (1977): 153.
    M. Charney, *JEGP* 76 (Oct. 1977): 549-50.
    R. Weimann, *MLR* 73 (Apr. 1978): 390-91.

1429.   Salomon, Brownwell. "Early English Drama, 975-1585:
A Select, Annotated Bibliography of Full-length
Studies." *RORD* 13-14 (1970-71): 267-77.

Contains fifty entries of this "century's most
authoritative and frequently cited book-length
critical and historical studies" (267). Does not
contain articles, superseded scholarship,
anthologies, editions, or studies of individual
dramatists.

1430.   Sanders, Barry.   "Who's Afraid of Jesus Christ? Games
        in the *Coliphizacio*."   *CompD* 2.2 (Summer 1968):
        94-99.

        Examines the use of buffeting--revealing the
        difference between its use in the play and its
        manifestation in the game Hot-Cockles.

1431.   Sanders, Norman.   "The Social and Historical
        Context."   In *The* Revels *History of Drama in
        English, Vol. II: 1500-1576*, 1-67.   (See next
        entry.)

        Treats "Drama and society" (1-6); "The suppression
        of the mystery cycles" (7-11); "Drama and
        Propaganda" (12-23); "The growth of control" (24-
        30); "Private playing and the court" (31-37); and
        a "Table: a calendar of plays, 1495-1575" (38-67).

1432.   ---, Richard Southern, T.W. Craik, and Lois Potter.
        The Revels *History of Drama in English, Vol. II:
        1500-1576*.   Ed. by T.W. Craik.   London and New
        York: Methuen, 1980.   xxxvii, 290 pp.

        Contains four parts, each by a different author:
        I. Sanders ("The Social and Historical Context,"
        previous entry); II. Southern ("The Technique of
        Play Presentation," entry # 1496 below); III.
        Craik ("The Companies and the Repertory," # 363);
        and IV. Potter ("The Plays and the Playwrights," #
        1322).   For contents of each part, see entries for
        each author.   With chronological table,
        illustrations, bibliography, and index.

        Rev. C. Belsey, *THES* 434 (Feb. 27, 1981): 17.
             G. Salgado, *BBN* (May 1981): 308.
             Choice 19 (Sept. 1981): 82.
             Paula Neuss, *TLS* (Sept. 11, 1981): 1045.
             Graham Barlow, *ThRI* 7.1 (Winter 1981/82): 62-
                63.
             RES 34 (Nov. 1983): 481.
             Ian Lancashire, "History of . . ." (see entry
                # 950 above).

1432a. Sarlos, Robert K.   "Computer Modeling in
        Reconstructing the Passion Play."   *FCS* 13 (1988):
        237-46.

1433.   Scally, William Arthur.   "Corpus Christi Drama: Four
        Versions of One World."   Ph.D. diss., U. of
        Maryland, 1982.

1434.   ---.   "Four Concepts of Time in *Corpus Christi*
        Drama."   *PPMRC* 6 (1981): 79-87.

        Distinguishes each cycle's notion of history from
        that of the others, along with varying
        relationships with their respective audiences, the
        differences relating to the cycles' dramatic
        content.

1435.   ---.   "Modern Return to Medieval Drama."   In *The Many
        Forms of Drama*, 107-14.   Ed. by Karelisa V.
        Hartigan.   Lanham, Maryland; New York; and London:
        U. Press of America, 1985.

        Mentions uses of the medieval plays by dramatists
        in the last two centuries, and uses Thornton
        Wilder's *Skin of Our Teeth* and other plays as
        examples.   Shows sources or analogues in several
        cycle plays.

1435a. Scattergood, John.   "*The Contention between
        Liberality and Prodigality*--A Late Morality Play."
        In *Early Drama to 1600*.   Ed. by Albert H. Tricomi.
        (See entry # 1589b below.)

1436.   Scattergood, V.J.   *Politics and Poetry in the
        Fifteenth Century*.   London: Blandford Press, 1971.
        415 pp.

        Covers the period 1399-1485.   Not on drama, but
        gives much background information on politics and
        events preceding and contemporary with the drama.

        Rev. *Choice* 10 (Mar. 1973): 98.
             AHR 78 (Apr. 1973): 419.
             Specu 49 (Apr. 1974): 372.

1437.   Schapiro, Meyer.   "'Cain's Jaw-Bone That Did the
        First Murder.'"   In *Late Antique, Early Christian,
        and Mediaeval Art, Selected Papers*, 249-65.   New
        York: Braziller, 1979.

        Not specifically on drama, but treats the
        iconography of the Cain/Abel incident and claims
        that the use of a jawbone was an English
        invention, and that "The affective connotations of
        both Cain and the jawbone for demonic and animal
        violence in English fantasy probably helped fuse
        these two elements into a single image" (259).
        Useful for interpreting the dramatic performances

of the story. [See also, in same volume, his
essay, "The Angel with the Ram in Abraham's
Sacrifice: A Parallel in Western and Islamic Art,"
288-306. Also not on drama, but with much
discussion on iconography, etc.]

1438. ---. *Words and Pictures: On the Literal and Symbolic
in the Illustration of a Text.* The Hague: Mouton,
1973. 108 pp.

Not specifically on drama, but offers insights
into the visual "reductions of a complex
narrative" (11). Looks at the use of symbols, the
relationship between the visual and the verbal,
and many themes of religious and secular art.

Rev. *NYRB* 21 (Nov. 14, 1974): 37.
     G.E. Yoos, *JAAC* 34 (Summer 1976): 506-07.
     S. Hindman, *Specu* 51 (Oct. 1976): 789-92.

1439. Schell, Edgar. "The Distinctions of the Towneley
Abraham." *MLQ* 41.4 (Dec. 1980): 315-27.

Points out how the Towneley play differs from the
Abraham plays in other cycles, "constructed in
imitation of an action all its own" (315). Shows
Abraham to be "presented as a heroic example of
obedience *in extremis*" (327).

1440. Schell, Edgar T. "*Scio Ergo Sum:* The Structure of
Wit and Science." *SEL* 16 (Spring 1976): 179-99.

On the play's three-part structure, complexity,
density, and transitional nature in the evolution
of moralities. [Partly reprinted in his book
Strangers and Pilgrims; see next entry.]

1441. ---. *Strangers and Pilgrims: From* The Castle of
Perseverance *to* King Lear. Chicago and London: U.
of Chicago Press, 1983. 214 pp.

Deals with five plays, including *The Castle* and
John Redford's *Wit and Science.* (The others not
applicable to this bibliography.) Focuses on "a
character who perverts his natural inclinations
and loses thereby his own identity" (1). Looks at
narrative and thematic elements, the form of man's
spiritual and temporal pilgrimage. Chap. 1 deals
with *The Castle* (a version of a paper already
published: "On the Imitation of Life's Pilgrimage
in *The Castle of Perseverance*," *JEGP* 67 [1968]:
235-48). Chap. 2 is on *Wit and Science* (part of
which appeared in article cited in previous
entry). Calls the plays examples of "didactic

theatrical allegory" (1). Looks at the
persistence of the plays' characteristics (single
action, characterization), their narrative and
thematic structures, and the pilgrimage elements
in their different uses. Contains notes and
index.

Rev. *LJ* 108 (June 1, 1983): 1140.
Choice 21 (Dec. 1983): 574.
RenQ 37 (Autumn 1984): 490.
VQR 60 (Winter 1984): 9.
ShakQ 37 (Spring 1986): 139.

1442. ---. "*Youth* and *Hyckescorner*, Which Came First?" *PQ*
45.2 (Apr. 1966): 468-74.

Agrees with Bang's theory that *Youth* precedes
Hyckescorner. Looks at the plays with respect to
the development of the morality genre. Concludes
that "The action of *Hyckescorner* is in the main an
elaborate version of the action of *Youth*" (472)
and posits that the author of *Hyckescorner* used
"the action of *Youth* as a framework for setting
out his own concerns" (474).

1443. Schiller, Gertrud. *Ikonographie der christlichen
Kunst*. Gütersloh: Gerd Mohn, 1966-1971. 4 vols.
Iconography of Christian Art. Trans. of the 2nd
German ed. of 1969 by Janet Seligman. Greenwich,
Connecticut: New York Graphic Society, 1971. 2
vols.

Not specifically on drama, but contains hundreds
of illustrations of Christian art, background to
the iconography of the plays. Vol. I covers the
Incarnation, Childhood, Baptism, Temptation,
Transfiguration, Works, and Miracles of Christ.
Vol. II covers Christ's Passion. Vol. I has 585
illustrations; Vol. II has 816. With bibliography
and index.

1444. Schmidt, Dieter M. *Die Kunst des Dialogs in den
Wakefield-Spielen*. Frankfurt am Main: Peter D.
Lang, 1980. Europäische Hochschulschriften, Reihe
14, Band 82. 191 pp.

Contains a catalogue of and commentary on the
Wakefield dialogues and what gives rise to them.
Analyzes where they come from, including a
character's entrance, the introduction of a
person, questioning, calling and fetching
characters, demands, and greetings. Analyzes
conversations of three or more people, setting,
and time. Contains bibliography, appendixes

paralleling Wakefield and York plays, number of
speakers, openings of plays, monologues to begin a
play or to begin a scene, dialogues, conversations
of three or more characters, addresses to the
audience, messengers' speeches, parallel or linked
speeches (e.g. Cain and Abel), forms of greeting
and leave taking, observing and listening, self-
introduction, the action of calling someone over,
and speeches.

Rev. Wolfgang Riehle, *Anglia* 104.3/4 (1986): 509-
10.

1445. Schmitt, Natalie Crohn. "The Idea of a Person in
Medieval Morality Plays." *CompD* 12 (Spring 1978):
23-34. Rpt. in *Drama in the Middle Ages*, 304-15.
Ed. by Davidson, Gianakaris, and Stroupe (see
entry # 409 above).

Claims that "while the object of the plays is
didactic, their effect is mimetic" and that "the
plays provide a phenomenological account of
existence" (23). Attempts "to recover the
psychology inherent in the medieval morality
plays" (23). Points out dramatic elements which
were once thought to be weaknesses but are now
seen "as representation of the human experience"
(23). Examines mimesis and the ways the plays
depict man in the world, allegory, personified
abstractions, and universalized types.

1446. ---. "*Perseverance.*" *ThSur* 18.2 (Nov. 1977): 96-98.

Answers several critics by clarifying her earlier
argument (in "Was There a Medieval Theatre in the
Round? . . ."; see next entry). Claims that "the
drawing accompanying . . . *The Castell of
Perseverance* indicates performance in the round
but provides no evidence of a theatre structure"
(96). Posits "production in the round on an open
field" (98).

1447. ---. "Was There a Medieval Theatre in the Round?:
Part II." *ThN* 24.1 (Winter 1969): 18-25. [Part I
(Stratman No. 2824a) is in *ThN* 23.4 (Summer 1969):
130-42. Both parts rpt. in *Medieval English
Drama*, 295-315. Ed. by Jerome Taylor and Alan H.
Nelson (entry # 1573 below).]

(Part I aimed at suggesting an interpretation of
the well-known illustration of the *Castle* which
contradicts Richard Southern's reading of it as
proof of a theater in the round.) Part II aims at
looking at evidence for such a theater. Examines

the Cornish rounds, the picture from the 1400
Terence ms, Jean Fouquet's "The Martyrdom of St.
Apollonia," Thomas Churchyard's *The Worthiness of
Wales*, Hieronymus Bosch's "The Seven Deadly Sins
and the Four Last Things" (all with
illustrations). Concludes that Southern's
"evidence . . . is interesting but certainly
questionable" (25), and that "the bulk of the
evidence so far seems to me to suggest more
flexible and intimate playing areas and
productions which were less formalized than such
specially constructed theatres would allow" (25).
(See response by Catherine Belsey, "The Stage
. . .," entry # 161 above.)

1447a. Schoell, Konrad. "Le Théâtre Erudit au Moyen Age."
FCS 13 (1988): 401-10.

1448. Schreiber, Earl G. "*Everyman* in America." *CompD* 9.2
(Summer 1975): 99-115.

Sketches the production histories of *Everyman* and
von Hofmannsthal's *Jedermann* in the United States.
Offers no criticism of the plays.

1449. Schroeder, Horst. "The Nine Worthies: A Supplement."
ASNSL 218 (1981): 330-34.

Discusses the popularity of the Nine Worthies
references in medieval literature. Supplements
his own earlier work with a list of 25 new
references, five of which are dramatic: a 1498
Dublin pageant; a masque of King Henry VIII at
Calais (June 24, 1520); two more Dublin pageants
of 1541 and 1557; and *England's Joy* (The Plot of
the play Called Englands Joy, November 6, 1602),
the last no longer extant.

1450. Schulz, Herbert C. *Catalogue of Middle English
Manuscripts in the Huntington Library: The
Towneley Plays.* Cited by A.C. Cawley and Martin
Stevens, eds. *The Towneley Cycle* . . ., p. xv, n.
1 (see entry # 19 above). Unpublished,
preliminary typescript. See C.W. Dutschke, R.H.
Rouse, et al., *Guide to Medieval* . . ., entry #
499 above.

1451. Seaton, Jean Q. "Source of Order or Sovereign Lord:
God and the Pattern of Relationships in Two Middle
English 'Fall of Lucifer' Plays." *CompD* 18.3
(Fall 1984): 203-21.

Compares the York and Chester plays; also compares
Rosemary Woolf's and Peter Travis's readings of

Satan and God (Woolf, *The English* . . ., entry #
1714 below; Travis, *Dramatic Design* . . ., #
1588). Claims that a careful reading of God would
explain the weaknesses of some scholars'
criticism. Examines God as creator; God in social
and metaphysical terms; as a part of a hierarchy;
as wisdom; as part of the Trinity. Looks at
"disjunctive" and "relational" portrayals (209).
Also assesses Lucifer and his relation to God.
Uses nominalism as a source of criticism.

1452. Sellin, Paul R. "The Hidden God: Reformation Awe in
Renaissance Literature." In *The Darker Vision of
the Renaissance: Beyond the Fields of Reason*, 147-
96. Ed. by Robert S. Kinsman. Berkeley: U. of
California Press, 1974. U.C.L.A. Center for
Medieval and Renaissance Studies Contributions: 6.

Looks at the medieval nature of *Everyman*.
Compares the play to "the utterances of the
Reformers" in northern Europe. Summarizes plot.
Looks at the differences in attitudes toward God
in the play and the Reformers with respect to the
benevolence of God, the nature of Everyman, and
grace. Considers cultural differences also
between the world and the world of the play.
Examines the world of the Reformation.

1453. ---. "An Instructive New *Elckerlijc*." *Comitatus* 2
(1971): 63-70.

Review article of R. Vos's edition of *Den spieghel
der salicheit van elckerlijc* . . .; Groningen:
J.B. Wolters, 1967.

1454. Selz, William A., ed. *Medieval Drama. A Collection
of Festival Papers*. Vermillion, South Dakota: The
Dakota Press, U. of South Dakota, 1969. Festival
Papers, Vol. III, 1968.

Contains nine essays, six on English drama: 1)
Rood ("Mystery . . .," entry # 1411); 2) J.W.
Robinson ("*Ad Majorem* . . .," # 1395); 3) Lewis
("The Complexion . . .," # 988); 4) Dunn ("The
Origin of the Saints' Plays," [see "The Origin of
the Middle English Saints' Plays," # 484]); 5)
Fifield ("'The Castle of Perseverance: A Moral
Trilogy," # 551); and 6) George R. Adams ("Comedy
and Theology . . .," # 90).

1455. Shapiro, Michael. "Three Notes on the Theatre at
Paul's, c. 1569-c. 1607." *ThN* 24.4 (Summer 1970):
147-54.

Discusses 1) the location of the theater in which
the Children of Paul's performed; concludes that
no evidence is extant to establish for certain,
but that St. Gregory's parish church or another
hall would have been possible; 2) the auditorium--
a general description of the type of interior of a
theater that the Children would have performed in;
posits that banqueting halls were the most likely
kind of performance places, like the halls at
Richmond, Windsor, or Hampton Court; 3) the
admission prices and the nature of the audience;
says that admission cost from twopence to
sixpence, and that "admission to private theatres
may have cost slightly more than admission to
public theatres until about 1610 or so" (153).
Concludes that "Performances in private theatres
originated as rehearsals for court performances
. . . . Spectators at these rehearsals tended to
be members of the aristocracy and gentry because
the performances were rehearsals for a courtly and
aristocratic occasion" (154).

1456. ---. "Toward a Reappraisal of the Children's
Troupes." *ThSur* 13.2 (Nov. 1972): 1-19.

Surveys the milieu in which children's troupes
acted, their "professionalism," their success, and
other features of dramaturgy (e.g. praise, insult,
satire). Concludes, "The satiric city comedies
acted by children's troupes struck at the very
roots of all authority and invited universal
participation in saturnalian mockery, representing
the last phase of a festal tradition that reached
back to the end of the Middle Ages" (15).

1457. Sharp, Thomas. *A Dissertation on the Pageants or
Dramatic Mysteries anciently performed at Coventry
. . . . .* Coventry: Merridew and Son, 1825; rpt.
Wakefield: E.P. Publishing; Totowa, NJ: Rowman and
Littlefield, 1973. Foreword by A.C. Cawley. 226,
[4] pp.

Contains a facsimile rpt. of Sharp's *Dissertation*,
with Cawley's new foreword. With illustrations
and bibliography. Foreword (vii-ix) discusses
Sharp's life and activities, and especially the
work he did on this *Dissertation*.

1458. Shatkin, Laurence. "Holiday Games in Early Tudor
Moral Interludes." Ph.D. diss., Lehigh U., 1978.

1459. Shawen, Edgar McDowell. "The Development of
Character in the English History Play." Ph.D.
diss., Yale, 1972.

1460. Sheeran, Janet Anne Watson. "The Corpus Christi
Plays and the City of York." Ph.D. diss., U. of
Nebraska, Lincoln, 1972.

1461. Sheingorn, Pamela. *The Easter Sepulchre in England*.
Kalamazoo, Michigan: Medieval Institute
Publications, Western Michigan University, 1987.
EDAM Reference Series, 5. 426 pp., 55 illus.

On the centrality of the liturgy in the religious
life of the middle ages. Relates the Sepulchre to
the fields of drama, liturgy, and art history.
Looks at rites, development, the rites in England,
the forms taken by the Sepulchre, iconography, the
Sepulchre in the religious life of England.
Contains "catalogue of Easter Sepulchres" (75-368)
by county and town. With bibliography and
illustrations.

1462. ---. "The Moment of Resurrection in the Corpus
Christi Plays." *M&H*, n.s. 11 (1982): 111-29.

Examines the Resurrection with respect to the
Visitatio, "the earliest medieval drama . . . a
para-liturgical play in which the Holy Women . . .
verify the fact of the Resurrection" (111). Looks
at the visual elements in the plays and aims to
investigate "the venerable tradition . . . behind
the plays in order to describe a theoretical
reconstruction of the staging of the Resurrection
scene" (112). Explains why the Resurrection plays
have been relatively neglected and shows the
Resurrection treatments in historic context in art
and literature. Points out the power of the
performance over the weakness of the scene on
paper. With two illustrations.

1462a. ---. "'No Sepulchre on Good Friday': The Impact of
the Reformation on the Easter Rites in England."
In *Iconoclasm vs. Art and Drama*., 145-63. Ed. by
Davidson and Nichols (see entry # 410a below).

Considers "the impact of the Reformation on art
and ritual in England" (145), with focus on the
Easter Sepulchre. Discusses the play's
suppression.

1463. ---. "On Using Medieval Art in the Study of Medieval
Drama: An Introduction to Methodology." *RORD* 22
(1979): 101-09.

Looks at medieval architecture, pictorial arts,
etc., "describing the two basic subfields of art
history, style and iconography" (101). Shows how

iconography is useful in studying drama (and *vice versa*). Talks of "the complex relationship between image and text" (103), regional variations, the availability of particular icons to different artists and playwrights, the "image in its original context" (104), and how to read a text visually.

1464. ———. "The *Sepulchrum Domini:* A Study in Art and Liturgy." *StudIcon* 4 (1978): 37-60.

Discusses the Holy Sepulchres and early evidence for the *sepulchrum Domini*. Gives examples of how these two forms blended. Describes the Holy Grave and Easter Sepulchre. Reviews the paraliturgical rites, showing how they were performed. Connects the *sepulchrum Domini* with "the people who made and revered them" (37). Not on drama, but useful in the study of the iconography of some New Testament plays.

1465. ———. "The Visual Language of Drama: Principles of Composition." In *Contexts for Early English Drama*, 173-91. Ed. by Marianne G. Briscoe and John C. Coldewey (see entry # 228 above).

Looks at the necessity of visualizing the drama in concrete terms and with respect to the iconography of the time. Uses "perception theory" to study the "ways of seeing" the artistic phenomena of the medieval period. Aims at a "visual analysis" based on the approach of art historians. Stresses the importance to drama critics of understanding all aspects of medieval art, thus enabling "us to see what they [the medieval audience] saw."

1466. ———, and David Bevington. "'Alle This Was Token Domysday to Drede': Visual Signs of Last Judgment in the Corpus Christi Cycles and in Late Gothic Art." In Homo, Memento Finis: *The Iconography of Just Judgment in Medieval Art and Drama*, 121-45. Ed. by David Bevington (see entry # 186 above).

Discusses the iconography and influence of the visual arts with respect to the plays. Sees the Last Judgment as functioning "to bind together seemingly unrelated episodes, to resolve the plot or plots, and . . . to pronounce a verdict . . . and thereby to interpret the moral significance of what the audience has seen" (122). Deals with the notion of completion or closure in this play.

1467. Shuchter, Julian David. "Man Redeemable, the Mankind Character in the English Morality Plays: A Study in Theatre and Theology." Ph.D. diss., U. of California, Berkeley, 1968.

1468. Silber, Patricia. "'The Develis Perlament': Poetic Drama and a Dramatic Poem." *Medi* 3 (1977): 215-28.

   Looks at the dramatic elements in the poem: plot, characterization, vocabulary, verse form, imagery. Suggests that the poem is so much like the plays "that some connection of authorship or source must be assumed" (215), and that it may have been "written for minstrel performance" (225-26) in a college or monastery, and would thus probably be familiar to the cycle playwrights.

1469. Simon, Eckehard, ed. *Medieval Theater: Research on Early European Drama Since the 1960's.* (Forthcoming.)

   Contains thirteen essays, the following of which are germane to the present bibliography: 1) Wickham ("Trends . . .," entry # 1698 below); 2) Flanigan ("Medieval Latin Music-Drama . . .," # 566); 3) Andrew Hughes ("Liturgical Drama . . .," # 783); 4) David Mills ("Modern Editions . . .," # 1153); 5) David Staines ("The English Mystery Cycles," # 1513); 6) Bevington ("*Castles* in the Air . . .," # 183); 7) Johnston ("*All the World* . . .," # 827); 8) Kahrl ("The Staging of Medieval English Plays," # 884). With bibliography and index.

1470. Simpson, Margaret Ann McCullough. "Doctrine Through Dramaturgy: A Study of Bale's Plays as They Relate to Tudor Polemic Literature and to the Evolution of English Drama." Ph.D. diss., Rice U., 1971.

1471. Sinanoglou, Leah. "The Christ Child as Sacrifice: A Medieval Tradition and the Corpus Christi Plays." *Specu* 48.3 (July 1973): 491-509.

   Claims the plays are specifically didactic, that they are visual proof of the doctrine of the Real Presence. Examines the transformation of the bread of the Eucharist into the Christ child, who is "then slain and dismembered" (491). Looks at this tradition (the child-host miracle) in the plays. Also points out the presence of the tradition in medieval art and in the liturgy, reaching fanatical cult proportions, and the

relation of the Corpus Christi cycles to this
tradition. Looks at this in several plays.

1472. Siy, Dennis. "Death, Medieval Moralities, and the
       Ars moriendi Tradition." Ph.D. diss., U. of Notre
       Dame, 1985.

1473. Skaggs, James Darrell. "King Johan and Elizabethan
       Drama." Ph.D. diss., Vanderbilt U.,. 1971.

1474. Skey, Miriam Anne. "Festival Waggons in Japan." *MET*
       2.2 (Dec. 1980): 74-79.

       Describes Japanese wagons. Suggests possible
       comparisons between Japanese wagons and those used
       in Corpus Christi drama in England. With eight
       photographs of Japanese wagons.

1475. ---. "Herod the Great: Biblical Villain or
       Historical Hero?" *ARS* 10 (1978): 119-41.

       Examines the figure of Herod historically and in
       literature. Reviews Herod's different reputations
       through a number of sources (Flavius Josephus and
       biblical and apocryphal texts). Points out the
       differences between the traditions of Herod and
       Pilate. Not specifically on the drama, but offers
       much background germane to the study of the plays.

1476. ---. "Herod the Great in Medieval Art and
       Literature." Ph.D. diss., U. of York, 1976.

1477. ---. "Herod the Great in Medieval European Drama."
       CompD 13.4 (Winter 1979-80): 330-64.

       Looks at the European depictions of Herod--"In the
       vernacular drama of the continent" (330), in which
       he is often "a courteous and sophisticated ruler
       . . . in a highly civilized and sumptuous medieval
       court" (330). Examines sources (biblical,
       apocryphal, patristic). Considers short plays,
       French Passion plays, German and Italian plays.
       Concludes that continental playwrights exhibit a
       clearer idea of the historical figure and
       emphasize more his regality than do English
       dramatists.

1478. ---. "Herod's Demon-Crown." *JWCI* 40 (1977): 274-76.

       Not on drama, but discusses the iconography of
       Herod's crown, which associates him with the
       devil; reveals this in many texts.

1479.   ---.   "The Iconography of Herod the Great in Medieval
        Art."   *EDAMN* 3.1 (Nov. 1980): 4-10.

        Offers a historical view from early
        representations, to twelfth-century art, to late
        medieval art, to fifteenth century English art.
        Concludes that the visual arts treat Herod in a
        way similar to his treatment in contemporary
        plays. Points out the European emphasis on
        nobility and the English emphasis on his tyranny.

1480.   Slights, William W.E.   "The Incarnations of Comedy."
        UTQ 51.1 (Fall 1981): 13-27.

        Defines and describes the genre. Looks at "the
        incarnational theme, the absurd flesh joined to
        the aspiring spirit" (16) in the Wakefield *Secunda
        Pastorum* (and in Swift's *A Modest Proposal*).

1481.   Slim, H. Colin.   "Mary Magdalene, Musician and
        Dancer."   *EM* 8 (Oct. 1980): 460-73.

        Considers the origins of the "music and dance in
        the legends about Magdalene" (460) in the middle
        ages--also the themes related to her. Looks at
        the visual arts as well as literature--glancing at
        the Digby *Mary Magdalene* play (462).

1481a. Smith, Donna Mary.   "The Uses of Narrative Drama: The
        English Mystery Plays."   Thesis, Harvard U., 1977.

1482.   Smith, Georgina.   "Chapbooks and Traditional Plays:
        Communication and Performance."   *Folklore* 92.2
        (1981): 208-18.

        Discusses the notion that chapbook plays are
        corrupted forms of traditional plays. Defines the
        term "traditional plays." Looks at mummings.
        Points out the complexities in trying to make such
        statements as which form of play (traditional or
        chapbook) is inferior to which.

1483.   Smith, M.Q.   "The Roof Bosses of Norwich Cathedral
        and their Relation to the Medieval Drama of the
        City."   *NA* 32 (1961): 12-26.

        Aims to prove the relationship between the bosses
        and the drama. Points out the close parallel
        between the two. Uses iconographic
        interpretations "to suggest a reconstruction in
        greater detail than before of the form and content
        of the cycle" (12). Shows how the bosses "provide
        a valuable picture of the methods of presentation
        on the players' pageants" (12). Calls the bosses

"a pictorial record of the plays as they were
produced in the streets" (25).

1484.   Smoldon, William L.   "The Melodies of the Medieval
Church Dramas and Their Significance." *CompD* 2.3
(Fall 1968): 185-209. Rpt. with extensive changes
in *Medieval English Drama* . . ., 64-80. Ed. by
Jerome Taylor and Alan H. Nelson (see entry # 1573
below).

Offers mostly a critical review of Karl Young's
work, focusing on church drama. Points up the
importance of having the musical notation as well
as the words to facilitate successful modern
revivals.

1485.   [---.]   "Music in Medieval Drama."   In *The Drama of
Medieval Europe*, 1-2. Ed. by Richard Rastall (see
entry # 1359 above).

Summarizes Rastall's presentation of Smoldon's
paper. Discusses only sung drama. Urges readers
to study the music of the plays; "music solves a
number of problems thrown up unnecessarily by
purely textual criticism" (1-2).

1486.   ---.   *The Music of the Medieval Church Dramas*.   Ed.
by Cynthia Bourgeault.   London and New York:
Oxford U. Press, 1980.

Contains an extensive study from early mss through
to the sixteenth century. Not specifically on
English drama, but offers a wealth of information
useful to the study of English dramaturgy. Has
many references to vernacular drama.

Rev. *Choice* 19 (Sept. 1981): 89.
TLS (Nov. 13, 1981): 1336.
Gerard Farrell, *EDAMN* 4.2 (Mar. 1982): 14-18.
Notes 38 (June 1982): 828.
Specu 57 (July 1982): 663.
MQ 69 (Winter 1983): 120.

1487.   ---.   "The Origins of the *Quem Quaeritis* Trope and
the Easter Sepulchre Music-Drama, as Demonstrated
by their Musical Settings." In *The Medieval
Drama*, 121-54. Ed. by Sandro Sticca (see entry #
1541 below).

Concerned "with the rise of the so-called
liturgical dramas of the medieval Church" (121)
and the musical nature of the trope. Not on
English drama, but covers much background
information on music in the drama and on oral

presentation. With illustrations and
transcriptions of musical passages.

1488. Somerset, J.A.B. "'Fair is foul and foul is fair':
Vice-Comedy's Development and Theatrical Effects."
In *The Elizabethan Theatre V: Papers Given at the
Fifth International Conference on Elizabethan
Theatre, University of Waterloo, July 1973*, 54-75.
Ed. by G.R. Hibbard (see entry # 745 above).

Discusses morality plays with respect to
performance history, use of low comedy, sources,
"the dramatic implications of [the plays']
theological insights into temptation . . ." (60).
Also assesses audience reaction and the requisite
quality of the actors. Aims at demonstrating "how
the morality plays concern themselves with evil"
(75).

1489. ---. "Local Drama and Playing Places at Shrewsbury:
New Findings from the Borough Records." *M&RD* 2
(1985): 1-31.

Looks at local dramatic activities in the
"complete and well-preserved" (1) records of the
borough. Considers only local plays. Delves into
legal records which preserve information on an
annual celebration, "Shearman's Tree." Recounts
the surviving titles of the more than 25 plays
known to have played there. Examines stationary
staging, probably in a semicircular amphitheater
(Shrewsbury quarry).

1490. ---, comp. *Records of Early English Drama:
Halliwell-Phillipps Scrapbooks: An Index.*
Toronto: Records of Early English Drama, n.d.
[1979]. 23 pp.

Contains index to dramatic records in the
Halliwell-Phillipps scrapbooks. Pamphlet is an
explanation of the way to use the enclosed
microfiche index. Scrapbooks contain local
dramatic records "organized under such headings as
companies, locations, dates and auspices" (from a
flier). Also gives information on volume and page
numbers and payments. Text on microfiche,
inserted into a pocket of pamphlet. Focuses
mostly on Renaissance materials.

1491. ---. "Scenes, Machines and Stages at Shrewsbury: New
Evidence." In *Atti Del IV Colloquio della Societe
Internationale pour l'Etude du Theatre Medieval.*
Ed. by M. Chiabo, F. Doglio, and M. Maymone.

Viterbo: 1984. (For full citation see entry #
405.1.)

1492. ---. "'this hawthorn-brake our tiring-house':
Records of Early English Drama and Modern Play-
texts." In *Editing Early English Drama* . . ., 95-
119. Ed. by A.F. Johnston (see entry # 828
above).

Looks at the usefulness of recent scholarship in
Elizabethan drama for the application to medieval
drama. Discusses recent editing procedures and
older practices. Reviews recent advances in the
approach to the plays. Mentions the kinds of
things editors should consider (e.g. place and
manner of performance, staging, ancillary
documents, etc.).

1493. Southern, Richard. *The Medieval Theatre in the
Round: A Study of the Staging of "The Castle of
Persevarance" and Related Matters*. 2nd ed.
London: Faber & Faber, 1975.

Part of foreword rewritten; second appendix added
(20 pp.) on his scheme for the action of the
performance of the Cornish Ordinalia at Piran
Round in 1969. Most of the text unchanged.
Ignores the published criticism of the first
edition.

Rev. *Choice* 12 (Sept. 1975): 857.
        B&B 21 (Nov. 1975): 49.
        R.T. Davies, *N&Q*, n.s. 23.1 (221) (Jan.
            1976): 26-27.
        B.D. Bills, *ETJ* 28 (Mar. 1976): 127-31.
        EDAMN 1.2 (Apr. 1979): 7.
        Sumiko Miyajima, *The Theatre of Man*, 33-46
            (see entry # 1165 above).
        William Tydeman, *English Medieval Theatre
            . . .*, Part Two, Chap. 3 (see entry # 1612
            above).

1494. ---. "Methods of Presentation in Pre-Shakespearean
Theatre." In *The Elizabethan Theatre V: Papers
Given at the Fifth International Conference on
Elizabethan Theatre* . . ., 45-53. Ed. by G.R.
Hibbard (see # 745 above).

Presents an extract from the author's book (*The
Staging of Plays Before Shakespeare*; see next
entry) since his talk at this conference was an
unscripted presentation using blackboard drawings.
Deals with *Apius and Virginia*.

1495.   ---.   *The Staging of Plays Before Shakespeare.*
         London: Faber & Faber; New York: Theatre Arts
         Books, 1973. 603 pp.

         Presents discussions and materials
         chronologically, using the periods 1466-1527,
         1527-1553, 1553-1560, 1560-1566, 1566-1576, and
         1576-1589. Has sections on "The Earliest
         Surviving Interludes" (19); "Contemporary Court
         Staging 1511 Onwards" (146); "Other Interludes to
         1527" (168); Heywood's plays (230); "New
         Technicalities" (257); "Presentation in Civic
         Halls" (329); mid-sixteenth-century developments
         (349); "Diversions from Interlude Tradition"
         (399); "Interludes into Drama" (486); "The Theatre
         Built" (543). Examines many plays individually.
         An influential and often cited study. With 45
         illustrations and six plates, and index.

         Rev. *Economist* 247 (June 9, 1973): 111.
              Drama (Summer 1973): 74.
              TLS (Aug. 24, 1973): 982.
              LJ 98 (Dec. 1, 1973): 3562.
              T.W. Craik, *ThN* 28.2 (1974): 86-88.
              Choice 10 (Feb. 1974): 1880.
              QJS (Oct. 1974): 403.
              G.C. Britton, *N&Q*, n.s. 22.9 (220) (Sept.
                1975): 416-18.

1496.   ---.   "The Technique of Play Presentation." In *The*
         Revels *History of Drama in English, Vol. II . . . ,*
         69-99 (see entry # 1432 above).

         Has sections on "Technicalities of presentation"
         (71-72); "Interludes and court pageants" (72);
         "Place and doors" (72-73); "The Tudor great hall"
         (73-75); "Conditions of performance" (75-76); "The
         'differentiation of acting areas'" (76-78); "Some
         features of plays of the first period 1500-1530"
         (79-80); "*Magnificence,* an interlude considered in
         detail" (80-89); "Further features of the first
         period 1500-1530" (89-92); "Some features of the
         middle period 1530-1550" (92-93); and "Features of
         the third period 1550-1576" (94-99).

1496a.   Spearing, A.C. "Mediaeval Religious Drama." In *The*
         Mediaeval World, 525-54. London: Aldus Books,
         1973. Literature and Western Civilization. Gen.
         eds. David Daiches and Anthony Thorlby.

         Offers the old view that the drama "developed
         . . . out of the liturgy" (525), from the simple
         quem quaeritis tropes to the fully developed

cycles. Discusses the mystery plays at length,
with only a quick glance at moralities (551-52).

1497. Specht, Henrik. "Peasants and Shepherds in Medieval
Literature and Art: A Comparison." In *Papers from
the First Nordic Conference for English Studies,
Oslo, 17-19 September, 1980,* 225-40. Ed. by Stig
Johansson and Bjorn Tysdahl. Oslo: Institute of
English Studies, U. of Oslo, 1981.

Warns against the casual use of study of the
visual arts and its application to literary
criticism. Cautions that the visual arts could
mislead a literary critic. Looks at the
shepherds' plays from the York, Chester, and
Towneley cycles with their "enlargement of the
original plot" (231) in a "veer towards realism"
(231). Not primarily on drama, but serves as a
warning of the inconclusive nature of the visual
arts as a reliable basis for literary scholarship.
Concludes "that where the visual treatment of the
rustic theme remains rather stereotyped and
homogeneously equivocal throughout the later
Middle Ages, the literature of the period abounds
in a far richer variety of approaches and
disparate, yet discernible, attitudes to the theme
of rustic life" (237).

1498. Spector, Stephen. "Anti-Semitism and the English
Mystery Plays." *CompD* 13.1 (Spring 1979): 3-16.
Rpt. in *Drama in the Middle Ages,* 328-41. Ed. by
Davidson, et al. (see entry # 409 above).

Discusses the "unrelenting hostility" of anti-
Semitism (3). Calls the drama "one of the most
vehemently anti-Jewish genres in the history of
English literature" (3). Proposes that this
attitude parallels that "of classic and clinical
anti-Semitism" (3), and that "it assigns to the
Jew the unwanted aspects of the Christian
community and consequently execrates him" (3).
Shows that the portrayal of the Jew in the plays
is impersonal and reveals more "of the world-view
of the plays than of the perceptions about actual
Jews" (13).

1499. ---. "The Composition and Development of an Eclectic
Manuscript: Cotton Vespasian D *VIII.*" *LSE,* n.s. 9
(1977, for 1976 and 1977): 62-83.

Examines the "disparate assortment of contiguous
parts" (62) of the ms of the N-Town Cycle. Says
that "layers of material were combined in the
development of a complex literary artifact" (62).

Argues "that the strata of the cycle . . . can be
sorted out according to prosodic tests; and that
the different strata were . . . often written in
characteristic prosodic forms" (62). Draws from
scribal and ms evidence, source studies,
expositors' speeches, incongruities within and
between the plays, and "an examination of verbal
and thematic parallels between the plays and
correlative Proclamation descriptions" (63).
Focuses on the "Marriage of Mary and Joseph" play,
the speeches of the expositor Contemplacio, and
Passion Play 2. "[C]onjectures, on internal
evidence . . . about the history of the
compilation of a composite text" (77). Concludes
that the cycle in its present form seems to be an
amalgamation of a "cycle of moderate size, three
once-independent sequences, several individual
plays, and occasional interpolations" (77).

1500.   ---. "The Genesis of the N-Town Cycle." Ph.D.
diss., Yale U., 1973.

1501.   ---. "Paper Evidence and the Genesis of the Macro
Plays." *Medi* 5 (1979): 217-32.

Uses watermark analysis and other tests to
"reconstruct the manner in which the three
manuscripts that constitute the [Macro] codex were
formed" (217). Discusses "the number, location,
and contents of leaves that have been displaced
from *Mankind* and the *Castle*" (217). Concludes
that *Mankind* is on paper which seems to date from
1487 to 1492--much later than 1475, "the date of
transcription that has been attributed to the
play" (219). Shows how a study of the paper can
help one identify lost leaves and interpolations.

1502.   ---. "The Provenance of the N-Town Codex." *Lib*, 6th
ser. 1.1 (Mar. 1979): 25-33.

Examines "various lines of speculation about the
cycle" (25) and discusses the ms's transmission.
Considers the various ways scholars refer to the
text (N-Town, Hegge, *Ludus Coventriae*, Cotton
Mystery Plays, Coventry Plays). Describes the
ms's physical attributes. (See reply by Norman
Davis, "Provenance of the N-Town Cycle," entry #
423 above.)

1503.   ---. "Symmetry in Watermark Sequences." *SB* 31
(1978): 162-78.

Proposes "a method of analyzing watermark
sequences which can not only discover the ways in

which gatherings were originally formed, but can
also identify and locate textual disruptions where
this might otherwise be impossible" (163). Aims
to elucidate the history of the Cotton MS.
Vespasian D.viii, which contains the N-Town Cycle.
Shows where interpolations and excisions were made
in the text.

1504. Speirs, John. *Medieval English Poetry: The Non-
Chaucerian Tradition.* London: Faber and Faber,
1957; rpt. 1971.

Contains a chapter on "The Mystery Cycle: Certain
Towneley Plays" (Chap. 5, 305-75). Recounts the
now-challenged theory of the development of the
cycles from the liturgy. Looks at the cycles in
general, the social conditions of the era, and
much more. Concentrates on Noah, Abraham and
Isaac, the two Shepherds', the Magi, and the Herod
the Great plays, as well as the Buffeting and
Conspiracy, the Harrowing of Hell and Last
Judgment, the Lazarus and Hanging of Judas plays.

1505. ---. "The Towneley *Shepherds' Plays.*" In *The
Pelican Guide to English Literature*, Vol. I, *The
Age of Chaucer*, 165-74. Harmondsworth and
Baltimore: Penguin Books, 1954; rev. ed. 1959.

Discusses the two "richly significant dramatic
poems" (165). Analyzes each play in terms of
humor, dialogue, characterization, plot.

1506. Sperk, Klaus. *Mittelalterliche Tradition und
reformatorische Polemik in den Spielen John Bales.*
Heidelberg: Carl Winter, 1973. *Anglistische
Forschungen,* 101. 151 pp. Originally presented
as a thesis, Mannheim.

Biographical and critical examination of Bale's
works. Discusses the plays "as protestant
adaptations of the medieval religious drama"
(139). Examines play structures, sources,
typology, dialogue, Bale's concept of history,
characterization, medieval thought and stagecraft.
Contains English summary, bibliography, and index.

1507. Speyser, Suzanne. "Dramatic Illusion and Sacred
Reality in the Towneley *Prima Pastorum.*" *SP* 78.1
(Late Winter 1981): 1-19.

Summarizes scholarship. Points out that the play
has not gotten "a consistent and coherent reading"
(2). Aims to give such a reading, showing that
the dramatist was expressing "a metaphysical tenet

of the Church" (2) in the use of illusion and
reality to dramatize and expatiate on the doctrine
of the reality of miracles and on the nature of
faith.

1507a. Spinalbelli, Rosalba. "The Eschatological Scene of
the *Last Judgement.*" *FCS* 13 (1988): 299-308.

1508. Spinrad, Phoebe S. "The Last Temptation of
Everyman." *PQ* 64.2 (Spring 1985): 185-94.

Reviews scholarly approaches. Says the play must
be seen on its own terms, not with respect to
other moralities, but with respect to the *ars
moriendi* theme. Anatomizes the theme into its six
parts; shows how *Everyman* uses this doctrine.

1509. ---. "The Summons of Death on the Medieval and
Renaissance English Stage." Ph.D. diss., Texas
Christian U., 1982.

1509a. Spivak, Charlotte. "Feminine vs. Masculine in
English Morality Drama." *FCS* 13 (1988): 137-44.

1510. Squires, Lynn. "Law and Disorder in *Ludus
Coventriae.*" *CompD* 12.3 (Fall 1978): 200-13.
Rpt. in *Drama in the Middle Ages*, 272-85. Ed. by
Davidson, et al. (see entry # 409 above).

Aims to "provide a new context" (200) for the
plays by looking at fifteenth-century legal
conditions exhibited in them. Considers "laws as
a religious ideal" (200) and discusses the legal
issues raised by the plays.

1511. Squires, Lynn Bahrych. "Legal and Political Aspects
of Late Medieval English Drama." Ph.D. diss., U.
of Washington, 1977.

1512. Stagg, Louis Charles. "The Concept of Creation in
Haydn's Oratorio *The Creation*, the Medieval
Mystery Cycles, and Bernstein's *Mass.*" *Inter* 7.1
(1975): 13-21.

Discusses how familiar plots can still hold an
audience's attention if they are imaginatively
played. Looks briefly at the Creation episode in
the English cycles and the Cornish plays.

1513. Staines, David. "The English Mystery Cycles." In
Medieval Theater . . . (forthcoming). Ed. by
Eckehard Simon (see entry # 1469 above).

1514.   ---.   "To Out-Herod Herod: The Development of a
        Dramatic Character." *CompD* 10.1 (Spring 1976):
        29-53. Rpt. in *Drama in the Middle Ages*, 207-31.
        Ed. by Clifford Davidson, et al. (see entry # 409
        above).

        Examines the Herod tradition, depicting him as a
        "raging braggart," a "ranting tyrant," a "bragging
        buffoon," a "tragic figure, the fatal victim of
        overreaching pride" (29). Shows the background
        and the development of the figure into a "comic
        braggart . . . tragic ruler . . . [or] a
        combination of comic and tragic hero" (29).
        Considers apocryphal works, biblical commentaries,
        liturgical drama, and the cycle plays. Reveals
        the two major views: comic and tragic.

1515.   Steadman, John Marcellus. *Nature into Myth: Medieval
        and Renaissance Moral Symbols*. Pittsburgh:
        Duquesne U. Press, 1979. xii, 308 pp.

        Not on English drama, but contains information on
        iconographic and lexicographic approaches to
        literature, specifically "the conversion of
        natural detail into moral symbol in . . .
        narrative and dramatic poetry" (1). With notes
        and index.

        Rev. *Choice* 16 (Oct. 1979): 1012.
             RES 32 (Aug. 1981): 314.

1516.   Steinberg, Clarence. "*Kemp Towne* in the Townley
        [sic] *Herod* Play: A Local Wakefield Allusion?" *NM*
        71 (1970): 253-60.

        Claims that hitherto, scholarship has found no
        Wakefield place names in the Towneley Herod play,
        but that the English Place-Name Society may have
        found an allusion to a Wakefield place in the
        phrase *Kemp towne*. Sees a "crude tampering" (255)
        with the stanza and claims that "the line
        containing *kemp towne* could have been added in
        late parody of the Archbishop" (255)--the absentee
        Archbishop of York from 1426-1452. Shows that
        "'Kemp towne' seems to be intended as some kind of
        territorial designation" (256). Posits a
        reference to a place in Yorkshire's West Riding.

1517.   Stemmler, Theo. "Entstehung und Wesen der englischen
        Fronleichnamszyklen." In *Chaucer und seine Zeit:
        Symposion für Walter F. Schirmer*, 393-405. Ed. by
        Arno Esch. Tübingen: Max Niemeyer, 1968.
        Buchreihe der *Anglia*, Zeitschrift für englische

Philologie 14. [This vol. is cited in Stratman (5183a, 5183b), but this particular essay is not.]

Says that the development of Corpus Christi plays is linked to the theological and liturgical aspects of the feast, instituted in 1264 by Pope Urban IV. Discusses the nature of salvation history and the Eucharist with respect to the choice of vignettes for plays performed on the feast day. Mentions also the liturgical influence in the selection of the plays and their content. Shows how the liturgy focuses on Christ typology in the Old Testament and on the ongoing series of God's miraculous deeds, from creation, to salvation, to the restoration of the kingdom expected at the end of the world.

1518.   ---. *Liturgische Feiern und geistliche Spiele: Studien zu Erscheinungsformen des Dramatischen im Mittelalter.* Tübingen: Max Niemeyer, 1970. Buchreihe der *Anglia* 15.   339 pp.

Discusses religious cults and quasi-dramatic celebrations; the typological origins and use of the *quem quaeritis* trope. Questions the logic of the theory of religious sources of the drama. Traces various sources (in the manner of Young). Points out the carryover of typological features from the religious to the secular drama (visitation typology, theophany typology, etc.). Discusses the origin and essence of English Corpus Christi cycles.   Links the English plays to the actual Corpus Christi feast.   Discusses "history" as liturgy; the necessity of the processional performance; the processions as the real expression of the phenomenon of the people's piety and reverence for the Eucharist.   Looks at old and new liturgical elements in the English cycle plays.   With bibliography, illustrations, and indexes.

Rev.   *Specu* 47 (Apr. 1972): 356.

1519.   ---. "Der Maulheld in englischen Spielen des Mittelalters und der Tudorzeit." In *Ares und Dionysos; Das Furchtbare und das Lächerliche in der europäischen Literatur*, 61-70.   Ed. by Hans-Jürgen Horn and Hartmut Laufhütte.   Heidelberg: Winter 1981.   Mannheim Beiträge zur Sprach- und Literaturwiss, 1.

Defines the term for braggart, partly in terms of one who manifests cowardice in battle, fearful speech, and rash retreats.   Points out the

similarity of this figure to the classical Roman
miles gloriosus character, but says that there is
probably no linear connection between the two,
despite the influence of Roman plays on medieval
drama; the plays of Terence and Plautus were read
as part of academic study but not performed in the
era. Says, however, that in the twelfth century
the *miles gloriosus* figure appears in religious
drama, and that authors did adapt heathen
characters in their own plays (especially in the
Passion plays; e.g. the soldiers who guard the
grave of Christ). Claims that the figure of the
braggart is not from the Bible or the Apocrypha
and is originally not in German or French works.
Looks closely at the Towneley plays and other
versions of the Herod play and reasserts that
there is no biblical precedent for this figure or
his men; concludes that there may be some Roman
influence here. Explains where the figure comes
from and why he is introduced. Concludes that the
figure probably has some Roman origins with many
local traditions influencing the medieval writers.
Shows the movement the character makes from having
a religious to having a secular function, critical
of society. But makes it clear that real soldiers
are never put into question through mockery--the
satirical element does not attack real warriors or
war *per se*; Christian participation in war was
regulated and not called into question. Says that
a fundamental critique of war was yet to be.

1520.   ---.   "Typological Transfer in Liturgical Offices and
Religious Plays of the Middle Ages."   *SLI* 8.1
(Spring 1975): 123-43.

Contains material revised and summarized from his
book *Liturgische Feiern* . . . (see entry # 1518
above). Defines *type, typology, typological*.
Claims that "typological transfer is a
characteristic constant of both Latin liturgical
offices and religious plays in Latin and in the
vernacular" (125). Distinguishes typological
exegesis ("invented by critics"--125) from
typological transfer (invented by authors).
Employs those definitions to examine religious
drama as well as the Ludus Coventriae *Lazarus*
play, the York and Ludus Coventriae *Assumption of
Mary* plays, the *Shrewsbury Fragments*, passages
from the Chester cycle, the shepherds' plays from
all the cycles, and other English plays.

1521.   Stephen, May.   "A Medieval Stage Property: The
Spade."   *MET* 4.2 (1982): 77-92.

Discusses the use of a spade in the Coventry
Cappers' records of 1544, 1567, and 1591. Points
out that the cycle lacked a Creation and Fall
play, but speculates that the play was probably
the Harrowing of Hell. Discusses the iconographic
use of the spade, with respect to Adam and God's
curse on Adam. Looks at other texts (*Liber
Apologeticus*, other play cycles, the Cornish
Ordinalia, the *Castle of Perseverance*, and
Mankind). Relies also on documents from York and
Beverley. With an illustration.

1522. Stevens, David. *English Renaissance Theatre History:
A Reference Guide.* Boston: G.K. Hall, 1982. 342
pp.

Contains chronological groups of references to
criticism, with many articles cited having
retrospective content, focusing on medieval
antecedants to Renaissance drama. Covers
criticism up through 1979. With index.

Rev. *Choice* 20 (Dec. 1982): 563.
ARBA 14 (1983): 452.

1523. ---. *Words and Music in the Middle Ages: Song,
Narrative, Dance and Drama, 1050-1350.* Cambridge
and London: Cambridge U. Press, 1986. xvii, 554
pp.

Not specifically on English drama, but covers a
great deal of background, including chapters on
the Sequence; *lai* and *planctu*; the dance-song;
speech and melody; liturgical drama; music,
action, and emotion in drama (looks at Herod,
inter alia), etc. With glossary, list of sources,
bibliography, and indexes.

1524. Stevens, John, with Jack Sage, III. "Medieval
Drama." In *The New Grove Dictionary of Music and
Musicians*, vol. 12, pp. 21-58. 6th ed. Ed. by
Stanley Sadie. London: Macmillan, 1980.

Contains much information; defines genres, surveys
scholarship, looks at "Elements and Traditions of
Medieval Music Drama" (21). Analyzes liturgical
drama, vernacular plays, eastern European drama,
the decline of medieval dramaturgy. With
illustrations, musical notation, and bibliography.

1525. Stevens, Martin. "Did the Wakefield Master Write a
Nine-Line Stanza?" *CompD* 15.2 (Summer 1981): 99-
119.

Inquires into the form of the stanza to see if it is possible to come up with some reliable measurement by means of which one can identify the "Wakefield Master" and his contributions to the cycle. Makes some generalizations about stanzaic poetry. Shows that some "stanzas" are editorially determined, and that there are three distinct formats within the Towneley ms. Compares the stanza to others in Middle English. Displays the three distinct formats of the Wakefield stanza. Considers the symbols in the ms used to separate lines. Discusses the possibility that it is a thirteen-line stanza ("a two-stress thirteener with a one or two-stress bob" [113]). Finds other thirteeners in medieval verse. Focuses on dialogue, "the dramatic and metrical qualities" (110) of the stanza, and the playwright's use of enjambment.

1526. ---. *Four Middle English Mystery Cycles: Textual, Contextual, and Critical Interpretations.* Princeton, NJ: Princeton U. Press, 1987. xv, 360 pp.

Contains chapters on "The York Cycle: City as Stage"; "The Wakefield Cycle: The Playwright as Poet"; "The N-Town Cycle: Dramatic Structure, Typology, and the Multiple Plot"; and "The Chester Cycle: The Sense of an Ending." Argues that the "cycles . . . are remarkably unified and powerfully developed" (323), are accurate representations of their times, and rely on and "preserve the ingredients of traditional festive folk celebration within a learned, finely structured, and self-conscious poetic drama of Christian salvation history" (323). Concludes that we can never know "what was actually performed" (323). Looks at ms evidence, audience, and genre. With bibliography and index.

Rev. *Choice* 25 (Nov. 1987): 479.
        Peter Happé, *CompD* 22.1 (Spring 1988): 86-89.

1527. ---. "Illusion and Reality in the Medieval Drama." *CE* 32 (1970-71): 448-64.

Challenges the notion that the actors were poor, inept amateurs. Notes that the plays were "expansive, lavish, and thoroughly professional entertainment" (448-49). Aims to look at "the aesthetic of the medieval drama in terms of present-day canons of criticism" (449). Shows the similarity in style and technique between medieval and absurdist drama. Applies "the Brechtian

aesthetic toward the interpretation of the popular
religious drama" (450). Claims that recent
(twentieth-century) criticism allows us to
understand medieval drama in showing us its non-
representational and multi-dimensional nature.

1528.   ---.   "The Johnston-Rogerson Edition of the York
Records: An Initial Reading." *Records of Early
English Drama: Proceedings of the First Colloquium
. . .*, 160-178. Ed. by Joanna Dutka (see entry #
497 above; the Johnston and Rogerson volume is
entry # 852 above).

Review article; points out the values and
weaknesses of the Johnston-Rogerson volume.

1529.   ---.   "Language as Theme in the Wakefield Plays."
Specu 52.1 (1977): 100-17.

Looks at the Wakefield Master "with a view toward
determining his major thematic contribution to the
. . . cycle as a whole" (100). Claims that he
"was essentially a reviser" (100). Uses the
Towneley *Judicium* (compared to its most probable
source, the equivalent play in the York Cycle) to
prove this assertion. Also looks at the
dramatist's use of other plays and says that he
"was a major redactor of the Towneley cycle who
composed or reworked from eleven to thirteen of
the thirty-two . . . plays" (101)--approximately a
fourth of the total cycle. Concentrates on the
playwright's language as proof. Concludes that
through the writer's particular use of language he
"makes an important statement about the limits of
art" (116), but that his brilliant use of language
"hinders communication" (116).

1530.   ---.   "The Manuscript of the *Towneley Plays:* Its
History and Editions." *PBSA* 67.3 (1973): 231-44.

Examines the document "as a historical artifact"
(231)--following its journey "from its place of
origin in the West Riding of Yorkshire to its
present home" (231), the Huntington Library. Also
looks at its editorial history.

1531.   ---.   "The Missing Parts of the Towneley Cycle."
Specu 45.2 (Apr. 1970): 254-65.

Looks at the textual and historical significance
of the major lacunae in the ms. Claims that the
cycle once contained a full set of banns and that
the biggest gap is "the result of editorial
tampering" (254) related to the Reformation.

Concludes that the cycle originally had 35 or 36
plays. Says that the lost plays were probably
"The Descent of the Holy Spirit," "The Death of
Mary," "The Appearance of Our Lady to Thomas," and
"The Assumption and Coronation of the Virgin"
(York plays # 44-47).

1532.   ---. "The Nativity Cycle at Irvine." *RORD* 29 (1986-
87): 95-97.

Recounts a performance of fall 1986.

1533.   ---. "Postscript." *LSE* 6 (1972): 113-15.

A postscript to Margaret Dorrell, "Two Studies
. . .," entry # 474 above. Stevens disagrees with
Dorrell's view that a full cycle of plays could
have been performed on a single day. Says that
". . . good sense dictates against the likelihood
that such a performance ever took place" (113).
Questions when the religious procession, which
Dorrell claims preceded the dramatic one, took
place. Claims that Dorrell ignores the underlying
and direct relationship between the two
processions.

1534.   ---. "*Processus Torontoniensis:* A Performance of the
Wakefield Cycle." *RORD* 28 (1985): 189-99.

Draws on performances of Toronto's *Poculi Ludique
Societas* to demonstrate the *Gesamtkunst* of the
medieval cycles, which kindle our awareness of all
the arts and cultural dimensions the plays
display: "music, art, theology, homiletics, folk
rituals, and social settings" (189). Reviews the
"Toronto Towneley" performance of May 1985.
Discusses "The Hypothesis and the Experiment"
(190), "The Stage Design" (192), "The Question of
Unity" (194), "The Missing Parts" (196), and "The
Modernized Text" (197).

1535.   ---. "The Theatre of the World: A Study in Medieval
Dramatic Form." *ChauR* 7.4 (Spring 1973): 234-49.

Discusses the drama in the context of its medieval
stage heritage--its "native tradition" (234).
Considers the tension between divine and human
will in the cycles, and claims that all medieval
drama contrasts good and evil. Examines this
native tradition--1) in opposition to the
tradition of neo-classical drama; 2) in terms of
its composite elements, drawing from dramatic and
non-dramatic forms; 3) with respect to the various
medieval dramatic genres; 4) with an eye to

staging; and 5) with the notion "of the medieval outdoor stage as a theatre of the world" (244).

1536. ---. "The York Cycle: From Procession to Play." *LSE*, n.s. 6 (1972): 37-61.

Offers "a new hypothesis accounting for the historical development of the Corpus Christi play at York and, by extension, elsewhere" (38). Points out that traditional views which claim a full performance of the whole cycle cannot be accurate since this would produce about nineteen hours of drama on a single day at a single station--not even accounting for performances at as many as fifteen stations. Discusses places of performance and doubling of roles for some actors. Suggests that instead of processional performance at one point, "a single continuous performance could have taken place in York after a processional riding" (41). Claims that "the York plays, as we have them, could not have been performed processionally" (41). Shows that most records of pageant processions are "ambiguous and obscure" (43). Claims that the plays changed in character over 150 years, and that it is possible that "theatrical performance did not bear a very close resemblance to the surviving manuscript" (43). Examines primary documents to propose that in the middle of the fourteenth century several guilds in York began to perform scenes on processional wagons, beginning as *tableaux vivants* and then performed with some dialogue; as late as 1426 "they were not independent plays" (44). By the second half of the fifteenth century the Corpus Christi plays had become established, taking place on consecutive holidays. Says that on Corpus Christi Day there were short enactments of scenes before the houses of burgesses, but eventually a "more detailed version of some or all of the cycle was given at the last stop on the route" (44). Says also that eventually professional actors took the major roles, while the guilds provided wagons; the plays--contents, actual texts, performers--changed year after year. Points out that this development from *tableaux vivants* to fully developed cycle plays is supported by the late dates of the surviving mss (mid-fifteenth century). "The evidence suggests that the . . . cycles . . . date from the fifteenth century, not the fourteenth" (45). Looks at historical and social conditions leading to the development of the cycles. Evaluates Roger Burton's *ordo paginarum* for 1415 in this connection, which proves that in that year the pageants were processional in York. Looks at the develpment of the full-fledged drama after 1426. Posits a "continuous, standing performance . . . for the last station" (54).

1536a. ---. "The York Cycle as Carnival." *FCS* 13 (1988): 447-56.

xxxx. ---, and Margaret Dorrell. "The *Ordo Paginarium* [sic] Gathering of the York *A/Y Memorandum Book*." (See entry # 79 above.)

1537. Stevenson, Benjamin H. "*Everyman:* A Creative Experiment in Church Music Drama." D.M.A. diss., U. of Southern California, 1971.

1538. Stevenson, Sharon Lynn. "An Introduction to the *Laud Troy Book*." Ph.D. diss., U. of Florida, 1971.

Shows the continuity between the *Laud Troy Book* and Renaissance revenge tragedies. Sees many dramatic elements in the former.

1539. Sticca, Sandro. "The *Christos Paschon* and the Byzantine Theater." In *Studies in Medieval Drama* . . ., 13-44. Ed. by Clifford Davidson, et al. (see entry # 410 above).

Not on English drama, but offers materials on liturgical backgrounds, theologically and historically.

1540. ---. "Drama and Spirituality in the Middle Ages." *M&H*, n.s. 4 (1973): 69-87.

Points up the importance of spirituality--along with the liturgy--as an important trait contributing to the drama's development. Focuses primarily on "affective and practical spirituality" (70) and its association with drama. Considers chronology, the drama of Hrotswitha, music, the "new mystical forces" (79) of the twelfth century, and the role of Mary in the Passion plays.

1541. ---, ed. *The Medieval Drama: Papers of the Third Annual Conference of the Center for Medieval and Early Renaissance Studies, State University of New York at Binghamton, 3-4 May 1969*. Albany: State U. of New York Press, 1972. 154 pp.

Contains six essays, only three of which are appropriate for this bibliography: Kolve ("*Everyman* and the Parable of the Talents," entry

927 above); Wickham ("The Staging of Saint Plays
in England," # 1697); and Smoldon ("The Origins of
the *Quem . . .,*" # 1487).

Rev. *Choice* 9 (Feb. 1973): 1609.
    Specu 48.2 (Apr. 1973): 435 (only lists
      contents).
    ChHist 42 (Jule 1973): 282.
    Neville Denny, *MedAe* 43.1 (1974): 84-87.
    CW 68 (Oct. 1974): 148.

1541a. ---. "The *Planctus Mariae* in the Medieval European
Theater: Theology and Drama." In *Early Drama to
1600.* Ed. by Albert H. Tricomi. (See entry #
1589b below.)

1542. Stock, Lorraine Kochanske. "Comedy in the English
Mystery Cycles: Three Comic Scenes in the Chester
Shepherds' Play." In *Versions of Medieval Comedy*,
211-26. Ed. by Paul D. Ruggiers. Norman: U. of
Oklahoma Press, 1977.

Reviews scholarship about the comic elements in
the plays. Defines the genre, gives views
contemporary to the plays about the comic, and
points up the difficulty of coming up with an all-
inclusive definition that will serve for all comic
plays. Shows how the Chester *Shepherds'* play is
underrated. Aims to show how the three comic
scenes in this play are seriously relevant
thematically. Concludes that the comic elements
may be "the *foundation* for the dramatic structure
rather than a gay frieze applied to the already
existing dramatic edifice" (226).

1543. ---. "Patience and Sloth in Two Middle English
Works: *Mankind* and *Piers Plowman C.*" Ph.D. diss.,
Cornell U., 1975.

1544. ---. "The Thematic and Structural Unity of *Mankind.*"
SP 72.4 (Oct. 1975): 386-407.

Surveys inaccurate or misleading scholarship on
the play. Counters these views by looking at the
play in terms of medieval exegesis "and the
septenary systems contained in medieval
penitential manuals, catechisms, and pulpit
literature" (387).

1545. Stokes, James D. "Robin Hood and the Churchwardens
in Yeovil." *M&RD* 3 (1986): 1-25.

Looks at the variety of places and forms in which
Robin Hood entertainments occurred in England.

Comments on the popularity of the subject matter.
Attacks the older notion that the performances
were under the strict eye of local authorities,
especially the wardens. Looks also at original
parish records (from Yeovil) which contain
"evidence of a well-established Robin Hood
tradition" (1). Discusses the Yeovil accounts to
show that "The Robin Hood entertainments . . .
were a complex mimetic process, unified by the
Robin Hood metaphor, that moved through a variety
of settings including the church, parish house,
streets, fields, and dwellings of Yeovil parish"
(8). Quotes from the records.

1546. Stokes, James David, Jr. "Roots of the English
History Play." Ph.D. diss., Washington State U.,
1979.

1547. ---. "The Wells Cordwainers Show: New Evidence
Concerning Guild Entertainments in Somerset."
CompD 19.4 (Winter 1985-86): 332-46.

Uses "a series of original guild accounts prepared
by the Wells Cordwainers" (332) to shed light on
performances. Discusses this recently found
document (with transcription--342-43) and the
performance it suggests.

1548. Stone, Charles Venable. "Dramas of Christian Time:
Temporal Assumptions and Dramatic Form in the
Medieval Mystery Cycle, the Morality Play, and
Shakespeare's Second Tetralogy." Ph.D. diss., U.
of Minnesota, 1971.

1549. Storrs, Peter Hamilton. "A Re-Evaluation of the
Dramatic Method of the Chester Cycle, with
Particular Reference to the Plays of the Fall of
Lucifer, Abraham and Isaac, the Passion, and the
Ascension." Ph.D. diss., U. of California,
Berkeley, 1975.

1550. Stouck, Mary-Ann. "A Reading of the Middle English
Judas." *JEGP* 80.2 (Apr. 1981): 188-98.

Examines the Judas story in the Middle Ages,
especially in the poetic version. Briefly
compares the poem to the N-town version (194-95).

1551. Stratman, Carl J. *Bibliography of Medieval Drama*.
2nd ed., rev. and enlarged. 2 vols. New York:
Frederick Ungar, 1972.

Adds more than 5,000 entries to the first edition.
Contains over 9,100 unannotated entries in main

listing and 81 in addenda. Covers medieval plays
in all western countries and languages which had
drama. With index.

Rev. *CLW* 44 (Feb. 1973): 405.
Choice 10 (Apr. 1973): 270.
Lorrayne Y. Baird, *Specu* 50.1 (Jan. 1975):
155-58.

1552. Strauss, Jennifer. "Grace Enacted: The *Secunda
Pastorum.*" *Parergon* 14 (1976): 63-68.

Reviews criticism about the play's structure.
Contends that "there is an element [in the play]
which works against the notion of antithesis
between secular plot and divine event" (63).
Concentrates on the shepherds' actions in Mak's
home; shows their actions to signify grace. Says
the characters are "imperfect figurations of
grace" (67).

1553. Strayer, Joseph R., ed. *Dictionary of the Middle
Ages.* New York: Charles Scribner's Sons, 1982-
1989. [Twelve vols. plus Interim Index; at the
time of preparation of this bibliography, only
vols. through 10 were in print.]

Contains original scholarship on a wide variety of
subjects, people, texts, ideas. Pertaining to the
drama, the following entries are now in print:
Beadle ("Mystery Plays," entry # 149 above);
Cawley ("*Everyman,*"# 281); Cosman ("Feasts and
Festivals, Western European," # 354); Michael T.
Davis ("Passion Cycle," # 414); Epstein ("Guilds
and Métiers," # 541); Ian Lancashire ("N-Town
Plays," # 953); Timothy J. McGee ("Drama,
Liturgical," # 1033); David Mills ("Chester
Plays," # 1137); David Mills ("Drama, Western
European," # 1146); Nelson ("Castle of
Perseverance," # 1193); Nelson ("Morality Play," #
1200); Rorem ("Corpus Christi, Feast of," # 1412).
Other articles planned but not yet in print:
"Second Shepherds' Play," "Towneley Plays," "York
Plays."

Rev. [N.B. Several of the reviews cover just
selected volumes.]

ANQ 21 (May 1983): 164.
WLB 58 (Nov. 1983): 225.
Commonweal 110 (Nov. 4, 1983): 604.
ARBA 15 (1984): 173, 174.
AL 15 (May 1984): 301.
RefSR 13 (Fall 1985): 9.

ARBA 17 (1986): 196.
ANQ 24 (Jan. 1986): 89.

1554. Streitberger, W.R. "Henry VIII's Entertainment for the Queen of Scots, 1516: A New Revels Account and Cornish's Play." M&RD 1 (1984): 29-35. (See entry # 144 above.)

Speculates about a play presumably by William Cornish, put on possibly by Children of the Chapel for Margaret, Queen of Scots.

1555. ---. "William Cornish and the Players of the Chapel." MET 8.1 (July 1986): 3-20.

Discusses the choral players of the royal household: the Chapel Royal. Not specifically on English drama, but offers background on court entertainments. Attempts to clarify from meager extant documents who Cornish was and what the Chapel's role was "in early Tudor secular entertainments" (4).

1556. Stríbrny, Zdenek. "Early Tudor Drama." In Acta Universitatis Carolinae. Philologica 1 (1963), 55-94. Ed. by Bohumil Trnka and Zdenek Stríbrny. Praha: Universita Karlova, 1963. Prague Studies in English 10.

In Czechoslovokian; with English summary (93-94) from which the following note is taken:

Explores the "new features of early Tudor drama" (93) which were apart from the elements of medieval heritage. Attempts "to show how the medieval patterns of religious symbolism and allegory were being replaced by a growing concern with earthly matters, which was accompanied by an increasingly realistic mode of expression" (93). Examines the works of Henry Medwall, John Rastell, and John Heywood.

1557. Strietman, Elsa. "The Middle Dutch Elckerlijc and the English Everyman." MedAe 52.1 (1983): 111-14.

Favorable review of E.R. Tigg's argument in his book (see entry # 1580 below). Summarizes the fine points of the debate.

xxxx. Studies in Medieval Drama in Honour of William L. Smoldon . . . . See under editors, Davidson, Gianakaris, and Stroupe (entry # 410 above).

1558.   Stugrin, Michael Andrew.   "Affective Spirituality and
the Epistemology of the Hegge Passion Plays."
Ph.D. diss., Pennsylvania State U., 1979.

1559.   Sullivan, Mark R.   "The Missing York *Funeral of the
Virgin.*"   *EDAMN* 1.2 (Apr. 1979): 5-7.

Discusses the missing play (called in civic
records *Fergus*).   Deduces information about the
play from York dramatic records and its portrayal
in literature and art.   Shows the unmannerly
responses of the audience to the play and the
goldsmiths' request not to have to perform it.
Describes some of the action in the play.
Establishes one line from the lost text--from its
music.

1560.   Sutermeister, Helen.   *The Norwich Blackfriars: An
Historical Guide to the Friary and Its Buildings
up to the Present Day.*   Norwich: 1977.

1561.   Sutton, Marilyn Phyllis.   "The Allegorical Mode and
the Medieval Dramatic Tradition."   Ph.D. diss.,
Claremont Graduate School, 1973.

1562.   ---.   "The Image of the Child in the English Mystery
Cycles."   *JRMMRA* 5 (1984): 69-81.

Attacks social historians who discuss the place of
children in medieval society for ignoring the
evidence presented in the cycle plays.   Presents
several children as possible exemplars, and
focuses on Isaac and Jesus.   Concludes that "the
figure of the child" has been established, by the
end of the cycle, "as an emblem of great value and
the death of the child as the epitome of
sacrifice" (79).

1563.   Swan, Richard Edward.   "An Investigation of Staging
Problems Involved in a Contemporary Production of
a Medieval Cycle Play."   M.A. thesis, California
State College, Stanislaus, 1975.

1564.   Swanson, Heather.   *Building Craftsmen in Late
Medieval York.*   York: U. of York, 1983.   Borthwick
Papers no. 63.   41 pp.

Contains references to Corpus Christi pageants and
pageant houses of the Masons, Sawers, Carpenters,
and Shipwrights.   Covers the period from 1350-
1450.   Draws evidence from buildings and from
civil and ecclesiastical accounts.   Says that
"there was certainly a fraternity responsible for
a play in the Corpus Christi pageant" (10) and

that "the sawers from at least the beginning of
the fifteenth century had been responsible for a
Corpus Christi pageant distinct from that of the
carpenters" (11). Along with other references to
the plays are several to purchases made by the
Corpus Christi Gild of tiles and wood (19).

1565. Taft, Edmund M. "Surprised by Love: The Dramatic
Structure and Popular Appeal of the *Wakefield
Second Shepherds' Pageant*." *JPC* 14.1 (Summer
1980): 131-40.

Looks at the popular nature of the play, the
heterogeneous audience, the didactic and
entertaining elements. Claims that the playwright
faced the problem of presenting the nativity in a
fresh light and solved the problem with the use of
surprise and innovation. Points up the use of
anachronism, the appearance of Mak, the unity in
theme in the two parts of the play, and so on.

1566. Tajima, Matsuji. "The Gerund in Medieval English
Drama with Special Reference to Its Verbal
Character." *SELL* 32 (Jan. 1982): 81-96.

1567. Takaku, Shinichi. "Disappearance of Death in
Everyman." *SEL*, English Number (1974): 232-34.

Offers an abstract of an article in the Japanese
Number (50.2 [Mar. 1974]: 217-27). Examines the
biblical depiction of death and shows how
"Everyman's repeated calling to Jesus Christ
reverberates on the stage as an anathema to Death"
(233); Everyman's purification makes "the stage
most uncomfortable and forbidding" for Death
(233). Claims that "Death . . . would be able to
lead Everyman into his grave" (234) if he (Death)
were not associated with the Devil.

1568. Tamburr, Karl. "The Dethroning of Satan in the
Chester Cycle." *NM* 85.3 (1984): 316-28.

Shows that this cycle makes the Fall of the Angels
the punishment for Lucifer's broken covenant with
God, while "His later dethronement during the
Descent completes Christ's victory begun during
His life on earth in *The Temptation*" (316).
Points out the originality and uniqueness of one
version of Satan's defeat in the Harrowing play,
where he is "forcibly dethroned by his own
henchmen, who acknowledge Christ's sovereignty
over them" (316). Shows how the defeat of Satan
through the cycle unifies the cycle's three parts
(before, during, and after Christ's life). Also

considers the cycle's emphasis on the concept of power.

1569.   ---.   "The *Harrowing of Hell* in the English Mystery Cycles: Perspectives on the Corpus Christi Drama." Ph.D. diss., U. of Virginia, 1974.

1570.   Taylor, Arnold.   "Royal Alms and Oblations in the Later 13th Century: An Analysis of the Alms Roll of Edward I (1283-4)."   In *Tribute to an Antiquary: Essays Presented to Marc Fitch by Some of His Friends*, 93-125.   Ed. by Frederick Emmison and Roy Stephens.   London: Leopard's Head Press, 1976.

Shows that this wardrobe book contains record of payment of 26s 8d. in December 1283 "for the clerks who performed the St. Nicholas miracle play and for their boy bishop" (123), probably at Gloucester.   Also gives evidence for festivals (e.g. for St. Agnes, Jan. 21 and 28, 1284) and other public festivities.

1571.   Taylor, David.   "'The Tyres that were Lost.'"   *MET* 6.2 (Dec 1984): 153-58.

Offers two interpretations for the word "tyres" from the Coventry Smiths' Account for 1450: either iron segments nailed to the rim of a wheel, overlapping the joints, "or complete iron hoops bound onto the wheels whilst extremely hot and then cooled very quickly to shrink onto the rims" (153).   Claims that the former definition is what was extant in the middle ages.   Offers the other reading that the "tyres that were lost" refers to caps worn by the actors, showing that "The amount paid out for the *tyrrys* is consistent with the outlay for two or three simple caps or hats" (156).

1572.   Taylor, Jerome.   "Critics, Mutations, and Historians of Medieval English Drama: An Introduction to the Essays that Follow."   In *Medieval English Drama* . . ., 1-27.   Ed. by Jerome Taylor and Alan H. Nelson (see next entry).

The opening essay in the volume.   Discusses trends and themes in criticism of early English drama and reviews the many areas of critical approach: the history/origin of the drama, its relation to liturgy and ritual, and its relation to Renaissance drama.   Gives a brief summary of the eighteen essays in the volume.   Discusses key terms: drama, ritual, rite, play, etc.

1573.   ---, and Alan H. Nelson, eds. *Medieval English Drama: Essays Critical and Contextual.* Chicago and London: U. of Chicago Press, 1972.

Contains eighteen essays on various aspects of medieval drama. Eleven essays in Stratman; two on non-English topics; five essays considered here are by Taylor ("Critics . . .," see previous entry); Nelson ("Some Configurations . . .," # 1206); Nelson ("The Temptation of Christ . . .," # 1208); Leigh ("The Doomsday . . .," # 973); and Kolve ("*Everyman* and the Parable . . .," # 927). See also Natalie Crohn Schmitt ("Was There a Medieval Theatre in the Round? . . .," # 1447) and William L. Smoldon ("The Melodies . . .," # 1484).

Rev. *LJ* 98 (Jan. 1, 1973): 71.
       Specu 43.2 (Apr. 1973): 435-36. [Only lists contents.]
       Choice 10 (June 1973): 625.
       ChHist 42 (June 1973): 282.
       WHR 27 (Autumn 1973): 415.

1574.   Theiner, Paul. "The Medieval Terence." In *The Learned and the Lewed: Studies in Chaucer and Medieval Literature*, 231-47. Ed. by Larry D. Benson. Cambridge: Harvard U. Press, 1974. Harvard English Studies 5.

Discusses the wide knowledge of Terence's drama in the middle ages, especially in the schools.

1575.   Thomas, Charles. *Piran Round and the Medieval Cornish Drama.* Perranporth, Cornwall; Newton Abbot, England: Nicholas Toyne for Piran Round Committee, July 1969: 6-9.

Souvenir program for the Cornish Cycle, presented by the Bristol University Drama Department; performance directed by Neville Denny. Discusses the Cornish drama in general, "The Plain-an-gwary" (6) presentation, the players, "Conventions of the Play" (8), and "The End of the Cornish Drama" (9).

1576.   Thomson, Peter. *Survey of Drama and Its Performance in Britain.* Guilford, Connecticut: Jeffrey Norton Publishers, 1977. Exeter Tapes on Linguistics and Language Usage, # E7667.

Offers "an introductory survey of drama and its theoretical context from its origins to the present day" (from flier). Presents a brief historical account of medieval drama, mentioning

only the old theory that the secular drama emerged
from the liturgy.

1577.   ---, and Gamini Salgado. *The Everyman Companion to
        the Theatre*. London and Melbourne: J.M. Dent and
        Sons, 1985.

        Gives "A Theatre Chronology" (1-19), and
        discussions of "Theatre, Theatres and Dramatic
        Genres" (21-124). Has entries on masque (100),
        theater in the round (119-20). Very little on
        medieval drama, The Christian Church and the
        Theatre (35 ff.), various staging practices (35
        ff.). Little on medieval English drama.

        Rev. Phyllis Hartnoll, *ThN* 41.1 (1987): 38-39.

1578.   Thornber, Robin. [Review.] *GW* (June 8, 1980).
        [Cited by Sheila Lindenbaum, *RORD* 23 (1980): 84.]

        Review of The York Cycle, performances of June 6-
        30, 1980, York Festival, St. Mary's Abbey, York.

1579.   Tidworth, Simon. *Theatres: An Illustrated History*.
        London: Pall Mall Press, 1973. 224 pp.

        Chap. III, "The Middle Ages: Theatre without
        Theatres" (35-45), briefly discusses English
        drama--methods of staging, mysteries and
        moralities, continuity between medieval and
        renaissance plays.

        Rev. *PW* 204 (Aug. 20, 1973): 76.
        NewRep 169 (Sept. 29, 1973): 33.
        Choice 10 (Feb. 1974): 1880.
        Werk 8 (1975): 750.

1580.   Tigg, E.R. *The Dutch Elckerlijc is Prior to the
        English Everyman*. London: Privately Printed,
        1981.

        Rev. Elsa Streitman, "The Middle Dutch *Elckerlijc*
             and the English *Everyman*." *MedAe* 52.1
             (1983): 111-14 (see entry # 1557 above).

1581.   Tiner, Elza Cheryl. "*Inventio, Dispositio,* and
        Elocutio in the York Trial Plays." Ph.D. diss.,
        U. of Toronto, 1987.

1582.   ---. "Treason and Court Language in the York Corpus
        Christi Plays." *Scintilla* 2-3 (1985-86): 101-17.

        Claims that the language in the court scenes
        "divides the characters according to their moral

nature [and] . . . creates in the plays the social and legal context of a fifteenth-century English court" (101). Demonstrates how the language depicts "opposing groups of characters, those who accept and those who reject Christ" (101); also, how "Christ's accusers make use of English common law to convict him [sic] of treason" (101). Discusses many court scenes, audience involvement in the judgment, themes in the cycle, the element of foreshadowing.

1582a. Tissier, André. "Le Role du Costume dans les Farces Medievales." *FCS* 13 (1988): 371-86.

1583. Tittler, Robert, ed. *Accounts of the Roberts Family of Boarzell, Sussex, c 1568-1582.* Lewes: Sussex Record Society, for 1977-1979. Sussex Record Society, 71. xxvii, 181 pp.

Contains farm and household accounts from as early as 1582 and as late as 1586. Notes payments for minstrels, pipers, and players. With indexes of 1) subjects and places, and 2) names. With a glossary.

1584. Tobin, Mary Lampland. "A Study of the Formation and Auspices of the *Ludus Coventriae.*" Ph.D. diss., Rice U., 1973.

1584a. Tomasch, Sylvia. "Breaking the Frame: Medieval Art and Drama." In *Early Drama to 1600.* Ed. by Albert H. Tricomi. (See entry # 1589b below.)

1585. *The Toronto Passion Play.* [Toronto]: *Poculi Ludique Societas* in Association with the Graduate Centre for Study of Drama and Records of Early English Drama, 1981. 16 pp.

Program for performances at the U. of Toronto, August 1-3, 1981. Contains information on the play, the text and its modernization, staging, set design, costumes, music, and directing methods. With illustrations.

1586. Trapp, J.B., et al., eds. *The Oxford Anthology of English Literature.* Oxford and New York: Oxford U. Press, 1973. 2376 pp.

Trapp's section, "Medieval English Literature" (3-500), contains his own introduction on drama (363-67), and modernized texts of "The Second Shepherds' Play" and "Everyman."

1587.   Travis, Peter W.   "The Credal Design of the Chester
        Cycle."   *MP* 73.3 (Feb. 1976): 229-43.

        Discusses the cycle plays' "recurring dramatic
        imperative":   "'Behold and believe'" (229).
        Focuses on the Resurrection group of plays
        (Christ's Resurrection through Thomas's
        conversion) and on audience perception, especially
        with respect to the Chester cycle and its
        playwright's artistry and didacticism.

1588.   ---.   *Dramatic Design in the Chester Cycle.*   Chicago
        and London: U. of Chicago Press, 1982.   310 pp.

        Attempts to elucidate the cycle's dramatic design
        based on all the new scholarship now available.
        Examines all 24 plays individually and the cycle
        as a whole.   "Design" means structure, strategy,
        and "idea" (xii).   Calls this "a multileveled
        formal, rhetorical, and thematic analysis" (xiv).

        Chap. 1--"Medieval Celebrations of Corpus Christi:
        A Formal Analysis"--discusses the plays with
        respect to "relevant cultural features" (1) by
        focusing on the eucharistic Host, celebrated
        through the Roman Mass, the Feast of Corpus
        Christi, the Corpus Christi procession, and the
        Corpus Christi play.

        Chap. 2--"The Development of the Chester Cycle: A
        Historical Analysis"--surveys criticism and extant
        documents; looks at the inception and early form
        of the cycle and the Whitsun amplifications of the
        cycle, its late manifestations, ms difficulties,
        and dramatic unity.

        Chap. 3--"The Dramatic Hermeneutics of Old
        Testament Time: Paginae I-IV"--claims "that the
        cycles' vision of history" (79) should not be seen
        primarily typologically, but "typology must be
        subordinated to a more complex view of Christian
        history" (79).

        Chap. 4--"The Comic Structures of Communal
        Celebration: Paginae VI-XI"--discusses the comic
        ritual, and sacramental elements of the Nativity
        pageants--plays that occasionally are "similar to
        ritual in both form and effect" (108); "these
        plays seek to achieve a unification of the cultic
        community with the incarnated presence of the
        newborn Christ child" (108).

        Chap. 5--"Christ's Neo-Romanesque Ministry:
        Paginae XII-XIV"--concerns the cycles' need to

represent Christ's ministry. Shows the cycle's
reliance on the Gospel of John, the playwright's
conservatism in sticking closely to his scriptural
sources, the emphasis on the divinity of Christ.

Chap. 6--"The Ritual Aesthetics of the Passion:
Paginae XV-XVI"--looks at the Passion as "the
center of Christian history" (174), "to be
understood best by a direct experience, of all the
sensational realities of the events" (174);
explains how the Chester Passion departs from the
realism and intensity of the other cycles. Shows
the Chester version to be "highly stylized in its
enactment" (184)--in characterization and
dialogue. Says that viewing the Chester Passion
was clearly "a painful yet purgative celebration"
(191).

Chap. 7--"The Credal Design of the Cycle: Paginae
XVII-XXI"--focuses on the pilgrimage aspect of the
Resurrection plays. Focuses also on the
"Harrowing of Hell" play to determine if it is of
the Passion or the Resurrection group. Shows how
the cycle incorporates the events of the
Resurrection--even the Apostles' Creed; hence he
sees a "credal design" in the whole cycle. Claims
that the cycle is "more than a Creed play in
disguise . . . . the episodes central to the
cycle's credal design are shaped to do much more
than simply to dramatize a single article of
faith" (216). The design reinforces the "emphasis
upon the need to recognize the power and authority
of Christ's truth" (216). Speculates on when this
emphasis was added to the cycle, concluding that
it was added in "the shift to Whitsuntide" (221).

Chap. 8--"Reformations in the Dramatic Image:
Paginae XXII-XXIV"--looks at the cycle's "dramatic
realizations" of salvation history and the
"oblique projection of Everyman's spiritual
education" (223), each of which "is predicated not
only upon time but upon the completion of time"
(223). Shows how this eschatological view forces
the audience to judge itself morally through the
cycle's aesthetic; "ideally each viewer will
discover . . . an image of his own state of
spiritual ill- or well-being" (224). Examines the
playwright's use of space and time, use of the
Antichrist and the two Antichrist pageants, and
"The Last Judgment" play. Claims that where the
other cycles depict Christ as "a human, vulnerable
and compassionate friend of man," Chester defines
"Christ as the divine king--aloof, powerful, and
even severe" (248). Speculates that because of

the consistently high sophistication of the drama, "it is tempting to believe that one highly sophisticated playwright had to be responsible for the finished achievement of the entire Chester cycle" (253).

Rev. *Choice* 20 (Oct. 1982): 271.
  Clifford Davidson, *MP* 80.4 (May 1983): 408-10.
  JEGP 82 (July 1983): 440.
  Meg Twycross, *English* 32.144 (Autumn 1983): 251-57.
  Specu 58 (Oct. 1983): 1095.
  Theresa Coletti, CompD 17.4 (Winter 1983-84): 390-94.
  Gail McMurray Gibson, EDAMN 6.2 (1984): 41-43.
  SewR 92 (Apr. 1984): 273.
  Stanley J. Kahrl, ELN 22.2 (Dec. 1984): 66-70.
  MLR 80 (Jan. 1985): 115.
  Alasdair A. MacDonald EngStud 66.2 (Apr. 1985): 162-66 (see entry # 1025 above).

1589. ---. "The Dramatic Strategies of Chester's Passion Pagina." *CompD* 8.3 (Fall 1974): 275-89.

Shows that generalized critical statements about elements of particular cycles should not be applied to all cycles. Examines the "unique . . . dramatic strategies of Chester's Passion" (276)-- the major devices the cycle uses, "the emotional parabola the patterning of those techniques describes" (276). Concludes that the cycle's "dramatic principles are controlled by a vision of Christ's mission" (276) differently from the way it is done in the other cycles. Claims that the other cycles heighten the audience's guilt and anxiety while Chester offers order and solace in its combination of sacred and profane ritual elements.

1589a. ---. "The Social Body of the Dramatic Christ in Medieval England." In *Early Drama to 1600*. Ed. by Albert H. Tricomi. (See next entry.)

1589b. Tricomi, Albert H., ed. *Early Drama to 1600*. Binghamton: Center for Medieval and Early Renaissance Studies, State U. of New York at Binghamton, 1987. Acta, 13. xvi, 167 pp.

Contains essays by Travis, "The Social Body . . ." (see previous entry); Johnston, "Cycle Drama . . ." (# 827c); Sticca, "The *Planctus Mariae*

. . ." (# 1541a); Kahrl, "The Texts . . ." (# 885a); Tomasch, "Breaking . . ." (# 1584a); Lampes, "The Magi . . ." (# 937a); Riemer, "The Dramatic . . ." (# 1387a); Fiondella, "Augustine's . . ." (# 558a); Hildahl, "Penitence . . ." (# 749a); Finkelstein, "Formation . . ." (# 557a); and Scattergood, "*The Contention* . . ." (# 1435a).

1590. Tristram, Philippa. *Figures of Life and Death in Medieval English Literature.* London: Paul Elek; New York: New York U. Press, 1976. 245 pp.

Looks at York, Towneley, and Chester Plays, *Ludus Coventriae*, and the moralities. Many plays and characters considered individually in the larger scope of the book (designated in the title).

Rev. *TLS* (Feb. 25, 1977): 224.
T.T. Tashiro, *LJ* 102 (July 1977): 1499.
Choice 14 (Oct. 1977): 1056.
B. Raw, *N&Q* 24 (Oct. 1977): 466-67.
D. Hamer, *RES*, n.s. 29 (Feb. 1978): 74-76.
Siegfried Wenzel, *Specu* 53 (July 1978): 638-40.
G.H.V. Bunt, EngStud 60 (Oct. 1979): 664-66.

xxxx. Tucker, Kenneth. (See Richard Levin, "The Acting Style . . .," entry # 986 above.)

1591. Turville-Petre, Thorlac. *The Alliterative Revival.* Woodbridge, Suffolk: D.S. Brewer; Totowa, NJ: Rowman and Littlefield, 1977. 152 pp.

Covers the so-called "alliterative revival" with respect to its origins and develpment, and focusing on specific literary texts. Cites the alliterative stanzas of some thirteen York plays (122 f.).

Rev. *Choice* 14 (Jan. 1978): 1501.
A.C. Spearing, *THES* 322 (Jan. 6, 1978): 16.
T.A. Shippey, *TLS* (Jan. 20, 1978): 68.
PS 52 (Spring 1978): 117.
E. Salter, *RES*, n.s. 29 (Nov. 1978): 462-64.
E.B. Irving, Jr., *ELN* 16 (June 1979): 322-24.
W.R.J. Barron, *EngStud* 62 (Jan. 1981): 56-58.

1592. Twycross, Meg. "'Apparell comlye.'" In *Aspects of Early English Drama*, 30-49, 142-44. Ed. by Paula Neuss (see entry # 1213 above).

Tries "to find out about fifteenth- and sixteenth-century English mystery-play costumes" (30). Aims to sketch what one can, ought to be able to, and probably cannot learn about wardrobes from material currently available. Considers scripts, account books, banns, the nature of contemporary materials (leather, canvas, buckram, saye [a twilled silk or wool], etc.), sources of the costumes (i.e. makers), traditional wardrobe items, and contemporary (i.e. non-dramatic) clothing. With three illustrations.

1593. ---. "The Chester Cycle Wardrobe." In *Staging the Chester Cycle*, 100-23. Ed. by David Mills (see entry # 1159 above).

Recounts the problems she faced in designing a set of costumes for the plays. Mentions that there are 357 named characters in the cycle, for whom she made 194 different designs. Explains her sources (the script, guild accounts, the banns), the kinds of costumes she made (biblical, "theatrical" [112]). With 22 drawings of costumes.

1594. ---. "The Chester Plays at Chester." *MET* 5.1 (July 1983): 36-42.

Reports on a "mini-Cycle of eight plays" (36) on June 26, 1983. With a map and seven photographs.

1595. ---. "The Flemish *Ommegang* and its Pageant Cars." *MET* 2.1 (1980): 15-41; 2.2 (1980): 80-98.

Analyzes the Flemish pageant wagons of the sixteenth and seventeenth centuries from published illustrations: their use, their relation to medieval English performances and pageants. With 41 illustrations.

1596. ---. "The 'Liber boonen' of the Leuven ommegang." *DC* 22 (Apr. 1984): 93-96.

Discusses the sixteenth-century illustrations by William Boonen of the Leuven *ommegang* and what the ms tells us about costume, pageant wagons, and their iconography. Not on English drama, but useful in showing how the visual arts impart information on the drama.

1597. ---. "*Mary Magdalen* at Durham." *MET* 4.1 (July 1982): 63-66.

Review of performances of June 27-28 and July 3-4, 1982. See Peter Meredith, "*Alia eorundem*" (entry # 1089 above).

1597a. ---. "My Visor is Philemon's Roof." *FCS* 13 (1988):
335-46.

1598. ---. "A Pageant-Litter Drawing by Dürer." *MET* 1.2
(Dec. 1979): 70-72.

Shows the drawing; claims the litter may be
similar to one used at Lincoln and Newcastle.
Discusses the odd distribution of weight, the
hanging cloths and ornamental canopy, etc.

1599. ---. "'Places to Hear the Play': Pageant Stations at
York, 1398-1572." *REEDN* 3.2 (1972): 10-33.
(Text, 10-26; map, 27; chart of locations, 28-33.)

Attempts to determine the playing stations of the
York plays by examining the lessees, in all
surviving lists, of the places mentioned in the
lessee lists. Points out that when several names
appear on several lists in the same order, we can
assume a continuity of place of performance from
one year to the next. Assumes that "if the same
person turns up for several years running at, say,
Stations 10, 8, 11, and 9, . . . the person and
the place are constants and that the numbering of
the station is a variable" (10). Says that
pageant routes tended to remain the same while
stopping-places varied. Also assumes that the
stations are in front of the houses of the people
named in the lists (with the exception of a
performance outside a religious house). Looks at
"external" documents (e.g. wills, mortgages, home
books, memorandum books, conveyances) to establish
precise locations. Discusses her charts and
sources (e.g. Council Minutes and the
Chamberlains' Books and Rolls of Account).
Concludes that, e.g., 1) stations did not always
follow the same pattern or exist in the same
number; 2) lessees' fees varied; 3) all the
identifiable stations are on the left hand side of
the route--a fact with implications about staging;
4) the lessees' professions "reflect the business
areas of medieval York" (21); 5) "many stations
were hired by more than one person" (21); 6)
"Family continuity is shown" (21); and so on.
Gives a 1398 map of York and Tables from 1398,
1416, 1454 . . . 1572 showing the stations.

1600. ---. "Playing 'The Resurrection.'" In *Medieval
Studies for J.A.W. Bennett* . . ., 273-96. Ed. by
P.L. Heyworth (see entry # 744 above).

Discusses a March 1977 performance of the play
from the York cycle, performed in the Nuffield

Theatre Studio of the University of Lancaster.
Considers "pageant-waggon staging" and "a standing
and potentially mobile audience" (273).
Concentrates "on what happens to the play in
performance" (273)--how physical circumstances
shape the play. With photographs of the
performance.

1601.   ---. "Report of a Meeting Held on Saturday 7th April
1979 in the University of Lancaster to Discuss the
Pageant Waggon." *MET* 1 (1979-80): 3-4.

At the meeting--topic divided into two sessions:
Evidence and Reconstruction. Discusses disparity
and range of information in the records, time span
of the performances (late fourteenth to late
sixteenth century), terminology, and actual
productions.

1602.   T[wycross], M[eg]. "Reports on Two Mystery Play
Productions in 1979: Three Mystery Plays: *Mactacio
Abel* (Wakefield), *Noah* (Chester), *Abraham*
(Northampton), Durham 7th July 1979." *MET* 1.1
(Oct. 1979): 43.

Discusses performances of three plays, "put on to
celebrate the 800th anniversary of the City of
Durum" (43). (For the other production see Peter
Meredith, "The Coventry Mystery Plays," entry #
1106 above).

1603.   ---. "The Toronto Passion Play." *MET* 3.2 (Dec.
1981): 122-31.

Reports on peformances of August 1-3, 1981, by the
Poculi Ludique Societas in Toronto.

1604.   ---. "'Transvestism' in the Mystery Plays." *MET* 5.2
(Dec. 1983): 123-80.

Discusses men in women's roles in several cities
and in many different plays. Also mentions young
girls or women in female roles. Explores some of
the implications of this phenomenon, based on
examination of texts, performances, and work done
by Lancaster Medieval Theatre students, 1982-83.
Examines historical evidence, other theatrical
events, continental parallels, ancient and modern
attitudes, voices and ages, "Representation and
the 'Dual Consciousness'" (147),
"Depersonalisation, Sexuality and Virginity"
(156), and "Should Women Act in the Mystery
Plays?" (172). Shows that "the 'beautiful woman'
roles . . . seem to be written so as to make it

possible for a man to play them. They are not aggressively feminine" (82). (See Happé, et al., "Thoughts . . .," entry # 689 above.)

1605. ---. [Untitled review.] *RORD* 20 (1977): 99-100.

Reviews performances of *The Resurrection of Christ*, March 9-11, 1977, at Nuffield Theatre Studio, Lancaster U., Lancaster, England.

1606. ---, and Sarah Carpenter. "Masks in Medieval English Theatre: The Mystery Plays." *MET* 3.1 (July 1981): 7-44. Pp. 29-36 of this article rpt. in *Medieval English Drama*, 171-80. Ed. by Peter Happé (see entry # 684 above).

Looks at the "far-reaching" (7) effects of masking in the plays, evidence for their use, and the different masking traditions. Part I of essay focuses on terminology: "maskes," "vezars," "face," "headpeces," and so on. Part II on the purposes and effects of masking. Shows "that there are several different masking traditions" (29)--as physical fact or as moral emblems (physical symbols for a spiritual state)--all "congruent with the whole medieval interest in emblem, sign, and figure" (33).

1607. ---, ---. "Masks in Medieval English Theatre: The Mystery Plays 2." *MET* 3.2 (Dec. 1981): 69-113.

Continues previous study with an examination of the characters who wore masks (figures of extreme good and evil--usually not ordinary human beings: Devils, very wicked human characters like Herod and the Tormentors, God and the Angels). With 25 illustrations.

1608. ---, ---. "Materials and Methods of Mask-Making." *MET* 4.1 (July 1982): 28-47.

Examines masks with brief references to their use in drama. With nine illustrations (see previous two entries).

1609. ---, and Peter Meredith. "Editorial." *MET* 1.1 (Oct. 1979): 1-2.

Explains the intent of this new journal. [Every issue begins (p. 1 or pp. 1-2) with an editorial by Twycross and Meredith. No others will be included here.]

xxxx.   Twycross-Martin, Henrietta. See Peter Happé, et al.,
        "Thoughts on 'Transvestism' by Divers Hands"
        (entry # 689 above; see also entry # 1604 above).

1610.   Tydeman, Bill. *"N-Town* Plays [sic] at Lincoln." *MET*
        3.1 (Dec. 1981): 131-34.

        Reports on performances of July 4-22, 1981, at
        Lincoln Cathedral.

1611.   ---. "Stanislavski in the Garden of Gethsemane: An
        Interlude." *MET* 5.1 (July 1983): 53-57.

        A dramatic presentation of how a director might
        guide his actors in a performance of the N-Town
        "Betrayal" play.

1612.   Tydeman, William. *English Medieval Theatre 1400-
        1500.* London, Boston, and Henley: Routledge &
        Kegan Paul, 1986. xiv, 221 pp.

        Focuses on *Mankynde,* the Croxton *Play of the
        Sacrament, The Castel of Perseveraunce,* the York
        Passion sequence, and Medwall's *Fulgens and
        Lucres.* Part One--"the Repertoire"--examines "the
        diversity of medieval religious plays in English"
        (9) and the five basic types of English drama
        (cycle mysteries, non-cycle mysteries, miracles,
        moralities, saints' plays); origins and the trend
        towards public performances; the nature of
        vernacular plays; the artistic achievements of the
        vernacular theater. Surveys several key plays and
        the cycles, and--in general--all the significant
        plays of the era.

        Part Two--"Plays in Performance"--in five
        chapters, aims "to reconstruct the original
        performances" (29) of the five plays mentioned
        above, "using . . . scholarly evidence and
        informed guesswork" (29). Chap. 1 discusses "The
        Booth Stage: *Mankynde,"* looking at staging and
        audience, and "how skilfully [sic] a relatively
        unsophisticated style of staging may . . . enhance
        the dramatic impact of a relatively sophisticated
        script" (52).

        Chap. 2--"Scenic Structures: the Croxton *Play of
        the Sacrament"*--looks at "the only true miracle
        play . . . which survives" in English (53); the
        possibilities of staging; its sources and actions;
        its banns and cast-list. Sums up the play's finer
        elements and the "deep sense of involvement . . .
        [and] the intensity of a theatrical experience"

(77) it renders with its "inventive use of scenic structures" (77).

Chap. 3, on "Theatre in the Round: *The Castel of Perseveraunce*," is on the play's staging. Examines Southern's book *The Medieval Theatre in the Round* (see entry # 1493 above), and adds his own criticism to that of others. Offers a hypothetical setting--"a roughly circular amphitheatre with possibly raked sides, with platforms set within its circumference at the four main compass points with a fifth to the North-East" (83). Talks of the banns, the phases of the play, blocking, plot and tableaux, and so on. Concludes with statements about the play's "complexity and diversity of medieval theatrical logistics" (102) and the play's use of "stimulating and theologically effective" (102) spectacle.

Chap. 4--"Processional Staging: the York Passion Sequence"--examines the facts about processional performance. Surveys scholarship on staging, the plays performed, the procession, the wagons' appearance, movement, and capacity. Reconstructs a full procession, then gets to the Passion sequence, play by play--stage action, distinctions of dress, stage mechanisms, and so on. (Draws on his own experience of producing a cycle sequence.)

Chap. 5--"Great Hall Theatre"--deals with "*Fulgens and Lucres*, an excellent example of a play specifically written with performance in the dining-hall or Great Chamber of some noble house in mind" (137). Gives historical background on the play and on possible performance styles. Looks at various internal and external data to try to reconstruct the play's earliest performance. Points up the importance of understanding the "intimacy between players and audience" (159), and the concomitant lack of need for scenery, using "only the standard furnishings of a Tudor dining-hall" (159).

Part Three examines the many forms of medieval "theatres" or production sites, indoor and outdoor; the reaction to various forms of drama by the clergy; the audience's influence; and the notion that "medieval theatre was designed for the community as a whole rather than for a privileged or educated section of it" (202).

Rev. *HistT* 36 (May 1986): 59.
    Choice 24 (Oct. 1986): 320.

Paula Neuss, *ThN* 41.2 (1987): 92-93.
RES 38 (May 1987): 239.
TLS (Aug. 14, 1987): 880.
C.W. Marx, *MedAe* 57.1 (1988): 123-24.

1613.   ---. *The Theatre in the Middle Ages: Western
European Stage Conditions, c. 800-1576.*
Cambridge: Cambridge U. Press, 1978. 298 pp.
Part of Chap on "The Performers"--pp. 209-17--rpt.
in *Medieval English Drama*, 180-89. Ed. by Peter
Happé (see entry # 684 above).

Contains chapters on "Ritual Survivals," "Classic
and Christian" influences, "Indoor Theatre,"
"Street Theatre," "Open-air Theatre," "Resources
and Effects," "The Performers," and "Financing the
Plays." With illustrations, map of Britain,
Chronological Table (800-1576), notes,
bibliography, Glossary of Technical Terms, and
index.

Rev. John H. Harvey, *AJ* 59.2 (1979): 468-69.
W. Temple, *Drama* 133 (Summer 1979): 75-77.
R. Morse, *BBN* (June 1979): 519.
Choice 16 (Oct. 1979): 1034.
Peter Meredith, *EDAMN* 2.1 (Nov. 1979): 5.
G.C. Britton, *N&Q* 27.6 (225) (1980): 541-42.
A.M. Nagler, *ThJ* 32 (Mar. 1980): 135-36.
D. Mills, *RES* 31 (Aug. 1980): 328-30.
R.B. Dobson, *History* 65 (Oct. 1980): 468-69.
S.J. Kahrl, *Specu* 55 (Oct. 1980): 851.
William A. Armstrong, *ThN* 37.2 (1983): 91-
93.

1614.   Tyson, Cynthia Haldenby. "Noah's Flood, the River
Jordan, the Red Sea: Staging in the Towneley
Cycle." In *Studies in Medieval Drama* . . ., 101-
11. Ed. by Clifford Davidson, et al. (see entry #
410 above).

Looks at four plays (*Noah, Jacob, Pharaoh*, and
John the Baptist) which refer to water as a prop.
Proposes that real water was used for the Towneley
plays, not draped cloth, as scholars have
suggested. Concludes that if water were really
used, the performance is surely stationary.

1615.   ---. "Property Requirements of *Purificacio Marie:*
Evidence for Stationary Production of the Towneley
Cycle." *StudMedCul* 8 and 9 (1976): 187-91.

Looks at stage directions and references early in
the incomplete ms, in corresponding plays of other
cycles, and elsewhere in the Towneley ms itself to

try to determine how the play was staged. Focuses
primarily on props (Simeon's vestment and beard,
two turtle doves, bells). Concludes from an
interpretation of the evidence that a fixed
location in production seems probable.

1616.   ---. "The Staging of the Towneley Plays." Ph.D.
        diss., U. of Leeds, 1971.

        Posits a stationary staging.

1617.   Uehling, Edward Martin. "Dimensions of Time in the
        Wakefield Pageants." Ph.D. diss., Pennsylvania
        State U., 1980.

1618.   Uéno, Yoshiko. "An Essay on the King John Plays:
        From History to Romance." *ShakStud* 12 (1973-74):
        1-30.

        Deals with John Bale's *King Johan* in terms of the
        genre of history plays. Speaks of Bale's "mixing
        historical with allegorical personages" (3), his
        use of current history and political problems, and
        characterization. Says that the play "is a kind
        of mirror using history to teach political lessons
        which are most pertinent to its own days" (5).
        Shows how Bale's aim was "to defend [Henry VIII's]
        claim of the royal supremacy over the Church of
        England" (6).

1619.   ---. "Robin Hood Plays and Pastoral--Two Huntingdon
        Plays and *The Sad Shepherd*." *SEL*, English Number
        (1979): 19-36.

        Looks at the plays written by Anthony Munday (*The
        Downfall of Robert Earl of Huntingdon*, 1598), by
        Munday and Henry Chettle (*The Death of Robert Earl
        of Huntingdon*, 1598), and by Ben Jonson (*The Sad
        Shepherd, or a Tale of Robin Hood*, 1635-38?; a
        fragment). Examines "the treatment of the Robin
        Hood legend" (21).

1620.   Umphrey, P.J. "*The Castle of Perseverance*, Line
        695." *PQ* 59.1 (Winter 1980): 105-07.

        Offers additional evidence to support the
        emendation of "prey" for "pley." Shows the
        appropriateness of the notion of evil as a
        predator in the play.

1621.   Utley, Lee, and Barry Ward. "The Folk Drama." In *A
        Manual of the Writings in Middle English, 1050-
        1500*, 1382-84, 1622-29. Ed. by Albert E. Hartung
        (see entry # 714 above).

Gives a general overview of Folk Drama: the
lateness of the plays, the likelihood that they
are derived from earlier medieval versions, lost
plays, Robin Hood plays, the relation of folk
drama to balladry and to other medieval drama, and
their "complex development in oral and in printed
versions" (1384). With a bibliography (1622-29).

1622. Valentine, Grace Evelyn Whysner. "A Study of the
Noun and Pronoun Inflections of the N-Town Plays."
Ph.D. diss., U. of Missouri, Columbia, 1971.

1623. Vance, Sidney Jerry. "Unifying Patterns of
Reconciliation in the *Ludus Coventriae.*" Ph.D.
diss., Vanderbilt U., 1975.

1624. Van Dyke, Carolynn. "The Intangible and Its Image:
Allegorical Discourse and the Cast of *Everyman.*"
In *Acts of Interpretation* . . ., 311-24. Ed. by
Mary J. Carruthers and Elizabeth D. Kirk (see
entry # 278 above).

Looks at the difficulty of acting, reading, and
viewing, at the role of Everyman, and at the
importance of an understanding of allegory.
Surveys criticism. Claims that theoretical
approaches may not prove useful, so "it may be
best to approach the dramatis personae of *Everyman*
through the text of the play" (314). Examines the
characters with respect to their "style of acting"
(322). Concludes that "*Everyman*'s allegorical
cast is in fact literal: its dramatis personae
are words, realized in many dimensions" (324).

1625. Van Waesberghe, Joseph Smits, et al. "Liturgical and
Secular Elements in Medieval Liturgical Drama."
In *Report of the Tenth Congress of the
International Musicological Society, Ljubljana
1967*, 271-83. Ed. by Dragotin Cvetko. Kassel,
Basel, Paris, and London: U. of Ljubljana, 1970.

Contains a panel discussion, chaired by van
Waesberghe, among Krzysztof Bieganski, Zoltán
Falvy, Walther Lipphardt, William L. Smoldon, and
Hélène Wagenaar-Nolthenius. Examines the *quem
quaeritis* trope--from its early appearance--as
dialogue. Considers origins and development. Not
on English drama, but offers background to later
dramatic developments.

1626. Vaughan, M.F. "Mak and the Proportions of *The Second
Shepherd's* [sic] *Play.*" *PLL* 18.4 (Winter 1982):
355-67.

Looks at the groups of threes in the play
(locales, characters, tones, etc.) and at entries
and exits of the characters. Recounts views of
the play's three-part structure. Claims the
play's "three-part division rests upon a
proportional arrangement of the action, or rather
of the dialogue which accompanies the action"
(358). Points out the "mathematical . . . [and]
dramatic sense" (358) that this proportion
produces. Counts lines and shows proportions of
the play as being significant. Offers a
numerological reading.

1627. Vaughan, Míceál F. "The Three Advents in the *Secunda
Pastorum.*" *Specu* 55.3 (July 1980): 484-504.

Discusses "the artist's and his contemporary
audience's world" (484). Considers the unity in
the separate parts of the play. Reviews
scholarship. Considers also a three-part
structure to the play, concentrating on the play's
threes (shepherds, locales, plot structure, the
"interweaving of past, present, and future" [495],
and the three Advents--"The playwright's triune
vision" [503]).

1628. Velz, John W. "Cosmic Irony in Medieval Tragicomedy
and Renaissance Tragedy." *CahÉ* 18 (Oct. 1980): 3-
10.

Reviews the notion that the conflict between
sinners and God "is prototypically tragic" (3) and
is a forerunner to Renaissance tragedy. Claims
that "The opponents of God . . . are too
monolithic for the most part to be fully tragic
. . . . But the tension between the World and the
Cosmos is one of the ingredients of great tragedy"
(3). Discusses the ironic nature of Corpus
Christi drama in that the audience knows the end
before the plays begin, and also because the
audience has a wider perspective on the actions
than do the plays' characters. Examines ways in
which these ironies are manifested and how they
are related to Renaissance tragedy.

1629. ---. "The Coventry Mystery Plays." *CahÉ* 20 (Oct.
1981): 121-22.

Reviews performance of the Belgrade Theatre
Company [under sponsorship of Coventry Cathedral,
directed by Michael Boyd]; at the Cathedral ruins
of the Church of St. Michael, Coventry, August 5,
1981.

1630.   ---. "Episodic Structure in Four Tudor Plays: A
        Virtue of Necessity." *CompD* 6.2 (Summer 1972):
        87-102.

        Deals with *Everyman, Tamburlaine* Pt. I, *Richard
        III,* and *Julius Caesar* in terms of how the
        personnel of traveling troupes affected the plays'
        structures. Claims "that though the prescribed
        structure must control dramatic art it need not
        defeat it," and that "the necessity of episodic
        structure could become a thematic virtue" (87).
        Shows how a small acting company can use the
        episodic structure to thematic advantage.

1631.   ---. "From Jerusalem to Damascus: Bilocal Dramaturgy
        in Medieval and Shakespearean Conversion Plays."
        CompD 15.4 (Winter 1981-82): 311-26.

        Stresses "the emblematic character of medieval
        stage space" (311). Aims to examine "the
        aesthetics and the semiotic implications" (311) of
        the moral world of the stage. Discusses the
        "bipolarity" (312) of the medieval stage: Old and
        New Testament, sin and righteousness, God and
        Satan, cosmos and world, and so on. Looks at the
        resulting possibilities for audience involvement.
        Claims that "the bifurcated world of a *conversio*
        play was sometimes symbolized" (315) by having a
        split stage and movement of the actors from one
        place to another. Focuses on "the metaphoring of
        moral change as spatial movement in conversion
        plays" (312). Examines several plays, including
        the Digby *Conversion of St. Paul, The Castle of
        Perseverance,* the Digby *Mary Magdalene,* and some
        of Shakespeare's plays.

1632.   ---. [Untitled review.] *CahE* 15 (Apr. 1979): 125-
        26.

        Reviews a production of The Coventry Cycle of
        Mystery Plays, directed by Ed Thomason; Belgrade
        Theatre and Coventry Cathedral, August 4, 1978.

1633.   ---. "The York Cycle of Mystery Plays." *CahE* 13
        (Apr. 1978): 49-52.

        Reviews the performance by the Poculi Ludique
        Societas in association with Records of Early
        English Drama and the graduate Centre for Study of
        Drama, University of Toronto--performance of
        October 1-2, 1977.

xxxx.   Villar, Mary del. See del Villar, Mary.

1634.　Vince, Ronald W. *Ancient and Medieval Theatre: A Historiographical Handbook.* London and Westport, Connecticut: Greenwood Press, 1984. xi, 156 pp.

Chaps. 1-3 consider origins and theater in Greece and Rome. Chap. 4 is on the medieval theater (89-129). Surveys scholarship. Looks at Production Documents (Prompt-Books, Stage Plans, archival documents, an eye-witness account, five performances [not English], and some questionable means of production), places of performance, written records, the extra-literary dimension, folk-drama, and art and theater. Has appendix: "A Review of Medieval Dramatic Texts." For information specifically on English plays see "English and Cornish Religious Drama," 143-45; and "The Secular Drama," 145-47. With bibliography and index.

Rev. J. Michael Walton, *ThRI* 10.3 (Autumn 1985): 227-28.
Oscar G. Brockett, *ThRI* 11.2 (Summer 1986): 152-54.

1635.　Vinter, Donna Smith. "Didactic Characterization: The Towneley Abraham." *CompD* 14.2 (Summer 1980): 117-36. Rpt. in *Medieval English Drama* . . . , 71-89 [with spelling *Characterisation*]. Ed. by Peter Happé (see entry # 684 above).

Shows Caiaphas to be an appropriate and an inappropriate voice to explain Palm Sunday. Considers the historical tradition and the use in the play of this character. Uses a Brechtian approach to analyze the dramatic aesthetic. Defends "the heuristic value of 'gest' as a tool for clarifying the relationship between idea and psychology in the mystery playwrights' elaboration of character" (122-23). Uses the Towneley Abraham and Isaac to show how an understanding of gest underlies the playwright's depiction of character in action. Concludes by showing the indistinguishability of drama and didacticism, and claims that with fixed conceptions of characters, "an audience-oriented dramaturgy" (134), and a focus on "the significant outline of attitude and action, or attitude *as* action" (134), the "plays . . . create speaking pictures in which didacticism and drama" (135) are one.

1636.　Voigts, Linda Ehrsam. [Untitled review.] *RORD* 23 (1980): 87-89.

Reviews performances of Heywood's *The Play of the Weather*, April 30 and May 3, 1980, Old Playhouse Patio, University of Missouri, Kansas City.

1637. Wade, Anna Lathrop. "The Relationship of the *Cursor Mundi* to the English Cyclic Dramas: The Old Testament Plays." Ph.D. diss., Auburn U., 1979.

1638. Walker, Lewis. "*Timon of Athens* and the Morality Tradition." *ShakS* 12 (1979): 159-77.

Points out the similarities between the renaissance play and *The Castle of Perseverance, Wisdom, Liberality and Prodigality*, and *Mankind*.

1639. Wall, Carolyn. "The Apocryphal and Historical Backgrounds of 'The Appearance of Our Lady to Thomas' (Play XLVI of the York Cycle)." *MedS* 32 (1970): 172-92.

Describes the structure of the play; gives plot summary. Recounts other accounts of the Assumption of the Virgin and speculates on sources/influences of the York version, with emphasis on the French Our Lady of the Cincture, "perhaps the oldest representation in Western graphic art of the legend which forms the 'plot' of the York weavers' play" (178). Traces the "cincture" version from legend to cult. Claims that the York playwright was probably familiar with "native sources" of the "cincture" versions, but used his sources "with a considerable degree of originality . . . [and] artistic inventiveness" (192); actual direct sources still in doubt.

1640. ---, Sister. "York Pageant XLVI and its Music." *Specu* 46 (1971): 689-712. With a "Note on the Transcriptions" by Ruth Steiner, 698-701.

Reviews the music for the cycle as a whole and specifically for "The Appearance of Our Lady to Thomas." Says that Jacobus de Voragine's *Legenda Aurea* is the source of the York songs' lyrics, but not a source of the play. Looks at "the general features of English polyphony" (689). With transcriptions of the music.

1641. Walsh, Martin W. "Performing *Dame Sirith:* Farce and Fabliaux at the End of the Century." In *England in the Thirteenth Century: Proceedings of the 1984 Harlaxton Symposium*, 149-65. Ed. by W.M. Ormrod. Grantham: Harlaxton College, British Campus of the Univeristy of Evansville, 1985.

Shows the relationship of the poem to drama,
especially in its heavy use of dialogue.
Summarizes criticism, showing its performability
as dramatic entertainment. Speaks of the
"dramatic conception" (156) of the work.
Concludes that the tale was originally written as
a play. Reconstructs its hypothetical dramatic
origin. With an appendix containing "A
Performance Analysis" (159-65).

1642. Ward, Barry J. "A Functional Approach to English
Folk Drama." Ph.D. diss., Ohio State U., 1972.

1643. Wardle, Irving. "Magnificent Production in the
Severest Test Yet." *The Times* (London), January
21, 1985.

Briefly reviews a performance of the National
Theatre's production of *The Mysteries* of January
19, 1985, in London's Cottsloe Theatre.

1644. ---. [Untitled review.] *The Times* (London), August
14, 1984.

Reviews a performance of Lindsay's *Ane Satyre of
the Thrie Estates*, August 1984, at the Assembly
Hall, Edinburgh, during the Edinburgh Festival.

1645. Ware, James Montgomery. "The Conversion Theme in
English Drama to 1575." Ph.D. diss., Claremont
Graduate School and University Center, 1970.

1646. Warning, Rainer. "On the Alterity of Medieval
Religious Drama." *NewLH* 10.2 (Winter 1979): 265-
92. Trans. by Marshall Brown.

Discusses the concept of the "foreignness" (265)
of the past. Aims to look at the "alterity" of
the drama by "Opening text theory to the pragmatic
correlate of the linguistic sign" (266). Claims
that "Religious drama is perhaps the genre which
demonstrates most forcefully the alterity of the
Middle Ages" (266). Concentrates primarily on
liturgical drama. Looks at typology, historical
phenomena, ritual. Claims that the drama's "unity
of play and reality is no longer accessible to our
experience" (285).

1647. Warren, Michael J. "Everyman: Knowledge Once More."
DalR 54.1 (Spring 1974): 136-46.

Examines the character Knowledge. Reviews
interpretations. Breaks discussion into 1) the
plot and the allegory, and 2) the problems of how

allegory works in the play and the relationship between characters and audience. Concludes that "Knowledge functions primarily as the knowledge of Christian teaching and conduct," and also, after Everyman's death, "as Christian knowledge that is always available to man" (145); she is also representative of the Church.

1648. Wasson, John. "Corpus Christi Plays and Pageants at Ipswich." *RORD* 19 (1976): 99-108.

Discusses the surviving court rolls, Domesday Book, and early charters of the Ipswich Guild of Merchants "to piece together a fairly clear notion of the constitution and development of the annual Corpus Christi procession" (99). Considers records from c. 1400 to 1530. Concludes that the records tell little about the play and nothing about which came first, the pageant or the play, though the records seem to show that the procession was more important.

1649. ---. "How to Read Medieval Manuscripts: A Guide for EDAM and Other Researchers." *EDAMN* 5.2 (Spring 1983): 47-84.

Offers detailed advice on paleography, signs and symbols, abbreviations, dates, Latin inscriptions, "types of useful documents and their locations" (55); gives many facsimiles with transcriptions, both for dramatic and musical texts.

1650. Wasson, John M. "Interpolation in the Text of *Everyman*." *ThN* 27.1 (Autumn 1972): 14-20.

Broaches the controversy of which came first, *Everyman* or *Elckerlijc*; does not take sides. Looks at "the artistic ineptitude of the second desertion episode" (14) and the following digression on priesthood in *Everyman*. Mentions some critics' justifications for these "weaknesses." Considers the background story, the staging, and the casting pattern, and concludes that the desertion episode (of Beauty, Strength, Five Wits, and Discretion) "was added later, by a writer more concerned with orthodox theology than with the number of actors at his disposal" (17); also claims that the present English and Dutch texts are made up of a simple, complete play "to which has been added a lengthy episode by someone concerned with the imperfect Catholic theology of the early version" (20), and this early version "looks suspiciously Protestant" (20). Claims that

the added episode seems to be aimed at "an
audience of clergymen" (20).

1651.   ---. "Karl Young and the Vernacular Drama." *RORD* 27
         (1984): 151-55.

         Assesses the work of Young on the fiftieth
         anniversary of the publication of *The Drama of the
         Medieval Church*. Examines some of Young's views
         on vernacular drama in the light of recent
         scholarship which uses contemporary public and
         private records. Points out that "Young was
         judging by the extant texts" and "that judgments
         based only on extant texts are likely to be
         misleading" (155).

1652.   ---. "The Morality Play: Ancestor of Elizabethan
         Drama?" *CompD* 13.3 (Fall 1979): 210-21.   Rpt. in
         Drama in the Middle Ages, 316-27.   Ed. by
         Davidson, et al. (see entry # 409 above).

         Questions the notion that the roots of Elizabethan
         drama are in the English moralities.   Also
         questions the idea that such plays as Bale's *King
         Johan* and Skelton's *Magnificence* are links between
         medieval and renaissance drama.   Does not deny
         parallels between the plays of the different eras.
         Points out the many lost plays which could have
         had more direct influence.   Suggests that miracle
         and folk plays may have also been a link.

1653.   ---. "Professional Actors in the Middle Ages and
         Early Renaissance." *M&RD* 1 (1984): 1-11.   (See
         entry # 144 above.)

         Looks at abundant evidence--from contemporary
         records--of the professional actors of early
         England, from at least as early as 1362, and
         probably as early as 1287.   Examines the
         "companies, their size, the conditions under which
         they played, their prosperity" (3-4).   Claims that
         there were performances at inns, guildhalls, and
         in churches.   Considers props, costumes, staging,
         and the plays performed.

1654.   ---. "Public Performances of Plays with Known Titles
         or Subjects."

         Unpublished paper presented at the Shakespeare
         Association of America Annual Meeting, Seattle,
         1987.   Cited by Barbara D. Palmer, "'Towneley
         Plays' . . .," entry # 1259 above.

1655.   ---.   "Records from the Abbey of St. Benet of Hulme,
         Norfolk." *REEDN* 5.2 (1980): 19-21.

         Recounts the dramatic contents of a few account
         rolls, one entry (of 1373) of which refers to a
         village play.

1656.   ---, ed. *Records of Early English Drama: Devon.*
         Toronto, Buffalo, and London: U. of Toronto Press,
         1986. lxxvi, 623 pp.

         Introduction contains information on "Historical
         Background" (xi); "Plays and Players" (xxiv); "The
         Documents" (xxix); and "Editorial Procedures"
         (lx); with notes, bibliography, maps, the records,
         five appendixes, translations, endnotes, "Patrons
         and Travelling Companies" (455), Latin and English
         glossaries, and index.

         Rev. *Choice* 24 (June 1987): 1550.
              CompD 21 (Winter 1987): 399.

1657.   ---.   "Records of Early English Drama: Where They Are
         and What They Tell Us." In *Records of Early
         English Drama: Proceedings of the First Colloquium
         . . .,* 128-44. Ed. by Joanna Dutka (see entry #
         497 above).

         Discusses these two "important aspects of
         collecting records of early English drama" (128).
         Also considers which records a researcher with
         limited time should ignore and which she or he
         should concentrate on. Discusses also borough
         records, parish records, cathedral and monastic
         papers, and records of guilds and manors. Also
         looks at terminology, Corpus Christi plays and
         processions, and "The nature of medieval drama"
         (139).

1658.   ---.   "The *St. George* and *Robin Hood Plays* in Devon."
         MET 2.2 (Dec. 1980): 66-69.

         Claims the plays "were not acted after 1541" (66).
         Looks at necessary props (sword, armor). Surveys
         primary documents from Devon and West Devon Record
         Offices. Mentions how they were rather simply
         produced plays, and the few expenses for some
         costumes, and, rarely, for a prop (e.g. an arrow).
         Shows that the Robin Hood play was generally acted
         in midsummer, though at Ashburton it seems to be
         connected with the Corpus Christi plays.

1659.   ---.   "Visiting Entertainers at the Cluniac Priory,
        Thetford 1497-1540."   *Albion* 9.2 (Summer 1977):
        128-34.

        Points out that priors' accounts from the priory
        reveal "104 . . . payments to minstrels" (129) and
        over seventy to players.   Mentions up to thirteen
        recorded plays from nearby towns.   Shows that the
        accounts discuss minstrels, acting companies
        (local amateur actors and professional companies),
        and a "mixed bag of entertainers" (133).

1660.   Watson, George, ed.   *The New Cambridge Bibliography
        of English Literature, Vol. I, 600-1600.*
        Cambridge: At the U. Press, 1974.   Cols. 727-742;
        1401-1424.

        Contains references to scholarship on "English
        Mystery and Miracle Plays" (§ 7); "Spectacles and
        Minstrelsy to 1485" (§ 8); "Folk Drama" (§ 9).
        Also has sections on "Moralities," "Early
        Comedies," and "Early Tragedies"--with references
        for John Bale, David Lindsay, Henry Medwall, John
        Rastell, John Redford, John Skelton, Richard
        Wever, Anonymous plays, Ulpian Fulwell, Thomas
        Garter, Lewis Wager, William Wager, George Wapull,
        Robert Wilson, and Nathaniel Woodes.

        Rev.   *RefSR* 2 (Oct. 1974): 140.
               WLB 49 (Dec. 1974): 316.
               Booklist 71 (Jan. 15, 1975): 516.
               Choice 11 (Jan. 1975): 1609.
               RefSR 3 (Jan. 1975): 24.
               P. Davison, *Library*, 5th ser. 30 (June 1975):
                  146-49.
               ARBA 7 (1976): 607.
               PBSA 71 (Apr. 1977): 237.
               Booklist (July 1, 1978): 1692-95.

1661.   ---, ed.   *The Shorter New Cambridge Bibliography of
        English Literature.*   Cambridge: Cambridge U.
        Press, 1981.   Cols. 75-78; 173-182.

        Contains references to scholarship in four
        sections on medieval drama: 1) "Bibliographies";
        2) "Histories"; 3) "Collections"; 4) [Criticism
        on] "English Mystery and Miracle Plays."   Also has
        entries on Moralities ("General Studies" and "Pre-
        Tudor Moralities").   With citations for John Bale,
        David Lindsay, Henry Medwall, John Rastell, John
        Redford, John Skelton, Richard Wever, Anonymous
        plays, Ulpian Fulwell, and Nathaniel Woodes.   Also
        cites works on "The Early Comedies" and "The Early
        Tragedies."

Rev. *TES* (Aug. 21, 1981): 19.
    LJ 107 (Jan. 1, 1982): 86.
    BBN (Mar. 1982): 142.
    TLS (May 7, 1982): 519.
    Library 4 (June 1982): 188.
    Choice 20 (Sept. 1982): 58.
    PBSA 76 (Oct. 1982): 501.
    ARBA 14 (1983): 566.

1662. Watson, Lois Jean. "The York Master." Ph.D. diss., U. of North Carolina, Chapel Hill, 1971.

1663. Watson, Thomas Ramey. "N Town [sic] *Death of Herod*." *Expl* 40.1 (Fall 1981): 3-4.

Disagrees with the traditional view that the death of Herod story is not biblical. Suggests that it is found in Acts 12:23.

1664. ---. "Redford's *Wyt and Science*." *Expl* 39.4 (Summer 1981): 3-5.

Answers John W. Velz and Carl P. Daw, Jr. ("Tradition and Originality in *Wyt and Science*," *SP* 65 [July 1968]: 631-46) who claim that Lady Science represents God. Says that she represents Christ.

1665. ---. "*The Second Shepherds' Play:* Daw's Place in the Augustinian Scheme." *ANQ* 21.3 and 4 (Nov.-Dec. 1982): 34-36.

Relates Daw's function in the play to St. Augustine's seven-age historical scheme in *De Civitate Dei*. Daw is youth--"the true member of the City of God" (34)--and is also the "revealer of the City of God . . . who prepares the audience to perceive the Age of Grace that invades the world in the incarnation" (35).

1666. ---. "The Wakefield *Noah*." *Expl* 40.3 (Spring 1982): 5-7.

Shows the Wakefield Master's linking of Old and New Testament patterns in two speeches--one by Noah and one by God--concerning the oil of mercy and anointing.

1667.   Webster, John M.   "The Allegory of Contradiction in
         Everyman and *The Faerie Queene*."   In *Spenser and
         the Middle Ages*, Proceedings from a Special
         Session at the 11th Conference on Medieval
         Studies, Kalamazoo, Michigan, 2-5 May 1976, pp.
         357-86. Ed. by David A. Richardson. Cleveland:
         Cleveland State U., 1976. Microfiche.

         Shows that many allegorical figures embody
         contradiction in their characterization. Compares
         The Faerie Queene to *Everyman:* "each work
         presents itself . . . as a fiction of character
         and motive" (359) in a realistic world while
         breaking "its narrative illusion" and forcing "its
         audience to recognize the work's necessarily non-
         dramatic thematic structure" (359). Looks at the
         nature of contradiction in *Everyman* (360-71).
         Claims that readers must take both narrative and
         allegorical approaches to understand the work.
         (For a critique of this article see Maureen
         Quilligan, entry # 1348 above.)

1668.   Wee, David L.   "The Temptation of Christ and the
         Motif of Divine Duplicity in the Corpus Christi
         Cycle Drama."   *MP* 72.1 (August 1974): 1-16.

         Examines the structural, dramatic, thematic, and
         theological interests of the Temptation. Looks at
         the medieval theory of it and discusses the
         implications of temptation in theological terms.
         Considers its use in York, Chester, and *Ludus
         Coventriae* plays. Shows how one can trace the
         ideas of temptation and the devil "in the neglect
         of the grammar of two biblical passages, in the
         suggestive power of another, and in the
         development of Christian apologetics" (16).

1669.   Weimann, Robert.   *Shakespeare and the Popular
         Tradition in the Theatre: Studies in the Social
         Dimension of Dramatic Form and Function.*   Ed. and
         trans. by Robert Schwartz. Baltimore and London:
         Johns Hopkins U. Press, 1978. xxii, 325 pp.

         "Originally published in German, in a somewhat
         different version, in 1967, by Henschelverlag
         Berlin, entitled *Shakespeare und die Traditions
         des Volkstheaters: Soziologie, Dramaturgie,
         Gestaltung*" (iv).

         Chap. I deals with mime and the character of the
         fool (1-14). Chap. II is on "The Folk Play and
         Social Custom" (15-48). Chap. III deals with "The
         Mystery Cycles" (49-97). Chap. IV covers
         "Moralities and Interludes" (98-160). The rest of

the book on renaissance drama. With appendix,
notes, bibliography, and index.

Rev. (of the German text):
     RES, n.s. 20 (May 1969): 220.
     JAAC 28 (Winter 1969): 260.

     (of the English text):
     Choice 15 (Dec. 1978): 1376.
     J.C. Trewin, *Drama* 132 (Spring 1979): 80-82.
     B. Erlich, *S&S* 43 (Summer 1979): 244.
     M. Shapiro, *JEGP* 78 (July 1979): 425.
     AB 64 (Oct. 1979): 2625.
     G. Wickham, *THES* 377 (Jan. 11, 1980): 15.
     Clio 9 (Spring 1980): 457.
     N. Rabkin, *SewR* 88 (July 1980): 447-62.
     A. Barton, *RES*, n.s. 31 (Aug. 1980): 343-46.
     Choice 19 (Oct. 1981): 213.

1670. Weld, John. *Meaning in Comedy: Studies in
        Elizabethan Romantic Comedy*. Albany: State U. of
        New York Press, 1975. x, 255 pp.

        Chap. I covers "Dramatic Exemplification and
        Metaphor" (21-55); Chap. II deals with "Dramatic
        Metaphor in Moralities and Other Entertainment"
        (56-75); and Chap. III is on "Semantic Complexity:
        Macrocosm and Microcosm" (76-97). These chapters
        deal with the morality plays and their traditions,
        with many references to the cycle plays. (The
        rest of the book is on renaissance drama.)

        Rev. *Choice* 12 (Feb. 1976): 1577-78.
             J.R. Brown, *TLS* (Mar. 12, 1976): 289.
             H.C. Cole, *JEGP* 75 (July 1976): 411-14.
             A.F. Kinney, *ShakQ* 29 (Winter 1978): 119-22.
             N. Sanders, *MP* 76 (May 1979): 398-401.

1671. Wells, Randall Anthony. "Stagecraft in Late Morality
        Plays." Ph.D. diss., U. of North Carolina, Chapel
        Hill, 1973.

1672. Wells, Stanley, ed. *English Drama (Excluding
        Shakespeare): Select Bibliographical Guides*.
        London: Oxford U. Press, 1975.

        Contains essays by John Leyerle ("Medieval Drama,"
        entry # 990 above) and T.W. Craik ("Tudor and
        Early Elizabethan Drama," # 364).

        Rev. *Library*, 5th ser. 30 (Sept. 1975): 261.
             G. Bott, *SchLib* 23 (Sept. 1975): 272.
             C.A. Bunge, *WLB* 50 (Oct. 1975): 119.
             Choice 12 (Dec. 1975): 1294.

J.C. Maxwell, *N&Q* 23 (May/June 1976): 253-54.
ARBA 7 (1976): 609.
PQ 55 (Fall 1976): 483.

1673. Wellwarth, George E. "From Ritual to Drama: The
       Social Background of the Early English Theatre."
       JGE 19.4 (Jan. 1968): 297-328.

       Shows how the political and social changes
       contemporary with the plays were concomitant with
       radical changes in the drama. Considers folk and
       traditional dramatic phenomena; compares Greek and
       medieval drama; discusses tropes and mysteries.
       Presents the old "Church to Market Place" (303)
       notion. Looks at plays in the Reformation,
       censorship, the move "From Popular to Coterie
       Drama" (315); and breaks down the drama into four
       periods. Also considers Elizabethan plays.

1674. Wenzel, Siegfried. "An Early Reference to a Corpus
       Christi Play." *MP* 74.4 (May 1977): 390-94.

       Points out that the earliest reference to a Corpus
       Christi play is in 1376; but discusses a record
       (from Robert Holcot, c. 1335) mentioning the
       Corpus Christi celebration. Quotes Holcot and
       comments on his reference to a play performed on
       Corpus Christi day. Looks also at the difference
       in York between the play and the procession.

1675. ---. "The Three Enemies of Man." *MedS* 29 (1967):
       47-66.

       Discusses the commonplace notion of the world, the
       flesh, and the devil. Shows the development of
       the notion and how the three are sometimes
       considered distinct, sometimes considered coeval.
       Considers its use in *The Castle of Perseverance*
       and *Mankind* (see especially 65-66), in which the
       role of the three has diminished in medieval
       thought.

1676. Wertz, Dorothy. "The Deadly Sins in a Changing
       Social Order: An Analysis of the Portrayal of Sin
       in the Medieval English Theater." *IJCS* 11.3
       (Sept. 1970): 240-45.

       Discusses the Seven Deadly Sins from their origins
       to their appearance and use in the middle ages.
       Comments on the sociological conditions of the
       era, and on the sins in several plays (*The Castle
       of Perseverance* and the cycle plays). Considers
       iconography, morality play emphases, the vices
       vis-à-vis the virtues.

1677. Wertz, Dorothy C. "Mankind as a Type-Figure on the
        Popular Religious Stage: An Analysis of the
        Fifteenth-Century English Morality Plays." *CSSH*
        12.1 (Jan. 1970): 83-91.

        Examines the development of the Mankind figure,
        which arose "partly from the individualist and
        voluntarist emphasis of nominalist thought and
        partly from the renewed emphasis on the individual
        associated with social changes of the time" (83).
        Focuses on *The Castle of Perseverance* among other
        dramatic exemplars, and also on the mystery
        cycles. Considers the influence of nominalism,
        "with its emphasis on man's free will and the
        possibility of his immediate access to God without
        the intervention of the sacraments" (91).

1678. ---. "The Theology of Nominalism in the English
        Morality Plays." *HTR* 62.3 (July 1969): 371-74.

        Looks at the three basic principles of the
        doctrine: "the sovereignty of God, the immediacy
        of God in the created world, and the autonomy of
        man" (371), and at how these relate to the
        morality plays--with special emphasis on *The
        Castle of Perseverance*.

1679. West, George A. "An Analysis of the Towneley Play of
        Lazarus." *PQ* 56.3 (Summer 1977): 320-28.

        Points out the play's uniqueness in its subject
        matter and its placement in the cycle. Shows how
        these two features are related. Aims to show that
        the play reaches "its full thematic potential"
        (320) at the expense of the cycle's chronology.
        Claims that in the Towneley cycle the play does
        not prefigure Christ's resurrection, but man's,
        and thus prefigures the Last Judgment. Claims
        also that the play has no "chronological or
        narrative connections in the cycle at all" (326),
        but has connections thematically to the Last
        Judgment.

1680. West, George Augustine. "The Last Judgment in
        Medieval English Mystery Plays." Ph.D. diss., U.
        of Nebraska, Lincoln, 1972.

1681. Westfall, Suzanne Ruth. "The Entertainment of a
        Noble Patron: Early Tudor Household Revels."
        Ph.D. diss., U. of Toronto, 1984.

1682. White, D. Jerry. *Early English Drama, Everyman to
        1580: A Reference Guide*. Boston: G.K. Hall, 1986.
        xx, 289.

Gives bibliographical entries--with brief
annotations--for many plays from c. 1495 to 1580.
Covers criticism through 1982 (and a few later
items). Excludes works on "folk drama, masques,
entertainments, and pageantry" (ix). Contains
nothing, also, on the cycle plays.

Rev. *Choice* 24 (Sept. 1986): 94.
  C&RL 48 (July 1987): 358.
  RRBN 2 (Winter 1987): 34.

1683. White, Eileen. "'Bryngyng Forth of Saynt George':
       The St. George Day Celebration in York." *MET* 3.2
       (Dec. 1981): 114-21.

       Using primary sources, speculates on the nature of
       the celebrations. Shows that "there was a
       procession, a mass with a sermon . . . and the
       Riding of St. George" (114). Explains that the
       "'procession' is linked with a mass and a sermon,
       and the 'riding' . . . is another element" (114-
       15). Discusses each and also the St. George Play,
       which itself was separate from the riding and like
       one of the Corpus Christi plays. Points out how
       little is known of the St. George play.

1684. ---. "The Disappearance of the York Play Texts--New
       Evidence for the Creed Play." *MET* 5.2 (Dec.
       1983): 103-09.

       Looks at original records--especially of William
       Revetour of York (a civic clerk) who claims to
       have bequeathed a Creed Play to the Corpus Christi
       Guild in 1446. Shows that there were three copies
       of the Creed Play. Traces other records and
       performances to try to locate the mss. Refers to
       a 24 March 1593 note at the back of the
       Chamberlains' Book suggesting that the play was
       loaned to Mr. Richard Hutton and probably not
       returned: "The Creed Play of York could . . .
       have disappeared because it was borrowed by a
       citizen . . . who died before he could return it"
       (107). Also points out that Dean Matthew Hutton
       advised the York City Council not to allow the
       play to be performed in 1568.

1685. ---. "The Girdlers' Pageant House in York." *REEDN*
       8.1 (1983): 1-8.

       Discusses the Bridgemasters' rolls in York, in
       which, in 1548, Girdlers are recorded "amongst the
       regular pageant house tenants" (2). Mentions
       rents and allowances and the "decayed tenements"
       (4); raises questions about the Girdlers' pageant

wagon. Shows how an understanding of the records "affords a possible glimpse of the organization of the pageant wagons during the setting forth of the Corpus Christi Play" (7).

1686. ---. "The Tenements at the Common Hall Gates: The Mayor's Station for the Corpus Christi Play in York." *REEDN* 7.2 (1982): 14-24.

Asserts that the mayor and his fellow councillors watched the Corpus Christi play from an upper chamber with removable windows in a tenement which the city leased to Richard Aynelay or Thomas Colthirst; the documents surveyed show "that plays in York did indeed take place in the streets, and that in 1575 the Mayor and his Council did not believe that this tradition had come to an end" (21).

1687. White, Patricia S. "*Everybody:* On Stage in New York." *RORD* 29 (1986-87): 105-07.

Recounts a performance of *Everyman*, April 17-19, 1986, at The Cathedral of St. John the Divine.

1688. Wickham, Glynne. *Early English Stages 1300 to 1660.*

Stratman (# 2755) cites this work as 2 vols. In fact, the work was published as follows:

Vol. 1: Subtitle *1300 to 1576.* London: Routledge and Kegan Paul; New York: Columbia U. Press, 1959. xliv, 428 pp.

Vol. 2, Pt. I: Subtitle *1576 to 1660, Part I.* New York: Columbia U. Press; London, Routledge & Kegan Paul, 1963. xxiv, 408 pp.

Vol. 2, Pt. II: Subtitle *1576 to 1660, Part II* London: Routledge and Kegan Paul; New York: Columbia U. Press, 1972. xii, 266 pp.

Vol. 3: Subtitle *Plays and Their Makers to 1576.* London and Henley: Routledge & Kegan Paul; New York: Columbia U. Press, 1981. xxvi, 357 pp.

Vols. 1 and 2, Pt. I in Stratman; only vol. 2, Pt. II and vol. 3 treated here. [N.B. a vol. 4 is planned.]

Vol. 2, Pt. 2--begins with Chap. IX--"From Gamehouse to Theatre"--"a brief précis of the arguments advanced in Part I" (3). Chap. X--"The Privy Council Order of 1597 for the Destruction of

London's Playhouses" (9)--discusses the order and why it was never carried out. Chap. XI--"Game or Playhouses, 1598-1660"--is in ten parts: 1) Introduction; 2) the notions of "Game" and "Play"; 3) "Gamehouses"; 4) "Games and Plays"; 5) "Cockpits"; 6) "Gamehouses for jousting and for the baiting of bulls and bears: Henslowe's Rose"; 7) "The Curtain and the Swan after 1597: the Hope"; 8) "The cockpits in Whitehall and Drury Lane before 1625"; 9) "The Amphitheatre: an unrealized projection"; and 10) "The Riding Academy of Monsieur Le Fevre." Chap. XII covers Inns; Chap. XIII is on Theatres; Chap. XIV covers "Houses for Plays, Masks and Banquets." Chap. XV is concerned with "Stages and Stage-directions" and deals with "Scene and Stage," stage managers, dressing rooms, stores, entrances and exits, and musicians. With appendixes, notes, illustrations, bibliography, and index.

Vol. 3--*Plays and Their Makers to 1576*--is divided into three books: Book One, "Drama and Occasion" (Chaps. I-III); Book Two, "Emblems of Occasion" (Chaps. IV-VII); Book Three, "Play-makers and Play Texts" (Chaps. VIII-IX). Chap. I--"Drama and Festival"--considers the occasions of drama and "Seasonal festivities." Aims to show that religious festivals retain many features and ideas "common to festivals that had fallen at approximately the same points in the calendars of pre-Christian religion" (20).

Chap. II--"Drama of the Christian Calendar"--covers "Festivals of the Christian year," "The drama of Easter and its vigil," "Christmas, its vigil and its aftermath," "Commemoration of Saints, prophets and martyrs," and "Corpus Christi and its sequels."

Chap. III--"Non-Recurrent Court and Civic Festivals"--focuses on works designed for particular occasions. Cites many kinds of festivities and specific examples of these.

Chap. IV--"Play-makers and Device"--discusses devices and "maker[s] of interludes" (70) who dealt with professional or semi-professional acting companies: the methods they employed in constructing a play.

Chap. V--"Device and Visual Figuration"--examines "the principal figurative devices invented by medieval and Tudor play-makers, and handed on from one generation to the next as a common storehouse

of visual and verbal emblems" (82). Considers
"Superimposition and typology," "Combat," "The
Tavern," "Changes of Name and Costume," and other
devices (e.g. make-up and, in general,
"disfigurement of faces" [116] and of physique,
the witch, the use of pillory or stocks, refereed
fights, the play within a play, trial scenes, gift
giving, and song).

Chap. VI--"Device and Verbal Figuration"--examines
biblical and other sources, types, use of
language, narrative styles and techniques, use of
"Disputation: argument and polemic," "Word games:
ludus and *jocus*," "Song and atmospherics."

Chap. VII is on "Practical considerations which
directly affected the making of plays."

Chap. VIII--"English comedy from its origins to
1576"--analyzes "Christian Attitudes and
Assumptions," the move "From *ordo* to *ludus*:
'earnest,' 'game' and 'play,'" "The genesis of
English comedy," and "The rationalizing of English
comedy."

Chap. IX considers "English Tragedy from Its
Origins to 1576"--its genesis and rationalization.
With appendixes, notes, bibliography, "List of
Plays Quoted from or referred to in the text,"
illustrations, and index.

Rev. Vol. 1. *TLS* (Oct. 17, 1980): 19.
          Choice 18 (Nov. 1980): 410.
          Donald C. Baker, *ELN* 18.4 (June 1981):
          294-95.
          F. Laroque, *CahE* 21 (April 1982): 69-70.
     Vol. 2, Pt. I. Richard Stoddard, *ANQ* 11.1
          (Sept. 1972): 12-14.
     Vol. 2, Pt. II. *AB* 49 (Apr. 3, 1972): 1297.
          Drama (Summer 1972): 70.
          B&B 17 (June 1972): 68.
          TLS (June 9, 1972): 662.
          ANQ 11 (Sept. 1972): 12.
          Choice 9 (Nov. 1972): 1146.
          AJ 52.2 (Winter 1972): 401.
          AHR 78 (June 1973): 678.
     Vol. 3. *AJ* 61.2 (1981): 398.
          M. Wakelin, *TES* (Apr. 24, 1981): 19.
          T.W. Craik, *BBN* (July 1981): 433.
          Choice 19 (Sept. 1981): 84.
          Paula Neuss, *TLS* (Sept. 11, 1981): 1045.
          Drama (Winter 1981): 50.
          Specu 57 (Apr. 1982): 441.
          Reavley Gair, *N&Q*, n.s. 29.6 (227) (Dec.

                   1982): 536-37.
         ThJ 35 (Mar. 1983): 132.
         RES 34 (Nov. 1983): 481.
         RenQ 36 (Winter 1983): 654.
         SewR 92 (Apr. 1984): 273.

1689. Wickham, Glynne W.G. "English Religious Drama of the
       Twelfth, Thirteenth and Fourteenth Centuries:
       Transition Revisited." *SMCOP* 2 (1985): 101-15.

       Recognizes "the scarcity of factual evidence . . .
       and inevitably hypothetical character of existing
       commentary and criticism" (101) of the drama in
       question. Selects this period for the
       transitionary information it sheds on later
       vernacular drama. Quotes from an August 9, 1352,
       letter of John Grandisson, Bishop of Exeter, to
       the Archdeacon of his diocese. Shows that the
       letter reveals much interest in dramatic activity.
       Discusses organizers and content of the 1352 play
       (which does not survive). Posits "the existence
       of an independent secular tradition of dramatic
       entertainment" (113) in the period in question.

1690. ---. *A History of the Theatre.* Cambridge: Cambridge
       U. Press, 1985. 264 pp.

       Contains a general overview of Western and
       Oriental drama. Looks only briefly at medieval
       English plays, guilds, genres, and so on.

       Rev. *GW* 133 (Dec. 8, 1985): 21.
            Drama 160 (1986): 48.
            PAJ 10.1 (1986): 116.
            BBN (Jan. 1986): 46.
            LJ 111 (Jan. 1986): 98.
            Economist 298 (Feb. 15, 1986): 84.
            ChrCnt 103 (Mar. 19, 1986): 306.
            TLS (May 30, 1986): 598.
            VQR 62 (Summer 1986): 103.
            BkR 5 (Sept. 1986): 52.
            ThJ 38 (Dec. 1986): 510.
            Phyllis Hartnoll, *ThN* 41.1 (1987): 38-39.

1691. ---. "Medieval Comic Traditions and the Beginnings
       of English Comedy." In *Comic Drama: The European
       Heritage*, 40-62. Ed. by W[illiam] D[river]
       Howarth. New York: St. Martin's Press, 1978.

       Talks about different and evolving notions of
       comedy. Mentions contrast and incongruity in the
       plays. Considers liturgical drama and also the
       Corpus Christi plays. Also focuses on morality
       plays and the works of later dramatists.

1692. ---. *The Medieval Theatre*. London: Weidenfeld and
       Nicolson; New York: St. Martin's, 1974. 245 pp.

       Aims to show "how dramatic art developed in Europe
       between the tenth and the sixteenth centuries" (1)
       and to show the influences on this development of
       religion, recreation, and commerce; hence the book
       is divided into three sections. Pt. I--"Theatres
       of Worship"--covers the Drama of Praise and
       Thanksgiving, looking at sources from Palestine,
       Rome, Liturgy and Ritual, and Christianity
       (Christ, Prophets, Saints, Martyrs). Pt. I also
       covers Drama of Repentance (Language and Drama,
       The Corpus Christi Feast, The Crucifixion, and
       Patron Saints), and the Drama of Moral Instruction
       (Popular Education, Sermons, Fine Arts, The Dance
       of Death, and the drama of Crime and Punishment).

       Pt. II--"Theatres of Recreation"--examines Drama
       and Nature (Climate, Seasons, Agriculture, Folk
       Festivals, the Mummers' Play) and Drama and
       Natural Man (Courtyard, Hall and Chamber, War
       Games, Sex-Games, Mummings, Disguisings, Masques,
       Civic Pageantry, Interludes).

       Pt. III--"Theatres and Commerce"--covers Amateurs
       and Professionals, Church and State. With
       appendix: "Calendar of Twentieth-Century Revivals
       of English Mystery Cycles and other major
       Religious Plays of the Middle Ages." Contains
       bibliography and index, and illustrtations
       (figures and plates).

       Rev. R. Temple, *Drama* 116 (Spring 1975): 81-83.
            R. Edwards, *Crit* 17 (Fall 1975): 364-66.
            Alan H. Nelson, *MedAe* 45.2 (1976): 223-26.
            B.D. Bills, *ETJ* 28 (Mar. 1976): 127-31.
            David M. Bergeron, *MLR* 71 (July 1976): 624-
            26.
            David Mills, *RES*, n.s. 27.107 (Aug. 1976):
            330-33.
            J.W. Robinson, *ThRI* 3.1 (Oct. 1977): 66-67.
            J.C. Trewin, *ContempRev* 236 (May 1980): 278-
            79.

1693. ---. *The Medieval Theatre*. 3rd ed. Cambridge,
       London, and New York: Cambridge U. Press, 1987.
       xv, 260 pp.

       Revision of preceding entry, with new materials in
       chaps. 1 and 2 "in the light of newly researched
       and recently published source materials" (8).
       Also adds a closing chapter "charting throughout
       Europe the transition during the sixteenth and

early seventeenth centuries from Medieval Gothic
methods of play-construction and theatrical
representation to those of neo-classical
revivalism" (8). With new, augmented
bibliography, notes, index, and illustrations.

Rev. *Choice* 25 (Feb. 1988): 918.
RRBN 3 (Apr. 1988): 21.

1694. ---. "No Heavens in the Early Theatres." In
"Abstracts of Papers at The International
Shakespeare Association Congress. The First Public
Playhouse: The Theatre 1576-1976." *ShakN* 26.3
(142) (May 1976): 27.

Claims that "at all playhouses before about 1590,
there were no heavens, no machinery above the
stage, no chair of state which could be let down,
and not even stage pillars holding up a roof
. . ." (27).

1695. Wickham, G.W.G. "The Romanesque Style in Medieval
Drama." In *Tenth-Century Studies: Essays in
Commemoration of the Millennium of the Council of
Winchester and Regularis Concordia*, 115-22, 233.
Ed. by David Parsons. London and Chichester:
Phillimore, 1975.

Looks at the religious origins of or influences on
the later English drama. Mentions the differences
between "the chanted Latin drama of the liturgy
. . . [and] the spoken vernacular drama of a later
epoch" (115), differences which appear in subject
matter and presentation. Shows the split into two
distinct genres, "liturgical music-drama and
vernacular didactic drama" (115). Distinguishes
Romanesque from Gothic styles, the former of which
is the focus of this essay.

1696. ---. "Stage and Drama till 1660." In *English Drama
to 1710*, 19-64. Ed. by Christopher Ricks (see
entry # 1385 above).

Provides one chapter in three parts: I. "Play,
Player, Public and Place"; II. "The Beginnings of
English Drama"; and III. "Reformation and
Renaissance." Pt. I deals with Game and Play,
actors, staging and areas of presentation, High-
days and Holy-days, and Roman and Celto-Teutonic
Preludes.

Pt. II looks at "The Drama of Christ the King,"
"The Drama of Christ Crucified," "The Drama of

Crime and Punishment," "The Drama of Social
Recreation," and "Amateurs and Professionals."

Pt. III deals with academic drama, censorship,
common players and their play-houses, stages,
costumes, and settings.

Examines terminology of game and play, actors, and
theater, and the implications of these. Considers
also social conditions leading to the emergence of
drama; the supposed church origins of English
drama; the different manifestations of this drama
and their social implications; the different
actors, costumes, props, companies, etc. of early
drama.

1697. ---. "The Staging of Saint Plays in England." In
Medieval Drama, 99-119. Ed. by Sandro Sticca (see
entry # 1541 above).

Explains the popularity of saint plays in medieval
England (of which there are only three non-cycle
exemplars extant: two plays in the Digby MS [St.
Paul and Mary Magdalene] and the Cornish play of
St. Meriasek). [Also in the Ludus Coventriae is a
play of St. Anne and one of St. Veronica in the
Cornish cycle.] Discusses the existence of other
now-lost saint plays. Notes how abruptly
references to these plays disappear, "coincident
with Henry VIII's break with Rome" (102), and the
"range and number of saints whose lives were
recreated in dramatic form" (103). Discusses the
summer and winter performances of the plays, their
patrons, and their cost. Considers the three
surviving English texts, their (almost certainly)
open-air performance, the ordering of the
production, and the staging. Concludes with notes
of a recent (1969) performance of St. Meriasek.

1698. ---. "Trends in International Drama Research." In
Medieval Theater . . . (forthcoming). Ed. by
Eckehard Simon (see entry # 1469 above).

1699. Wierum, Ann. "'Actors' and 'Play Acting' in the
Morality Tradition." RenD, n.s. 3 (1970): 189-
214.

Treats characters which take on disguises or play
other roles to deceive, showing how this is
accomplished with name changes, costume changes,
masks, and affectation. Looks at "the play-acting
metaphor" (190) in the morality plays, especially
with respect to Vice/Satan/Lucifer disguised as
good. Shows the relationship between play-acting,

disguise, and vice. Comments on "the organic association of play acting with disguised evil" (214) which comes from a medieval theological inheritance.

1700. Wightman, Carolyn L. "The Genesis and Function of the English Mystery Plays." *StudMedCul* 11 (1977): 133-36.

Discusses economic conditions relative to the Black Death and other plagues, which lowered the population and increased per capita wealth (especially between 1349 and 1375). Shows how the crafts gained in wealth and how there was "luxurious living in England" (134), manifest in several ways, including dramatic activity of various kinds. Speculates on costs and dates of plays in Beverley, York, Coventry, Chester, and London.

1701. Wiles, David. *The Early Plays of Robin Hood.* Cambridge: D.S. Brewer, 1981. 97 pp.

Looks at the Robin Hood legends through their literary manifestations with focus on "the custom of performing plays of dramatic games based around the outlaw" (2). Calls Robin Hood plays "a wholly indigenous, wholly secular cultural tradition--a spring equivalent to the Christmas plays of St George" (2). Gives a systematic description of plays, tracing their folk origins, their courtly and popular traditions. Contains chapters on "Robin Hood as Summer Lord," "The Combat Play," "Game and Ballad: The Courtly and Popular Traditions," and "The Symbolic Language of Carnival." Appendixes contain a "Gazeteer of References to Robin Hood Plays before 1600" (64-66), "Extracts from the Church-wardens' Account Book . . ." (68-70), "Original Play-texts" (71-79), "May-games in Elizabethan Drama" (80-90), and "The Kempsford Mumming Play" (91-93). [Appendix 2 (p. 67) is labeled "map," but the page is essentially blank (it has two notes "locations mentioned in the earliest ballads" and "locations of Robin Hood plays"; nothing else is on the page.]

Rev. *TLS* (Jan. 1, 1982): 9.
C. Belsey, *THES* 483 (Feb. 5, 1982): 18.
K. Stern, *BBN* (Apr. 1982): 229.
Choice 19 (July 1982): 1563.
Specu 58 (July 1983): 857.
RES 35 (Nov. 1984): 587.
MLR 80 (Apr. 1985): 415.

1702. Williams, Arnold. "The Comic in the Cycles." In
       Medieval Drama, 108-23. Ed. by Neville Denny (see
       entry # 442 above).

       Defines the medieval notion of comedy. Discusses
       such elements as disguise, mistaken identity,
       discovery, plot, burlesque, "punishment" of
       villains, stereotypical characters, the illogical
       or impossible, the use of farce, anachronisms, and
       other sources of humor. Deals with satire and the
       use of comic irony in the cycle plays.

1703. Williams, Peter Neville. "Satan and His *Corpus*:
       Cultural Symbolism in the English Mystery Plays."
       Ph.D. diss., U. of Delaware, 1976.

1704. Willis, Paul. "The Weight of Sin in the York
       Crucifixio." *LSE*, n.s. 15 (1984): 109-16.

       Examines the crucifixion scene in terms of its
       humorous and doctrinal elements, with specific
       reference to the weight of the cross, the cross as
       burden. Observes analogues and sources of the
       incident, with an awareness of the parallel notion
       of atonement.

1705. Wilson, F.P. *The English Drama, 1485-1585*. Ed. by
       G.K. Hunter. New York and Oxford: Oxford U.
       Press, 1969. The Oxford History of English
       Literature, IV, pt. 1. 244 pp.

       Chap. I--"The Earlier Tudor Morality and
       Interlude" (1-46)--deals with "Medwall and before
       Medwall," Skelton and Lindsay, Rastell and
       Heywood, the Papist and Protestant influences, and
       John Redford.

       Chap. II--"The Late Tudor Morality Play" (47-77)--
       covers "Authors and Actors," the two primary
       themes of the era ("the upbringing of the young
       and . . . the evils of social corruption"--(52),
       "The Vice," "Metre and Rhetoric," and the nature,
       characters, and performance of the morality plays.

       Chap. III is on "Tudor Masques, Pageants, and
       Entertainments" (78-84). Chap. IV--"Sacred Drama"
       (85-101)--deals with academic, sacred, and
       prodigal son plays. Chap. V is on "Comedy, *c.*
       1540-*c.* 1584" (102-25). Chap. VI discusses
       "Tragedy, *c.* 1540-*c.* 1584" (126-50). Chap. VII
       concludes with "The Theatre before 1585" (151-72).
       With a chronological table of public and private
       events; English and Scottish texts; Greek, Latin,

and Continental vernaculars. With bibliography
and index.

Rev. *Drama* (Spring 1969): 54.
    VQR 45 (Spring 1969): R54.
    Choice 6 (May 1969): 346.
    SoAQ 68 (Summer 1969): 441.
    TLS (July 3, 1969): 725.
    PBSA 64 (Apr. 1970): 256.
    RES, n.s. 21 (May 1970): 197.

1706. Wilson, Katharina. "Hagiographic (Dis)play:
Chaucer's 'The Miller's Tale.'" In *Auctor Ludens:
Essays on Play in Literature*, 37-45. Philadelphia
and Amsterdam: John Benjamins Publishing Co.,
1986. Cultura Ludens: Imitation and Play in
Western Culture. Gen. eds. Giuseppe Mazzotta and
Mihai Spariosu.

Looks at "The rise of miracle plays" (37), and
play elements in Chaucer's tale, especially with
respect to the tale as hagiographic play.

1707. Wilson, Richard Middlewood. *Early Middle English
Literature*. 3rd ed. London: Methuen and Co.,
1968. 309 pp.

Contains a chapter on the drama (chap. 12, 275-
87), with the usual old information on liturgical
origins, contents of the cycles, differences
between the cycles, etc.

Rev. *Choice* 6 (Feb. 1970): 1756.

1708. ---. *The Lost Literature of Medieval England*. New
York: Philosophical Library, 1952. 2nd ed. rev.
New York: Barnes & Noble, 1970. xiv, 272 pp.

Chap. XI is on drama (215-40). Discusses plays
known only by reference, both in English and in
Latin. Looks at the twelfth-century liturgical
origins.

Rev. (of 1970 ed.)
    Choice 6 (Dec. 1969): 1402.
    TLS (Sept. 25, 1970): 1078.
    RES, n.s. 22 (Aug. 1971): 322.
    Choice 8 (Sept. 1971): 837.
    MLR 66 (Oct. 1971): 849.

1709. Wimsatt, James I. *Allegory and Mirror: Tradition and
Structure in Middle English Literature*. New York:
Pegasus, 1970. 224 pp.

Aims to define the two modes (allegory and mirror). Discusses them with respect to several works, including *Everyman* (46-49).

Rev. *LJ* 95 (Aug. 1970): 2685.
Choice 7 (Dec. 1970): 1378.

1710. Winser, Leigh. "*Magnyfycence* and the Characters of *Sottie*." *SCJ* 12.3 (Fall 1981): 85-94.

Examines "The French origin of Skelton's knaves" (85). Aims to show the influence on Skelton of "the Sottie--a French dramatic form that . . . provided him with at least three different models or [sic] his scheming knaves" (85).

1711. Witte, Stephen Paul. "The Typological Tradition and *Beowulf*, the York cycle, and Milton's Nativity Ode." Ph.D. diss., Oklahoma State U., 1977.

1712. Woehlk, Heinz D. "The Staging of *Wisdom*." Ph.D. diss., U. of Colorado, Boulder, 1977.

1713. Wolff, Annastatia Maria. "Dynamics of Drama in the Old Testament Plays of the English Cycles." Ph.D. diss., U. of Oregon, 1973.

1714. Woolf, Rosemary. *The English Mystery Plays*. Berkeley and Los Angeles: U. of California Press, 1972. 437 pp. Chap. IX rpt. in *Medieval English Drama* . . ., 89-95. Ed. by Peter Happé (see entry # 684 above).

(One of the most cited and influential books on medieval English drama in the past 20 years.) Chap. I covers Latin Liturgical Drama. Chap. II on Twelfth-Century Knowledge of Plays and Acting. Chap. III deals with Drama in the Twelfth Century. Chap. IV looks at The Development of the Cycle form. Chap. V explains Attitudes to Drama and Dramatic Theory. Chap. VI discusses Plays of the Fall. Chap. VII considers Types and Prophecies of the Redemption. Chap. VIII and IX are on Nativity Plays. Chap. X discusses The Life of Christ between the Nativity and the Passion. Chap. XI is on The Passion. Chap. XII covers Triumphs and Eschatological Plays. Chap. XIII is a Conclusion. Chap. XIV deals with The Decline of the Plays. With appendixes on The Shrewsbury Fragments, The Plays of the Burial and Resurrection, and French Influence on the Mystery Plays. With notes, bibliography, and index. Focuses primarily on the four cycles. Essentially little on the moralities or other forms of dramatic entertainment.

Rev. *LJ* 97 (Sept. 1, 1972): 2735.
Choice 10 (June 1973): 625.
VQR 49 (Autumn 1973): R152.
WHR 27 (Autumn 1973): 415.
Barbara Raw, *N&Q*, n.s. 29.9 (218) (Sept. 1973): 344-45.
Neville Denny, *MedAe* 43.1 (1974): 84-87.
RES, n.s. 25 (Feb. 1974): 70.
Stanley J. Kahrl, *ELN* 11.3 (Mar. 1974): 210-13.
MP 71 (May 1974): 409.
MLR 69 (July 1974): 614.

1715. ---. "The Influence of the Mystery Plays upon the Popular Tragedies of the 1560's." *RenD*, n.s. 6 (1973): 89-105.

Says that the tragedies of the 1560s contained elements from Senecan and native dramatic traditions, which created "plays more vigorous but also more crude than the formal imitations of Seneca" (89). Shows that the main trait of native dramatic tradition that was used was personification, especially the kind of the morality plays which presented good and evil, virtue and vice. Looks at *Apius and Virginia, Cambises,* and *Horestes,* and also glances at the mystery plays, from which certain "striking effects" (105) are taken for use in the later tragedies.

1716. ---. "Later Poetry: The Popular Tradition." In *History of Literature in the English Language,* Vol. 1, The Middle Ages, 263-311. Ed. by W.F. Bolton. London: Barrie and Jenkins in Association with Sphere Books, 1970.

Discusses "romances, lyrics, and mystery and morality plays . . . the literature of the unlearned of all classes of society" (263). Treats drama relatively briefly (299-309). Considers the mystery plays' "devotional purpose" (299), staging, playwrights, audience, actors; the cycles, themes, plots, relation to lyrics, etc. Looks also at moralities (304-09). With bibliography.

1717. Worsley, Alice Feeney. "Three Medieval Studies: An Index of the Visual Content of 5000 Medieval Manuscript Illuminations in the Bodleian Library; A Glossary to the *Towneley Plays;* A Study of the Staging Requirements of the *Towneley Plays* in Relation to Three Modes of Performance, to Evidence Concerning Other Cycle Plays, and to

Medieval Manuscript Illuminations." Ph.D. diss.,
U. of California, Santa Cruz, 1973.

1718. Wortham, C.J. "*Everyman* and the Reformation."
Parergon 29 (Apr. 1981): 23-31.

Looks to history to discuss "the religious and
political significance of the changes made in the
process of translation" (23) from Dutch to
English.

1719. Wortham, Christopher John. "An Existentialist
Approach to *Everyman*." *AULLA* 19 (1978): 333-40.

1720. Wright, A.P.M., ed. *A History of the County of
Cambridge and the Isle of Ely*. Vol. VI. The
Victoria History of the Counties of England. The
University of London: for the Institute of
Historical Research by Oxford U. Press, 1978.

Contains hundreds of citations from historical
documents. Mentions "visiting players" (98) at
Pembroke College. Other references to fairs,
guilds, etc. throughout the volume.

For other historical data on medieval drama, see
also the other volumes in this series; e.g.:

A History of the County of Essex, vol. VIII, ed.
by W.R. Powell, 1978. *A History of the County of
Oxford*, vol. V, ed. by Alan Crossley, 1979. *A
History of the County of Somerset*, vol IV, ed. by
R.W. Dunning, 1978.

1721. Wright, Jackie. [Untitled review.] *RORD* 23 (1980):
89-90.

Reviews performances of *A Mery Play Betwene Johan
Johan the Husbande, Tib his Wife, and Sir Johan
the Preest* and *Moses and Pharaoh* (York Play of the
Hosiers), June 6-30, 1980, West End of York
Minster, in the Dean's Park, York, by The Lords of
Misrule, Centre for Medieval Studies, University
of York.

1722. Wright, Michael J. "*Ludus Coventriae* Passion Play I:
Action and Interpretation." *NM* 86.1 (1985): 70-
77.

Shows that the play works allegorically toward
explicitness and historically, dramatizing the
conspiracy against Jesus. Says that the two modes
interact and play off one another to reveal the

historical yet timeless significance of Jesus'
actions.

1723.	Wright, R.A. "Mediaeval Theatre in East Anglia." M.
Litt. thesis, U. of Bristol, 1971.

1724.	Wright, Robert. "Community Theatre in Late Medieval
East Anglia." *ThN* 28.1 (1974): 24-39.

Examines source materials, primarily in the Great
Dunmow Churchwardens' Book and in other sources
from East Anglia, which record "dramatic or semi-
dramatic events" (24). Summarizes the Dunmow
material and emphasizes items which are evidence
of play performance. With two maps.

1725.	---. "The Medieval Theatre in Some Essex Towns:
Dunmow, Chelmsford, Maldon, Heybridge, and
Braintree." *EJ* 9.4 (Winter 1974-75): 110-21.

Concentrates mostly on Corpus Christi drama, but
also looks at Lord of Misrule, Plough, Boy Bishop,
and other forms of plays. Draws from newly
consulted primary documents to depict "a more
complete picture of rural theatre in late medieval
times" (111). Examines the Dunmow Churchwardens'
Book for 1526-1547. Tries to reconstruct what
theatrical performances were like from the
records.

1726.	---. "Parnell and Burles." *EAM* 33 (Apr. 1974): 324-
26.

Discusses theatrical activity in Dunmow--
activities such as "The boy Bishop, the Lord of
Misrule, the Plough Day, May Day, *Corpus Christi*
and other feast days" (324). Finds evidence in
the account book of the churchwarden of Great
Dunmow St. Mary's. Points to dramatic activity in
King's Lynn, Snettisham, Heybridge, Rayleigh,
Yarmouth, Walberswick, Bassingborne, Bishop's
Stortford, Bungay, Norwich, Bury St. Edmunds,
Thetford, Ipswich, and Chelmsford. Discusses
Burles and Parnell, two renowned and accomplished
performers.

1727.	Wright, Stephen K. "The Durham Play of Mary and the
Poor Knight: Sources and Analogues of a Lost
English Miracle Play." *CompD* 17.3 (Fall 1983):
254-65.

Posits the theory that "the English Marian miracle
play is an all but vanished species" (254), the
existence of which can only be surmised. Looks

for such a play in all available evidence,
including the "Durham Prologue," the 36 lines of
which "constitute . . . the complete spoken
prologue to a Marian miracle play" (255). Reviews
scholarship. Says that the lost play may come
from the legend "The Knight Who Denied Christ but
Not the Virgin" in the *Dialogus Miraculorum*
(compiled c. 1223 by Caesarius of Heisterbach);
details of action and dialogue in both correspond.
Speculates on the staging, scope, and complexity
of the lost play.

1728.   ---.   "'The Historie of King Edward the Fourth': A
Chronicle Play on the Coventry Pageant Wagons."
M&RD 3 (1986): 69-81.

Claims that "the Coventry cycle was the last to
disappear" (69), and that the citizens of that
town were reluctant to drop such outdoor
entertainment. Discusses the 1584 performance on
pageant wagons of the "Destruction of Jerusalem"
by John Smith (1563-1616), and another performance
of the same or another play in 1591. Also
discusses the Hock Tuesday play the "Conquest of
the Danes," and the "Edward the Fourth" play, the
latter played "at least once before 1591" (72).
Tries to reconstruct the contents of the play.
Compares what we know of it to Thomas Heywood's
King Henry the Fourth. Concludes that the
Coventry play is "a final attempt to preserve the
staging practices of the Corpus Christi cycles"
(78), and that the attempt was unsuccessful.

xxxx.   Wyatt, Diana. See "Thoughts on 'Transvestitism' by
Divers Hands"; Happé, et al. (entry # 689 above).

1729.   ---.   "The Pageant Waggon: Beverley." *MET* 1.2 (Dec.
1979): 55-60.

Examines primary Beverley records which reveal
dramatic activity, specifically a pageant wagon.
Considers wheels, movement of wagons, curtains,
decorations, floats, and materials. Highly
speculative.

1730.   ---.   "Two Yorkshire Fragments: Perhaps Dramatic?"
REEDN 3.1 (1978): 17-21.

Examines and quotes two ms fragments which could
be from an early fifteenth-century play--from an
area known for its dramatic productions but from
which no known text survives (the Hull/Beverley
area). Points out words which have parallels in
the York and Towneley Harrowing of Hell plays.

Discusses the date and the poetic nature of the fragments. Speculates on their relationship and content. Asks for help in identification.

1731. ---, and Pamela King. "Chanticleer and the Fox/The Shepherds' Play." *MET* 6.2 (Dec. 1984): 168-72.

Reports on performances at Westfield College, November 22-24, 1984, by The Medieval Players on Tour. Discusses a dramatized version of "The Nun's Priest's Tale" and a translation of the Wakefield *Second Shepherds' Play*.

1732. Yamakawa, Tamaaki. "The Ideal Woman in Henry Medwall's *Fulgens and Lucrece.*" *ELR* (Kyoto) 14 (Dec. 1970): 45-59. In Japanese.

Aims to show the new image of woman created in the new era, eighty years before Shakespeare. Points out the revolutionary nature of the plot in which a young girl insists on the freedom of choice in selecting a mate. Shows that the meaning of the play lies in the fact that the play was written, audience in mind, to depict a new, free woman. Says the play is "anti-noble" and satirical.

1733. ---. "The Plowman in *Of Gentylnes and Nobylyte* (1)." *ELR* (Kyoto) 19 (Dec. 1975): 31-40. In Japanese. (See next entry.)

Speculates on who authored the play, John Rastell, who appears in the colophon, or John Heywood, who is depicted on the lining paper. Also says the author may have been Thomas More, or possibly all three. Focuses on the plot and the Plowman's satire and cynicism. Claims that the concluding words of the play are definitely Rastell's.

1734. ---. "The Plowman in *Of Gentylnes and Nobylyte* (2)." *ELR* (Kyoto) 21 (Dec. 1977): 1-15. In Japanese. (See previous entry.)

Says that three characters of the play clearly suggest the writer's critical position against the class structure of the society. Points out that the playwright's approval of diligence and hatred of idleness marks him as one sympathetic to More's *Utopia*. Points out the similarities between this work and others by Heywood, technically and thematically. But says also that these traits are not Heywood's alone. Does not agree with Bevington that the work is clearly by Rastell. Analyzes Plowman's role in the play as master of

ceremony, especially with relation to his role as
becoming Vice.

1735. Yamomoto, Hiroshi. "Igirisu Chusei Engeki no
Fukkatsu Joen." ["Re-creation of Performances of
English Medieval Drama."] *Sophia* 30 (1981): 336-
42. In Japanese.

Concerns the re-creation of performances of the
plays in the twentieth century. Claims there were
only nine recorded performances until the
beginning of World War I. Of these nine, Monck
was responsible for five. Points out the drastic
change in this situation since World War II, with
performances by church groups, at local festivals,
and in schools. Mentions that most of the
performances are done by amateurs, but a few were
done by professionals. Discusses the most
commonly performed and most important of the
plays, "The Nativity," with performances at the
National Theatre. Discusses the modernized,
abridged version, adapted to a modern audience.

1736. York Cycle. Toronto: U. of Toronto, 1978.

C. a 12-hour-long videotape of the complete cycle
(47 plays). [Cited in *REEDN* 3.1 (1978): 21. Also
listed in their brochure "The Medieval Drama Video
Collection, Presented by University of Toronto
Media Centre and the Poculi Ludique Societas."
The brochure shows each play individually, with
running times and purchase and rental figures.]

[N.B. This is one of a number of videotapes
produced at the U. of Toronto. The 47 plays are
available individually on separate cassettes.
Other plays offered from the same source are: *The
York Cycle in the Fifteenth Century; The Castle of
Perseverance:* A Perspective (abbreviated version
with analysis); *Castle of Perseverance* (full-
length version); *Coronation of Henry V*
(abbreviated version); *The Killing of Abel; Robin
Hood and the Friar; The Toronto Passion Play* (N-
Town version); *The Origins of Liturgical Drama.*
Also scheduled for the series are *The Staging of
Medieval English Drama* and a performance of the
Second Shepherds' Play.]

1737. Young, Abigail Ann. "Plays and Players: The Latin
Terms for Performance." *REEDN* 9.2 (1984): 56-62.

Presents research to give scholars of early drama
a useful lexicon of dramatic terms with
translations and discussions.

1738.   ---.   "Plays and Players: The Latin Terms for
        Performance, (part ii)."   *REEDN* 10.1 (1985): 9-16.

        Continues lexicon from previous article.

1739.   Young, Alan R.   *The English Prodigal Son Plays: A
        Theatrical Fashion of the Sixteenth and
        Seventeenth Centuries.*   Salzburg: Institut für
        Anglistik und Amerikanistik, U. of Salzburg, 1979.
        Salzburg Studies in English Literature, Jacobean
        Drama Studies 89.   Ed. by Dr. James Hogg.   345 pp.

        Has chapters on "The Parable and its
        Interpretation" (Chap. I, 1-54); "The Christian
        Terence and the Moralities" (Chap. II, 55-102);
        "Later School Plays" (Chap. III, 103-40); and
        later drama.   Contains much on *Acolastus* by John
        Palsgrave, as well as on *Mankind, The Castle of
        Perseverance, Wisdom,* and other late medieval
        English plays (see especially chap. II).

        Rev. *SevCN* 39 (Summer 1981): 54.

1740.   Young, M. James.   "The Unity of the English Mystery
        Cycles."   *QJS* 58.3 (Oct. 1972): 327-37.

        Complains about scholars who present and critique
        individual plays out of the context of their
        cycles.   Says that the plays' scope creates unity
        within each cycle.   Looks at "the unifying nature
        of the cycles" (328) from three perspectives:
        their scope, the characterization, and "the
        'depth' or intensity of the central action" (328).
        Claims that all of the cycles are "unified in
        conception and execution" (337).

1741.   Zapatka, Francis E.   "'East Coker, IV' and *Everyman.*"
        ANQ 18.1 (Sept. 1979): 7-9.

        Sees *Everyman* as the source for "the wounded
        surgeon" (7) reference in T.S. Eliot's poem.
        Cites lines 744-46 of the play.

1742.   Zarrilli, Phillip.   "From Destruction to
        Consecration: Covenant in the Chester *Noah* Play."
        ThJ 31.2 (May 1979): 198-209.

        Reviews the work of other critics on the relation
        between Corpus Christi plays and the religious
        feast and on the selection of the plays in the
        cycles.   Looks at the mythic and dramatic action
        in the Chester cycle to seek "out the deeper
        significance of interplay between the sacred
        history enacted and the dramatic action itself"

(198), and at the "consecration of the covenant of grace" (209) in the *Noah* play.

1743. Zimbardo, Rose A. "Comic Mockery of the Sacred: *The Frogs* and *The Second Shepherds' Play*." *ETJ* 30.3 (Oct. 1978): 398-406.

Claims that mockery of the sacred allows an audience to "transcend the realm of the seemingly sacred to glimpse the truly sacred" (398). Calls the two plays "supreme renderings of the comic perspective" (398). Says that comic mockery of the sacred is aimed at man, not at God. Concludes that "the vision of comedy is . . . redemptive" (406).

1744. ---. "A Generic Approach to the First and Second Shepherds' Plays of the Wakefield Mystery Cycle." *FCS* 13 (1988): 79-90.

Appendixes

I. The Cycle Plays

    A. Chester Cycle

    B. N-Town Cycle

    C. Wakefield Cycle

    D. York Cycle

II. Plays by Known Authors and Anonymous plays

    A. By Title

    B. By Author

III. Records of Early English Drama: Projected
     Volumes

Appendix I

The Cycle Plays

Though authorities tend to vary somewhat on the ordering of
these plays and the ways they designate the titles, the
following lists present the full content of the four cycles.
(Some variant title designations are given in parentheses.)

A. Chester Cycle

1. Fall of Lucifer
2. Creation and Fall; Death of Abel
3. Noah's Flood (Deluge)
4. Lot; Abraham and Isaac (Sacrifice of Isaac; Histories
        of Lot and Abraham)
5. Balaam and his Ass (Balaam and Balak [Balaak])
6. Salutation and Nativity
7. Shepherds (Adoration of the Shepherds)
8. Coming of the Three Kings (Adoration of the Magi)
9. Offering; Return of the Three Kings (Magi's Oblation)
10. Slaughter of the Innocents
11. Purification
12. Temptation; Woman Taken in Adultery (Christ; The
        Adulteress; Chelidonius)
13. Lazarus [or Christ's Visit to Simon the Leper]
14. Christ's Entry into Jerusalem
15. Betrayal of Christ
16. Passion
17. Crucifixion
18. Harrowing of Hell (Christ's Descent into Hell)
19. Resurrection
20. Pilgrims of Emmaus (Christ Appears to Two Disciples)
21. Ascension
22. Descent of the Holy Spirit (Sending [Emission] of the
        Holy Ghost)
23. Ezechiel
24. Antichrist
25. Judgment (Doomsday; The Last Judgment)

B. N-Town Cycle
[Ludus Coventriae; Hegge Plays]

1. Creation of Heaven and the Angels; Fall of Lucifer
2. Creation of the World and Man; Fall of Man
3. Cain and Abel

451

C. Wakefield Cycle
[Towneley Cycle]

1. Creation
2. Murder of Abel (Mactacio Abel)
3. Noah and His Sons (Noah and the Ark; Processus Noe cum Filiis)
4. Abraham and Isaac
5. Isaac
6. Jacob
7. Prophets
8. Pharaoh
9. Caesar Augustus
10. Annunciation
11. Salutation of Elizabeth
12. First Shepherds' Play (Prima Pastorum)
13. Second Shepherds' Play (Secunda Pastorum)
14. Offering of the Magi
15. Flight of Joseph and Mary into Egypt
16. Herod the Great (Magnus Herodes)
17. Purification of Mary
18. Pageant [Play] of the Doctors
19. John the Baptist
20. Conspiracy
21. Buffeting (Coliphizacio)
22. Scourging
23. Crucifixion
24. Talents
25. Harrowing of Hell (The Deliverance of Souls)
26. Resurrection
27. Pilgrims to Emmaus
28. Thomas of India
29. Ascension (of the Lord)
30. Judgment
31. Lazarus [sometimes placed after John the Baptist]
32. Hanging of Judas [sometimes placed after the Scourging]

D. York Cycle

1. Creation; Fall of Lucifer
2. Creation, to the Fifth Day
3. Creation of Adam and Eve
4. Adam and Eve in Eden
5. Fall of Man (Man's Disobedience and Fall)
6. Expulsion from Eden (Adam and Eve Driven from Eden)
7. Sacrifice of Cain and Abel (Sacrificium Cayme and Abell)
8. Building of the Ark
9. Noah and His Wife; The Flood (and Its Waning)
10. Abraham and Isaac (Abraham's Sacrifice of Isaac)
11. Departure of the Israelites from Egypt; Ten Plagues; Crossing of the Red Sea

12. Annunciation and Visitation (Visit of Elizabeth to
        Mary)
13. Joseph's Trouble about Mary
14. Journey to Bethlehem; Birth of Jesus
15. Shepherds (The Angels and the Shepherds)
16. Coming of the Three Kings to Herod
17. Coming of the Kings; Adoration
18. Flight into Egypt
19. Slaughter of the Innocents
20. Christ with the Doctors (in the Temple)
21. Baptism of Jesus
22. Temptation
23. Transfiguration
24. Woman Taken in Adultery; Lazarus
25. Christ's Entry into Jerusalem
26. Conspiracy
27. Last Supper
28. Agony and Betrayal
29. Peter's Denial; Jesus Before Caiaphas
30. Dream of Pilate's Wife; Jesus before Pilate
31. Trial before Herod
32. Second Accusation before Pilate; Remorse of Judas;
        Purchase of the Field of Blood
33. Second Trial before Pilate (and The Judgment of Jesus)
34. Christ Led to Calvary
35. Crucifixion (Crucifixio Christi)
36. Mortification of Christ (Mortificacio Christi); Burial
37. Harrowing of Hell
38. Resurrection (and The Flight of the Jews)
39. Christ's Appearance to Mary Magdalene
40. Travellers to Emmaus
41. Purification of Mary; Simeon and Anna
42. Incredulity of Thomas
43. Ascension
44. Descent of the Holy Spirit
45. Death of Mary
46. Appearance of Mary to Thomas
47. Assumption and Coronation of the Virgin
48. Judgment

Appendix II

Plays by Known Authors
and Anonymous Plays

Part A: By Titles

The following appendix lists plays considered throughout the annotated entries of the main bibliography. That is, works other than mysteries and moralities and related liturgical drama generally discussed in the canon of medieval English drama are presented here.

I am indebted to D. Jerry White (entry # 1682) and many others for the citations in this appendix. The plays here and many others are treated at some length in *A Literary History of England*, 2nd ed. Ed. by Albert C. Baugh (Englewood Cliffs, NJ: Prentice-Hall, 1948). Other valuable sources are Glynne Wickham's *Early English Stages . . .* (entry # 1688) and the Stratman bibliography (entry # 1551).

These works are generally transitional between the morality and mystery plays of the middle ages and the drama of the renaissance. Dates offered here are approximate-- there is a good deal of disagreement among sources. Sometimes authors cite dates of composition, sometimes of publication, sometimes of performance; and most often the sources do not designate which of these (or some other date) is indicated. When there is a wide divergence in the dates given by the sources, the date I quote is accompanied by a question mark. There is also some confusion as to attribution (indicated by a question mark).

I have included--in brackets--brief citations to sources for many of the entries below. The attempt has not been to be definitive, but to offer a starting point for scholarship. Citations to Salgado and Southern refer to entries # 1427 and # 1495 respectively in the bibliography. Many of the plays listed here are treated by works in the bibliography; see the index by title.

Abraham's Sacrifice (1575); Arthur Golding, trans. (from the
        French play by Theodore Beza) [Malcolm W.
        Wallace, ed., *A Tragedie of Abrahams Sacrifice*
        . . . . Toronto: U. of Toronto Library, 1906. U.
        of Toronto Studies: Philological Series, extra
        vol.]

Absolom (1540); Thomas Watson [John Hazel Smith, ed.
    "Thomas Watson's *Absolom:* An Edition . . . ."
    Ph.D. diss., U. of Illinois, 1958.]

Acolastus (1540); John Palsgrave [P.L. Carver, ed. *The
    Comedy of Acolastus.* London: Oxford U. Press,
    1937. E.E.T.S., o.s. 202.]

Aesop's Crow (1552); lost play [Lily B. Campbell, "The Lost
    Play of Aesop's Crow." *MLN* 49 (Nov. 1934): 454-
    57.]

Albion Knight (c. 1537) [W.W. Greg, ed. Albion Knight: *A
    Fragment of a Morality Printed by T. Colwell, c.
    1566.* Malone Society Collections 1, part 3
    (1909): 229-42.]

Alcestis (1543) [P. Sharratt and P.G. Walsh, eds. *The
    Tragedies of Buchanan.* Edinburgh: Scottish
    Academic Press, 1983.]

All For Money (1577? or 1578?); Thomas Lupton [J.O.
    Halliwell. *Literature of the Sixteenth and
    Seventeenth Centuries Illustrated.* London: 1851.
    See also Southern.]

Ap[p]ius and Virginia (c. 1564); R.B. (Richard Bower)
    [Ronald B. McKerrow and W.W. Greg, eds. Apius and
    Virginia, *1575.* London: Malone Society, 1911.
    See also Southern.]

Archipropheta (1547); Nicholas Grimald [LeRoy Merrill. *The
    Life and Poems of Nicholas Grimald.* New Haven:
    Yale U. Press, 1925. Yale Studies in English 69.]

Arraignment of Paris (c. 1581-83); George Peele

Baptistes sive Calumnia (1541); George Buchanan [See
    citation at *Alcestis.*]

Battle of Alcazar (1589?); George Peele

Brief Comedy or Interlude Concerning the Temptation of Our
    Lord; see Temptation of Our Lord

Brief Comedy or Interlude of John the Baptist's Preaching in
    the Wilderness (see John Baptist's Preaching in
    the Wilderness)

Bugbears (1564); John Jeffere [James D. Clark, ed. The
    Bugbears: *A Modernized Edition.* New York:
    Garland, 1979. Renaissance Drama: A Collection of
    Critical Editions.]

Calisto and Melebea (also called Celestina, The Beauty and
     Good Properties of Women) (c. 1525-27); John
     Rastell (?) [Albert J. Gerlitz, comp. "Recent
     Studies in John Rastell." See # 619 above. See
     also Southern.]

Cambises (c. 1561); Thomas Preston [Robert Carl Johnson,
     ed. "Thomas Preston's *Cambises:* A Critical
     Edition." Ph.D. diss., U. of Illinois, 1964.
     Published in Elizabethan Studies 23. Salzburg:
     Institut für englische Sprache und Literatur,
     Universität Salzburg, 1975. See also Salgado and
     Southern.]

Celestina, the Beauty and Good Properties of Women (see
     Calisto and Melebea)

Chief Promises of God (see God's Promises)

Christ's Resurrection (1545); John Bale [See citation at
     Temptation of Our Lord.]

Christus Redivivus (1540); Nicholas Grimald [Ruth H.
     Blackburn, "Nicholas Grimald's *Christus Redivivus:*
     A Protestant Resurrection Play." *ELN* 5 (June
     1968): 247-50.]

Christus Triumphans (1556); John Foxe [Warren W. Wooden,
     "Recent Studies in Foxe." *ELR* 11 (Spring 1981):
     222-32. See also Wooden, *John Foxe.* Boston:
     Twayne: 1983. Twayne English Author Series, 345.]

Clyomon and Clamydes (c. 1570-75); Robert Greene (?) or
     George Peele (?) [Betty J. Littleton, ed.
     Clyomon and Clamydes: *A Critical Edition.* The
     Hague and Paris: Mouton, 1968. Studies in English
     Literature, 35.]

Cobbler's Prophecy (1580-94?); Robert Wilson [Irene Rose
     Mann, "The Text of the Plays of Robert Wilson."
     Ph.D. diss., U. of Virginia, 1942. See also
     H.S.D. Mithal, "The Two-Wilsons Controversy."
     N&Q, n.s. 6 (1959): 106-09.]

Comedy Concerning Three Laws (see Three Laws)

Common Conditions (c. 1576) [C.F. Tucker Brooke, ed.
     Common Conditions. New Haven: Yale U. Press,
     1915. Elizabethan Club Reprints, no. 1. See also
     David M. Bevington, *From Mankind to Marlowe.*
     Cambridge: Harvard U. Press, 1962. See also
     Southern.]

Conflict of Conscience (1575-81); Nathaniel Wood[es]
        [Herbert Davis and F.P. Wilson, eds. *The Conflict
        of Conscience, 1581.* Oxford: Malone Society,
        1952. See also Celesta Wine, "Nathaniel Wood's
        Conflict of Conscience." *PMLA* 50 (Sept. 1935):
        661-78. See also Southern.]

Contention between Liberality and Prodigality (see
        Prodigality)

Courage, Kindness, Cleanness (1539); John Redford   [See
        citation at Wit and Science.]

Cradle of Security   [David M. Bevington. *From Mankind to
        Marlowe.* Cambridge: Harvard U. Press, 1962.]

Cruel Debtor (1565); William Wager   [Mark Eccles, "William
        Wager and His Plays." *ELN* 18 (June 1981): 258-
        62.]

D, G, and T[om] (1539); John Redford   [See citation at Wit
        and Science.]

Damon and Pithias (1565 or 1566); Richard Edwards
        [Leicester Bradner. *Life and Poems of Richard
        Edwards.* New Haven: Yale U. Press, 1927. Yale
        Studies in English, 74. See also Southern.]

Darius, King (see King Darius)

Disobedience, Temperance, and Humility; see Temperance and
        Humility

Disobedient Child (c. 1560); Thomas Ingelend [James Orchard
        Halliwell(-Phillipps), ed. *The Interlude of the
        Disobedient Child.* London: Richards, 1848. Percy
        Society Publications, 75. See also Southern,
        Staging . . ., entry # 1495 above. See also
        Southern.]

Enough is as Good as a Feast (c. 1564); William Wager   [See
        citation at Cruel Debtor. See also Salgado and
        Southern.]

Ezekias (1539); lost play by Nicholas Udall   [William L.
        Edgerton. *Nicholas Udall.* New York: Twayne,
        1965. Twayne English Author Series, 30.]

Ferrex and Porrex (1562); Thomas Norton and Thomas Sackville
        [See citation at Gorboduc.]

Four Cardinal Virtues (1542?); only last 4 leaves survive
        [W.W. Greg, ed. "*The Four Cardinal Virtues:* A
        Fragment of a Morality Play Printed by W.

Middleton between 1541 and 1547." *Malone Society Collections* 4 (1956): 41-54. See also Southern.]

Four Elements (c. 1517-25); John Rastell [See citation at Calisto and Melebea. See also Salgado and Southern.]

Four Ps (1544?); John Heywood [Robert Carl Johnson. *John Heywood*. New York: Twayne, 1970. Twayne English Author Series, 92. Also see Edmund Milton Hayes, "John Heywood and the Play within the Play." Ph.D. diss., U. of Massachusetts, 1972. See also Salgado.]

Free Will (1568); Henry Cheke [Leicester Bradner, "Henry Cheke's *Freewyl*." *PMLA* 49 (Dec. 1934): 1036-40.]

Fulgens and Lucres [Lucrece] (1497); Henry Medwall [M.E. Moeslein, ed. *The Plays of Henry Medwall: A Critical Edition*. New York: Garland, 1981. Renaissance Drama: A Collection of Critical Editions. See also Salgado and Southern, and also Wickham, *English Moral Interludes*, entry # 86 above.]

Gammer Gurton's Needle (c. 1553); William Stevenson (?) or John Bridges (?) [Henry Bradley, ed. *Gammer Gurton's Nedle* [sic]. In *Representative English Comedies*, I, 195-261. Ed. by Charles Mills Gayley. Vol. I, *From the Beginnings to Shakespeare*. New York: Macmillan, 1903. See also Salgado and Southern.]

Gentleness and Nobility (c. 1527); John Rastell (?) or John Heywood (?) [See citation at Calisto and Melebea. See also David M. Bevington. *From Mankind to Marlowe*. Cambridge: Harvard U. Press, 1962, 42-43. See also Salgado and Southern.]

Gismond of Salerne (1566-67); Robert Wilmot (also cited as by Robert Stafford, Henry Noel, G.N., Christopher Hatton, and Robert Wilmot) [Iriye Kyoko, "A Stylistic Comparison of *Gismond of Salerne* and *Tancred and Gismund*." *ShakStud* 4 (1965-66): 1-35. See also John Murray, "*Tancred and Gismond*" [sic] *RES* 14 (Oct. 1938): 385-95. See also Southern.]

Glass of Government (1575); George Gascoigne [Richard Geldart Barlow, ed. "The Complete Works of George Gascoigne (Volumes I-III)." Ph.D. diss., U. of Michigan, 1976. See also Ronald C. Johnson. *George Gascoigne*. New York: Twayne, 1972. Twayne English Author Series, 133. Also see Samuel A. Tannenbaum. *George Gascoigne: A Concise*

Bibliography. New York: S.A. Tannenbaum, 1942.
Elizabethan Bibliographies, no. 26. With
supplement by Robert C. Johnson, ed. "George
Gascoigne: 1941-1966." In *Minor Elizabethans.*
London: Nether Press, 1968: 19-25. Elizabethan
Bibliographical Supplements.]

Godly Queen Hester (c. 1527) [W.W. Greg, ed. *A New
Enterlude of Godly Queene Hester.* Louvain: A
Uystpruyst, 1904. Materialen zur Kunde des
älteren englischen Dramas 5. See also Southern.]

Godly Susanna (see Virtuous and Godly Susanna)

God's Promises (1538); John Bale [See citation at
Temptation of Our Lord.]

Good Order (c. 1500); John Skelton (?); only last 131 lines
survive [See citations at Magnificence. See also
George L. Frost and Ray Nash, "*Good Order.* A
Morality Fragment." *SP* 41 (Oct. 1944): 483-91.]

Gorboduc (the second edition is called Ferrex and Porrex, c.
1570) [Normand Berlin. *Thomas Sackville.* New
York: Twayne, 1974. Twayne English Author Series,
165. See also Southern.]

Grissil, Patient and Meek (see Patient and Meek Grissel)

Herodes (1572); William Goldingham [Warren E. Tomlinson.
Der Herodes-Charakter im englischen Drama.
Leipzig: Mayer & Müller, 1934.]

Hester, Godly Queen (see Godly Queen Hester)

Hickscorner (or Hick-Scorner; Hyckescorner) (c. 1510) [W.W.
Greg, "Notes on Some Early Plays," *Library* 11
(1930-31): 44. Called by Baugh "perhaps the
earliest printed English play"--Baugh, p. 359,
note 4.]

Horestes (c. 1567); John Pickering [Daniel Seltzer, Arthur
Brown, and G.E. Bentley, eds. *The Interlude of
Vice (Horestes), 1567.* Oxford: Malone Society,
1962. See also Salgado and Southern.]

Impatient Poverty (c. 1560) [Leonard Tennenhouse. *Two
Tudor Interludes. Entry # 80 above. See also
Southern.]*

Interlude of Minds (1574) [Marshall Theodore Keys, ed. "An
Enterlude of Myndes: A Critical Edition." Ph.D.
diss., Vanderbilt U., 1976.]

Interlude of Vice (see Horestes)

Interlude of Youth (see Youth)

Iphigenia in Aulis (1558); Jane Lumley, trans. [Harold H.
        Child and W.W. Greg, eds. *"Iphigenia at Aulis,"*
        Translated by Lady Lumley. (London): Malone
        Society, 1909. See also Nancy Cotton, entry # 356
        above.]

Irish Knight (1577); lost play [W.F. McNeir, "A Possible
        Source for *The Irish Knight."* *MLN* 58 (May 1943):
        383-85.]

Jack Juggler (1555?); Nicholas Udall (?) [W.H. Williams,
        "The Date and Authorship of *Jacke Jugeler."* *MLR* 7
        (July 1912): 289-95. See also Salgado and
        Southern.]

Jacob and Esau (c. 1553-54); Nicholas Udall (?) [See
        citation at Ezekias. See also Southern.]

Jephthes (or Jephthah) (1544); John Christopherson [Francis
        Howard Fobes, ed. and trans. *Jephthah.* Intro. by
        Wilbur Owen Sypherd. Newark: U. of Delaware
        Press, 1928.]

Jephthes (or Jephthah) sive Votum (1542); George Buchanan
        [See citation at Alcestis.]

Jocasta (1566); George Gascoigne (with Francis Kinwelmarshe)
        [See citations at Glass of Government.]

Johan Johan (1533); John Heywood [See citations at Four Ps.
        See also Southern.]

Johan, King (see King Johan)

Johan (or John) the Evangelist (c. 1520) [W.W. Greg and
        Arundell Esdaile, eds. *The Interlude of Johan the*
        Evangelist. London: Malone Society, 1907.]

John Baptist's Preaching in the Wilderness (1538); John Bale
        [See citations at Temptation of Our Lord]

Juli (or July) and Julian (1550-70) [Giles Dawson and
        Arthur Brown, eds. *July and Julian.* Oxford:
        Malone Society, 1955.]

King Darius (c. 1565) [James O(rchard) Halliwell
        (-Phillipps), ed. *A Preaty New Enterlude . . .*
        the Story of King Daryus . . . . London: Thomas
        Richards, 1860. See also Southern.]

King Johan (1536 or 1538); John Bale   [See citations at
          Temptation of Our Lord]

Knack to Know a Knave (c. 1594)   [Paul Esmond Bennett, "*A
          Knack to Know a Knave. A Critical Edition.*" Ph.D.
          diss., U. of Pennsylvania, 1952. See also G.R.
          Proudfoot. *A Knack to Know a Knave.* London:
          Malone Society Reprints, 1963.]

Liber Apologeticus de Omni Statu Humanae (A Defense of Human
          Nature in Every State) (c. 1460)   [Enright-Clark,
          "*Liber Apologeticus . . . :* Edited with an
          Introduction and Notes." Ph.D. diss., Columbia
          U., 1954; published: entry # 35 above.]

Liberality and Prodigality (c. 1567-68); lost play, possibly
          revised as The Contention between Liberality and
          Prodigality (1601)   [W.W. Greg. *The Contention
          between Liberality and Prodigality, 1602.* Oxford:
          Malone Society, 1913. See also Southern.]

Life and Repentance of Mary Magdalene (see Mary Magdalene,
          Life and Repentance of)

Like Will to Like (c. 1568); Ulpian Fulwell   [John S.
          Farmer, ed. *The Dramatic Writings of Ulpian
          Fulwell.* London: Early English Drama Society,
          1906. See also Edward Clarence Wright, "The
          English Works of Ulpian Fulwell." Ph.D. diss., U.
          of Illinois, 1970. See also Southern.]

Lincolnshire Plough Play   [E.H. Rudkin, "Lincolnshire Plough
          Play." *Folk-lore* 50 (1939): 88-97.]

Longer Thou Livest (also Longer Thou Livest the More Fool
          Thou Art) (1559 or 1564); William Wager   [See
          citation at Cruel Debtor. See also Southern.]

Looking Glass for London and England (c. 1590); Thomas Lodge
          and Robert Greene   [C.R. Baskerville, "A Prompt
          Copy of *A Looking Glass for London and England.*"
          MP 30 (1932): 29-51. See also R.A. Law, "*A
          Looking Glass* and the Scriptures." *U. of Texas
          Studies in English* (1939): 31-47.]

Love, A Play of (see Play of Love)

Love Feigned and Unfeigned (c. 1550)   [W.W. Greg and Arundel
          Esdaile, eds., "*Love Feigned and Unfeigned:* A
          Fragmentary Morality." Malone Society Collections
          1, pt. 1 (1907): 16-25.]

Lucrece (c. 1530); a fragment of a morality [E.K. Chambers.
    The Medieval Stage, vol. 2. London: Oxford U.
    Press, 1903, p. 458.]

Lusty Juventus (c. 1550); Richard Wever [J.M. Nosworthy,
    Arthur Brown, and G.R. Proudfoot, eds. *Lusty
    Juventus*. Oxford: Malone Society, 1971. See also
    Helen Scarborough Thomas, ed. (entry # 81 above).
    See also Southern.]

Magnificence (c. 1515); John Skelton [John Scattergood.
    John Skelton: The Complete English Poems.
    Harmondsworth: Penguin, 1983. See also Southern.]

Maister Benet's Cristemasse Game (< 1483); Benedict Burgh
    [F.J. Furnivall, *N&Q*, ser. iv, I (1868): 455-56
    (16 May), and 531 (6 June).]

Marcus Geminus (1566); lost play [Leicester Bradner, "The
    Play of *Marcus Geminus* and Its Source." *MLR* 22
    (July 1927): 314-17. See also citation at Progne,
    below.]

Marriage between Wit and Wisdom (c. 1575-79); Francis
    Merbury [Wickham, entry # 86 above. Also see
    Lennam, # 51. And see Southern.]

Marriage of Wit and Science (see Wit and Science, The
    Marriage of)

Mary and the Poor Knight; lost Durham miracle play [See
    Wright, entry # 1727 above.]

Mary Magdalene, The Life and Repentance of (c. 1558); Lewis
    Wager [See Frederic Ives Carpenter, ed. "*The
    Life and Repentaunce of Marie Magdalene*": A
    Morality Play Printed from the Original Edition of
    1566-67. Chicago: U. of Chicago Press, 1902.
    Also see Southern.]

Medea (1543); George Buchanan [See citation at Alcestis.]

Meleager (c. 1572?-90?); a preliminary sketch for a play
    [Arthur Freeman, "The Argument of *Meleager*." *ELR*
    1 (Spring 1971): 122-31.]

Minds, An Interlude of (see Interlude of Minds)

Misogonus (c. 1565); Laurence Johnson (?) (Johnson was also
    called Laurentius Bariona) [G.L. Kittredge, "The
    Misogonus and Laurence Johnson." *JEGP* 3.3 (1901):
    335-41. See also Southern.]

Most Virtuous and Godly Susanna (see Virtuous and Godly
        Susanna)

Mundus et Infans (c. 1510)   [Henry Noble McCracken, "A
        Source of *Mundus et Infans.*"   *PMLA* 23.3 (1908):
        486-96.   See also Mallory Chamberlain, Jr., ed.
        "*The World and the Child,* Otherwise Called *Mundus
        et Infans:* A Critical Edition."   Ph.D. diss., U.
        of Tennessee, 1969.   See also Southern.]

Nature (1495?); Henry Medwall (?)   [See citations at Fulgens
        and Lucres.   Also see Southern.]

Nature of the Four Elements (see Four Elements)

New Custom (c. 1560)   [Leslie Mahin Oliver, "John Foxe and
        the Drama *New Custom.*"   *HLQ* 10 (Aug. 1947): 407-
        10.   See also David Bevington.   *From Mankind to
        Marlowe.*   Cambridge: Harvard U. Press, 1962, esp.
        pp. 54-55, 146-49.   And see Southern.]

Nice Wanton (c. 1550)   [Leonard Tennenhouse, entry # 80.
        Glynne Wickham, entry # 86.   See also Southern.]

Old Custom (1533); lost play   [Albert Feuillerat, "An
        Unknown Protestant Morality Play."   *MLR* 9 (Jan.
        1914): 94-96.   See also C.R. Baskervill, "On Two
        Old Plays."   *MP* 14 (May 1916): 16.]

Palamon and Arcite, I and II (1566); Richard Edwards   [See
        citation at Damon and Pithias.]

Pardoner and the Friar (1519); John Heywood   [See citations
        at Four Ps.   See also Salgado and Southern.]

Pater, Filius, et Uxor (see Prodigal Son)

Patient and Meek Grissel (c. 1566); John Phillip[s]
        [Charles Walter Roberts, ed.   "An Edition of John
        Phillip's *Commodye of Pacient and Meeke Grissill.*"
        Ph.D. diss., U. of Illinois, 1938.   See also
        Southern.]

Pedlar's Prophecy (c. 1561); Robert Wilson (?)   [W.W. Greg,
        ed. *The Pedlar's Prophecy, 1595.*   Oxford: Malone
        Society, 1914.   See also G.L. Kittredge, "The Date
        of *The Pedlers Prophecie.*"   *HSNPL* 16 (1934): 97-
        118.   See also Southern.]

Perseus and Andromeda (1574); lost play   [G.K. Hunter, "Sir
        Edmund Chambers and *Perseus and Andromeda* (1572)."
        N&Q 202 (Oct. 1957): 418.]

Play of Love (1533); John Heywood [See citations at Four
        Ps. Also see Salgado and Southern.]

Play of the Weather (c. 1527 or 1528); John Heywood [See
        citations at Four Ps. Also see Salgado and
        Southern.]

Play of Theano (see Theano, Play of)

Pride of Life (c. 1400); fragment, now lost [Norman Davis,
        entry # 29 above.]

Prodigal Son (Pater, Filius, et Uxor) (c. 1530); fragment on
        a single leaf [W.W. Greg, ed. "*The Prodigal Son:
        A Fragment of an Interlude Printed c. 1530,*"
        Malone Society Collections, 1, pt. 1 (1907): 27-
        30.]

Prodigality (see Liberality and Prodigality)

Progne (< 1566); lost play [W.Y. Durand, "*Palaemon and
        Arcyte, Progne, Marcus Geminus,* and the Theatre in
        Which They Were Acted, as Described by John
        Bereblock (1566)." *PMLA* 20.3 (1905): 502-28.]

Promos and Cassandra, I and II (1578); George Whetstone
        [George Wilfred Amos, ed. "A Critical Edition of
        George Whetstone's *Promos and Cassandra.*" Ph.D.
        diss., U. of Arkansas, 1968.]

Ralph Roister Doister (c. 1550 or 1553); Nicholas Udall
        [See citation at Ezekias. See also Salgado and
        Southern.]

Rare Triumphs of Love and Fortune (c. 1589) [W.W. Greg, ed.
        The Rare Triumphs of Love and Fortune. Oxford:
        Malone Society, 1931.]

Respublica (or Res Publica) (1553); Nicholas Udall [See
        citation at Ezekias. See also Southern.]

Resurrection of Our Lord (see Christ's Resurrection)

Richardus Tertius (1580); Thomas Legge [Robert J. Lordi,
        ed. *Thomas Legge's "Richardus Tertius": A
        Critical Edition with a Translation.* New York:
        Garland, 1979. Renaissance Drama: A Collection of
        Critical Editions.]

Sapientia Solomonis (1566); English adaptation of a Latin
        text [Elizabeth Rogers Payne, ed. "*Sapientia
        Solomonis,*" Acted before the Boys at Westminster
        School, January 17, 1565/6 . . . . New Haven:
        Yale U. Press, 1938.]

Satire of the Three Estates (Satyre of the Thrie Estaitis)
        (c. 1540); David Lindsay [Joanne S. Kantrowitz,
        entry # 888 above. See also James Kinsley, ed.
        Ane Satyre of the Thrie Estaites. Critical Intro.
        by Agnes Mure Mackenzie. Foreword by Ivor Brown.
        London: Cassell, 1954. Also see Salgado.]

Sir Clyomon and Sir Clamydes (see Clyomon and Clamydes)

Sir Thomas More (c. 1590-93); Anthony Munday [Peter Happé,
        entry # 43 above.]

Somebody, Avarice, and Minister (or Somebody and Others, or
        The Spoiling of Lady Verity) (1547-50?); fragment
        [Peter J. Houle, entry # 775a above. Also W.W.
        Greg, ed. *"Somebody and Others."* Malone Society,
        Collections 2, no. 3 (1931): 251-57.

Supposes (1566); trans. of Ariosto's *Gli Suppositi*; George
        Gascoigne [See citations at Glass of Government.
        See also Southern.]

Susanna, The Most Virtuous and Godly (see Virtuous and Godly
        Susanna)

Synedrii sive Concessus Animalium (1555); Ralph Worseley

Tancred and Gismund (1591); Robert Wilmot [See citations at
        Gismond of Salerne]

Temperance and Humility (or Disobedience, Temperance, and
        Humility) (1528?) [W.W. Greg, ed. *"Temperance
        and Humility:* A Fragment of a Morality Printed c.
        1530." *Malone Society Collections* 1, pt. 3
        (1909): 243-46. See also T.W. Craik, "The
        Political Interpretation of Two Tudor Interludes:
        Temperance and Humility and *Wealth and Health."*
        RES, n.s. 4 (Apr. 1953): 98-108.]

Temptation of Our Lord (or A Brief Comedy or Interlude
        Concerning the Temptation of Our Lord) (1538);
        John Bale [John S. Farmer, ed. *The Dramatic
        Writings of John Bale, Bishop of Ossory.* London:
        Early English Drama Society, 1907. See also
        Wickham, *English Moral Interludes;* entry # 86
        above.]

Theano, Play of (1550-54); lost play [Edwin W. Robbins,
        "The Play of Theano." *MLN* 58 (June 1943): 417-
        22.]

Thersites (or Thersytes) (1537); Nicholas Udall (?) [See
        citations at Ezekias. See also A.R. Moon, "Was

Nicholas Udall the Author of *Thersites?" Lib* 7
(Sept. 1926): 184-93. See also Southern.]

Three Estates (see Satire of the Three Estates)

Three Ladies of London (c. 1581); Robert Wilson (?) [See
citations at Cobbler's Prophecy. Also see
Southern.]

Three Laws (or A Comedy Concerning Three Laws; or Three Laws
of Nature, Moses, and Christ) (1538); John Bale
[See citation at Temptation of Our Lord.]

Three Lords and Three Ladies of London (1589); Robert Wilson
[See citations at Cobbler's Prophecy. Also see
Southern.]

Tide Tarrieth No Man (1576); Geogre Wapull [J. Payne
Collier, ed. "The Comedy of the *Tyde Taryeth No
Man,* 1576." In *Illustrations of Early English
Popular Literature,* vol. 2. London: n.p., 1863.
See also David Bevington. *From Mankind to
Marlowe.* Cambridge: Harvard U. Press, 1962. See
also Southern.]

Titus et Gesippus (sometimes with the word 'Comoedia'
following the main title) (1544); John Foxe [See
citations at Christus Triumphans.]

Tom Tyler and His Wife (1560) [Felix E. Schelling, ed.
"Tom Tyler and His Wife." PMLA 15.3 (1900): 253-
89. See also G.C. Moore Smith and W.W. Greg, eds.
"Tom Tyler and His Wife," 1561. London: Malone
Society, 1910. See also Southern.]

Tragedy or Interlude Manifesting the Chefe Promise of God
(see God's Promises)

Trial of Treasure (1565 or 1567); William Wager (?) [See
citation at Cruel Debtor. See also Leslie Oliver,
"William Wager and *The Trial of Treasure." HLQ* 9
(Aug. 1946): 419-29. See also Southern.]

Vice, The Interlude of (see Horestes)

Virtuous and Godly Susanna (c. 1569); Thomas Garter [B.
Ifor Evans and W.W. Greg, eds. *"The Most Virtuous
and Godly Susanna," by Thomas Garter, 1578.*
Oxford: Malone Society, 1937. See also Southern.]

Wealth and Health (1554?) [W.W. Greg and Percy Simpson,
eds. *The Interlude of Wealth and Health.* London:
Malone Society, 1907. See also citation at

Temperance and Humility. Also see Ebihara, entry # 502 above, and Southern.]

Weather, The Play of the (see Play of the Weather)

Wily Beguiled (1602); lost play, possibly a revision of Wylie Beguylie (q.v.)

Wit and Folly (see Witty and Witless)

Wit and Science (c. 1530); John Redford [Arthur Brown, F.P. Wilson, and Charles Sisson, eds. *Wit and Science*. Oxford: Malone Society, 1951. See also Salgado and Southern.]

Wit and Science, The Marriage of (1567 or 1568) [Arthur Brown, John Crow, and F.P. Wilson, eds. *The Marriage of Wit and Science*. Oxford: Malone Society, 1961. See also Trevor Lennam, entry # 53 above. And see Southern.]

Wit and Wisdom, The Marriage between (see Marriage between Wit and Wisdom)

Witty and Witless (or Wit and Folly) (1533); John Heywood [See citations at Four Ps. Also see Salgado and Southern.]

World and the Child (see Mundus et Infans)

Wylie Beguylie (1567); possibly revised as Wily Beguiled (1602) [W.W. Greg, ed. *"Wily Beguiled," 1606*. Oxford: Malone Society, 1912.]

Youth (or Interlude of Youth) (c. 1520) [A(dam) L(uke) G(owans), ed. *The Interlude of Youth*. Intro. by John Drinkwater. London: Gowans & Gray; Boston: Leroy Phillips, 1922. See also Schell, entry # 1442 above.]

Part B: Authors

Authors whose plays are known are listed below with short
titles of the plays they wrote. Question marks preceding
titles indicate uncertain attribution.

Bale, John (1495-1563)
      Christ's Resurrection
      God's Promises
      John Baptist's Preaching in the Wilderness
      King Johan
      Temptation of Our Lord
      Three Laws

B[ower], R[ichard] (fl. 1564)
      Appius [Apius] and Virginia

Bridges, John (d. 1618)
      ? Gammer Gurton's Needle (possibly by William
            Stevenson)

Buchanan, George (1506-1582)
      Alcestis
      Baptistes sive Calumnia
      Jephthes sive Votum
      Medea

Burgh, Benedict (d. < 1483)
      Maister Benet's Cristemasse Game

Cha[u]ndler, Thomas
      Liber Apologeticus de Omni Statu Humanae Naturae (A
            Defence of Human Nature in Every State)

Cheke, Henry (c. 1548-1586?)
      Free Will

Christopherson, John (c. 1520?-1558)
      Clyomon and Clamydes
      Common Conditions
      Jephthes

Edwards, Richard (1524-1566)
      Damon and Pithias
      Palamon and Arcite, I and II

Foxe, John (1516-1587)
    Christus Triumphans
    Titus et Gesippus, Comoedia

Fulwell, Ulpian (fl. 1568-1586)
    Like Will to Like

Garter, Thomas (fl. 1565-1580)
    Virtuous and Godly Susanna

Gascoigne, George (c. 1539-1578)
    Glass of Government
    Jocasta (with Francis Kinwelmarshe)
    Supposes

Golding, Arthur, trans. (1536-1606)
    Abraham's Sacrifice

Goldingham, William (c. 1540?-c. 1589)
    Herodes

Greene, Robert (1560?-1592)
    ? Clyomon and Clamydes (possibly by George Peele)
    Looking Glass for London and England (with Thomas
        Lodge)

Grimald, Nicholas (1519-1562)
    Archipropheta
    Christus Redivivus

Heywood, John (c. 1497-1580?)
    Four Ps
    Johan Johan
    Pardoner and the Friar
    Play of Love
    Play of the Weather
    Witty and Witless (Wit and Folly)

Ingelend, Thomas (f. 1560)
    Disobedient Child

Jeffere, John (fl. 1564)
    Bugbears

Kinwelmarshe, Francis
    Jocasta (with George Gascoigne)

Legge, Thomas (1535-1607)
    Richard Tertius

Lindsay, David (1486-1555)
    Satire of the Three Estates

Lodge, Thomas (1558?-1625)
    Looking Glass for London and England (with Robert
        Greene)

Lumley, Jane (c. 1537-1577)
    Iphigenia in Aulis

Lupton, Thomas (fl. 1577-1584)
    All for Money

Lydgate, John (1370?-1451?)
    Mumming at Bishopswood
    Mumming at Hertford

Medwall, Henry (fl. 1490-1514)
    Fulgens and Lucrece
    Nature

Merbury, Francis (1555-1611)
    Marriage between Wit and Wisdom

Norton, Thomas (1532-1584)
    Gorboduc (Ferrex and Porrex) (with Thomas Sackville)

Palsgrave, John (c. 1483?-1554)
    Acolastus

Peele, George (1558?-1597?)
    ? Clyomon and Clamydes (possibly by Robert Greene)

Phillip(s), John (fl. 1566-1594)
    Patient and Meek Grissil

Pickering, John (1544-1596)
    Horestes (The Interlude of Vice)

Preston, Thomas (fl. 1561)
    Cambises

Rastell, John (c. 1457-1536)
    ? Calisto and Melebea (Celestina, the Beauty and Good
        Properties of Women)
    Four Elements
    Gentleness and Nobility

Redford, John (c. 1485-1545)
    Courage, Kindness, Cleanness
    D,G, and T[om]
    Wit and Science

Sackville, Thomas (1536-1608)
    Gorboduc (Ferrex and Porrex) (with Thomas Norton)

Skelton, John (c. 1440-1529)
    ? Good Order
    Magnificence

Stevenson, William (c. 1521-1575)
    ? Gammer Gurton's Needle (possibly by John Bridges)

Udall, Nicholas (1505-1556)
    Ezekias
    Jacob and Esau
    Ralph Roister Doister
    Respublica (Res Publica)
    Thersites

Wager, Lewis (fl. 1558-1566)
    Mary Magdalene (The Life and Repentance of)

Wager, William (fl. 1559-1569)
    Cruel Debtor
    Enough is as Good as a Feast
    Longer Thou Livest the More Fool Thou Art
    ? Trial of Treasure

Wapull, George (fl. 1571-1576)
    Tide Tarrieth No Man

Watson, Thomas (1513-1584)
    Absolom

Wever, R[ichard?] (fl. c. 1549-1553)
    Lusty Juventus

Whetstone, George (1544?-1587?)
    Promos and Cassandra, I and II

Wilmot, Robert (fl. 1566-1608)
    Gismond of Salerne
    Tancred and Gismund

Wilson, Robert (d. c. 1600)
    Cobbler's Prophesy
    ? Pedlar's Prophecy
    ? Three Ladies of London
    Three Lords and Three Ladies of London

Wood[es], Nathaniel (b. c. 1550?)
    Conflict of Conscience

Worseley, Ralph
    Synedrii sive Concessus Animalium

Records of Early English Drama
Projected Volumes

With the publication in 1979 of the Johnston and Rogerson
volumes on York and the Clopper volume on Coventry (see
entries # 852 and 306 respectively), the University of
Toronto Press inaugurated a series in what I would like to
call the New Drama Criticism. Along with the EDAM work at
Kalamazoo and elsewhere, which also looks outside the drama
for information about dramatic production, the Records of
Early English Drama (REED) volumes provide a wealth of
information useful to scholars of the early plays.
   There are presently eight entries in the series already
in print. Along with the two already mentioned are those by
Reginald Ingram (Coventry); J.J. Anderson (Newcastle upon
Tyne); David Galloway (Norwich 1540-1642); Audrey Douglas
and Peter Greenfield (Cumberland, Westmorland,
Gloucestershire); John Wasson (Devon); and Alan Nelson
(Cambridge).
   The press projects the publication of several other
volumes. This is a long-range program, and the publication
of some of these may be a decade or more off. At present,
as the list below indicates, there are plans to seek out and
publish the dramatic records of a good portion of Great
Britain. The list is drawn from a number of sources, but
primarily from the *Records of Early English Drama
Newsletter*. The proposed editors may change or be added to,
or the volumes may never see the light of day. But at
present, these are the volumes presumably under way, listed
by place, followed parenthetically by the designated
editors.

   Bath (Robert Alexander)
   Berkshire (Alexandra Johnston)
   Beverley (Diana Wyatt)
   Bristol (Mark Pilkinton)
   Buckinghamshire (Alexandra Johnston)
   Cornwall (Evelyn Newlyn and Sally Cross)
   Derbyshire (John Wasson)
   Dorset (Rosalind Hays and Ted McGee)
   Durham (Thomas Craik, John McKinnell, Anna Spackman,
        and Clare Lees)
   Essex (John Coldewey)
   Herefordshire and Worcestershire (David Klausner)
   Ireland (Alan Fletcher)
   Kent (east of Medway) (James Gibson)

Lancashire (David George)
Leicester and Leicestershire (Alice Hamilton)
London Guilds and Corporations (Anne Lancashire and Ia
    Lancashire)
Middlesex and London Parishes (Mary Erler and Anne
    Lancashire)
Norwich to 1540 (JoAnna Dutka)
Nottinghamshire (John Coldewey)
Oxford University and Town (John Elliott and Marianne
    Briscoe)
Oxfordshire (Marianne Briscoe)
Salisbury (Audrey Douglas)
Scottish Royal Court (Meradith McMunn)
Shropshire and Staffordshire (J.A.B. Somerset)
Somerset (James Stokes)
Southeast Yorkshire (Diana Wyatt)
Southampton (Thomas James and John Marshall)
Surrey (Sally-Beth MacLean)
Sussex (Cameron Louis)
Westminster (Sheila Lindenbaum)

Index

The following index contains titles of plays and names of playwrights, names of characters often cited by critics, prominent scholars mentioned in the criticism, cities, towns, and counties in which dramatic activities have been discussed, and common themes or topics of the scholarship. Individual cycles are indexed only when the full cycle or groups of plays are treated, not individual plays mentioned in an article; these can be found under the title of the play. Single plays appearing in the following works are not indexed: Bevington (entry # 14); Brock and Byrd (# 16a); Brown (# 17); Davies (# 28); Davis (# 29, 30); Happé (# 41); Lumiansky and Mills (# 55 ff.); Moeslein (# 64), and Collins (# 336).

This is a straightforward alphabetical list. Numbers refer to the entry numbers in the bibliography.

475

Allegory   161,   174,   182,   267,   272,   273,   298b,   369,   411,   431,
      449,   503,   552,   554,   667,   732,   742,   746,   750,   860,   886,
      888,   889,   898,   1191,   1208,   1280,   1348,   1388,   1427,
      1441,   1445,   1556,   1561,   1618,   1624,   1647,   1667,   1709,
      1722
All's Well That Ends Well (Shakespeare)   1217
Amateur drama, actors, or dramatists   184,   321,   525,   558,
      649,   860,   886,   1069,   1418,   1527,   1659,   1692,   1693,   1696
      (see also Professional drama or actors)
Anachronisms   666,   1051,   1121,   1240,   1265,   1307,   1320,   1343,
      1394,   1565,   1702
Ane Satire . . ., see under *Satire . . .*
Annas, the character   310,   1232,   1343,   1370
Annunciation, the play   108,   1258
      (Liturgical play)   336
      (Wakefield)   118,   131,   934,   1001
Annunciation and Nativity (Chester)   230
Anselm, Saint   805
Antichrist   95,   96,   259,   538,   539,   804,   1071,   1275
Antichrist (Chester)   82,   1029,   1076,   1588
Anti-Semitism in the plays   764,   1343,   1498
Antitheatrical sentiment   122a,   141,   222a,   227,   381.1,   383b,
      392b,   410a,   584,   611,   612,   789,   860,   886,   1134,   1154,
      1163,   1178,   1202,   1223,   1431,   1462a,   1684,   1688,   1697
      (See also Censorship)
Apius and Virginia (Appius . . .; R[ichard] B[ower])   43,
      211a,   648,   1494,   1715
Appearance of Our Lady to Thomas (York)   1639,   1640
      (See also *Assumption of the Virgin* [York])
Aquinas, Thomas   405a
Arena theaters   440,   443,   549,   1493
      (see also Theaters; Playhouses)
Ars moriendi   479,   589,   634,   1170,   1472,   1508,   1509
Ascension play   230a
      (Chester)   308,   961,   1549
      (York)   334
Ashmole Fragment (*Caesar Augustus*)   1128
Assembly of Gods (pseudo-Lydgatean)   958
Assumption of the Virgin   (N-Town)   885,   1102
      (York)   9,   74,   1367
      (see also *Appearance of Our Lady to Thomas* [York])
Audience; audience involvement   28,   32,   88,   126,   127,   153,
      188,   213,   219,   231,   235,   272,   278a,   304,   325,   330,   331,
      333,   382,   402,   412,   440,   446,   463,   477,   513,   547,   558a,
      588,   591,   606,   607,   609,   614,   628,   630,   652,   655,   664,
      665,   666,   667,   672,   679,   685,   752,   753,   757,   780,   824,
      827a,   842,   865,   866,   883,   898,   961,   963,   973,   977,
      1012,   1043,   1083,   1117,   1121,   1122,   1125a,   1182,   1183,
      1191,   1195,   1204,   1206,   1212,   1230,   1231,   1233,   1281,
      1285,   1295,   1307,   1308,   1309,   1378,   1386,   1391,   1394,
      1427,   1434,   1455,   1488,   1526,   1559,   1565,   1582,   1587,
      1588,   1612,   1624,   1631,   1647,   1650,   1716
      Children as audience   678

Augustine (*City of God*), influence on the plays   222, 558a,
   709, 750, 1074, 1248, 1665
Authorship   22, 31, 49, 51, 54, 67, 81, 112, 121, 135, 137,
   150, 163, 224, 243, 299, 307, 316, 355, 356, 606, 734,
   792, 883, 909, 949, 990, 1016, 1023, 1031, 1115, 1121,
   1233, 1322, 1688, 1705, 1716, 1733
   (see Wakefield Master; York Realist)
A/Y Memorandum Book   11, 79, 157, 1114, 1408

B., R. [Richard Bower]   43
Baitings   102, 318, 1688
Balaak and Balaam (Chester)   59, 1020
   Balaam and Balak   1162
Bale, John   1, 40, 42, 86, 126, 158a, 198, 252, 272, 502,
   503, 545, 560, 686, 688, 737, 984, 1081, 1324, 1418,
   1425a, 1470, 1506, 1618, 1652, 1660, 1661
Banns   953, 1592, 1593, 1612
   (Chester)   41, 1016, 1148, 1154
   (Croxton *Play of the Sacrament*)   1612
   (N-Town)   14, 506
   (Wakefield)   1531
Baptism   18
Baptism of Christ (York)   333, 334
Barking Abbey; the Barking Ordinale   355, 356, 743
Bassingbourne, dramatic records   1726
Bath, dramatic records   97
Berkshire, dramatic records   830, 836, 840
Bernard of Clairvaux   118, 750, 807, 1184
Bernstein, Leonard (*Mass*)   1512
Betrayal play (N-Town)   1611
Beverley, dramatic records   252a, 860, 1199, 1521, 1700,
   1729, 1730
Bewnans Meryasek, see *Meriasek, The Life of* (Cornish)
Bishop's Lynn, dramatic activity   166
Bishop's Stortford, dramatic records   1726
Boethius   1247
Booth stage   286, 773, 1613
Bosch, Hieronymus   372, 734, 815, 1447
Bower, Richard, see B., R.
Boys, as actors   184, 205, 206, 363, 594, 678, 679
Braggart, the character   1519
Braintree, dramatic records   1725
Brecht, Bertholt, influence on scholarship   555, 1527, 1635
Bristol, dramatic records   142, 143, 558, 596, 1311, 1311a,
   1311b, 1312
Britten, Benjamin   639, 1086
Brome Hall Commonplace Book   422
Brome play   603
Bruegel, Peter (Brueghel)   734
Buffeting, see *Coliphizacio* (Wakefield)
The Bugbears   22
Bungay, dramatic records   1726
Burgess Court Records   578, 579
Burton, Roger   79, 1536

Bury St. Edmunds, dramatic activity   620, 621, 624, 637,
    1041, 1726
    (see Rickinghall Fragment)

Caesar Augustus, see Ashmole Fragment
Caesarius of Heisterbach (*Dialogus Miraculorum*)   1727
Cain, the character   209, 235, 432, 463, 660, 670, 709, 734,
    820, 894, 901, 1087, 1136, 1308, 1372
Cain and Abel   93, 209, 233, 463, 1122, 1232, 1417, 1437
    (Chester)   232
    (N-Town)   1227
    (Wakefield)   76, 370, 709, 1177, 1393, 1444
Caiaphas, Caiphas, see Cayphas
Calisto and Melebea (Rastell)   5, 617
Cambises (Preston)   211a, 1715
Cambridge, dramatic records and activity   192, 1204a, 1720
Cambridge Fragment   1128
Candelmes Day and the Kylling of the Children of Israelle
    6, 7
Capgrave, John (*Solace of Pilgrimes*)   147
Carols, see Songs
Carpenter, Alexander (*Destructorium Viciovum*)   227
Castle of Perseverance   13, 23, 31, 42, 69a, 70, 77, 79a,
    147, 161, 163a, 187, 211a, 230, 249, 278a, 280, 379,
    407a, 432, 445, 446, 515, 546, 549, 550, 551, 581, 675,
    690, 749, 749a, 756a, 814, 860, 896, 897, 898, 921,
    1001, 1088, 1113, 1135, 1143, 1165, 1190, 1193, 1201,
    1222, 1266, 1279, 1280, 1281, 1314, 1332, 1342, 1351,
    1378, 1388, 1427, 1440, 1446, 1493, 1501, 1521, 1612,
    1620, 1631, 1638, 1675, 1676, 1677, 1678, 1739
Cayphas (Caiphas, Caiaphas), the character   10, 310, 1232,
    1343, 1370, 1635
Censorship   1673, 1696
    (see Antitheatrical sentiment)
Chambers, E.K.   134, 555, 584, 613, 887, 1236
Characterization   13, 77, 83, 121, 156, 160, 167, 182, 193,
    194, 211a, 214, 216, 218, 219, 230, 232, 254, 272, 273,
    288, 298a, 310, 328, 330, 332, 336, 346, 379, 381, 385,
    391, 403, 412, 480, 493, 539, 540, 552, 554, 617, 625,
    652, 667, 672, 676, 688, 734, 752, 781, 820, 860, 886,
    898, 964, 973, 1136, 1148, 1163, 1165, 1182, 1183,
    1187, 1219, 1296, 1320, 1324, 1340, 1396, 1410, 1417,
    1441, 1459, 1468, 1505, 1506, 1514, 1588, 1618, 1635,
    1667, 1740
Charter Fragment (Cornish)   795
Chaucer, Geoffrey   456, 533, 657, 672, 759, 827b, 929, 938,
    958, 1247, 1341a, 1706
    (see also *Miller's Tale; Nun's Priest's Tale;
    Pardoner's Tale; Physician's Tale*)
Chaundler, Thomas   35
Chelmsford, dramatic records   314, 1725, 1726
Cheltenham, dramatic records   558
Cheshire, dramatic records   307, 477, 1134

Crow, Robert (playwright, actor, . . .) 792
Croxton play, see *Play of the Sacrament*
Crucifixion (Chester) 1148
    (Wakefield) 328, 391, 805
    (York) 10, 38, 110, 162, 391, 509, 886, 1133, 1704
Cumberland, dramatic records 476
Cumbria, dramatic records 475
Cursor Mundi 971, 1637

Dame Sirith 478, 1167, 1641
Damon and Pythias (Edwards) 648
Dance 15, 102, 125, 126, 127, 191, 245, 366a, 480, 483,
    915, 1067, 1117, 1481, 1523
    (see also Morris dance; Sword dance)
Dante (*Commedia*) 759
Death and Burial of Christ 365
    (York) 333
Death of Mary play 677
Death of Robert Earl of Huntingdon (Munday and Chettle) 1619
Decline of the drama 77, 107, 149, 195, 196, 231, 316, 484,
    496, 556, 584, 789, 882, 886, 964, 988, 1119, 1163,
    1418, 1431, 1524, 1575, 1714
Destruction of Jerusalem (John Smith) 1728
Destructorium Viciovum (Carpenter) 227
Devon, dramatic records 1656, 1658
Dialogue 117, 119, 392, 424, 478, 481, 552, 562, 627
Didacticism of the plays 28, 77, 240, 266, 270, 282, 283,
    303, 311, 333, 427, 440, 462, 511, 540, 547, 571, 609,
    610, 612, 664, 667, 679, 681, 720, 753, 836, 860, 889,
    893, 1001, 1021, 1030, 1054, 1171, 1191, 1230, 1232,
    1244, 1251, 1307, 1308, 1325, 1384, 1387, 1427, 1441,
    1445, 1471, 1565, 1587, 1588, 1635, 1647, 1692, 1693,
    1695
Digby plays 6, 7, 16a, 33, 136, 166, 314, 315, 324, 397,
    964, 1128, 1333
Disguise 126, 292a, 339, 441, 593, 707a, 731, 785a, 1280,
    1699, 1702
Disguisings 107, 145, 211a, 231, 496, 860, 911, 1202, 1692,
    1693
A Dissertation on the Pageants or Dramatic Mysteries . . . .,
    see Thomas Sharp
Doctor Faustus (Marlowe) 781, 1214, 1059
Doomsday 44, 388, 392, 394, 406, 948, 973
Doomsday Pageant (York Mercers) 849, 853
Doubling 40, 42, 686, 1199, 1536
Downfall of Robert Earl of Huntingdon, see *Death of Robert
    Earl of Huntingdon*
Dürer, Albrecht 1598
Duk Moraud (Dux Moraud) 29, 747, 766, 1128
Dunmow, dramatic records and activity 1724, 1725, 1726
Durham Corpus Christi play 29, 100, 1128

East Anglia, dramatic records 147, 148a, 379, 506, 595,
    621, 1222, 1298, 1723, 1724

"East Coker" (T.S. Eliot) 1741
Easter, play or dramatic activity 197, 243, 260, 355, 386,
    501, 547, 565, 870, 1196, 1268, 1311, 1461, 1462a,
    1464, 1487, 1688
Edinburgh, see Herod, Hammerman's play

Editing of drama and dramatic records [see introductions to
    editions, entries # 1-8, 20, 49, 55], 185, 344, 417,
    422, 449, 462, 471, 476, 505, 598, 703, 828, 844, 850,
    852, 876, 882, 940, 952, 956, 957, 1016, 1017, 1044,
    1094, 1108, 1153, 1160, 1163, 1266, 1492
Edward the Fourth 1728
Edwards, Richard 648
Elckerlijc 8, 25, 343, 345, 346, 435, 589, 1085, 1263,
    1453, 1557, 1580, 1650, 1718
Eliot, T.S. (*Murder in the Cathedral*) 435
    ("East Coker") 1741
Elucidarium (source of *Lucidus and Dubius*) 971
England's Joy (lost play) 1449
Enough Is as Good as a Feast (Wager) 77, 1217
Eschatology 259, 973, 1076, 1248, 1507a, 1588, 1714
    (see also Time)
Essex, dramatic records 315, 316, 1720, 1725
Ethelwold 243
Eton, dramatic records 205, 206
Eton College, dramatic records 842
Eusebius 1074
Eve, the character 402, 432, 489, 530, 746, 755, 1232
Everyman 3, 8, 25, 26, 38, 54, 70, 76, 77, 128, 178, 204,
    211a, 278, 278a, 281, 343, 344, 345, 346, 347, 348,
    353, 360a, 379, 400, 435, 445, 459, 479, 544, 546, 572,
    588, 589, 631, 634, 635, 643a, 704, 752, 781, 797, 798,
    799, 800, 807, 860, 878, 924, 927, 931, 1001, 1009,
    1048, 1051, 1059, 1085, 1088, 1165, 1170, 1184, 1191,
    1283, 1324, 1332, 1348, 1352, 1356, 1378, 1393, 1427,
    1448, 1452, 1467, 1508, 1537, 1557, 1567, 1580, 1586,
    1624, 1630, 1647, 1650, 1667, 1682, 1687, 1709, 1718,
    1719, 1741
Exegesis 96, 112, 222, 310, 390, 539, 576, 741, 803, 804,
    1007, 1073, 1369, 1384, 1394, 1520, 1544
Exeter, dramatic activity 350, 1689
Expositors in the plays 127, 266, 547, 719. 1021, 1499

Fabliau(x) 130, 586, 625, 931, 1237, 1641
Faerie Queene (Spenser) 1348, 1667
Fall of Lucifer plays 681, 1232
    (Chester) 718, 933, 1282, 1308, 1451, 1549, 1568
    (N-Town) 1308
    (Wakefield) 1308
    (York) 412, 1308, 1451
Fall of Man (Chester) 721, 1175, 1714
    (Wakefield) 721, 1175, 1714
    (York) 10, 530, 721, 1175, 1374, 1714
    (see also Norwich Grocers' Play)

Holcot, Robert 1674
Homecoming (Pinter) 298a
Hone, William (*Ancient Mysteries Described*, 1823) 1401
Horestes 4, 211a, 1715
Horologium Sapientiae (Suso) 1386
Hull/Beverley area, dramatic records 252a, 1730
    (see Kingston upon Hull)
Humanist drama and thought 14, 106, 753, 768, 807, 825,
    1184, 1194, 1251, 1253, 1254
Humor 23, 77, 118, 168, 194, 234, 284, 298, 429, 462, 481,
    625, 729, 764, 806, 866, 886, 983, 1071, 1124, 1258,
    1375, 1417, 1505, 1702, 1704
    (see also Comedy; the comic)
Hyngham, Richard (scribe of Macro ms) 152, 624

Iconography 132, 174, 186, 279, 286, 325, 326, 329, 336,
    337, 338, 339, 372, 381, 382, 390, 391, 393, 394, 397,
    399, 401, 404, 407, 407a, 408, 408a, 411, 412, 434,
    453, 457, 487, 509, 536, 539, 569, 610, 741, 743, 755,
    760, 784, 1035, 1061, 1062, 1078, 1083, 1123, 1190,
    1221, 1297, 1316, 1317, 1320, 1343, 1365, 1413, 1423,
    1437, 1443, 1461, 1463, 1464, 1465, 1466, 1478, 1479,
    1483, 1515, 1521, 1596, 1606, 1676
    (see Typology; Visual arts)
Idley, Peter (*Instructions to His Son*) 380
Impatient Poverty 80
Interlude of the Student [Clerk] and the Girl (*Interludium
    de Clerico et Puella*) 30, 86, 478, 904, 951, 1128, 1167
Interlude of Youth, see *Youth*
Interludium de Clerico et Puella, see *Interlude of the
    Student and the Girl*
Interludes 4, 32a, 43, 49, 65, 77, 78, 80, 86, 109, 111a,
    123, 126, 231, 245, 286, 322, 419, 421, 427, 490, 548,
    580a, 596, 664, 665, 684, 712, 753, 768, 824, 826, 860,
    865, 886, 888, 904, 931, 969, 1046, 1214, 1296, 1345,
    1418, 1427, 1458, 1495, 1496, 1669, 1688, 1692, 1693
Iphigenia in Aulis, see Jame Lumley
Ipswich, dramatic activity 1199, 1648, 1726
Irish drama and dramatic activity 560, 569a, 573, 593, 632,
    638, 1093, 1449
Irony 602, 871, 983, 1628, 1702
Isaac, the character 1562
Isaac and Jacob (fragment) 108
Isabella's Triumph (1615) 966
Islington, dramatic records 242

Jacke Jugeler (*Jack Juggler*) 4, 53
Jacob (Wakefield) 1614
Jacob and Esau (Udall) 648
Jacobus de Voragine, see *Legenda Aurea*
Jedermann 589, 878, 1263, 1448
Jeu d'Adam 886
Jewell, Simon (actor) 507a, 1045

Johan Johan (Heywood)   1, 32, 40, 42, 71, 530, 824, 1233, 1427, 1721
Johan Baptystes Preachynge   40
John the Baptist (Wakefield)   874, 1614
Jonson, Ben   891, 1619
   (*Sad Shepherd*)   1619
Jordan, William (author of Cornish plays?)   66
Joseph, the character   10, 130, 131, 213, 622, 796, 886, 1308
Joseph's Return (N-Town)   130, 625, 886
Joyce, James   631, 1009, 1347
Judas   660, 858, 1550
Judgment   186, 187, 235, 411, 457, 741, 781, 1125, 1234, 1248, 1378, 1582
   (see Justice)
Judgment play (Chester)   935, 1248
   (York)   10, 333, 390, 399
Judicium play (Wakefield)   602, 821, 1529
Julius Caesar (Shakespeare)   1630
Justice   295, 298, 445, 1323, 1378
   (see also Judgment)

Katherine of Sutton (playwright)   355, 356
Kenilworth Castle, dramatic activity   342
Kent, dramatic records and activity   342, 1400
Killing of Abel (*Mactacio Abel;* Wakefield)   76, 234, 235, 298, 602, 676, 694, 734, 820, 1372, 1393, 1394, 1602
Killing of the Children, see *Slaughter of the Innocents*
King Henry the Fourth (Thomas Heywood)   1728
King Johan (Bale)   1, 40, 42, 158, 272, 502, 503, 545, 688, 984, 1080, 1081, 1344, 1425a, 1472, 1618, 1652
King Lear (Shakespeare)   402, 1441
King's Lynn, dramatic records   1726
Kingston upon Hull, dramatic records   252a
Kingston upon Thames, dramatic records   1043
Kolve, V.A.   227, 231, 305, 357, 486, 584, 610, 989, 1245, 1313, 1427

Lamech, the character   1227, 1320, 1371
Last Judgment   973, 1313, 1507a, 1679, 1680
   (Chester)   1588
   (Wakefield)   1211, 1504
   (York)   10, 333, 390, 411, 1232, 1466
Last Supper (N-Town)   1102
Laud Troy Book   1538
Lazarus, the character   117, 166, 336, 407, 501, 1313, 1387a, 1504, 1520, 1679
Legal issues in the plays   80, 135, 137, 211a, 216, 235, 301, 305, 464, 607, 702, 921, 936, 1059, 1226, 1323, 1326, 1510, 1511, 1582
Legenda Aurea (Jacobus de Voragine)   642, 677, 719, 1016, 1640
Leicester, dramatic activity   673
Lemegeton (or *Lesser Key of Solomon*)   869

Processions, Processional performance; Processional staging
14, 79, 100, 102, 129, 252a, 286, 308, 358, 361, 366a,
426, 439, 443, 474, 477, 490, 613, 628, 674, 778, 822,
831, 838, 843, 848, 877, 960, 970, 1128, 1132, 1163,
1190, 1196, 1199, 1204, 1206, 1209, 1256, 1285, 1329,
1354, 1355, 1518, 1533, 1536, 1588, 1599, 1612, 1648,
1657, 1674, 1683, 1686
Processus Satanae 1001
Processus Talentorum, see *Play of the Talents* (Wakefield)
Prodigal Son theme and plays 80, 158a, 1705, 1739
Prodigality, see *Liberality and Prodigality*
Professional drama; Professional actors 135, 170, 184, 245,
321, 525, 649, 664, 839, 860, 886, 1069, 1204a, 1418,
1427, 1456, 1527, 1536, 1653, 1659, 1688, 1692, 1693,
1696
(see also Amateur drama, actors, or dramatists; Wages,
for actors)
Prophets, see Procession of Prophets in the cycles
Props 28, 83, 249, 286, 300, 314, 321, 336, 412, 526, 686,
792, 853, 898, 1083, 1098, 1117, 1204a, 1379, 1427,
1521, 1614, 1653, 1658, 1696
Proverb play 1217
Proverbs 444, 459, 796, 1217
Prudentius 870
Punch and Judy plays 904
Puppets; Puppeteers 142, 146, 396, 904, 951, 1400
Purification and Doctors (Chester) 84, 1031
Purification of Mary play (Chester) 286, 1031
(Liturgical) 336
(N-Town) 286
(Wakefield) 286, 1615
(York) 334

Quem quaeritis 197, 555, 562, 626, 801, 870, 917, 968,
1034, 1036, 1349, 1487, 1518, 1625
(see also Tropes)

Ralph Roister Doister (Udall) 278a, 739
Rapper dance 857
Rastell, John 5, 24, 106, 126, 452, 465, 618, 619, 753,
860, 886, 935, 1233, 1252, 1392, 1556, 1660, 1661,
1705, 1733, 1734
Rastell, William (*Good Order*) 1392
Rayleigh, dramatic records 1726
Realism in the plays 167, 270, 272, 298a, 330, 331, 382,
390, 403, 440, 462, 495, 540, 580a, 591, 613, 633, 664,
667, 709, 734, 753, 768, 886, 897, 1005, 1012, 1121,
1182, 1309, 1318, 1321, 1363, 1365, 1417, 1427, 1445,
1497, 1507, 1527, 1556, 1588, 1667
Redford, John 12, 14, 43, 1440, 1660, 1661, 1664, 1705
Respublica (*Res publica*; Udall?) 43, 77, 211a
Resurrecio Domini (Cornish drama) 1120

Resurrection, as a topic; Resurrection plays   6, 7, 10, 16a,
     158, 202, 221, 279, 396, 500, 664, 792, 919, 1121,
     1128, 1313, 1426, 1587, 1588, 1600, 1605, 1714
Resurrection of Lazarus   117, 1313
     (see also Lazarus)
Revesby Sword Play   292, 1334
Revetour, William (York civic scribe)   1184
Rex Diabole (Interlude)   1214
Reynard (Caxton)   1085
Reynes Extract (*Speech of Delight*)   29, 1001, 1128
Richard II, pageants   910
Richard III (Shakespeare)   1630
Rickinghall (Bury St. Edmunds) Fragment   1128
Ritual   237, 245, 247, 261, 291, 292a, 305, 311, 440, 508,
     514, 593, 610, 611, 627, 664, 765, 809, 870, 902, 910,
     972, 1004, 1119, 1163, 1292, 1301, 1305, 1324, 1377,
     1411, 1424, 1427, 1534, 1572, 1588, 1589, 1613, 1646,
     1673, 1692, 1693
Robin Hood, the character and the plays   15, 30, 160, 181,
     468, 762, 763, 836, 894, 904, 985, 1043, 1046, 1163,
     1210, 1261, 1291, 1294, 1335, 1545, 1619, 1621, 1658,
     1701
Robin Hood and the Friar   15, 468, 1177, 1261
Robin Hood and the Potter   468, 1261
Robin Hood and the Sheriff   30, 468, 1261
Rogers, David (*Brevarye . . .*)   301, 307, 308, 425, 684,
     1064, 1066, 1190, 1329
Royal entries   107, 171, 231, 286, 655, 908, 909, 1173, 1361

Sachs, Hans (*Ein comedi von dem reichen sterbenden menschen
     . . .*)   878
     (*The Stolen Shrovetide Cock*)   1177
Sacrifice of Isaac (Chester), see *Abraham and Isaac* plays
Sad Shepherd (Jonson)   1619
St. Anne (N-Town play)   1697
St. Catherine (Katherine) plays   142, 397, 1049, 1056, 1126
St. George, plays and depictions   392a, 397, 904, 960, 1219,
     1658, 1683
St. John's College, dramatic activity   192
St. Nicholas play   1570
St. Paul (Digby saint play)   1697
St. Veronica (Cornish saint play)   1697
Saints' plays   14, 28, 385, 397, 404, 437, 438, 439, 483,
     484, 485, 628, 641, 817, 957, 1202, 1612, 1688, 1697
     (in art)   411
Salisbury, Palm Sunday processional 426
Salutation (Wakefield)   230, 934, 1001
Salutation and Conception (N-Town)   1140
Salutation of Elizabeth   108
Satire   67, 216, 229, 235, 304, 379, 607, 665, 680, 688,
     768, 821, 866, 886, 983, 1046, 1229, 1233, 1251b, 1323,
     1456, 1702, 1732, 1733
Ane Satire of the Thrie Estatis (Lindsay)   42, 271, 725,
     785a, 888, 890, 1019, 1290, 1644

Sawles Warde 1056
Scaffold, see Place-and-scaffold presentation
Scale of Perfection (Hilton) 182
Scenery 28, 111a, 231, 526, 655
Scottish drama 286, 358, 490, 1046, 1047, 1049, 1126, 1129,
    1130, 1183, 1705
Second Shepherds' Play (*Secunda Pastorum*) 17, 38, 76, 90,
    114, 125, 177, 203, 222, 230, 255, 256, 264, 270, 298a,
    348, 372, 373, 543a, 602, 604, 653, 661, 687, 732, 734,
    754, 804, 819, 823, 937a, 974, 976, 991, 1039, 1058,
    1071, 1088, 1309, 1336, 1374, 1375, 1393, 1397, 1410,
    1416, 1417, 1480, 1504, 1505, 1520, 1552, 1565, 1586,
    1626, 1627, 1665, 1731, 1743, 1744
Secunda Pastorum, see *Second Shepherds' Play*
Seinte Resurreccion 886
Sermons, plays' relation to or use of 77, 125, 131, 263,
    316, 427, 572, 576, 675, 741, 747, 766, 818, 838, 860,
    898, 1053, 1079, 1100, 1165, 1178, 1283, 1325, 1544,
    1683, 1692, 1693
    (see also Preaching)
Shakespeare 140, 255, 367, 374, 386, 392a, 402, 447, 448,
    450, 451, 526, 629, 643, 728, 740, 751a, 756, 858, 918,
    1050, 1050a, 1059, 1172, 1249, 1254, 1356, 1391, 1428,
    1548, 1631, 1669
Sharp, Thomas (*A Dissertation on the Pageants . . .*) 307,
    388, 406, 1066, 1127, 1245a, 1457
Shepherds, Adoration of (N-Town) 276, 1183
Shepherds, non-cycle, unspecified, or composite plays 89,
    111b, 125, 260, 264, 270, 336, 1258, 1497, 1520
Shepherds' Carol 373
Shepherds' Play (*De Pastoribus*, Chester) 36, 91, 462, 651,
    659, 716, 1183, 1520, 1542
Shepherds (York) 155, 1183, 1520
    (see also *First Shepherds' Play; Second Shepherds'
    Play*)
Sherbourne, Dorset, dramatic records and activity 1132
Shrewsbury, dramatic records and activity 1355, 1489, 1491,
    1520
Shrewsbury Fragments 29, 30, 373, 1128, 1345, 1346, 1520,
    1714
Sir Gawain and the Green Knight 857
Sir Thomas More (Munday) 43
Skelton, John 42, 67, 103, 252, 643a, 1324, 1652, 1660,
    1661, 1705, 1710
Slaughter of the Innocents (*Killing of the Children*) 10,
    194, 259, 269, 298, 336, 365, 432, 697, 1049, 1096,
    1105, 1403
    (Hammermen's, Edinburgh) 1049
Smith, John (*Destruction of Jerusalem*) 1728
Snettisham, dramatic activity 1726
Solace of Pilgrimes (Capgrave) 147
Soliloquy 374, 604
Somerset, dramatic activity 1335, 1547, 1720

Suffolk, dramatic activity 146, 595, 600, 623
Susanna 240a
    (see also *Virtuous and Godly Susanna* [Garter])
Sussex, dramatic records and activity 1583
Swift, Jonathan ("A Modest Proposal") 1480
Sword dances 292a, 664, 731, 857, 904, 1219, 1292
Sword play 237, 1334
    (see also Revesby Sword Play)

Tableaux vivants 412, 611, 811, 1423, 1536, 1612
Tamburlaine, I (Marlowe) 1630
Tamworth, dramatic records 948
Temptation of Jesus in the Wilderness (York) 10, 530
Temptation of Our Lord (Bale) 86
Temptation plays 1208, 1668
Terence 192, 1046, 1339, 1447, 1519, 1574, 1739
Tewksbury, dramatic records 558
Theater in the round 137, 147, 161, 220, 237, 425, 439,
    526, 534, 549, 664, 867, 970, 1005, 1040, 1195, 1206,
    1218, 1285, 1414, 1446, 1447, 1493, 1577, 1612
Theaters; playhouses 143, 147, 242, 243, 252a, 286, 439,
    526, 549, 595, 596, 770, 771, 772, 773, 866, 886, 945,
    969, 970, 1312, 1419, 1427, 1431, 1455, 1489, 1495,
    1496, 1577, 1579, 1612, 1613, 1653, 1688, 1696
    (Open-air theater 32a, 137, 147)
    (see also Arena theaters; Mansion stages; Theater in
        the round)
Thersites (Udall?) 4
Thetford, dramatic activity 151, 1659, 1726
Thomas of India (Wakefield) 222
Three Kings (Chester) 1403
Three Laws (Bale) 40, 545
The Tide Tarrieth No Man (Wapull) 77, 278a
Time, as a theme; playing time 111, 156, 234, 269, 333,
    405, 431, 463, 474, 501, 614, 666, 670, 676, 734, 748,
    815, 886, 927, 973, 1012, 1121, 1165, 1228, 1248, 1321,
    1434, 1548, 1588, 1617, 1627, 1679
Timon of Athens (Shakespeare) 1356, 1638
Titivillus (Tutivillus) 119, 380, 821
Tom Tiler (Tyler) *and His Wife* 360, 648, 1177
Torturers, in the plays 368, 805, 1061, 1062, 1607
Tournament of Tottenham 350
Tournaments 107, 231, 286, 585, 655, 1220, 1280
Tourneur, Cyril (*The Atheist's Tragedy*) 756
Towneley Cycle, see Wakefield Cycle
Tragedy 163a, 190, 232, 234, 252, 278a, 379, 383, 402, 456,
    652, 858, 1046, 1157, 1247, 1254, 1421, 1514, 1538,
    1628, 1660, 1661, 1688, 1705, 1715
Tragicomedy 140, 602, 1628
Transvestism 689, 1604
A Tretise of Miraclis Pleyinge 141, 398, 417, 418, 684, 782
Trial and Flagellation (Chester) 1148
Trial of Christ (York) 1226, 1581
Trickster figures 114, 193, 368

Tropes   197, 243, 270, 561, 562, 627, 784, 801, 870, 968,
     1034, 1036, 1487, 1539, 1625, 1673
     (see also *Quem quaeritis*)
Tudor drama; the Tudor period   4, 43, 49, 65, 78, 80, 106,
     107, 123, 126, 170, 172, 174, 188, 195, 198, 302, 322,
     364, 480, 753, 824, 825, 826, 866, 911, 1251, 1256,
     1257, 1296, 1344, 1415, 1427, 1458, 1470, 1555, 1556,
     1612, 1630, 1681, 1688, 1705
Tutivillus, see Titivillus
Typology   156, 209, 214, 218, 234, 259, 284, 340, 348b,
     580a, 610, 715, 734, 755, 804, 963, 1007, 1014, 1071,
     1121, 1122, 1182, 1229, 1341a, 1352, 1369, 1379, 1394,
     1506, 1517, 1518, 1520, 1526, 1588, 1646, 1677, 1688,
     1714
     (see also Iconography)
Tyrants   310, 665, 868, 1082

Udall, Nicholas   1324
     (*Jacob and Esau*)   648
     (*Ralph Roister Doister*)   278a, 739
     (*Respublica*)   43
Ulster, dramatic records   573
University of Glasgow, dramatic activity   490

Van Eyck, Jan (painter; "Last Judgment")   823
Versification; Stanza forms; Prosody   1, 7, 8, 9, 20, 22,
     26, 28, 60, 79a, 121, 153, 164, 180, 200, 333, 334,
     339, 435, 462, 483, 509, 638, 683, 752, 898, 962, 979,
     1016, 1102, 1191, 1278, 1397, 1499, 1504, 1525, 1705
Vestiarian Controversy   316
Vice; The Vices   99, 211a, 381a, 431, 451, 550, 551, 665,
     688, 700, 701, 704, 707, 738, 753, 768, 785a, 865, 982,
     1165, 1421, 1488, 1676, 1699, 1705, 1715, 1734
Vincent of Beauvais (*Speculum Historiale*)   677, 1144
Violence   82, 194, 365, 449, 764, 886, 1437
Virgin Mary, the character   128, 131, 202, 213, 252a, 270,
     276, 325, 390, 402, 463, 643, 1013, 1042, 1540
Virtuous and Godly Susanna (Garter)   85, 682, 683, 769, 991,
     1139
Visitatio sepulchri   14, 197, 243, 743, 1169, 1235, 1236,
     1241, 1353, 1354, 1462
Visitation (N-Town)   1102
Visual arts, related to drama   163a, 182, 186, 187, 230a,
     285, 326, 329, 381, 382, 383, 384, 386, 387, 388, 390,
     391, 392, 393, 394, 397, 399, 401, 403, 405, 406, 407,
     408, 408a, 411, 412, 434, 446, 457, 509, 536, 580a,
     589, 612, 621, 623, 705, 734, 741, 742, 743, 755, 764,
     770, 773, 815, 823, 899, 901, 909, 966, 1041, 1042,
     1061, 1062, 1068, 1078, 1123, 1166, 1190, 1195, 1220,
     1221, 1222, 1260, 1303, 1304, 1343, 1350, 1395, 1413,
     1423, 1437, 1438, 1443, 1447, 1461, 1462, 1464, 1465,
     1466, 1471, 1476, 1478, 1479, 1481, 1483, 1497, 1534,
     1559, 1584a, 1595, 1596, 1639, 1692, 1693, 1717
     (see also Iconography)

Vocabulary of the plays   17, 108, 113, 119, 132, 135, 137,
        138, 153, 180, 200, 201, 209, 235, 343, 344, 345, 347,
        348, 444, 489, 496, 533, 534, 576, 587, 603, 735, 738,
        788, 861, 898, 927, 983, 1085, 1102, 1150, 1163, 1191,
        1212, 1337, 1338, 1339, 1370

Wager, Lewis   1660
Wager, William   77, 252, 383b, 1217, 1660
Wages, for actors   84, 97, 102, 148, 151, 184, 205, 206,
        252a, 286, 321, 614, 649, 664, 790, 839, 853, 941, 942,
        1069, 1204a, 1490, 1570, 1583, 1659
Waits   320, 476, 811, 812, 1257, 1368
Wakefield Cycle (Towneley Cycle)   17, 19, 108, 115, 138,
        217, 223, 250, 258, 274, 285, 286, 377, 393, 429, 433,
        454, 463, 499, 501, 558a, 578, 579, 583, 601, 602, 635,
        676, 691, 854, 871, 964, 977, 978, 1028, 1074, 1121,
        1125a, 1128, 1161, 1207, 1209, 1216, 1238, 1259, 1331,
        1444, 1450, 1504, 1526, 1529, 1530, 1531, 1534, 1590,
        1616, 1617, 1717
        (Language of)   108, 341
Wakefield, dramatic activity   288b, 578, 579, 1161, 1199,
        1209, 1259, 1516
Wakefield Master   17, 108, 298, 298a, 393, 581, 590, 622,
        676, 680a, 681, 733, 734, 871, 981, 1331, 1336, 1525,
        1529, 1666
Walberswick, dramatic activity   1726
Wales, dramatic records   802, 1398
        (see Welsh plays)
Wapull, George (*The Tide Tarrieth No Man*)   77, 278a, 1660
War, in the plays   432, 1519, 1692, 1693
Wealth and Health   502
Welsh plays   670
        (see Wales, dramatic activity)
Wescott, Sebastian   53
Westmorland, dramatic records   476
Wever, Richard (*Lusty Juventus*)   68, 81, 1660, 1661
Whit Monday   496, 1202
Whitsun(day), procession and feast   246, 301, 673, 1016,
        1063, 1065, 1202, 1291, 1588
Wilder, Thornton (*Skin of Our Teeth*)   1435
Wilson, Robert   1660
Wiltshire, dramatic activity   1335
Winchester, dramatic records   205, 206, 220, 243, 244, 424
Winter's Tale (Shakespeare)   643
Wisdom   6, 7, 13, 16a, 70, 135, 152, 182, 330, 379, 407a,
        546, 607, 624, 695, 736, 750, 785a, 842, 860, 898, 929,
        930, 1001, 1067, 1079, 1165, 1222, 1267, 1332, 1386,
        1388a, 1389, 1638, 1712, 1739
Wit and Science (Redford)   12, 14, 43, 77, 480, 1251, 1440,
        1441, 1664
Wit and Science, The Marriage of (Anon.)   53
Wit and Wisdom, The Marriage of (Merbury), see *Marriage
        Between Wit and Wisdom*
Witney, Oxfordshire, dramatic activity   396

Witty and Witless (Heywood)   1427
Woman Taken in Adultery (N-Town)   513, 923, 1100, 1318,
    1374, 1402
Women, in the plays; on the stage   109, 184, 298, 390, 402,
    407b, 433, 583, 586, 1129, 1301, 1604, 1731
    (as playwrights)   355, 356
Woodes, Nathaniel (*Conflict of Conscience*)   77, 1660, 1661
Wooing ceremony; wooing plays   237, 238, 292a, 731, 1219,
    1292
The World and the Child (see *Mundus et Infans*)
Wymondham, dramatic activity   595
Wynnere and Wastoure   534

Yarmouth, dramatic records   147, 1726
Yeovil, dramatic records and activity   1545
York, dramatic records and activity   252a, 270, 294, 361,
    381a, 382, 384, 399, 411, 463, 466, 467, 471, 472, 473,
    474, 778, 779, 780, 822, 829, 831, 837, 838, 843, 844,
    846, 847, 848, 849, 852, 853, 1011, 1092, 1101, 1114,
    1123, 1167, 1171, 1199, 1209, 1255, 1256, 1257, 1257a,
    1287, 1345, 1346, 1409, 1521, 1528, 1559, 1564, 1599,
    1674, 1683, 1684, 1685, 1686, 1700, 1730
York plays   9, 10, 11, 45, 60, 120, 139, 150, 154, 157, 189,
    241, 287, 293, 297, 332, 333, 334, 381, 390, 474, 528,
    592, 601, 626, 635, 645, 655, 668, 672, 691, 757, 765,
    813, 816, 833, 843, 844, 845, 851, 855, 872, 873, 907,
    959, 962, 964, 983, 1003, 1023, 1112, 1114, 1128, 1204,
    1228, 1230, 1250, 1269, 1270, 1289, 1345, 1346, 1355,
    1406, 1408, 1409, 1422, 1444, 1460, 1526, 1536, 1536a,
    1578, 1582, 1590, 1591, 1599, 1633, 1640, 1711, 1736
York Realist   150, 382, 390, 403, 1662
York Register   157, 471, 1095, 1408
    (see John Clerke)
Young, Karl   134, 185, 555, 561, 584, 1236, 1485, 1518, 1651
Youth   43, 49, 77, 158, 446, 753, 958, 1442

missed: Dutton Book/CD articles.
Bourgeault on Hildibrand

Smedlen in New Oct. Hist.

Diane Dolan

Viterbo Collog.
Peter Herrm's Bale tribling. in ELK

John Edwards see p. 135.
Fletcher on "Coveytyse Copbard" in
Castle — ES 1987.
gamer — p. 161.

Covette descripi.
framley # 640.

Mathilen Harris
Merionseh 1977